Major
European
Governments

Major European Governments

9th edition

■ *JORGEN S. RASMUSSEN*
Iowa State University

■ *JOEL C. MOSES*
Iowa State University

Wadsworth Publishing Company
Belmont, California
A Division of Wadsworth, Inc.

Political Science Editor: Brian Gore
Editorial Assistant: Jennifer Dunning
Production: Lifland et al., Bookmakers
Design: Quica Ostrander
Print Buyer: Barbara Britton
Copy Editor: Janice Ostock
Illustrator: Gail Magin
Cover: Bruce Kortebein/Design Office
Compositor: Williams Studio
Printer: Arcata Graphics/Fairfield

This book is printed on acid-free recycled paper.

 International Thomson Publishing
The trademark ITP is used under license.

Printed in the United States of America
1 2 3 4 5 6 7 8 9 10—99 98 97 96 95

Library of Congress Cataloging-in-Publication Data

Rasmussen, Jorgen Scott.
    Major European governments / Jorgen Rasmussen, Joel Moses. — 9th ed.
       p.   cm.
    Commonly referred to as MEG.
    Rev. ed. of: Major European governments / Alex N. Dragnich, Jorgen S. Rasmussen, Joel C. Moses. 8th ed. c1991.
    Includes index
    ISBN 0-534-22212-9
    1. Europe—Politics and government.   2. Comparative government.
I. Moses, Joel C.   II. Dragnich, Alex N.   Major European
governments.   III. Title.   IV. Title: MEG
JN12.D7   1995
320.3—dc20
                                      94-17290
                                        CIP

Brief Contents

Contents

List of Figures

List of Tables

Preface

Although neither of us were involved in the birth of this "child," we both, to varying degrees, have helped to guide it into adulthood. At thirty-three years old it is on the brink of middle age. Of the comparative politics textbooks currently in print, *MEG* has proven to be the most long-lived. Why has it been so durable? Because it has remained true over the years to its original basic approach and style. The basic aim always has been to present the essential features of government and politics in major European political systems, to strike a balance between excessive detail and superficial generalities. Since most of the students using *MEG* were assumed to have little previous knowledge of foreign political systems, much of the contents have been descriptive. Previous editions, however, never neglected interpretation and analysis. Furthermore, since some matters are intrinsically complicated, explaining them requires involved accounts. The material covered has never been oversimplified just to make reading the book easier. Studying a new subject often requires learning a new vocabulary, as well as becoming familiar with new concepts. Here again *MEG* has sought balance, has endeavored to keep unfamiliar terms to a minimum and to avoid needless jargon. A clear, relatively untechnical prose style has been the goal.

To say that *MEG* is nearly middle-aged is not entirely accurate. The revisions in this ninth edition are so extensive that the book could be regarded as a babe in arms or, at least, a toddler. Those familiar with previous editions will see the family resemblance to its older siblings (it has its sister's eyes, its brother's hair, and so forth), but *MEG* the ninth is an individual in its own right. How could it be otherwise for the first edition written after the collapse of Communism in the Soviet Union? That momentous event has produced the main change in organization in this edition.

In previous editions the three European democracies covered were examined in detail. Only after the discussion of democratic systems had been completed did attention turn to the Soviet Union. On that gloomy note of dictatorship, the book ended. In some senses, there was no conclusion; alternatively, the conclusion came not at the end of the book but before the Soviet section—in the concluding comments on the democracies. In this edition, the section on the post-Soviet systems of Russia and Central Eurasia comes after the section on Germany. A subsequent two-chapter concluding section gives the book for the first time a real conclusion.

This shift in placement for Russia and Central Eurasia was not done because we are naive optimists about the prospects for democracy among these fifteen successor states. Nonetheless, the attempts being made by many of these countries to institute democratic and free-market reforms make comparison with the major powers of Western Europe relevant to a far greater extent now than was true for nearly a half century after World War II. To a significant extent, efforts are being made to domicile the new countries of Russia and Central Eurasia in the common European home already dwelt in by Britain, France, and Germany.

Therefore, we examine the government and politics of these fifteen successor states *before* we shift from an individual system focus to comparative analysis. This is not to say that we offer no comparative comments prior to Part Six. Although each of Parts Two through Four deals with a particular country and Part Five concentrates primarily on Russia, we don't discuss these countries in complete isolation. In particular, we comment on similarities and contrasts with the American system to provide perspective on the political practices likely to be most familiar to students. In this way, study of foreign governments should help identify those aspects of American politics that are unique products of our particular culture and those that are common across national boundaries. Nonetheless, in each country section our main concern is a particular system in the context of its history, political culture, geography, economic circumstances, and demographic configuration. What sort of institutional arrangements has each context produced, and how do those institutions operate? Every political system exists in a context, and those who ignore these details are likely to misapprehend that system's politics.

As far as possible, however, we wish to go beyond particularistic analysis to generalize about government and politics. That is what we do in the first chapter of Part Six, stressing in particular the ability of political systems to adapt to changing circumstances. How much stress of what type can a system endure, and why do some seem to handle the challenge better than others? The new organization of this edition—with Russia and Central Eurasia *before* this discussion—helps to provide stronger insight into the problems of transition to democracy currently being experienced there.

In the concluding chapter of the book we shift to yet a higher level of political relations—the international dimension. Whatever the current problems and reverses in the process of integrating the residents of the common European home into some sort of overarching, coordinated system, the endeavor continues. In a significant sense, no matter how far off it may be, *this is* the wave of future. Therefore, it is entirely appropriate that *MEG* concludes on that note.

The other major change in organization for this edition is that each country section concludes with a short summary chapter. In the past each part simply came to an end when the last of that country's governmental institutions had been discussed—a paragraph or two sufficed as summary for that country's political system. Now, just as the book itself has a full-blown conclusion, so does each country section. We hope that these changes help students to pull the material together and obtain a better grasp of the key points.

This is a jointly authored book—we have been integrated even if Europe has not been. The division of labor was for Moses to make some sense out of events in Russia and Central Eurasia and for Rasmussen to do everything else. We each read and commented on the other's work, however, and revised in light of the suggestions.

As in the past, we have chosen not to cover a number of countries superficially, but to concentrate on major political systems in the European region. This concentration is somewhat diluted in this edition because of the splintering of the Soviet

Union into fifteen different countries. Nonetheless, our stress on Russia, with less attention to the remaining countries of Central Eurasia, still enables us to give thorough attention to our selections. Given these countries' geographic propinquity, they are more likely to have some common elements in their political heritages than would be the case for countries selected from each of the corners of the world. Whatever their similarities, however, they differ sufficiently to make comparisons interesting.

We've divided Parts Two through Four into chapters that focus primarily on a particular structure or institution (governmental or political), describe its formal status, and explain how it operates in practice. We lack sufficient space for a detailed account of the content of public policy. To that extent, we emphasize political and governmental machinery more than output. Nonetheless, we are also concerned with the performance of functions. Thus, we analyze the role each structure plays in the country's total system. Some of our chapter titles indicate the main purpose, or principal function, of a given institution. After discussing the channels for political inputs—that is, electoral arrangements, interest groups, and political parties—we examine the legislature and the executive and the relation between them. Our attention is then directed to the officials involved in implementing policies, with emphasis on responsiveness and efficiency and, finally, to the procedures for adjudicating conflict.

Although Russia and the countries of Central Eurasia are endeavoring to reform their governmental and political institutions into greater conformity with those prevailing in the established Western European democracies, we must admit that this process has not advanced sufficiently far for us to be able to use the same chapter organization for Part Five as for the previous parts. Therefore, the first two chapters on Russia and Central Eurasia compare and contrast the two major figures—Mikhail Gorbachev and Boris Yeltsin—who have been the colossi of recent Soviet and post-Soviet politics. We then turn to the context of that politics—to the peoples, the history, and the geography—and then to the legacy of the Communist period. All of this is essential for understanding the nature of the economic and nation-building problems addressed next. Finally, political institutions and policy options are surveyed and prospects for the future outlined.

A French cliché, thought to be an apt summary of that country's politics, says that no matter how things change, they remain the same. No matter how *MEG* has changed in this edition, it remains the same—only better. In part this is because of the advice we received from Margaret Haupt, Coe College; Andrew Milnor, SUNY-Binghamton; W. David Patterson, Southern Methodist University; and Martin A. Schain, New York University. Their reviews helped us to keep focused on the book's main themes and to develop important substantive points. We also were happy to work once again with Jane Hoover and Janice Ostock of Lifland et al., Bookmakers.

Jorgen S. Rasmussen
Joel C. Moses
June 1994

About the Authors

Jorgen S. Rasmussen received his Ph.D. in political science from the University of Wisconsin–Madison, following an A.B. with highest honors in government from Indiana University. Currently he is Distinguished Professor of Political Science at Iowa State University, having served as chair of that department from 1972 to 1976. He has also taught at the University of Glasgow, Vanderbilt University, Columbia University, and the University of Arizona. One of the founders of the British Politics Group, he has been its executive secretary for two decades. From time to time he comments on American political developments for BBC Scotland news broadcasts. Dr. Rasmussen is the author of three other books: on British politics, on the British Liberal party, and on the study of comparative politics. In addition, he has co-authored or contributed to several other works. His scholarly articles have been published in journals both in the United States and abroad, as have many of his book reviews.

Joel C. Moses received his Ph.D. in political science from the University of Wisconsin–Madison in 1972. A professor of political science at Iowa State University since 1982, he has also taught as a visiting faculty member at Cornell University; the University of California, San Diego; and the University of Wisconsin–Madison. He is the author of *Regional Party Leadership and Policy-Making in the USSR* (1974) and *The Politics of Women and Work in the Soviet Union and the United States* (1983) and coeditor of *Political Implications of Economic Reform in Communist Systems: Communist Dialectic* (1990). A frequent contributor to journals and edited volumes on contemporary Soviet politics, he is a managing editor of the journal *Soviet and Post-Soviet Review* and a member of the board of trustees of the journal *The Current Digest of the Post-Soviet Press.*

Major
European
Governments

...... Part One

Introduction

". . . poor, nasty, brutish, and short."

■ THE ESSENCE OF POLITICS

You are starting to learn about the government and politics of the major European countries. You know what government is, but your idea of politics may differ somewhat from ours. We like the definition offered many years ago by an eminent political scientist: politics is "who gets what, when, and how." This definition is helpful because it indicates that politics involves conflict. If everyone agreed about everything, politics wouldn't exist. Those who deplore the clash of political groups and believe that disagreement should be eliminated from government are either naive or potential dictators; people *will* disagree on virtually any issue.

People who dislike political conflict, however, are justified to some extent. Human beings create governmental structures to channel (not eliminate) conflict, to keep it manageable, to keep it from erupting into violence. A seventeenth-century political philosopher trying to imagine what life would be like without government envisioned a "condition called Warre; and a warre, as is of every man, against every man—[a life] solitary, poor, nasty, brutish, and short." Although the study of politics does not leave out war, riots, and other disruptive acts, its main concern is how societies organize to resolve conflicting and competing interests in ways that will not tear those societies apart. The aim is not to avoid conflict but to manage unavoidable conflict, not to produce universal agreement on issues but to produce policies that most members of a society can tolerate, even if many think the policies are mistaken or undesirable.

During the twentieth century each of the countries included in this book has failed at one time or another in varying degree to keep domestic conflict within peaceful bounds. In Russia the autocratic rule of the tsar was terminated at the time of World War I by a revolution and civil war, only to be replaced by an even more coercive and repressive regime. The Communists systematically executed countless opponents and purged hundreds of thousands of members of their own party. Since 1985 reformers have openly admitted in the Soviet media that the terror and violence against millions of people under Stalin equaled or surpassed even the worst atrocities of Hitler's regime.

In Germany the brief experience with democracy during the Weimar Republic, after World War I, was marred by street fighting between political groups and political assassinations. But even this was better than what followed the Nazi seizure of power. Through their secret police and concentration camps, the Nazis practiced terror and violence on a scale so vast as to be unbelievable. More recently, disruptive student demonstrations in the late 1960s and extralegal protests against the military and nuclear power in the 1980s caused some people to fear that Germany might be returning to the Weimar days. In the 1990s attacks on residents of non-German ethnic backgrounds caused concern about a possible revival of Nazi sentiment.

In France in 1958 the likelihood that French paratroopers might invade Paris to seize power brought one governmental system to an end and started the process for a new regime. Ten years later this regime found itself besieged by students and workers who battled police in the streets from behind barricades. These events helped to drive the President from office within a year, even though he had served little more than half of his term.

Britain has been the most stable, the least turbulent, of the four countries studied in this book. Even there, however, politics has involved violence. Women fighting for their political rights prior to World War I broke windows and set fire to mailboxes. Although the forced feedings administered to many of these women while they were in prison were not designed to be torture, physically they had much the same effect.

Full-scale violence was required for Ireland to become independent of Britain after World War I. In Northern Ireland—which remained joined to Britain—the virus of religious discrimination and bigotry remained dormant until the late 1960s, when it erupted anew. Snipings, fire bombings, and street fighting became common occurrences. A Catholic woman was even tarred and feathered because she planned to marry a non-Catholic British soldier who was part of the peace-keeping force in Northern Ireland. In 1984 a bomb planted in a hotel in England by Irish nationalists nearly killed the British Prime Minister while she was attending her party's conference and did kill several others, including a member of Parliament.

In the spring of 1990 mass protest against the newly instituted poll tax erupted into rioting in central London, producing extensive property damage and looting. Elsewhere in Britain demonstrations in council chambers disrupted the meetings of local government bodies.

■ DEMOCRATIC AND AUTOCRATIC POLITICAL SYSTEMS

We have commented that social conflict is common and that dealing with it nonviolently is a constantly pressing concern. Why is this? An ultimate answer would turn on how you conceive of human nature. Are people fundamentally good but corrupted by malignant social structures, as Communists assert? Or are they essentially and incorrigibly sinful, as Christians believe? We don't need, however, to dig that deeply for an answer. You know that even in a prosperous country such as the United States, resources are limited, and, therefore, not everybody will be satisfied with his or her share. If deceit and brute strength are not to be the chief means of trying to satisfy desires, if there is to be any community among humans, then some rules, behavioral boundaries, and accepted practices must exist to constrain the struggle for redistribution of limited resources.

Someone has to make the rules; someone has to assign the benefits; someone has to be able to apply the sanctions necessary to implement these decisions. A society's government is composed of the structures in the society that are widely recognized as being properly engaged in these activities and possessing as well the exclusive authority to set the limits within which force may be used legitimately. Political struggle among various segments of society involves their use of whatever power they may possess to try to control the government. Those segments that succeed will be able to make authoritative decisions—ones that are binding throughout the society—or alter the procedures for making them.

Thus, all forms of government share the same initial concern. Given conflicting individual goals, wants, and needs, how is it possible to get people to obey authoritative decisions they do not like? To what extent must power be concentrated in the hands of public officials in order to maintain social order and avoid the war of all against all? Devising governmental structures to solve this problem creates a new one. And it is here that forms of government begin to diverge.

Key Aspects of Democracy

If the authoritative power created to maintain order is unlimited, then it becomes a new threat of injury and violence. In ancient Rome this idea was put as a question: *quis custodiet ipsos custodes?* (who will guard against those who themselves are guards?). How can we ensure that those to whom we entrust the power to settle conflicts nonviolently do not abuse that power and tyrannize everyone?

The first step in a response is constitutionalism—the idea of creating limits on governmental power. These limits are of two types: substantive and procedural. That is, government is prohibited from doing certain things. And within the permitted sphere, some actions are allowed only if performed in a particular way. Thus, society initially concentrates power to maintain order and prevent injury of one person by another, but then—in a democracy—it limits that power to avoid tyranny by those who wield it.

Democracies establish the rule of law. This means that sanctions must not be applied arbitrarily. The rules must be clear and generally known. Convictions for criminal offenses must conform with due process; that is, they must be obtained fairly—any based on confessions obtained by torture are not permitted, for example. Everyone must be subject equally to the law. And government is not above the law; it must be able to cite authorization for all its actions.

Although constitutionalism is essential to democracy, democratic systems involve more than limitations on power. They also must focus on how authoritative decisions are to be made and by whom. Merely because certain actions are permitted doesn't mean that all of them will be taken. Of the many things a government can do, the benefits it can bestow, how are we to decide which will be done? Is government to be something of a lady bountiful in that a well-off elite will decide out of the goodness of its heart what shall be granted to the rest? Or shall we as a community decide? Furthermore, shall the actual implementation of such decisions be left to the elite, or shall the community have a voice in determining to whom the task will be entrusted?

At the center of the democratic ideal is the belief that individuals are important, that political institutions exist to serve the people rather than the reverse, that the government, therefore, exists by virtue of the people's consent. Closely related is the belief that individuals can manage their own affairs better than someone else could do it for them. Of course, people make mistakes, and at times they fail to recognize their own best interests. Democracy assumes not that the people are always right, but that in the long run they are good judges and can distinguish sensible policies from shortsighted ones and capable leaders from incompetent ones.

Furthermore, the mistakes in judgment that the people do make are preferable to paternalistic government, however efficient it might be. Without the opportunity to make mistakes and learn from them, human beings would be unable to grow. People not permitted to think and decide for themselves, allowed only to act on command, would no longer be human beings, but animals or robots.

The emphasis on the worth of the individual is expressed in democracies not only through the rule of law, but also by toleration of dissent and by the principles of political equality and majority rule. Often democracy is defined as government by the people. Obviously no country of any size can be run by a mass town meeting of the citizens, however; representative government is necessary. Nor is it possible to ensure that everyone has exactly the same amount of political influence. Therefore, efforts to attain political equality normally focus on eliminating all extraneous obstacles, such as requirements concerning religion or occupation, to the right to vote and hold office and on giving the same weight to each vote.

The practical test of democracy is whether the people can change by regular, legal procedures the holders of governmental power, replacing one set of leaders with another. Differences over who should hold office and what policies should be implemented are resolved in favor of those persons and policies gaining the most votes in honest and frequent elections.

If the procedures for involving the community in governing are to be more than a charade, those holding office must be accountable for their actions. Their policies must be subject to criticism, and they must justify their behavior. Should their service be judged unsatisfactory, they must be subject to removal. Whether political decision makers are accountable is a fundamental test for distinguishing among types of political systems. Systems in which decision makers are accountable, where power is responsible, are democracies; those where they aren't are autocracies.

Despite the high value democracy places on the people's preferences, some limits must be placed on majority rule; otherwise we would be back to the brute strength free-for-all that governmental systems are intended to eliminate. The tyranny of the majority is no better than that of an individual dictator. Concern for individuals becomes the basis for limiting individual behavior. In seeking to develop themselves, in attempting to realize their potential, individuals can't be permitted to infringe on the rights of others. This is why democratic government is always in dynamic tension. Individual freedom is tempered by the need for authority to protect the rights of other individuals. Someone once put it this way: my right to swing my fist stops where your nose begins.

Although the majority is to prevail, it must not oppress the minority. Minority opinion should not be dismissed cavalierly. Dissenting groups and parties should be free to organize, to assemble, to speak and write freely as they seek to persuade people to support their programs and policies. At the next election they can offer an alternative set of leaders for approval by the voters.

A democratic society is a flexible one, constantly readjusting the balance between freedom and constraint, rather than a fixed order; it is an open society that allows, even welcomes, change. To some this is an agreeable idea, for they believe that people should be the masters of their fate. But to others even the prospect of constant change produces anxiety. They cannot adjust readily to new ideas and new ways of doing things and, therefore, feel threatened by innovation. Taken to an extreme, such feelings may culminate in an authoritarian personality, one that would be more at home in an autocratic, rather than a democratic, system.

Stable democracy requires consensus on procedures, on the fundamental rules for making political decisions. Beyond the basic principles and procedures we've outlined, democracy makes no substantive demands on a country. Specifying goals or requiring particular institutional arrangements is more characteristic of utopian or millenarian dictatorial systems. Democracy leaves the choice of particular political, social, and economic structures up to each country. Some of the resulting combinations work better than others. But, as we have said, one of the hallmarks of democracy is to allow people freedom to make their own decisions and then to assess the results of their choices.

Some countries, such as Britain and France, have instituted a considerable amount of government ownership of economic enterprises and, along with other countries, such as Sweden, have established an extensive system of social welfare benefits. Implementing such policies does not make a country less democratic. Some people argue that doing so strengthens commitment to democratic values. Such an assessment, however, talks of "social" or "economic" democracy and loses sight of the point made above that democracy is a method.

Since democracy requires providing choices among leaders and policies, systems in which only one political party can operate freely are not fully democratic. Yet these single-party systems do vary in the extent to which they can be classified as autocracies. In some countries, especially some in the Third World, a degree of governmental accountability and of choice among alternative officeholders exists even though the right to organize politically is limited.

Some single-party systems are more open to diverse views; others are more monolithic. The nature of the single party and the extent to which it must compete with other influential domestic groups and forces help to account for the differences in these systems. In Syria, for example, the ruling Ba'th (Renaissance) single party is dominated by a particular ethnic or religious group—the Alawite, or Shi'a Muslims, who constitute 15 percent of the population. The party's intolerance of political dissent coincides with its determination to exclude the other ethnic-religious groups (Sunni Muslims and Ismaili), which comprise 85 percent of Syria's population, from power. In Syria's neighbor to the north, Iraq, a similar pattern prevails, but with exactly the opposite groups being in and out of power. The Iraqi Ba'th Party is dominated by the minority Sunni Muslims and bases its autocratic rule under Saddam Hussein on the need to suppress the majority of the Iraqi population, Shi'a Muslims and Kurds.

In many African and Middle Eastern single-party systems, the military is the most powerful institution and the one with the fullest sense of identity. Of course, the military also can be the chief potential rival to ruling autocrats because of its ability to command weapons and soldiers. In many Third World countries the leaders of the ruling single party must share power uneasily with military officers; their continuing rule is contingent on responding satisfactorily to the military's desire for resources and commitment to preserving public order. Should this arrangement break down, the disgruntled military officers are likely to stage a coup against the single-party leaders and impose martial law.

Variety among single-party systems also occurs because any given system may be forced by circumstances to become less oppressively monolithic and to tolerate some dissent. In 1989 the Communist rulers of Poland had to concede free competitive elections for the national legislature. Candidates of the independent trade union movement, Solidarity, which had been outlawed until that year, were elected in a landslide over Communist-backed candidates and chose a non-Communist and co-chair of the Solidarity movement, Tadeusz Mazowiecki, as Prime Minister of the Polish government.

For seven decades the leaders of the Soviet Union were severely intolerant of opposition, but in the late 1980s they were compelled to bargain with, rather than repress, ethnically based political groups in all regions of the country. By 1990 many independent ethnic national popular fronts had formed in the fifteen republics of the Soviet Union. They competed for and won offices against candidates of the conservative Communist establishment. By 1991 several national popular fronts had become so powerful that the central Soviet government could no longer impose its autocratic decisions on the republics. By December of that year the national popular fronts brought about the collapse not only of the Soviet Communist system, but of the entire Soviet Union. Official tolerance of political opposition—a concept institutionalized in Britain for centuries under the label "the loyal Opposition"—proved to be crucial in the transition from autocracy to post-Soviet independence for the fifteen new countries that have emerged out of the former Soviet Union.

In summary, democracy makes concentrated power accountable to the people. Not only does it limit the powers and procedures of government through a constitution, it also constrains and directs the uses of power by calling government to account. Democratic government is responsible, constitutional government.

Varieties of Autocratic Rule

In having had firsthand experience with democracy, you are very uncommon. For most of history, even for most people today, living under some form of autocratic or authoritarian regime has been typical. Perhaps the earliest form of autocratic rule was by the chief of a tribe or clan. Such rulers are still to be found in places where tradition-bound societies exist in relative isolation. Societies much larger than primitive tribes have been ruled over by potentates who used such titles as king, emperor, and sheik.

In the modern world the last remaining vestiges of this type of traditional autocracy are found in some Muslim countries in the Middle East, such as Jordan and Saudi Arabia. Their rulers base their legitimacy on their alleged descent from the family or close followers of the Prophet Muhammed, who founded the religion of Islam in the seventh century. Elsewhere in the region, in Iran, the Ayatollah Khomeini was obeyed because of a widespread belief that he was the modern-day equivalent of the Prophet in Shi'a Islam and that he had inherited from Allah (God) the state of "holiness" that was first granted to Muhammed and enabled him to set forth Allah's revelations in the *Koran*.

Although autocratic monarchies governed European countries for many centuries, the modern versions have become constitutional. That means that virtually all of the power previously exercised by the monarch has been transferred to popularly elected officials and that governmental powers are limited. Outside of Europe, however, some monarchs continue to exercise almost unlimited power.

The oldest form of dictatorship occurred in ancient Rome. A leader often would be given extensive and unchallenged powers to deal with a certain crisis. Unlike most modern dictators, he was elected rather than self-designated and served for only a limited time, never more than six months. Modern democracies frequently allocate special reserve powers to handle crises. During the time the executive is granted the extraordinary powers, the system may be labeled "constitutional dictatorship."

In the modern world autocratic regimes are of several types. Some, including the quasi-military, strong-man type found in some Latin American countries, can be labeled dictatorships, or traditional autocracies. In such regimes the dictator completely controls the political and military establishments; censorship and the police are used to suppress internal opposition, and the people are permitted only a minor, formalistic role in decision making. In some instances the old social elite may need to concede some power to the military or a rising professional middle class, but that is as far as the system opens to new groups. The dictator not only permits little political change, but also is little interested in economic development, which might unleash new and uncontrollable pressures for reform. If the economy grows at all, the benefits are channeled to the traditional social elites—these autocratic regimes aren't interested in redistributing a society's wealth. Although the people in general enjoy little say in or benefit from such a system, they tend to be left to pursue their own goals unhindered, so long as these do not threaten the dictator or encroach on the economic interests of the traditional elites backing the regime.

The typical twentieth-century autocratic system, however, takes one or the other of two forms. In one form—the modernizing autocracy—the old elite no longer retains power and has been replaced by well-educated and highly trained elements of the society, such as military officers, bureaucrats, business executives, and professionals. Economic development has high priority, and the people share some of the benefits. With the land-holding oligarchs banished, land reform is common. Furthermore, political change is not entirely ruled out. Some of the trappings of democracy—the procedures and the forms—are adopted. This is largely a matter of appearances, however, since no real political competition is permitted. Mexico since 1929 under the leadership of the Institutional Revolutionary Party (PRI) and Iran from 1953 until 1979 under the Shah (Mohammed Reza Shah Pahlavi) typify modernizing autocracies in the twentieth century.

The other common twentieth-century form is the mobilizational autocracy. Here the same new technocratic elites have come to power as in the modernizing regime. And, as in that regime, economic development is sought, and some redistribution of the benefits to the people is allowed. In the political sphere, however, these two forms of autocracy differ markedly. The mobilizational regime doesn't just permit some political activity; it requires it. The people are virtually forced to participate in various political activities. Not to do so, or even to do so without the proper show of enthusiasm, suggests lack of commitment to the regime and is likely to incur punishment.

Mobilizational autocracies seek to create the appearance of popular legitimacy. It is not uncommon for them to call themselves "people's democracies" or "people's republics." One of the tools frequently used to mobilize the people is an official ideology—a system of ideas about the nature, operation, and goals of society. No other beliefs are permitted to compete for public support. The official ideology, proclaimed and interpreted by those who rule the system, is the only one. This ideology guides an effort to remake people and society. Mobilizational autocracies concern themselves with everything in the society. Politics comes to include personal, social, and cultural behavior, and all other aspects of life. The rulers seek to eliminate all private spheres of activity. To penetrate all levels of society, the regime spawns and directs a variety of groups and activities so that no independent organizations exist.

If the ideology is the guide to transforming society, the typical instrument for this process is the single, elite party, which is to protect, propagate, and implement the ideology. Thus, mobilizational autocracies are sometimes called "party dictatorships." All other political groups are outlawed, and the pronouncements of the party must be accepted without question. Assisting the party are a variety of auxiliary agencies, such as youth groups, women's organizations, and sport clubs. These groups help to ensure that the people are occupied with acceptable activities and can be easily kept track of and mobilized to carry out the will of the state. Nazi Germany from 1933 to 1945, the former Soviet Union from 1917 to 1991, and some contemporary Communist countries such as China and North Korea all typify these defining attributes of a mobilizational autocracy.

These three forms of autocracy should not be thought of as stages in a sequence of political change, even though the traditional form frequently does give way to either the modernizing or mobilizational version. On the other hand, some countries of the former Soviet Union show evidence of reverting to traditional autocracies since the collapse of Communism. In countries such as Uzbekistan, Tajikistan, Turkmenistan, and Azerbaijan, the new autocratic regimes seek to justify the absolute power of their rulers by the need to protect the majority ethnic group—the modern version of the tribe or clan—against the other ethnic and religious minorities.

▪ TYPOLOGIES AND TYPES OF VARIABLES

We have been presenting a simple classification scheme, or typology, whose main categories are democracy, monarchy, and autocracy (the latter with three subtypes: traditional, modernizing, and mobilizational). The criteria for distinguishing among these five categories are the extent of popular distribution of political power, the security of fundamental rights, the origins and policies of the wielders of power, and the scope of governmental penetration into the society. Classifying political systems according to basic type is a good way to compare them.

In addition to the typology just discussed, several others are frequently used in comparative politics: one-, two-, or multiparty systems; presidential or parliamentary systems; and federal or unitary systems. The differences among the categories in the typology based on the number of parties are self-evident, although applying them to particular countries can be difficult, as you'll see when we discuss the British system in Chapter 4.

In the second typology mentioned, presidential systems, such as that of the United States, separate the executive and legislative structures of government, with officeholders in each being elected independently by the people for set terms. In a parliamentary system, such as that of Britain or Germany, the two branches are fused; the legislature can vote the executive out of office without any need for a national election by the people.

The federal/unitary typology focuses not on how power is distributed at the national level (as is true of the parliamentary/presidential typology), but on how power is allocated between the national and subnational units of government. In a unitary system all power is in the hands of the central government, which decides what regional and local units of government shall exist and grants them whatever power it wishes. These subnational units can be eliminated by the central government; for example, Britain abolished the major metropolitan governmental structures in the mid-1980s. In contrast, in the federal system of the United States, the states exist independently. The people have given some power to the central government and some to the states. This division of powers can be altered only through a procedure involving both the central government and the states or by the people. The essence of federalism is establishing two levels of government, neither of whose powers can be altered unilaterally. The federal arrangement allows greater diversity within a society than the more centralized unitary system.

When the typologies we've discussed are applied to the countries in this book, Britain usually is classified as a two-party parliamentary democracy with a unitary division of powers. Never in modern times has Britain had an autocratic government. Germany is a multiparty parliamentary democracy with a federal system. From 1933 to 1945, however, Germany was a classic example of the mobilizational autocracy. And for virtually all of the twentieth century, the one-party system of the Soviet Union was another. France, which had some experience with autocratic regimes in both the nineteenth and twentieth centuries, clearly is a multiparty democracy at present, but whether it is parliamentary or presidential is unclear, as we will discuss in detail in Part Three.

As this difficulty in labeling France suggests, applying a classification system is not an automatic process, but one calling for informed judgments. Some people would argue that Britain has not really been a two-party system for most of the last two decades, and others would question whether Germany was a multiparty system for much of the 1970s. Indeed, it is difficult to state criteria that can distinguish between the party systems of these two countries (again, we will discuss this for each country in its part of the book).

The problem is that any classification system admittedly sacrifices some detail by grouping together for the sake of generalization things that are not exactly the same. Given such distortions, why bother trying to classify systems? Although no two persons are alike, they clearly have enough in common to be grouped together and distinguished from horses. In fact, it is only when we begin to group things according to one or more criteria that we can discover just how much they have in common and in what respects they differ from each other and from other objects not grouped with them. Similarities and differences spring into view. If placing items in the various categories of a typology is not to be a haphazard search for information, however, systematic procedures need to be followed. Therefore, we need to discuss some of the basic principles of scientific research.

■ COMPARATIVE POLITICS AS A SCIENTIFIC STUDY

As you begin to learn something about the government and politics of other countries, you are likely to be struck by the differences between political life there and what you are familiar with in the United States. You may be sufficiently intrigued to try to explain these differences. Can some pattern of events be discovered, an association or link among them be found, that might suggest a causal relation? Can this hunch (or hypothesis, to give it its more formal name) be supported by evidence that you are able to dig out by detailed study?

The Scientific Method

Such inquiry is the process of scientific discovery, which is simply a new way of thinking about familiar things. Scientific discoveries are desirable for their practical uses or simply because they satisfy curiosity about why things happen as they do. The familiar things explained are observed regularities—for example, whenever the weather is sufficiently cold, puddles of water freeze. Such observed regularities are only *descriptive* reports and do not *explain* anything. The mere fact that two things always have occurred together or in sequence is no guarantee that they will continue to do so. The process of scientific discovery goes beyond description to analysis.

Analysis separates an event into its component parts to help reveal relations, especially those that might not be readily apparent. This process helps to generate hypotheses—tentative solutions to problems, or suggestions for interpreting data so that they make sense. Experiments or further observations test the usefulness of these tentative solutions. Experiments are preferable because they tend to minimize the errors or distracting factors that are inherent in unplanned and unmanipulatable observations. By this process of verification, hypotheses are either rejected or transformed into scientific laws.

A scientific law states the form and scope of a regularity. It tells how things known to be connected are related: whether, for example, they increase in size together or whether one gets larger as the other gets smaller. A law tells the circumstances in which it applies: whether, for instance, it is true only when the temperature is above freezing. The significance of a law is that it implies that the stated relation is a necessary one, thus going beyond the mere reporting of an observed regularity.

When a number of laws whose scope has been established can be interrelated, the result is a system of knowledge called a theory. A theory's validity depends on its ability to account for the known data simply and economically. The geocentric theory of the universe, for example, was abandoned not because it was disproven—

it was not known for certain that the sun did not revolve around the earth—but because increasingly complex and elaborate explanations were required to make this theory conform with newly acquired information about the movements of heavenly bodies. As the explanations became more cumbersome, the theory became less helpful. A new theory was needed that could explain the available data more simply and was more likely to suggest useful subsidiary laws.

At this point we have come full circle in describing the process of scientific investigation. A theory helps make a generalization a law by providing reasons for the regularities observed. Furthermore, one can deduce from a theory what relations should prevail if the theory is correct and thus search for regularities not previously discovered. Should these regularities then be found, they can be established as laws, further buttressing the theory's validity.

The Comparative Study of Politics

As we noted, experimentation is a key method in the process of scientific discovery. Unfortunately, it is rarely possible in political science; people, unlike laboratory rats, are not expendable and do not tolerate being manipulated. Therefore, political scientists usually have to settle for observation, for gaining their data from the study of uncontrolled situations and events. In an effort to avoid being misled by the presence of extraneous factors in the research sites they are forced to use, political scientists endeavor to compare political phenomena across national boundaries. If they can discover the same regularity in more than one country, they feel more certain that there is some link between the associated events or objects and that the relation is not just an accidental one, due to mere happenstance. Thus, cross-national generalizations are essential for an empirically grounded theory of politics.

We are not talking about the useless study of a lot of abstract, irrelevant information. No country has devised a perfect set of political institutions. (Winston Churchill, Prime Minister of Britain during World War II, once said that democracy is the worst form of government—except for all other forms.) But all political systems have valuable lessons to teach. Virtually every political system does at least some things effectively. Even if one didn't, it could provide examples of things to be avoided. By studying other political systems, we can gain some idea of which political reforms we might wish to adopt in this country and which we would be wise to avoid.

Comparing political systems is hardly new. Aristotle, the Greek philosopher who lived over two millennia ago, sometimes is regarded as the founder of political science because he attempted to classify the constitutions of the Greek city-states. (He was constructing and applying typologies, the same process suggested previously as a useful starting point for comparative studies.)

In the 1950s some political scientists complained that the study of politics had advanced little since Aristotle's time. They felt that the prevailing practice of concentrating on laws, constitutions, and formal governmental structures, rather than on political processes and group interaction, resulted in mere comparative description, with little analysis. They advocated more systematic and rigorous research with as great precision—typically involving the use of quantitative measures—as existing research techniques would permit. Furthermore, they wished to push the scope for comparison as far as possible, arguing that comparing only three or four countries left open the possibility of mistakenly attributing causality to mere accidental relationships. (To express the problem more technically, N—the number of cases—was too small to permit the use of methods measuring statistical significance, which would indicate the probability that an association was due simply to chance.)

Perhaps the greatest stimulus for comparing political systems has been the emergence during the past four decades of many new countries, formerly colonies of European powers, in Africa, Asia, and the Middle East. Not only has the emergence of these countries more than doubled the total number of sovereign units that can be compared in a search for political generalizations, but these new countries also have provided a unique "political laboratory" in which to study and try to explain universal dynamics and processes in country formation and development. Too often the very longevity of old established systems and the ready acceptance of their legitimacy by their citizens obscure such dynamics and processes, especially at crucial stages of development. New systems must demonstrate to their citizens their effectiveness and justify their right to exist; they have no reserves of loyalty on which to draw. As a result, the key elements in the struggle over "who gets what, when, and how" often are easier to observe. Meeting needs, generating a sense of national identity, resolving group conflict—all must have high priority in a context of little popular affection for the system or its leaders. The essence of the political process could hardly be more starkly highlighted.

Whether political scientists choose to study new countries or old established ones, certain topics have been of particular interest to them. We need next to discuss what it is about the process of governing, of seeking to resolve conflict that has drawn their attention. What things are worth knowing about a political system?

■ CONTEXTUAL CONSIDERATIONS

One of the intellectual battles that has long raged in psychology is whether an individual's behavior is affected primarily by circumstances or heredity—nurture or nature, as the choice is put concisely. Is one's personality shaped mostly by those abilities and capacities with which one is born or by the situations experienced and the training received after birth? Most psychologists probably would agree that neither can be ignored. Similarly, in studying a political system, we need to consider not only the structures themselves but also the context in which the system operates. This needs to be stressed because political science has tended to slight geographic factors, largely as a reaction against geopolitics. This late nineteenth- and early twentieth-century approach to international relations argued that the country that controlled Eastern Europe would dominate the heartland—the Eurasian land mass—and, therefore, the world. The fact that this approach has been largely discredited and is now considered a pseudoscience should not be allowed to eliminate geographic considerations from politics.

A country's location can affect its politics. If its boundaries are natural ones—rivers, oceans, mountains—rather than an arbitrary line drawn across an open plain, it may feel less threatened by its neighbors and be less likely to build up a strong military establishment and to accept militaristic values. Geographic barriers within a country's borders can hamper communication and thwart the development of a sense of national unity. Finally, a country's location and geographic characteristics will determine its supply of natural resources, which will have a major impact on both its domestic and foreign policies.

The supply of natural resources is an element in a country's level of economic development. In recent years many political scientists have tried to relate various measures of economic development to type of political system. Some have argued that a high level of development in a country affects its politics by making political conflict less ideological and more practical, thus reducing the heat and bitterness of political battle. When the great majority of the people are relatively well-off, the conflict over the allocation of resources is presumed to be less sharp, thus facilitating compromise.

Level of economic development also affects the class structure in politically important ways. Industrialization requires a large class of manual, production-line workers, whose values and behavior are likely to differ markedly from those of the rest of the population. But as industrialization becomes fully mature, the proportion of manual workers in the work force begins to decline, and the share composed of service workers rises sharply. In both their lifestyle and economic situation, such workers are likely to have much more in common with the middle class than are manual workers. Thus, the relative change in these two groups' sizes would seem likely to contribute to greater homogeneity of outlook in a society and help to reduce the sharpness of political conflict.

Technological advance both requires and contributes to improving a country's communications network. This creates an opportunity for wider circulation of more information about governmental actions and eases communication of popular political preferences to governmental officials. Improved communications also can help to unify a country through the nationalizing effects of mass media on public opinion. In a more prosperous country more money can be spent to provide mass public education. Raising the educational level makes possible an intelligent use of the greater volume of information supplied by the improved communications network. Mass public education can contribute significantly to a common socialization process through which the predominant values of the society—both political and nonpolitical—are inculcated.

An advanced level of economic development, with its necessary concentration of workers in major urban areas, also gives rise to a host of complex problems unknown in the simple society of a pastoral economy: problems of transportation, health care, pollution, crime. Many of these can be dealt with effectively only by collective action through government, thereby expanding the load of demands and wants that the political structures must process.

The changes we've been discussing are important not only because of their separate impacts on politics, but also because they interrelate to form a phenomenon known as modernization. The growth of cities, technological and industrial advances, more widely available and more extensive education, and easier and more comprehensive communication through elaborate mass media "modernize" a country, significantly altering the environment in which its political system operates. Rapid modernization often generates great pressure on governments by creating tensions and conflicts among recently emerged or newly articulate groups. As these groups make demands—often mutually exclusive ones—on the government, a crisis of participation can develop. Many new interests want a voice in the decision-making process—and have the level of education, the crucial positions in the industrial economy, and the concentration of residency and ease of communication with others of their type to be able to compel a response.

The complexity of modern life requires individuals and social structures to specialize; certain abilities and knowledge are needed to cope with contemporary problems. Efficiency demands that personnel be recruited, retained, and promoted on the basis of merit, rather than kinship or caste. This need to bureaucratize structures is not confined to the economic sector of a society, but is present as well in the political.

Not only do particular structures become more complex, but the entire group system becomes more elaborate as new occupational and economic groups are created and grow with economic development. Many of these groups will have political objectives and, therefore, obviously will affect the nature of a country's politics. The advance of technology, coupled with the changes in the bureaucracy just mentioned, enhances the capabilities of governments to control their environments and thus to achieve their goals more readily. Depending on the orientation of the government, this can mean either greater material prosperity and fuller social services for the people or more repressive control of their lives.

Context can play a major role in shaping political values. The American political system developed in the geographic context of a vast continent. The ever-receding frontier had a major impact on American society. Those who weren't successful in the settled areas or who were looking for new challenges could move west into a less structured way of life. Elaborate social distinctions meant little there; all that mattered were drive, imagination, and ability (along with a bit of luck, of course). This produced a sense of self-reliance, a culture in which little help was expected from the governmental authorities (such as they were). Limited government that kept out of people's way and let them get on with their lives was preferred. The combination of both social and geographic mobility undermined collective values, such as social solidarity. The preference for individualism over collectivism had a significant effect on the type of political parties that developed in the United States.

All this is to say that the American experience differed profoundly from the European. A prominent social historian once termed the United States "the first new nation." Although he was stressing the uniqueness of American history, the context in which that history occurred was crucial. Although we've included many comparisons with U.S. government and politics in this book, it is essential for you to understand that our focus is on *European* government and politics—which have a fundamentally different, probably unfamiliar, tradition. Don't allow the many links, both past and present, between the United States and Britain lead you to think that

that country, the first on which we're going to focus, is basically the same as the United States. Although Britain, France, Germany, and Russia and Central Eurasia differ among themselves in many ways, they all share certain European characteristics and possess a mix of values and political institutions that contrast with those produced by the American experience.

▪ HISTORY AND POLITICAL CULTURE

At the start of the preceding section, we used the analogy of psychologists' interest in individuals' circumstances and heredity. Having talked about some aspects of political systems' context, in this section we examine aspects that are more like heredity.

The major events of a country's history produce a particular mix of values, beliefs, and attitudes, which are passed on from one generation to the next. Of course, you don't inherit these the way you do brown or blue eyes. But you do acquire them from family, friends, schools, religious groups, and the mass media — all of which are among the leading agents of political socialization.

Thus, talking about a national heritage of feelings about politics does make sense. You can no longer find any American who lived through the Civil War, and those alive at the time of the Revolution are long since dead. But both these events continue to have significant effects on how Americans think about politics. The American experience made thinking of government as derivative from monarchical divine right impossible. Government emanated from the people. Many European countries no longer have monarchs, and even in those that do, few people think of the ruler as God's agent. Nonetheless, Europeans' views about the source of government power are likely to differ from those held by most Americans because of their countries' contrasting courses of historical development.

If you've ever lived in another country, you may well have noticed how the political ideas of its people differed from those you were familiar with in the United States. In some countries government is regarded as a hostile force and contacts with it are to be avoided as much as possible; in other countries it is seen as a beneficial agency of considerable use in improving the quality of life. In Britain the police are widely respected and generally thought to be incorruptible; in much of the United States the reverse attitudes and beliefs prevail.

Over the years a people begins to build up out of its experiences a body of what may be called "folk wisdom" about government and politics. Political scientists refer to this as political culture, which may be defined more precisely as the sum of (1) individual evaluative attitudes and emotive feelings toward politics and the existing political system and (2) perceptions, feelings, and evaluations of the role of the individual in the political process. In other words, what do people know about the political system, what is their gut reaction to it and their considered judgment about it, and how do they feel about the political activity and influence they see the system permitting to them?

Although, as we have said, you are not born with values and beliefs, they are handed down from generation to generation, often without any conscious effort. If you want to "get the government off our backs," it may be because of comments around the supper table when you were growing up about red tape and foolish bureaucrats way off in Washington. The process of transmitting political values and beliefs is called political socialization; it helps to provide continuity in ideas about politics from one period to another. The belief system into which you are socialized is important because it disposes you to regard the political system in a particular way before you have had any firsthand contact with it. Not surprisingly, when that contact does occur, you tend to interpret it according to what you expected. Of course, the values and beliefs you acquire while young only predispose you toward certain views, they do not automatically determine your behavior. Political socialization is a lifelong process; your values and beliefs constantly evolve in response to your experience with political institutions.

Although the main elements of a country's political culture can be described, regarding it as uniformly present throughout a country would be a mistake. To one extent or another, subcultures exist in all political systems. The political culture is the set of values and attitudes that is most common; probably no single individual's political outlook will match this mix precisely. More important, certain groups within a country may differ sharply from the common denominator in their ideas about politics. The Jews in Nazi Germany are an example. Any study of political culture needs to examine the values and beliefs of major subgroups, whether religious, ethnic, occupational, geographical, or whatever, to find out just how typical the prevailing political culture is.

Let's consider three contrasting patterns of political culture to see what different effects they might have. A country with widespread consensus on political values and beliefs shows a pattern like example A in Figure I–1. Political conflict probably can be waged relatively peacefully there, since political opponents share the same basic values. Political differences are matters of degree, not of fundamental principle, and losing is not too bad since it won't cost you a great deal. The pattern in example B is the reverse; a sharp cleavage divides the country into two separate, virtually mutually exclusive political cultures. The potential for hostility and violent disruption of the political system is high. No national political culture exists in example C; each of the various subcultures into which the country is fractionalized encompasses roughly equal segments of the population. Political leaders in such a country will need considerable skills in coalition building as they seek to piece together majority support for some action. Failure to do so may stalemate the political system and, in turn, produce political apathy and alienation among many citizens.

The actual, as distinct from the potential, effect of each of these patterns is influenced to a considerable extent by the political style that prevails in the country, especially among the political leaders. Style turns on how people conceive of the political process, which affects their disposition toward participating in politics and their behavior in doing so.

When people's views of the proper political structures, procedures, and policies not only differ but are mutually exclusive, when they prefer a politics of redemption to one of convenience, then an explosive situation results. The political style characteristic of those who regard politics as the procedure for establishing the true faith is exhortation as they seek to convert the lost souls. Those who see

Figure I–1

Patterns of Political Culture

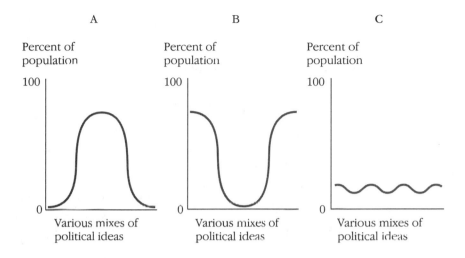

politics as an instrumental process are more likely to employ a political style of bargaining and negotiation as they seek to adjust conflicting desires by a compromise that will satisfy most people at least temporarily. For them governing is not the process of choosing between good and evil, but of distinguishing among varying shades of gray. They are not so much trying to be certain to do what's right as they are hoping to avoid the wrong mistake.

Political style and patterns of political culture tend to be reciprocally related. A pattern like that of example A in Figure I-1 helps to encourage an instrumental view of politics—a politics of convenience. The stakes are relatively limited (penny-ante poker can be enjoyable, but when the cheapest chip costs a dollar, anxiety sets in); losing the political struggle is no catastrophe, and next time your side may win. But where the pattern resembles example B, the political process may turn into a holy war in which the stakes are survival; lose this time and the game is over forever with no chance to recoup your losses. The results are dogmatism and distrust—the politics of redemption. The reciprocal aspect is that if most of the population practices an instrumental style, this helps to distribute opinions around a single point, as in example A; if the prevalent style is one that regards politics as a battle for Truth, the society may be polarized into two separate camps, as in example B.

The content and pattern of political culture and the political style of a country are shaped to a considerable extent by the order and magnitude of political or social conflicts. Some of the fundamental historical cleavages that have shaped the politics of Western Europe are the conflicts between church and state, between primary and secondary producers, and between workers and employers. Whether these crises could be faced one at a time or had to be dealt with simultaneously also has made a considerable difference.

Even if these crises did occur sequentially, if an earlier one had not been resolved by the time the next appeared, then the two would be intermingled in the political process, making it that much harder to deal with either one. The political load to be carried by the transformers of the political system—the magnitude and complexity of the issues to be processed—would be more likely to exceed the capacity of the system. Furthermore, newer issues seldom would be considered on their own merits, since the injection of the still fervent disputes of the past would produce an unthinking (conditioned) pro or con response. For much of the twentieth century, one had only to raise the question of the church when discussing any issue in French politics, and most of the political participants, like Pavlov's dogs, would froth at the mouth. The result of such intermingling of crises is that nothing is accomplished very well.

These are some of the reasons why you need to examine a country's history to see what cleavage patterns and political culture it has produced. This study is essential to discovering why one people holds one type of political values and another holds another, why one type of political structure is viable and effective in one country and another in another, or why the same type of structure is functional in one system and not in another.

■ STRUCTURES FOR POLITICAL PARTICIPATION

If everyone were self-sufficient, could meet his or her needs unassisted and wanted nothing from anyone else, a political process wouldn't exist. Since that is not the case, we can begin by focusing on needs and wants—inputs, as they are termed by some political scientists. This is not to argue that people are constantly clamoring for action. In any political system relatively few people make specific demands on the government. Typically, most people do not want to be bothered by political matters; they prefer to turn over to someone else the job of seeking to devise social arrangements that make life livable. Yet *some* people do wish to be involved actively in political decision making, and many of the rest wish to be heard on the few occasions when they feel particularly strongly about a matter. The type and amount of political participation that a person feels is proper for him or her is influenced, of course, by the society's political culture and by the subculture of the groups to which the individual belongs.

In turn, a society's political culture and the nature of politically conscious subgroups will be affected by the broad changes in style of life described in an earlier section as modernization. Economic growth, urban life, education, and exposure to the mass media tend to raise the level of what people expect government to do for them and to encourage them to regard the opportunity to participate in political decision making as a right. Those belonging to racial or religious minorities are much more likely to share a sense of group identity and make political demands as a group when they are educated and concentrated in urban areas. Political culture and modernization do affect the type and amount of political participation that people come to demand, but also important is whether the political structures and practices themselves encourage or discourage participation, whether obstacles exist that make access to decision makers difficult.

Making demands, however, is only one of two types of political participation; the other is expressing support for the system and its agents. Such expressions may be positive endorsements of particular leaders and policies, or they may be indirect. For example, when people vote in an election not only are they expressing their preferences among the contending candidates, but also, unless they vote for anti-system candidates, they are supporting the existing political system. Just as there would be no need for a political system if there were no demand inputs, a political system could not exist unless there were support inputs.

Demands and supports may originate with the public or be stimulated by governmental agencies or by political structures whose apparent primary purpose is simply to communicate public opinion. But almost never is public opinion transmitted in its original form to decision makers; instead, as demand and support inputs travel through the channels for political communications, they are altered. The extent to which they are distorted, and public influence on government thereby lessened, is a key factor in the analysis of a country's political process.

Electoral Systems

Three subsystems of the main political system deal primarily with various forms of participation: the electoral system, the group system, and the party system. In studying the electoral system, you can't be satisfied simply to know the legal regulations; you also need to discover the related behaviors and practices. If night riders call on blacks who vote, if priests can instruct parishioners on how to vote, then neither group of voters really has access to decision makers even if the law provides for universal suffrage.

Access can be drastically affected by the method used to convert the popular vote into officeholders. You will be amazed to learn how inventive the human mind has been in thinking up different kinds of electoral systems. The same percentage of votes can yield a considerably different share of the seats in a legislature depending on whether a country employs a single member/simple plurality system, as do the United States and Britain, or a proportional representation system, as does Germany, or the double ballot system used in France.

The electoral system may do more than affect access. Some political scientists regard it as the major determinant of the type of party system a country has. Others have gone so far as to claim proportional representation weakened democracy in Weimar Germany and helped to encourage the rise of dictatorship. Although these views are extreme, party strategies and campaign practices necessarily vary from one type of electoral system to another, and people do decide how to cast their vote differently, depending on the electoral system used in their country.

Interest Groups

Voting is only one of the ways in which individuals participate in politics. You may communicate your views to your legislative representative or protest a regulation to a bureaucrat. Most people, however, find that their access or influence as individuals is so limited that they are much more likely to be successful if they combine their efforts with those of others. So people sharing a common interest form an organization to advance it. Although everyone is familiar with interest groups of this type, they are not the only groups involved in the political process.

Another type of group is organized for purposes other than influencing the government and yet may devote some of its time to doing just that. Religious bodies are not organized for political purposes, yet many of them seek to influence government on a variety of issues. At times, to cite another example, a government agency itself may operate as an interest group. Some people regard the Army Corps of Engineers as one of the most effective interest groups in the United States, given its success in lobbying Congress for financial support of the various projects it wishes to undertake. Such governmental interest groups may establish close ties with the more familiar type of interest group; this gives the one the aura of popular support and the other the appearance of official endorsement.

Somewhere between the two common types of interest groups are the "corporatized" relations that have developed to a considerable extent in Europe between government and nongovernmental organizations. Because of certain groups' significance in the society, the government regularly consults with them before taking action that would affect their interests. In some instances the procedure is formalized, and special boards are created with membership composed of, for example, representatives of the government, the leading unions, and the principal manufacturing organizations. The quasi-governmental status of these groups obviously gives them considerable opportunity to influence the government.

Curiously, we also need to mention under the heading of interest groups those segments of the population that are hardly organized at all. In this case people do not consciously come together to further a shared interest. Instead, they have something in common; they share certain characteristics. They belong to the group by virtue of what they are; they don't have to join anything. The influence of such groups on public policy often is more potential than explicit. In deciding what laws to pass, legislators may consider how certain segments of the society would react, even though no officer of any such group has sought to influence them.

Given the limited organization of such groups, their leaders tend to be self-appointed or created by the mass media. The influence of Martin Luther King was based not simply on the fact that he headed an organized racial equality group (the Southern Christian Leadership Conference) but on the willingness of the public to recognize him as a major voice for the unorganized interest group consisting of the black segment of the American population. The influence of blacks on public policy extends beyond the efforts of groups organized around the shared interest of racial equality.

Interest groups differ not only in their nature but also in their means of contacting and influencing governmental officials. The common view of a lobbyist as an agent of an interest group calling on a legislator in an effort to affect the content of a law is much too narrow a perception of interest group activity. Interest groups devote a good deal of effort to developing contacts with bureaucrats. They seek to influence the content of any new regulations these officials might issue and to affect the way in which the existing rules and policies are applied in individual cases. A group that appears to have lost a battle in the legislature may be able to salvage a good deal through contacts with the appropriate bureaucrats when the law is put into effect.

Not every group enjoys the benefit of access channels to decision makers. A group's aims or the type or size of its membership may deny it legitimacy in the eyes of officials. Such groups may feel that they must resort to protests and demonstrations. These tactics may help to stimulate public awareness of their cause and may encourage decision makers to grant them access in order to defuse turmoil and disruption.

Political Parties

Political parties obviously have a good deal in common with interest groups. The principal difference is that, whereas interest groups seek to win the support of governmental officials for their views, parties offer candidates in an effort to win control of the government so as to be able to make policy decisions and to supervise putting them in effect.

Visualizing a modern democratic government without political parties is virtually impossible. So many groups proclaim their views that voters can't possibly examine the merits of all proposals and decide which are best. If you have ever had a problem in an ice cream store deciding which of the dozens of flavors you wanted, you can multiply that by a thousand to get some idea of how impossible democratic government would be unless parties existed. Parties weed out and filter group proposals so as to produce a coherent set of alternatives rather than a jumble of diverse, even contradictory, ideas. Parties simplify and focus policy issues so that voters are presented with a clear choice of contrasting programs and alternative leadership teams to implement them.

Once the electorate has made its choice in an election, parties carry out their function in contrasting ways. A party in power, by defending the policies and actions of its leaders, seeks to convince the people that the country is being governed in the best possible way; a party out of power, by criticizing the policies and actions (or inactions) of those running the country, tries to convert the people to the idea that it would do a better job. Whether this effort is limited to attacking those in power or includes as well detailed proposals for alternative policies is a matter of tactics. Democratic government is party government.

When discussing typologies in an earlier section, we noted that a frequently used one is based on the number of parties in a country. You can easily see that politics in a country where only one party legally may offer candidates and communicate with the citizens differs sharply from that in a country where two or more parties compete for support. But why distinguish between two-party and multiparty systems? The answer involves the basic function we've just been discussing.

In a multiparty system, especially one fractionalized into several sizable competitors, parties are unlikely to focus the alternatives for the voters very well. No single party is likely to hold a majority of the seats in the legislature; therefore, a coalition will have to be formed. The executive body, the cabinet, will have to be composed of people from more than one party. Obviously, the different parties in the coalition will agree on only some policies. Each party may well have presented the electorate with a set of integrated proposals, but only bits of each will be enacted. Forming a majority coalition may require including a policy from a splinter party's program that is at odds with the rest of the coalition's objectives. Furthermore, conflicts within the cabinet may cause its members to resign after only a short time in office, to be replaced by another tenuous collection of executive leaders. All coherence in policy is likely to be lost, and the choices offered to the voters will be confusing and ambiguous rather than being contrasting alternatives. France, Germany, and Italy have experienced such problems with multiparty systems during the twentieth century; however, the Scandinavian experience with such systems has been much more positive.

As we explained above, the American experience tended to nourish individual, rather than collective, values. In contrast, in Europe feelings of community solidarity and group distinctiveness have been common. The European value system has been conducive to religious, class, occupational, regional, and ethnic parties. The relative absence of pressures supporting such organizations in the United States has made maintaining a two-party system easier than in Europe, where such pressures have encouraged a fractionalized system. The contrasts between European and American value systems affect not only the nature of the party system, but also that of the parties themselves.

Parties may be pragmatic and able to work together in devising a coherent compromise program, or they may be rigidly dogmatic and refuse to cooperate with each other at all. Pragmatic/consensual parties can lower social tensions by encouraging many conflicting groups to feel that their causes are being effectively championed. Conversely, dogmatic/conflictual parties tend to worsen social divisions. Instead of seeking to bridge opposed groups, they often become the voice for a single segment and keep its fervent support by exaggerating its disagreements with other groups. Society is polarized, conflict becomes ideological, and disputes can't be resolved by bargaining. The result in this case is likely to be either a weak and ineffective minority cabinet—one in which the governing party or parties hold fewer than half the seats in the legislature—or a divided, and also ineffective, coalition.

Parties may be highly unified, or they may be loose collections of individuals and local or regional political machines. When parties are organized in the latter way—as the Democratic and Republican parties are in the United States—it is hard to argue that the alternatives have been focused so as to present a clear choice to voters. Although distinguishing two-party systems from multiparty ones is worthwhile, you can't automatically assume parties in every two-party system perform their basic function effectively. Conversely, if each party in a multiparty system of only three or four parties is relatively nonideological and highly unified, the task of simplifying and focusing the policy issues likely will be performed at least as well as in a two-party system with loosely organized parties.

As you study parties, you need to focus on four main aspects: doctrines and policies, supporters, strength, and organization. What does a particular party want to do, what views and actions does it want to make authoritatively binding on the entire population by having them sanctioned by government? Does it have a vision of totally transforming society and human nature or merely a list of preferred policies over which it is willing to bargain and compromise? Is it simply a personal following of an attractive leader, dedicated to attaining power largely for its own sake with little concern for policies? Elaborate intellectual analyses of society have had little appeal in the United States; American parties have not been ideological. European parties have tended to be ideologically based, that is, have offered the electorate an integrated set of proposals derived from a particular conception of society, rather than a collection of policies directed toward whatever issues seem currently most pressing.

Once you have discovered a party's program or objectives, you will want to know to whom this type of party appeals. From what groups, segments of society, and kinds of individuals does it get most of its support? Is it able, for example, to cut across the main social divisions of the society and thus help to moderate political conflict (a pragmatic/consensual party), or does it tend to reinforce and perpetuate existing divisions by drawing support from only one narrow segment (a dogmatic/conflictual party)? Remember that, as we suggested earlier, the absence of an explicit social hierarchy in the United States has helped to produce parties that are a collection of diverse groups. The adherents of one American party generally resemble the supporters of the other. In contrast, Europe's rather rigid social structure has produced parties of a different type.

Are most of a party's adherents so bound to it by socioeconomic factors that they will continue to support it come what may? Most Americans do have a sense of party identification; however, this doesn't prevent many of them from voting for the other party's candidates fairly often. Americans, unlike most Europeans, don't feel bound to the party with which they identify. If party loyalty is high, as it has been in Europe, how does this affect responsiveness? Since a party can count on continued support regardless of whether it attempts to ascertain or even listen to the policy preferences of its supporters, why should it bother?

Among the type of people to whom a party appeals, how many are willing to vote for it, join it, donate money to it? Is the party just a minor fringe one with no hope of influencing the government, much less controlling it, or is it a main competitor for political power? In most cases a party's strength is a good measure of its influence in the policy process.

Although a party's organization is important because of its impact on the party's strength, it also deserves study in its own right as a crucial factor in governmental accountability—one of the basic democratic characteristics. The way power is distributed within a party determines whether it can serve as a channel for communicating views of political activists to the government or it is so dominated by its leaders that communication is almost entirely from the top down, with party members serving simply to implement the leaders' views. In his Iron Law of Oligarchy, Roberto Michels maintained that the latter situation must necessarily prevail in all parties, however democratic they claim to be. If this were true, the policy-making process would be even more elite-dominated than it is.

Whether a political system with oligarchic parties can be termed democratic depends on whether you feel that in a democracy the people must have an influential role in the policy-making process as well as in the selection of leaders. Some would argue that the latter is sufficient—that the role of parties is not so much to assist people in formulating policies as to maintain competing sets of leaders who have been tested, apprenticed, and provided with political experience. By offering the electorate a choice among such potential officeholders, parties make democratic politics possible. Such a restrictive view, however, seems to lose sight of the point that those who have had some role in the making of a decision are more likely to accept the outcome, without having to be coerced, even if they don't like the substance of the decision. They may feel that they had a fair hearing and, since they were unable to convince enough others to support them, should gracefully accept defeat for the time being. Perhaps participating in the decision-making process may have helped them understand better the alternatives to their position and realize that those and the people who hold them aren't so bad after all. Whether such benefits can be obtained when participation involves little more than deciding for whom to vote is questionable.

Involving millions of people meaningfully in the policy process, however, is a formidable task. No country has yet been able to devise political structures capable of doing this satisfactorily. Even in democracies popular participation in policy making is limited.

▪ GOVERNMENTAL STRUCTURES AND PROCESSES

Electoral systems, groups, parties—these are the principal structures through which people can support the governmental system and its agents and make demands on them. The institutions of government are set forth in constitutions, which usually have little to say about parties and interest groups. A country's constitution almost invariably is written—Britain's is the best-known exception—but commonly is augmented by certain traditionally established political practices known as usages or conventions (not to be confused with gatherings of people to draw up constitutions or to nominate candidates). Although unmentioned in the written constitution, these are, nonetheless, an essential part of the country's political system. The U.S. Supreme Court's power to declare a law unconstitutional is an example of such a convention.

Although constitutions have existed since ancient times, the growth of the idea of limited government a few centuries ago was the main stimulus to the proliferation of such frameworks. The idea was to restrain royal power through a document spelling out the requirements of natural law. The early constitution makers did not assert that they were devising new procedures or admit to seeking legal support for their political preferences. They claimed only to be making explicit certain precepts of justice and of right that were said to be divinely established and, therefore, immutable and eternal.

Subsequently, constitutions were justified more pragmatically: an ordered political system with agreed-on procedures and specified rights seemed likely to minimize arbitrariness and discourage revolutionary disruptions, and thus produce greater stability. This defense came to be questioned as well. Obviously, merely putting words on paper doesn't guarantee anything if the ruling officials refuse to abide by them.

Nonetheless, evidence of the continued importance of constitutions and symbols in politics is that even nondemocratic countries feel compelled to have constitutions appearing to be democratic. Also notable is the flurry of constitution writing that occurred in the quarter century after World War II as national boundaries changed and former colonies gained independence. New countries were not the only ones to engage in such activities. Many people in Germany and Italy felt that defects in their countries' constitutions had permitted dictators to gain power. If only they could get the right procedures on paper, perhaps they could ensure against another lapse into dictatorship. Although such a view may put too much trust in the effectiveness of constitutions, constitutions can state a country's ideal political values and, thus, can influence political behavior.

The governmental structures that constitutions establish process the inputs from the channels for participation that we've discussed and convert them into authoritative rules binding on the entire society. The separation-of-powers ideal—well known to all high school civics students—encourages the belief that this process has three main subroutines: legislatures, with some help from the executive, make the rules; bureaucrats, under the direction of the executive, implement the rules; courts adjudicate the conflicts that arise under the rules. Unfortunately, reality is not this simple.

The law is not just the formal statutes passed by a legislature, but the entire body of binding rules for a society. Thus, administrators and judges make law just as surely as legislators do. Legislatures often draft statutes in general language, leaving detailed provisions to be filled in by administrators, whose power to make rules thus is expanded. The vast expansion of governmental activities over the past several decades has given administrators the job of deciding to whom and in what circumstances laws shall apply, since statutes often are ambiguous and the severity of enforcement varies, as you know if you have ever tried to talk your way out of a ticket at a highway speed trap.

The power of the courts to formulate authoritative rules is most obvious in a country such as the United States, where they have the power to void a rule made by the legislature by declaring it unconstitutional. When discussing democracy early in this chapter, we identified two key themes: constitutionalism and accountability. Although all democracies possess these characteristics, the balance between them varies from one system to another. The United States has emphasized the constitutional theme, and European democracies have tended to stress accountability. The United States has sought to impose legal limits on power and prevent its abuse by fractionalizing it among several governmental institutions. In Europe greater trust has been placed in political limits or sanctions on the abuse of power. Power has been concentrated but those wielding it have had to account for their actions. American office holders are accountable to the electorate periodically in elections. In Europe accountability has been carried further by making those entrusted with formulating and implementing public policy responsible *on a daily basis* to representatives of the people.

Even in democracies that do not put primary emphasis on the constitutional theme—Britain, for example—courts still are involved in rule making. Judges must interpret the law to apply it to particular cases. In doing so, they give meaning to the specific details of its provisions in practice.

Any delegation of legislative authority, intended or de facto, poses problems for democracy, since few judges or administrators are elected and most have permanent tenure, except in cases of malfeasance. How are these wielders of political power to be made accountable so as to maintain responsible government? The elected and accountable legislators and executives have the job of surveillance and control of administrators. In your study of any particular governmental system, you need to discover whether the arrangements for doing this provide sufficient power to control administrators without being so intrusive that efficiency is destroyed. Although everyone hates red tape, remember that that is simply a negative name for the procedures used to ensure that administrators are accountable.

In the case of the courts the matter is further complicated by the fact that no one in a democratic system wants to see the courts become partisan organs. Yet doesn't strict independence of the judiciary threaten to insulate judges from popular preferences so that all accountability is destroyed? Although what is right is not necessarily what the majority wants, a strong argument can be made that the courts should follow the election returns to a considerable extent.

Some countries use courts of quasi-judicial officials and procedures to try to control administrators. France, for example, has a separate system of courts purely for the adjudication of conflicts arising from challenges to administrative action. Britain and a few other countries have established the office of ombudsman, an official to whom complaints about administration can be referred and who will investigate whether citizens have been treated improperly in their contact with governmental officials. In either case the objective is to provide an opportunity for people to appeal or seek redress in situations where administrative power may have been abused.

The idea of using one governmental structure to control another is an element in both the separation-of-powers and the fusion-of-powers systems, which we defined earlier under the labels *presidential* and *parliamentary*. The difference is that in the first system no branch has the power to act alone, and in the second system the branch with the power (typically the executive) must explain its actions and seek frequent approval for them. In the presidential, or separation-of-powers, system, the legislature can refuse to enact the program favored by the executive and may have some power to block executive appointments. Neither branch of government may end the term of the other simply because of a clash over policy preferences. Thus, each branch has an element of independent power, which it can use to limit the action of the other. In the parliamentary, or fusion-of-powers, system, the legislature's power to control the executive extends to the ability to remove the executive from office simply because of a disagreement over programs and policies. In effect, the executive branch runs the government only so long as it satisfies, or retains the confidence of, its controller—the legislature.

In addition to these basic differences, legislative-executive relations are affected by the organization of the legislature. The rules of procedure may facilitate the passage of laws and create few, if any, obstacles to enacting the executive's legislative program. Alternatively, a number of procedural roadblocks may exist, as in the U.S. Congress, providing ample opportunity for ambushing proposed policies. Legislatures may have extensive information-gathering facilities that enable them to examine executive actions knowledgeably, or they may be dependent on the executive structures for expert knowledge, with a consequent lessening of the executive's accountability.

The personal characteristics and political style of leaders are important factors as well. Charles de Gaulle was able to dominate the French legislature for many years not so much because of the power vested in the office of President of France as because of his personality, background, and operating procedures. No other political figure in France at the time would have dared to decide the major issues on his or her own authority, as de Gaulle often did.

How legislative-executive relations operate in practice and the extent to which systems of either basic type achieve the goal of making power accountable depend to a considerable extent on the nature of the party system and the way in which parties operate in the legislature. Both this influence and that of leaders' personalities make clear that, important as the governmental structures themselves are, it is the system as it functions—the living body, rather than the bare bones of its skeleton—that matters most.

■ SYSTEM INSTITUTIONALIZATION AND DURABILITY

The fundamental purpose of the governmental system as it performs its basic function of making authoritative rules is to enable a society to adapt to, and thus cope successfully with, changes in its setting. The ability of a society to do this can be termed political development. Development is more than mere haphazard change; it is a purposive process. The focus on the goal sought makes development a normative, or at least an evaluative, concept.

The most fundamental concern in coping with changing circumstances must be simply to survive, to be durable. A political system with staying power is said to be institutionalized. This means that its structures are valued for themselves rather than for the popularity of those who hold positions in them. Charlemagne's attempt to revive the Roman Empire several centuries after its demise did not outlast his lifetime. The political system he created was divided among his grandsons, and Europe soon was more fragmented than it had been prior to his rule. Similarly, England descended into virtual anarchy following the death of William the Conqueror, and a few centuries later the republic created by Cromwell endured only a few years beyond his death. None of these rulers managed to institutionalize the governmental structures he initiated.

In contrast, Kamal Attaturk's work in modernizing Turkey early in the twentieth century did outlast him. He was able to transfer support for himself as a magnetic leader to support for the system he launched. His reforms became institutionalized. In the United States, the ability of the constitutional system to endure beyond Washington's service as President demonstrated that popular support was more than adulation of an extraordinary leader. The American system was becoming institutionalized.

In an institutionalized system, society employs known, regular procedures to grapple with public problems. Since conditions are constantly changing, however, commitment to these procedures must be tempered with flexibility. Institutionalizing a system does not require engraving it in stone; such monuments are erected to the dead, not the living. A living system needs to be dynamically stable, needs to maintain itself through change, in accord with established procedures, to meet new conditions. Change in any other way becomes a contest of brute force and defeats the purpose of creating a political system, which is to make possible human self-government in a civilized fashion.

Basic as durability is, survival alone isn't enough of an accomplishment. Why maintain a system able to do nothing other than perpetuate itself? A system must be able to achieve some other goals in order to provide various benefits to its people. Nonetheless, some systems prove able to endure for a time even if they are not very successful in meeting the challenge of their circumstances and are able to satisfy only a few of the demands made upon them. Poor performance can be offset by legitimacy; that is, people may feel that a system is morally sound and conforms to the basic values of the prevailing political culture. Most parents don't throw their children out of the house for coming in an hour late fairly often. Persistent severe malfunction, however, can exhaust the supply of legitimacy, forcing a major over-haul of the system and threatening violence. To speculate about a political system's prospects, you will need to have some idea how much legitimacy it has "in the bank," how institutionalized it is, in addition to knowing how well it is meeting the needs of its population.

Meeting popular needs might seem relevant to the durability of democratic sys-tems only; after all, autocratic regimes can maintain themselves by force and don't need to worry about whether people are satisfied with the government. In some senses, however, repression is self-defeating—the more a government uses it, the more it is likely to need to do so. Repression destroys those feelings of legitimacy that are the best buttress for the political system. When much of the public lacks such feelings, maintaining the system becomes a matter of force virtually all of the time. Although we are not suggesting that people armed with rocks can overthrow a regime armed with tanks, successful autocracies do recognize that force has its limits. As you will see in Part Five, Communist leaders under Mikhail Gorbachev came to recognize that political repression had a self-defeating effect through its negative impact on the Soviet Union's economy. They conceded that the repressive measures of seven decades directly contributed to the climate of widespread cyni-cism, indifference, and disaffection among many Soviet workers and inevitably pro-duced economic decline.

In the final decade of the twentieth century, the most prominent challenges to political system durability involve possible or actual fragmenting. To understand why this is occurring requires distinguishing between the terms *country* and *nation*. A country is a legal entity recognized to have jurisdiction over a given terri-tory. The various political systems that have existed and currently are established are countries. A nation is a group of people holding a common sense of identity, typically produced by such shared characteristics as customs, culture, language, ethnic background, and history.

Countries and nations often aren't coterminous, resulting in significant strains and tensions. Most people living in northern Belgium are Flemish; they have a Germanic heritage. Most people living in southern Belgium are Walloons and have links with France. The sense of separate identities held by these two groups, but-tressed by linguistic differences, has troubled Belgian politics for many years and has fragmented the party system into two sets of parties. Tension between the French population of Quebec and the rest of Canada has caused concern that the country may not continue to exist in the twenty-first century. As we'll discuss in Part Two, Britain is one country, but is composed of four nations—English, Scots, Welsh, and Irish. This ethnic diversity has been a major issue in British politics in recent years. In spite of the strains, Belgium, Canada, and Britain have managed to handle the problem of non-coincidence of country and nation better than some other political systems have.

Communism denied ethnic-national differences, or at least proclaimed that they were trivial compared to a political system's economic arrangements. An individual's status in the productive process mattered much more than his or her ethnicity. Communism was unable to eliminate national differences, however, and once its oppressive regimes crumbled, nationalism reasserted itself. One result has been a horrendous civil war among Serbs, Croats, and Bosnians in the former Yugoslavia. Similarly, a number of civil wars and widespread unrest have marked the passing of the former Soviet Union. By 1993 there had been 125 different ethnic disputes in the fifteen countries that used to make up the single country of the Soviet Union. At least 25 of those disputes were armed conflicts, in which tens of thousands died and hundreds of thousands were forced into exile to seek asylum in other countries as refugees. Some of those armed conflicts even threatened to escalate into major regional wars involving several countries bordering the Middle East and Central Europe.

Despite decades of belonging to the same country, various post-Soviet nations —including Russia, Ukraine, Azerbaijan, and Armenia—have found since 1991 that they have very little in common to bind them together now that Communism no longer imposes a form of community. Even within Russia, Ukraine, and several other of these post-Soviet countries, the ethnic groups that make up the majority of their populations confront challenges from numerous ethnic-religious minorities to break away and form their own countries. The minorities consider themselves nations and feel that the majority nation in their countries discriminates against and persecutes them.

The distinction between nation and country has become a major source of conflict among the newly emerging countries of the former Soviet Union. Over 25 million ethnic Russians live outside what has been since 1991 the country of Russia. The Russian government of President Boris Yeltsin has continuously protested the perceived mistreatment of these ethnic Russians by their countries of residence. The war of words between Russia and these countries at times has threatened to escalate into war. We'll discuss all these matters more fully in Part Five.

Whether a multi-nation country proves durable or breaks up into its component ethnic groups involves such a unique configuration of circumstances that providing a generally valid explanation is difficult. Clearly, repression can hold diverse people together in a single political system for some time. In more democratic systems, a key question is whether a component nation feels threatened. Are what the nation believes to be basic rights—the power to make French the language of instruction in Quebec's schools, for example—guaranteed? Does the nation have an influential voice, perhaps even a veto, in the making of public policy? Does the nation receive significant economic benefits, including regional subsidies, by remaining a part of the country? Would it be economically viable as a separate country? Although a material cost/benefit analysis may help to keep a nation within its current country, rationality doesn't always triumph. To take another post-Communist example, Czechoslovakia divided into the Czech Republic and Slovakia despite the fact that the latter nation became worse off economically than if it had remained part of the existing bi-national country. Feelings of ethnic diversity were so great that they overcame economic calculation. That is, symbolic gratification mattered more than material satisfaction.

Although breakup of political systems is the dominant trend toward the close of the twentieth century, there are a few instances of the pursuit of broader political systems. One of the most prominent examples is an effort to make country and nation coincide more closely; in another the trend has been toward an ever more nationally diverse political system. Once Communism collapsed, the dream of reuniting the divided nation that had been enshrined in the West German constitution for forty years could be realized. For both East and West Germans a shared sense of Germanness, of a cultural heritage, provided a feeling of community despite many regional differences in dialect and customs. Furthermore, East Germans could anticipate economic benefits, an improved standard of living, from reunion with the West, and West Germans were willing, at least initially, to pay the bills. We'll discuss German unification more fully in Part Four. The relevant point here is that in this instance, in contrast to the others we've discussed, nationalism has produced union rather than disunion.

The other example of countries combining into a larger political system is the European Union (EU). This development has taken place in the face of nationalism, which is precisely why the process has been rather halting. Whether Europeanness can provide sufficient shared values to overcome centuries of national differences and create a political community rather than a cooperative association will be discussed in Part Six. Whatever the result, the EU is evidence that not all nations are seeking ever smaller, more homogeneous political systems. It provides some countervailing influence to the force of national particularism. Somewhat similarly, several of the countries that used to make up the Soviet Union and its Eastern European empire are attempting to form new international economic and political communities. We discuss some of these early efforts toward regional integration in our analysis of the relations among Russia and countries in Central Eurasia following the collapse of the Soviet Union.

■ WHERE DO WE GO FROM HERE?

We have set forth for you some of the principal concepts and topics in the comparative study of politics. We have pointed out how these topics relate to each other and why they deserve your interest. Our aim is to help you understand what political scientists specializing in comparative politics do and why.

Over the last half century scholars have offered a number of theories or approaches as frameworks for organizing information so as to reveal and make understandable patterns of political behavior. None of these has won acceptance by a majority of political scientists. We are not going to propose yet another elaborate set of abstract concepts. We do need, however, to give you an overview of how we have organized the material in this book and explain why we have included some topics and omitted others.

Rather than covering a lot of countries superficially, we examine four major international powers—Britain, France, Germany, and Russia—in some detail and also take a look at the other fourteen post-Soviet countries. Britain, France, and Germany are all European countries. Since Russia and the other fourteen post-Soviet countries are both European and Asian, we'll refer to them collectively as Russia and Central Eurasia to acknowledge that the one-sixth of the world's land mass they occupy overlaps two continents.

Britain, France, and Germany do differ from the United States in many ways, but you should find them less exotic than you would African, Asian, or, perhaps, even Latin American countries. Studying them should be most useful in gaining perspective on American political practices. And since these three are from the same relatively small region, they are more likely to have common elements in their political heritages than would be the case for countries from different corners of the world. Such similarity makes comparative study easier. The fifteen countries of Russia and Central Eurasia are much less similar, but a majority of them share a common European cultural and historical origin. The various countries of Russia and Central Eurasia have consciously sought to one extent or another since 1991 to model themselves politically on the parliamentary democracies of Western Europe, thus producing some similarity with the other three countries included in this book.

Despite sharing the European tradition, the countries we'll discuss differ sufficiently to make comparisons interesting. Although none of them has been able to devise a set of governmental institutions capable of processing all opposed demands for action without experiencing some resort to violence, they differ in the frequency and level of such violence. Russia and Central Eurasia underwent two full-scale revolutions in the twentieth century; Britain has not experienced even one. Britain's political system has altered relatively little in the past century. Some people argue that the reforms required to meet the current needs of the British people demand at least extralegal, perhaps violent, action. Why, then, has resort to violence been much less common in British politics than in Russian politics in the twentieth century? Why do governmental institutions in one country prove much more capable of winning popular support than do those in another? During the past two centuries a single constitutional system has sufficed for the United States; why has France needed over a dozen different regimes?

Although each country has its own part in this book, we don't discuss it in complete isolation. In particular, we comment on similarities or contrasts with the American system. So your study of foreign governments should help you to see which aspects of politics in the United States are unique products of its particular culture and which are common across national boundaries.

The most straightforward way to organize the material would be to focus on one governmental or political institution after another. The problem with such an approach is that it suggests that all governmental bodies labeled, for example, legislatures do basically the same thing. As you'll learn from this book, the functions of the British legislature are quite different from those of the U.S. Congress, and the functions of both of them differ considerably from those performed by the legislature of the former Soviet Union. Furthermore, structures change over time and come to perform different functions from those they once did. The Soviet legislature is a prime example. As our chapters on Russia and Central Eurasia will explain, a major goal of political reform under Gorbachev's leadership in 1985–1991 was to transform the country's legislature into the most influential political institution. Political functions traditionally monopolized by the Communist Party bureaucracy and unelected government officials were to be transferred to full-time legislative deputies elected by the people through competitive secret balloting. Gorbachev's successors in the countries of Russia and Central Eurasia have found their own new legislatures to be too powerful. Many of their members are actually holdovers from the former Soviet Union, elected to their national legislatures despite their lack of sympathy with the goals of instituting market economies and democracies in their countries. The national political leaders in Russia and Central Eurasia have sought to curtail legislative power, and some have actually reinstituted autocracies. Others, for example, President Yeltsin in Russia, have attempted only to reduce the power of their national legislatures along lines similar to that on which Charles de Gaulle sought to push France some three decades earlier.

An alternative way of presenting the material would be to focus on the basic functions that must be performed in every political system and explain how the mix of institutions involved in performing a particular function varies from one country to another. Although this functional approach is informative, it has a drawback. If you were asked after reading such a book what the purpose and powers of the House of Commons were, you might have some difficulty in answering, since you would have to pull together material from several different chapters. You might well have learned something about an abstract concept known as the interest aggregation function or the rule-making function, but probably only at the cost of being rather uncertain about what real institutions such as the Commons and the Cabinet actually do.

We have tried to combine these approaches. We've divided each part into chapters that focus primarily on a particular structure or institution (governmental or political), describing its formal status and explaining how it operates in practice. What structures and procedures have been devised in each of the countries to resolve conflict, to make authoritative (not to be confused with authoritarian) decisions concerning the distribution of benefits and values? What channels exist for individuals and groups seeking to participate in politics and to secure the backing of the government for their policy preferences?

We lack sufficient space for a detailed account of the content of public policy in most specific areas. Thus, we must emphasize political and governmental machinery more than output. The basic research question in the study of politics can be put like this: who governs by what means for what purpose? We are placing least emphasis on the last part of this question. We will not be discussing individual motivation to any great extent, nor will we proceed very far in examining the impact of societal goals on the quality of life, except where this has particular relevance for the maintenance of the political system.

Despite our focus on structures, we are also concerned with the performance of functions. We analyze the role each structure plays in its country's total system. Some of our chapter titles indicate the main purpose, or principal function, of a given institution. You will want to note, as your study moves from one country to another, how the significant political functions are discharged in contrasting ways involving different structures.

As we set forth the various structural arrangements and allocation of functions in these countries, you may well become lost in details. You certainly need to learn a good bit of new information. Do not lose sight, however, of the twin underlying concerns of the concentration of power and its accountability. If power is too fractionalized, too dispersed within a political system, then accomplishing anything is difficult. Concentrated power, however, facilitates not only doing good for the citizens, but also doing ill—depriving them, perhaps, of their basic liberties and freedoms. Where power is dispersed, people may enjoy freedom and liberty. But when the system fails to deliver the goods, to produce the policy output to meet the people's needs, then eventually they will become disillusioned and their commitment to the system will weaken. Power must be concentrated, but it also must be accountable. The final assessment of any system turns on whether its structures provide for effective power constrained by constitutionalism and accountability.

We start first with the political system that, because of historical ties and a shared language, is likely to seem less exotic to Americans. You'll see that in Britain the power to govern has long been concentrated. In the twentieth century the growing strength of parties and the declining influence of Parliament, however, have undercut accountability. On the other hand, France for most of this century suffered from dispersed power; little capacity to deal with pressing problems existed. In the last three and a half decades, that flaw has been remedied, but in a fashion still rather controversial. Part of the remedy was a major constitutional transformation, but equally important were personal leadership and decreased party fractionalization. The same comments apply to Germany as well, except that the German solution has proved less controversial.

Surprisingly, given our comment about Britain being less exotic, you may find the French system and, especially, the German one more similar to the American than the British is. France has a strong, popularly elected President, something that you will look for in vain in Britain. As for Germany, relations between the executive and legislative branches and between the central and subnational units of government are more balanced—more American, if you will—than is the case in either Britain or France. Although you will find familiar features in each of these three countries, try to focus on the ways in which they differ from the United States and on how they are fundamentally like each other. Look for the basic contrast between the American and the European political traditions.

In the parts on Britain, France, and Germany, we begin by discussing the context in which the political system operates—geography, demographics, economic conditions, and so forth. Then we briefly summarize each country's history. That leads logically (to us, at any rate) to examining the fundamental political values that that history both has produced and illustrates. How have those values been embodied in basic constitutional principles?

The remaining chapters for each of these three countries describe the system as it exists currently, along with information on how it has developed since World War II. The organization of these chapters follows a simple model of the political process. First are political inputs, the channels through which people, by themselves or in cooperation with others, can get their needs and desires into the policy-making process. That is, we start with discussion of electoral arrangements and interest groups. Next come political parties, the structures whose job it is to process and focus the myriad of demands the people make for governmental action. How are these parties organized, and what policies do they offer? How much support do they have and from whom?

The next chapters in each part deal with the governmental institutions. The next stage of the political process is for the legislature and the executive to enact into public policy some of the popular demands that the parties have helped to identify. How do these two branches, especially the former, go about doing this? What is the relative balance of power between them? And what do these arrangements mean for responsiveness to the people, for accountability of power?

Next the bureaucrats have to implement the policies. Who are those entrusted with this most important task of all? How responsive are they likely to be to popular sentiments, and how accountable? Do the procedures that seek to ensure accountability impede efficiency? Finally, what about conflicts between the individual and the government or among individuals themselves? Perhaps policies or the way in which they are implemented produce conflicts. Perhaps policies fail to resolve the conflicts they were intended to, and yet another cycle of the policy-making process is needed. Again, who are the people entrusted with settling conflicts about the law, and how accountable are they? What role do they have not just in settling disputes, but in actually making policy?

In Part Five on Russia and Central Eurasia, we begin with an evaluation of the bold efforts made by Gorbachev and Yeltsin to transform the Soviet system from a rigid single-party autocracy into a Western-type parliamentary democracy. We focus on underlying trends, factors of importance for understanding the politics of this area, regardless of who currently leads it or how governmental institutions change. Familiarity with the broad sweep of Russian history and an understanding of the various forces contending for change are essential for this purpose.

By the early 1990s political changes in Russia and Central Eurasia had blurred the previous sharp contrast between the democratic Western European countries and what had been the autocratic Soviet system. The Western democracies of Britain, France, and Germany, as well as the United States, are exactly the systems on which democratic reformers in Russia and Central Eurasia are basing their attempts to alter their governments. They have spoken openly of their intention to erect a political system on a foundation of majority will, minority rights, the rule of law and supremacy of a constitution, a separation of powers with checks and balances among the three branches of government, equal rights and civil liberties for the citizens, and political pluralism. Locke, Montesquieu, Jefferson, and Madison have been cited frequently as the inspirational sources for the current democratic reforms.

Part Two

The United Kingdom of Great Britain and Northern Ireland

Democracy in Russia and Central Eurasia still has a very uncertain future and confronts numerous problems and obstacles. Democracy obviously is more firmly established in Britain, France, and Germany. But there as well it is tested by severe strains and challenges. Therefore, the first chapter in Part Six seeks to evaluate the prospects for European democracy. How durable will this form of government prove to be? To what extent can it adapt to changing circumstances without losing its distinctive political values, beliefs, and attributes?

The final chapter differs from the rest of the book in that it doesn't deal with a particular country. Although it might be seen as focusing on international relations, the better view is that it focuses on system building. We discuss the extent to which a growing number of European democracies are relinquishing some sovereignty to a new governmental entity. Is the EU merely a trade and commercial organization or is a United States of Europe being born? Are the supranational organs whose functions have been expanding yet another example of remote bureaucratic government? Do they attenuate democracy by impeding Europeans' ability to control those who exercise significant power to regulate their lives? Or can enhanced cross-national services and standards be obtained without homogenization? Can the benefits of unity be realized without sacrificing the virtues of diversity? Whatever the answers, they won't produce lives that are "poor, nasty, brutish, and short," but they most certainly will determine "who gets what, when, and how" for millions of Europeans.

Tho' much is taken, much abides; and tho'
We are not now that strength which in old days
Moved earth and heaven; that which we are, we are;
One equal temper of heroic hearts,
Made weak by time and fate, but strong in will
To strive, to seek, to find and not to yield.

Tennyson

.....1

The Setting of British Politics

■ THE INFLUENCE OF GEOGRAPHY

First, where is this place? More than two-fifths of adult Americans don't know. If you look at a map of Europe, you can easily find Italy because it is shaped like a boot. Moving up and to the left from there, you'll see some islands off the northwest coast of Europe. The largest of these is Britain.

The twenty miles of water between southern England and the Continent certainly have been a geographic feature of major significance in British history. Britain has frequently intervened in continental conflicts to maintain a balance of power such that no country or alliance would be strong enough to threaten it. Nonetheless, the English Channel has enabled Britain to escape being fully involved in a number of European wars and has saved the country from invasion since the Norman Conquest in 1066. France and Poland—to mention only two examples—doubtless would have liked twenty miles of water separating them from their neighbors.

Not surprisingly, then, it is only recently that a tunnel under the English Channel to connect Britain with the Continent has been constructed, after having been discussed for over a century. If you enjoy the type of book known as alternate history, you will be fascinated to learn about the rash of books that appeared in Britain toward the close of the nineteenth century.[1] The first story of an invasion of Britain through a Channel tunnel (successfully by the Germans) appeared in 1876. From 1882 to 1883 at least eight books were published on this theme, with the French usually being depicted as the invaders. While British imaginations were running riot in this fashion, the French showed not the slightest interest in speculating about a British invasion of France. These "alarums" eventually blew over, although such stories continued to trickle out in Britain until 1901.[2]

---

[1]I. F. Clarke, *Voices Prophesying War 1763–1984* (London: Oxford University Press, 1966), pp. 109–113.
[2]On the other hand, the creator of Sherlock Holmes, Arthur Conan Doyle, published a story favoring a tunnel only a month before World War I. In his story Britain lost a war because a naval blockade of submarines cut off the food supply. Ibid., p. 103.

Although hardly isolationist, the British have not thought of themselves as being an integral part of Europe. They have felt that their history of stable government and their basic liberties have produced a political tradition and demonstrated a competence different from and superior to those of most European nations. When in the 1960s President Charles de Gaulle of France barred Britain from the European Economic Community (EEC), saying that the British were not really Europeans, there was some truth in his position. Britain's traditional aloofness from the Continent helps to explain why the country has been so skeptical about the EEC. Had it not been for twenty miles of water and the history associated with it, Britain almost certainly would have been a charter member. As it is, not only was Britain late in joining, but the question of whether the country should pull out remained an issue in British politics for some time after it became a member.

British public opinion on the EEC and its successor, the European Community (EC), has fluctuated almost at random. At the start of the 1960s, two-fifths of Britons favored British membership, one-fifth opposed it, and one-third didn't know. At the start of the 1970s, only one-fifth favored, three-fifths opposed, and one-fifth didn't know. Nonetheless, Britain became a member in 1973. In 1975 a referendum was held (the first time such an outrageous innovation had been tried) on whether Britain should remain a member. One-third of the electorate didn't bother to vote, but among those who did, the split was two to one in favor of retaining membership. By the 1980s, however, opinion had shifted again, and fewer than one-third supported continued membership. In the mid-1980s only a quarter said they would be very sorry if the whole EC was terminated; a third said they were indifferent to such an event; another third said they would be relieved if it happened. The public's views continue to be volatile. Some polls find more people in favor of continued membership than against; others find the reverse to be true. A bill aimed at integrating Britain more fully into the EC was an extraordinarily contentious issue in the legislature in the mid-1990s. Many members of the political elite, as well as of the public, are very reluctant to cede any more power from their country to the EC.

Being an island has been important for British history in other ways as well. No Briton ever is farther than 75 miles from tidal water or 110 miles from the ocean proper. Birmingham, in what the British call the Midlands, is only 95 miles from the sea (see Figure 1–1). What could be more natural, then, than Britain's being a maritime country? Britain has long been the home of world explorers and traders, which made it a center for world commerce. As its international trade grew, so also did its industries, cities, and commerce. Furthermore, international trade and the need to control the sea lanes went hand in hand. On the other hand, since an island does not need to worry about defending land frontiers, Britain rarely saw the need for a large standing army. (Early in the nineteenth century it had only 11,000 soldiers, an army smaller than the Chicago police force in 1968.) Instead, Britain developed its naval power. The navy, not the army, has been known as the Senior Service.

This sea power helped Britain to obtain a worldwide empire. Although an important weapon in international relations, a navy is of limited assistance in combating domestic challenges to governmental authority. For most of Britain's history, royal absolutism has been easier to combat than it was on the European continent,

Figure 1–1
Travel Times by
Regular Rail Service
from London to
Other Cities

where large armies were common and could be used by rulers to put down dissent. The deemphasis of the army in Britain has helped to keep the country free of the militarism that often has been a problem in German history.

Don't call the country we've been talking about England. The island you located earlier is composed of three nations: England, Wales, and Scotland. Scots, in particular, do not appreciate being called English. Furthermore, there is more to the country than the one island. To the left of Britain, you'll see another sizable island, which is composed of two countries. The southern and larger part is Eire, or the Republic of Ireland. At one time it was linked to Britain. For about two-thirds of a century, however, it has been a separate, independent country. The upper right-hand corner of the island, Northern Ireland, broke away when the rest of Ireland became independent and continues to be linked with Britain.

Thus, the full, official name for this political system is the United Kingdom of Great Britain and Northern Ireland. In order to have a less cumbersome label, some people use just United Kingdom or the abbreviation U.K. Britain is accepted as correct for semi-official purposes, but strictly speaking that term includes only England, Scotland, and Wales.

As you can see from Table 1–1, England is by far the largest—both in area and population—of the four nations making up the United Kingdom. This accounts for the common error of calling the entire system England. (People made the same mistake in referring to the former Soviet Union as Russia.) Nonetheless, each of the four has its own distinctive features and importance, and what is true in England frequently is not in the other three.

© King Features. Reprinted with permission of King Features Syndicate Inc.

Table 1–1

Size of Component
Nations of the United
Kingdom

	Population (millions)	Area in square miles (thousands)	Population density per square mile
England	47.7	50.4	946
Scotland	5.1	30.4	168
Wales	2.9	8.0	363
Northern Ireland	1.6	5.5	287
Total	57.2	94.2	607

By American standards the United Kingdom is small—from the northern tip of Scotland to the southern coast of England is just under 600 miles; California's length is a third greater. As for area, the United Kingdom is about the size of the state of Oregon. Although the United Kingdom has a population only a quarter as large as that of the United States, it is one of the world's more populous countries—only a dozen have more people.

Having so many people in such a small area means that the United Kingdom is very densely populated (see the figures in Table 1–1). The United Kingdom is nearly ten times more densely populated than the United States and more densely populated than India. Parts of Scotland are relatively sparsely populated, which lowers the density for the United Kingdom as a whole. England by itself has more people per square mile than Japan does.

Dense population almost of necessity means high urbanization. More than four times as many people in England and Wales live in urban districts (one of the subdivisions of local government) as in rural districts. Much more so than Americans, Britons are city dwellers. Surprisingly, however, one city is preeminent. London is the political, cultural, and commercial hub of the country; the concentration of these various activities is not split among a number of cities as it is in the United States. An eighth of the entire population of the United Kingdom lives in London and its suburbs. No other city has as many as a million people, although Birmingham is nearly that large. Next come Leeds and Glasgow in Scotland, the first somewhat over and second a bit under 700,000. Fourth is Sheffield at about a half million.

High urbanization tends to strain governmental capabilities because of increased demand for public services. Crime control, transportation, health and sanitation, food distribution, recreational facilities, and so forth, which can be handled on a private basis when most people live in rural areas, become pressing public concerns when the population is concentrated in urban settings. Whatever the political philosophy of the party in power, government must play a more active, interventionist role in a highly urbanized society than in one that is more rural.

The smallness of Britain and the concentration of population in urban areas are a great aid to communication, especially given the extensive rail network that has existed for many decades. As Figure 1–1 indicates, from London a train ride of only an hour and a half takes you to Birmingham. With a journey of two and a half hours, you can reach most of the principal English cities, including Exeter in the West Country (the peninsula that juts out to the southwest into the Atlantic Ocean) and

Manchester and Leeds to the north. Even Newcastle, about forty-five miles from the Scottish border, can be reached in three and a half hours. This rail network enables England to have a national press, something that has not developed in the United States. People who live in the north or west can read with their breakfast an earlier edition of the same newspaper that Londoners read. Papers published in the capital city circulate widely throughout the country and help to nationalize opinion. Unlike the United States, England has no important regional news media centers.

The smaller a country's area, the less likely it is to have regional differences in such features as geography, climate, lifestyle, occupational structure, and social relations. Add to this the national press just mentioned and you'd be justified in guessing that Britons are likely to react similarly to political events regardless of where they live. You shouldn't expect the contrasts in attitudes from one region of the country to another that you know to be common in the United States. The differences between the U.S. and U.K. environments long led American students of British politics to stress the great homogeneity of Britain and its people. This point has been greatly overemphasized. The fact that the United Kingdom is composed of four separate nations suggests, in itself, considerable diversity.

Wales was joined with England in 1535 and had been an English possession for two and a half centuries before then. You might think this would be sufficient time for Wales to be fully integrated into the political system. Nonetheless, many people in Wales do not feel any great sense of association with England. The Welsh have a distinctive culture, which is reinforced by having their own language. You need only know that the name of the town Pontypridd is pronounced something like "Ponta-preeth" to understand that Welsh has little similarity to English. In rural parts of Wales, printing election campaign material in Welsh or speaking Welsh at campaign rallies is not unusual.

About a quarter of all the people in Wales can speak Welsh (virtually all of them can speak English as well), but in northwest Wales the proportion rises to nearly two-thirds. The number of children in Wales who could speak Welsh had been declining for over a half century, but has been rising in recent years. Welsh is a required subject for all schools in Wales. Furthermore, more than 12 percent of all primary school children in Wales are taught all their subjects in Welsh, and an additional 7 percent are taught some courses in Welsh. Thus, for a fifth of the children, Welsh is a language of instruction.

The Scottish sense of a separate national identity has little to do with language. Less than 2 percent of the Scots can speak their language, Gaelic, although most do speak English with a distinctive accent (one of several accents, in fact, depending on whether the person comes from Glasgow, the Highlands, or elsewhere in Scotland). Scotland was joined to England more recently (in 1707) than was Wales, and its long earlier history and battles with the English have helped to produce a sense of national identity.

We hope you noticed that our comments about a national press referred to England, not Britain. Although most London-published papers can be obtained at breakfast time in Scotland, their circulation there tends to be limited. The typical Glaswegian is unlikely to read the same paper as a Londoner. The existence of a distinctive Scottish media system significantly limits the homogenizing effect of the press on political opinion in the United Kingdom.

As an example of Scottish separateness, look at the TV listings below for the day in 1987 when England was playing Brazil in a major international football (soccer) game. While the English were glued to the tube cheering on their team, Scots were viewing a seven-year-old movie of less than classic quality. Appearing with the TV listings is a wrapper from a sugar cube typically found in restaurants in Scotland. Can you imagine traveling across the United States and finding restaurant sugar wrapped especially for Texas or Kansas?

Discovery and exploitation of oil in the North Sea in the 1970s and 1980s reinforced separatist feelings by suggesting that Scotland could be economically viable as an independent country. Thus, although for contrasting reasons, in the 1970s support erupted for Welsh and Scottish nationalist movements wanting their nations to break away from the United Kingdom and become independent. These groups' continued impact on the politics of these sections of the country clearly demonstrates the importance of regional factors in British politics.

Northern Ireland presents yet another situation. All of Ireland was joined to Britain in 1800. The Irish never ceased to agitate for their independence. The conflict frequently was violent and culminated in a major insurrection immediately after World War I. Most of Ireland, the predominantly Catholic southern part, was granted independence. The northern six counties, which were mainly Protestant, preferred to remain linked with Britain. This partition of Ireland into two segments—one within and one outside of the United Kingdom—failed to settle the conflict. Although Catholics are in a minority in Northern Ireland, they account for about a third of the population. Discrimination and retaliation have been rife for generations. Most Catholics would like to be part of the Republic of Ireland, and most

Scottish

1	0	News.
1	20	Scottish News.
1	30	Family Theater.
2	30	As Granada.
5	15	Emmerdale Farm.
5	45	News.
6	0	Scotland Today.
6	25	Crossroads.
6	50	Take the High Road.
7	20	Carry on Laughing.
7	50	Film: Bear Island. 1980 Arctic adventure with Richard Widmark Donald Sutherland Vanessa Regrave
10	0	As Granada.

English

7 50 INTERNATIONAL FOOTBALL SPECIAL: England v. Brazil. Live from Wembley, with Nick Owen introducing live coverage of the first Rous Cup match, the 14th encounter between the two national sides. Kevin Keegan joins Brian Moore in the commentary box.

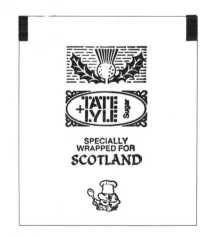

SPECIALLY
WRAPPED FOR
SCOTLAND

Protestants are adamantly opposed to such a change. Beginning in the late 1960s, political assassinations, bombings, riots, armed conflict between Protestants and Catholics, and extended use of military troops by the U.K. government to maintain order amply demonstrated that sectarian factors play a much greater role in politics in Northern Ireland than they do in the rest of the United Kingdom.

Thus, this kingdom may well be united, but it certainly is not homogeneous. Despite its smallness, the United Kingdom has considerable diversity. However, it does lack one characteristic of diversity found in the United States—a sizable minority group. About 8 percent of the population is Catholic and less than 1 percent is Jewish, each proportion being less than a third as big as in the United States. The proportion of nonwhites—called "coloureds" by some Britons and "blacks" by others (even though they are referring to Indians and Pakistanis as well as Africans and West Indians)—is around 5 percent of the population. The small numbers of nonwhites have not, however, prevented race relations from becoming an important issue in British politics, as we'll discuss in the next chapter.

■ ■ ■

In summary, then, geography has had an immense impact on both the domestic politics and the international relations of the United Kingdom. It has made the country both outward-looking and yet separate from Europe. Its maritime setting made the seas not only commercial highways, but also avenues that led to discovery, exploration, empire building, and naval supremacy. This meant great national power but without the lengthy history of absolute rule common in many continental countries. Britain's dense population and urbanization facilitated the Industrial Revolution—another element in its rise to world power—and encouraged an expanded role for government. Despite its smallness, the country has a number of regional diversities, many of which are significant for its politics.

■ ASPECTS OF THE ECONOMY

As the home of the Industrial Revolution, Britain has long been a world economic power. Coal, iron, good harbors, and urbanized population all helped to make it the first industrial nation. This economic strength was a major source of its world power in the nineteenth and early twentieth centuries.

Prior to the Industrial Revolution, Britain had a strong agricultural economy. Moderate temperatures (hard freezes are rare and anything over 70 degrees Fahrenheit is considered a heat wave), easily accessible fertile land, and abundant rainfall (the country averages only about four hours of sunshine a day) enabled Britain to produce the great bulk of its needed foodstuffs until about a century and a half ago.

As Britain industrialized and its population grew, it began importing large quantities of food. Advances in ocean transportation and Britain's unsuitability, relative to countries such as Canada and the United States, for raising wheat meant that, increasingly, food products could be imported more economically than they could

© King Features. Reprinted with permission of King Features Syndicate Inc.

be produced at home. Britain's strength in manufactured goods made the doctrine of free trade attractive, so tariffs were eliminated to give the population inexpensive imported food.

By the middle of the nineteenth century, British agriculture was little protected or encouraged. Only between the world wars did British farmers again receive some tariff protection, and only during World War II was an elaborate farm subsidy system developed. As a result, Britain is not self-sufficient in food production and must engage in international trade to feed its people. Furthermore, since it lacks many natural resources, it has to import raw materials for its industries.

Thus, Britain's international balance of payments is a matter of national survival. A country must sell sufficient manufactured goods to obtain the foreign currencies needed to pay for necessary imports of foodstuffs and raw materials. Whatever the political philosophy of the party in power, considerable intervention in economic affairs is likely to be necessary. Inflation and low productivity are not just domestic problems; they carry the danger that Britain will price itself out of its international markets. The British government often must use taxes, currency controls, export/import regulations, and similar devices to affect the domestic economy and alter consumption patterns.

Paradoxically, having been a pioneer of the Industrial Revolution proved in the long run to be something of a liability for Britain. As technology advanced, more efficient methods of production were invented. British industry hesitated to modernize, reluctant to abandon the old methods that had made it a world leader. Consequently, for much of the latter part of the twentieth century, British industry suffered from obsolete equipment and made little use of modern management techniques.

During the 1960s and 1970s the annual percentage increase in gross domestic product (GDP) in the United Kingdom was only a half, or even a third, of that in other major Western countries. Double-digit inflation and balance of payments deficits made the economy Britain's most pressing problem in the 1970s. The country's currency (the pound sterling) had to be devalued by more than 14 percent in 1967 and then began an alarming drop in value in the mid-1970s. By 1976 it was worth only about two-thirds as much as it had been a decade earlier. Further declines by 1984 had reduced its value to less than half of what it had been twenty years before.

Britain's fear that it would lose many of its traditional markets eventually forced it to seek membership in the EEC. This step freed British products intended to be sold in much of Europe from the EEC's common external tariff. Those supporting British membership hoped that the economies of scale involved in producing for a continental-sized market and the heightened competitive challenge of no protection from the output of continental countries would help to strengthen British industry.

Although the government eventually managed to get inflation under control, this appeared to have been done at the cost of rising unemployment. Traditionally, Britain had regarded a half million unemployed as normal. By the mid-1980s the number of people out of work had soared to above 3.25 million. This was a greater number than had been without jobs even in the Great Depression of the 1930s, although the growth in the size of the population since then meant that the unemployed were not as large a percentage of the work force.

As Britain's oil fields in the North Sea began full production toward the close of the 1970s, the country moved rapidly toward self-sufficiency in oil. Thus, the United Kingdom (sometimes referred to as the sheiks of Europe) was not affected as greatly as were many other countries by the huge increases in the prices charged by OPEC countries. This good fortune put the British balance of payments in surplus from 1980 through 1985 and eventually reversed the declining value of the pound. "All's Well That Ends Well," you might have said were you a British Prime Minister given to quoting your country's most illustrious literary figure. But you would have been speaking too soon, for the next events seemed to call for an old American saying, "Sometimes you can't win for losing." The pound recovered too much and became overvalued compared to other international currencies. As a result, British manufacturers faced problems when competing in foreign markets against goods from other countries. The balance of payments was kept in surplus only by Britain's ability to sell services (such as shipping insurance) to foreigners, and, at times, even the large sums of foreign currency earned in this way proved insufficient to avoid a deficit. Furthermore, the royalties from development of North Sea oil failed to give the government a big bonus with which to cut taxes or launch new programs because most of the money had to be spent on payments made to the greatly increased numbers of unemployed.

Then a ray of light broke through this unmitigated gloom. In the latter part of the 1980s, unemployment began to decline (although some spoilsports claim that this was largely due to the government's having changed the way in which the records were kept). Furthermore, the annual percentage increase in productivity in the United Kingdom outstripped that of major continental countries and was not far behind that of Japan. Unfortunately, these successes proved to be short-lived.

The British economy went into recession in the 1990s. GDP *declined* (that's known as "negative growth" to Pollyannas) by more than 2 percent in 1991 and by 0.6 percent the following year. Unemployment began to rise once again, moving ever closer to the intolerable 3 million mark. Early in 1992, 10 percent of the work force was unemployed, a rate half again as high as only two years earlier.

About the only positive aspect of the British economic situation was inflation. The inflation rate had been rising since the mid-1980s, climbing to around 10 percent at the start of the 1990s—double that of either France or Germany. The government decided to fight inflation no matter what the cost in unemployment and lack of growth. Although the government, unlike Mary Poppins, didn't use a spoonful of sugar to help the medicine go down, it could boast of having prescribed the proper treatment. Inflation declined to only 4 percent early in 1992 and not only fell below 2 percent in 1993, but was nearing a rate of only 1 percent. The need to maintain low inflation while combating unemployment and encouraging economic growth will keep economic issues a major concern for British political leaders.

The structure of the British labor force is typical of many advanced economies. Only about 1 percent of the workers are employed in agriculture, and fewer (about a quarter) work in manufacturing than in service occupations (more than two-thirds). These proportions are not markedly different from those for the United States, but in two other respects the British labor force does differ. In the United States less than a fifth of the labor force is employed by national, state, or local governments. This percentage has increased little during the last forty years. In Europe governments are likely to employ a much larger share of the workers. Nearly two-fifths of Swedish workers are employed by the government. The figure is not that high in Britain, yet at about a third it is considerably larger than in the United States. Some people have argued that the next major division in British politics will be between those who, because of wages or welfare payments, are dependent on the government and those who are not.

As for the other difference, Britain always has been more heavily unionized than the United States. Union membership grew steadily in Britain, reaching a peak of about 13 million in 1979. Since then membership has declined constantly, and by the latter part of the 1980s unions had lost about a fifth of their members. The decline was due in part to the growth of unemployment in the first part of the 1980s, but the Thatcher Government's determination to reduce the power of unions also was a factor. Here, as in other ways, economic affairs and politics are closely intertwined in Britain. Even with the decline, close to two-fifths of the British labor force belongs to unions—a proportion well over twice that for the U.S. labor force.

■ HISTORICAL BACKGROUND

The original population of the British Isles was not, as you might think, Anglo-Saxon, but Iberian. The Iberians, however, are of little importance in Britain's history. Early on, various Celtic groups invaded Britain; one of these was the forerunner of the Scots, another of the Welsh, and a third of the Irish. These groups formed the ethnic composition of the population the Romans found when they invaded in A.D. 43. (You may find it helpful to follow along in Table 1–2 as you read this section.)

Although the Roman occupation of Britain lasted nearly four centuries, it has had surprisingly little effect on modern British political institutions. The rugged Welsh and Scottish countryside prevented the Romans from controlling the entire island. In northern England and southern Scotland, they simply built walls stretching across the countryside from one body of water to the other to protect themselves from attacks originating in the areas they didn't dominate. The Romans occupied Wales, but their presence was little more than a system of forts linked by good roads, and in the mountainous areas their control was even more tenuous. Except for the bulk of the peninsula jutting out into the Atlantic, however, the Romans fully settled that area of the island that is now England. The differences in Roman control contributed to the regional differences that continue to exist.

Table 1–2
Some Key Dates and Events in British History

43	Roman invasion
circa 410	Roman withdrawal
1016–1042	Danish rule
1066	Norman Conquest
1215	Magna Carta
1295	Edward I's Model Parliament
1535	Wales incorporated
1642–1648	Civil War
1649–1660	Cromwell's republic
1688	Glorious Revolution
1707	Scotland incorporated
1800	Ireland incorporated
1832	Great Reform Act
1922	Irish independence

As their empire crumbled under various barbarian invasions, the Romans were forced to withdraw all military forces from the British Isles, leaving the population to see to its own defenses. These people—Romanized Celts—were the Britons. When the Roman legions were gone, the more militant Celts surged back from the fringe areas into which they had been driven. The Britons hired the Saxons, people living in what is now northern Germany, to help defend against this threat. The resultant upheavals—civil war among the Britons, rebellion by the Saxon mercenaries, and resurgence of the Celts—virtually destroyed the culture that Roman rule had established. Even before the Romans withdrew, Germanic raiders had been attacking along the coasts. These people—Angles, Saxons, and Jutes—capitalized on the political chaos and gained control by around 600 of virtually the same areas the Romans had dominated. The Britons retired in disarray to the fringe areas of the British Isles, as the last remnants of Roman civilization were destroyed.

Why do you need to know this? Because these events are why Britain did not follow the tradition of Roman law prevalent on the Continent, but developed instead the common law system. (We will examine this contrast in more detail when we discuss the British legal system in Chapter 8.) So, in the final analysis, about the only lasting contribution of the Romans to British life was a network of roads; few new ones were built in Britain during the thirteen centuries following the Romans' departure.

The Germanic invaders proved to be more than just raiders, since they began to settle in the country. From them comes the ethnic stock of most contemporary inhabitants of the United Kingdom. That is, the Anglo-Saxons became what we now call the English, and the Celtic Britons became the Welsh, Scots, and Irish.

Next the Vikings, or Norsemen, got into the act. (Why do you think this part of the book has all these "Hagar, The Horrible" cartoons? Have you considered the name of one of the authors?) Before 800 they began raiding Britain and in less than a century controlled a considerable portion of what is now northeast England. They established a thriving commercial center in York. The struggles between the Saxons and the Danes surged back and forth—the Danes actually ruled the entire country from 1016 to 1042. This contest was still unresolved when another group of Norsemen intervened. Viking raiders had terrorized the Continent as well as the British Isles. They were given territory in what is now France (called Normandy in recognition of their being north-men) in an effort to buy them off. These Normans crossed the Channel in 1066 to defeat the English at the Battle of Hastings.

One of the reasons that William the Conqueror, the Norman leader, was able to establish his rule was that the population of England and Wales was only 1.75 million—less than that of Minneapolis and St. Paul today. The importance of the Norman Conquest lies first in the fact that it united the country by eliminating the various dukedoms that formerly comprised it. Thus, a major step in the essential process of nation building was taken under William's centralized rule. The other important result of the Conquest was introduction of the feudal system into Britain. Under the feudal system the rights as well as the duties of the nobility were specified. Although obligated to render certain services in exchange for the lands they were granted by the king, nobles also enjoyed certain rights so long as they remained loyal. Should disputes arise concerning these rights and duties, they were to be settled in a council of the king and his leading lords. Thus, foundations were laid that eventually supported constitutionalism and parliamentary government.

The gains made under William's rule were almost lost in a period of virtual anarchy following his death. Eventually, however, central control was established. Perhaps the most important fact of English history for several centuries was the country's ability to maintain a balance between feudal anarchy and tyrannical kingship. At any given time one or the other might be ascendant, but equilibrium was achieved much more consistently than in any other European country.

This equilibrium was not so much the product of wise rulers' policies purposefully directed toward such an end as the serendipitous outcome of variously motivated actions. For example, in the twelfth century the Crown developed a policy of sending judges throughout the kingdom to settle disputes without resort to arms. The aim was to help unify the country and to increase central revenues by collecting legal fees. The result, however, was to lay the foundation for the common law, one of Britain's major contributions to constitutional government. In deciding the controversies presented to them, the itinerant judges tended to rely more on tradition, the customs of the local people, and on precedent than on formal edicts or statutes. This practice gave rise to the idea that the judges were bit by bit elaborating a "higher law" more valid than that embodied in any written legal code. This in turn suggested that The Law was above the monarch and that any rules he or she made that clashed with it were unjust and invalid. The concept of limited, or constitutional, government developed from such thinking. The concept was reinforced in 1215 when the leading barons forced King John to accept Magna Carta, a list of arbitrary actions that he promised (a promise not always kept) never to engage in.

Another fortuitous development that became a major factor in controlling royal power was the growth of what became Parliament. Lacking sufficient revenue to finance his policies, King John decided in 1213 to tax the lower nobility, who previously had not had to bear this burden. Since there were too many of them to summon to the Great Council that would approve the tax, John ordered that a limited number of knights be chosen to attend, to represent the many holding such a title. This was the initial step in representative government: until that time those who participated in the decision-making process were included simply because of their personal eminence and spoke only for themselves. Later in the same century the brief parliament of the rebel Simon de Montfort included representatives of the townspeople as well as of the knights. This practice was legitimated in 1295 when a legal ruler, Edward I, repeated it.

From these feeble beginnings a body of representatives known as Parliament was established. It had very little authority, was not popularly elected, and met only when the monarch called it. Sometimes several years passed between meetings. Moreover, it was not really a legislature but served as a kind of high court of justice concerned with judicial and administrative matters. The commoners from the counties and the boroughs were not permitted to meet with the monarch and nobles to take direct part in making decisions. In time the gathering of those representing the commoners was allowed to present grievances to the monarch. But not until the fourteenth century were they told to elect a speaker (to communicate their collective decisions to the monarch), and not until the reign of Henry V

(1413–1422) did they begin putting their petitions in the form in which they wished them enacted, thereby initiating a crude legislative process.

Parliament had not been intended to be a means of controlling the monarch's government. Gradually, however, this is what it came to do. This process was furthered as the House of Commons acquired the right of originating all bills for raising or disbursing revenue. This power made the support of the Commons essential to the Crown.

Nonetheless, Charles I attempted to rule without Parliamentary support and declined to call Parliament into session from 1629 to 1640. Such high-handed government, which was also characterized by illegal taxation, martial law, and arbitrary imprisonment, combined with religious conflict between Protestants and Anglicans to culminate during the 1640s in the English Civil War.

Despite the name, this conflict is better understood as a revolution. To a considerable extent it pitted the rising commercial middle class against the landed gentry. Even more important, it transformed English government. The king was executed, and the monarchy was replaced by a republic with a written constitution. In practice, the republic tended to be an autocracy under General Oliver Cromwell, as Lord Protector. Cromwell's rule lasted only five years, until his death in 1658. This was too short a time to institutionalize (see our discussion of this topic in the Introduction) what was essentially a system of personal rule. Within two years of Cromwell's death, the republic crumbled, undermined by factional conflict within the army, and the monarchy was restored. This period of little over a decade more than three centuries ago is the only experience Britain has had with republican government.

Less than three decades after the restoration of the monarchy, England was suffering from arbitrary government once again. The rule of James II raised once more the questions of whether Britain was to be a Catholic or Protestant country and whether ultimate power was to reside with the monarch or Parliament. The result was another revolution, this time bloodless, which in 1688 drove James from the throne. Given recent experience, few wanted another republic. So Parliament invited James's Protestant daughter Mary and her husband William to become monarchs. Since Mary was not the immediate heir to the throne, Parliament had demonstrated its power to determine who the monarch would be. By accepting Parliament's offer, William and Mary were acknowledging its supremacy.

The experience under Cromwell suggested that written constitutions had little to offer. The English opted, instead, for action similar to that which had produced Magna Carta. A Declaration of Rights (much of which was later enacted into law) was drawn up. Parliament's offer to William and Mary required that they accept the Declaration, thereby forswearing arbitrary actions that violated basic freedoms.

Thus, at a time when continental feudal kingdoms were turning into absolute monarchies, limitations on the royal prerogatives in Britain were developing into parliamentary restrictions on the exercise of the powers of the Crown. What makes Britain even more distinctive is the fact that these restrictions weren't enshrined in a constitution. Although the limits on royal power were written down, no single framework document set forth the allocation of powers among various governmental organs, the procedures for exercising these powers, and the criteria for governmental offices, as well as the means by which officeholders were to be selected.

The crucial question resolved by the seventeenth-century constitutional settlement was whether the monarch could make laws autonomously without approval by Parliament. The Civil War confirmed yet again the idea that the monarch was not above the law. The common law that was being "found" and applied by judges could be amended only in Parliament. Technically speaking, the term *Parliament* encompasses both the legislature *and* the monarch. Nonetheless, since William and Mary in 1689, no monarch has challenged the supremacy of the legislature, which has come to be regarded as synonymous with Parliament. This doesn't mean that the monarchy lost all governmental influence after 1689. On the contrary, several British monarchs have been powerful. They had to depend on Parliament, however, for funds and for deciding what would be the law. Nonetheless, the long-term development of the monarchy since 1689 has been a peaceful decline in power and influence.

Parliamentary supremacy meant that the monarch would have to govern through political leaders—ministers—who were acceptable to Parliament. William sought to reduce problems with the House of Commons during a conflict with France (which was supporting the deposed James II) by giving some of the principal governmental offices to four leaders who had a sizable following in the Commons. Eventually, such maneuvering developed into the practice of selecting chief ministers exclusively from an alliance of leaders able to control the Commons. Although these ministers were supposed to assist the monarch, the advice they could give was affected by the views of the group they led in Parliament. Until these groups developed into political parties, the monarch could play one faction off against another, but could not prevail against a united majority in Parliament.

The monarch's small group of chief advisors became known as the Cabinet. During the eighteenth century the monarch stopped meeting with them as a group. Although this temporarily reduced the power of the Cabinet, the ministers remained significant. Since they, as well as the monarch, had to sign all official acts, they came to be regarded as being responsible for such laws.

The Cabinet gradually came to be the executive committee of the party that held a majority in Parliament. As the power of the House of Lords declined during the second half of the nineteenth century and through the twentieth, the political situation in the House of Commons became the more important. The Cabinet's policies had to be those that could command support there. A Cabinet advised the monarch what actions its party would accept. The monarch could not take some other action, since then there would be no supporting majority in Parliament and the result would be a constitutional crisis of monarch defying Parliament, which had led to the revolution of 1688.

As power within Parliament shifted from the Lords to the Commons, the latter also became more democratic. Beginning in 1832, in a process that went on for almost a century, Britain permitted more and more of the population to participate in choosing the members of the Commons. Thus, the country's political leadership became more accountable to the people.

Political parties developed along with the expansion of voting rights. The Whigs and Tories of the seventeenth century can be called parties only in the loosest sense, since they were little more than factions based primarily on personal connections rather than on shared policy preferences. But they were the start of the process of developing the unified leadership and definite principles that were to characterize their successors. Not until the nineteenth century, however, did a modern party system, resting on extensive grass-roots organization and coherent programs of policies, appear.

At several points in this brief summary of British political history, we have noted that a basic reform occurred gradually—in stages—and without each change being consciously planned. We want to stress how important this evolutionary process has been in giving Britain continuity in its political development and a durable political system. The only real break in this history was the English Civil War and the republican form of government that resulted from it. But this brief hiatus proved to be of little lasting effect. The point is that in Britain, in contrast to the situation in many other countries, reforms have been neither sharp nor sudden. As a result, they have more readily won acceptance and have seldom produced enduring extreme political cleavages. This has been the genius of British politics.

Recently some British historians have tended to emphasize instead the discontinuities, the breaks in British political development. Although Britain's political history couldn't be graphed as an ascending straight line, such a graph would be less jagged than one for France or the United States. British history lacks major watershed events that compare, for example, with the French Revolution. Furthermore, despite periods of reversal or stagnation, British political history exhibits a long-term trend of greater constraint on governmental power, a trend toward increased responsibility or accountability. During the half century from 1870 to 1920, however, several events occurred that suggested that this long-term development may not have just taken a temporary downturn, but rather have been reversed. Ironically, this apparent reversal occurred as democracy, in terms of voting rights, was being fully realized. We will discuss the factors involved in this paradox in the following chapters.

■　■　■

Britain's location left it free to develop its own distinctive system largely independent of (although not uninfluenced by) events on the Continent, and to do so at a deliberate pace. Change has been slow and slight enough to be virtually unnoticeable at any given time. As a result, British institutions appear to be tried and true, to have withstood the test of time. Life in the twentieth century is much less placid than in the past, is almost frenetic. Technological change proceeds at an astounding pace. The question is whether organic adaptability—piecemeal, evolutionary change—remains suitable for the closing decade of this century. Do the values that have grown out of Britain's context, out of its geography and history, equip it to deal with the challenges it now faces? We next examine the nature of those values and the way in which they have been embodied in the fundamental governmental framework.

2

The Foundations of British Politics

■ BASIC VALUES: UNITING AND DIVIDING

In part because of Britain's smallness, ruling power became concentrated relatively earlier than in most other countries. The key question was not so much whether rulers had sufficient power to deal with problems as it was how to constrain power, to keep it from being arbitrary and oppressive.

For restraints on power to be effective, they must be enshrined not only in a constitution, but also (perhaps even more so) in the hearts of the people. Therefore, we need to examine Britain's political culture. As you learned in the Introduction, political culture is the values and attitudes concerning government and politics that are most prevalent in a country. This mixture of beliefs varies a great deal from one country to another and greatly influences the way in which the legal, constitutional structures function.

You may think of Britons as very proper, sedate, and unemotional people, perhaps a bit arrogant, even snobbish. Visualize an Englishman and you almost can hear "Pomp and Circumstance" (the music they used when you graduated from high school) begin to play. Many people hold such a stereotype of the British. We have a few surprises for you. Prior to the nineteenth century, Europeans regarded the English as a volatile nation of brawlers. European sports fans may still hold such a view. English soccer fans have become infamous for hooliganism; at times the country's teams have been banned from international competition out of fear that their supporters would maim and kill fans from other countries.

In the nineteenth century, lawlessness in Britain was at a level now hard to believe. When the House of Commons ends its business each night, the police officers on duty pass through the building shouting a traditional cry, "Who goes home?" What seems a quaint custom (the police do not hail taxis for the Members) has a serious origin. As recently as a century and a half ago, people were so likely to be mugged on the London streets at night that police escorts had to be formed to get Members of Parliament home safely.

But what of political, as distinct from criminal, violence? The Houses of Parliament were destroyed in an accidental fire in 1834. One of the reasons they

© King Features. Reprinted with permission of King Features Syndicate Inc.

were rebuilt in the same location, according to one of the leading political figures of the day, Robert Peel, was "the facility which the [River] Thames offered for escaping from inflamed mobs."[1] Incidents of violence and riots accompanied the campaign at the start of the 1830s to expand the right to vote. The violence practiced both by and on the women suffragists in Britain early in the twentieth century far exceeded that which occurred in the United States. And we mentioned in the Introduction the riots in response to the new poll tax in 1990.

How did such a people get a reputation for being sedate, or, as the British would say, unflappable? The British response to two major historical events that occurred within about a half century of each other is the answer. When France was convulsed by a revolution toward the close of the eighteenth century—a revolution that claimed to be advancing the cause of the oppressed everywhere without regard to national boundaries—British society and its political system remained intact and unaltered. An analogy would be if Canada had a bloody communist revolution and the United States hardly noticed. Similarly, in the middle of the nineteenth century, revolutions swept the Continent but created far less turmoil in Britain. Out of such tranquil responses grew the British reputation for political stability and decorum.

Although this reputation has been overstated, we wouldn't want you to think that it is completely false. Compared to a country in which any psychotic can buy a gun for less than a day's pay, walk to within ten feet of the President, and shoot him, Britain is remarkably nonviolent. The number of murders in New York City alone in a single year is well over one and a half times the number that occurs in all of the United Kingdom. In England and Wales there is about one homicide each year for every 100,000 people; in the United States there are nearly ten.

Furthermore, since guns are tightly controlled, less than 10 percent of all murders are shootings (if you read British murder mysteries, you already know that—the murder may be caused by poison, an "accident," blunt object, etc., but never a gun), and an even smaller percentage of robberies involve guns. This is despite the fact (or maybe due to it) that the British police, except in rare, specially authorized circumstances, do not carry guns. Only about one police officer a year is killed in

---

[1] Quoted in M. H. Port, ed., *The House of Parliament* (New Haven, Conn.: Yale University Press, 1976), p. 20.

the line of duty. Britons do not believe that owning a gun is a basic right—three-quarters of them favor a total ban on private possession of guns.[2]

Low levels of violence are also typical of political and economic conflict. Political demonstrations, riots, and industrial confrontations do occur in Britain and often involve physical conflict and injuries, but virtually never is anyone killed. Only one British Prime Minister has ever been assassinated, and that occurred in 1812.

Northern Ireland is another matter. There adherents of one religion regularly shoot and bomb those supporting the other. In 1984 the Irish Republican Army (a quasi-military organization seeking to join Northern Ireland to the Republic of Ireland) bombed a hotel in southern England in an almost successful attempt to kill Prime Minister Thatcher. By the standards of the rest of the country, however, such behavior clearly is an aberration.

The British have little sympathy for extreme political action. Even though about nine-tenths of them believe that public meetings and the publishing of pamphlets to protest against the government should be allowed and three-quarters aren't opposed to protest marches, less orthodox behavior is less acceptable. Little more than a tenth would allow occupying a government office and stopping work there for several days (behavior similar to that which has occurred on many American college campuses). Virtually no one—only 2 percent—would condone serious damage to government buildings.

Related to this characteristic are attitudes toward the police, which contrast sharply with those in the United States. During the 1960s and 1970s many Americans engaged in rather violent confrontations with the police. Not only were such events less common in Britain, but there four-fifths approved of courts' giving severe sentences to protesters who disregard the police, and nearly as many favored the use of force by the police against demonstrators. When Britons were asked to assess the honesty and ethical standards of those in various occupations, they rated the police second only to doctors, with half believing police standards were high. In contrast, less than a fifth thought the same of business executives. Surprisingly, Britons of your age—those fifteen to twenty-four—also had a positive view of the police. When asked which two or three of a list of occupations they most respected, over half mentioned the police—again, second only to doctors. Only a quarter of the young people surveyed had the most respect for teachers.

Although highly positive, Britons' evaluations of the police are not as high as they once were. It used to be thought that the British police were absolutely incorruptible, but recently cases of police dishonesty and abuse of authority have come to light. Britons now are more likely to believe that some police are corrupt.

---

[2]Much of the information in this section comes from various surveys of British public opinion conducted by Social Surveys (Gallup) and by Market & Opinion Research International (MORI). I wish to thank Robert Wybrow and Robert Worcester of these two organizations for making available the findings of their surveys. Additional sources were Roger Jowell, Sharon Witherspoon, and Lindsay Brook, eds., *British Social Attitudes: the 1986 Report* (Aldershot, England: Gower, 1986), *British Social Attitudes: the 1987 Report* (Aldershot, England: Gower, 1987), and *British Social Attitudes: Special International Report* (Aldershot, England: Gower, 1989); and Roger Jowell, Lindsay Brook, and Bridget Taylor with Gillian Prior, eds., *British Social Attitudes: the 8th Report* (Aldershot, England: Dartmouth, 1991).

Nonetheless, of those who sought aid from the police, three-fourths felt they were very or fairly helpful. Even among those whom the police questioned about a possible offense, two-thirds found them to be very or fairly polite. Four-fifths of those surveyed said they had a great deal or quite a lot of confidence in the police—the army was the only social institution receiving greater support. Finally—and this is really an acid test—nearly two-thirds would be pleased if their son became a policeman.

By now the British may sound so conventional that you may be wondering whether they have any attachment to basic freedoms. On questions of the powers to be allowed to the police and the exercise of basic civil liberties, however, the views of Britons and Americans are quite similar. For example, in both countries, three-quarters do not think the police should be allowed to open the mail of even a suspect with a long criminal record, and half think that people who want to overthrow the government should be allowed to hold public meetings.

Britons and Americans do differ, however, in their attitudes toward government. Britons are more supportive of interventionist government; they show greater enthusiasm for social welfare activities and are more likely to think that the government should do something to deal with social problems. Nearly nine-tenths of Britons think the government has a responsibility to provide health care for the sick (only a third of Americans think so), four-fifths believe it should provide a decent standard of living for old people (about two-fifths in the United States), three-fifths believe it should control prices by law (two-fifths of Americans), and half believe it should reduce income differences between rich and poor (only a sixth of Americans).

On the other hand, Britons are less likely than Americans to feel that they can influence the government and get political leaders and representatives to respond to their views. Four-fifths of them feel that the public has little control over what politicians do in office, and nearly three-fifths say that you get nowhere by talking to public officials (in the United States, little more than two-fifths say that).

People in the two countries also differ in their attitudes toward reform. The typical British view is that if something has been done a certain way for some time, that is sufficient reason for continuing to do it that way. At the very least, it is a strong argument for regarding proposed changes warily and examining them thoroughly. Unlike Americans, Britons do not believe as a matter of faith that the newest is necessarily the best. And when a convincing case has been made in favor of reform, the British still prefer to implement it gradually, bit by bit over an extended time period.

Nonetheless, the British are open to reason and practical considerations. Their approach to politics is much more pragmatic than ideological. They are not much impressed by grand, abstract social theories—Marxism has had little appeal in Britain. The British do not care that something may have illogical aspects; their main concern is whether it works. Practice, not theory, is the key consideration. They have piled new political institutions on old and altered the original purpose of others—all very untidily but, nevertheless, effectively. By retaining old institutions while shifting power around, they have maintained continuity in political development.

The practical, empirical approach that prevails in Britain is reflected in the school of philosophy known as British empiricism. This group of thinkers, including Locke, Berkeley, and Hume, rejected the rationalism of the French philosopher Descartes in favor of a philosophy grounded in experience. This tradition has helped to make it possible in Britain to discuss political ideas with respect to their concrete merits rather than their supposed logical virtues.

A pragmatic attitude in politics helps to support tolerance for opponents and a willingness to compromise. When your opponents are simply arguing the value of limited, practical reform rather than advocating the virtues of transforming the entire system, you feel less threatened by their possible victory. And when you feel less threatened, you are more willing to tolerate differing views and to attempt to work out some course of action that will be mutually agreeable.

Some observers felt that British politics became more ideological in the 1980s, with the leading parties polarizing their positions. The election of 1983 may well have given British voters their most clear-cut choice in a generation. To some extent this impression is a matter of political rhetoric. Certainly changes in party control of the government have not produced dramatic changes in policy in the past.[3] The scramble of the Labour party to get back to the center of the political spectrum in the late 1980s hardly suggests a basic ideological cleavage in British politics.

Perhaps some commentators were influenced by an apparent growth of dogmatism in British politics in the 1980s. The Leader of the Conservatives during this decade, Prime Minister Margaret Thatcher, labeled herself a "conviction politician." Her confrontational style contributed to a perception that partisan differences were sharpening. Gallup opinion surveys during the mid-1980s found that about half of those interviewed believed it was better to stick firmly to one's own beliefs rather than trying to meet political opponents halfway, compared to two-fifths preferring the more accommodating approach (a tenth had no opinion). Interestingly, those who supported the Conservative party were much more likely to favor sticking to one's own beliefs—nearly two-thirds of such respondents preferred that to meeting opponents halfway.

Before the end of the decade, however, fervent advocacy seemed to pall for the British public. Late in 1989, as Thatcher entered what would be her final year in office, less than two-fifths favored sticking to one's own beliefs, and nearly three-fifths were willing to try to meet opponents. In the long run, then, any change in the nature of political debate was more a matter of temporary rhetoric than of permanent divisive cleavage.

However remarkable the confrontational intransigence of the 1980s, it hardly was completely foreign to British life. In the seventeenth century, religious conflicts produced a civil war, just as regional conflicts did in the United States in the nineteenth century. We mentioned earlier how religious cleavages currently spawn violence in Northern Ireland. Despite these and other such examples, the British have a well-deserved reputation for tolerance. They have been more willing than Americans to allow unpopular minority views to be expressed freely in their coun-

---

[3]Richard Rose, *Do Parties Make a Difference?*, 2d ed. (Chatham, N.J.: Chatham House, 1984).

try. They have neither sought to outlaw the Communist party nor felt the need to create an Un-British Activities Committee. Around half of the public believes that people who want to overthrow the government by revolution should be allowed to hold public meetings and publish books. Nearly a third would permit television to broadcast and newspapers to publish interviews with terrorists. But to what extent does such toleration of those who are outside the political mainstream extend to those who are different in other ways?

Racial Relations

Toleration consists of not only how you react to other people's opinions but also how you respond to them as individuals. Events of the 1960s and 1970s made clear that British toleration of diverse political views did not extend as readily into racial matters. Although fewer than one in twenty-five Britons were nonwhite, their growing number and concentration in a relatively few areas produced many negative reactions. White neighbors forced some "coloureds" (remember that the British lump Indians, Pakistanis, Bangladeshis, West Indians, and Africans together under this label) to move from their homes; some employers discriminated against these "immigrants." Some politicians urged banning nonwhite immigration into Britain and even suggested that the government pay "coloureds" to return to their native countries.

During the past three decades, British policy concerning race relations has moved in two directions that might seem contradictory but that the British hope are complementary. Immigration into Britain is now much more tightly restricted than it was, and racial discrimination against nonwhite residents in Britain is more widely prohibited than it had been. The aim is to assimilate nonwhites more easily and protect their rights by keeping their numbers relatively low. Although the main political parties agree in general on this approach, many average Britons want more government action to control immigration and keep "blacks" out of their neighborhoods.

The importance of this emotional issue has varied considerably from time to time. Race was of some importance during the 1979 election but of little significance in elections during the 1980s. Early in 1990, however, the Government's proposal to permit some of Hong Kong's residents to emigrate to Britain caused controversy in Parliament. The idea was to provide a means of escape, if needed, from any persecution by Communists that might occur when this former British possession is acquired by China. Several right-wing Conservative legislators opposed their own party's proposal to relax the immigration law because that might result in as many as a quarter of a million people coming from Hong Kong to Britain.

Gallup found in June 1988 that four-fifths of its respondents thought that people were discriminated against in Britain because of their "colour" or race. A more recent survey asked people to speculate about what would happen if two people, one white and the other black, were to appear in court charged with a crime that they had not committed. Although half thought the two would have the same chance of being acquitted, more than two-fifths thought that the black was more likely to be found guilty.

Contributing to the potential for worsening relations is the fact that, on the average, nonwhites are younger than the rest of the British population. As they marry and have families, their numbers will increase more rapidly than the white population. Furthermore, since unemployment in Britain is especially prevalent among those under twenty-five, the relative youth of the nonwhite population (even without considering the effect of job discrimination) means that it has been particularly hard hit. The potential for fear, resentment, and conflict is great. Add to this the fact that half of the nonwhites, although perceived by many Britons to be immigrants or foreigners, were born in Britain. By any reasonable definition of citizenship, Britain is their country; yet some other Britons talk of sending them "home." The sun may have set on the British Empire, but that empire's effect on British politics lingers on in that Britain's imperial past has ill equipped it to deal with its nonwhite population.

The British don't seem to be very optimistic about the future of race relations. Surveys have found that about two-fifths think there is more racial prejudice than there was five years ago (only one-fifth think there is less) and about two-fifths think there will be more five years in the future. More positively, however, most Britons do know what's right. Two-thirds of them thought it should be illegal to discriminate against people on the basis of race or colour and three-fourths claimed they would not mind having nonwhites for neighbors. In fact, when it came to listing the people those surveyed would not want to have as neighbors, drug addicts (66 percent) and heavy drinkers (48 percent) were more often rejected than were immigrants. In 1985 two-fifths had not wanted to have immigrants as neighbors, but eight years later less than a tenth objected to them. Also encouraging is the decline in the number of people seeing conflict between whites and blacks as a major source of antisocial activity in Britain. In 1985 more than two-fifths regarded such racial tensions as a very important cause for the increase of crime and violence in the country, but eight years later less than a fifth thought so.

On the other hand, and here one can understand why British policy has had two contrasting thrusts, the proportion of the public wanting controls on immigration has declined only slightly. In 1983 around two-thirds wanted nonwhite immigration to be reduced. Seven years later three-fifths favored less settlement of immigrants in Britain. As you've seen, Britain is very densely populated, and one might argue that it needs no more immigration at all. The point is the clear racial bias in British attitudes toward immigration. Only two-fifths wanted less settlement in Britain from European countries, and only three-tenths wanted less settlement from Australia and New Zealand.

The emotionalism that race or immigration occasionally has raised isn't typical of British politics. Britain has had charismatic leaders, notably Winston Churchill during World War II, but demagogues have been rare. Churchill's grandson (also named Winston) went over the top in an extraordinarily racist speech in 1993, asserting such patently false claims as that some cities in Britain were half black. Most people were perplexed by what had caused this outburst; some felt that he was venting his spleen at having been passed over for a position in the executive branch. Several politicians and newspapers denounced his remarks. This attempt at racial demagoguery engendered little approval.

Demagoguery of any type is a high-stakes gamble in Britain because the people do not engage in mass enthusiasms bordering on hysteria. (They are inclined to find the hoopla of American nominating conventions rather amusing.) The rather low-key image of bulldog determination is accurate. The chief exception with respect to this trait is the Welsh, who tend to favor a more florid and rhetorical style. Most English people are uncomfortable with such profuseness and suspect it. The Welshness of Neil Kinnock, the Leader of the Labour party during the latter part of the 1980s and early 1990s, was a liability for him; many English people referred to him as the Welsh windbag and dismissed him as lacking political substance in part because of his ornate style of public speaking. As we'll see in examining the 1992 election campaign, this may have been a crucial factor in Labour's defeat.

Social Class and Education

Individualism is valued in Britain. British society, more than American, is willing to make room for the individual eccentric, the screwball. At a more subtle level, you might think at first glance that each residence in a series of London rowhouses was exactly like all the others. On close inspection you would see that each front door was painted a different color and each window box held a different mix of flowers. In contrast to the United States, however, individualism is overshadowed by a social characteristic that puts Britain in the European tradition—class solidarity and social division. Social class tends to separate Britons into distinct groups and for most of the twentieth century has been the basic cleavage in British politics. A Briton can tell within a few minutes of beginning to talk with strangers what their social position is, because their speech patterns and accent identify them. Gallup has found that nearly three-quarters of Britons think that people are very or quite aware of class differences. Unlike in the United States, where a southern drawl may get you labeled a redneck in other parts of the country, in Britain it is the accent of the northerner that stigmatizes one as lacking the proper background, breeding, and education.

Not only do Britons notice class differences, they act on them. How Britons treat others depends on whether they are above or below the social position of those with whom they are dealing. Well over a quarter say they would be bothered if their child had a friend from another class; little more than half say they would not mind. Two-thirds think that class affects one's opportunities a great deal or a lot. Any change in class attitudes seems limited. A quarter believe that the effect of class is greater than it was ten years earlier, and only slightly more than that think that it has lessened. As for the future, a fifth think class will have more effect than it now does, and about a quarter expect it to have less.

Americans are aware that titles are used in Britain—Lord this or Lady that or Sir whatever. Although these titles do carry some social prestige, many of them were created relatively recently and were awarded to self-made businesspeople or successful politicians. Some titles are not even hereditary. So a title does not necessarily imply centuries of luxury and a home in a castle. In any event aristocrats and the nobility have not run the country in the twentieth century.

The true governing class in Britain is the upper middle class. Many such families are financially better off than those having titles and often feel a need to justify their success by serving society. (An American parallel would be the Rockefellers or the Kennedys.) The political relevance of this sense of duty is heightened in Britain by the view—sharply contrasting with American attitudes—that politics is a much more suitable and honorable career than is business for someone of high social status.

Within the middle class, occupations and wealth vary considerably. An upper and a lower middle class can be distinguished, but the dividing line is rather imprecise. The sharpest social break, the point at which a gulf separating contrasting lifestyles exists, is between the middle class and the manual workers. The latter comprise the social class whose accent gives them away the instant they speak. Feelings of class solidarity are most fully developed among manual workers. This has generated an us/them view of society that has had considerable impact on the British party system.

Traditionally most Britons have held little prospect of advancing from the class into which they were born. The American experience, in contrast to the British, has supported a belief that hard work will be rewarded and might easily result in a change in social status. Americans did not so much want government to provide an elaborate program of benefits, as to keep out of the way and let them take care of themselves. As mentioned earlier, Americans are less likely to see the need for interventionist government.

Class structure affects not only views on the role of the government, but also views on the role of the citizen. Class solidarity tends to lessen interest in individual activism. Given the feelings of community and the network of social interrelations, any effort to formally organize a group is likely to seem unnecessary or, even, divisive. Any initiative should come from within the community rather than from the individual. As we'll see in the next chapter, interest groups have existed in Britain for some time and play a significant role in the policy process. In contrast, public interest and community service groups haven't been as prevalent as in the United States.

One of the key elements that perpetuate social divisions in Britain is the educational system. In the United States education and occupation tend to determine social status; in Britain social status tends to determine education and occupation. Although the government provides education up to age eighteen, until recently most students left as soon as they reached the compulsory schooling age of sixteen. Not until 1990 did more than half of those reaching sixteen opt to continue in school. The 61 percent who stayed on in 1992 constituted the highest proportion ever, but this was surpassed by 71 percent continuing their education in 1993. Furthermore, in 1993 the proportion of seventeen-year-olds continuing their education rose sharply from 33 percent to 55 percent. Until recently Britain has been a nation of high school dropouts, but high levels of unemployment appear to be changing that.

The government-supported schools used to be of two main types: secondary modern schools provided a general education with some vocational emphasis for the great bulk of the students, and grammar schools offered an academic, college-preparatory education for the more able few. To bridge the gap between this elite education and the mediocre offerings of the secondary moderns, the comprehensive school was devised. Comprehensives were similar to American high schools in taking all types of students, but even their curriculum distinguished between those students who were planning to go to university and those who were not.

The Labour party, in keeping with its egalitarian principles, strongly favored such schools and passed legislation requiring all local school boards to "go comprehensive." (The fact that the national legislature could order this is a good example of how a unitary system differs from a federal one.) The Conservative party opposed this policy, arguing that to abandon the grammar schools would dilute the quality of education. When the Conservatives returned to power in 1979, one of their first actions was to repeal Labour's requirement for comprehensives.

Nonetheless, the great majority of British children attending government-supported schools (nearly nine out of ten) go to comprehensives, and fewer than one in twenty go to grammar schools. The grammar school remains important, however, because it is a significant entry route to higher education. In contrast to students in comprehensives, the great majority of students in grammar schools not only stay until they are eighteen, but then go on for higher education.

If you have been reading carefully, you may have wondered why we have been using the awkward term "government-supported schools." Why not just say "public schools"? Because what the British call public schools are in fact private. British public schools are not owned and operated by the government. Although they may receive a financial grant, the bulk of their money comes from sizable fees charged to their students. Unless you can win one of the few scholarships offered by such schools (remember, we are talking about secondary schools, not universities), you can attend only if your parents can afford the fees. Room and board (public schools typically are boarding schools, although some take day pupils, who live at home) plus tuition at a top public school can run well over $18,000 a year.

Although about sixteen times as many students attend government-supported schools as public schools, the public schools are immensely significant politically and socially. Attending the proper public school enhances (or perhaps we should say attests to) your social status much more than does graduating from Oxford or Cambridge University (the British equivalent of the Ivy League). Controversy over the role and status of the public schools exceeds even that concerning the comprehensives and the grammars. The public schools are at the heart of class cleavage in Britain.

The most illustrious of all British public schools is Eton, founded in 1441. Although it has a student body numbering little more than a thousand, Eton has produced eighteen Prime Ministers over the years. In the first half of the twentieth century, nearly three-fifths of all the Conservative Cabinet ministers and about a quarter of all Conservative members of Parliament were Old Etonians.[4] The old school tie is the bond that men (public schools are not coeducational, and those

---

[4]W. P. Buck, *Amateurs and Professionals in British Politics* (Chicago: University of Chicago Press, 1963).

that exist for females do not have the same prestige) who have attended the same public school, however many years apart, feel for each other. A significant factor in relations among the British political elite, this tie has no American parallel; the link among fraternity brothers is only a pale imitation.

Some members of the Labour party would like to abolish the public schools. The party usually, however, has concentrated less on attacking the privileges of the elite and more on providing opportunities for those who merit it among the less well-off. Labour's view is that those who have demonstrated intelligence should not be prevented by financial constraints from realizing their potential. This means that even in the Labour party few people hold the belief common in the United States that virtually everyone has a God-given right to attend a university. In Britain, higher education is not mass education; only about 600,000 students attend colleges and universities full-time.

Of those who are admitted, however, the overwhelming majority (about 90 percent) receive financial aid from the government. Tuition charges are quite low—lower than those for public schools, and even lower than the cost at a state university in the United States. The grants that students receive from the government vary according to the financial circumstances of their parents, who may be expected to contribute to their children's support. The idea that British university students might work at part-time jobs while going to school, however, is regarded with horror. Students may complain about trying to live on their grant and the money from their parents, but almost never get a job. Rather than spend their time in a way familiar to most American students, British students prefer to lobby the government for larger grants.

Despite the government's generous (by American standards) financial assistance, British higher education is not egalitarian. Students from working-class families account for only about a fifth of all those pursuing higher education. The British educational system at all levels serves primarily to train a social elite. Because of the divisive effect that education has had on British society, it will continue to be an important political issue.

Income inequality increased considerably in Britain during the 1980s. The average household's real disposable income rose by about 25 percent, while that of households in the top tenth went up by 30 percent. Households in the bottom tenth, on the other hand, suffered a decline of about 6 percent. The share of total income going to the poorest tenth dropped during the decade from 4 percent to only 2.5 percent. The bottom half of households saw their share of income fall from 32 to 27 percent. As a result, the proportion of households with less than half of the average income more than doubled, from around 8 percent to nearly 20 percent. Thus, although the 1980s overall were a time of prosperity for Britain, the gains were shared very unequally. Those unemployed or on pensions found themselves worse off.

Wealth, as distinct from income, is even less equally distributed. The top 1 percent of the population owns a fifth of the wealth, and the top 10 percent nearly three-fifths. (These figures are little different from those for the United States.)

Customs and behavior matter more than money in producing social cleavages. Skilled workers, for example, may think of themselves as working class, and clerks or teachers may label themselves middle class; yet the best-paid skilled workers earn considerably more than many teachers and clerks and do not have the financial burden of trying to maintain a middle-class lifestyle, such as by paying for children to go to public schools. Furthermore, increased income cannot readily be translated into the manners, speech, social habits, and other attributes essential for winning acceptance as an equal by the social elite.

At the heart of social divisions in Britain is the way in which people treat each other and how they feel about their place in society. As you have seen, Britons are much more aware of and feel more separated by social divisions than Americans do. Differences in lifestyle have separated the manual workers from the rest of society and frequently given them an embattled sense of class solidarity—us against them. Class barriers will continue to exist until a person can relate comfortably to someone from another class as a fellow human being. In Britain that time remains in the future.

Thus, Britain is a country divided into two contrasting lifestyles, almost two subcultures: middle class and working class. Despite the differences between these classes in customs, behavior, and outlook, they share many fundamental values. Antipathy toward extremism and emotionalism and support for a pragmatic approach prevail across class lines. In short, the British tend to be conservative (with a small c), regardless of where they are located on the partisan spectrum. This has immense significance for government and politics.

■ CONSTITUTIONAL ELEMENTS AND PRINCIPLES

The essence of constitutionalism is restraint of political power. This restraint deals with both substance and procedure. Not only are the powers given to government limited, but those that are granted are to be exercised according to stated rules or principles, not according to the whim of the power-holder. As you have already seen in the summary of British history in Chapter 1, limitations on power have been a feature of British government for some time.

Despite the close link between constitutionalism and democracy, you should not confuse the two. The former focuses on restraints on powers and procedures; the latter emphasizes the source of legitimate power and the way in which that source is manifested. A country can have a constitutional system without being democratic; that is, the government's powers and procedures may be limited, and the people still have little say in selecting those who decide policy for the country. This, in fact, was exactly the British situation until about the middle of the nineteenth century. Constitutionalism had been firmly established, but the people weren't recognized as the source of power and the unreformed electoral system permitted few of them any role in selecting government leaders. Britain simply wasn't democratic.

Although both Britain and the United States practice constitutionalism, they do so in such contrasting ways that their constitutional structures differ fundamentally. Britain does not have separation *or* division of powers. And, oddest of all from an American perspective, Britain doesn't even have a written constitution. Pick up any textbook on U.S. government and turn to the back and there it is: the Constitution. Do the same with a text on British government and you will find nothing. Imagine, no Founding Fathers, no history-making constitutional convention (or, alternatively, just to confuse you a bit, a permanent, continuing constitutional convention).

Clearly, something is not quite right here. Britain practices constitutionalism? Yes. But it lacks a written constitution? Yes. The point is that in Britain the limitations on governmental power do not derive from a single, framework document that allocates powers and functions among the various organs of government, prescribes procedures for making decisions, and establishes limits on governmental action. The absence of a single document means that governmental structures and procedures have been altered not by formal amendment but by shifts in customary practices.

Americans weren't happy under this vague system; they sought redress for their grievances in the latter part of the eighteenth century and failed to obtain any. Their claim that their rights as Englishmen were being violated won no vindication. After the American Revolution, therefore, they resorted to a written constitution (and even then they needed more than a decade of problems under the Articles of Confederation before drafting a full-fledged constitution). England's unhappy experience with a written constitution more than a century earlier did not cause Americans to hesitate about the need for explicit constitutional arrangements.

Not only did Americans depart from English constitutional tradition—written, rather than unwritten—but they also opted for a new form. The means they chose for restraining leaders' exercise of power was checks and balances, not accountability. Checks and balances fit with the "trendy" view of how to restrain power when the American Founding Fathers convened in Philadelphia. The writings of Locke (although he had lived nearly a century earlier) and of the more nearly contemporary Montesquieu were popular with intellectuals. Thus, an up-to-date written constitution should provide for checks and balances, for separation of powers. The irony was that while Montesquieu influenced the Founding Fathers to create a form of constitutionalism that put the United States on a different path from Britain, his writings contained his interpretation of *English* constitutional arrangements.

In developing their contrasting forms of constitutionalism, the English and the Americans were working from contrasting diagnoses of the basic political problem. Both recognized that power could be abused and result in arbitrary government. The English were more influenced, however, by the understanding that power could be beneficial, that in some circumstances strong government offered the only satisfactory solution to public problems. Therefore, they did not so much want to weaken governmental power as to see that it was used properly. Thus, the appropriate remedy was for power to be accountable. The Americans, on the other hand, given their recent experience with the English monarch, were convinced that the dangers of concentrated power far outweighed any possible benefit that it might provide. Thus, the appropriate remedy was to fractionalize power, to realize Montesquieu's separation-of-powers system, with each element able to check and to balance the others.

Britain's lack of a single, framework document doesn't mean that the limits and prescriptions required for constitutionalism don't exist. Nor are the allocation of powers among various governmental organs and the procedures for selecting and criteria for holding various offices left to chance. The British unwritten constitution is more than just a state of mind. It is composed of four basic elements, only one of which is, in fact, not written. The four are historical documents, acts of Parliament, judicial decisions, and conventions of the constitution.

Heading the list of historical documents is Magna Carta, or Great Charter, which was not the result of a popular revolution (how un-English that would have been) and, frankly, contained little that was new at the time. In 1215 a handful of barons forced King John to sign what they regarded as primarily a statement of existing feudal law, in the hope that the king would feel honor-bound to stop abusing their rights by autocratic rule. So what importance does this little skirmish have centuries later? Magna Carta is a constitutional landmark. First, it contributed to the idea that the monarch was not above certain principles of law, and should he or she disregard them, the nation had the right to force him or her to follow them. Second, although the chief motivation that produced the charter was to protect the barons' privileges, some of its provisions went further: towns were guaranteed their ancient liberties, and a basic fairness was proclaimed ("to no one will we sell, to no one will we refuse or delay, right or justice"). Third, such provisions became ideals. Over the centuries whenever Britons felt that a monarch was exceeding royal authority, they invoked Magna Carta in protest. Totally apart from its original purpose or specific provisions, Magna Carta came to serve as the perfect embodiment of constitutionalism. Other historical documents play a similar role, but they cannot match the prestige attached to Magna Carta because of its great age. (You must never forget The Importance of Being Ancient in British affairs.)

As for the second constitutional element, not every act of Parliament becomes part of the constitution. Only statutes dealing with fundamental matters, such as the distribution of power among various governmental organs, the procedures for making authoritative decisions, or the basic rights of the people, are included. Among the acts of Parliament typically considered part of the constitution are the Reform Acts, which extended voting rights during the nineteenth century, and the Parliament Acts of 1911 and 1949, which reduced the powers of the House of Lords. We say "typically considered part" because nothing explicitly distinguishes such constitutional legislation from other laws. Nothing in the statute itself says anything about amending the constitution, and no special procedures like the extraordinary majorities required to amend the U.S. Constitution are involved. The fact that Parliament can alter the constitution through its normal procedures is the reason for our earlier comment that Britain has a permanent constitutional convention.

Judicial decisions, the third element, form part of the constitution despite the fact that no British court has the power of the U.S. Supreme Court to declare laws unconstitutional. Nonetheless, judges must interpret the law as they apply it to the cases that come before them. When these cases involve the kinds of fundamental matters noted in connection with constitutional statutes, then the judges are modifying the constitution. Their role can be significant because of the tradition that, in matters of basic liberties, they will interpret the law as narrowly as possible so as to preserve basic rights.

Important as these judicial interpretations are, judicial decisions make an even greater contribution to the constitution through the common law. The common law, one of the world's most influential law systems, is a body of legal rules and principles deriving from judicial decisions, which developed apart from any action by Parliament. Early in English history judges often were presented cases that did not come under any of the statutes enacted by the monarch and Parliament. Since these cases had to be decided to prevent people from taking justice into their own hands, judges looked for a fair solution that embodied the customs and values of the local community. (Centuries later the U.S. Supreme Court, in essence, suggested that the same approach should be used in deciding what is obscene.)

As you learned in Chapter 1, these judges were itinerant, sent out by the monarch to travel throughout the country and establish law and order by deciding conflicts. From time to time these travelers would return to London and get together to discuss their interesting experiences. When, in their subsequent travels, they encountered a case similar to one they had heard about in those conversations, they were likely to settle it the same way another judge had said he had done. Thus, the elaborate body of legal rules that developed was common not only because it was based on the practices of the commoners—the people—but also because it became uniform throughout the country.

The development of the common law was aided by the medieval notion that law was divinely ordained. Governments did not make law but were simply to discover God's law and state it explicitly. (Even though common law sometimes is referred to as judge-made law, to distinguish it from the statutes passed by a legislature, the judges who developed the common law would have rejected any thought that they were making law.)

Note that the common law was written down—just like the other two elements of the British unwritten constitution that we have discussed so far, historical documents and fundamental statutes. The records of the various courts stated what judges had decided and why. What didn't exist was any coherent summary of the various cases in a topic-by-topic form. As you can guess, someone eventually got the bright idea that such a summary might perhaps be of use at times. Noted jurists, such as Glanville, Coke (pronounced Cook), and Blackstone, attempted to summarize all the decisions courts had made on a particular subject and based on similar facts. These collections, or commentaries, as they usually were called, served to codify (that is, to make uniform and systematic) much of the common law. It is in this body of legal practice and comment that most guarantees of British civil rights are rooted. For that matter, the same can be said about American rights. When the Fifth and Fourteenth Amendments to the U.S. Constitution say that you cannot be put in jail without due process of law, the required procedures stem from the common law.

Conventions of the constitution—the fourth element—are basic practices or traditions; in the United States these are known as custom and usage. Although most of these conventions are not written, this is not the key factor in distinguishing them. The basic criterion is whether a particular practice is enforceable, whether it can be the basis for a legal judgment. If so, then the practice is common law rather than a convention. For example, the principle of *stare decisis*—

that the courts will decide a current case according to the rulings made in previous similar cases—is common law. So also is the supremacy of Parliament—the rule that any law passed by the legislature is valid and cannot be declared unconstitutional—since the courts do enforce it. Practices that the courts do not enforce are conventions.

The mere fact that something has been done a certain way for some time does not by itself create a convention. A traditional practice must also have logical and normative support; that is, doing things that way makes sense and people feel bound to continue the practice. For example, if the monarch refused to accept as Prime Minister the person preferred by a majority of the House of Commons, the government could not function, since no other person would have the support necessary to get any legislation approved by the Commons. Thus, it is sensible for the monarch to accept the Commons' preference. The Prime Minister must have a seat in the House of Commons not because the law says so, but because in the twentieth century it is felt that it would be wrong for him or her to be in the non-elective House of Lords. The prevailing democratic political values provide normative support for this practice and help to make it a convention.

Being used to a formal Constitution with a Bill of Rights, you may not regard the British constitution as offering much protection of basic liberties. This conclusion is especially likely if you recall that the second of the four elements means that Parliament can amend the constitution at will in the same way it passes ordinary legislation. Despite this apparent vulnerability, more Britons feel secure than do Americans, Canadians, or Germans. An international survey in 1990 found that 85 percent of Britons thought that citizens' rights were very or fairly well protected, compared to 73 percent of Americans who thought that.[5]

Nonetheless, concern seems to have grown in recent years. Talk about the need for some sort of written bill of rights that could not be altered by Parliament has become common. Some of the concern is the product of partisan politics, the knee-jerk reaction of Colonel Blimps (the British term for right-wing, extremely stuffy traditionalists who believe that nothing should ever be done for the first time). They fear that if the Labour party won an election, it might do fearsome things. A Labour Government could abolish the House of Lords and then there would be nothing to check a left-wing majority in the Commons.

But civil libertarians have had cause for concern as well. The government in Britain has considerably more control over the media than is true in the United States and in recent years has been using it much more intrusively. The government has been concerned that too much information about the secret intelligence services has become public—spies, both retired and current, are writing memoirs and talking to journalists and Members of Parliament. The government has tried to prevent the publication and sale of some books and to censor various newspapers by preventing them from publishing secret information. Perhaps the most incredible event occurred early in 1987, when the police ransacked the offices of the BBC in

---

[5]Roger Jowell, Lindsay Brook, and Bridget Taylor with Gillian Prior, eds., *British Social Attitudes: the 8th Report* (Aldershot, England: Dartmouth, 1991), p. 176.

Glasgow and carried away boxes of material to prevent the televising of a program about a spy satellite.

Although such dramatic events cause some unease, basic liberties have long been firmly grounded in Britain, despite the fact that its constitution is unwritten. Committing some of these liberties to writing in some sort of fundamental document may seem increasingly attractive, but it is not clear that this would add much of significance to British constitutionalism. As you will see in Part Five of this book, an extensive written catalogue of rights failed to protect liberties in the Soviet Union. For that matter, the U.S. Constitution could not prevent a strong, determined group from establishing a dictatorship in this country. The success or failure of such an attempt would depend on the public's response. Ultimately, written constitutions rest on political, not legal, sanctions and supports—just as the British unwritten constitution does. Limited government, fair play, and justice have been part of British political culture for some time, and enshrining such principles in some document seems unlikely to increase support for them beyond its current high level.

This is a good time to summarize the basic principles of the British constitution—both those concerned with liberties and those underlying other aspects. Given the nature of the British constitution, you must understand that no two books on the subject will give exactly the same list.

Liberty of the citizen   The rule of law prevails in Britain. This means, among other things, that the government is not above the law; it cannot do whatever it pleases but must be able to cite legal authorization for its actions. All citizens are equal before the law. Convictions for breaking the law must conform with due process; torture, for example, may not be used to secure confessions. The law must be publicly known in advance before it is enforced.

Democracy   Citizens have the opportunity to participate in authoritative decision making. The government is to do what the majority, not some elite group, desires. In Britain, as in most democracies, this means universal suffrage, buttressed by the right to form parties and pressure groups and to communicate with one's representatives.

Parliamentary supremacy   The ultimate legal authority in Britain is Parliament. Since Parliament can alter the constitution at will, its actions can never be declared unconstitutional by any court. In contrast to the situation in the United States, a strong judiciary is not established to check the power of the legislature.

Constitutional monarchy   Given the liberty of the citizen and the supremacy of Parliament, the British monarchy must be a constitutional, limited one, rather than an arbitrary or autocratic one. Although a hereditary monarch continues to reign over Britain, the occupant of this position does not rule, as we will discuss in Chapter 6. You could almost go so far as to label the British system a symbolic monarchy.

Unitary government   Unlike the United States and Germany, Britain lacks division of powers. In Britain the subnational units of government owe their power and existence to Parliament, which can alter or abolish them at will. Instead of being a federal system, Britain is a unitary one. The existence of a separate parliament in Northern Ireland, with power to legislate on matters relevant to that region, created an element of federalism, although that legislature's actions could be overridden by the national Parliament in London. In 1972, however, conflict between Catholics and Protestants in Northern Ireland grew so severe that the national government suspended the parliament there and assumed direct rule from London.

The rise of nationalistic feelings in Scotland and Wales has encouraged efforts to qualify the unitary system by devolving some powers to these areas. When a referendum on these proposals was held in 1979, 80 percent of those voting in Wales rejected them. A bare majority of those voting in Scotland were in favor, but more than a third of those eligible to vote there stayed home. Thus, only a third of the Scottish electorate voted yes. The proposals had to be abandoned because they failed to get the support of 40 percent of the electorate, a criterion those opposed to devolution had managed to write into the legislation. Even had the devolution proposals been implemented, Britain would have remained a unitary system. Not only were the powers that the central government intended to delegate to the subnational units limited, but it could have reclaimed them whenever it wished, regardless of the desires of those units.

A final example should help to underline the centralized nature of the British system. In the mid-1980s the national government abolished the Greater London Council, turning the city's governmental functions over to various boards and subcity units of government. Similar action was taken against the metropolitan counties, the units of government for the country's major cities. Clearly, the national government in Britain has powers that its counterpart in the United States lacks.

Parliamentary government/cabinet government   Also in contrast to the United States, Britain does not have separation of powers. As we noted in discussing parliamentary supremacy, although the courts are separate, they are not intended to check Parliament. Britain goes even beyond this in fusing powers. The executive structures are not separated from the legislature but are intertwined with it in both their origin and continuance. The Cabinet system is related to the principle of constitutional monarchy. Historically, the Cabinet developed to serve as a buffer, or mediator, between the ruler and those political leaders empowered to make authoritative policies for the country. In the twentieth century the Cabinet has become the most powerful element in the British system. Chapters 5 and 6 will explain that although legally Parliament is supreme, in practice the Cabinet is.

Party government   If parliamentary government is to produce stable cabinets, well-organized, disciplined parties are essential. The life of British Cabinets was much more tenuous when political groups were based on personal attachments rather than loyalty to party principles. Furthermore, it is difficult to conceive of a political process in a mass democracy (the second principle mentioned above) that would not give rise to a fairly well-developed party system to channel and stimulate demands for governmental action.

■   ■   ■

What this adds up to is a form of constitutionalism that seeks to constrain power not in the American way—through the use of checks and balances—but through accountability. The idea is to leave power sufficiently untrammeled and undispersed that something can be done (remember the support for interventionist government), but to guard against abuse by requiring the wielders of power to justify their behavior and to be subject to removal from office should they not perform satisfactorily.

This summary of basic principles should make it clear that in the remaining chapters of this part you'll find some familiar practices but many others that initially seem unusual. We will try to make clear for you why these different arrangements have developed out of the setting and foundations of British politics, as well as the extent to which they result in a system that functions differently from that of the United States. We will begin with those arrangements and procedures relating to what for most people—in Britain or any other country—is the only form of political activity.

......3

Channels for Individual and Group Political Activity _____

◼ THE ELECTORAL SYSTEM

In a democracy the most popular—that is, the most widely practiced—political activity is voting. For many people, in fact, occasionally going to the polls is their only political activity. Casual and infrequent as this behavior may be, it is the final link in the chain of accountability. Given the particular importance in Britain of accountability as a constraint on concentrated power, beginning our examination of Britain's political system with electoral regulations and procedures is entirely appropriate.

In the twentieth century, before the civil rights movement removed many racial bars to voting in the United States, Britain was more democratic as far as the ability of the people to participate in electoral politics was concerned. Virtually no legal bars to voting existed in Britain: no literacy test had to be passed; no poll tax had to be paid; no period of local residency had to be established. Furthermore, social and racial pressures against voting were unknown, and legislative districts were much more fairly and equally drawn than in the United States. During the nineteenth century, however, the United States was more democratic as far as the breadth of voting rights was concerned. To see why this is true, you need to know how the British electoral system developed. Reviewing this process will also give you an excellent insight into the way in which change occurs in Britain.

The rules that determined who could vote were confused and chaotic in early nineteenth-century Britain. In some towns many adult males could vote; in others not even 1 percent could. In some places, property of a certain value had to be owned for a person to be entitled to vote; in others, the right was obtained through membership in the municipal corporation—membership that could be bought or acquired by marriage or inheritance. Moreover, representation in the legislature was not allocated according to population. Each county and each borough (town or city), regardless of its size, had two members in the House of Commons.

This inequitable situation was worsened by the Industrial Revolution. The new factory towns, such as Manchester and Birmingham, grew rapidly in population but were unrepresented in Parliament because they had not been boroughs at the time when legislative seats were allocated. Many previously thriving rural market towns had become virtually deserted, yet they retained their representation. Dunwich, despite having slid into the sea, still had two members in the Commons; so did Old Sarum, although it had become merely a pasture for sheep. The fish at Dunwich and the sheep at Old Sarum were better represented than the people of Manchester. The representatives from such "rotten boroughs" often were selected by a mere handful of "freemen," usually nonresidents, who owned a few dilapidated buildings there. Membership in the House of Commons literally was bought and sold; a few men of wealth controlled the balance of power in the legislature by having many members "in their pockets."

The first step in the process toward democratic government was the Reform Act of 1832. This law redistributed the seats in the legislature and extended the right to vote. Although representation still was not proportional to population, many rotten boroughs were eliminated and about 150 seats were allocated to the new industrial towns. Uniform voting requirements were established in the towns, and about 200,000 voters were added to the electorate. This was a dramatic change, as you can see in the right-hand portion of Figure 3-1, because it increased the electorate by about 50 percent. On the other hand, as the left-hand portion of the figure shows, only about 7 percent of the total adult population was entitled to vote even after this reform. In contrast, at that time the United States was in the period of Jacksonian democracy, when universal suffrage for adult white males was widely established.

Although the franchise was broadened further in 1867, not until 1884 could most men vote in Britain. And universal manhood suffrage had to wait until well into the twentieth century—until 1918—when the vote also was extended to women, but only to those over thirty. Only then could a majority of the adult population vote. Finally, in 1928 women between twenty-one and thirty were given the vote. Electoral reform required five installments (six, if you count the introduction of the secret ballot in 1872) spread out over a century. There is no better example of the British approach to political reform—incremental change over an extended period of time. Nor was the process of broadening the franchise completed in 1928, for in 1969 the voting age was lowered to eighteen.

The requirements for eligibility to vote are now basically the same in Britain as in the United States, but the countries differ considerably in voter registration. In Britain the government takes the initiative in seeing that those eligible are registered and, therefore, able to vote if they wish to do so. Every October each household receives a form on which the head of the household is to list all residents at that address who meet the voting requirements. Failure to return the completed card makes one subject to a small fine, although this is rarely collected. The registration officer in each constituency compiles a list of registered voters from the information returned and posts the list on bulletin boards in public buildings or other public places. People not on the list, who believe that they should be, may protest to the registration officer and, if the decision is unsatisfactory, may appeal to

Figure 3–1

Expansion of Voting
Rights in Britain

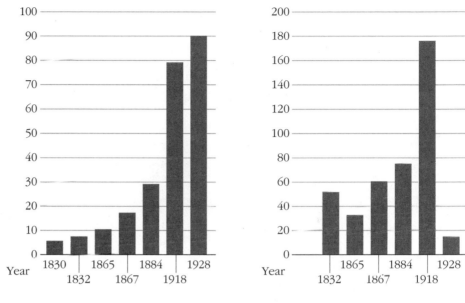

Percentage of adult population enfranchised

Percent increase

the county court. Similarly, anyone may protest the inclusion of persons he or she considers ineligible.

The British approach to voter registration is of great significance because low voter participation in U.S. elections is due more to people not being registered than to those who are registered not bothering to vote. Since the British government accepts the initiative for registering voters, fewer citizens are, in effect, disenfranchised there than in the United States.

The poll tax enacted in Britain at the end of the 1980s was not intended to prevent some groups from voting, as was a similar tax used for many years in parts of the United States. Britons were not required to pay the tax to be permitted to vote; the poll tax simply was an unrelated means of raising local revenue. Nonetheless, the tax adversely affected voter registration. The lists of people required to pay the poll tax were compiled from the voting register. People who regarded the poll tax as unjust (because it was a flat rate tax and unrelated to ability to pay) tried to evade it by keeping their names off the voting register, hoping that this would keep them off the poll tax register as well. The number of registered voters probably would have been about 2.5 percent larger for the 1992 general election had it not been for the poll tax.

Britain has lagged behind the United States in making absentee ballots available. Until 1985 only those clearly unable to get to the polls (such as the physically infirm) could get an absentee ballot. Now the convenience of an absentee ballot has been extended to those who are away from home on election day on business or vacation. If a voter desires, he or she can authorize another person to cast his or her vote, rather than asking for an absentee ballot. The new law also gave the vote to Britons living outside the country. For twenty years after moving away from Britain, they remain on the list of registered voters in the constituency where they last lived. During this time they may vote by absentee ballot or by proxy.

Shortly before an election, registered voters receive a card from the government reminding them of the election and telling them where their polling place is located and the hours it will be open (see Figure 3–2). Clearly, the British government does everything it can to encourage and facilitate participation in elections. Voter turnout in Britain is considerably higher than it is in the United States. Only once in the twentieth century—the first election in which women could vote—has turnout fallen below 70 percent. In one post–World War II election, it reached 84 percent. In 1992, 78 percent of the registered voters participated in the election.

Types of Elections

Britain has two types of national elections: general elections and by-elections. General elections, in which every Member of the House of Commons stands for reelection, must occur at least once every five years. Unlike in the United States, the term of office is not specified, so elections may occur at any time. Twice—in 1910 and in 1974—Britain has had two general elections in a single year. On the other hand, the five-year limit can be ignored, if both the House of Commons and the House of Lords approve doing so. This happened during both of the world wars in this century; the country did not want partisan politics to get in the way of its fight for survival.

Despite the flexible schedule, general elections have been no more frequent in Britain in the twentieth century than have presidential elections in the United States: through 1992 Britain had 25 and the United States 24. So does that mean that whichever practice is followed makes little difference? No, because in Britain the scheduling of an election can be an important factor in the governing party's strategy. The party in power can delay until unemployment is low, prosperity is growing, or new programs have been implemented effectively before calling an election—in the hope that the voters will reward it.

The British practice for scheduling elections also makes the mandate theory of elections more plausible. According to this concept, an election presents the voters with a choice between alternative policy programs. The winning party then can be said to have a mandate—voter approval—for its policies. This theory makes an election resemble a referendum.

The popularity of the mandate theory in Britain (along with the traditional preference for limited, rather than mass, democracy) helps to explain why referenda were unknown in Britain until the 1970s. In 1975 a referendum was held on whether Britain should remain a member of the European Community (EC). British politicians had not suddenly been converted to a belief in the virtues of participatory democracy. The referendum was entirely a matter of political expediency. The Labour party was split on whether Britain should withdraw from the EC; the only way Prime Minister Harold Wilson could think of to hold the party together was to pass the buck to the electorate. The side that lost was supposed to stop agitating, since the people had spoken. Those who wanted Britain to pull out were beaten decisively, but did not throw in the towel. They did lick their wounds for a while, however, so Wilson's strategy paid off in the short run.

Figure 3–2
A Poll Card

ON HER MAJESTY'S SERVICE — OFFICIAL POLL CARD

YOUR POLLING STATION WILL BE:

FCLLOKSHIELDS BURGH HALL
70 GLENCAIRN DRIVE
GLASGOW G41 4LL

POLLING HOURS
7 AM TO 10 PM

POLLING DAY

11TH JUN 1987

GLASGOW POLLCK

CONSTITUENCY

NUMBER ON REGISTER, NAME AND ADDRESS
PK43 / 920

SANDY MACTAVISH
1905 GLENCAIRN DRIVE
GLASGOW   G41 4PR

IF UNDELIVERED RETURN TO RETURNING OFFICER,

PARLIAMENTARY ELECTION

You need not take this card with you when you go to the polling station, but it will save time if you take it and show it to the clerk there.

When you go to the polling station, tell the clerk your name and address, as shown on the front of this card. The presiding officer will give you a ballot paper; see that he stamps the official mark on it before he gives it to you.

Mark your vote on the ballot paper secretly in one of the voting compartments. Put one X in the space to the right opposite the name of the candidate for whom you wish to vote. You may vote for only one candidate. If you put any other mark on the ballot paper your vote may not be counted.

Then fold the ballot paper so as to conceal your vote, show the official mark on the back to the presiding officer and put the paper into the ballot box.

If you spoil the ballot paper by mistake, do not destroy it; give it back to the presiding officer and ask for another.

If you have appointed a proxy to vote in person for you, you may nevertheless vote at this election if you do so before your proxy has voted on your behalf.

If you have been granted a postal vote, you will *not* be entitled to vote in person at this election; so please ignore this poll card.

ISSUED BY THE RETURNING OFFICER

The EC referendum was supposed to be a special case—one time and one time only, according to the Wilson Government. Those who objected to referenda on principle, knowing that what matters in Britain is getting something done for the first time, did not have long to wait until their fear seemed justified. A year and a half later, the Government announced that before devolution was implemented, referenda would be held in Scotland and Wales. As you may remember from Chapter 2, the result of these votes was to kill that measure.

During the decade and a half after the devolution referenda, no others were held, although now and again some politician would urge that the people be consulted on some issue. Not until ratification of the Maastricht Treaty, integrating Britain more fully into the EC, did the issue again become a major one. Some people argued that because of the potential loss of sovereignty involved in the treaty, the public should be consulted. Most of those favoring this step were opponents of the treaty and, aware of the negative public opinion toward the EC, saw this as a means of preventing ratification. Prime Minister John Major adamantly opposed holding a referendum. He argued that Parliament, as the people's representatives, had the authority to legitimate a decision even on such a fundamental matter. Resort to a referendum would undermine that authority and suggest that Parliament was not competent to decide some matters. As was mentioned in Chapter 2, parliamentary supremacy is one of the basic principles of the British constitution. Thus, both in legal theory and in practice, referenda can hardly be considered an essential feature of the British political system. Given the importance of precedent in Britain, however, their use in the future would not be surprising.

At the beginning of this section, we mentioned that Britain has not only general elections, but also by-elections. Whenever a seat in the House of Commons becomes vacant through death or resignation, an election is called to fill it. Although several by-elections may occur on the same day, only a fraction of the country will be voting; in contrast, in a general election everyone goes to the polls.

General elections and by-elections (both for legislative offices) are the only elections for national political office in Britain. Britain does not use primary elections to nominate candidates. Holders of executive office are never elected by the voters. As for the local elections, these are not held at the same time as the national legislative elections (1979 was the one and only exception). As a result, the British ballot is quite simple. No referenda or bond issues clutter the ballot as often happens in the United States. Only one office—representative of the particular constituency in the national legislature—is to be filled; the voters do not have to wade through an American-style list of candidates for county supervisor and dog catcher. The voter's only task is to decide which of three to five candidates he or she wishes to represent the constituency. On the other hand, this does mean that only the few thousand people living in the Prime Minister's constituency have any chance to vote for or against him or her. And those electors are voting for him or her only as a legislative representative and not as Prime Minister.

The ballot lists candidates' addresses and occupations, but, until 1969, party labels could not appear. Now candidates are permitted to use up to six words to describe their party affiliation. Some independents use this provision for some last-minute electioneering. For example, one candidate during the Vietnam War styled herself "Stop the SE Asian War." Some prefer a lighter touch, like the candidate who labeled himself as belonging to the "Science Fiction Loony Party." Naturally, the press referred to him as the loony candidate.

Such candidates do little harm; few people are willing to vote for them. Nonetheless, some Britons have been concerned about their making a travesty of elections. This is a legitimate concern in Britain because, as noted previously, primary elections are not used to weed out fringe candidates. To get on the ballot, a candidate needs only the signatures of ten qualified voters in the constituency.

This is so incredibly easy compared to the United States that you might guess there is a catch—and there is, in the form of a deposit. From 1918 to 1986, any candidate failing to win an eighth of the vote, lost his or her deposit; the government keeps the money.

When the deposit was first required, the sum was £150. Over the years inflation so reduced the value of this sum that the requirement of a deposit ceased to eliminate loony or eccentric candidates (some of whom contested more than two dozen elections even though they knew that they were virtually certain to lose their deposits). Therefore, prior to the 1987 election, the deposit was increased to £500.[1] The proportion of the vote a candidate must win to get the deposit back was reduced to 5 percent. The effect of this change was slight and temporary. The number of candidates in 1987 dropped by about a tenth compared to the previous general election. In the next general election, in 1992, however, nearly 3,000 candidates stood (the British don't run) for election—almost 400 more than in any previous election. That Britain should seek to control candidature by means of a financial penalty is curious, given the country's efforts to reduce the importance of money in the electoral process. Whether the British arrangement eliminates only frivolous candidates, without impeding serious—even if unorthodox—ones as well is open to question.

Candidates are not required, either by law or by custom, to live in the constituency they represent. Remember that Britain is a unitary, not a federal, system. Someone who lives in southern England may well contest a constituency in Scotland. Some candidates do promise that if elected they will move to the constituency. And at times candidates with local roots will refer to opponents who come from outside the area as "carpetbaggers" (perhaps in ignorance of the American origins of this term). Such strategies probably do not win many votes; what matters is the amount of time a representative spends in a constituency and the effort devoted to working for its interests.

Campaign Activities

In contrast to U.S. campaigns, British election campaigns are brief, lasting about three or four weeks. Candidates speak at various meetings, sometimes talking to three or four gatherings in schools or other public facilities during the course of an evening. Sometimes a national political figure will attend one of these meetings in an attempt to boost attendance. Typically, if forty or fifty people show up, that's a good turnout. Most of those who do come probably have already decided to vote for the candidate, although a few may be trying to make up their minds and some may be looking for amusement in the shape of shouting embarrassing comments or raising difficult issues.

Since relatively few voters attend these meetings, the campaign must go to the voters. One of the most traditional electoral activities in Britain is canvassing. Candidates and their supporters go door to door throughout the constituency seeking to

---

[1]The value of the pound sterling (£) fluctuates a good bit from one year to another. In the mid 1990s, £500 was about $750.

Figure 3–3
Portion of a
Conservative Election
Address

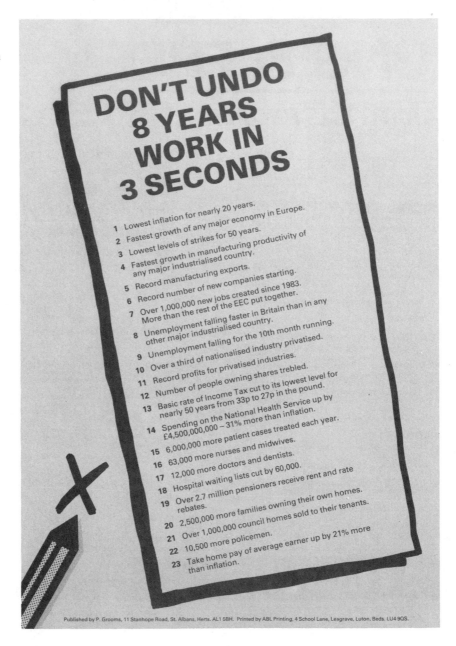

identify favorable voters. These contacts may require candidates to answer questions about their policies, but they try to avoid lengthy debates on doorsteps, in order to cover as many houses as possible. All that the candidates really want to know is who intends to vote for them. On election day, party workers can check the official record of who has voted and contact those voters who said they would support the candidate but have not yet gone to the polls.

Figure 3–3
(continued)

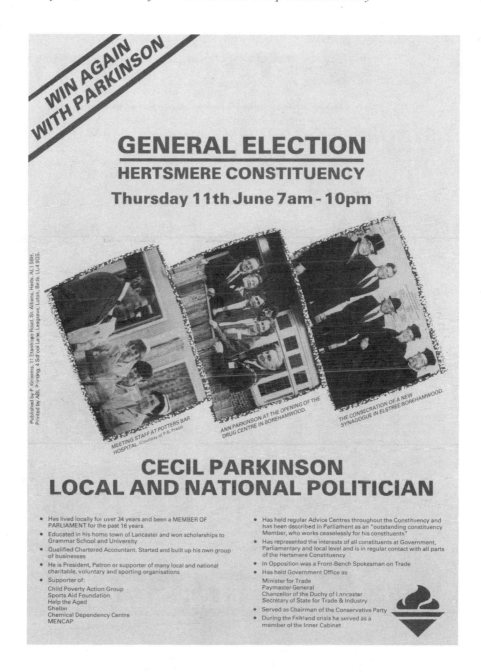

The post office delivers free of charge one communication from a candidate to every voter in the constituency. Typically this "election address" includes the candidate's picture, some biographical information, and a statement of the policies he or she thinks are especially important. (See Figures 3–3 through 3–6.)

Each candidate is required by law to appoint a campaign manager (called an election agent) who must account for *all* campaign expenses (excluding the candi-

Figure 3–4
Portion of a Labour
Election Address

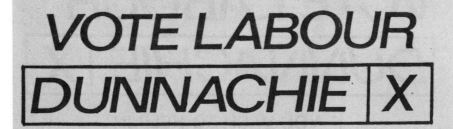

**A PERSONAL MESSAGE FROM JIMMY DUNNACHIE
YOUR LABOUR CANDIDATE IN POLLOK ...**

Dear Elector,

I live with my wife in Pollok and for many years I have represented parts
of the Pollok constituency in local government: on Glasgow Corporation,
Glasgow District Council and, since 1978, on Strathclyde Regional
Council.

I have served on the policy making Executive Committees of the
Councils and I am currently Senior Vice Chairman of Strathclyde
Region's Social Work Committee.

Throughout my local government service I have at all times been
available to my constituents. I work hard and I fight well for the people I
represent. I now seek your vote to continue my fight for you at
Westminster when Labour wins this election.

I know that the next Labour Government will end the hardships that
Thatcherism has imposed on our people because Labour will once more
invest in our people. Together we will build a better future.

I will never rest until my fight for the people of Pollok has won a better
environment and secured a decent standard of living for everyone in
Pollok.

This is my pledge to you.

                          Yours sincerely,
                          JIMMY DUNNACHIE

VOTE LABOUR

DUNNACHIE │ X

Published by: Wm O'Rourke, Election Agent,
259 Peat Road, Glasgow G53.

Printed by: T.F. Dryden Printing Ltd (T.U.)
147 Howard Street, Glasgow G1 4HF.

date's personal expenses). Any campaign spending for a candidate (or against an
opponent) must be authorized by this agent. Expenditure is limited by law. The
maximum varies according to the type of constituency and the size of its electorate.
For a typical constituency in 1992 the maximum was under $13,000. Small as that is
by U.S. standards, candidates for the two main parties spent only about three-

Figure 3–4
(continued)

fourths of the maximum in the 1992 election, and the typical Liberal Democrat laid out well under half the limit.[2]

---

[2]David Butler and Dennis Kavanagh, *The British General Election of 1992* (New York: St. Martin's, 1992), p. 245.

Figure 3–5
Portion of a Liberal
Democrat Election
Address

A PERSONAL MESSAGE FOR

FROM

WILLIAM GOODHART
Liberal Democrat for
Oxford West & Abingdon

Election Communication

Sir William Goodhart
Liberal Democrats

William and his wife, Celia, have lived in the constituency with their family for more than 20 years. Celia is herself a former Parliamentary candidate and now a headmistress of a girls' school. Their eldest daughter works for the NHS as a child psychologist. Their two youngest children, Laura and Benjamin, are at University.

William Goodhart was brought up in Oxford, where his father was a professor. After National Service in the Oxford and Bucks Light Infantry, William studied law at Cambridge University, gaining first-class honours.

William was appointed a Q.C. in 1979 and is an eminent lawyer. He is Chairman of the all-party human rights organisation "Justice", which works to prevent miscarriages of justice.

William Goodhart is a leading member of the Liberal Democrats and is a member of the Party's Policy Committee, working together with party leader Paddy Ashdown

The contest in this constituency is between William Goodhart and the Conservative. Labour have always done badly here. Labour came third in 1983, 1985, 1987, 1989 and 1991 in local and national elections. Make your vote count!

For more information, to help William Goodhart's campaign, display a poster or for a lift to the polling station, please ring (0865) 204106.

Spending by parties at the national level is not limited. In the 1992 election the national organization of the Conservative party spent nearly $18 million, that of Labour spent $12.5 million, and that of the Liberal Democrats less than $4 million.[3] The national organizations must be careful that nothing in their campaign materials appears to appeal for votes for a specific candidate—including even their party Leader and potential Prime Minister. This limitation does not preclude using pic-

---

[3] Ibid., p. 260.

Figure 3–5
(continued)

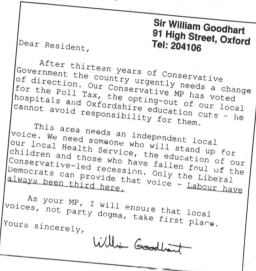

"Oxford West & Abingdon urgently needs a change of MP. After a year of recession, we need an MP who will fight for the Health Service, against local education cuts and get more police for our area."

Sir William Goodhart
91 High Street, Oxford
Tel: 204106

Dear Resident,

After thirteen years of Conservative Government the country urgently needs a change of direction. Our Conservative MP has voted for the Poll Tax, the opting-out of our local hospitals and Oxfordshire education cuts - he cannot avoid responsibility for them.

This area needs an independent local voice. We need someone who will stand up for our local Health Service, the education of our children and those who have fallen foul of the Conservative-led recession. Only the Liberal Democrats can provide that voice - Labour have always been third here.

As your MP, I will ensure that local voices, not party dogma, take first place.

Yours sincerely,

William Goodhart

Sir William Goodhart

● William Goodhart has fought against local hospitals opting-out of the local Health Service.

● William Goodhart has fought for more police - Thames Valley is one of the most understaffed police forces in the country.

● William Goodhart has fought against the cuts to local education forced by the Conservative Government.

● William Goodhart wants to see small business given a chance to grow - not sacrificed by the Government as part of their national economic strategy.

It's a Straight Choice

It is a straight choice in this election between local Liberal Democrat William Goodhart and the Conservative. Labour have always been third here, and still are.

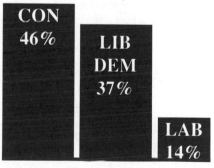

tures of the Leader in election leaflets, as an example (Figure 3–7) from the 1980s shows. Notice, however, that the cover of the leaflet did not urge the electorate to vote for Prime Minister Thatcher as an individual candidate (nor did anything inside the leaflet). Had it done so, the cost of printing it would have had to have been included in the official account of her campaign spending for her constituency. That cost alone might well have exceeded the maximum that she could spend on her campaign.

In order to avoid possible legal complications, British parties refused for many years to advertise in newspapers during election campaigns. In 1974, however,

Figure 3–6
Portion of an SNP Election Address

We're going to <u>win</u> Scotland a better deal

● **AN INDEPENDENT SCOTTISH PARLIAMENT.**
The SNP believes in an independent Scottish Parliament, safe-guarded by a written constitution, elected by proportional representation, within the E.E.C. Self-government is the only constitutional answer to the social and economic problems facing Scotland.

● **280,000 JOBS FOR SCOTLAND.**
The SNP has produced a 280,000 jobs plan, costed by experienced economists, to be carried out by a Scottish parliament within 5 years. The plan includes a national apprenticeship programme and a legally enforced national minimum wage.

● **A NUCLEAR FREE SCOTLAND.**
The SNP believes that armed neutrality, with strong conventional weapons, is the safest and most stable defence for a small country like Scotland. Over 120 countries already reject the immorality of nuclear weapons. A Scottish parliament will do likewise.

> *YOU CAN HELP ANDREW TO BECOME YOUR M.P. BY PHONING:—*
> **FRANK HANNIGAN: 638 0713**
> OR **IAN HUNTER: 649 1093**
> *AND BY USING THIS ELECTION ADDRESS AS A WINDOW POSTER.*

A PRIORITY FOR POLLOK
As MP for Pollok, Andrew would sponsor a European Expenditure Bill which would compel the UK to match EEC grants to help bring jobs and industry to Strathclyde in general and Pollok in particular.

play the Scottish Card... Vote SNP!

Figure 3–6
(continued)

ELECTION COMMUNICATION: GLASGOW POLLOK CONSTITUENCY.

FROM
ANDREW DOIG
YOUR SCOTTISH NATIONAL PARTY CANDIDATE

Andrew Doig is a young man who is both able to communicate with, and campaign for, the people of Pollok, where his parents lived for over a decade. He was President of Glasgow University SNP, has been an elected member of the Party's National Council, and is a founder-member of the SNP Trade Union Group.

Dear Electors,

I am Standing as your Scottish National Party candidate because I know that the SNP is the only hope for Scotland. The Tory party is anti-Scottish, the Alliance are pro-Tory, and Labour can't win.

If my Labour opponent is elected on June 11th, his campaign against Thatcherism will end. If I am elected, my campaign against Thatcherism will just begin!

Andrew Doig

Figure 3–7
Conservative Party
Election Leaflet

the Liberal party broke with this practice. Since all of its ads in the national press
urged support for the *party* rather than for individual *candidates*, it did not allocate this advertising expense to the official spending accounts of any of its candidates. Nonetheless, no account of a Liberal candidate was challenged in court.
Therefore, during the next election campaign, the Conservative and Labour parties

followed suit with ads in the national press, and this has been the practice ever since.

Television plays a major role in British elections. The news programs, of course, cover the campaign. We say "of course," but, surprisingly, this was not true until the 1959 election. Before that, you would not have known from watching newscasts that an election was in progress. The British, you see, wanted to believe that elections are a time for rational choice between policy alternatives and to avoid the hype and hoopla that they felt had debased the U.S. electoral process. Furthermore, the broadcast media were worried that no matter how objective their coverage, they would be criticized for favoring one party or the other. Despite such concerns, the British finally recognized that ignoring elections was journalistically absurd. Now, in addition to news coverage, television provides various public affairs programs that comment on the campaign and discussion or interview programs that give party leaders, and even some of the less prominent candidates, an opportunity to express their views and respond to questions.

On most weekday mornings during the campaign, each of the main parties holds a press conference in London. Various party leaders are present to make short statements on the issues the party wants to emphasize and to answer questions from the press. The parties hope that clips from these sessions will appear on the evening TV news programs. The parties' leading figures usually spend little time campaigning in their own constituencies, preferring to tour the country. Although they may make major speeches on this tour, they are more concerned with visiting a prosperous farm or an efficient factory so that the TV cameras can get some apparently interesting, but basically irrelevant, footage for the evening news.

None of this is terribly different from American practices, but one aspect of the role of television in elections differs considerably in Britain. Neither parties nor individual candidates are permitted to buy any TV time for special programs or even ads. Instead, free broadcast time is officially allotted to the main parties. The parties prepare at their own expense whatever type of program they wish; these programs are carried by both the government-owned BBC (British Broadcasting Corporation) and the commercially operated ITV (Independent Television).

Even though British election campaigns are short, you will be surprised to learn that the total time provided for all the parties combined for election broadcasts in 1992 was only about two and a half hours. The two leading parties, Labour and the Conservatives, each had five broadcasts of about ten minutes each. The Liberal Democrats, the main third party, were allocated only four broadcasts. Two other parties, the Greens and the Natural Law party, offered enough candidates (at least fifty) to earn some TV time, but were given only a single broadcast each. The allocation of two broadcasts within the Scottish viewing area to the Scottish Nationalist Party and one in Wales to the Welsh nationalists was evidence of the importance of regionalism in British politics.

The free TV time, along with the free postage and the short duration of the campaign, does much more to keep down the cost of British elections than does the spending limitation, which applies only at the constituency level in any event. Campaigns also cost less than in the United States because British constituencies have much smaller electorates. As in the United States, each constituency elects only one representative, the candidate who receives the most votes, regardless of whether this is a majority of all the votes cast. Because Britain's population is only about a quarter that of the United States and the House of Commons has half again as many members as the House of Representatives, the typical English constituency has fewer than 70,000 voters and the typical Scottish or Welsh one well under 60,000.

The British have tried harder than Americans to maintain relatively equal constituencies. Boundaries are updated every ten to fifteen years, with the most recent changes occurring prior to the 1983 election. Despite these efforts, the size of electorates varies from under 23,000 to nearly 100,000. On the other hand, more than two-thirds of all constituencies have electorates between 52,000 and 81,000.

Despite all the expense and effort of election campaigns, most constituencies are won by the same party election after election. As you can see from Figure 3–8, only once since World War II have as many as a third of the seats in the House of Commons changed hands from one party to another in a general election. (The 1950, February 1974, and 1983 elections are omitted because extensive changes in constituency boundaries make any comparisons between them and previous elections impossible.) Most of the time, fewer than a tenth of the constituencies shift. The primary reason for this stability has been the traditional loyalty of British voters to particular parties. Most voters have tended to vote for the party they supported in the past, regardless of who the candidate is. As one voter told an interviewer back in the 1950s, "I'd vote for a pig if my party put one up." Although attachment to parties is declining in Britain, few candidates can expect to win even as many as 1,000 votes on a personal basis, that is, not because of their party affiliation.[4]

Thus, as is true for most aspects of the British electoral process, the contrast with the United States is notable. The countries share the same basic electoral system—single-member, simple-plurality constituencies—but differ in virtually everything else about campaign practices and electoral regulations. In some instances the British seem to have the best of it (short and relatively inexpensive campaigns, for example); in other cases the American procedure provides greater citizen involvement (for instance, the use of primary elections to select candidates). Although neither country's system can be said to be clearly superior to the other, the essential point is that British electoral arrangements are quite appropriate for, and conducive to, their basic function of calling power to account.

■ THE INTEREST GROUP SYSTEM

Most people are content simply to vote occasionally, but a few are quite concerned about some specific issue or the benefits available for those having certain characteristics or positions in society. They want a more active role, in conjunction with others, as they seek to make power accountable.

The British were slow to admit the importance of interest groups in their political process. In the nineteenth century special interests in the United States fre-

[4]Ibid., p. 340.

Figure 3–8
Percentage of Seats
Shifting from One
Party to Another at
General Elections

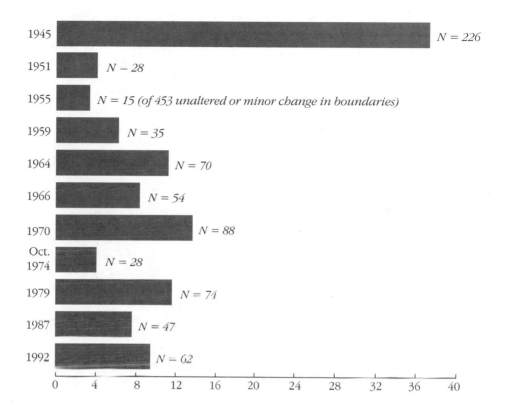

quently were politically corrupt and perverted the common good for the benefit of a narrow segment of society. Although quite ready to recognize that such disreputable influences flourished in the United States, the British wanted to believe that their lengthy governmental experience and concern for proper behavior kept their politics free from such defects. In fact, however, interest groups existed in Britain even before the United States gained its independence. And today the role of interest groups in public policy making is at least as great in Britain as in the United States.

Interest groups are somewhat like the criminal Willie Sutton, who, when asked why he robbed banks, replied, "Because that's where the money is." Similarly, groups focus their efforts where the power is. One of these concentrations of power in Britain, as in the United States, is the electorate. So British groups, like American ones, devote some time to trying to influence public opinion, using ads, public meetings, demonstrations—the range of techniques familiar to any American. For example, the National Association of Local Government Officers (NALGO) ran more pages of political advertising in newspapers during the 1992 election campaign than either the Labour or Conservative party.

Another locus of power is the national legislature; when they think about interest groups, most Americans probably picture a lobbyist talking with a member of Congress. Federal law requires legislators in the United States to be very discreet in their financial relations with groups. (Yes, the law at times is broken.) In Britain, however, a direct financial connection between an interest group and a member of the House of Commons is quite acceptable.

More than half of all the Labour Members of the House of Commons elected in 1987 were sponsored by one or another of Britain's trade unions. Unions that sponsor candidates typically pay some or all of their election expenses. Since this frees the party organization in the constituency from bearing the cost, anyone who is seeking a Labour party nomination and can tell the local selection committee that he or she is sponsored has a much better chance of being chosen. Sponsored legislators also may be given money to help pay their expenses and even have their salaries supplemented.

Sponsorship as such doesn't exist on the Conservative side of the House of Commons. Some of the many Conservative legislators who serve as company directors, however, receive a stipend for little more than the use of their name on company stationery and may be able to shift some of their constituency party's expenses to the company. In addition, many Conservative legislators serve as honorary officers for some interest group or are linked with one in some other way such that when they speak in the Commons on matters of concern to that group, they are effectively serving as its spokesperson.

Neither sponsoring organizations nor other groups can order a legislator to vote a particular way on a bill. Some Labour legislators have at times irritated their sponsors with their voting record, and some unions have withdrawn sponsorship from legislators they felt were not sufficiently loyal to policies favored by the unions. These facts demonstrate that even sponsored legislators are not willing to be mere puppets and that a sponsoring organization does expect "its" legislators to voice its views during debates in Parliament.

You'll be surprised to learn that even though such relations—much closer than those that typically exist in the U.S. Congress—are of some use to British interest groups, they are not of fundamental importance. Strong party discipline in voting, the limited role of the legislature in initiating and shaping legislation, and the comparatively narrow functions of legislative committees (all of which we will discuss in Chapter 5) combine to make Parliament less than the primary focal point for interest group efforts in Britain.

In Britain, policy making is dominated by the executive branch. An interest group favoring some new law will make little headway through influencing legislators. Instead its task is to convince the minister (the top politician) of the appropriate executive department to seek the backing of the Government (the Administration, we would say in the United States). If the desired law involves spending money, then the group also must try to convince the Chancellor of the Exchequer (the politician similar to the U.S. Secretary of the Treasury). Of course, if a group could win the Prime Minister over to its position, it would most certainly get the action it desires, but doing that is likely to be quite difficult.

Interest groups are not concerned solely with getting new laws enacted. Modern government intervenes in so many aspects of life that groups are more likely to be concerned with how existing laws are administered—whether they are applied rigorously or implemented casually, to better serve their spirit or to assist a favored group. Furthermore, much contemporary legislation provides only a framework of aims and procedures and gives to administrators (the dreaded bureaucrats) the job of making detailed regulations. In many instances administrators are the most important actors in the making of a particular policy program. To be effective, an interest group must concentrate on the bureaucracy.

It is at this key point in the policy process that interest groups play a more important role in Britain than they do in the United States. So closely involved in the policy process are the leading British interest groups that they do not even need to take the initiative. Prior consultation of interests by ministers and administrators is standard operating procedure. Before an important bill is sent to Parliament, the governmental department involved will discuss the purpose and general content with leading interest groups. Although the groups don't get to see a draft of the bill (that would infringe on Parliament's rights), they are fully briefed.

The Government is willing to maintain such close relations with groups because it wants to know how such key organizations will respond to the proposed legislation—will their members cooperate in implementing it, or do all they can to hinder putting it into effect? If the latter, can anything be done to make the proposed action sufficiently palatable that they won't be recalcitrant? Furthermore, in many instances these groups have expertise derived from practical experience, which the bureaucracy lacks. Administrators may want some advice on whether the proposed bill is likely to achieve its aims if it is enacted. Have those who drew it up overlooked some crucial aspects?

Such contacts give interest groups their greatest opportunity to influence policy making. The Government has not yet committed itself in public to all the details of the proposed legislation; it can change them without loss of face. Once the bill has been introduced in Parliament and is a matter of public record, the Government is much less willing to back down or reverse direction. Parliament will debate the bill but will rarely make any changes that the Government opposes. An interest group may get "its" legislator to make a fuss in Parliament, but that is more a tantrum than a serious tactic. At that point a group cannot hope for any real concessions and is left with only the possibility of creating a bit of unpleasantness that won't bother the Government much more than a mosquito bite.

Only major interest groups representing key elements in British society enjoy the valuable contacts with the bureaucracy. Contacts were narrowed in 1993 when the head of the trade and industry department announced that his department would deal only with "lead trade associations." This meant that a large number of smaller trade associations ceased to enjoy access. Any groups unable to obtain preferential recognition by the executive are forced to focus on Parliament because such contacts are all they have. The visibility of an interest group's activities in Britain probably is inversely related to its strength and effectiveness. The fact that so much interest group activity occurs behind the scenes helps to explain why the role of interest groups in British politics was overlooked for so long.

World War II greatly enhanced contacts between interest groups and civil servants. Many private groups—for example, producers' associations—became quasi-governmental during those years as Britain sought to ensure the most efficient use of scarce resources. The productive capacity of the country had to be integrated into the Government's war plans as tightly as possible without going through the upheaval of taking industry into full ownership by the state. The extensive consultation to which both administrators and group officials became accustomed during the war carried over into the postwar period.

By the 1970s recognition of the role of interest groups in Britain had grown to the extent that many people wondered whether they had made the country ungovernable. The unions, in particular, were widely criticized for preventing the government from dealing with the problems of inflation, balance-of-payments deficits, and miniscule productivity growth. Prime Minister Edward Heath decided to confront the problem head on and fought the February 1974 election on the question "Who governs?"—meaning the Government or the coal miners' union. Not only did he lose the election, but he eventually failed to retain the leadership of the Conservative party.

The basic issue was still unresolved when Margaret Thatcher came to power in 1979. You might expect that Heath's experience would have made her quite cautious, but not a bit. Instead her view was that Heath and his supporters had been too "wet" (wimpy is an equivalent American term), and she was determined to show that she had the backbone he lacked. The conflict came to a head in 1984, when the coal miners opposed the Government's plans to shut down the least productive mines. The head of the miners' union, Arthur Scargill, was every bit as dogmatic and inflexible as Thatcher. His goal was as much political (to drive Thatcher from office) as it was economic (to protect union members' jobs). This clash between the irresistible force and the immovable object produced a strike that dragged on for months. Police and pickets frequently clashed, and property damage, personal injuries, and even deaths occurred.

Although the Government eventually conceded on minor matters, it was widely regarded as having triumphed; in some sense Thatcher had obtained the answer that Heath had wanted to the fundamental question he had raised. As unemployment mounted in Britain, union membership declined, and many workers were sufficiently grateful to have a job that their capacity for militancy was curtailed. Thus, by the end of the 1980s few people thought any longer that the unions had too much power or doubted that it was the Government that ran the country.

Nonetheless, a change in attitude seems to have occurred in Britain. In the past many people believed that "the man from Whitehall [the civil servant] knows best"; today few Britons are likely to accept that view. Although more willing to question governmental actions, Britons still do not tend to think of using group strategies in politics to the same extent that Americans do. Two-thirds say they would sign a petition to protest Parliament's consideration of a law that they thought was unjust and harmful; none of the group actions suggested—demonstrating, forming a group to protest, raising the issue in a group to which one already belonged—attracted the support of more than a tenth.[5] This low interest in group strategies is not surprising given that only a fifth to a third regard such strategies as likely to be

---

[5] Roger Jowell, Sharon Witherspoon, and Lindsay Brook, *British Social Attitudes: the 1987 Report* (Aldershot, England: Gower, 1987), p. 56.

effective; in contrast, nearly three-fifths think that contacting the media is a good means of protest.

Thus, although "movement" politics is not unknown in Britain and powerful interest groups are prevalent, participation in the interest group system remains confined to a small minority. Narrowing the focus to those groups most influential in the making of public policy makes this political activity even less of a mass behavior. Nonetheless, interest group activity remains a channel by which the public seeks to influence officeholders and thus is a highly important complement to voting behavior as a means of enforcing accountability. In the next chapter we consider a structure involving even fewer people than are associated with interest groups—the party system. There accountability and power merge in the sense that many of those involved in parties perform more than one role: at times they call power-holders to account; at other times they themselves wield power.

4

Policy Alternatives

■ *THE PARTY SYSTEM*

Although the origin of political parties in Britain can be traced back several centuries, many scholars go no further than the early eighteenth century, when two major groups—Whigs and Tories—can be distinguished. And some experts contend that "real" parties did not develop until a century and a half later. Only in the latter part of the nineteenth century did loyalty to party doctrines begin to replace personal relations as the basis for political organization. The need to mobilize the new voters as the electorate expanded (as we explained in Chapter 3) required more elaborate party organization. Factions in Parliament became more stable in their membership and more tightly linked with expanding political organizations outside of the legislature. Party membership grew beyond just a handful of people elected to public office and a small number of political activists. The founding of the Labour party at the turn of the century accelerated this trend toward mass membership parties. Thus, by the start of the twentieth century, Britain had a fully developed modern party system, one involving grass-roots activity throughout the country and not confined merely to interactions of officeholders.

Type of System

As you learned in the Introduction, countries often are classified according to whether they have a one-party, two-party, or multiparty system. Now you might be expecting us to say which one Britain has—a simple matter for anyone who can count, right? Unfortunately, no; although Britain has long been called a two-party system, that label is misleading and has become increasingly questionable.

Toward the close of the nineteenth century, the Liberals and the Conservatives were the only parties of importance throughout the country, although a nationalist party dominated Ireland (part of the British political system then, remember). The Liberal party began a series of splits that almost destroyed it, and in the process some new parties developed that had a range of lifespans. Meanwhile the Labour party was founded and eventually managed to displace the Liberals as one of the leading parties. The Liberals took an unconscionably long time in dying, staggering around the stage like a wounded Wagnerian soprano in her death throes. During the past two decades, sectarian conflict in Northern Ireland (the rest of Ireland is now independent, remember) and the rise of nationalist sentiment in Wales and Scotland have generated additional parties of importance. So instead of simply sticking a label on the British party system, we need to look at some specific information that more precisely indicates its basic type.

In the fourteen general elections in Britain from 1945 through 1992, nearly two-fifths of all candidates for the House of Commons were from neither of the two leading parties, Conservative or Labour. In the most recent election (1992), these two parties provided only 43 percent of the candidates. Voters have a choice from among more than two candidates in many constituencies. Figure 4—1 shows the dramatic change that has occurred in the nature of electoral contests for the House of Commons over the last forty years. In the 1950s voters in most constituencies had a choice between only two candidates. In the 1960s three or more candidates were on the ballots in most constituencies. By the end of the 1970s no constituency was contested by only two candidates, and most had choices among four or more. In the first election of the 1990s, nearly half of the constituencies were contested by five or more candidates.

The many independent and third-party candidates might, of course, have won only a handful of votes and made little difference to the result of the election. A third of all the legislators elected to the House of Commons since 1945, however,

Figure 4–1

Prevalence of Candidates in Recent Elections

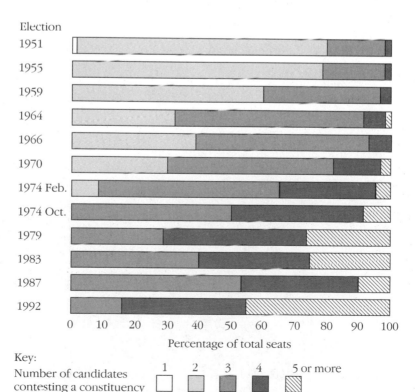

have been minority winners, that is, have received fewer than half of the votes in their particular constituency. In 1992 two-fifths of legislators were minority winners. Clearly, third-party candidates have been gaining a significant share of the vote.

What claim can a country with this pattern of electoral competition have to being designated a two-party system? The answer appears in Figure 4–2. Since the end of World War II, the two leading parties have consistently held well over nine-tenths of the seats in the House of Commons. Since it is strength there that determines which party will control the executive branch, the Labour and Conservative parties have been the only two in the last half century that have had any prospect of forming a Government.

If you think a bit about what we've been saying, you may be puzzled. We say that there are a lot of third-party candidates, right? Right. And they gain a significant share of the vote, right? Right. But they get virtually no seats in the legislature, right? Right. So how can this be? To answer that question we must explain certain aspects of the electoral system that we didn't discuss in Chapter 3.

Constraints Favoring a Two-Party System

As you'll remember, Britain's electoral system is the same as that of the United States in that the candidate who gets the most votes in a constituency wins, regardless of what share of the vote that is. By far the most important effect of such a system is that the share of seats in the legislature that a party wins *has no necessary relation* to the proportion of the popular vote it received. To elect representatives, a party must concentrate its votes in some constituencies so as to beat out everyone else there. Having a substantial share of the total popular vote spread out evenly over the entire country only dilutes the party's support and may not win it any seats at all.

This has been the Liberal party's problem since Labour displaced it as one of the leading parties. In October 1974 the Liberals received over six times as many

Figure 4–2

Percentage of the Seats in Parliament Won by the Two Leading Parties in Twentieth-Century General Elections

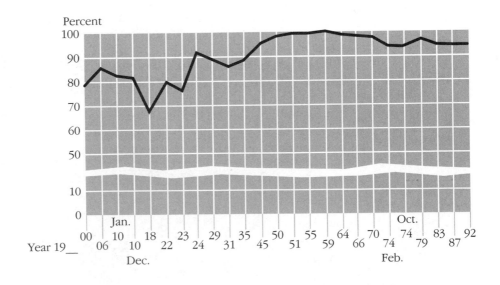

Figure 4–3

Relation between Share of Vote and Number of Seats in Parliament

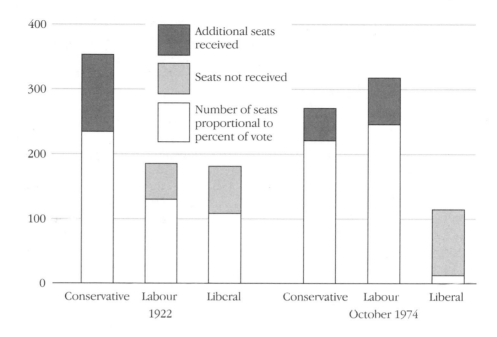

votes as the Scottish Nationalist Party did— more than 5.3 million compared to less than 850,000. Yet the Liberals won only two seats more in the House of Commons—thirteen versus eleven. The Liberal party spread its support across more than 600 constituencies throughout the country; the SNP concentrated its in Scotland's 71 constituencies.

Figure 4–3 provides two examples, from before and after World War II, of how the single-member, simple-plurality electoral system confers benefits and imposes penalties. Typically, the strongest party gets a substantial "bonus" of seats in the legislature—its strength there will be considerably greater than its popularity among the voters. The second strongest party does not benefit as much, either it is penalized or it simply doesn't receive as big a reward. The third party (assuming that it is a nationwide, and not a regional, one) is the one that is really victimized. In 1974 the Liberals received half as many votes as the Conservatives did and nearly half as many as Labour. Yet the Liberals won less than one-twentieth as many seats as either of the leading parties did.

But, you may say, if this is the effect of the electoral system, how did the Labour party, which was a third party early in the twentieth century, manage to replace the Liberals as one of the two leading parties? One reason was that the Labour vote then, unlike the Liberal vote subsequently, was concentrated in certain areas—urban working-class districts and mining constituencies. As a result, Labour could manage to beat all comers in a number of places.

The electoral system, then, is a major influence in giving Britain a two-party system with respect to the national legislature, whatever it may be with respect to the distribution of the popular vote and the pattern of partisan competition. Another aspect of electoral regulations—the electoral deposit—also tends to support a two-party system. In addition to campaign expenses, parties must risk a good deal of money in deposits if they are contesting every constituency. Third parties, in trying to get their electoral challenge to the leading parties off the ground, are most likely to have trouble winning the share of the vote necessary for the deposit to be refunded. For such a party, whose finances are likely to be constrained in any event, this is a major impediment.

The Liberal party lost so many deposits in 1950 that it was forced to go from contesting three-fourths of all the constituencies to fighting only a sixth of them in the next election. You may remember from Chapter 3 that the share of the vote required to save a candidate's deposit was lowered from one-eighth of the votes cast to only 5 percent. And you might think that the leading parties decided to do the Liberals a favor. The Liberals certainly didn't see things that way. By the mid-1980s their strength had revived to the extent that they no longer feared losing deposits. In fact, in the 1983 election the Labour party lost more deposits than the Liberals did. What worried the Liberals was the increase in the size of the deposit. In order for them to contest all the constituencies, they would have to tie up the equivalent of well over a half million dollars in deposits, which would be unavailable for spending during the campaign. They would have preferred an increase in the number of signatures required for nomination to raising the deposit. The only concession the Liberal party received was that the Government increased the deposit to only half as much as it originally had intended to do. The point is that even a party that has no fear of losing its deposit is constrained by this requirement, and those hurt most are parties with limited finances—third parties, not the leading ones.

Another factor that reinforces a two-party system is the arrangement for campaign broadcasts. Prohibiting parties from buying media time does reduce the cost of elections drastically. But it also raises questions of fairness. In Britain the great bulk of the time allocated to parties goes to Labour and the Conservatives. Other parties receive considerably less and thus have less opportunity to use the most powerful channel of mass communication to get their message across. Only in 1987 did the Liberals (cooperating with the Social Democrats in what was called the Alliance) receive the same number of broadcasts as did each of the two leading parties. The allocation of broadcasts is important not only in itself, but also because the TV companies use it as the guide for the amount of coverage they need to give each party on news programs. Furthermore, the allocation of broadcasts carries with it a subtle message: third parties aren't as important as the leading two; if they were, they would be given equal time.

In addition to the obstacles created by electoral regulations and procedures, third parties face yet another obstacle—the pragmatism of the British voter. Recall our comments in Chapter 2 about the relative unimportance of ideology in British politics. The Liberals have long had to fight against the wasted vote argument. The leading parties tell the voters that since the Liberals have no hope of gaining the more than 300 new seats they would need to obtain a majority in the House of Commons, voting for them is irrelevant. Much better to choose between the realistic alternatives—should Labour or the Conservatives run things? Many British voters find this argument persuasive. Thus, even though they may prefer the Liberals' policies, they don't vote for them.

In Britain the deck is stacked against third parties, particularly those campaigning on a nationwide basis. This has not, however, discouraged third parties from continuing to try. In fact, the range of choice available to the British voter today is considerably more varied than it was thirty years ago. Hope springs eternal, and there is a precedent in the Labour party—the third party that managed to become one of the two leading parties, just as the Republican party did in the United States. History may repeat itself, and some new third party may replace Labour as one of the leaders. Or there might be a transformation, not just a realignment, and three or four parties might compete on relatively equal terms for power. For that to occur, however, almost certainly would require major change in the British electoral system, given the extent to which it buttresses the two-party system.

Thus, Britain may be a multiparty system as far as electoral inputs are concerned; but once these have been processed by the electoral system, the output is a two-party system as far as the control of governmental power is concerned.

■ THE LEADING PARTIES

Although a number of parties exist in Britain, two—Labour and Conservative—clearly have been preeminent for the past half century. The rest of this chapter, therefore, concentrates primarily on these two. We discuss, first, the policy alternatives offered by them and, then, the segments of the population preferring the one policy mix to the other. Next, we examine the parties' strengths and weaknesses—their level of support and prospects. Doing so requires some evaluation of the effectiveness of their organization. Party organization gets fuller treatment, however, when we turn to the distribution of power within each party and the implications of this for participation in the democratic process.

Party Programs and Policies

The Conservative party Outlining the Conservatives' program is difficult because many Conservatives would question whether such a thing exists. They certainly would object to a study of Conservative ideology because they feel free of the doctrinaire constraints they regard as a defect of socialism. They regard conservatism as more of an attitude toward society than a coherent set of doctrines. Conservatives present themselves as the traditional party of government, the party composed of society's leaders, obviously best suited by heredity and experience to run the country. At times they almost seem to say to the electorate, "Never mind our policies, simply trust our capable leaders, who will know what's best to do, whatever may happen."

The Conservatives have supported the traditional elements of British society: the monarchy, the established church, the military, the existing social structure, and the public school system. Theirs has been a party of the elite and of the status quo. Yet they have not been reactionary or, from an American perspective, even very conservative. They are able to adapt to change. Although at times they have opposed their opponents' reform measures, they have introduced some welfare policies and have accepted socialized medicine, claiming that they can operate it better than other parties could. Beginning in the 1980s Conservative Governments returned a number of government-owned enterprises to private ownership. On the other hand, some of the businesses owned by the British government were taken over not when Labour was in power but when the Conservatives were.

Conservatives want to avoid the extremes of either individualism or collectivism. They prefer individual freedom to bureaucratic direction; they believe that widespread ownership of property is essential to a healthy democracy. They recognize, however, that social considerations often necessitate qualifying these beliefs. The Liberals, not the Conservatives, were the traditional party of laissez-faire. The idea that the government may need to act to correct economic abuses or stimulate the economy is not foreign to a Conservative.

What makes Conservatives conservative is their feeling that not much needs reforming or, indeed, can be reformed. Social inequality, for example, is not bad and can't be eliminated in any event. People contribute to society in various ways; it is only natural that their rewards and political influence should vary as well. Despite this view of social diversity, Conservatives try to appeal to feelings of community by stressing national unity. They see themselves as the only truly national party, representative of all interests rather than just those of a single section, as they charge Labour is. In fact, as we'll discuss shortly, Conservatives have won the support of many working-class voters. Conservatives berate socialists for emphasizing class divisions and needlessly stirring up divisive feelings. Whatever our station in society, we are all British, say the Conservatives. They almost seem to feel that they are the only true patriots. The British flag is often displayed prominently at Conservative party meetings.

One of the ironies of British politics is that a party with such strong nationalistic views was the one to arrange for British entry into the EC, while Labour, traditionally the more internationalist party, became increasingly hostile to this step. Labour worried, more than the Conservatives did, about what would happen to the Commonwealth (the contemporary descendant of the British Empire, which always made Conservative hearts quicken with pride). Although some Conservatives were unhappy with British membership in the EC, conflict among them on this issue was not nearly as sharp as it was in the Labour party, at least until the 1990s.

After being out of office for a few years, the Conservatives returned to power in 1979 with a campaign that stressed two themes: the weakness of the British economy and the Labour Government's unwillingness to stand up to the trade unions. Linking these themes was the argument that allowing unions to get the huge wage increases they were demanding would fuel a disastrous rate of inflation. Labour had managed to cut inflation from a truly horrendous 22 percent in July 1975 to under 10 percent by the time of the 1979 election. Widespread strikes during the winter preceding the election, however, seemed to indicate a new period of union unreasonableness that might drive the rate back up. In any event, when things literally had reached the point that people could not bury their dead because the gravediggers were on strike and picketing the cemeteries to prevent anyone else from digging graves, Conservatives were not the only ones thinking that things had gone too far. This "Winter of Discontent" did a great deal to lose the 1979 election for Labour.

What was the Conservative solution? Cuts in government spending, which would reduce government borrowing and get the money supply under control. Heavily influenced by the theories of the American economist Milton Friedman, Conservatives believed that the money supply was the key element in controlling inflation. Spending cuts also would permit lowering the income tax. Doing that would restore the incentive for hard work and business competition, since people would keep more of what they earned. A tight money supply would force employers to make more efficient use of their workers and to resist excessive wage demands, since they could not easily borrow money to finance their businesses. The Conservatives believed that the free enterprise system, along with unfettered collective bargaining, could be relied on to limit wage demands and prevent any need for governmental intervention to control prices and wages. The problems of low productivity, inefficiency, and international lack of competitiveness that had bedeviled the British economy would thus be solved.

In 1987 the Conservatives won a third consecutive election, using a double-barreled campaign. On the one hand, they stressed their accomplishments over the past eight years, in particular, the strength of the economy. They had kept inflation lower than in most other countries, and the economy was growing at a higher rate than that of France or Germany. And, best of all, unemployment was beginning to decline. Indeed, opinion polls showed that people were much more optimistic about the state of the British economy than they had been only a couple of years earlier. The other prong of the Conservative attack in 1987 is summed up in their slogan, "Britain Is Great Again. Don't Let Labour Wreck It." (Figure 4–4 shows a newspaper ad featuring this slogan.) The Conservative argument was that the Labour party was not only incompetent but so dominated by extremists that it was downright dangerous. In foreign affairs Labour could not be trusted to keep Britain's defenses strong; in domestic matters its support for libertines, homosexuals, and minorities was destroying all aspects of British society that right-thinking people held dear.

Some people would say that the policies implemented in Britain during the 1980s expressed not so much Conservatism as Thatcherism. For the first time in Britain's history, a Prime Minister was so dominant that that person's name could be used as a label for a set of policies and a style of governing. From the beginning Margaret Thatcher proclaimed her determination to stick to her principles no matter what. She refused to alter the economic policies she felt necessary even when they were accompanied by a shocking growth in unemployment. Many of the party's traditional elite were appalled by what they regarded as her insensitivity to the personal degradation involved in long-term unemployment. They feared she was diverting the party from its traditional adaptability and concern with national community. In both her abrasive style and the substance of her policies, Thatcher was out of step with traditional Conservatism. Late in 1990 she was driven from office by a revolt within the party (discussed later in this chapter).

John Major became the Conservatives' Leader and the new Prime Minister. In 1992 he managed to lead the party to a fourth consecutive victory. Since the economy had gone into recession, the campaign appeals of 1987 had to be modified. As you can see in Figure 4–5, the Conservatives virtually pretended that they had noth-

Figure 4–4
Conservative Newspaper Ad for the 1987 Election Campaign

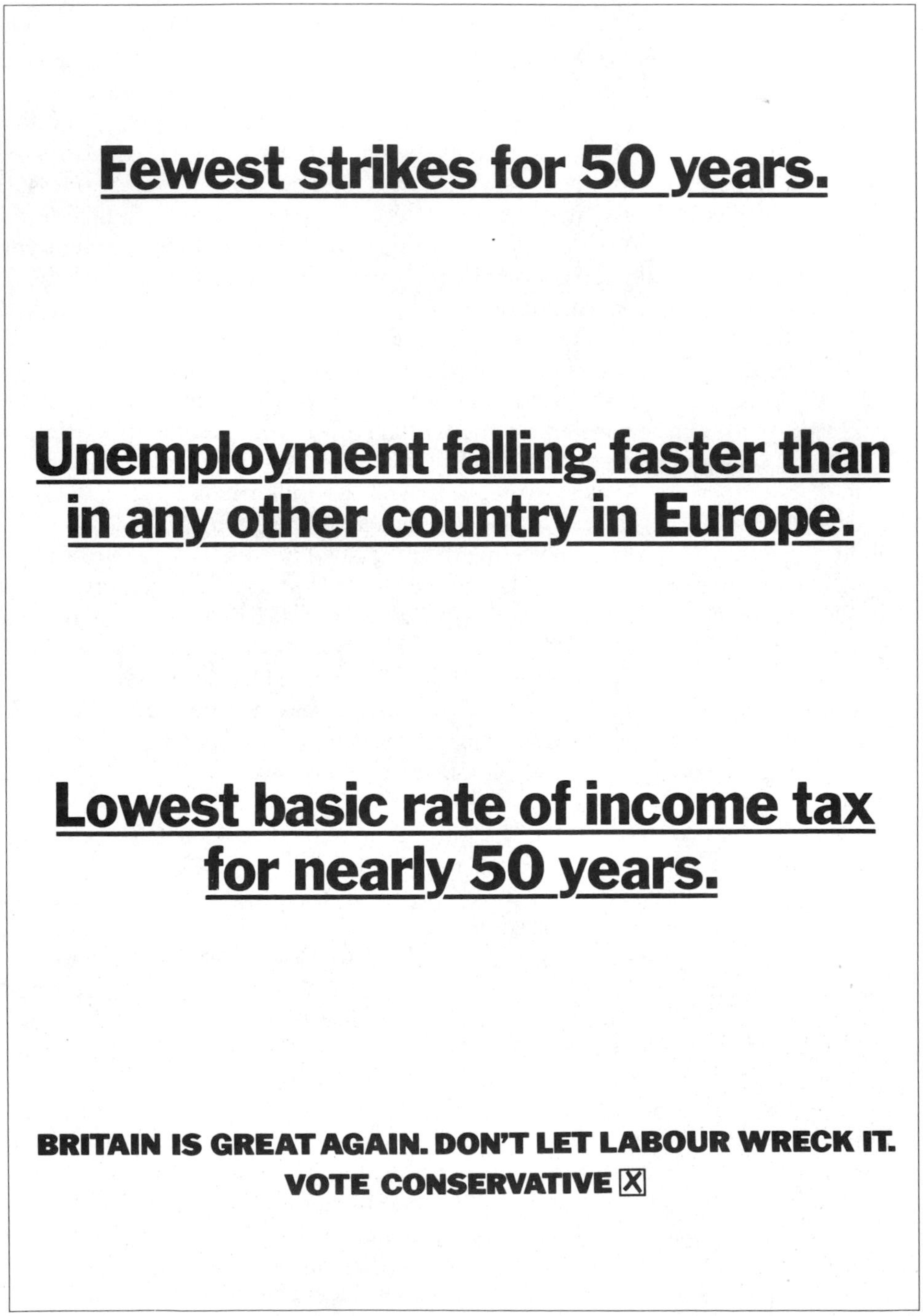

Fewest strikes for 50 years.

Unemployment falling faster than in any other country in Europe.

Lowest basic rate of income tax for nearly 50 years.

BRITAIN IS GREAT AGAIN. DON'T LET LABOUR WRECK IT.
VOTE CONSERVATIVE ☒

Figure 4–5
Conservative
Newspaper Ad for
the 1992 Election
Campaign

Just as recovery is under way, Labour would start a new recession. A Conservative win will end uncertainty, raise confidence and speed Britain ahead. Labour would put taxes up, mortgages up, inflation up and strikes up. That's why 90% of business leaders say that Britain needs the Conservatives to keep Britain moving forward.

ing to do with Britain's economic problems, despite having been in power for the previous thirteen years. They proclaimed that they had the solution and, as in 1987, putting Labour in office would make things worse. Despite being Thatcher's preference as her successor, Major was her opposite in many regards. An emollient, some would say bland, personality, he campaigned on making Britain "a classless society, a country at ease with itself." He was seeking "a Britain where everyone has the chance to succeed." Government was to become more responsive to the citizen. The hated poll tax that Thatcher would not alter would be dropped. Major also took a more conciliatory attitude toward Europe, saying that Britain's place was at the heart of the EC. He stressed the national unity theme of traditional Conservatism by strongly opposing the devolution of power to Scotland. Thus, under Major the Conservatives were moving back toward their traditional policies and attitudes.

The Labour party   The basic doctrine of the Labour party is socialism. No doubt you're grateful for such a clear-cut statement after the ambiguity concerning conservatism. Unfortunately, Labour has its own lack of clarity. The party has been little influenced by Marxism (although you will find Marxists among its members); its intellectual heritage derives instead from Christian socialists of the social gospel school and the Fabian Society. As one of the leaders of the Labour party once wrote about its forerunner, its "socialism was derived far more from the Methodist Church and a Christian approach than from Continental revolutionaries."[1] As for the Fabians, this elite group of intellectuals wanted nothing to do with Marxist revolutionaries; the society's statement of purpose begged "those socialists who are looking forward to a sensational historical crisis, to join some other society."[2]

Sidney Webb, one of the most influential of the Fabians and a Labour activist during the party's formative period, asserted that four conditions were essential if political and social reform were to occur in Britain: (1) change must occur democratically; (2) it must occur gradually, causing no dislocation; (3) it must not be regarded as immoral; (4) it must be achieved constitutionally and peacefully.[3] Hardly a cry to man the barricades against the capitalist oppressors! Fabians believed that sound factual research would be sufficient to establish the case for socialism in the minds of all reasonable people.

Fabians were living proof that you could be a socialist without having to use Marxist jargon or swallow an abstract, elaborate theory of history. They made advocacy of modern reform respectable by showing that you could be for extensive change without having to be a revolutionary. Their enormous influence on the development of Labour reinforced the practical bent of the party that derived from being based in the trade union movement. This organizational core focused the party on seeking to ameliorate living conditions for the average person now, not in some future millennium when the state would wither away.

Despite these strong influences, the Labour party for much of its history has been torn between two contrasting views of socialism. The left wing, which believes that it alone is true to the party's principles, sees the essence of socialism as nationalization—government ownership of "the commanding heights of the economy." Labour has been officially committed to such a policy since 1918. The left wing argues that in a democracy large concentrations of economic power must be controlled by government to ensure that social ends, rather than the benefit of a few, are served. The working class, through its representatives, must control all forms of power.

Labour moderates do not regard nationalization as a panacea for social ills. They admit that the extensive program of nationalization that the party implemented from 1945 to 1951 did little to promote greater equality by redistributing wealth;

---

[1]Hugh Gaitskell, *Recent Developments in British Socialist Thinking* (London: Cooperative Union, n.d. [circa 1960]), p. 4.
[2]Quoted in Margaret Cole, *The Story of Fabian Socialism* (London: Mercury Books, 1963), p. 92.
[3]G. Bernard Shaw, ed., *Fabian Essays in Socialism* (Garden City, NY: Doubleday, n.d.), p. 51.

this will necessarily be true unless a government seizes private enterprises without compensating their owners—action the moderates would reject as tyrannical. So socialism for them is not a matter of government ownership of the means of production, distribution, and exchange, but a quest for social justice (not that the left wing is uninterested in this). Government's task is to maintain a floor of basic benefits for all as a right while ensuring that everyone really does have equal opportunity to rise above that floor to the maximum of his or her ability.

According to Labour, the quest for equality is not just a matter of correcting disparities in wealth and income. The values of British society must be transformed to eliminate snobbery and privilege. Class barriers and social inequalities that prevent people of differing status from associating easily with one another must be destroyed. The father of the Labour party, Keir Hardie, observed, "Socialism is at bottom a question of ethics or morals. It has to do mainly with the relationships which exist between a man and his fellows."[4]

As we noted earlier, Labour has an international perspective, a belief that workers share a common bond whatever their nationality. Thus, the party has been much less nationalistic (Conservatives would say less patriotic) than the Conservative party, has opposed colonialism, and has taken a dim view of the British Empire. Why, then, has Labour been so suspicious, indeed, at times hostile, to the EC? The left wing of the party sees the EC as an alliance of capitalists and faint-hearted socialists; British membership prevents the country from controlling its own economy and thereby forecloses socialist reform. Furthermore, the EC's Common Agricultural Policy penalizes the British working class with higher food prices.

In 1980 the Labour party conference voted for the Government to pull Britain out of the EC once Labour returned to power. Although the party's leaders did all they could to soft-pedal this stand, the Labour manifesto for the 1987 election still said that the party rejected EC "interference with our policy for national recovery and renewal."

Although never a majority position, pacifism traditionally has been strong in the Labour party. (If all workers are brothers and sisters, regardless of nationality, then they should not kill each other in wars, which only enrich the capitalists, anyway.) At times such feelings combine with the left wing's distrust of the capitalist United States to produce neutralist sentiments. In the early 1980s the party conference opposed any defense policy based on nuclear weapons and wanted not only the withdrawal of all cruise missiles from Britain, but also the closing of all U.S. bases there. Nonetheless, a proposal for Britain to withdraw from NATO was defeated.

Labour's attempt to regain power from Margaret Thatcher in 1983 was one of the most disastrous and incompetently waged campaigns in the history of British politics. The party's policies were so extreme and out of touch with the electorate that a disgruntled moderate Labour leader labeled the party's extraordinarily lengthy manifesto "the longest suicide note in history." The party's choice for Prime Minister, Michael Foot, was a former darling of the left wing, who was so far past his

---

[4]Quoted in Socialist Union, *Twentieth Century Socialism* (Harmondsworth, Eng.: Penguin Books, 1956). Despite the fact that this statement now seems sexist, Hardie was quite supportive of women in politics.

Figure 4–6
Labour Newspaper
Ad for the 1987
Election Campaign

TRY TELLING HER THAT SHE'S WRONG.

 THE COUNTRY'S CRYING OUT FOR LABOUR.

Figure 4–7
Labour's New Image

prime that virtually no one could take him seriously as a contender for the highest office.

Labour's campaign in 1987, however, was extremely professional, generally regarded as having outshone the Conservatives. Thinking that eight years of Thatcher's abrasive dogmatism was all that most people could stand, Labour attacked her as insensitive and uncaring. Figure 4–6 shows the "punch line" to a four-page sequence of ads. Each of the first three pages pictured a person such as a teacher and said, "Try telling him that education [or whatever government service was relevant to the picture] is adequately supported"; the last page pointed at Thatcher's inflexibility. Labour argued that government services were deteriorating under the Conservatives and that even if unemployment was declining (which was not certain since the methods by which it was estimated had been changed by the government), it still was far beyond any acceptable level.

Figure 4–7 shows what Labour believed the country wanted. This simple sticker has a fascinating story. Several socialist parties on the Continent had adopted party logos that include a rose. The French Socialists' logo depicted an almost virile dark-red rose clutched in a clenched fist, nicely suggesting both toughness and tenderness. The Labour party apparently was so stung by charges that it had been hijacked by left-wing extremists that it felt it could not go that far. Its logo omitted the fist entirely and the rose, a soft-focus pastel pink, looked like the sort of thing that might appear on a container of dishwashing liquid.

Despite Labour's slick campaign the party suffered from two great liabilities. First, the economy *had* improved. If you weren't one of the unemployed—and even at 3 million the unemployed constituted only a fraction of the electorate—you didn't have much to complain about. Second, there was the albatross of Labour's defense policy. The party was committed to unilateral nuclear disarmament, that is, getting rid of Britain's nuclear weapons regardless of what the Soviet Union did. Although Labour Leader Kinnock was willing to tone down Labour's other policies, on defense he remained a committed unilateralist.

During the campaign a TV interviewer pressed Kinnock on how Labour could defend Britain without nuclear weapons. If the Soviet Union said it was going to invade and Britain resisted, then it would nuke Britain—how could Kinnock protect the country if he had gotten rid of its Polaris missiles within two weeks of coming into power, as he had said he would? Kinnock gave one of his usual rambling answers and seemed to say that in the end passive resistance and guerilla warfare from the hills was all that could be done to make such an invader decide to withdraw. To the Conservatives this sounded like surrender. They quickly prepared a

Figure 4–8
Conservative Newspaper Ad on Labour Defense Policy for the 1987 Election Campaign

classic ad that knocked Kinnock out of the ring (see Figure 4–8). From that point on, everything that Labour said to clarify its position on defense only made matters worse.

Clearly, Labour's policies and image had to be revised further for the party to again become a credible challenger to the Conservatives. Under Kinnock's direction Labour not only laid to rest its hostility to the EC, but also, despite Kinnock's past views, abandoned unilateralism. Furthermore, those most responsible for Labour's economic policies met with bankers and business leaders to assure them that a Labour Government wouldn't be radical. It wouldn't take back into government ownership all the enterprises that Thatcher had sold to the public. It wouldn't impose a siege economy with control on investment abroad and high taxes. And it wouldn't give in to every desire of the trade unions, although it obviously would not be as hostile to them as Thatcher had been.

Labour's campaign appeal in 1992 was essentially the same as in 1987: "It's time for change. It's time for Labour." Party advertising (see Figure 4–9) rang a variety of changes on this theme, hitting at various Conservative vulnerabilities. Until the final week of the campaign, the transformed Labour party seemed certain to regain power after thirteen years out of office. Then Labour held a major campaign rally in Sheffield. Kinnock's natural ebullience caused him to seem offensively overconfi-dent of victory. He was widely accused of the sin of "triumphalism"—as we said in Chapter 2 many English people find the florid rhetorical style of the Welsh hard to take. Many voters apparently concluded that Kinnock was just as unsound as they had feared, certainly not as trustworthy as that nice Mr. Major. Beyond this, the Conservatives' claims that Labour's spending plans would cost the average person about $2,000 more in taxes began to have an impact. The certain victory evaporat-ed. Despite all its efforts, Labour still faced the task of devising a program both dis-tinctive and attractive, which grew out of its basic philosophy, rather than a random collection of policies thought to be electorally expedient.

The Bases of Party Support

Social structure   Landed interests were the traditional core of Conservative support. Around the turn of the century, many industrialists left the Liberal party and joined the Conservatives. To these two segments of society, the Conservatives added professionals and farmers. Labour's main strength, as its name suggests, has been among the working class. Some people in the lower middle class, teachers, for example, have also supported this party. Typically, about a fourth of the middle class voted Labour. Since the Conservatives won a fourth to a third of the working class and since that segment of British society has been larger than the middle class, Labour has usually been a net loser on these shifts across class lines.

Cross-class voting is common in the United States. In Britain, however, the sharper class distinctions that we discussed in Chapter 2 made such behavior unusual for many years. Furthermore, no major party in the United States claims by its very name to represent the workers' interests, as the Labour party does. For most of the post–World War II period, therefore, social class was by far the strongest influence on voting behavior in Britain. In the 1970s, however, Britain entered a period of dealignment; that is, attachment to parties became much less

Figure 4–9
Labour Newspaper Ad for the 1992 Election Campaign

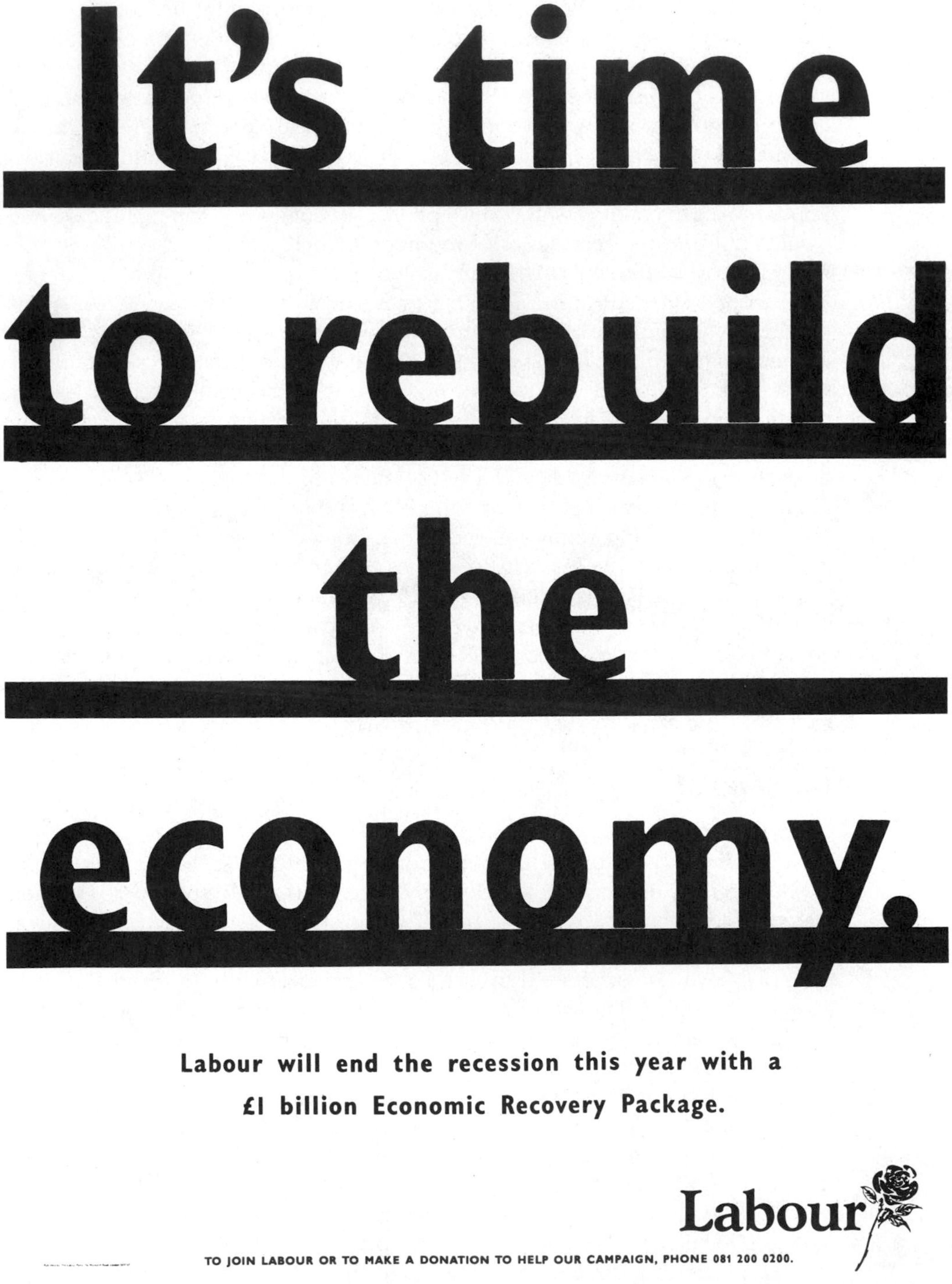

It's time
to rebuild
the
economy.

Labour will end the recession this year with a £1 billion Economic Recovery Package.

TO JOIN LABOUR OR TO MAKE A DONATION TO HELP OUR CAMPAIGN, PHONE 081 200 0200.

automatic, and feelings of class solidarity no longer affected voting as they once had. Voters became more inclined to weigh the issues in a campaign and to assess party performance. Election campaigns became not so much a matter of parties' getting "their" voters to turn out on election day as of convincing uncommitted or wavering voters to choose them.

About 11 million people, around a quarter of the electorate, changed their voting intention from the start to the end of the 1992 campaign, considerable flux for a period of less than a month. Most of this change was people shifting to or from "don't know." Shifts to and from Liberal, Conservative, and Labour involved around 4.5 million people, about a tenth of the electorate. Thus, although voting has ceased to be automatic, people don't drift randomly from one party to another. The impact of class has declined, but not disappeared.

In the 1992 election, over half again as many unskilled workers voted Labour as voted Conservative.[5] Nonetheless (because of votes cast for other parties), Labour fell just short of winning a majority of even the group from which it could expect maximum support. Among skilled workers, Labour's strength declined considerably during the 1980s, until more of this segment of the working class voted Conservative than supported Labour. Labour managed in 1992 to regain some of its former strength among skilled workers, but could do no better than equaling the share of this group's votes won by the Conservatives. As for those in the rest of the social structure—white-collar workers on up—two to three times as many of them voted Conservative in 1992 as voted Labour. No wonder Labour failed to dislodge the Conservatives from office.

Various elaborate theories have been suggested to explain why class became less important, why many British workers turned their back on the Labour party. One fairly straightforward idea was that as manual workers became more prosperous, they could afford middle-class consumption patterns. Becoming like the middle class in this respect might affect political attitudes and thus party allegiance. Whatever the validity of this theory, certain elements of lifestyle clearly are related to political behavior. For example, in 1992 manual workers owning their own homes were as likely to vote Conservative as to vote Labour. Those who lived in public housing, however, favored Labour over the Conservatives by a margin of more than two and a half to one.

Membership in a trade union also affects the tendency to vote along class lines. As mentioned previously, the Conservatives and Labour were equally strong among skilled workers. Among skilled workers belonging to unions, however, Labour won twice as many votes as did the Conservatives. Union membership increased Labour support even more among unskilled workers.

Other characteristics affecting partisan preferences   As social class declines in influence on voting behavior, other factors become more important. The 1992 election showed a modest gender gap. The proportion of women voting Conserva-

---

[5]Much of the information in this and following paragraphs is from David Butler and Denis Kavanagh, *The British General Election of 1992* (New York: St. Martin's, 1992), pp. 276–279, and from various Gallup and Market & Opinion Research International polls.

tive was about 10 percentage points greater than the share favoring Labour. Among men the Conservative lead was less than half as large.

A similar age gap also was evident. Support for the Conservatives rose by about 10 percentage points from those eighteen to twenty-four compared to those fifty-five and older. Labour's support declined by about half that much between the two groups. The youngest age group, people about your age, was the only one to give more support to Labour than to the Conservatives. Even here, however, Labour's position was weaker than it had been. At the end of the 1970s, it was far ahead of the Conservatives among those eighteen to twenty-four; in 1992, it led by only a few percentage points.

Gender and age combine to produce some interesting voting patterns. Women over sixty-five are half again as likely to vote Conservative as to favor Labour, whereas men of that age give the Conservatives only a slight edge. At the other end of the age spectrum, however, women are more "left" in party preference. Men under twenty-five slightly favored the Conservatives in 1992, whereas women of that age were nearly half again as likely to vote Labour.

As for regional patterns of party support, for some time the Conservatives have dominated England from a bit south of Manchester to the southern coast, except in inner London and the urban industrial areas. The Labour party has been virtually obliterated as a significant political force in southern England; the Conservatives won 95 percent of the constituencies in this section of the country in both 1983 and 1987, declining only slightly to 91 percent in 1992. In London and central England, Conservative domination is not as overwhelming—the party won close to three-fifths of the seats in these areas in 1992. On the other side of the political divide, in northern England, Scotland, and Wales, the Conservatives won only a quarter of the seats in 1992. The contrast in partisan preference between the north and the south is stark.

Until the 1970s Northern Ireland was virtually an exclusive Conservative preserve; that party regularly won all the seats there. Religious conflict has so affected Northern Ireland's politics, however, that now no British party can win even a single seat there; usually they don't even bother to try.

Party Strengths and Weaknesses

Electoral success   The results of all general elections since 1945 in Britain appear in Table 4–1. After winning an overwhelming victory in 1945, the Labour party just managed to retain power in 1950. And then it lost control of the Government in 1951, despite the fact that it not only received more votes in that election than the Conservatives did, but received more than any other party before or since, until the Conservatives topped 14 million in 1992. (As we noted in Chapter 3, peculiar things can happen with a single-member, simple-plurality election system.) During the 1950s the Conservatives won three consecutive general elections, an unprecedented accomplishment. Returned to power by a narrow margin in 1964, Labour won a substantial victory in 1966, but, surprisingly, was defeated by an unusually large shift of seats to the Conservatives in 1970. Although the Conservatives received more votes than Labour did in February 1974, they did not win quite as many seats and, thus, were put out of office (tit for tat for 1951). Labour, although the largest party in the House of Commons, had to form a minority Government since it was several seats short of an absolute majority. Several months later this Government called another election in hopes of winning firm control of Parliament. It was successful but just barely, gaining only one seat more than an absolute majority.

In the 1979 election, the Conservatives swept back to power on the largest shift of votes from one of the two leading parties to the other in the entire postwar period. Despite their gains the Conservatives polled only 44 percent of the popular vote. (Note that in only one election in more than forty years has any party managed to get half of the popular vote.) Although the Conservatives' support declined slightly in 1983, the collapse of the Labour vote gave the Conservatives a landslide victory in number of seats won—the greatest triumph for any party since 1945. Labour lost a quarter of the support it had received only four years earlier. In terms of number of votes it was that party's worst result since 1935, and in terms of share of the vote the worst since 1918.

In 1987 the Conservatives' support remained stable, and Labour recovered somewhat. Nonetheless, Labour's popular support and its strength in the House of Commons were lower than they had been at any time from 1945 to 1983. Labour strengthened further in 1992. Even so, the number of seats it won was lower than its total in nine of the previous thirteen elections, and its share of vote was lower than in eleven.

From 1983 through 1992 the Conservatives won majority control of the legislature with little more than two-fifths of the popular vote. These disproportional

Table 4–1
Party Strengths since World War II in General Elections

	1945	1950	1951	1955	1959	1964	1966	1970	Feb. 1974	Oct. 1974	1979	1983	1987	1992
Seats in House of Commons:														
Conservative	213	229	321	345	365	304	253	330	296	276	339	397	375	336
Labour	393	315	295	277	258	317	363	287	301	319	268	209	229	271
Liberal*	12	9	6	6	6	9	12	6	14	13	11	23	22	20
Others	22	2	3	2	1	0	2	7	24	27	17	21	24	24
Percentage of popular vote:														
Conservative	40	44	48	50	49	43	42	46	38	36	44	42	42	42
Labour	48	46	49	46	44	44	48	43	37	39	37	28	31	34
Liberal*	9	9	3	3	6	11	9	7	19	18	14	25	23	18
Others	3	1	1	1	1	1	2	3	5	7	6	5	4	6

*The Alliance in 1983 and 1987.

results were due not solely to the British electoral system, but to a split in anti-Conservative sentiment as well. As we suggested when discussing party policies, Labour in 1983 especially, and in 1987 in some respects, seemed to have moved far to the left on the political spectrum. Many moderate progressives felt unable to continue supporting the party and either stayed home on election day or voted for the Alliance, a political group we will discuss in the last section of this chapter. Similarly, in 1992 the Conservatives' won because their opponents were divided. A unified opposition could have swept them from office.

Internal divisions   The Labour party has a long history of factionalism. Usually this pits the left wing against the right. The left berates the party's leaders for being insufficiently committed to socialism, by which it usually means government ownership of business. The leaders, recognizing that government ownership is not a vote winner, try to soft-pedal commitment to such a policy, which further fuels the left's suspicion that the leaders are closet Conservatives. Labour also has been sharply divided over unilateral nuclear disarmament and British membership in the EC. These three contentious issues have tended to divide the party the same way: left-wing socialists being for unilateralism and against the EC. Those favoring the minority position did change somewhat, however, from one issue to another, so no constant dissident bloc existed.

All parties have internal differences. What has been notable about Labour's disputes is the fervency and vituperation involved in dissent. Opponents are not seen as just mistaken, they come close to being regarded as evil conspirators. Perhaps this strength of feeling accounts for the other two notable characteristics of Labour's factionalism. First, dissidents within the party tend to organize formal groups with recognized membership that endure for a considerable time. Second, Labour never has been able to cover up these internal differences; the battles always are fought in public view. As a result, many voters have concluded that the party can't even run its own affairs, much less direct the whole government. Thus, when the Conservatives campaign on the charge that Labour is incompetent and can't be trusted with power, a number of voters are inclined to think this is true.

The electoral disaster of 1983 caused the Labour party to suppress internal differences for a short time. Squabbles soon broke out once again, however, especially after the party made only modest gains in the 1987 election. Nonetheless, the party was more united for its 1992 campaign than it had been in many years. When it nevertheless managed to lose the election, the Leader did not have to be told that he would have to resign; he immediately announced that he was doing so. The new Leader is John Smith from Scotland. Although quite able, Smith is cautious and colorless. He has had to deal with the other principal source of Labour's internal divisions—conflict over relations with the trade unions. We'll discuss this shortly when we examine party organization.

Internal disputes usually are much less visible in the Conservative party. Attacks are made "in code"; that is, critics don't actually fault an opponent by name, but those in the know understand who is being criticized. The two leading parties differ markedly in ethos. The rank-and-file Conservative is disposed to follow; the typical

Labour activist to criticize and berate. Thatcher's domineering style created a number of dissidents among prominent Conservatives, politicians who either had been dismissed from the Cabinet by her or had resigned in protest of her actions. These opponents took potshots at her from time to time, but caused her little inconvenience during the 1980s.

Conflict within the Conservative party is rather decorous. You should not think, however, that this means that Conservative politicians simply fight mock battles and then retire to the clubhouse for drinks and good fellowship. Despite their unobtrusive and proper behavior, the Conservatives can be considerably more ruthless than Labour. Once the party decides that the Leader is not doing the job, out he or she goes without any sentimentality. It might seem like the Labour party is constantly brawling with chains and broken bottles in the alley, but meanwhile the Conservatives smile, jab the stiletto between the ribs, and furtively dump the body in the river.

The Conservative Leader is secure only as long as he or she looks like an electoral asset, as Thatcher learned to her surprise in 1990. Here was someone who had led the party to three consecutive election victories and had served as Prime Minister longer than anyone else in the twentieth century. In the Labour party anyone who had managed to keep the party in power for more than a decade would be a virtual monarch. Yes, some dissidents might find something to grumble about, but the party would feel such an immense debt of gratitude to this hero that no one would dare to dump him or her in the river. In the Conservative party, however, by the start of the 1990s a number of legislators were beginning to regard Thatcher as a liability. The chief fiasco that concentrated their minds—just as Dr. Johnson once said that the prospect of hanging tends to do—was the poll tax, Thatcher's remedy for extravagant spending by left-wing local governments. Voters who normally supported the Conservatives were up in arms when they discovered that they soon would have to pay considerably higher local taxes. Since this change in the way local revenue was raised was enacted by the national legislature (remember that Britain is a unitary system), angry voters knew who to penalize—their representative in London. Many Conservatives feared that Thatcher's intransigent support for the poll tax would cost them their seats in the legislature (horrors!). She would have to go and out they chucked her.

Although the person selected to replace her, John Major, was the candidate she most preferred, she soon disapproved of his policies. In particular, she proclaimed that he was much too willing to concede British sovereignty to the EC, something that she never would have permitted. Furthermore, some Conservatives were sufficiently sentimental to feel that those who had deposed Thatcher were ingrates; these loyalists were determined to defend her honor, even if after the fact. Public feuding of unprecedented level erupted in the Conservative party. Major seemed unwilling or unable to combat dissent and came to be regarded as indecisive.

Thus, during the first part of 1993 neither party had its house in order. For several months polls typically found that only two-fifths of respondents thought that Labour was united, with slightly more thinking it was divided. This was a much more positive view, however, than the reaction to the spectacle of the Conservative ruckus. Little more than a quarter of respondents thought that the Conservatives were united, while about three-fifths regarded them as divided. Even this low level was an improvement over the depths to which the Conservatives had sunk. At the end of October 1992, only one person in eight had seen the party as united. The British have a saying for mind-boggling incompetence: "unable to run a whelk stall," which means that you lack the ability to manage even a small, sidewalk seafood business. If neither party was up to this task in the mid-1990s, for whom would the electorate vote?

Party finances   Even in Britain, politics is an expensive activity. Substantial funds can buy an advantage over poorer rivals. The Conservative party's financial resources are usually greater than Labour's. Conservatives claim that this edge merely offsets the volunteer assistance that Labour receives from the unions. In both the 1983 and 1992 election campaigns, the Conservative party at the national level spent about half again as much as Labour did, and in 1987 it spent well over twice as much.

In the closing stages of the 1987 campaign, the Conservatives spent nearly $3.5 million on advertising. Every day on the last five days before the election, they ran a sequence of three full-page ads in virtually every national newspaper. Labour was able to respond to this blitz on only one day, when it managed a sequence of four full pages in most papers. Its campaign seemed to be washed away by the Conservative tidal wave. In 1992, however, the Conservatives advertised little in papers until the final week of the campaign. Although Labour also reduced its ads, it bought about a third again as many pages during the entire campaign as did the Conservatives. On the other hand, large posters were more widely used in 1992 than in previous campaigns and the Conservatives spent three times as much for this purpose as did Labour.[6]

Despite a financial connection with the trade unions—the main source of its income—the Labour party lives a hand-to-mouth existence. It seems always to be hatching some new fund-raising scheme, which soon proves a failure. In a nonelection year, Labour's income is only about two-thirds of that of the Conservatives at the national level and only about one-third at the constituency level. In the days when voting was largely an automatic expression of class status, such a financial imbalance might not have been a serious obstacle to electoral success. With an increasingly volatile electorate that must be wooed, however, financial constraints are a serious impediment.

Labour is unable to operate a national headquarters as well organized as that of the Conservatives. The Conservative party's headquarters is only a short walk from the Houses of Parliament, and Labour's is located in an obscure spot south of the River Thames. Indicative of Labour's problems are its staff's complaints that it is a bad employer, paying substandard wages. If the party that is supposed to represent the workers' interests fails to remunerate its employees properly, then financial constraints must indeed be severe. Lack of money adds further weight to the pack that Labour has to carry in any electoral race.

---

[6]Butler and Kavanagh, op. cit. pp. 116–117 and 205.

Politics appears to be getting too expensive, however, even for the Conservatives. In 1992 (an election year, which boosts both income and expenditure), the party received about $33 million, but unfortunately spent around $42 million. As a result, it found itself with an accumulated deficit of nearly $30 million. Perhaps Labour with a total deficit of only about $3 million was not so badly off financially after all. Both parties found themselves having to make deep cuts in staff at national headquarters and take other steps to economize.

Party Organization and Power Structure

The modern British party system is the product of the gradual expansion of the electorate that began in 1832. Before then, parties were groups of men in Parliament who thought, talked, and, for the most part, voted alike on the key issues. Even within Parliament, however, party organization in the modern sense didn't exist. The reason was that none was needed. The right to vote was so limited that Parliamentary seats could be controlled by a few people; an organized effort to persuade the public to vote for particular candidates was unnecessary. When the Reform Act of 1832 enlarged the electorate, however, lists of qualified voters had to be compiled. Each political group needed to be certain that all of its supporters who were qualified did in fact register and that any of its opponents' supporters who were unqualified were not included on the voting lists. To do this, registration societies were formed—the start of party organization at the constituency level.

More than a third of a century passed, however, before the registration societies were coordinated in a national party organization supporting groups of candidates and offering a program of policies. The second Reform Act, by expanding the right to vote still further in 1867, made national organization an absolute necessity. The National Union of Conservative and Unionist Associations (the official name of the Conservative party) was soon formed and continues today.

Although party organization in Britain originated at the grass-roots level, both of the major British parties are more highly centralized than their American counterparts. Labour tries harder than the Conservatives do to operate democratically, but both parties concentrate considerable power in the hands of the national Parliamentary leaders.

The Conservative party   The Conservative party's leaders intended from the beginning that the volunteer, mass organization outside of Parliament should not control the party in Parliament but should be its servant. To ensure that, the national headquarters of the party was put under the command of the Parliamentary Leader. The Leader appoints the party's top officers, who direct the professional staff and handle finances. Key party committees are responsible not to these officers but to the Leader.

The party organization, therefore, is confined to being an aid to the winning of elections and to publicizing the party's position on public issues. The channel of communication that it provides between the Parliamentary elite and the rank-and-file members in the country flows primarily downward. Only rarely does what percolates back up have much influence on party policy.

The local constituency association is the basic organizational unit of the mass party. Party membership is more formal in Britain than in the United States. Just declaring a preference isn't enough; one must join a local association and pay a small sum annually for dues. The Conservatives are one of the most successful parties in any democracy at recruiting members. During the 1950s they had around 2.75 million members; even now, when membership has declined to only about 0.5 million, the number is quite substantial compared to other parties in democratic countries.

The most significant role of the local association—the function that gives it its only real power—is to decide who will be the Conservative candidate for Parliament in the constituency. The association's selection committee interviews potential candidates and recommends two or three of them to the executive council. After hearing these make speeches and answer questions, the executive council recommends one to a general meeting of the association's members. This meeting almost invariably approves the choice.

Early in this selection process, the chair of the association usually requests Conservative national headquarters to suggest names of potential candidates. The selection committee may gather names on its own as well. Although these names are supposed to be cleared with national headquarters, that doesn't always happen. The associations are very protective of their power to choose whomever they wish as candidates. If they feel that national headquarters is trying to impose someone on them, that is the last person they will select. National headquarters is empowered to veto an association's choice of candidate, but never does so. Given the many safe seats in Britain (those consistently won by the same party), the few people on the association's executive council and selection committee wield considerable power in determining who holds national legislative office.

At the national level the party's most visible organ is the Conference. This meeting, held each year for about three and a half days, somewhat resembles an American Presidential nominating convention. Like those, the Conference is a gathering of delegates from the local party associations. Early each fall, several thousand party activists converge on some seaside resort. Even though elections may be held only once in five years, the Conference meets annually because, in contrast to an American political convention, it has nothing to do with nominating anyone for anything—its sole purpose is discussing policy. Earlier in the year, the associations send various resolutions to party headquarters, some of which are selected for "debate." After a couple of hours of delegate speeches on a given resolution, it typically is passed without amendment, and often without dissent.

Parliamentary leaders see little harm in letting the delegates talk and pass resolutions—these merely express the delegates' opinions and do not bind the leaders in any way. Nonetheless, occasionally the proceedings reveal such enthusiasm for a particular policy that the Parliamentary leaders feel compelled to support it so as not to alienate their followers.

The advisory nature of the Conference is underlined by the fact that it is the Central Council that is designated as the mass party's governing organ. The Council is, in effect, a smaller and briefer version of the Conference. Since it does not meet much more frequently than the Conference, however, direction of the party's affairs falls mostly to the Executive Committee, which typically convenes every other month. Since this committee has about 150 members, most of the detailed work is in fact performed by subcommittees.

The Conference, the Central Council, the Executive Committee—all are organs of the mass, volunteer party, the party in the country. The more powerful, elite portion of the party is the party in Parliament. The key body here is the Conservative Private Members Committee. No one calls it by that name, however, referring to it instead as the 1922 Committee. In that year a revolt among Conservative Members of Parliament drove the party Leader from his position. The committee then was created to help ensure that the Parliamentary leaders were aware of the views of the average members of the Parliamentary party and did not get so far out of step with these that they would again be forced to walk the plank.

The 1922 Committee does not make policy, but provides Conservative Members of Parliament with a forum in which to question leaders' actions and policies. Votes are rarely taken; the chair of the group must interpret the "sense of the meeting." The chair has direct access to the Parliamentary Leader so as to be able to alert him or her when views are beginning to diverge. Sometimes the Leader may even attend a 1922 Committee meeting in order to answer criticism and try to convince the legislators that his or her policies are the right ones.

Through the 1922 Committee, Conservative legislators are organized into subject-matter committees. (These party committees should not be confused with the legislative committees of the Parliament.) The scope of these committees corresponds to that of the various governmental departments. The committees discuss current political issues and government policies and help to crystallize the party's position on them. Ideally, internal party policy differences can be settled in private through this process.

We have been referring to the Parliamentary Leader using a capital L in order to be certain that you understand the distinction between the mass and the Parliamentary parties. The Leader, as the person actually is known, is the head of the entire party, not just of the Parliamentary portion, although he or she invariably is a Member of Parliament. Whether in or out of power, the Conservative party is headed by a single, formally chosen, Leader. In the United States, since only one party controls the Presidency at any given time, the party out of power lacks an ex-officio head. Furthermore, the President and Congressional leaders may disagree even when they belong to the same party, raising the question of who really does lead the party. In Britain, the Leader of a party, who becomes Prime Minister if his or her party controls the House of Commons, always is clearly designated.

The Conservative Leader is preeminent. National party headquarters is his or her personal machine. He or she is the authoritative voice for the party's policies and is not bound by any policy resolution of the mass party. He or she appoints the chief whip of the Parliamentary party and selects whomever he or she wishes for the Shadow Cabinet, the top leadership group in the party when it is out of power. The Labour Leader has none of these powers. The Conservative Leader also has enormous authority over the party's legislators because, as either the current or the potential Prime Minister, he or she can greatly affect the course of their political careers.

Despite these powers, the Leader is accountable. Prior to 1965 each Leader "emerged"; that is, when the position was vacant because of a voluntary retirement or forced resignation, the new Leader was chosen in behind-the-scenes negotiations before the party meeting that formally made the choice. Many prominent Conservatives were unhappy when this procedure produced Lord Home as Leader in 1963. Although Home was the second choice of many, few liked him best. Lack of consensus on a first choice, however, boosted Home into the position of Leader. As a result, the process for choosing a Leader was changed to an election among Conservative legislators. Special majorities and multiple ballots are provided to help ensure that the person selected has broad support. The legislators' choice must be confirmed by a meeting of all Conservatives in both Houses of Parliament, prospective Parliamentary candidates, and members of the Executive Committee of the mass party. This gathering of about a thousand people is unlikely to do anything other than rubber-stamp the selection.

The first use of the new procedures went smoothly; the next produced surprising results. Having led the party in 1974 to two electoral defeats in a single year, Edward Heath, the Leader, was quite vulnerable (remember what we said earlier about the Conservatives and stilettos). Few anticipated, however, that Margaret Thatcher, a not especially prominent member of the Shadow Cabinet, would receive more votes than Heath. That a party as committed to tradition as the Conservatives should become the first British party to choose a woman as Leader was amazing. Most Conservative Members of Parliament weren't seeking a change in party policy; they simply were determined to rid themselves of Heath, because he was aloof (and seemed arrogant) and a loser. Thatcher had the courage to risk her political career by standing against Heath in the Leadership contest, when more prominent Conservatives, who were widely considered to be his possible successors, did not. Thus, the only way to jettison Heath was to embrace Thatcher. Little did any Conservative legislator think when voting for her that she would become the longest-serving Prime Minister of the twentieth century.

As we mentioned earlier in discussing the parties' internal divisions, Thatcher's domination of British politics for over a decade ended unexpectedly. The poll tax and high interest rates for home mortgages made her so unpopular that Conservative legislators feared losing the next general election. Geoffrey Howe, who had served as Chancellor of the Exchequer and Foreign Secretary, resigned from the Cabinet. He came to think that Thatcher's adamant opposition to tighter integration of the EC risked Britain's being left behind by the other eleven members of that organization. So mild-mannered is he that a prominent Labour politician once said that being attacked by Geoffrey Howe was like being savaged by a dead sheep. Howe's speech in the House of Commons, however, explaining why he had resigned, was regarded as the most vicious attack in memory on a Prime Minister.

The next day Michael Heseltine, who had resigned from Thatcher's Cabinet in 1986 (see Chapter 6), challenged her for the position of Leader. When the party tried in the mid-1970s to rid itself of Edward Heath, the rules for choosing a Leader were revised to provide for annual elections. No one had thought that anyone would seriously challenge a Leader who was also Prime Minister. Thatcher outpolled Heseltine by a substantial number of votes—204 to 152 (with 16 Conservative legislators abstaining)—but failed to win by the required 15 percent margin. If only two of those who had voted for him had voted for her instead, she would have led by 56 votes and would have been confirmed as Leader. Her colleagues convinced her that many of those who had voted for her on the first ballot would not do so on the second. To block Heseltine (whom she did not want to become Prime Minister), she would have to withdraw and let some of her loyalists be nominated.

Once she had done so, the two members of her Cabinet who had nominated and seconded her, Douglas Hurd and John Major, became candidates. The results were Major 185, Heseltine 131, and Hurd 56. Clearly, a number of Conservative legislators had originally voted for Heseltine simply to get rid of Thatcher. Although the rules drop the 15-percent provision for the second ballot, they continue to require a majority of all those eligible to vote. Major was two votes short; nonetheless, both Heseltine and Hurd immediately withdrew. Major was the new Leader and, thus, Prime Minister.

The son of a trapeze artist, Major was a high school dropout. He was unemployed for a while and lived on welfare before working his way up in a bank to a position of importance. A more unlikely candidate for Leader of the Conservative party would be hard to imagine. Thatcher had appointed him Chancellor of the Exchequer about a year before he became Prime Minister. In short order, she decided that she had made a mistake in supporting him (not nearly as big a one, of course, as the party had made in getting rid of her). Her attacks and those of her friends soon made Major the most unpopular Prime Minister in the history of opinion polling in Britain. So weakened was Major that Thatcher had to back off and urge Conservatives to rally to him and stop tearing the party apart.

In summary, the Conservative party is very hierarchically structured, with the Leader at the apex. Despite possessing great power even when the party is out of power, the Leader can be driven from his or her post by determined opponents in the Parliamentary or mass party. In fact, in the twentieth century Conservative Leaders have suffered this fate more frequently than Labour Leaders have. No one would ever think that the Conservative party is democratic, yet the Leader is responsible to the followers. His or her power ultimately is checked by the need to convince the party to accept the policies he or she prefers.

The Labour party   Unlike the Conservative party, the Labour party was organized from outside, not from within, Parliament. As you have seen, it was Conservatives in the national legislature who felt the need to combine various local registration associations into a countrywide organization. Labour gained representation in Parliament, however, only after the party had been organized in the country, so the initiative did not come from legislators. This contrast in development helped to give the Labour party a structure and organizational values greatly at odds with those of the Conservative party.

The Labour party regards itself as a movement aimed at voicing the people's interest in the political process. This makes the Parliamentary Labour Party (PLP) merely the means to that end; the PLP is to serve the mass party by seeking to carry its principles into law. This is the exact opposite of the Conservatives' organizational ethos; their mass party is to serve the Parliamentary one by raising money and recruiting activists so that elections can be won.

The Labour party was founded in 1900, when representatives of the Independent Labour Party, the Fabian Society, various socialist groups, and several trade unions met to form the Labour Representation Committee (LRC). Their key decision was that legislators elected with their support should be entirely independent of either the Conservative or the Liberal party. The next crucial step, three years later, was the unions' increasing their nominal financial support to a substantial and regular levy. Three years after that, the LRC changed its name to the Labour party. Within twenty-two years of its founding, this party had driven the Liberals into third place; within twenty-four years, it gained the office of Prime Minister; within forty-five years, it won an absolute majority of seats in the House of Commons at a general election.

Labour's organization is more complex than that of the Conservative party. The mass party not only coordinates the activities of the local associations but also seeks to integrate various related organizations, primarily trade unions and cooperative societies. These organizations affiliate with Labour at both the national and the local levels.

Labour's semifederated structure allows for two types of members: direct and indirect. Just as with the Conservative party, an individual can join Labour directly by paying dues to a local association. Only about a quarter of a million people (many fewer than for the Conservatives) do this. The bulk of the Labour party's members, about 5 million, join indirectly; they are members simply because the union to which they belong has affiliated with the party and has paid a political levy for each of its members. Thus, many of the Labour party's indirect members may not really support it at all and may, in fact, vote for its opponents.

Indirect members who dislike Labour can "contract out," that is, sign an official form saying that they do not want any of their union dues paid to the party. Very few do so, however. The amount per person that goes to Labour is so small that alienating one's workmates by contracting out doesn't seem worth it. When the small individual sums are multiplied by millions of people, of course, the total involved is substantial. In a sense, Labour's finances are based on apathy and inertia.

Each local constituency party is governed by a General Management Committee (GMC) composed of delegates from ward committees and the affiliated organizations, primarily local branches of unions. Since the GMC usually meets only once a year, effective power is wielded by the executive committee, which is chosen by the GMC and meets monthly. When a candidate for Parliament was to be selected, the executive committee prepared a short list (the leading applicants) and the GMC chose one of them.

Candidate selection is one of the most important powers of constituency Labour parties, just as is true of the Conservative party. Toward the end of the 1970s, this power became a major battleground between the left and right wings of the party. The procedure had been that a Labour legislator currently holding office as the constituency's representative could not be dumped as a candidate in the next election unless the local party passed a motion of no confidence. The left wing complained that this allowed legislators so much independence that they could refuse to work for the policies that "true socialists" wanted. Leftists sought a procedure that would make it easy to get rid of those who refused to do their bidding. Thus, the party rules were changed to require every constituency Labour party to select candidates afresh during each Parliament. A sitting legislator could no longer continue automatically as the candidate but had to win specific approval to be able to run for reelection. Furthermore, this reselection process had to be open to new applicants.

By American standards this seems a modest reform, but British legislators had been remarkably well-insulated from popular accountability. A handful of local party activists decided who the party's candidate would be, and, once elected, a legislator had virtual life tenure, never having to fear the bruising primary election fights that have ended the careers of some American politicians.

The change of rules did make Labour legislators more accountable, but certainly not to the voters. Their accountability was to local party officials, who are not representative of the electorate or even of that portion of it that votes Labour. Remember that the change was sought by the left wing of the party, trying to get people who shared its views into office. Somewhere between two and three dozen Labour legislators had their careers ended prior to the 1983 election as a result of the new procedures. Only seven were "deselected," that is, dumped by their local party, but many more retired rather than trying to win reselection.

The widespread fear that Labour was being taken over by extremists led to a further change of rules in 1987. An electoral college composed of all party members in a constituency, along with delegates from local trade unions, was given the power of selecting candidates. By enlarging the group that makes the choice, the party leaders hoped to dilute the strength of extremists and to field candidates acceptable to the electorate.

Although the local Labour party selects its candidate, the national party organization is more active in the process than is true in the Conservative party. The national party must be given an opportunity to comment on the short list before the local party makes its choice. Furthermore, the choice is not final until endorsed by the national party, which doesn't always do so. And in by-elections the local party must share the power to select with the national party.

The governing body of Labour's national mass party is the Conference. Well over a thousand delegates from local parties and affiliated organizations attend these annual gatherings to discuss and vote on various policy resolutions that their groups have submitted. Voting strength is allocated according to the number of party members an organization has, so a total vote of over 5 million on some issues is not uncommon.

The power of Conference has been a contentious issue between the left and right wings. Various party documents and leaders have said from time to time that Conference is the ultimate authority and controls Labour legislators. If this were the case, they would be accountable not to the voters but to a party organ, which certainly would seem to be a short-circuiting of democracy. Conference is prohibited, however, from telling Labour legislators how they must vote on a specific bill. Principles endorsed by Conference are to be carried out as soon as practicable, but—major loophole—the party's constitution doesn't say who determines what is practicable. Labour leaders can't openly defy Conference, but they have some freedom in deciding when and how to implement its decisions; in practice, "when" may turn out to be never. Procrastination is risky, however, since the Leader must report to each year's Conference on the work of the PLP. During the debate on this report, delegates may challenge the Leader if Conference resolutions have been ignored.

Between Conferences the mass party is run by the National Executive Committee (NEC), which can expel party members and disaffiliate local parties. National headquarters and its professional staff are directed by the NEC. Thus, in contrast to the Conservative party, the Labour party has a headquarters that is not the Leader's personal machine, but the servant of Conference and the NEC.

The Leader, Deputy Leader, and Young Socialist delegate are ex-officio members of the NEC. The remaining twenty-six members are chosen at Conference. The trade union delegates elect twelve members, delegates from constituency parties elect seven, and delegates from socialist and cooperative organizations elect one. Five places are reserved for women, and all Conference delegates vote on these. The same is true for the party treasurer, who is another ex-officio member of the NEC.

Since the trade unions always can control Conference—even with the most recent reform they hold 70 percent of the votes—they are able to select a majority of the NEC. In addition to the twelve seats reserved to them, they have the major voice in Conference's selection of the five women and the treasurer. Furthermore, by longstanding Conference procedure, each delegation casts all its votes as a single block. The combined block votes of the four largest unions comprise well over a majority of Conference's total voting strength. Thus, when the main unions agree, they determine the policies Conference supports and who controls the NEC.

During the 1940s and 1950s, union leaders usually were politically moderate and not very assertive. They accepted the Parliamentary leaders' policies with little question. The Parliamentary leaders, in fact, found the union leaders useful allies in fending off attacks by extremist delegates from the constituency parties. Furthermore, since most union leaders were interested mainly in industrial relations and not in a political career, the majority of the NEC's members were legislators, not union officials.

Beginning in the 1950s, struggles over policy so divided the PLP that the fact that most members of the NEC were legislators was no guarantee that the Parliamentary leaders could control it. More important, the new generation of union leaders was less deferential than its predecessors had been and often leaned more to the left on policy. Further worsening the relations between union and Parliamentary leaders were Britain's economic troubles, which at times forced Labour Governments to pursue policies that the unions opposed. Instead of being able to count on the union block vote to save them from defeats at Conferences, Parliamentary leaders found some unions giving aid and comfort to left-wing enthusiasts from the constituency parties. Leading the Labour party, a difficult job in the best of circumstances, became an even more onerous task.

The left's success in getting Conference to vote for left-wing policies failed to satisfy, however, because party leaders tended to ignore extreme policies during election campaigns. Therefore, the left was determined to gain control over the party's "manifesto" (what American parties call a platform). The tide of victory in this bitter battle flowed back and forth in the early 1980s; eventually a truce was called with nothing having been resolved. A new Leader and a commitment to winning for a change combined to produce little conflict over the 1987 manifesto, even though it was much more moderate than the 1983 one. If Conference resolutions are treated as cavalierly in future elections as they were in 1979, the battle will be renewed. On the other hand, Parliamentary leaders do have some room for maneuvering and can soft-pedal some policies they think will alienate voters.

As for the organization of the Parliamentary party, the PLP has two overlapping sets of committees. Area groups help to ensure that Labour legislators attend important debates and vote as the party wishes. Subject groups resemble the Conservatives' subject-matter committees, giving the rank-and-file Labour legislators some input into policy making. These committees' influence is rather marginal when the party is in power (the Cabinet dominates the policy process then), and even when it is not, a committee's influence depends to a considerable extent on the status within the party of its chair.

The PLP chooses a chairman, whose function is similar to that of the chair of the 1922 Committee. When Labour is in power, this person heads a specially created liaison committee intended to keep the Labour Government informed of the views of the average Labour legislator. When Labour is out of power, the PLP elects a Parliamentary Committee each year. Its twelve members, along with three Labour members from the House of Lords, the PLP chairman, the chief whip, the Deputy Leader, and the Leader, are in effect the party's Shadow Cabinet. The Leader may add others to the Shadow Cabinet but basically has to work with advisors chosen by the party's legislators more than the Conservative Leader does.

Given its self-image as a democratic movement of the people, the Labour party was slow to designate someone Leader. The PLP had a chairman in its early years, but this was simply because someone had to preside at meetings. The chair did not exercise any special authority or power. During the party's first two decades, the post passed among six men, with four years being the longest unbroken period of service. Eventually the party reconciled itself to having a Leader; the result was one of its greatest traumas. In 1931 Ramsay MacDonald (the first Labour politician to be called Leader) replaced his minority Labour Government with a coalition government dominated by the Conservatives. The bulk of the Labour party refused to follow MacDonald and excoriated him for betraying his followers. The combatants in that conflict are long dead, but the idea that one can't trust the party's leaders, that they are scheming to sell out the movement, continues to flourish within the Labour party. A taste of power is thought to so besot a leader that he or she will jettison principle for personal gain and glory. One of the ways in which a Labour Leader can try to counteract these suspicions is to demonstrate that he or she is a true socialist. Usually this means strident advocacy of government ownership. Unwavering support for unilateral nuclear disarmament also can serve to establish one's left-wing credentials.

When Labour is not controlling the Government, the Leader is supposed to be elected annually. Since in most years no one stands against the incumbent, no election is held. Until 1981, only Labour legislators could vote for the Leader. Here again the left wing sought to expand its power within the party by depriving the PLP of this power. Now, when an election is needed, it is held during Conference, if convenient, or at a specially called gathering. The PLP is granted only 30 percent of the votes. The same proportion is allocated to the constituency parties, and the remaining 40 percent, the largest share, belongs to the unions. Having to please the electorate every few years is likely to make Labour legislators somewhat moderate or at least realistic. Denying them the sole power to select the Leader by bringing into the process people not subject to such a constraint seems likely to produce Labour Leaders more inclined to the left; that, at least, was the left wing's goal in securing this change in procedure.

The current Leader, John Smith, and his supporters (frequently referred to as modernizers) want to curtail the power of the unions within the party. They favored a shift to one member, one vote (OMOV) for the selection of Parliamentary candidates and election of the party Leader. Most union leaders opposed OMOV, arguing that the long history of party/union association and the fact that the unions bankroll the party entitled them to a major voice in significant party decisions. In the summer of 1993 a frantic search was underway to find some compromise that would avoid a major confrontation between the Leader and the unions. Instead of "fudging" the issue (the typical means of dealing with conflict in the Labour party), Smith stood firm. Even the day before the decision was to be taken, his defeat appeared likely. After much lobbying and arm twisting, however, sufficient votes swung to OMOV to give it a narrow victory: 47.5 percent of the votes to 44.3 percent (some delegates abstained). Henceforth, Labour candidates would be chosen by vote of all party members in a given constituency. Those who are indirect members through their trade union can participate in candidate selection by paying the constituency Labour party where they live an annual membership fee under $5. This is only a fifth as much as dues cost to join directly without any union connection. Thus the link between the unions and the party was recognized to some extent; however, the thrust of the reform was to loosen union dominance of the party.

Smith's problems in trying to "modernize" the party indicate that despite the similarity in title, the Labour Leader lacks the power typically wielded by the Conservative Leader. The two positions differ in several notable respects: (1) the Labour Leader does not choose the bulk of the Shadow Cabinet or appoint the chief whip, the Labour legislators do; (2) party headquarters is not the Labour Leader's personal machine, but is directed by the NEC; (3) the Labour Leader can't make policy on his or her own authority; (4) the Labour Leader must report to the Conference annually on the work of the Parliamentary party, whereas the Conservative Leader doesn't; (5) the Labour Leader is elected by a diverse group, only a minority of which has any experience of serving with him or her in the legislature.

Nonetheless, the Leader is the most powerful single person in the Labour party. When Labour is in power, the Leader, who is then Prime Minister, functions essentially as a Conservative Prime Minister would. A Labour Prime Minister picks the Cabinet members he or she prefers and, along with that Cabinet, runs the country. A Labour Prime Minister can't ignore strongly held views in the party, but neither can a Conservative one. Finally, if the most distinguishing evidence of power is the ability to retain one's office, then the Labour Leader is actually stronger than the Conservative Leader. As we noted previously, in the twentieth century, intraparty revolts have driven Leaders from power more often in the Conservative party.

■ *OTHER PARTIES*

Nationwide Parties

Until the 1920s the Liberals were one of Britain's two main parties. Once they were displaced by Labour, they soldiered on as a third party. From time to time they would revive—score an unexpected victory in a by-election or win four or five new seats in a general election. These accomplishments always proved to be false dawns, but in 1974 it appeared that the sun really was coming up for the Liberals as they won nearly a fifth of the vote.

A few years later prospects were greatly enhanced by a split in the Labour party. A number of Labour moderates finally despaired of redeeming their party and broke away in 1981 to found the Social Democratic Party (SDP). The SDP and the Liberals cooperated in an association called the Alliance. Both parties maintained their distinct identities—separate officers, party rules, policies, and so forth. But they arranged an electoral pact for the general elections in both 1983 and 1987 (and for by-elections during this period as well). The two parties divided all the constituencies between them, deciding which of them would offer a candidate in each so that they would not oppose each other. Rather than issue separate policy statements, they presented a joint manifesto. And their press conferences each morning of the campaign included leaders from both parties. They also shared the officially allocated TV time. For electoral purposes, they were a single alternative.

For a brief time these two parties appeared to be on to something. In December 1981 more than half of those interviewed by Gallup said they intended to vote for one or the other of the two parties. But before the election occurred, Prime Minister Thatcher sent a task force to retake the Falkland Islands from Argentina and skyrocketed in popularity. Even so, the Alliance almost pushed Labour into third place in 1983, managing to win a quarter of the popular vote. Another 4 percentage points would have put them ahead of Labour, and the subsequent political history of Britain might have been strikingly different (the saddest words, "might have been"). In 1987 the Alliance did nearly as well, but expectations had risen so high that this level of achievement seemed a setback.

The fundamental question for the Alliance was whether the two parties should continue to cooperate as they had in the past or should merge to form a single, new party. Policy and personality differences made merger a contentious issue. The Liberals and most of the SDP merged in 1988 to create the Liberal and Social Democrats. Paddy Ashdown, who had been a Liberal legislator, became the first Leader of this new party. Unfortunately, the Leader of the SDP, David Owen, had been one of those opposed to merger, and he determined to carry on with his little band of followers. Thus, the SDP continued to exist. What might have been a golden opportunity for a transformation of the British party system degenerated almost to the level of farce. Eventually, in 1990, after one of its candidates did even worse in a by-election than the Raving Monster Loony candidate, the SDP threw in the towel. Owen didn't stand for reelection in 1992, and the only two remaining SDP legislators who did were defeated. In the meantime the Liberal and Social Democrats had changed their name to become the Liberal Democrats.

Whatever the name has been, the Liberal Democrats have a long history of advocating governmental reform. They want to cut back government secrecy (much more prevalent in Britain than in the United States) and establish a written bill of rights to protect basic freedoms. They seek to make government more effective and responsive by devolving many powers and functions to a new tier of regional governments (virtually converting Britain into a federal system) and by changing the electoral system to proportional representation (which, as we suggested in Chapter 3, would greatly expand their representation in the legislature).

The Liberal Democrats assert that the two larger parties are so hostile to each other that campaigns degenerate into name-calling with neither side being willing to consider any policy proposed by the other. As a result, the real issues aren't debated, as an ad (see Figure 4–10) that the Liberal Democrats used in the 1992 campaign emphasized. Down each side of the ad are copies of Labour and Conservative billboard ads, while the question in the middle notes the issues being ignored—issues the Liberal Democrats implied they were discussing.

Education, the issue heading the list, was a major theme in the Liberal Democrats' 1992 campaign. The party advocated reducing class size, buying more books and equipment, and constructing new buildings. In a shocking departure from the practice of most parties, the Liberal Democrats actually stated how they would pay for this. (No wonder they are sometimes regarded as amateurs.) Polls suggested that the electorate not only approved of the proposed educational improvements, but appreciated the party's honesty in specifying the necessary tax increase. Unfortunately, the electorate seemed to forget these positive feelings in the voting booth; the Liberal Democrats received a smaller share of the vote in 1992 than the Alliance had in either of the two previous elections (see Table 4–1).

Like their predecessors, the Liberal Democrats would claim that—in contrast to the two larger parties—they are not beholden to any segment of society. Their pattern of electoral support tends to bear this out. However the electorate is analyzed—by age, gender, home ownership, or social class—the level of support for the Liberal Democrats varies by only a few percentage points from one subgroup to another.

Nonetheless, the Liberal Democrats' electoral victories in 1992 were concentrated (about three-fourths of their seats) in the Celtic Fringe—Scotland, Wales, Devon, and Cornwall. Furthermore, the bulk of the nine seats won in Scotland were on the rural fringes of that region. Since two of their seats were in spa (resort) towns, only three of their twenty legislators represented constituencies that could be considered urban. Thus, the Liberal Democrats often seem irrelevant to British politics not only because their representation in the national legislature is tiny, but also because they seem to represent the atypical periphery.

You have already seen that Labour can't match the financial resources of the Conservatives. Other parties have even greater difficulty. During the late 1950s the Liberals were trying to run their national party machinery on an annual budget of only $50,000; the party nearly went bankrupt. Eventually, in the 1970s, the party managed to get its budget up to around a third of a million dollars. The Alliance's funds were so constrained that it could afford no national press advertising in 1983 and only a few ads in 1987. Had it not been for the free TV time, the Alliance would have had great difficulty in communicating with a national audience. The same was

Figure 4–10
Liberal Democrat
Newspaper Ad for
the 1992 Election
Campaign

largely true of the Liberal Democrats in 1992. They could afford only about a seventh as many pages of newspaper advertising as the Conservatives and a tenth as many as Labour.

Both the Liberals and the SDP allowed the rank-and-file members to participate in electing the parties' Leaders (there never was a single Alliance Leader). The Liberal Democrats have done the same. Their first (and thus far only) Leader, Paddy Ashdown, was elected in a mail ballot of all party members. Like the larger parties, the Liberal Democrats hold annual conferences. These gatherings lack the constitutional status of the Labour Conference but have somewhat more influence over party policy and leaders than the Conservative Conference usually does. Constituency parties are virtually independent in selecting candidates for Parliamentary elections. The Liberal Democrats' national headquarters has such limited resources that little pressure could be brought to bear on a local party thought to have made an undesirable choice.

The Liberal Democrats aren't the only party in addition to the Conservatives and Labour to be organized on a nationwide basis. The ecology-oriented Green party was amazingly successful in the elections for the European Parliament in 1989. The Greens came in third with 15 percent of the vote, nearly three times as much as the Liberal Democrats. Given the British electoral system, however, they received no seats. The Greens offered more than 250 candidates for the 1992 legislative elections; all of them lost their deposits, and they averaged only 1.3 percent of vote. Similarly, the Natural Law party of Maharishi Mahesh Yogi offered more than 300 candidates in 1992; all of them lost their deposits, and they averaged only 0.4 percent of the vote. The Natural Law party is a quasi-religious organization whose position can be summarized, perhaps not too facetiously, as believing that right thinking will solve all the world's problems and permit personal levitation as well. Given the Maharishi's wealth, the party did not lack money. It bought nearly as many pages of newspaper ads as the Conservatives did.

Regional Parties

The only other parties worth mentioning are regional ones. The Welsh nationalists (Plaid Cymru, pronounced "plied come-ree") and the Scottish nationalists (SNP) seek complete independence from the United Kingdom for their nations, not just Welsh and Scottish assemblies set up under some sort of regional governmental system. The extent to which such a goal has enjoyed support in each area in elections during the last few decades can be seen in Table 4–2.

Plaid Cymru is especially concerned with defending the Welsh language and culture. The SNP shows little interest in such issues, emphasizing instead economic policy, particularly measures to fight the poverty that exists in many parts of Scotland. Both parties have been divided at times between those who want to concentrate almost exclusively on the issue of nationalism (independence) and those who want to focus on socialist-type economic policy.

Nationalist movements have existed in Wales and Scotland throughout the twentieth century. Why is it only in recent years that nationalists have ceased to be politically insignificant? Does this development suggest the breakup of the British state? A more useful way of posing the first question is to ask "Why not?" instead of "Why now?" Recent decades have seen the growth of ethnic interests and tensions around the world. Why should Britain be any different, especially when its structure of government makes responding to regional concerns difficult? Regionalism is not ignored entirely; the executive has its Scottish Office and Minister for Welsh Affairs, and Parliament has various committees for Scottish and Welsh matters. Nonethe-

Table 4–2

Liberal and Nationalist Strength in Wales and Scotland in Recent General Elections

	Wales				Scotland			
	Seats		Percent of vote		Seats		Percent of vote	
	Liberal*	PC	Liberal*	PC	Liberal*	SNP	Liberal*	SNP
1966	1	0	6	4	5	0	7	5
1970	1	0	7	12	3	1	6	11
February 1974	2	2	16	11	3	7	8	22
October 1974	2	3	16	11	3	11	8	30
1979	1	2	11	8	3	2	9	17
1983	2	2	23	8	8	2	25	12
1987	3	3	18	7	9	3	19	14
1992	1	4	12	9	9	3	14	22

*Alliance in 1983 and 1987

less, Britain, unlike the United States, is not a federal system. Any desire for regional diversity can't be accommodated as readily as in the United States.

Regional interests may be willing to tolerate a lack of responsiveness to their special concerns as long as the entire system seems to be functioning well. When that is not the case, they are more likely to want to handle their own affairs. It is hardly a coincidence that both nationalist parties saw their greatest popular support during the 1970s, a time when politicians in London seemed not to have a clue about how to manage the economy. Furthermore, if North Sea oil belonged to Scotland (as the SNP asserted), then the nation had a good chance of running an economy healthier than that of the United Kingdom. In short, it would have been amazing if calls for Scottish independence had not been made and had not fallen on many receptive ears.

Until such a time as the United Kingdom seems to be operating as well as it did during the 1950s, the nationalists are likely to enjoy significant support. And the longer restoring "normal service" takes, the more likely it will become that the nationalists can establish an appeal beyond a simply economic protest vote. Whatever might account for initial support, feelings of ethnicity are likely to become compelling. Strength of support, however, is only one consideration, because the nationalists must contend with the curious results Britain's electoral system can produce when more than two parties are serious contenders. Note, for example, in Table 4–2 that in Wales in 1992 the Liberal Democrats received more of the popular vote than the PC did, but won fewer seats. That same year in Scotland, however, the SNP received half again as much support as did the Liberal Democrats and yet won only a third as many seats. The electoral system tends not to penalize regional parties as much as it does national third parties, like the Liberal Democrats. Even so, the nationalists can't count on converting their popular support into equivalent strength in the House of Commons.

■ *PROSPECTS FOR BRITAIN'S PARTY SYSTEM*

Scotland, Wales, and Northern Ireland account for a fifth of the seats in the United Kingdom's national legislature. In those areas the party strengths (share of vote/share of seats) are as follows: Conservatives, 24 percent/13 percent; Labour, 37 percent/60 percent; Liberal Democrats, 11 percent/8 percent; Nationalists, 14 percent/6 percent; and others, 14 percent/13 percent. Whether this pattern of partisan support is termed a multiparty system or a one-party-dominant system is immaterial. Clearly, it is impossible to label it a two-party system.

In England, on the other hand, the pattern runs like this: Conservatives, 46 percent/61 percent; Labour, 34 percent/37 percent; Liberal Democrats, 19 percent/2 percent; and others, 1 percent/0 percent. With a bit of pushing, this configuration could fit into the two-party pigeonhole. How likely is the pattern to change in the heart of the party system, regardless of what occurs in the Celtic periphery?

Despite the weaknesses of Labour and the Conservatives, the Liberal Democrats seem unlikely to win more than 25 percent of the vote in a general election. From time to time the party will achieve sensational by-election results, overturning huge majorities to win a single interim victory. Retaining all of these triumphs, however, in a general election, when the Liberal Democrats have to spread their limited resources over the entire country, will prove difficult. Any possibility for change in the party system doesn't lie with them.

The majority of Labour party leaders still believe that the party can return to power unassisted. These people sometimes are referred to as the "one last heavers." As you can see from Table 4–1, Labour advanced slightly in both elections following its 1983 disaster. The party's optimists think that at the next general election, expected to take place in 1996 or 1997, a third such modest gain will be enough to put them back in office. Therefore, they are unwilling to seriously consider any deal with the Liberal Democrats. But if the next election gives Labour its fifth successive defeat, despite everything the party has done to make itself more attractive to the electorate, then even optimists are likely to concede that something must be done to stop splitting the anti-Conservative vote. Surely allowing the Conservatives to wield power uninterrupted for two decades despite winning only two-fifths of the vote is more than enough.

Should that view spread, Labour would be likely to seek some electoral arrangement with the Liberal Democrats in order to drive the Conservatives from power. The payoff that the Liberal Democrats would demand would be some change in the electoral system to make their share of seats in the legislature more comparable to their share of the popular vote. That would transform the British party system, clearly moving it from something that partially resembles the American system to a form that has more in common with Continental ones. Thus, a significant change in British politics is foreseeable, but don't look for it prior to the start of the next millennium.

....5

Representation and Accountability _____

Political parties present policy alternatives to the people. British voters decide who will represent each of the constituencies into which the country is divided and, more important, thereby determine which party will control the House of Commons. The Commons, more than any other political institution, seems to embody the essence of British government. It appears to be the focal point of the political process, the showcase of democracy in action. Many students of British government assert, however, that the Commons has become virtually all show and very little substance, that what happens there is irrelevant to the governing of the country, to the making of national policy. In this chapter we emphasize form and procedure, to give you a feel for the atmosphere of Parliament—its show—and an understanding of how it works. In the first part of the next chapter, we will do the same for the executive. Then, in the latter part of that chapter, we will be able to build on this information to discuss power relations between the executive and the legislature and, therefore, to assess the balance between show and substance in the Commons.

■ THE HOUSE OF COMMONS

The Chamber

The House of Commons meets in a small room—only sixty-eight feet by forty-five feet. Although the Commons has half again as many members as the U.S. House of Representatives does, its meeting room is only about a fourth as large. The Commons' chamber is too small, in fact, to seat all of its members; less than two-thirds of them can squeeze onto its green leather-covered benches at any one time. The members do not have desks or even assigned seats. The benches rise in tiers, with members of the two main parties facing each other across a wide aisle running lengthwise down the center of the chamber. You can see the detailed arrangements in Figure 5–1, which presents an aerial view of the main floor of the Commons and its balcony, as though you were looking straight down from the roof.

Figure 5–1

Arrangement of
Seating in the
House of Commons

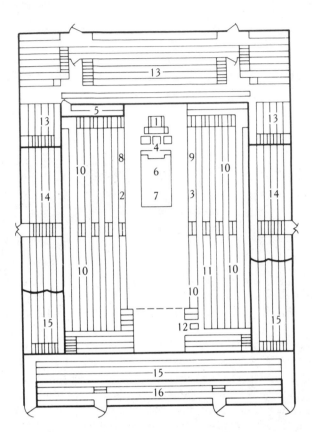

1. The Speaker
2. Prime Minister or Government spokesperson
3. Leader of the Opposition or Opposition spokesperson
4. Clerks at the table
5. Civil servants in attendance
6. The table
7. The Mace
8. Government front bench, occupied by ministers
9. Opposition front bench
10. Back benches
11. Other opposition parties
12. Serjeant-at-arms
13. Hansard and press gallery
14. Members' side galleries
15. Special galleries, including peers', "distinguished strangers," diplomatic, and Commonwealth galleries
16. The public gallery

The Commons has met at the same site since 1852. The original chamber was destroyed, however, in May 1941 by a Nazi bomb. (During the next several years the Commons met in the House of Lords chamber, and the Lords met in a room known as the monarch's Robing Room. This sequence of displacements tells you something about the hierarchy of power in Britain.) After World War II, the Commons chamber was rebuilt, generally along its original lines. The interior decoration was made less ornate, and some modernizing was done, including better lighting, a voice-amplification system, air conditioning, and foam-padded benches. Why, you must wonder, given such an opportunity, would any sensible people build a meeting room for their legislature too small to hold all its members?

A small chamber was thought to be essential to preserve the conversational style of speaking that had characterized Commons' debates. A large chamber would encourage bombastic rhetoric rather than reasoned discussion. Furthermore, if the chamber had seats for every Member, most debates would seem poorly attended unless virtually everyone was present. (Many first-time visitors to the U.S. House of Representatives are shocked to see what appears to be a virtually empty chamber.)

The floor plan of facing rows of benches was retained to reinforce a two-party system with clearly distinct parties. Crossing the floor (that is, switching parties) would require a more decisive move than in a semicircular seating arrangement, where one party's seats would shade into another's. This seems a strange argument to Americans, since both houses of the U.S. Congress and most state legislatures seat their members in a semicircle and still maintain a two-party system, with few legislators switching parties. The British, however, were thinking of continental political systems, where multiple parties and semicircular seating coincided.

At the head of the chamber is a large, canopied chair, the seat of the presiding officer of the Commons, the Speaker, who wears the traditional garb of knee breeches, wig, and long black gown. That is, the Speaker was so attired until 1992 and the unprecedented selection of a woman for the position. She declared that the wig was much too hot and uncomfortable and she certainly wasn't going to wear knee breeches. (Just as the British always fear: you make one change and there's no telling where it will end.) In front of the Speaker at a long table sit the clerks of the House, wearing wigs and gowns, recording the proceedings. On the table are receptacles to hold the Mace, the jewel-encrusted club that symbolizes the monarch's authority.

The Members

Certain types of people may not serve in the Commons. (They could be nominated, but could not hold a seat if elected.) Among these are leading judges; clergy of the Church of England, the Church of Scotland, and the Roman Catholic Church; persons holding an office of profit under the Crown; those guilty of corrupt or illegal election practices; and criminals. Although Members of Parliament (MPs) can be as young as twenty-one, most are well into middle age. The median age of the Conservatives elected in 1992 was forty-eight; for new Labour MPs it was forty-nine; Liberal Democrats were only slightly younger at forty-five. Only one Member (a Liberal Democrat) from the three largest parties in 1992 was under thirty; on the other hand, only two (both Conservatives) were seventy or older. Most MPs are experienced legislators; only a fifth of those seated in 1992 either were entering the Commons for the first time or had done so in a by-election between 1988 and 1992. At the other extreme, only a dozen Members had first entered the Commons before 1960.[1]

Following the 1992 election, sixty Members were women. Although this was less than 10 percent of the total membership, it was the highest number ever. The parties differ in gender mix. The Conservatives had twenty female MPs, and Labour had nearly twice as many—thirty-seven. During the election the Liberal Democrats had offered more women candidates (143) than any other party. Because of the party's electoral weakness, however, only two of these were elected. Ethnic minorities were even more poorly represented than women were after 1992; only six MPs were nonwhite.

The occupational background of Members differs considerably between the major parties. Among Conservatives the largest group is company officials (a third of all Conservative MPs), with lawyers next (not quite a sixth). Journalists and other

---

[1] The information on Members' backgrounds is from David Butler and Dennis Kavanagh, *The British General Election of 1992* (New York: St. Martin's, 1992), pp. 219–227. That section of the book was written by Bryon Criddle.

businesspeople are the other main groups. Among Labour MPs the largest single group (more than a quarter) is teachers, at whatever level in the educational system. Next come skilled manual workers, followed closely by white-collar workers, each group about half as prevalent as teachers.

Over the long term the proportion of Conservative MPs with business backgrounds has declined (although it increased slightly in both 1987 and 1992), while the proportion from the professions has increased. The proportion of Labour MPs from the working class has dropped over the years, while the percentage from professions has increased. Thus, with respect to the occupational background of their MPs, both parties have moved away from their traditional class base, and their Parliamentary parties are becoming more like each other. People from the professions accounted for about two-fifths of both party's Members in 1992. Some occupational contrasts still remain, however. Although nearly two-fifths of Conservative MPs in 1992 had occupational backgrounds in business, only 8 percent of Labour MPs did. And more than two-fifths of Labour MPs had been manual workers, but only four Conservatives had been. (Despite their substantial numbers in 1992, manual workers comprised the smallest share of the PLP that they ever had in its entire history.)

Educational differences are more notable. Well over two-fifths of the Conservatives elected in 1992 went to Oxford or Cambridge, but only a sixth of the Labour MPs did. Even more striking, especially if you recall our comments in Chapter 2 about education and the class system, are the differences in secondary schooling. Three-fifths of all Conservative MPs attended public schools, but only a seventh of Labour MPs did. Furthermore, more than an eighth of Conservative MPs went to the elite schools of Eton, Harrow, or Winchester; only three Labour MPs attended one of these schools. Even among what could be called the political elite, social class differences between the two parties are deeply etched.

Remuneration

Prior to 1911, Members of Parliament were not paid. Although the salary established then has been increased over the years, the British have been niggardly in helping MPs meet the expense of public service. They feared that if MPs were paid a decent salary, some rotter would try to make a good thing of it and stand for Parliament just for the money. An MP's salary is about $45,000. Those who do not live in London are given a supplement of $14,000 to pay for the cost of accommodations while attending Parliament.

Not until 1969 could MPs respond to their constituents' letters without having to pay postage personally. And only then did they get money to cover the cost of secretarial assistance. They now receive about $60,000, which is to cover not only clerical help but also research staff. Clearly, no MP can afford the large number of research assistants that a U.S. Congressperson enjoys. Expenses of traveling to and from an MP's constituency are reimbursed. And, in a show of great munificence, the British provide fifteen travel vouchers a year for an MP's spouse and children (under eighteen years old) to come to London for visits.

Incredibly inadequate as this level of compensation is, you have not yet heard the topper. For many years MPs could not even count on having office space. It used to be that when you visited the Palace of Westminster (the large building in which Parliament meets, shown in Figure 5–2), you would see MPs sitting on the stone benches dictating letters to secretaries whose salaries they paid out of their own pockets. If they managed to ferret out an empty room somewhere in the Palace, they could establish squatter's rights, or they might share an office (and perhaps a secretary) with another MP. But office space was not available for everyone. Although the situation has been improved through acquisition of space in nearby buildings, MPs have nothing like the elaborate suites enjoyed by members of the U.S. Congress.

The material rewards of being a Member of Parliament are hardly great. A person must have either a high sense of public service or a strong desire to be near the seat of power to undertake this career. And unless an MP is independently wealthy, some other source of income, such as part-time journalism or partnership in a legal firm, may well be necessary. Perhaps this is why a number of Conservative MPs sought to make a comfortable living by investing in the insurance brokerage, Lloyd's of London. An unexpected number of disasters, such as hurricanes and wrecked oil tankers, produced huge claims on coverage provided by Lloyd's. As a result several Conservative MPs faced serious financial losses in the mid-1990s.

Powers and Procedures

The powers of the House of Commons can be stated briefly: Parliament is supreme. This means that the Commons—given the concurrence of the Lords or the overriding of its opposition—literally can do whatever its Members want. No matter how outrageous it may be, any law passed by Parliament is valid.

Sessions and sittings   Each fall a new session of Parliament begins (unless a general election has occurred at such a time as to require altering the usual schedule) with the Speech from the Throne. The monarch delivers this speech from a throne in the House of Lords, with the Lords seated as usual and Members of the

Figure 5–2
The Palace of Westminster, Site of the Meetings of Parliament

Commons standing crowded together at the foot of the chamber. The Cabinet decides what will be in the speech; the monarch has no say about its contents. The speech outlines the Government's plans for the coming Parliamentary session. Thus, it is the equivalent of the U.S. President's State of the Union Address, although it is much shorter than that speech usually is.

For about the next week the Commons discusses the content of the speech. Then it begins to consider specific bills that the Government has submitted to it. With various holiday recesses the session continues until the following fall. The Commons usually returns from summer vacation for about a week to wrap up loose ends. Again, the monarch delivers a speech in the House of Lords, this time summarizing the accomplishments of the session. The session formally closes, and all bills and motions that weren't acted on die. Then a new session of Parliament is opened, and the cycle begins again.

Daily sittings of the Commons begin at 2:30 in the afternoon Monday through Thursday and usually end at 10:30. Longer sittings are possible, however, and sometimes the Commons does not adjourn until the wee hours of the morning. In fact, a sitting can last for more than twenty-four hours, thus running over into the next day's business and forcing it to be rescheduled. On Fridays the Commons meets from 9:30 in the morning to 3:00 to enable MPs to leave London early enough for weekend visits to their constituencies.

As we noted in describing the rebuilding of the Commons' chamber, the ideal procedure is reasoned debate. A number of customs have grown up over the years concerning such things as how MPs are to refer to each other. They cannot address other MPs by name and instead use phrases such as "the learned lady" to refer to a female MP with a university degree or "my gallant friend" to indicate a member of their party with a distinguished military record. In addition, an MP may not refer to another MP as a swine, jackass, stool pigeon, or guttersnipe, among other things.

The Speaker   The Speaker is responsible for seeing that name calling does not occur and that Members do not get carried away with emotion. Lacking the gavels or bells used by presiding officers in other legislatures, the Speaker merely stands up when tempers flare and says, "Order, order." This usually is sufficient. If an individual MP is the cause of a disturbance and refuses to obey the Speaker, then the Speaker can bar him or her from the Commons for several days. If the disorder is more general, the Speaker can suspend the sitting for a while until Members calm down. Such steps are rare because most MPs accord the Speaker great respect and authority; one of the few exceptions is Labour MP Dennis Skinner, who seems to specialize in getting himself "named" (suspended), thereby demonstrating, no doubt, that he is a true man of the people.

The Speaker's salary indicates the importance of the position. At close to $100,000 a year, it surpasses that paid to most of the top members of the executive branch. One of the main reasons for the honored status accorded to the position is that, unlike the Speaker of the U.S. House of Representatives, the Speaker of the House of Commons is nonpartisan. Although Speakers traditionally were selected by the leaders of the governing party, they have been formally elected by the Commons, usually without dissent from opposition parties.

Following the 1992 election, a new Speaker had to be chosen because the incumbent one had decided to retire. The leaders of both leading parties decided not to be involved in the process, leaving the choice entirely to the Commons. One of the candidates nominated was a Conservative; the other was a Labour MP, who not only was a woman but was nominated by a Conservative. Furthermore, the Labour MP was elected Speaker even though Labour had fewer seats in the Commons than the Conservatives did. Thus Betty Boothroyd became the first woman Speaker in the history of Parliament.[2]

As this selection process suggests, those chosen to be Speaker rarely have been prominent partisans. Whatever their previous activity, once elected, Speakers divorce themselves from their party. This means, for example, that a Speaker may not even make a partisan speech in his or her own constituency when standing for reelection to the House of Commons. In a spirit of fair play, the custom had been that parties would not offer candidates to oppose the Speaker in a general election. This practice began to lapse in the mid-1960s, however.

Since the daily sittings of the Commons run without break for at least eight hours and frequently longer, the Speaker obviously needs assistance in presiding over the meetings. Also, the custom is that the Speaker does not preside when the Commons meets in Committee of the Whole. When the Speaker is not in the chair, the Commons is presided over by either the chairman or one of the two deputy chairmen (despite this title, women—Betty Boothroyd, for example—have held one of these positions) of the Ways and Means Committee. Although these three officers of the House, unlike the Speaker, do not sever their ties with their parties, they are expected to be just as impartial as the Speaker is. To help ensure this, they do not vote in any of the divisions (a type of voting procedure) in the House of Commons. Since everyone understands that those who preside over the House must be absolutely impartial and fair to all, it is not surprising that the Speaker and the other three officers are selected from the opposition parties as frequently as from the Government party, a practice that would never occur in the United States.

The Speaker is to maintain order and fair play in the Commons' deliberations, but MPs are not to be prevented from expressing their views fully. To be certain that they do not feel constrained, MPs have no legal responsibility—cannot be sued for slander—for statements they make in the House of Commons. And to prevent them from being hampered in their duties, MPs are immune from arrest arising from civil suits and exempt from jury duty.

Procedure for enacting laws   The legislative process begins when a member of the Government introduces a bill (the typical way) or an ordinary MP does. In the latter case the bill is referred to as a private member's bill. Bills of limited application or of relevance only to specific localities are known as private bills; those of general application and public importance are termed public bills. We will be con-

---

[2]Even more incredible than the fact that the British Prime Minister (John Major) is a high school dropout whose father was a trapeze artist is the fact that the Speaker of the House of Commons was, in her youth, a chorus line dancer.

cerned only with the procedure for passing public bills; the procedure for private bills differs in some ways. (Referring to Table 5–1 will help to make the various stages clear.)

All bills must go through three readings, committee consideration, and, usually, a report stage. First reading is merely a formality to get the bill started in the legislative process; no debate occurs at that time. Second reading, when the basic purpose is discussed, is the major stage for most bills. No amendment can be proposed during a second reading; the Commons must either kill the bill or continue it on its way as it stands. If a bill passes its second reading, it is highly likely to be enacted. It goes next to a committee—either a standing committee or the Committee of the Whole—for discussion of details and possible amendment in light of the views expressed in the Commons during the second-reading debate.

Note that the committee stage comes *later* in the legislative process than is true in the United States. In the U.S. Congress, bills are sent to committee as soon as they are introduced on the floor, *before* the legislature as a whole has had any opportunity to express its views on the bill. When a committee receives a bill in Britain, however, the legislature already has approved it in general. A U.S. Congressional committee may spend weeks working on a bill only to see it killed on the floor when it is finally reported out of committee. This virtually never occurs in Britain; committees there revise bills guided by suggestions for change already voiced in legislative debate and by the knowledge that the aim of the bill has majority support.

The committee stage for the most controversial bills usually occurs in Committee of the Whole, made up of the entire House of Commons. The rules of procedure in Committee of the Whole are more informal than in regular meetings of the Commons and permit more Members to participate. As a result, this procedure is more time-consuming than is sending a bill to a standing committee. Occasionally, opposition parties may be able to force the Government to concede significant changes in a bill or abandon a bill entirely in Committee of the Whole in order to avoid excessive delay in its program of legislation.

If a bill has not been amended in Committee of the Whole, it goes to third reading. When, more typically, it has been amended or has been considered by a standing committee, a report stage occurs before third reading. This stage offers the last

Table 5–1

Steps in the British Legislative Process

First reading	Formality, no discussion
Second reading	Debate on the substance or purpose of the bill as a whole
Standing committee or Committee of the Whole	Consideration of the detailed provisions of the bill; specific amendments are in order
Report stage	Further chance for specific amendments (skipped if bill is unamended in Committee of the Whole)
Third reading	Debate on the bill as a whole, only technical amendments are in order

opportunity for amendments of substance, since on third reading the vote is on the entire bill (except for minor technical changes).

The structure and functions of Parliamentary standing committees differ from those of Congressional ones, in part because the committee stage occurs at a different point in the legislative process. Commons' committees are designated not by a subject area but simply by a letter of the alphabet. Although they are called standing committees, they have no permanent membership. When a bill is sent to committee, the Committee on Selection appoints sixteen to thirty MPs to serve on the committee—formed to consider that bill only. During a given session of Parliament, Standing Committee A may deal with several bills, totally unrelated to each other in subject matter, and have a complete turnover in membership from one bill to the next.

The Committee on Selection is chosen annually by the Commons. In staffing a standing committee, it tries to appoint MPs having knowledge relevant to the particular bill being assigned to that committee. Length of service in the Commons is not directly linked to committee membership; nothing like the seniority system of the U.S. Congress exists. This also is true of committee chairmanships. The Speaker of the House selects the chairs. Since they, like the Speaker, are to preside impartially, an MP from an opposition party may be appointed.

Unlike Congressional committees, Commons' standing committees do not gather information. They do not hold public hearings on proposed legislation; they do not call expert witnesses to testify for or against a bill. All that a person with expert knowledge can do is contact an MP on a committee and hope that he or she will relay the information to the committee.

Since a bill can get to a Commons' standing committee only if it has been approved in principle by the Commons, the committees do not have to weed out hundreds of legislative proposals as U.S. Congressional committees do. To make the point another way, British committees cannot kill a bill or mutilate it out of recognition—the whole House already has accepted it. Thus, the sole function of a committee is to consider the details of a bill—the Commons doesn't have time to do that—and make any changes recommended during the second-reading debate.

What might seem to be trivial differences in legislative procedure between Britain and the United States have some significant effects. First, since the power of Commons' standing committees is limited, MPs usually do not compete for appointment. Second, interest groups do not mount extensive campaigns to galvanize public opinion when a bill of concern to them is in committee, as frequently happens in the United States. A British interest group might want to have an MP who was linked to it serve on a committee considering the bill, but primarily just to be certain that it was kept informed about the new legislation.

The absence of permanent subject-matter legislative committees also means that Britain lacks the constant surveillance of executive actions and proposals by small groups of expert legislators, which occurs in the United States. You already have learned that most MPs cannot afford a sizable personal research staff; now you see that they cannot even call on such assistance collectively. Thus, the Commons frequently is not well informed on the subjects it must consider; it is unable to challenge the Government's proposals effectively because they appear to be justified by superior knowledge, being based on the expertise of the civil service.

Select committees   To alleviate the problem of Members' lack of special knowledge, the Commons in the late 1960s began experimenting with specialist select committees. Unlike the standing committees, these committees can call expert witnesses and hold public hearings. These committees are, however, not comparable to Congressional ones. Information gathering is their sole function; no bills are sent to them. In effect, the British have divided the functions of Congressional committees in two: one set of committees works on the detailed content of bills, and another set gathers information on which to base a report to expand the legislature's expertise.

The current set of specialist select committees is about a decade and a half old. Sixteen committees, each with eleven members, focus on subject areas corresponding to government departments. Each committee is able to hire a few people, typically three or four, to serve as expert advisors—again, hardly the extensive staff support prevailing in the U.S. Congress.

The select committees operate under several constraints. Although they can call Government ministers and civil servants to testify, they do not have any statutory right to compel these officials to provide information. The problem came to a head in 1987. In the so-called Westland Affair, the Cabinet was divided over whether a particular defense contract should go to a company linked to an American firm or to one involved in a consortium of European companies. Information was leaked that was detrimental to Michael Heseltine, the Defence Secretary, who opposed Prime Minister Thatcher's position on this issue. Heseltine eventually resigned from the Cabinet in protest, as did the minister from whose department the leak had come.

When select committees tried to find out what had happened, they encountered a Catch-22 situation. The minister who had headed the leaking department refused to answer key questions on the grounds that he no longer was in office and therefore wasn't responsible and, in any event, it was civil servants who had misbehaved in leaking the information. When committees then sought to question the civil servants involved, they were barred from doing so because civil servants are answerable to their ministers, not to the House of Commons. As the head of one of the committees observed, this logic created an accountability gap. To make matters worse, neither the former nor the current head of the leaking department would penalize the civil servants involved, despite blaming them for what had occurred. (There was good reason to believe that, in leaking the information, the civil servants were only doing what the Prime Minister and the department minister wanted them to do.)

This affair produced a lengthy debate that led to a good bit of hair splitting. The select committees were acknowledged to have the right to question civil servants about their "actions" (that is, behavior consistent with ministers' desires) but not about their "conduct" (that is, misbehavior). The top civil servant issued a memo telling civil servants that, should any select committee question them about their conduct or that of any other civil servants, they should refuse to answer. The Commons' Liaison Committee (composed of the chairs of the various select committees) maintained that such instructions violated the rights of the select committees, but the Government refused to concede the point. Whatever the Iran-Contra hearings may have indicated about the ability of the U.S. Congress to get to the bottom of devious, illegal behavior in the executive branch, the fact is that Congressional committees have stronger weapons with which to compel testimony than the Commons' select committees do.

Although the select committees supposedly were created to strengthen the legislature, the Commons has not been able to decide exactly how to utilize them effectively. No procedure has been established to ensure regular discussion by the full House of the reports that the committees make. Thus, the investigations may end up informing only the dozen MPs who are on a given committee.

The British have not moved very far in reforming the Commons' committees, in part because, as you have learned, they believe in altering things bit by bit over the years. More importantly, a fundamental issue about the ultimate location of power in the British system is involved. The Commons wants to be better informed, so that it can play a more influential role in the policy process; the executive does not want to give up any of its power and opposes any change that would make it more subject to legislative control. The basic issue is one of legislative-executive relations, which, as we indicated at the start of this chapter, will be discussed more fully in Chapter 6.

Limits on debate   Every democratic legislature must devise procedures that can limit debate in order to prevent dogmatic obstructionism while not denying a full hearing to those voicing unpopular views. Closure, the procedure for ending a debate and taking a vote, requires only a simple majority vote in the Commons, provided that at least 100 Members vote in favor. The Speaker may refuse to accept a motion for closure, if he or she feels that some significant views have not been adequately heard. Thus, the Speaker's impartiality, mentioned previously, is an essential element in ensuring that neither the will of the majority nor the rights of the minority are violated in the legislative process.

The Speaker also helps the Commons to transact its business efficiently by ignoring amendments proposed by small, atypical groups of Members. This power is known as "kangaroo closure." During the report stage for a bill, the Speaker, in effect, hops over insignificant amendments, calling for votes only on those seeming to have substantial backing. The chairs of the Ways and Means Committee and the standing committees possess this power as well.

Still another form of closure is known as the "guillotine," or, more formally, an allocation of time order. When a bill is likely to arouse lengthy and fierce opposition, a guillotine is used to set time limits for each stage (committee, report, third reading) of its passage through the Commons. A guillotine also makes dilatory motions out of order and removes possible impediments to quick action (such as time regularly set aside for dealing with recurring subjects). To prevent the guillotine motions themselves from being obstructed by delaying tactics, debate on them can't exceed three hours.

The rules discussed so far limit the debating time of the Commons as a whole; other rules constrain individual Members. Except when the Commons is in Committee of the Whole, MPs may speak only once on any motion. Furthermore, their comments must be relevant to the topic or the Speaker can order them to stop. Unlike former U.S. Senator Huey Long, an MP cannot filibuster by reading recipes for creole cooking. The only actual time limit is that the Speaker may restrict back-benchers (MPs not part of the two main parties' leadership groups) to ten minutes during second reading and other major debates (such as that on the Speech from the Throne). MPs may not completely write out a speech in advance and read it word-for-word to the Commons. Managing to remain relevant while speaking from only a few notes is difficult enough that it probably helps to limit the length of speeches.

Voting procedures   At times the Commons simply votes by voice. When a record of each Member's vote is desired, however, as on major legislation, the method used contrasts sharply with the roll call of legislatures in the United States. The Speaker calls for a division of the House. Members have six minutes to enter one or the other of the two "division lobbies" around the Commons' chamber. Each party's whips make certain that late-arriving MPs enter the proper lobby. As MPs file out of the lobbies, they give their name to clerks, who check them off the list of Members, and are counted by tellers. After all the Members have left the lobbies, the tellers and the clerks make certain that their totals for the ayes or noes agree, and the results are reported back in the chamber to the Speaker.

You may regard calling a division as another of those quaint practices that by now you have come to expect of the British, one that any sensible country would abandon for more up-to-date methods. The procedure does give rise to snide comments about Members being herded through the lobbies like sheep. Nonetheless, a division in the Commons consumes only about twelve to fifteen minutes, less than it takes for a roll call vote in the U.S. House of Representatives, even though the latter has only two-thirds as many members. The apparently silly, traditional ways do have something to be said for them at times.

Calling the Government to Account

The House of Commons devotes more floor time to its business than any other legislative body in the world. In a typical year it meets for 150 to 180 days and averages well over 1,500 hours of sittings. This is almost five times as long as the German Bundestag sits and one-third longer than the U.S. Senate does. Yet, not counting the time spent in discussing financial matters, the Commons devotes only about two-fifths of its time to debating and passing legislation. Furthermore, as you will see in Chapter 6, strong party discipline has moved the locus of decision making from the Commons to the Cabinet. In Britain, the Cabinet—that is, the executive—makes policy; the legislature does little more than ratify.

In basic function, then, the British and U.S. legislatures differ fundamentally. As we discussed in Chapter 2, constitutionalism in Britain takes a different form from that in the United States. In Britain, power is concentrated, restrained primarily by accountability for its use. The primary function of the Commons—and a key one it is, given Britain's form of constitutionalism—is to call the Government to account. The Government must defend and justify its actions and policies in the Commons. The Commons provides an arena for debate of the Government's program and for ventilating grievances produced by its management of the country.

Question time   One of the best-known means of calling the Government to account is question time. Four days a week (no questions on Friday), one of the first activities of the Commons' sitting is replies by Cabinet ministers to questions that have been submitted at least two days in advance by nonministerial Members. Each MP may submit two questions, directed to those ministers in whose sphere of responsibility the matter falls. The Prime Minister replies to questions twice each week. Questions may be designed to embarrass a minister, call attention to minor injustices in bureaucratic action, or obtain information.

Expert civil servants in each department prepare answers for their ministers. A minister may refuse to answer a question on the grounds that to do so would injure the national interest—if there were delicate foreign negotiations in progress, for example. Ministers try to avoid overuse of such a response, however, since it may seem to suggest that they are hiding something.

Once a minister gives an answer in the Commons, any Member may ask a supplementary question, provided that the Speaker considers it related, and this must be answered immediately. At this point the minister is on his or her own, although civil servants may be in the box (a row of seats at the end of the House to the right and behind the Speaker, labeled 5 in Figure 5–1). The box is separated from the chamber proper by a low partition and technically is not part of it. Conversation and notes may pass over the partition if the minister needs help. A minister inadequately informed or unable to think on his or her feet can be a liability to the Government. Careers may be jeopardized and reputations broken by consistently poor performances during question time. In the hands of skilled MPs, question time often has been a potent weapon.

Recently, however, the power of question time to control the Government has been suspect. Ministers and their civil servants are very skilled in not telling the Commons anything they do not wish MPs to know. Although question time is useful, American observers often overrate it as a means of calling the Government to account. Some MPs devote a great deal of time to questions; during the 1979–1980 session of Parliament, one MP submitted nearly 1,400 questions. The typical MP, however, submits fewer than 100. The specialist select committees may be able to breathe new life into question time by providing MPs with the detailed information necessary to ask more searching questions that ministers cannot evade so easily.[3]

Adjournment debates   In addition to question time, MPs have a special opportunity to call the Government to account at the end of each sitting. At 10 P.M., the Commons' regular business is halted for an adjournment debate. (If a sitting is

---

[3]For a thorough discussion of the role of questions, see Philip Norton and Mark Franklin, eds. *Parliamentary Questions* (New York: Oxford University Press, 1993).

to continue beyond the usual 10:30 closing, the adjournment debate does not occur until just before the end of the sitting.) During the half-hour before the House adjourns automatically, MPs can discuss a particular grievance or aspect of Government policy. At times an MP dissatisfied with a minister's reply during question time will have an opportunity to pursue the matter further during an adjournment debate.

The end-of-sitting adjournment debates, like question time, provide individual MPs with a chance to call the Government to account on detailed matters, probably of limited interest to most other MPs. Another type of adjournment debate deals with issues of wider concern. Following each sitting's question time, any MP may move that the Commons adjourn on "a specific and important matter that should have urgent consideration." If the Speaker agrees that the subject meets these criteria and the request (if opposed) is supported by forty MPs, a special three-hour debate is scheduled for the following day immediately after questions. Alternatively, if the Speaker feels it is necessary, he or she can schedule the debate for 7 P.M. on the day of the request. When this kind of adjournment debate occurs (typically one to four times each session), the House does not argue the merits of whether it should go home, but discusses the urgent topic that the MP raised.

Immediately after questions the Government itself may move that the House adjourn. This is not because the Cabinet ministers are unprepared and want a day off. Under the Commons' rules of procedure, virtually any topic is relevant under a motion to adjourn. Such a motion, therefore, permits a wide-ranging debate on some topic of current interest without the Speaker having to exclude some MP from the debate because the relevance of his or her comments is not immediately apparent. The Government consults with the Opposition in arranging such debates, giving the latter some influence over the topics that are discussed.

The Opposition has even more control over the topics for the twenty Opposition Days that occur during every session. On these days opposition parties decide what subject will be debated and what form the motion on which debate is based will take. Seventeen of these days are controlled by the largest opposition party, with the other three allocated to the second largest opposition party.

When the Government's opponents want to pose the most aggressive challenge, they submit a motion of censure against or of lack of confidence in the Government. Such motions usually cite an alleged failing of the Government, but the resultant debates are often broad in scope. We will discuss such motions in more detail in Chapter 6.

Assessing accountability procedures   As you have seen, the House of Commons possesses a number of means for calling the Government to account, but to what purpose? Party discipline in Britain is so strong that the outcome of any major vote in the Commons is hardly ever in doubt. (The 1992 reduction in the Conservatives' majority to under two dozen and the splits in the party in attitudes toward Europe did, however, make ratification of the Maastricht Treaty rather more "exciting" than Prime Minister Major would have preferred.) The Opposition does not expect that the force of its argument will convert the Government or its MPs. You should not be too quick to conclude, however, that it is another meaningless British charade. The Opposition actually is playing to the public, hoping that its challenges to the Government will win over enough voters to return it to power in the next election. If, as occasionally happens, the Government does modify or even withdraw a proposal because of sharp criticism in the Commons, that is an unexpected bonus for the Opposition.

The British procedures facilitate, much more than the American system does, public, face-to-face discussions among the leading politicians of current political issues precisely at the time those subjects are of greatest importance. By criticizing the Government's policies in the Commons, the Opposition publicizes policy alternatives during the period between elections and does not have to rely on election campaigns alone to present its distinctive appeal to the electorate. In having to explain and defend its actions, the Government has a chance to clarify its program for the public. Thus, each side has an opportunity to work out a coherent set of policies and to stimulate some public response to them.

The fact that the Government cooperates with the Opposition in arranging these debates is evidence of the great importance attached in Britain to fair play, free speech, and responsible government. For those in power to help provide their opponents with opportunities to drive them from power is remarkably rare among the world's political systems. Further evidence of this concern is the financial aid provided out of public revenues for opposition parties. The amount received varies according to number of votes and seats that a party received in the preceding general election.

The Government expects the Opposition to challenge it in the Commons, but debate may also reveal complaints from and doubts among MPs of the Government party. Unless the Government responds promptly to such discontent, it may grow into a major defection (as, for example, occurred following Prime Minister Major's refusal to allow the electorate a referendum on the Maastricht Treaty). Dissent among "its own" MPs is taken much more seriously by the Cabinet than is attack by the Opposition. (Major would not have had to worry about what the Labour party and the Liberal Democrats were going to do on the Maastricht Treaty if he could have counted on the votes of all the Conservative MPs.) Thus, such dissent is more likely to produce changes in Government policies and be more effective in calling the Government to account.

Many students of Parliament and some MPs themselves fear that the ability of the Commons to call the Government to account has declined drastically. Procedures that were effective in the nineteenth century seem to have lost their bite in the twentieth, with the increasing complexity of public problems and altered political circumstances. Accountability clearly has attenuated, and public esteem for Parliament has declined. Less than a third—30 percent—of Britons questioned in an opinion poll early in 1993 said they had a great deal or quite a lot of confidence in Parliament. Restoring some of the legislature's former power and significance poses an important problem, given the form that constitutionalism takes in Britain. If accountability is ineffective, then the only check on abuse of power is the politicians' personal values.

■ THE HOUSE OF LORDS

Although the House of Commons, even in its reduced status, clearly is the more important house of Parliament, the British legislature does consist of two chambers, and we need to say something about the "upper" house.

The Members

The House of Lords is a potentially unwieldy legislative body with a formal membership of around 1,200. None of the members are elected (that is, accountable to anyone), and most are entitled to belong simply because they have inherited a title from a forebearer. Those who have not inherited membership have been appointed because of their eminence in various fields or for faithful political service to the party in power. In addition, the Lords includes twenty-six archbishops and bishops of the Church of England and eleven Lords of Appeal in Ordinary, who serve as the country's highest judges. Some of those eligible are excused because they indicate they do not wish to attend; this reduces the body's effective size to around 900. The working size—the number of active members—is even smaller, about 300.

To improve the quality of the membership, the Life Peerages Act was passed in 1958. The Act permits appointment to the Lords for a person's lifetime only; the title and membership do not pass to his or her descendants. Prior to then, capable people who objected in principle to a hereditary aristocracy would refuse a title and, thus, could not be appointed to the Lords. Life peers now make up about a third of the total membership and an even larger proportion of the active membership.

Powers and Procedures

The House of Lords meets less frequently than the Commons does and for a shorter time, about six and a half hours a sitting on average. Procedure is more informal than in the Commons; there are no standing committees and no closure. The Lord Chancellor, a member of the Government, presides over the Lords and, unlike the Speaker in the Commons, takes an active part in debate.

Although many lords are not affiliated with any party, enough of them support the Conservatives to give that party a permanent majority in the Lords. This political situation makes the Lords' power of some importance. A major constitutional crisis early in the century led to limitations on the Lords' powers in 1911. These powers were curtailed further by the Parliamentary Act of 1949. Both houses must pass a bill for it to become law. When they disagree, no joint conference committee of members from both houses, such as is used in the U.S. Congress, is set up to work out a compromise. Instead, the bill is shuttled back and forth in an attempt to revise it sufficiently to be acceptable to both houses.

If these attempts fail, the bill cannot be enacted, unless the Commons wishes to override the Lords. To do this, the bill must be reintroduced in exactly the same form the following year and passed by the Commons. Thus, the Lords can delay, but not block, the will of the popularly elected house. This power to delay can be important at times, especially near the end of a Government's term. If the Government loses the election, it will not be able to reintroduce the bill, and the Lords' suspensive veto will, in effect, become a permanent one.

For financial bills—the Speaker of the Commons decides which bills meet this criterion—the Lords' powers are much more limited. Such bills become law thirty days after passage by the Commons, regardless of any opposition from the Lords.

Such constraints usually do not come into play; the Lords and the Commons are not constantly at odds. Typically, if the Commons insists on certain legislation and will not accept the changes the Lords favors, then the Lords gives in and does not block passage of the bill. Nonetheless, Government defeats in the Lords have become more prevalent. On the other hand, these totaled about 100 during the 1980s, which hardly makes them an everyday event. Slightly more than half of the time, the Government accepts the Lords' wishes and does not utilize the Commons to override the upper house.

A couple of specific examples should help make the Lords' impact less vague. When the Government was abolishing local governmental organs in the metropolitan areas, many people in the left wing of the Labour party were surprised to find themselves applauding the Lords—hardly their favorite organ of government. One of the Lords' concerns was that the proposed transitional arrangements would undercut accountability to the voters. The compromise the Lords managed to wring out of the Government was to extend the life of the existing metropolitan councils for an additional year. Thus, the Lords could not prevent the Government from implementing the policy but could induce the Government to modify it in such a way as to help maintain a measure of popular control over local government. The House of Lords is not accountable, but that doesn't mean that it is unresponsive. Certainly, some left-leaning local governments thought it worth the effort to produce ads and banners egging their Lordships on. (The offices of London's local government were right across the river from the Houses of Parliament and anything displayed there was easily visible. The picture of the Parliament building that appears in Figure 5–2 was taken only a short distance away from the building that housed that local government.)

In another instance the Government planned to require local government to sell public housing accommodations to elderly tenants. Although this might seem like a reasonable idea, interest groups working for adequate housing and for the elderly were concerned that such action would result in a shortage of low-rent housing for retirees who could not afford to buy. Here again a popular movement made common cause with the hereditary chamber. Because the relevant legislation contained other provisions that the Government was anxious to have enacted without delay, it gave way in the face of the Lords' opposition and did not try to restore the right-to-buy provision, which the Lords had cut from the bill.

Such incidents, along with the declining influence of the Commons that we discussed earlier, have led one authority on the House of Lords to comment, "By 1987 the impact of the Upper House in amending the actual content of bills was widely recognised to be greater than that of the House of Commons."[4] Although this is an

---

[4] Donald Shell, *The House of Lords* (Totowa, N.J.: Barnes and Noble, 1988), p. 151.

expert assessment, it remains a minority opinion. Most people would be more inclined to believe that Gilbert and Sullivan (nineteenth-century composers) were right when they wrote of the Lords' action during the Napoleonic Wars, "The House of Lords did nothing in particular and did it very well."

A convincing case can be made, however, for the continued existence of the House of Lords. First, the Lords' diverse membership enables it to hold informative debates by nonpartisan experts on topics of public interest. Even more useful is the time the Lords spends discussing legislative amendments that the Commons was too busy to consider. Such supplementing of an overloaded Commons helps to prevent possible abuses and arbitrary action in the case of delegated legislation, provisional orders, and other such executive decrees. Much contemporary legislation in any democracy simply sets forth general provisions and procedures and leaves to the bureaucracy the details of implementation. The framework law authorizes the executive branch to issue detailed regulations to achieve the goals determined by the legislature. The power to issue such rules, typically called statutory instruments in Britain, must be controlled to ensure that the executive does not become a law unto itself. Parliament must be certain that the executive does not abuse this grant of power.

The Commons lacks time to discuss more than a handful of the approximately 2,500 statutory instruments issued each year. The Joint Committee on Statutory Instruments (composed of seven Members from each house) and the Commons' Standing Committee on Statutory Instruments do manage to examine a good number of them, but most receive little scrutiny by Parliament before going into effect. The House of Lords' consideration of some of them helps to improve this situation somewhat. The Lords has more free time than the Commons does, it has people with legal training, and, since its members need not be concerned with attracting attention to help them get reelected, it has people willing to work on matters generally regarded as dull.

▪ ▪ ▪

Perhaps the best brief assessment of the Lords is that offered by Herbert Morrison, a prominent figure in Labour's 1945–1951 Government, who wrote, "The fact that the House of Lords has many irrational features is not in itself fatal in British eyes, for we have a considerable capacity for making the irrational work; and if a thing works we tend rather to like it, or any rate to put up with it."[5] A more quintessentially British comment would be hard to find.

---

[5]Lord Morrison of Lambeth, *Government and Parliament,* 3d ed. (London: Oxford University Press, 1964), p. 205.

6

The Executive and Policy Making

As you have seen, the idea of limited government has had a long history in Britain. One of the reasons the struggle to establish this doctrine in Britain was so protracted is that, although many of the royal powers were derived from acts of Parliament, many powers, rights, immunities, and privileges of the monarch were based on common law, on legally enforceable custom and tradition. Rather than try to abolish all of the royal prerogatives, some of which were essential to the proper functioning of any government, the British instead eventually established the doctrine that the decision to exercise these powers must be made not by the monarch, but by the Government's ministers. The ministers in turn were made answerable to Parliament for their acts. Thus, the Cabinet is the center of power in the British political system, and its relation with Parliament is the key aspect of accountability. Before dealing with these topics, however, we need to explain the role and powers to which the monarch now is limited.

■ *THE SYMBOLIC EXECUTIVE*

If you were to judge simply by statutory law, you would conclude that Queen Elizabeth II can veto legislation, designate whomever she chooses as Prime Minister and make other key Government appointments, summon and dissolve Parliament at will, and, having received advice from her ministers, decide what her Government's policy and actions will be. As so often is the case in Britain, however, the reality differs. Should the Queen attempt to exercise any of these powers, she probably would be regarded as acting unconstitutionally, even though she would not be violating any statute.

The British, in typical fashion, have shifted power around within the governmental system by custom rather than by statute. Dissolution of Parliament, for example, remains a Crown power, but the monarch uses the power only when told to do so by the Prime Minister. Not for more than a century has a monarch refused to dissolve Parliament when the Government desired it. A monarch has not vetoed a bill for well over two and a half centuries. No monarch for almost a century and a half has dismissed a Government because he or she disliked its policies.

Furthermore, the monarch has no discretion in designating the Prime Minister. General elections determine who will be Prime Minister; the Leader of the party with the largest number of seats in the House of Commons is entitled to that office. Each party, as you learned in Chapter 4, has a formal procedure for choosing a new Leader when the current one dies or resigns. And when a party comes to power, its current Leader becomes Prime Minister. The parties would not permit the monarch to select their Leader for them by picking a Prime Minister.

Nor does the monarch have any greater involvement in selecting other members of the Government. The Prime Minister assigns Government offices without any assistance from the monarch. As for the Government's policies, the monarch does not ask the Cabinet for advice and then decide what to do. The Cabinet decides; the monarch, at best, can only suggest to the Cabinet what it might do.

Should a Government be defeated in Parliament and resign instead of dissolving the Commons, the monarch must call the Leader of the Opposition to let that person attempt to become Prime Minister by forming a Government. The monarch cannot consult other politicians before doing this because to do so would appear to be an attempt to keep the Leader of the Opposition out of office.

Any of these actions would aid one party and harm others. Doing them would involve the monarch in partisan politics and violate the conventions of the constitution. The monarchy has survived in Britain and become a respected institution because it is widely recognized to be politically neutral. Maintaining this stance must be the overriding concern of every British ruler.

The monarch's political neutrality is the culmination of changes begun by the Reform Act of 1832. This and subsequent legislation expanding the right to vote made Cabinets dependent on the will of the people, not on the favor of the monarch. Collective responsibility (which we will discuss later in this chapter) enabled the people's representatives in the Commons to call the Government to account for the way in which the country was being run. Thus, the monarch was spared responsibility for any shortcomings and was relieved from being involved in political struggles.

If Queen Elizabeth were to identify herself with any particular group of politicians or specific set of policies, she would herself become a politician, subject to criticism and attack like all other politicians. She could not appeal to the people against the Cabinet without expecting the Cabinet to appeal to the people against her. Not only must the monarch be impartial, but he or she must be believed by the public to be so. Until the twentieth century this rarely was the case. Queen Victoria, for example, was perceived (and rightly so) as a political partisan during many years of her reign.

Although the monarchy is expected to remain aloof from politics, the monarch is not entirely divorced from the policy process. Official documents such as Cabinet papers and Foreign Office telegrams are sent daily to Buckingham Palace (see Figure 6–1). In addition, the monarch may ask for information and may talk with experts and foreign dignitaries. A diligent monarch can be very well-informed, always in a strong position for exerting influence.

Figure 6–1

Buckingham Palace, the London Residence of the British Monarch

A sensible Prime Minister will welcome nonpartisan opinions from someone with long experience and sound knowledge. Queen Elizabeth, by the start of the 1990s, had been served by nine different occupants of the office of Prime Minister. She provides continuity and an active recollection of previous decisions not available from anyone in the Cabinet. None of those in the Cabinet had even won their first election to the Commons when she became queen in 1952. The impact of the Queen's opinions should not be exaggerated. No Government will abandon a major policy just because the Queen has a notion to do so. To the extent that her views are sound and do not clash with the governing party's program, however, she can influence her ministers.

The monarch's most important role is not policy maker, but ceremonial or symbolic head of state. In this capacity Queen Elizabeth relieves the political head of state (the Prime Minister) and his or her colleagues from many time-consuming duties, such as meeting foreign dignitaries on their arrival in Britain, dedicating important buildings or monuments, and other such functions. The symbolic role has a more important aspect; the monarch provides an apolitical focus for national loyalty. The Queen personifies the state; she is a *living symbol* of the nation and thus is able to stir patriotic feelings of national pride more successfully than a flag or a song can do.

Over a century ago, in a classic commentary on British government, Walter Bagehot argued that the head of state—the monarch—played a dignified role, and the Government—the Prime Minister and Cabinet colleagues—performed an efficient function. The Cabinet ran the country behind the scenes, while public ceremony suggested that the monarch actually was in charge. Monarchical pomp was needed to awe the public into accepting laws and regulations; if the people discovered that the decisions were made by mere politicians, they would be less disposed to obey. Such an argument seems pretty farfetched in the closing years of the twentieth century. Yet, as recently as the 1960s, a public opinion poll suggested that it still had some validity. Asked whether the views of the Queen or of the Prime Minister *would* prevail in a conflict over policy and which views *should* prevail, a substantial majority believed not only that the Queen's would, but that they should.[1] Apparently, the monarch still helps to legitimate the political system.

In the United States, where the President combines the roles of head of government and head of state, criticizing him in his partisan capacity without appearing to be attacking him in his symbolic status is difficult. The former behavior is legitimate; the latter is not. Thus, Americans are forced to make such comments as "I respect the office, but not the man."

The British system clearly offers a symbolic focus for loyalty, a constant presence whatever the shifts in partisan control of the government. By providing such a focus, the monarch also serves a lightning-rod function. Many people want some personal magnetism, or charisma, in their politics. If an unscrupulous politician with such an attribute were to gain power, he or she would pose a serious threat to democracy—Americans are not unfamiliar with the dangers of populist demagogues. Rather than try to banish charisma from politics, the British seek to channel it through the monarchy. Doing so presents no danger because the monarch's powers have been reduced to virtually nothing. Thus, the monarchy can help to discharge popular passions that otherwise might jeopardize democracy. The role of the monarchy in system maintenance should not be overlooked.

Few people in twentieth-century Britain have been republicans, have wished to abolish the monarchy. Nonetheless, in recent years criticism of the institution has become considerably more vocal. The royals often seem frivolous and out of touch with the people. Everything seemed to go wrong in 1992. The carryings on of the heir, Prince Charles, and his wife Diana and of his brother Andrew and his wife Fergie would not have been believed had they been part of the script for a TV soap opera. In addition, a major fire caused substantial damage to Windsor Castle, the monarch's principal English residence outside of London. Queen Elizabeth despaired that 1992 was an "*annus horribilius*" (a horrible year).

Assuming that the wealthy hate taxes just as much as everyone else, the Queen had another reason for being depressed by 1992. More than two centuries ago, the monarch agreed to turn over to the government the income from Crown lands in exchange for an annual stipend. This stipend was not so much a salary as it was funds to operate the royal establishment. By the early 1990s this so-called Civil List totaled around $15 million a year. The Queen's ancestors owned a variety of personal property and wise investment over the years produced a considerable personal fortune. Although previous monarchs had paid taxes on this personal wealth, at some time during the reign of Queen Elizabeth's father, a deal was made that exempted the monarch from all taxes. As the monarchy became less sacrosanct, it became quite vulnerable on the issue of tax avoidance. A Liberal Democrat MP, for example, introduced a bill (which made no further progress) in 1991 to require the monarch to pay taxes.

Queen Elizabeth apparently decided that the best way to reburnish the monarchy was to offer to pay taxes, which she did late in 1992. She also said that she

---

[1]*The Queen* (Harmondsworth, England: Penguin Books, 1977), p. 13.

would take over payments to most of her relatives who had received funds through the Civil List so that this stipend would cost the government less. Thus beginning in April 1993 the Queen paid taxes at the top rate of 40 percent on her personal income.

How much the Queen actually is worth is a matter of considerable controversy. *Fortune* magazine said in 1993 in its annual list of billionaires that her fortune had decreased by a third in 1992 due to the decline in value of the British pound sterling and fall in the value of various art and property holdings. Even so, that publication claimed she was worth $7.4 billion. A few months earlier Prince Edward (her youngest and, fortunately, unmarried son), reacting to other reports that she was worth £6.5 billion, erupted, "Absolute crap! If *only* she had £6.5 billion." When Prime Minister Major announced the details of how the Queen would be taxed, he commented on various estimates of her private funds, which had ranged from £100 million to billions. He said, "Her majesty has authorised me to say that even the lowest of these estimates is grossly overstated." Since the Queen's tax returns are to be given the same confidentiality as those of any other citizen, that information probably is as specific as any the public is likely to get.

How much has all this affected the public's views of the monarchy? At the end of 1992 nearly half of those polled said that their opinion of the Royal Family had gone down during the year (only 5 percent said it had gone up). Even more, three-fourths, felt that the Royal Family was not setting the British people a good example. Half believed that the events of the year had inflicted a great deal of damage on the monarchy. As a result, although in July 1991 two-thirds had professed affection for the Royal Family, a year and a half later only half felt that way.[2]

Somewhat surprisingly, despite all the scandalous stories, Princess Diana has become more popular. At the close of the 1980s only a tenth chose her as their favorite member of the Royal Family, but twice as many did so in 1993. On the other hand, there was little contest about royals' service to the nation. Respondents could rate eight members of the Royal Family on a scale from 0 to 10. Nearly a third gave Queen Elizabeth the top rating on service. Her average score was 7.7. Next was the Queen's only daughter, Princess Anne, who averaged 7.3 (a fifth gave her top marks). Prince Charles didn't fare very well—an average rank of 5.7.

The public's view of Charles is crucial for the future of the monarchy. In 1988 a fifth chose him as their favorite member of the royals—he was more popular than any other member. By 1993 only 4 percent selected him, putting him well behind not only his mother and grandmother, but also his wife and his sister. Only a fifth of the public wants Queen Elizabeth to relinquish the throne while she is still alive so that Charles can become King now. A substantial minority—close to two-fifths—feels that when the Queen dies Charles should be skipped over and his son made King. Nonetheless, well over two-thirds believe that the monarchy and the Royal Family will exist in the next century. The institution remains an important element in the British political system.

---

[2]The information in this and following paragraphs is from *Gallup Political & Economic Index,* Report No. 390, February 1993.

■ *THE EFFECTIVE EXECUTIVE*

Unlike the American separation-of-powers system, the British system fuses the legislature and the executive. The electorate votes only for legislative representatives, never for any executive officers. The leaders of the party with the largest number of seats in the House of Commons, along with the leaders of the same party in the House of Lords, take all the top political offices in the executive branch. This group of about a hundred people, all of whom continue to serve in Parliament, is called the Government. The Government is responsible for making all the policy and administrative decisions involved in running the country.

The Cabinet

The Government is directed by the Cabinet. Despite its dominant position, the Cabinet is scarcely mentioned in British law. Its powers, functions, and membership are almost wholly a matter of custom (the unwritten constitution again). There is no list of offices whose holders must be included in the Cabinet, nor is its size specified. The law does not even require that Cabinet members have a seat in Parliament.

In practice, Cabinet members have numbered from eighteen to twenty-four, depending solely on the Prime Minister's wishes. In selecting a Cabinet, the Prime Minister is influenced by political considerations. Several of his or her party colleagues will have to be included because of their experience and popularity within the party. Many of those chosen will have served in the Shadow Cabinet (the term used to designate the Parliamentary leaders of a party when it is out of power). Thus, the Prime Minister's choice will be somewhat circumscribed; people whom he or she really would prefer to leave out may have to be included to ensure unified support from the party in Parliament. In fact, because of collective responsibility (more about this in a moment), including a known dissident in the Cabinet may be a more effective strategy for a Prime Minister than leaving that person to run free in Parliament stirring up dissent.

The Prime Minister's choice also is somewhat constrained by the Ministers of the Crown Act, which, in effect, requires a minimum number of Cabinet members to be from the House of Lords. If a major department is headed by someone from the Lords, then that department's minister of state or undersecretary (these are politicians, not clerical staff) must be appointed from the Commons so that he or she can present and defend the Government's policies in the chamber containing the people's elected representatives. Such appointment does not, however, entail membership in the Cabinet.

Those appointed to certain key offices, such as the Foreign Secretary (the equivalent of the U.S. Secretary of State), invariably are included in the Cabinet. Most Cabinet members head one or another of the various executive departments, but not all heads of departments are included in the Cabinet. It all depends on the Prime Minister's wishes.

By now you should not be surprised to learn that the Cabinet has no legal, statutory power. It makes decisions, which, because of custom and party discipline, are implemented by those who do have legal authority. The Cabinet decides what the country's policies will be and what legislation Parliament needs to pass to implement these policies. The Cabinet tries to coordinate Government action so that policies that are desirable in themselves do not prove to be at cross-purposes with each other.

Traditionally, the Cabinet operated very informally; there were no agendas, no minutes, no record of decisions other than a letter sent to the monarch by the Prime Minister reporting on the meetings. The result, as you would expect, frequently was confusion. The British managed to put up with such a system in peacetime, but they found it intolerable during World War I. A Cabinet secretariat was created in 1916 and now is firmly institutionalized in the Cabinet Office. The secretariat issues notices of meetings of the Cabinet and of Cabinet committees, prepares the Cabinet agenda (under the Prime Minister's direction), circulates memoranda and documents relevant to items on the agenda, and takes minutes of Cabinet discussions and decisions.

This latter record, called Cabinet Conclusions, outlines the main points made during a discussion, without attributing these to any particular member, and then summarizes what the Cabinet agreed on. All ministers (the term for those holding the top executive positions) receive copies of the Conclusions, regardless of whether they are members of the Cabinet. This is the means of informing them of any action required by their departments. The Cabinet Office verifies that the various executive departments implement Cabinet decisions.

The Cabinet meets regularly for about two to three hours one morning each week, although the Prime Minister can summon it at any time and additional meetings are not uncommon. Since the relevant ministers or members of a Cabinet committee are expected to have discussed an issue in some detail before it comes to the Cabinet, lengthy debates on a single topic are unusual. Thus, the Cabinet is able to cover a number of matters in a typical meeting.

The Cabinet does much of its work through a variety of committees. Technically, all of these had been secret until recently: not only was there no list of who served on any of them, but they were not even acknowledged to exist. Nonetheless, journalists and scholars managed to obtain some information about Cabinet committees from time to time. A legislation committee, for example, was responsible for monitoring the progress of Government bills through Parliament on schedule. Other committees handled subjects such as defense and education. In 1992 Prime Minister Major, who had proclaimed a commitment to less secret government, released a list of some of these committees and their members.

Formal voting in the Cabinet is extremely rare. When the Prime Minister feels a subject has been discussed sufficiently, he or she will "collect the voices." Cabinet members in turn briefly state their conclusions. The Prime Minister sums up by stating what he or she takes to be the sense of the comments (not necessarily the same thing as just counting the number for and against) and that becomes Government policy.

Collective Responsibility

Although they may differ in opinion behind the closed doors of the Cabinet room, all Cabinet members are obligated to tell the public the same story. Unless any member is so opposed to a decision that he or she is willing to resign, all those opposed to a policy become as responsible for it as those who supported it. Even ministers outside the Cabinet, who have had no direct voice in making most of the Government's policies, must resign if they are not willing to defend all Cabinet decisions. No one remaining in the Government can later defend themselves from criticism by saying they had argued against the policy. This is the doctrine of collective responsibility.

This united front means that when Parliament challenges a minister on his or her department's policies, it is attacking the entire Government. To censure the minister would be to drive the entire Government from office. The Cabinet need not, however, defend a minister's errors of judgment or faulty administration. Collective responsibility is concerned only with matters of policy. If a minister resigns for failure to operate his or her department properly, the Cabinet remains in office.

The doctrine of collective responsibility was widely regarded as a constitutional principle. Events in the 1970s, however, called it into question. Although the Labour Government favored continuing British membership in the EC, many Labour supporters—including some Cabinet members—wanted Britain to withdraw. As the 1975 referendum on the issue approached, Labour's leaders decided to permit Cabinet ministers to oppose the Government's policy in speeches around the country and even to vote against it in the House of Commons. They were prohibited, however, from speaking against the Government's position in the Commons; thus, the fiction that the Government had a single official view was maintained. Clearly, collective responsibility was violated.[3] This departure from collective responsibility was defended on the grounds that the issue was unique and thus would create no precedent. But only two years later exactly the same violation of collective responsibility was permitted on the issue of direct election of the EC Parliament.

Controversy over the doctrine arose again in the mid-1980s, during the Westland Affair (mentioned in Chapter 5). The Cabinet had decided that a British manufacturer of helicopters seeking a defense contract should be allowed to decide for itself whether to be linked with an American company or with a European group of companies. The Defence Secretary, Michael Heseltine, strongly favored the latter option. Prime Minister Thatcher did not demand his resignation, but she colluded in an effort to discredit him. He resigned, complaining that Cabinet meetings that were to have been held weren't and that no chance had been given to settle the matter on the basis of full information. Collective responsibility, Heseltine asserted, requires collective decision making, not Prime Ministerial domination. In response, Thatcher claimed that she was the true defender of collective responsibility. In her view Heseltine was violating it by working for the European option when the Cabinet had taken a hands-off stance.

Collective responsibility seems to have become a weapon for dealing with relatively manageable dissent within the Government. If the dissidents are few or

---

[3]For the relevant documents, see Harold Wilson, *The Governance of Britain* (New York: Harper & Row, 1976), pp. 191–197.

insignificant, they must accept the majority view or resign. But the doctrine no longer has much force when there are sharp cleavages within the Government. When the dissident minority is sizable or includes prominent party leaders, collective responsibility is modified or ignored so as not to split the party and drive the Government from office.

Furthermore, certain behaviors common enough in the United States but previously unusual in Britain are beginning to occur: people who did not resign from the Government later seek to divorce themselves from its shortcomings. They suggest that they tried at the time to convince their colleagues that certain policies were undesirable and, when they couldn't do so, simply went along with the majority. They grant that they were part of the Government that took the unpopular action, but deny that they were to blame for it. Political expediency seems to have triumphed over collective responsibility, and, in practice, the United States and Britain no longer differ greatly on this aspect of executive policy making.

The Prime Minister

The Cabinet is headed (some would say dominated) by the Prime Minister. This office, however, does not exist in British law. The law states no qualifications that one must possess to be Prime Minister. Not until 1937 was a law passed to provide a salary for the post. Currently, the Prime Minister is paid about $115,000 a year. In practice, becoming the Leader of a major party makes one a potential Prime Minister. The Leader of the party with the largest number of seats in the House of Commons is invited by the monarch to form a Government. Doing so makes that person the Prime Minister. Constitutional convention requires the Prime Minister to have a seat in the House of Commons.[4]

Given the fusion of executive and legislative branches in Britain, you will not be surprised that British Prime Ministers have considerable legislative experience before attaining that office. The shortest time that any of the eighteen people who have become Prime Minister in this century had served in Parliament prior to becoming the chief executive was nearly twelve years, with the mean length of prior service being twenty-four years. As for twentieth-century U.S. Presidents through Bill Clinton, more than half (ten of seventeen) had not served in Congress at all. The seven that had been in Congress averaged under thirteen years of service—a little more than the shortest period of prior legislative service for Prime Ministers.

Presidents and Prime Ministers also differ in the way they get to the top political office; in Britain the route is much more narrow. An ambitious British politician must work his or her way up in the party through service in the national legislature. Alternate routes, such as being governor of a large state, a war hero, or a prominent businessperson (which often have been the means to a Presidential

---

[4]This has been the case since 1902, with one exception. In 1963 the Earl of Home became Prime Minister. It was understood, however, that he would give up his title, as the Peerage Act of 1963 allowed. He then quickly won a by-election to enter the Commons, so it was only for a few weeks that Britain had a Prime Minister not in that house.

nomination), do not exist in Britain. Thus, a British political career seems much more dependent on the favor of party leaders. Those who rebel against the leaders are unlikely to receive appointment to the subsidiary offices in which they can demonstrate that they have the abilities necessary for top office; just as damaging to one's career is getting a reputation for being a troublemaker, for being "unsound." Nevertheless, four of the ten Prime Ministers since the end of World War II had been rebels at earlier stages in their careers. Despite stepping out of line, they were able, for a variety of reasons, to survive and advance.

Their long prior service in Parliament means that most Prime Ministers aren't especially young when they become chief executive. The mean age on entering office in the twentieth century has been nearly fifty-nine. John Major, not yet forty-eight when he assumed the office, is the youngest Prime Minister in this century. American twentieth-century Presidents through Clinton have had an average age of fifty-five at inauguration. (Reagan, especially, and Bush—the two oldest at inauguration in this century—make the gap closer than it otherwise would be.)

The Prime Minister appoints, and can dismiss, the top executives, presides over Cabinet meetings, and coordinates and directs Government policy. Traditionally, the Prime Minister was said to be *primus inter pares*—first among equals. Whether that phrase ever described the Prime Minister's position accurately, many think it is now totally misleading. The prestige and authority of the Prime Minister have become so dominant that ultimate power seems to have passed to the chief executive, just as earlier it had passed from Parliament to the Cabinet. The essence of the British system, according to these experts, is not Parliamentary supremacy or even Cabinet supremacy, but Prime Ministerial government.[5]

The basis of the Prime Minister's power is domination of the Cabinet, the bureaucracy, and the party machine. By dismissing ministers from the Cabinet or shifting them to less important departments, a Prime Minister can affect colleagues' careers drastically. By controlling the Cabinet agenda, a Prime Minister determines what issues will be discussed and when. The Prime Minister formulates the Cabinet Conclusions. The Prime Minister creates Cabinet committees, decides who will serve on them, and determines their scope of action and rules of procedure. If the Prime Minister announces a new Government policy, the Cabinet must support it, regardless of whether the Prime Minister bothered to consult with them beforehand. Ministers, on the other hand, are likely to get the sack (be removed from office) if they initiate a change in policy without having received the Prime Minister's approval.

The Prime Minister also decides which civil servant will be the top bureaucrat in each department, called the permanent secretary. This power is especially important in the case of the Treasury because of its great influence in policy making throughout the executive branch. Furthermore, the Prime Minister also selects the civil servant who functions as secretary of the Cabinet, a job that involves controlling the flow of the documents essential to decision making.

---

[5]For a brief statement of these views, see Richard Crossman, *The Myths of Cabinet Government* (Cambridge, Mass.: Harvard University Press, 1972), especially Lecture II.

Figure 6–2
Conservative Poster for the 1979 Election Campaign

In recent years the personality of party leaders has come to play a larger role in British elections. Posters and leaflets such as those in Figures 6–2 and 6–3 are much more common than in the past. Being an electoral asset strengthens a Prime Minister's position as party Leader. No sensible party would want to lose or weaken someone who can help it gain votes. Thus, a popular Prime Minister is likely to have firm control of the party machine.

Strong as this evidence for Prime Ministerial government is, a contrary case can be made. To begin with, the dominance of the Prime Minister begins to pale

Figure 6–3
Conservative Election
Leaflet for the 1992
Campaign

when the office is compared with the American Presidency. The Prime Minister lacks the huge staff of the U.S. chief executive. The total number of employees in the Prime Minister's private office, counting not only clerks and typists but messengers and cleaners as well, is under 100. Including those who work in the political office, the policy unit, and the press office would add only a handful more. Nor is the Prime Minister serviced by anything equivalent to the Executive Office of the

President. The U.S. National Security Council, for example, is part of the Executive Office of the President; the similar Defence Committee is under the Cabinet in Britain.

Prime Ministers lack the constitutional position of Presidents. A Prime Minister does not enjoy a fixed term of office. In the twentieth century the term served by Prime Ministers has ranged from only half a year to eleven and a half, with the average being little more than four years. Thatcher is quite exceptional in having served an unbroken term of more than a decade. From Theodore Roosevelt through Bush, Presidents have served from two and a half to twelve years, with the mean being more than five and a half years.[6] Since they can be forced out of office at any time, Prime Ministers must work constantly to retain the support of colleagues and followers. A President can ignore dissent within the Cabinet with relative impunity; a Prime Minister cannot. Should key members of the British Cabinet resign, the Government might fall.

Government under Prime Minister Thatcher provides a good example of the constraints on the British chief executive. On the one hand, she dominated her colleagues to a greater extent than any other peacetime Prime Minister in the twentieth century. She was the only Prime Minister in Britain's entire history to shape Government policy so completely to her own values and goals that her name became an "ism." On the other hand, she probably lost more battles in Cabinet (there's no way yet to get sufficient information to be certain) than any other twentieth-century Prime Minister. Despite all her public rhetoric about sticking to her guns, she sometimes found it necessary to alter her policies in response to dissent within the Cabinet or even from her followers in the House of Commons. To mention only a few instances, she had to retreat on admitting the "boat people" (refugees from Vietnam) to Britain, give way in her opposition to a teachers' pay increase, and abandon a desire to reduce the size of a pension increase.

After her military response to Argentina's attempt to seize The Falklands was successful, however, her dominance over the Cabinet increased. Eliminating some of her critics from the Cabinet also helped her to get more of the decisions she wanted. Fiascos such as the Westland Affair and the poll tax helped to undermine her authority, however, allowing her to be forced from office.

The point is that Prime Ministers lack Presidents' security of tenure, and this fact may encourage them to be more cautious in exercising power. An intransigent President may see his legislative proposals voted down in Congress; an intransigent Prime Minister could see himself or herself voted out of office. Furthermore, a Prime Minister has less time than a President does to have some impact on the political process by implementing a policy program fully. This, as well, implies a limit on the Prime Minister's power.

Although control of the party machine was certainly wielded by Margaret Thatcher, this hardly was the case for James Callaghan, the Labour Prime Minister of the late 1970s. The left-leaning National Executive Committee of the Labour

---

[6]Were it not for assassinations and deaths in office of Presidents, neither of which has occurred to Prime Ministers, the greater longevity of Presidents would be even more marked.

party persistently opposed his views and frequently defeated his proposals. Nor did Callaghan enjoy any greater success in controlling Labour's Conference. In short, some Prime Ministers do wield great power within their party, but this is not automatically true of all of them.

Thus, whatever the strengths of the Prime Minister and however much these may have grown in recent years, Prime Ministers still have a long way to go to dominate the executive branch to the extent that U.S. Presidents do. Paradoxically, however, the British executive branch as a whole occupies a stronger position within the political system than does the U.S. executive branch. The absence in Britain of the U.S. separation-of-powers system with its checks and balances gives the executive a dominance over the legislature unknown in the United States. The final section of this chapter explains why this is true.

■ *LEGISLATIVE-EXECUTIVE RELATIONS*

Policy Making

The Government dominates the legislative process. The Cabinet decides on the legislative program to be presented to Parliament and how the available time will be allocated to the various bills and other matters demanding Parliamentary action. Those matters that the Cabinet selects for action always get first priority. Although the Government at times permits the Opposition to decide what the subject of a Commons debate will be, the Opposition does not introduce bills and attempt to pass them.

As for individual Members, they can introduce bills but have little hope of getting them enacted. Only twelve Fridays a session are set aside to deal with all stages after first reading of bills introduced by backbenchers. Remember that in Britain a bill does not go to committee until after it has passed second reading. Thus, unless an MP can get his or her bill on the agenda for a second reading, there is no hope for its survival. So scarce is the available time that MPs actually hold a lottery to determine which of them will be able to use some of the time on the twelve Fridays for their bills. Furthermore, even those bills lucky enough to win a time slot can be impeded so easily that none of them ever pass unless the Government decides to assist in some way.[7] The laws that Parliament enacts are those that the Cabinet has proposed or is willing to accept.

The Government's power is enhanced further because, in contrast to American practice, only ministers can propose measures to spend or raise money. A bill authorizing expenditure, even if it doesn't appropriate money, requires the Government's recommendation. Motions by backbenchers to increase expenditures are prohibited by the Commons' rules. Although a motion to reduce expenditures would be in order, it is regarded as the equivalent of a motion of censure. Such motions—for example, one to cut a minister's salary by an amount equivalent to a

---

[7]David Marsh and Melvyn Read, *Private Members' Bills* (Cambridge, England: Cambridge University Press, 1988).

few dollars—are used as a means of holding a debate on the success or failure of Government policy in the field for which that minister is responsible. If such a motion passed, its significance would not be that the minister would be paid a bit less, but rather that he or she would have to resign because, in effect, the Commons had voted no confidence in him or her.

Although the Government as a whole is responsible for public finance, the major role is played by the Treasury and its head, the Chancellor of the Exchequer. All departmental requests for funds must undergo Treasury scrutiny. Cabinet members will know generally the plans for taxes and spending, but they will not learn the exact details until the Chancellor makes the Budget speech in the Commons. Nonetheless, everyone in the Government must support the proposals because of collective responsibility. The Chancellor works closely with the Prime Minister in developing the key financial policies. The frequent complaints that other Cabinet ministers make about this process are cited as evidence in support of the argument that the British system has become Prime Ministerial government.

The job of seeing that the Government's legislative program progresses expeditiously through the Commons falls on the Leader of the House, an appointee of the Prime Minister. The detailed day-to-day arrangements are handled by the Government party's Chief Whip. He or she discusses with the Opposition Chief Whip the arrangements for the Commons' agenda. These contacts, referred to in the Commons as the "usual channels," help the Government get its proposals through the Commons without denying the Opposition a chance to criticize them and to make a case for alternative policies.

The Government Chief Whip is assisted by a deputy and a number of junior whips. All the whips are members of Parliament. The Chief Whip has an office at 12 Downing Street (No. 10 is the Prime Minister's residence), which accommodates the junior whips as well. The Opposition has several whips also. So strong is the belief that a loyal Opposition prepared to challenge the Government and offer alternatives is essential to democratic government that three of the Opposition whips are paid a salary out of public funds.

Party Discipline

The Government whips try to ensure that their party's Members are present in the Commons to support the Government when votes on its proposals occur. In addition to transmitting the leaders' orders to their Parliamentary followers, the whips also communicate the backbenchers' complaints and misgivings to the leaders. Keeping the leaders in tune with the mood of the backbenchers helps to avoid unexpected rebellions caused by introducing unacceptable proposals.

Each Thursday when the Commons is in session, the Leader of the House announces the business that will be brought before Commons the following week. The next day, each party mails to all of its MPs a document called the whip. This document includes the schedule announced by the Leader of the House, indicates some of the main speakers for important debates, and, most significantly, designates the relative importance the party assigns to each item on the agenda. A matter of limited concern will be underlined once. Fairly important matters are underlined twice. A three-line whip means that the party expects (read "requires") an MP to be present, unless ill or unavoidably detained, to vote the party line. Sometimes even those two excuses are insufficient. MPs have been brought from hospital beds on stretchers to the precincts of the House of Commons so that their votes could be counted in crucial debates, and ministers have had to break off negotiations in foreign countries to fly to London for a key division. Votes on motions of censure are always designated as three-line whips, as are the principal items in the Government's legislative program.

Strictly speaking, a whip only tells MPs when they should be certain to attend the Commons. In fact, of course, their party is not really interested in the pleasure of their company, but intends for them to vote as it instructs them to do. MPs are expected to vote the party line, regardless of personal views or any arguments made during the debate. Abstaining is about as far as an MP can go in refusing to support the party line and even that can get him or her in trouble. On some issues involving morals or conscience—such as the death penalty—parties usually permit a free vote; that is, they do not take a position and let MPs vote as they wish. On the great majority of issues, however, the parties do take stands, and MPs must fall in line or suffer the consequences.

An MP who rebels on a crucial vote or who does so persistently on matters of less importance is likely to have the whip withdrawn. The Conservative party vests this power in the Leader; in the Labour party a majority vote of the Parliamentary Labour Party (PLP) is required. Withdrawal of the whip expels the rebel from the party in Parliament. In the Labour party the action is reported to the National Executive Committee (NEC), which can expel the offender from party membership. Neither the Conservative nor the Labour party would permit one of their constituency parties to adopt an expellee as a candidate. Therefore, rebels risk an end to their political careers.

To Americans, used to seeing a coalition of Democrats and Republicans passing legislation in opposition to a group of other Democrats and other Republicans, such a draconian concern with party discipline may seem almost totalitarian. You may conclude that British MPs simply are a group of cowardly sheep terrorized by their leaders through their brutal whips. The whips rarely bully or coerce, however; reasoned persuasion is their typical approach. This method can be quite effective because of the fundamental difference in legislative-executive relations in Britain and the United States. Remember, the British Prime Minister has no fixed term; he or she can be voted out of office at any time by the House of Commons. If enough MPs fail to support their party when it is in power, the Government will have to resign, thereby permitting its opponents to gain control of the executive branch. Whatever quarrel MPs may have with their own party, they must regard bringing their opponents to power as a worse alternative—otherwise they would be members of that party.

Another buttress to party discipline is the British MP's different conception of the role of legislator. The typical MP recognizes that he or she has not been elected because of personal abilities or magnetism, but largely because of the party label. The electorate votes to give a party enough seats in Parliament to carry out its policies; the individual candidate is largely incidental to the process.

The whips do not need to do anything to the MP who persistently rebels; his or her constituency party is likely to warn that, unless this behavior ceases, another candidate will be found for the next election. Usually dissent is tolerated only when an MP is moving toward the fringe of the political spectrum, away from the party's opponents. Local activists tend to be farther from the center of the spectrum than are the party's national leaders. An MP who voted against the party's policy because it was too moderate might well survive (although he or she could not expect executive office), but one who refused to support it because it was too extreme would be likely to be disciplined by the local constituency party.

Another aid to maintaining party unity in legislative voting is the backbench committee system. In committees Government MPs are able to express their views on possible legislation before the debate in the Commons. Input at that stage is more likely to be effective. As you saw in Chapter 5, the executive consults closely with relevant interest groups in working out the details of proposed legislation. Thus, by the time a bill is introduced into the Commons, it is likely to be an elaborately worked out set of compromises; major changes at that stage are highly unlikely. Since no person can be expert on more than a few matters, most MPs will be uninformed on any given issue. Why, in such circumstances, should MPs do anything other than vote as the whips tell them to do? What is the sense in jeopardizing one's career by being a troublemaker in what is probably a lost cause?

The result of all these factors is extremely high party cohesion—disciplined voting of MPs in the same party in the same way. The party winning a working majority of seats in the Commons in a general election can count on getting its legislative program through Parliament. Its proposals do not have to hurdle a number of obstacles or face ambush by a hostile committee chairperson. The Government knows that it has the votes to pass the bills. This is why, as we discussed in Chapter 5, interest groups, although regarding contacts with MPs as of some use, are concerned mainly with developing their links with various executive departments.

Exceptional cases do arise from time to time. The Conservative party whips had to work quite hard from 1992 through 1993 to mobilize the votes needed for Parliament's approval of the Maastricht Treaty. In contrast to the United States, where a Senate vote is required to ratify treaties, in Britain the Crown (that means, in practice, the Cabinet) ratifies treaties. The changes in Britain's relation with the EC that were encompassed by the Maastricht Treaty required, however, certain changes in British domestic law. Passage of that bill was drawn out over several months and involved a few minor defeats, in the form of either formal divisions in the Commons or Cabinet retreats on proposed amendments. This unusual situation arose because the legislation involved such a fundamental question (Britain's international status), the Government's majority in the Commons was rather small (less than two dozen over all other parties), and a number of dissidents in the majority party felt more loyalty to the recently deposed party Leader and Prime Minister than to the current one. Obviously, such a configuration of circumstances occurs but rarely. Even at that, Prime Minister Major was able to stonewall and refuse to concede to the popular referendum on the treaty that some of his opponents desired.

A strong case can be made for a political system that concentrates power as the British system does. Such a system concentrates responsibility as well. A British Government can never argue that its program was thwarted by the perversity of a handful of strategically placed legislators. In the British system, not only does the same party control both executive and legislative branches, but the same section of the party controls both. Unlike in the United States, there are not Congressional Democrats and Presidential Democrats responsible to contrasting constituencies and thus perpetually at odds with each other, despite nominally belonging to the same party. Thus, in Britain, when things do not get done or when what does get done is objectionable, the voters know whom to blame. And at the next election they can remove them from power and give their opponents a chance.

The cost of such a system, however, is that the legislature is reduced to little more than a rubber stamp for the Government's decisions. The typical MP has little freedom in deciding how to vote, little chance to introduce legislation, and not much chance to participate in debates. Given the large number of Members in the Commons and the priority that the Speaker gives to speeches by party leaders, backbenchers are relegated to activities something like social work.

Votes of Confidence

The power to remove the executive from office might seem to make the Commons the ultimate authority in the British system. In practice, however, that power is rarely used. In the past century only four votes of confidence or censure have been carried against the Government. On a few other occasions, votes in the Commons have changed the Government. In 1940, for example, the Government won on an adjournment motion by 81 votes but resigned anyway because its potential majority was around 200. Since many of those who previously had supported the Government had abstained or even voted against it, Prime Minister Neville Chamberlain felt that he no longer had the confidence of the Commons. Therefore, he resigned and Winston Churchill became Prime Minister. Such displays of the Commons' power are so dramatic that they are long remembered. Nonetheless, they are extremely rare, certainly not typical of the day-to-day relations between the legislature and the executive. Strict party discipline is the norm, and that means that the Commons' power in fact has atrophied.

By the 1960s many scholars and politicians had become sufficiently concerned to offer a variety of proposals for reform. Of the various experiments that were tried, the one that seemed to win the most support was the reform of the Commons' committee system to create specialist select committees. The idea was that Members' lack of expertise was the root of the problem. The reformers seemed to believe that MPs could swallow a few select committee reports like Popeye gobbling a can of spinach and then be ready with bulging muscles to deliver a knockout punch to the Government. The flaw in this approach was its concentration on institutional change, ignoring behavior. The reformers failed to understand that the real problem was not that MPs were ignorant, but that they were not motivated to oppose the Government, for the reasons we discussed earlier in explaining party cohesion. No matter how much information MPs have, if they are not willing to vote against their own party's Government more often, the Commons will remain weak.

More significant, then, than institutional reform of the Commons has been the change in Members' behavior that developed during the 1970s. Although not to the extent found in U.S. legislatures, MPs did begin to vote against their party's line more frequently than in the past. Discovering the reasons for this change is difficult. Some evidence suggests that new MPs (who lack years of socialization into the old ways of not making a fuss about anything) and MPs with middle-class backgrounds (who may be less likely to see membership in the Commons as an activity to occupy the time of the idle rich or to provide a pleasant retirement for elderly trade union officials) are more likely to dissent. The personality and policies of Prime Minister Edward Heath have been suggested as key factors triggering the change.[8] Heath's failure to communicate adequately with his backbenchers and his unyielding commitment to policies that were unpopular with them caused many Conservative MPs to vote against their own party's Government. Dissent even reached the point of defeating the Government on a three-line whip. Such an event was unprecedented, especially since the Government did not resign.

Until that time most scholars and politicians had believed (they had no way of knowing for certain since Britain has an unwritten constitution) that a defeat on major legislation would force a Government to resign just as surely as a defeat on a motion of censure or no confidence would. Suddenly the scales fell from Members' eyes, and they realized that only a defeat on a question of confidence or censure would drive the Government from office. The whips' argument that MPs must support the Government on key legislative votes or it would have to resign no longer had much strength. The Government, it was seen, could tolerate some defeats and continue in office; the danger of permitting the other side to gain office receded.

The correct form of the relevant rule was clarified further during the Labour Governments of the 1970s. Admittedly, these Governments lacked a majority in the Commons most of the time, and therefore some have argued that they were not expected to meet the same requirements as were Governments with a working majority. Nonetheless, the fact that they remained in office despite losing a number of votes in the Commons demonstrated that resignation was not an automatic consequence of legislative defeats. Only when Prime Minister James Callaghan's Labour Government was defeated by a single vote on a motion of confidence in March 1979 did it call an election and, after being defeated in that election, leave office.

Not since the Chamberlain vote of 1940 had a Government been driven from office by a vote in the Commons, and not since 1924 had a Government been defeated on a matter of confidence or censure. The House of Commons demonstrated that, despite the many years since it had last exercised the power, it could

---

[8]Philip Norton, *Conservative Dissidents: Dissent within the Parliamentary Conservative Party 1970–74* (London: Temple Smith, 1978), pp. 217–255.

still determine the fate of the Government. Nonetheless, the infrequency with which votes of confidence are carried against the Government in the Commons exposes a paradox at the heart of the British system. Without disciplined, cohesive two-party competition, the executive is unlikely to enjoy a reliable majority in the Commons. This would produce weak and ineffective government, unable to deal effectively with public problems. The result would resemble the gridlock that many commentators have identified as the bane of American government. Furthermore, when the executive lacks the power to act decisively, where to place responsibility for failures to cope with public problems becomes ambiguous, and calling power wielders to account is impeded. But if parties are so disciplined that their members automatically toe the party line and unthinkingly vote together as opposing blocks whatever the issue, then the executive can do as it pleases, secure in wielding power. Clearly, that severs the accountability link as well.

Fortunately, dissent does not have to defeat the Government to be effective. Although the form of the parliamentary system makes the ability of the House of Commons to vote the Cabinet out of office appear to be the key aspect of legislative-executive relations, in Britain the accountability mechanisms are more significant in practice. Remember that the main purpose of debate in the Commons is to force the Government to justify its actions. A Government unable to make a convincing case for its policies is likely to be considered incompetent or callous. Since MPs do not enjoy appearing to be blind loyalists, support for such a Government can dwindle rapidly. At times, Commons' debates may seem to have limited influence on the Government, but that is precisely because it was careful to draw up proposals that could be defended as logical and fair in the face of the toughest challenge. If accountability has attenuated, as was suggested in Chapter 5, then the Government would not need to exercise as much care in drafting its proposals.

Despite the grounds for concern about the Commons' performance of its most significant function, some reassuring evidence can be found. When the Thatcher Government came to power in 1979 with a majority of more than forty over the combined strengths of its opponents in the Commons, some observers expected a return to the party cohesion of the 1960s. The strengthening of the Commons during the latter part of the 1970s would be a short-lived aberration produced by minority Government, a mere hiccup in the inevitable trend toward legislative impotence. Conservative MPs soon showed, however, that they had not lost their willingness to vote against their own Government and that they were able in some instances to get it to change its plans. When both the 1983 and 1987 elections gave the Conservatives even larger majorities in the Commons, dramatic legislative defeats for the Government could no longer be expected. But dissident voting still did not die out. During the first part of 1988, for example, some Members from its own party voted against the Thatcher Government on fifteen separate divisions. Nearly a quarter of all Conservative MPs voted against their Government one or more times.

As described previously, Thatcher's successor as Prime Minister, John Major, was vexed by dissidents within his party on the Maastricht Treaty legislation in 1992–1993. Nor was this the only issue to stimulate significant dissent. Grumbling of backbench Conservatives on closure of coal mines and educational reform, to mention only two items, was sufficiently loud to force the Government to modify its plans. As a result, by 1993 the main theme of political commentary didn't concern a dominant, unresponsive Prime Minister lording it over a supine legislature, but rather a weak, vacillating chief executive, uncertain where he was headed and hardly capable of getting there even if he knew.

■   ■   ■

The British executive branch dominates the legislature to a much greater degree than the typical President does Congress; the picture we have painted here of power relations in the British political system remains fundamentally valid. At any given time, however, the balance may be tilting toward or away from the executive. A further qualification of any assessment of relative power is the fact that the Commons' influence often is greater than it seems on the surface. The Commons' decline appears to have been halted in the 1970s, giving it a more significant voice in calling the executive to account than it possessed at mid-century. Whether the course of development for the first half of the twentieth century actually has been reversed, however, remains unclear. As always in Britain, change takes a long time to manifest itself.

7

Policy-Implementing Structures _____

■ THE CIVIL SERVICE AND ITS POLITICAL SUPERVISORS

The parties have presented their programs, the voters have made their choices, the legislators have been elected, and the Cabinet has presented a coherent legislative package, which has been enacted. That's it, right? Hardly. Somebody has to decide what the rather generally worded laws are intended to accomplish when applied to specific cases—cases involving not hypothetical beings, but real people. At this point the governing process directly affects you and me. Yet we have no direct voice at all in selecting these somebodies who are going to do this to us. How can this be in a democracy?

But reflect for a moment. Do you really want the extent to which the law is applied to someone to depend on whether he is a buddy of the chief of police? Do you really want someone's tax to be assessed on the basis of whether she has a friend in the IRS? Do you really want someone who is a nice guy and, perhaps, has some good ideas but lacks the ability to organize a bake sale to administer the law? We need the law to be applied fairly, impartially, efficiently, and competently. We need administrators selected for ability, not popularity or connections. Once selected, they need to be protected from powerful interests that would pressure them to apply the law unfairly.

The problem is that these needs are mutually exclusive to some extent. Take efficiency and accountability, for example. The well-known bureaucratic red tape is nothing other than the detailed records that must be kept to justify administrative action in case the legislators—functioning as watchdogs for the people—demand that particular actions be explained. The endless forms that governmental agencies fill out and file away could be disposed of almost entirely if bureaucrats were never to be called to account for their behavior. In that case, however, democracy—popular control over government—would be weakened greatly.

An effective way to obtain popular control is to replace all administrators each time one party replaces another in power. But then the prospects for efficient, experienced administration would not be bright. Since responsibility can be obtained only at the cost of efficiency, and vice versa, political systems must attain some sort of compromise between the two. The balance struck in Britain differs significantly from that reached in the United States.

Staffing the Bureaucracy

In the United States the Jacksonian period in the early nineteenth century popularized the slogan "To the victor belong the spoils" and established the procedure of rotation in office—bureaucrats came and went in accord with election outcomes. The result was not only considerable administrative incompetence but also appalling political corruption. Although Jacksonian ideas had no influence on British politics, Britain, as well as the United States, had governmental staff employed on the basis of patronage for much of the nineteenth century. Merit or ability had nothing to do with getting a government job. Government employment in Britain served as unemployment relief for otherwise unoccupied aristocrats. So far were the British from notions of rotation in office that the holder of a governmental position acquired property rights to his job. He could sell it or will it; if it were abolished, he was entitled to compensation.

Overcoming this obstacle to establishing a merit system was not as difficult as in the United States, where both patronage and rotation in office were impediments. Once Britons were convinced that administrators should be an aristocracy of *talent* rather than of *inherited title*, support was available for a professional civil service system. Thus, in 1870, thirteen years before similar action in the United States, the principle of open competition for governmental jobs was established, and the various governmental departments were unified into a single civil service system.

The British civil service system was created by an Order in Council under the prerogative powers of the Crown. These powers are the residue of discretionary authority legally remaining to the Crown.[1] The civil service operates under regulations authorized by various such Orders. Parliament has passed few laws regulating the structure and procedures of the civil service. Thus, restructuring the bureaucracy is relatively easier in Britain than in the United States, since the executive branch can simply decide to do so and does not need to obtain legislative approval.

When Margaret Thatcher became Prime Minister in 1979, she was not especially interested in the details of the organization of the bureaucracy; she simply wanted to cut its size—the British version of "getting the government off our backs." By 1984 she had reduced it to its lowest level since World War II. Five years later, having been in power for a decade, she had eliminated about a fifth of the bureaucracy, lowering the number employed by the national government to around 600,000. Most of the cuts, however, have been of the so-called industrial civil servants, people working for government enterprises such as the Royal Ordnance factories and the Royal Dockyards.[2]

---

[1]As Chapter 6 noted, the exercise of Crown powers rests with the Cabinet; despite their name, these powers are not subject to the personal decision of the current sovereign.
[2]Workers in nationalized industries (such as the railroads) are not counted as civil servants.

Cutting the number of bureaucrats is always popular with the public. Especially when, as was the case under Thatcher, the cuts are primarily the result of increased efficiency rather than a cutback in services. The net saving from Thatcher's efforts, however, was less than 0.5 percent of the annual governmental expenditure.

Britain's nonindustrial civil servants—the people that readily come to mind when you think of bureaucrats—number about a half million. The organizational skeleton for this portion of the civil service is provided by the administrative group. Lower-level staff, who do manual or clerical work, are recruited separately by the various departments. Middle- and upper-level personnel for all agencies are hired by the Civil Service Commission. The level at which a civil servant enters depends on the extent of his or her education. Opportunities for promotion are better than they used to be. People with limited education, who have entered at the bottom of the civil service, can, given suitable abilities, progress up the ladder.

Recruitment for higher-level positions in the civil service involves both a written examination and an oral interview. The written examination tests general knowledge, proficiency in English, and command of two or three academic subjects, which the applicant selects from a large number of alternatives. The British recruit civil servants on the basis of general ability rather than on the basis of technical expertise and training for a specific position. In their view, top minds can learn quickly the specific requirements of a position after being appointed to it. They remain convinced that a knowledge of classical Greek excellently prepares one for life and is admirable training for being in charge of public affairs.

This bias in recruiting is responsible for the most frequently heard criticism of the British civil service—that it is obsessed with the cult of the amateur. The subject-matter expert, it is charged, too often is relegated to simply supplying technical information to the amateur or generalist, who is the one empowered to make the decisions that shape policy.

In an attempt to respond to this criticism, the top five grades of the civil service, regardless of the particular duties associated with a specific post, were made part of an open and unified structure. This change was intended to facilitate the shifting of civil servants from one ministry to another, leading to an integrated, rather than a narrowly segmented, civil service. Top civil servants would thereby gain greater breadth and become sensitized to the impact of a policy beyond their particular department. Despite such structural reforms, tradition has prevailed. Those relatively few bureaucrats playing an influential role in policy making continue to be generalists and rarely are trained in the substantive fields they administer.

The other principal criticism of the civil service concerns its class composition. A disproportionately low number of people from working-class backgrounds are recruited into the civil service. The typical civil servant at an influential level has gone from a public school to Oxford or Cambridge. Many people, particularly supporters of Labour, feel that the oral interview is the culprit. They believe that the interviewers are easily impressed by applicants with the proper social background. Even lack of knowledge and shallow thinking may be excused if an interviewee, because of the right background, is thought to be suitable for the civil service. Similar shortcomings in a person from the working class would be treated as grounds for rejection, and an able person with that background may be passed over because he or she lacks some of the social graces.

Few would deny that the top British civil servants are highly intelligent and extremely able. The concern is whether their academic preparation provides them with too little knowledge of science and technology and of management techniques. To the extent that this is true, efficiency is undermined. And to the extent that the class base of the civil service is narrow, accountability is jeopardized. Calling any bureaucracy to account without harming efficiency and introducing undesirable partisanism is difficult. In Britain the problem is compounded further: how can a civil service, so few of whose most influential members have had direct experience of the type of life lived by most people, adequately consider the population's needs and concerns? Is not such a bureaucracy likely to need to be called to account even more frequently than one that is more representative of the population? Thus, although Britain could be labeled the mother of civil services—even more aptly than calling it the mother of parliaments—serious problems of both efficiency and accountability have yet to be solved in its governmental bureaucracy.

Treasury Control

Although the Civil Service Commission recruits administrators, the Treasury actually controls the civil service. A 1920 Order in Council empowered the Treasury to supervise the standards and conditions of work in the civil service. Much of this power was shifted to a newly created Civil Service Department (CSD) in 1968. As part of her effort to cut the bureaucracy and government spending, however, in 1981 Prime Minister Thatcher abolished the CSD and returned much of its powers to the Treasury.

Some of the CSD's responsibilities are now discharged by the Office of the Minister for the Civil Service, located in the Cabinet Office. This office develops policies concerning recruitment and training of civil servants (the Civil Service Commission and the separate departments are simply the agencies that implement these policies) and the duties and standards of the civil service.

The Treasury controls not only staffing and pay but, even more importantly, financial management. It designates an accounting officer in each department, usually the chief financial officer of the permanent secretary. This officer is responsible, through the political head of the department (the secretary of state), to Parliament for departmental expenditures. Moreover, he or she is personally and pecuniarily liable to the Treasury for irregular expenditures (those unauthorized by Parliament), unless he or she has protested to the political department head in writing and has received permission to incur such expenditures.

What's important about all this? The Treasury is preeminent within the British administrative structure. Its powers earlier in the century made other departments seem subordinate to it. This perceived superiority has lingered, despite shifts in power; the agencies with which the Treasury has had to share responsibilities more recently lack its great prestige. The Treasury is perceived as having virtual veto power over proposals for new policies anywhere within the government.

This does not mean that the Treasury is the real center of power in British government. The Prime Minister is both First Lord of the Treasury and Minister for the Civil Service. Although Prime Minister Thatcher delegated day-to-day supervision of the civil service to another Cabinet minister, she remained ultimately in charge.

Furthermore, the Prime Minister appoints not only the permanent secretary of the Treasury but also the secretary of the Cabinet, who serves as the head of the civil service as well. (Both secretaries are career, professional—that is, nonpolitical—personnel.) All of this helps to ensure that the civil service complies with the Prime Minister's wishes. These arrangements provide further support for the position described in Chapter 6—that British government has ceased to be Cabinet government and has become Prime Ministerial government.

Organizing the Bureaucracy

The Government's policies are implemented by some two dozen departments, whose political heads are responsible to the House of Commons. Each department is staffed by civil servants headed by the permanent secretary (see Figure 7–1). Above this hierarchy are a handful of political appointees—typically, the secretary of state and two to four associates—who give political direction to the department. The secretary of state serves at the pleasure of the Prime Minister, as do the associates, who are picked by the Prime Minister in consultation with the secretary.

Policy and administration fuse at the secretary's level. As Members of Parliament and of the Government, secretaries both make policy and administer a department. They must spend much time in the Commons for debates, must keep in touch with their constituents, and must be involved in party activities. In addition, a fair amount of time is consumed by meetings of the Cabinet and its committees. Clearly, secretaries can devote only part of their time to directing the activities of their department. Nonetheless, they are responsible to the Commons for its functions.

Figure 7–1
Typical
Administrative
Structure of a British
Department

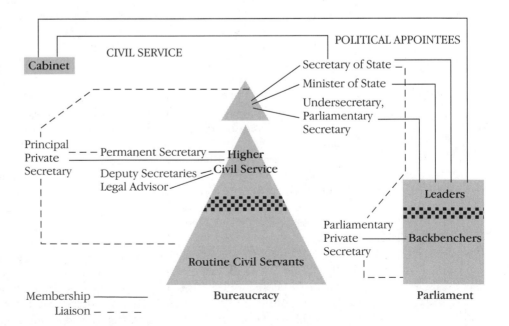

Secretaries can delegate some of their tasks to their political assistants—who are titled minister of state, undersecretary of state, and parliamentary secretary. Holders of these positions are also members of the Government and have seats in either the House of Commons or the House of Lords. When a secretary of state is in the Lords, his or her immediate assistant must be in the Commons, so that there will be someone present to defend the department's policies in the legislative chamber that can censure the Government. Unlike the other assistants, ministers of state have some discretionary powers. The parliamentary secretaries and the undersecretaries relieve their superiors of less important duties. By learning the business of a department, these assistants gain the experience that will help to qualify them for eventual promotion to the rank of secretary of state—if their careers prosper. But in the meantime they cannot decide policy on their own. They cannot even override civil servants, but must refer any problems or questions from them to the secretary of state.

Also assisting the secretary is a Parliamentary private secretary (PPS), who is a Member of Parliament but technically not part of the Government. He or she (unlike the other assistants we've mentioned) receives no salary for administrative duties in addition to an MP's pay. PPSs perform a variety of tasks for their secretaries. They are expected to know the temper of the House so that secretaries do not encounter unexpected revolts against a department's policies. They convey both the secretaries' views to the party's backbenchers and the backbenchers' grievances to the secretaries.

Only the secretary is responsible to the Commons for what happens in a department. Civil servants do not have to answer publicly for administrative errors or misjudgments. The British do not believe that civil servants should be dragged into the political arena; only politicians should face that occupational hazard. The secretary, therefore, is to shield the civil servants from blame and, in return, receive from them faithful service and absolute loyalty. This is why, for example, civil servants called to testify before the Commons' specialist select committees are instructed not to reveal anything about the advice they have given to their secretary.

The head of the civil service, in a note of guidance concerning duties and responsibilities, told civil servants that they could not refuse to take an action merely because it conflicted with a personal opinion. Only if they felt the action "to be directly contrary to deeply held personal conviction on a fundamental issue of conscience" could they consider declining to act. A civil servant feeling that way was instructed to consult with his or her superior. If that did not resolve the matter, then "he or she must either carry out his or her instructions or resign from the public service —though even after resignation he or she will still be bound to keep the confidences to which he or she has become privy as a public servant." In other words, whistle-blowers are even less welcome in Britain than they are in the United States.

Individual Responsibility

Civil servants who make mistakes will be criticized and, perhaps, disciplined by their secretaries, but in private. Publicly, the secretary must accept the blame personally. A grave failure of administration may force a secretary to resign as political head of a department and leave the Government. If he or she can assure the Commons that knowing about the action before it occurred was impossible and that steps have been taken to ensure that it cannot happen again, then simply an apology to Parliament may be sufficient to allow the secretary to remain in office. These customary procedures are known as individual ministerial responsibility, which differs from the doctrine of collective responsibility discussed in Chapter 6. Individual responsibility focuses on shortcomings in administering the government; collective responsibility is concerned with the content of policy.

Although the requirements of individual ministerial responsibility are well known to those to whom they apply, they have seriously attenuated in recent years. In the half century since the end of World War II, fewer than two dozen secretaries have resigned on grounds of individual responsibility. Furthermore, recent cases have been more likely to involve personal misjudgments than bad administration. For example, the Secretary for National Heritage was driven from office in 1992 by newspaper revelations of an affair he was having. One paper eavesdropped on a phone call in which he told his mistress that he was too tired to prepare for an important speech in the House of Commons because of having spent the previous night with her. In 1993 the junior minister for security in the Northern Ireland office resigned because of his links with a foreign businessman who had fled his British residence to avoid prosecution for financial corruption. The minister not only had given the fugitive an inscribed watch but had contacted the attorney general about his case, perhaps seeking to restrain prosecution.

Even in those instances involving faulty administration, individual responsibility has received only ambiguous support. In 1982 Lord Carrington, the Foreign Secretary, and two of his associates resigned because they had failed to perceive the seriousness of the Argentine threat to The Falklands (and thus had done nothing to discourage the invasion that occurred). Although they clearly were accepting blame for having run things badly, this was hardly a case of an error by civil servants for which supervising politicians had to pay the cost.

We've mentioned a couple of times the row in the Cabinet in the mid-1980s over a defense contract. Michael Heseltine resigned to protest what he regarded as the Prime Minister's high-handed way of determining policy without adequate consultation of her Cabinet colleagues. That clearly was a case of collective responsibility, since he was unwilling to support the position the Prime Minister had set forth. The other secretary who resigned in this episode had been head of the department from which came the leak that aimed to undercut Heseltine's position. This second resignation appeared to be a clear case of individual responsibility. The secretary endeavored, however, to escape blame by saying that it was all the fault of his civil servants. Furthermore, contrary to traditional practice, the civil servants involved were publicly identified rather than being accorded the usual anonymity. When the secretary resigned, he commented that he felt he had to do so because he no longer enjoyed adequate support among the party's MPs. He was well aware that many of them were so disgusted with the devious way in which this affair was conducted and had sufficient admiration for Heseltine that a sacrificial victim had to be found.

The doctrine of individual ministerial responsibility also has been made less compelling by instances in which a secretary did not resign despite failures in administration. For example, in 1983 thirty-eight members of the terrorist Irish Republican Army, in jail for various criminal activities, escaped. Although the subsequent investigation cited a wide range of failures at the prison and recommended seventy-three improvements in security, the relevant secretary declined to resign. Furthermore, in contrast to previous practice, he did not even argue that he was remaining in office because he had made changes that would ensure that such a thing could not happen again; he specifically said that he couldn't guarantee that it wouldn't.

These instances pose serious questions about whether individual responsibility is still a convention of the British constitution. Cabinets now seem inclined either to treat a secretary's poor administrating as a matter of collective, rather than individual, responsibility or to overlook it entirely, thus sparing the secretary the embarrassment of resigning. This development weakens the accountability of administrative power. If the secretary is not, in fact, responsible and the civil servants are insulated from public criticism in order to maximize their efficiency, then no one is accountable. Abandoning the doctrine of individual ministerial responsibility destroys the effective solution the British had devised for the basic problem of public administration—how to reconcile efficiency with accountability.

The Official Secrets Act

Questions about the role and political neutrality of the career civil service were raised in the mid-1980s when a civil servant was prosecuted for violating the Official Secrets Act. Parliament was investigating whether the Argentine ship, the Belgrano, had been sunk unnecessarily—for political rather than military reasons—during the Falklands conflict. The civil servant gave some relevant confidential documents to an MP who had been one of those charging that the Prime Minister had authorized the attack primarily to gain political capital from a dramatic success.

Taking an American perspective on this, you might say, "Fine, what can be wrong with helping the legislature in an investigation?" We mentioned in an earlier section the note of guidance that the head of the civil service issued to instruct departmental staff about their responsibilities. It observed that "civil servants often find themselves in situations where they are required or expected to give information to a parliamentary select committee." In deciding how to respond, a civil servant was to remember that his or her "first duty is to his or her [secretary]. Ultimately the responsibility lies with [secretaries], and not with civil servants, to decide what information should be made available, and how and when it should be released, whether it is to Parliament, to select committees. . . ." If civil servants are not to divulge information even when Parliament has asked for it, they certainly mustn't hand it over when it hasn't been directly requested.

The civil servant was unwilling, however, to be a party to what he regarded as a cover-up, so he gave the information not to a journalist, but to a public official, who would seem to have a right to know. Nonetheless, as night follows day, the government prosecuted him. Although the jury acquitted him, the case does not provide a robust precedent for open government. The jury apparently was unwilling to stomach the judge's instruction that the interests of the Government were synonymous with the national interest. A more reasonable charge to the jury might well have resulted in a conviction. Other civil servants who have turned information over to journalists have found themselves convicted and sent to jail.

Since Watergate, few people in the United States are willing to condone governmental cover-ups. In Britain, however, secrecy is still the rule. Prime Minister Thatcher seemed obsessed with it. When Peter Wright, a retired intelligence officer, decided to publish his memoirs (which contained little that wasn't already public knowledge and dealt with events many years in the past), Thatcher was not satisfied with having the book banned in Britain but prosecuted it to the Antipodes, spending huge sums of public money to fight the book all the way to the highest court of Australia (where Wright resided). Not only did Wright win the case, but in the process the head of the British civil service, who had been sent to Australia to testify, was made to look devious. During cross-examination he was forced to concede that he had been "economical with the truth" in earlier testimony. In plainer terms, he hadn't lied but had given less than full answers in the hope of misleading the court.

On the other hand, most people will grant that some matters (many aspects of national security, for example) must be kept secret. If civil servants feel no constraint about revealing confidential material, then the floodgates will be opened, releasing a torrent of revelations, not just a few leaks. But if everything is confidential (strictly speaking, revealing what kind of tea is served in civil service cafeterias violates the Official Secrets Act), then the constraints seem an abuse of power. Furthermore, since British constitutional doctrine gives Parliament a key role in securing accountability, what justification can the executive branch have for withholding as much as it does from the legislature? Surprisingly, for a system that seemed to have solved the problem effectively, British government faces serious accountability issues.

The Policy Role of the Civil Service

Each department has both a political head, the secretary of state, and a nonpolitical head, the permanent secretary (see Figure 7–1). The latter is a career civil servant, who is the true administrative chief of the department. He or she is responsible for the organization and efficiency of the department and for the advice given to the secretary of state by the career staff. Subordinate civil servants may not deal directly with the secretary of state without the knowledge and approval of the permanent secretary. Since the permanent secretary will, in most cases, have been at the top of the department much longer than the secretary of state, the former is excellently placed to influence policy.

The British believe that really capable people cannot be recruited into public service and be motivated to make it a career unless they see some prospect of eventually reaching a position of influence. The structure of the British civil service facilitates this because, in contrast to the structure of the American executive, top positions—often referred to as the higher civil service—are much nearer to the locus of policy making.

The officials working most closely with a secretary of state are the permanent secretary and the principal private secretary. The latter is a promising young civil servant (called a "high flyer") whom the secretary of state has designated as a special assistant. The principal private secretary shields the secretary from unnecessary engagements and needless paperwork. He or she also has the delicate task of maintaining good relations with both the permanent secretary and the medium-level civil servants in the department. In attempting to make the department seem in complete agreement on a particular policy or to make decisions easier by limiting the range of options, the permanent secretary may not wish to report conflicting views. The private secretary, on the other hand, must try to ensure that contrasting views and doubts are not filtered out but reach the secretary of state. Medium-level civil servants may speak more freely to the private secretary because he or she, unlike the permanent secretary, is not their superior in the chain of command and has no direct control over their career prospects.

Although the position is a coveted appointment, a principal private secretary must endure the tension of divided loyalties. The role is to be the secretary of state's personal assistant, but that secretary soon will move on to some other position. The permanent secretary, however, will continue to serve as part of the network of elite civil servants. If a high flyer has been so assiduous in reporting activities within the department to the secretary of state that he or she has crossed the permanent secretary, a crash is entirely likely and a promising career may never again take wing. Those who can serve two masters without irritating either one deserve any subsequent promotion they receive.

A department's legal advisor and its few deputy secretaries also have some contact with the secretary of state. All of these civil servants we have mentioned are expected to serve each succeeding secretary of state loyally, whatever their own political views. Only by keeping out of the political arena and performing as faceless mandarins can they play this role. British practice contrasts sharply with both American and French. In the United States, turnover in top posts within a department is high from one Administration to another because most of the jobs are political and not career positions; in France, a political executive brings along to a department a personal group of trusted advisors, many of whom are career civil servants. Thus, in both France and the United States, the political head of a department has his or her trusted colleagues to run things. In Britain, the politician must make do with assistants already in place, who owe little to him or her for having advanced to where they are and who can expect little help in furthering their careers in the future. Thus, the tradition of loyal service to all masters is all that the British secretary of state can count on in trying to direct his or her department.

When the Labour party came to power in 1945, having won a majority of seats in the Commons for the first time, many of its adherents feared that an unsympathetic civil service would sabotage the party's nationalization program. This did not occur; the civil servants loyally assisted their political supervisors in implementing Labour's economic and industrial policies. Six years later, when the Conservatives had returned to power, the same civil servants with equal loyalty helped to denationalize the iron and steel industry, which had been taken under public ownership by the Labour Government with their assistance.

One might have thought that this demonstration of civil servants' political neutrality and willingness to serve whoever wins elections would have put Labour's fears to rest. But concern continues to linger. Almost invariably the top civil servants, as career merit personnel, will have been with a particular department considerably longer than the secretary of state, whose service depends on shifting electoral fortunes and changing power relations within a party. Thus, the civil servants may know more about a topic than does the secretary; they certainly are likely to think that they know the practical complexities better.[3] Furthermore, since secretaries come and go, the civil servants feel that they will be the ones who will have to clean up any mess resulting from a mistake in policy.

As a result, the civil service tends to be cautious and suspicious of innovation. Such an attitude poses a particular problem for a reform party such as Labour. The difficulty is not so much that civil servants are Conservative partisans as that they resist change simply because it is inconvenient. Change disrupts the comfortable existing pattern of activities. Thus, top civil servants are likely to respond to any new proposal with reasons why it shouldn't be implemented rather than trying to figure out how it can be. Only a determined secretary can avoid having reforms shunted onto a side track. For probity, loyalty, discretion, and intelligence, the British civil service probably is unsurpassed. Whether it provides the ideal instrument for reform—of whatever type—is another question.

■ CONTROL OF ADMINISTRATIVE DISCRETION

Implementing the laws has always involved administrators in rule making. As modern government has expanded its activities in social and economic areas, such activity has increased dramatically. Parliament has tended to pass laws in skeletal form, entrusting administrators with filling in the details. Two major problems have arisen as a result: (1) how to ensure that rule-making authority is exercised in conformity with the basic statute, and (2) how to protect citizens' rights from being abused by administrative boards and tribunals, especially when their actions cannot be challenged in the courts.

Parliament has little alternative to delegating rule-making authority to administrators; it cannot cover in legislation all the details of every situation that may arise. Furthermore, as you have seen, time pressures on the Commons usually do not permit full discussion of technical details, and, in any event, the Commons is not organized in such a way as to scrutinize such aspects of bills. The Commons' strength lies in debating the general policies that lie behind particular bills.

Even if it were possible for laws to detail individual cases, this would not be desirable. Such laws would be too rigid; some flexibility to deal with changing circumstances and human variability is desirable. So bureaucrats must be given some

---

[3] If you have seen even one or two episodes of the funny and highly accurate British TV series "Yes, Minister," you have a good idea of the way in which civil servants are likely to regard politicians.

leeway to make rules adapting the general principles of the law to the practical circumstances of everyday life.

On the other hand, administrators' discretion must be limited. They are not elected; there is no way of replacing them if the people do not like the rules they are making. The problem is more acute in Britain than in the United States because no constitution limits the British legislature and the role of the courts is far more modest than in the United States. British courts cannot inquire whether Parliament has the right to legislate and, consequently, to bestow rule-making power. They can only decide whether or not the rule-making body is acting in accordance with the procedural framework prescribed by law.

The British have attempted to deal with the problem by establishing certain safeguards. First, administrators are able to make rules and regulations that have the effect of law only when authorized to do so by statute. Second, all rules made in a department must be confirmed by its secretary of state. Third, an increasing number of statutes require the department to consult advisory committees before issuing regulations. All departments in the economic and social sphere use advisory committees. The effectiveness of these committees depends, however, on how willing the secretary is to consult them and also on how representative of the interests affected they are.

As an additional safeguard, Parliament is given a role in the process. We explained in Chapter 5 that the Joint Committee on Statutory Instruments and the Commons' Standing Committee on Statutory Instruments manage to discuss some of the rules made by administrators; on occasion, so does the House of Lords. Parliament's control over administrative rules varies. In some cases a rule goes into effect unless the Lords or the Commons votes against it within a stated period of time. In other cases a rule can't be implemented unless Parliament has voted in favor of it. In practice, however, this check probably serves to catch only blatant abuses of administrative discretion. So great is the number of regulations that some that are unwise or undesirable are bound to get through.

The increased number of rules made by administrators has caused concern about individual rights. To resolve conflicts between governmental agencies seeking to implement regulations and citizens alleging that their rights have been violated, various departments have established administrative tribunals. These are staffed by experts with experience or training in the relevant field. Because procedures are less formal in tribunals than in courts, the former tend to be cheaper and quicker. Tribunals have been criticized, however, precisely because they do not follow all the procedures that courts do. For example, the lack of any right to cross-examine those who testify at a tribunal may make refuting them difficult. Furthermore, since the secretary of state for a department appoints the members of the tribunal that deals with controversies caused by that department's actions, the department (and the secretary, since he or she is the one accountable under individual ministerial responsibility) appears to be a judge in its own case.

The courts can scrutinize any points of law involved in tribunals' findings. And a special council reviews and reports on the workings of many tribunals. Nonetheless, in 1967 it was thought necessary to add a further safeguard similar to one pioneered by Scandinavia and New Zealand—to establish an ombudsman, formally known as the Parliamentary Commissioner for Administration. Since, as you know by now, the British never want to move too far too fast, the Commissioner's powers were more limited than those of the typical ombudsman in other countries. The Commissioner is an officer of Parliament and is permitted to consider only those complaints channeled through its Members. When people write to the Commissioner directly, he (or she) will pass on to the MPs those that appear to be the most worthwhile cases, asking them to consider referring the matter back to him for action.[4]

The Commissioner can investigate cases where administrative action is so "thoroughly bad in quality" that it suggests bias or perversity. Should considerable hardship or injustice have been caused, the Commissioner can examine the case, even if the rules have been applied correctly, to ascertain whether the department concerned had reviewed adequately the applicable rule with the aim of making changes to prevent such results in the future.

Unfortunately, most of the complaints referred to the Commissioner have to be rejected because they fall outside the post's authority. The Commissioner can't, for example, deal with complaints about general policy, and certain subjects, such as nationalized industry and foreign policy, are ruled out entirely. An even greater limitation is that the Commissioner can only investigate and report to Parliament—that is, can only recommend redress, not order it.

Nonetheless, the Commissioner has enjoyed some success. In some instances departments respond to the Commissioner's investigation by making the necessary corrections. In other cases Parliament has passed special legislation to compensate those who were improperly treated. And in many cases—the majority, in fact—the Commissioner finds that there really was no justification for a complaint. Although some individuals who receive such a finding may feel shortchanged, others may be satisfied that their complaint was investigated thoroughly—or perhaps misunderstandings were cleared up. The Commissioner provides a useful supplementary safeguard, but not a complete solution to the problem of abuse of administrative power.

■ *ACCOUNTABILITY IN THE NATIONALIZED INDUSTRIES*

Governmental control of the economy and regulation of business are not synonymous with direct management and ownership of specific enterprises. Nationalized industries, that is, government-owned concerns, are not part of Britain's regular administrative structure. Nevertheless, they are administered by governmental agents. How are these industries managed; how are they made accountable? This is no trivial question since the basic motivation for nationalization is accountability. Those who challenge capitalism complain that it permits entrepreneurs and managers to wield economic power (which often can be transformed readily into polit-

---

[4]The one exception to this procedure is for the National Health Service. Complaints about its operation can be made directly to the ombudsman.

ical power) subject to little popular constraint. That is, in capitalism the power-holders are not accountable to the people. Therefore, anticapitalists argue, government should own the major enterprises to ensure that they function in the people's interest.

Although the Labour party has long been identified with nationalization, it did not originate government ownership of business in Britain. In the six years after it won majority control of the House of Commons in 1945, however, it did greatly extend public ownership. Even at the height of nationalization, Britain remained a private-enterprise economy: less than a tenth of the work force was employed by government-owned firms, and only about a tenth of the GDP was produced by such industries. Labour wanted the government to acquire only the essential enterprises, the so-called commanding heights of the economy.

Having acquired these enterprises (by paying their owners), the Government faced the question of how to operate them. What type of administrative structure should run them? Unlike government departments dealing with defense or foreign relations, these were commercial operations. A product or service was being made available for purchase by those wishing to obtain it. A government department must keep extensive records of all decisions to be able to respond to any official inquiries about its actions. Such a practice seemed likely to impede the operational flexibility and efficient management required in commercial enterprises. But if there were no responsibility to Parliament for nationalized industry, how could taking these enterprises under government ownership solve the problem of unaccountable power?

To reconcile these conflicting aims, the public corporation was created. Such corporations (which run the various nationalized industries) are under the jurisdiction of various secretaries of state, who, in turn, are responsible to Parliament. The managers of the corporations can make many decisions without reference to their secretary. Parliament can question the relevant secretary about a corporation's broad policy, but that secretary is not accountable for every detailed decision of the corporation.

All public corporations share certain basic features. Their finances are self-contained; that is, their accounts are kept separate from those of the regular government. They are run by specially appointed boards, whose members are not civil servants. The boards do not seek to make a profit for their industries, but to provide the best service at a break-even price. No politician exercises day-to-day control over a board's managerial activity. The appropriate secretary appoints and can remove members of the board and can be questioned in Parliament about the appointments. The secretary has to approve any borrowing or capital investment that the board wishes to undertake, as well as any program of research and development. Each year, the secretary submits to Parliament the annual report and accounts of the corporation.

Secretaries can issue general instructions or policy directives to boards, but rarely do so because that would be regarded as questioning the board's competence. Secretaries typically express their wishes informally, and boards comply to avoid receiving a directive. This may sound like a satisfactory compromise, but it obscures responsibility. Since no directive is issued, Parliament cannot question the secretary about the action, and the corporation's annual report need not disclose anything about why the decision was made.

The public corporation significantly altered the old convention that secretaries were accountable for every act in their departments. Only if their consent was required (for example, for borrowing) or they could have voided a decision can they be held accountable.

Parliament debates some of the annual reports of nationalized industries but can find time for only about two or three a year. Given the number of nationalized industries, several years usually pass between debates on any particular industry. Although the Commons' Public Accounts Committee can examine the finances of public corporations, it can't devote much time to this since it is responsible for scrutinizing the full range of government spending. A corporation's board has to respond to inquiries from the Treasury concerning income and expenditures. This means that public enterprises are subject to some financial control and Government direction. This fails, however, to get to the heart of the problem—which is not that public corporations are a power unto themselves, but that the Government may manage to escape having to answer to Parliament for the policies it instructs them to pursue.

A satisfactory solution to the problem of attaining both commercial flexibility and political accountability has yet to be devised. Margaret Thatcher used Alexander the Great's approach to the Gordian knot—don't try to untie it, just slash through it with a sword. While Prime Minister, she vigorously pursued a program of privatization, that is, selling government-owned enterprises back to the public. Sales of gas, banking, and telecommunications enterprises transformed the pattern of private investment in Britain. In only four years during the mid-1980s, the proportion of the population owning shares more than tripled, going from about 6 percent to more than 20 percent. And more was to come: the Thatcher Government began selling water services to the public. The proportion of shareholders increased to 25 percent before declining to 22 percent in 1992.

Although the total value of government enterprises sold off during the 1980s surpassed $50 billion, not everything that the government owned was privaitized. Whatever other policy differences they may have had, Major shared Thatcher's commitment to privatization. In the early 1990s his Government was working on plans to sell the railroads. For enterprises remaining in government hands, the problem of finding a structure to reconcile flexibility with accountability still remained. In the meantime other developments of an entrepreneurial nature were beginning to raise more pressing problems of accountability.

One means initiated under Thatcher for reducing the size of government was to require competitive tendering for many activities. Private businesses would have to be allowed to bid on jobs currently being performed by government employees (these employees could also bid) to see whether the work could be done more cheaply. When a private business won the bid, one might argue that the market was the control device—either the business provided value for the money or it didn't. If the latter was the case, when the contract expired, it could be granted to someone else. Here is an example of the sort of accountability question that such arrangements could raise: "What could an MP do to respond to a constituent's complaint that the hospitals in her town weren't being properly cleaned, if a private cleaning firm had won the contract for this work?"

Even more significant was the growth of executive agencies. Thatcher's advisors argued that government had become so bloated and overburdened that mere reorganization offered no solution. Government had to divest itself of some functions—and, yet, people had come to depend on certain services. The solution was to make bureaucracy responsible for policy formulation and remove it from policy implementation, or the actual delivery of services. To accomplish this, a number of executive functions have been hived off to quasi-autonomous agencies. These agencies operate largely independently, each with its own executive head and separate budget. For example, the office responsible for publishing and selling governmental materials, such as the transcripts of the debates in the House of Commons, became an executive agency. By mid-1990, thirty-three such bodies with a total staff of 80,000 had been established. The following year, when a Benefits Agency was created, the number of people employed by the Department of Social Security plummeted from 80,000 to only 2,600.

Whether this development made government more efficient and businesslike is not the issue. Perhaps the British people were better served at lower cost. The problem is that the line of responsibility from the executive head of such agencies through the relevant secretary of state and on to Parliament is even more vague and unenforceable than the links for nationalized industry. Those providing government services are becoming increasingly difficult to call to account. And since calling people to account is, as you saw in Chapter 5, one of the main functions of Parliament, this trend raises serious questions about the value of Parliament. Finally, recall that Parliament is assigned the task of calling people to account not just so that it can have something to do. Having to account for actions in a public forum lends legitimacy to the actions, makes what government does tolerable even when it isn't palatable. We don't wish to push this point too far. The British executive still *makes* policy, with the assistance of the bureaucracy, and Parliament retains some procedures for enforcing accountability in this sphere. When the focus turns to *implementing* policy, however, Parliament is finding it increasingly difficult to perform one of its central functions.

8

Resolving Conflicts

As we suggested in the Introduction, the entire political process—the election of representatives to make rules and to supervise those entrusted with implementing them—is an effort to resolve conflicting needs and desires without resort to violence or coercion. The political process does not end with passage of a law; nor does implementation of a law complete the process. Furthermore, conflict is not just a matter of the individual against the government. Equally significant is conflict between individuals. There the government's role is to provide a means of resolving disputes that is fair to all. The government maintains a system of courts so that the people do not have to engage in feuds and vendettas. Any assessment of a political system's success in achieving its fundamental purpose of resolving conflicts fairly and peacefully is incomplete without considering the legal system.

■ THE ROLE OF COMMON LAW IN BRITISH JUSTICE

In Chapter 1 we referred briefly to the early development of the English judicial system and the evolution of the common law. We touched on the common law again in the discussion in Chapter 2 of the constitutional foundations of British politics. In this chapter we give common law the detailed attention it deserves as one of the two most extensively copied and influential legal systems (the other is the Roman law system). The common law system spread from Britain through most of the areas it controlled, including, of course, the United States. The Roman law system is preferred on the European Continent and in Japan and Turkey. Interestingly, Scottish law is in the Roman tradition, and, therefore, Scotland's judicial system and procedures differ from those of England and Wales.

You will recall that common law is based on judicial decisions; Roman law is founded on legal codes. Of course, legislatures pass laws in common law systems, and judges decide cases in Roman law systems. Statutes tend to be more elaborate and detailed in the latter, and judges expect to find in the statutes the rules to cover the cases they hear. In the common law system judges seek the correct decision for a current case by examining the decisions of judges for similar cases in the past.

Centuries ago, royal courts were only one of several courts. Various feudal lords operated their own systems of courts distinct from those of the state. Because they tended to be more just, the royal courts were more popular and eventually super-seded the others. By the end of the fourteenth century, the royal courts were staffed by professional judges appointed by the monarch from among the practic-ing lawyers. The aim of these courts was to mete out justice in the cases brought to them. Strictly speaking, a decision applied to only the case at hand; the judges did not attempt to elaborate extensive rules to cover the subject in general. Common law had little or nothing to say about many topics because few cases had arisen in those areas. In essence, the law developed fortuitously, although it grew most rapidly in the areas of greatest concern to the people because these were where the most cases were generated.

To produce some order out of this haphazard pattern of development, leading legal scholars, such as Coke and Blackstone, grouped together the decisions in sim-ilar cases and indicated what the typical ruling was. These commentaries revealed obvious defects in the law. In some instances cases that were only slightly similar were not adequately differentiated in existing common law rules; in other instances cases that were virtually indistinguishable were covered by conflicting rulings. Furthermore, centuries of following the doctrine of *stare decisis* (pronounced "star-ay-dee-sigh-sis," Latin for "let the decision stand"—that is, the holding in a pre-vious similar case should determine the decision in subsequent cases, regardless of whether that produced a just result) had cost the common law a good bit of its flex-ibility. Excessive devotion to precedent was becoming a cause of injustice.

For example, under common law, contracts made under threat to life and limb were invalid, but those made subject to other improper influences (such as getting someone drunk before hoodwinking them) were valid. The chief remedy available under common law was to seek damages. But payment of money cannot restore circumstances to what they were. What was needed was a legal procedure that could stop an action *before* it did damage.

How could the law be kept sufficiently flexible to provide justice without becoming so variable as to be arbitrary and capricious? The Lord Chancellor was charged with functioning as the monarch's conscience to prevent any miscarriages of justice resulting from rigid devotion to precedent. An entire system of legal rules gradually developed out of the Lord Chancellor's decisions in cases where people had appealed to the monarch for relief from injustices of the common law. By the early part of the nineteenth century, equity (also known as chancery) had taken its place alongside the common law as a humanizing element. Equity dealt with civil controversies (that is, conflicts between private individuals), rather than criminal cases (conflicts between an individual and the government). It established the prac-tice of granting an injunction (an order prohibiting certain action) to prevent possi-ble injury or nuisance before it occurred.

Note that equity, like common law, is judge-made. All British courts apply both equity and common law. Where the two sets of rules conflict, equity takes prece-dence. Any applicable statutes supersede both common law and equity. Increasingly, Parliament has legislated in areas previously covered only by common law or equity. This has occurred not so much in an attempt to repeal judicial precedents as to provide rules to cover rapidly expanding governmental activities. Despite the growth of statute law, judge-made law remains fundamental in most areas of British jurisprudence.

■ THE ORGANIZATION OF THE JUDICIARY

Like many other institutions in Britain, the court system has been shaped and altered by many years of usage. Itinerant royal commissioners, who were originally concerned mainly with looking after William the Conqueror's financial affairs, were transformed into itinerant judges by Henry II early in the twelfth century. They visited each county three or four times a year to determine whether charges of serious crimes were accurate (lesser offenses were left to sheriffs and justices of the peace). Thus, the practice of trying almost all criminal cases in the county where the crime was committed became well established.

In civil cases of importance, however, proceedings were held at Westminster, which meant that the litigants, witnesses, and others with an interest in the case had to travel to London for the trial. Travel in those days not only was time-consuming and quite wearing, but could be positively dangerous. So Justices of the Assize Courts were sent to the counties to hear cases. The points of law continued to be argued mainly at Westminster, however, and formal judgment was rendered there.

Despite these and other measures that have decentralized the courts over the centuries, the British legal system remains unified in a national system in both its structure and its appointment procedures. The United States, as a federal system, has two separate court systems: the state courts and the federal courts. The intertwining of these two systems is very complex, but with respect to appointments they are completely distinct. Although in this respect the British legal system is unified in a way the American one isn't, the British courts are divided in a way the American ones aren't. Britain has separate judicial hierarchies for civil and for criminal cases.

Figure 8–1 provides an overview of the British court system; refer to it as you read the following description. In the criminal courts, virtually all—95 percent—of the cases begin in magistrates' courts. Summary offenses (minor violations not requiring an indictment or trial by jury and having a maximum sentence of six months in prison or a fine of about $3,000) are tried here. Criminal cases are the primary concern of magistrates' courts, but they also hear some civil cases, primarily on matters of family law. Magistrates' courts also perform the function allocated to grand juries in the United States: they decide whether sufficient evidence exists for an indictment (a formal accusation that must be defended in court) to be issued for a serious crime.

The approximately 700 magistrates' courts are staffed by about 28,000 magistrates (judges), largely unpaid laypersons appointed by the Lord Chancellor. Three magistrates hear each case; they are advised on points of law by a legally trained clerk (pronounced "clark"). In large urban areas, however, a few magistrates are full-time, legally trained judges, who sit alone in hearing cases.

Figure 8–1
The British Court
System

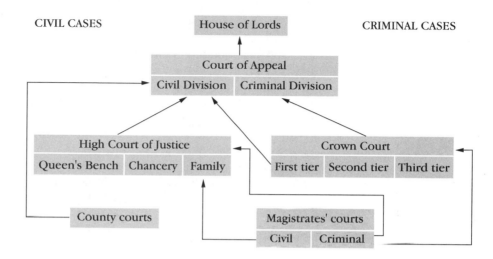

Appeals from the magistrates' courts in civil cases go to the Family Division of the High Court of Justice. Appeals in criminal cases go to the High Court only when a point of law is involved. If the question is whether the verdict was correct or the sentence too severe, then the appeal is to the Crown Court.

In addition to hearing appeals from the magistrates' courts, the Crown Court serves as the original court for serious crimes. For the most important of these cases, such as murder, a judge from the High Court of Justice sits alone. In other cases, such as assault or forgery, a circuit judge, or even a part-time recorder, presides and is assisted by two or four magistrates. In either instance a jury is used.

Crown Court sessions are held in about ninety locations around the country. Those in the largest cities are designated as the first tier. This tier has some limited civil jurisdiction in addition to its main responsibilities for criminal cases. The second tier is located in smaller cities, and the third tier, comprising about half of the total number of locations, in towns. The latter courts try serious crimes of lesser importance, such as assault with intent to rob or wounding. Appeals are taken to the Court of Appeal, Criminal Division, except for any civil cases heard by first tier Crown Courts.

In the civil courts the lowest level is the county court, of which there are about 300. As long as the damages sought do not exceed about $7,500, the county court can try the case. The Lord Chancellor assigns circuit judges to these courts. No juries are used, and judges typically preside alone. Appeals go to the Court of Appeal, Civil Division.

The more serious civil cases start in the High Court of Justice, which holds sessions in London and a couple of dozen other cities. The High Court has three divisions: Queen's Bench, for commercial law; Chancery, for wills and estates; and Family, for divorces and guardianships of minors. One of the eighty judges presides alone when a case is being heard for the first time, but judges sit in twos and threes for appeals from lower courts. Appeals from the High Court go to the Court of Appeal.

The Court of Appeal links to some extent the separate criminal and civil court systems yet has two separate divisions, one for each type of law. The Court of Appeal has twenty-eight judges.

You probably will be surprised to see in Figure 8–1 that the court of last resort in Britain, the one to which any appeals from the Court of Appeal go, is the House of Lords. Although, technically, all peers are entitled to hear cases, by custom the Lords' judicial function is performed by only eleven of its members. As vacancies among this group occur, people who have demonstrated outstanding legal ability are designated by the Prime Minister to receive a life peerage. These lords of appeal in ordinary (or law lords, for short) try the cases reaching the House of Lords. Should the workload be too heavy for these eleven to handle promptly, the Lord Chancellor, retired law lords, or peers who have held high judicial positions can try cases as well.

Since, formally, the entire House of Lords is the court, the law lords cannot hear cases when the Lords is meeting for legislative business. To get around the problem of inadequate time for judicial work, appellate committees were created. Cases are actually heard by only three or five of the law lords. Whatever such a committee decides is accepted by the other law lords as though all eleven of them had been involved, just as the Lords treats the law lords' decisions as though made by the entire House. The appellate committees decide cases on the basis of majority vote. Just as is true for the U.S. Supreme Court, a case may produce concurring and dissenting opinions in addition to the main one explaining the reasons for the decision.

Appeal to the Lords is not automatic; at whatever level a case began, at least one rehearing occurs before a case can get to the Lords. Cases reach the Lords, therefore, only when the Court of Appeal chooses to refer them or the Appeals Committee of the Lords requests them. Cases before the Lords deal only with questions of law, never with matters of fact. The lower courts are responsible for clarifying what actually happened in a case. The Lords, then, can consider how to interpret the law and apply it to the facts that prior judicial proceedings have established.[1]

Although the House of Lords is the final authority for legal interpretation, you should remember that, as we explained in Chapter 5, Parliament is supreme. All laws passed by Parliament are valid; not even the law lords can declare them unconstitutional. Furthermore, the law lords' interpretation of the law is not final; Parliament can reverse any of their decisions simply by passing a new law. Unlike the situation in the United States, in Britain an elaborate process of constitutional amendment is not needed when the highest court interprets basic governmental powers and duties in a way that many people dislike. On the other hand, British judges cannot protect people from arbitrary government to the same extent that American ones can. Until a law is amended, its provisions are what the British judges say they are. But a majority of Parliament (which typically follows the will of the Cabinet) can alter the law. As we discussed in Chapter 2, the nature of this rela-

---

[1]As we already noted, the Scottish legal system differs from that of England and Wales. Only civil cases can be appealed from Scottish courts to the House of Lords. For criminal cases the High Court of Justiciary (located in Scotland) is the court of last resort.

tion between the legislative and judicial branches has made some Britons concerned about the adequacy of protection for basic freedoms.

■ JUSTICE IN BRITAIN: POLICE AND TRIAL PROCEDURES

The British legal profession is divided into solicitors and barristers. Solicitors advise clients and prepare material for the trial, but usually do not appear in court. They give the material to a barrister whom they have selected, and he or she argues the case. One cannot be both a solicitor and a barrister, nor can lawyers of the two types be partners in a law firm.

The atmosphere of British courts tends to be more formal and sedate than that of most American courts. The Perry Mason stereotype may have little validity in the United States, but it is even less accurate in Britain. Blustering or hectoring is rare. Both judges and barristers are attired in robes and wigs to lend dignity to the proceedings. A more important contrast, however, concerns the role of judges. In both countries the burden of proof is on the prosecution, but a British judge, unlike an American one, is not just a referee but an active participant in the trial. British judges may comment on the evidence as it is presented as well as on the failure of the defendant to testify.

Despite a reputation for fairness, British justice has had some flaws. Legislation during the 1980s corrected some, but not all, of these. Although the police have no legal power to hold a person for questioning, they frequently do so. People taken into custody for this purpose are said, in a classic British phrase, to be "helping the police with their inquiries." As Michael Zander, professor of law at the London School of Economics, has said, this really means "being held illegally by the police while they decide whether there is enough evidence to charge [them] with some offence."[2] The police need not make clear to such detainees that their presence is entirely voluntary and they have the right to leave at any time.

Those who are formally arrested have no choice about "helping the police with their inquiries." Being arrested, however, is not the same as being charged with an offense. The key question concerns how long the police may detain and question a suspect without making a charge. Under the Police and Criminal Evidence Act, the limit is twenty-four hours, except that those suspected of a serious offense may be held without charge for thirty-six hours. The police can obtain an additional thirty-six hours if a magistrate approves (in a full hearing with the detainee present and legally represented). And at the end of seventy-two hours, a further extension of twenty-four hours is possible, again after a full hearing. About three-quarters of all suspects are charged within six hours, and virtually all—around 95 percent—within twenty-four hours. Nonetheless, a suspect could be held for as long as four days without ever having been charged with committing any crime.

Obviously, someone who is in police custody needs a lawyer. The British police were not very good about protecting the right to counsel. Suspects often were held incommunicado. Even if a friend or relative knew that a person had been arrested

---

[2]*The Guardian,* 16 December 1977, p. 5.

and sent a lawyer to the police station, the police did not have to tell the suspect that legal help had arrived. Since reforms in the mid-1980s, the law requires that police must tell those who are arrested that they have a right to a lawyer. Suspects may call their own lawyer or may obtain one free of charge from the pool of those on call at the police station. The right to counsel is not absolute, however. With serious crimes the police need not inform the suspect of this right, if they believe that doing so would have injurious effects (for example, if allowing a suspect to call a lawyer would alert confederates in the crime to the fact that the police were on to them). The police cannot delay allowing a suspect to contact a lawyer for more than thirty-six hours, since the suspect is entitled to a lawyer at the hearing to determine whether he or she can continue to be held without charge.

As we mentioned earlier in this chapter, a magistrates' court decides whether the evidence against a person accused of a serious crime is sufficient to justify a trial. A lay magistrate, assisted by a legally trained clerk, presides over the hearing. If the defense argues that there is too little evidence for a trial, weeks or even months will go by before the issue is settled. The defendant will have to spend this time in jail, unless he or she is granted bail. Given most magistrates' limited legal knowledge, they tend to commit people for trial almost automatically; only about 2 percent of those brought before them are discharged from further proceedings.

Close to half of the cases tried in the Crown Court, however, result in acquittals. Apparently, magistrates fail to review the evidence properly and impose the cost and stigma of a trial on many people who should not have to endure them. Even worse, the magistrates' behavior tends to encourage slipshod police work; police are not deterred from seeking committals despite a lack of sufficient evidence to obtain a conviction.

Deciding whether to prosecute someone had been primarily the responsibility of the police in Britain; there was no official comparable to the District Attorney in the United States. In the late 1980s, however, a national Crown Prosecution Service (CPS) was established to take over this function. The CPS is headed by the Director of Public Prosecutions (DPP), who is appointed by the Attorney General. The DPP decides whether to prosecute in a few of the most difficult and serious cases, but the bulk of these decisions are made by Crown prosecutors at the local level. The new system is intended to provide greater consistency in decisions to prosecute, without losing sight of local circumstances that may counsel some variation from one area to another. In addition, it is hoped that there will be less inclination to proceed with weak cases than when the police were in charge of prosecutions.

The CPS has had a number of problems in getting established. Inadequate funding has left it woefully understaffed and unable to discharge its responsibilities effectively. Also, conflicts with the police have been common. The police complain that the CPS frequently fails to prosecute the cases they submit to it. As a result, they say, those the police accuse of crimes go free, and law enforcement efforts are discouraged. The CPS complains about lack of cooperation from the police and their failure at times to appear in court when they are scheduled to give evidence. In the long run these accusations and suspicions probably will disappear, but they have made the early years of the CPS difficult. Shifting to a prosecution structure more akin to the American one has not been a smooth process.

A person committed for trial may have to wait some time before the case is heard. The number of prisoners awaiting trial doubled between 1979 and the mid-1980s. Delays of over a year were not unknown. The cost of defending against a serious criminal charge is so great that virtually all defendants in the Crown Court had qualified for legal aid, a government-financed program administered by the legal profession. The Lord Chancellor, the head of the British legal system, ordered severe cuts in the program, however, as a government economy measure. So harsh were these and so seriously would they restrict access to legal proceedings for millions of people that the Law Society, the solicitors' professional association, sued the Lord Chancellor in 1993. The Law Society charged that the Lord Chancellor had acted *ultra vires*, beyond his legal powers, in making the cuts. The Law Society lost its case, however, because the High Court held that since many people still would receive legal aid, the cuts could not be said to be so inconsistent with the purpose of the program as to be invalid.[3]

Once a case gets to trial, the accused may be disadvantaged by the rules of evidence. Search warrants authorize looking in specific places for specific types of evidence. Although the police may fail to turn up any of the specified evidence in searching someone's home, they may find evidence of a totally unrelated crime and decide to seize it. Even more of a problem is the fact that many searches are conducted without a warrant. At times the police simply fail to get one, even though it is required by law. In most cases this occurs because the law permits the police to search the home of someone arrested and any premises that he or she occupied immediately before arrest. In such searches any evidence possibly related to any crime can be seized. Thus, not uncommonly the police will have evidence obtained by questionable means.

Can such tainted evidence be used against the accused? In the United States an exclusionary rule applies in federal prosecutions: illegally obtained evidence will not be admitted. In Britain the rule is discretionary. Judges can exclude any evidence that they feel is unfair—involuntary confessions, for example. This means, however, that the defendant's fate turns on the views of the particular judge who happens to hear the case.

In sum, the rights of defendants and suspects clearly are better protected under the American legal system than under the British. Some would argue that this means that criminals are coddled in the United States; others would say that in Britain people enjoy less protection from arbitrary police action. This lack is of some importance because many people in Britain feel that judges are biased.

This charge of bias is not primarily a matter of partisan politics. Many judges at the state level in the United States serve for limited terms and must stand for reelection. This ensures that they are subject to popular control, that they are accountable to the people, as democracy requires. Most people, however, want judges to

---

[3] The situation has been even worse for civil cases. In 1950 the great majority of the population qualified for civil legal aid, but now only a minority are within the disposable income and capital limits. Many middle-class and skilled working-class people must bear legal costs unassisted and find that they simply can't afford to go to court, no matter how strong their case is.

be objective; they do not want them to be swayed by partisan influences. The law should not be a matter of transient majority opinion. Although British judges are not elected, this does not guarantee that they are free from partisan influences. The head of the legal system, the Lord Chancellor, is appointed to the Cabinet by the Prime Minister. He or she does not serve for a specified term and is replaced immediately when the Opposition comes into power. British judges are selected by the Prime Minister or the Lord Chancellor. These appointments do not require any legislative approval.

Judges are appointed on the basis of professional competence, however, not for political opinions or activities. Barristers are much more likely to win appointment as circuit judges than are solicitors. The justices in the magistrates' courts, however, are unlikely to be either solicitors or barristers, since legal training is not required for appointment. Judges serve "during good behaviour," which means, in effect, that they have lifetime tenure. A vote by both Houses of Parliament is required to remove a judge from office. This has occurred only in 1830, when a judge had misappropriated funds.

The charge of bias is related to judges' class background. Just like British civil servants, British judges clearly are unrepresentative of the public. Even if they do not consciously favor one segment of society over another, their background may dispose them to believe those with similar status and to look askance at those unfamiliar with the social graces. Britons were asked in an opinion survey to speculate about two people—one rich, one poor—appearing in court charged with a crime they did not commit. Less than two-fifths thought there would be an equal chance of their being found guilty; nearly three-fifths thought the poor person was more likely to be found guilty.[4]

Freeing judges from electoral considerations in Britain does not appear to have produced a reputation for fairness. Little has been gained in return for the loss of accountability. A Gallup poll early in 1993 found that little more than a third of the public professed a great deal or quite a lot of confidence in the legal system.[5] To put this result in perspective, the response was the same for the civil service and the Anglican Church, and Parliament generated even less confidence. Public views on another institution pointed up contrasts between Britain and the United States. Despite some recent damaging revelations about police corruption, 70 percent of Britons had a great deal or quite a lot of confidence in the police—twice as many as felt that way about the legal system. Guess what response you might get to such a question in the United States!

■ ■ ■

The seriousness of low confidence in the courts is somewhat lessened by the limited power of the British judiciary. No judge in Britain can declare a law unconstitutional, or overturn what the representatives of the people have enacted into

---

[4]Roger Jowell, Lindsay Brook, and Bridget Taylor with Gillian Prior, eds., *British Social Attitudes: the 8th Report* (Aldershot, England: Dartmouth, 1991), p. 190.
[5]*Gallup Political & Economic Index*, Report No. 390, February 1993.

law. The holdings of British courts may well have political impact, but their effect is not as great as it would be if they possessed the American power of judicial review.

This point has not been adequately considered by those in Britain who have been advocating a written constitution. Such a document would end Parliament's supremacy; it would confine the legislature to certain specified powers and prohibit it from acting in certain matters. Something like the U.S. Supreme Court would have to be established to determine whether Parliament had abided by these constraints. Questions on this issue would be raised in the form of judicial proceedings, as in the United States, yet one person's legal/constitutional question is another's political issue. Some judges would wield significant political power. If the American system were followed, not just a few top judges would exercise this power. Although the Supreme Court is the final authority on the meaning of the U.S. Constitution, even lower courts can refuse to enforce a law because they hold it to be unconstitutional. If circuit judges in Britain were able to make such rulings, concern about bias probably would become even more widespread. Reforming the British constitution requires further thought about the dilemma of how to balance judicial accountability and objectivity.

Perhaps these considerations explain the relative uncertainty about and lack of support for constitutional guarantees of rights in Britain. Asked their views on a bill of rights that "would give the courts rather than Parliament the final say on any laws or government actions which threaten basic freedoms," little more than a quarter definitely favored such a change, with only slightly more saying they probably supported it. Thus, only about half regarded it as a good idea. Although only about a fifth were opposed, nearly a quarter were unable to decide whether they preferred such a change or thought it was "better to leave things as they are."[6] Despite its heritage as one of the world's most estimable legal systems, the British system still has flaws that require attention.

---

[6]Jowell et al., op. cit., p. 198.

9

Contemporary Trends in British Politics: The Ratchet and the Pendulum

In the first half of the twentieth century, Britain had two charismatic and decisive Prime Ministers. David Lloyd George served nearly six years, from 1916 to 1922. Winston Churchill served five years, from 1940 to 1945; he subsequently returned in his dotage (at age 77) for a term of three and a half years from 1951 to 1955. If you are familiar with twentieth-century history, you'll have noticed that Lloyd George served during World War I and Churchill during World War II. Dominant, larger-than-life leaders often are required when a nation is fighting for survival. It is hardly a coincidence that the man many people regard as the greatest U.S. President—Abraham Lincoln—served during the Civil War.

In the second half of the twentieth century, Margaret Thatcher was the one who overshadowed all others who served as Prime Minister. She was unique not only in being Britain's first female Prime Minister, but also in serving for eleven and a half years—twice as long as Lloyd George and several years more than Churchill's combined total. And she did it during peacetime, not when war threatened the country's future. (The Falklands conflict between Britain and Argentina early in her period in office can hardly be compared with either world war, although her success as a military leader did contribute to her political longevity.)

In their day both Lloyd George and Churchill *were* British government and, yet, neither became, as Thatcher did, an "ism." Although she was a person of action, rather than an intellectual or a political philosopher, she seemed to embody such a coherent package of policies and attitudes toward government and economics that "Thatcherism" soon came to be understood as meaning much more than that Maggie was still in charge.

Titanic leaders stir up strong popular emotions. Some people almost worship them; others loathe them. Ask your grandparents for their views on Franklin Roosevelt, who served as President of the United States even longer than Thatcher later did as Prime Minister, and compare notes with classmates. You'll find a wide range of reactions. An Englishman involved in the effort to raise funds for a major gift to Churchill on his eightieth birthday told me that he had received a letter with a razor blade taped to it. It said, "Give this to the old goat and maybe he'll cut his throat."

That would never have happened in the case of Thatcher only because she doesn't shave. The bulk of the British electorate never regarded her as a warm, compassionate leader ready to listen and respond to their concerns. They did see her as an insightful, decisive leader ready to administer strong medicine even if that cost her her popularity. Once a war has been won, the dominant leader's skills may not be the most appropriate ones for returning a country to "normalcy." That is, a dominant leader's influence may be situationally specific—more temporary than long term. What, then, of Thatcher? No war called her into office, and no military victory meant that her services no longer were needed. Running a country for more than a decade during peacetime certainly would seem to offer sufficient time to have lasting influence on government and politics. Does British government continue to be "Thatcherite" even though she fell from power several years ago? In this chapter we examine the pattern of British politics in order to answer this question.

As soon as World War II was over in Europe, Britain held a general election. Surprisingly, Churchill was voted out of office. More accurately, the electorate rejected the Conservatives. The party's failure in the 1930s to ameliorate the effects of the economic depression and its identification with appeasement of Hitler cost it many votes in 1945. Had Britain had the American separation-of-powers system, which would have permitted a vote on Churchill independent of his party, he almost certainly would have remained Prime Minister. Instead he was swept from office along with the other Conservatives. For the first time in British history, the Labour party held a majority of the seats in the House of Commons.

The Labour Government under Prime Minister Clement Attlee created the template for the next three decades of British government and politics. An extensive welfare state was established. The most notable feature was universal medical care, financed primarily out of taxes, rather than from fees for service. Second, Labour took a number of enterprises—for example, the coal mines, the railroads, and the gas industry—under government ownership. This action was linked to the third important element: the government was to play a major role in directing the economy, with the primary objective to be low unemployment. Despite this enhanced role for government, policy making became increasingly corporatist. That is, the fourth important element was active consultation by government with major business interests and unions in devising its economic policies. Some eventually argued that these private economic interests acquired a veto over government action.

Even though corporatism affected the substance of policy, it is best seen as a procedure or a style of decision making. It focused on the Government's relations with external groups. As a style, it had some affinity with the way in which decisions were reached *within* the Government. Dominant Prime Ministers—the Lloyd Georges and the Churchills—are policy initiators, who seek to mobilize government to move toward the goals they desire. A Prime Minister also can lead, however, by being a consensus builder. Such a leader employs a collegial style in trying to synthesize the diverse aims and means of his or her associates into a coherent set of policies that enjoys widespread support. This was Attlee's style. He was not unique in that respect; most Prime Ministers have preferred this approach. Given the British emphasis on a collective executive—the Cabinet—rather than on a chief executive (recall the way in which the office of Prime Minister simply evolved from that of presiding officer), the collegial style as standard operating procedure is only to be expected. You should not be surprised that the Lloyd Georges and the Churchills are the exception.

The key point, however, is that in the crucial period from 1945 to 1950 Britain *didn't* have that dominant type of leader. Recovery from the damage of World War II would have necessitated a major effort in any circumstances. But, beyond that, Britain had a reform government that was determined to transform social and economic life. Surely this called for the mobilizing leader. Despite Attlee's being instead a consensus builder, the Labour Government was quite successful. In the 1980s and 1990s, as Labour sought to make itself attractive to the electorate and relevant to Britons' concerns, it would have given anything to have been the party it was nearly a half century earlier. How much stronger its appeal to the electorate would have been if what most people remembered about Labour in power wasn't the "Winter of Discontent" (see Chapter 4), but the achievements of the Attlee Government.

Although the Conservatives managed to push Attlee and Labour from power after six years, they perpetuated the fundamental characteristics of that Government. Over the decades, the Conservatives have proven more adaptable to social change than have the Liberals. The Conservatives recognized after their defeat in 1945 that their only hope of survival was to embrace, in effect, the essentials of social democracy as established by the Attlee Government. Given this basic consensus, the two leading parties alternated in power, not surprisingly, as the pendulum of public opinion swung from one to the other. From 1945 to 1979, Labour had three periods in power, for a total of about seventeen years; the Conservatives had two, also totaling seventeen years. When each party returned to power, it didn't reverse its predecessor's programs.[1] The Attlee Government had, in effect, advanced a ratchet and locked Britain in a new mode of society and politics.

The template underlying this mode implicitly presumed economic growth. Prosperity meant that extensive governmental benefits and services could be provided without inflicting much pain in the form of the taxes necessary to finance such provision. The economic interests that the government consulted might disagree on how to divide the pie, but everyone could expect a generous serving. Furthermore, as long as business was booming, keeping unemployment low was easy.

The world changes, however; policies appropriate at one time cease to be effective if they aren't adapted. A major recession in the international economy, caused to a considerable extent by a huge jump in oil prices, slowed economic growth just about everywhere. That Britain was especially hard hit was, to some extent, its own fault. Having been a major world economic power for so long, Britain assumed it always would retain a dominant position without having to put in

---

[1] Richard Rose, *Do Parties Make a Difference?* 2d ed. (Chatham, N.J.: Chatham House, 1984).

much effort. Third World countries that formerly had produced only raw materials and food products began to industrialize, however, and their output started to compete with Britain's manufactured products. Too slow in developing concern about quality, service, and price, Britain lost many foreign markets. By the latter part of the 1960s, Britain no longer was able to support itself in the style of life to which it had become accustomed.

British politics in the 1970s indicated that neither leading party could devise a solution. The Conservatives tried in the first part of the decade and Labour in the second, but the economic malaise only worsened. Britain did not fear a foreign aggressor in 1979, as it had in 1916 and 1940. Nonetheless, to a considerable extent, the country was engaged in a similar fight for survival. Another back or forth of the pendulum to this party or that wouldn't suffice. During the prosperity of the 1950s, many Britons came to adopt an "I'm-Alright-Jack" attitude. The title of a popular 1960 film comedy, the phrase meant that one's standard of living was quite comfortable and expected wage increases would continue to make life even better. To some extent, the contrast mentioned in Chapter 2—that Britons are more likely than Americans to see government as a necessary provider of benefits—lessened.

When the economic downturn occurred during the late 1960s and into the 1970s, many Britons returned to their previous views about the role of government. The only problem was that, realistically, government lacked the funds to provide extensive benefits. The social democratic consensus appeared to have run its course. Nor was it only politicians on the right of the spectrum who questioned whether it remained feasible. As one of Labour's leaders was forced to admit, "The party's over." A new approach, a new template, was needed. And advancing the ratchet probably would require a different kind of leader.

Admittedly, this account makes the process sound more purposeful than it actually was. What became known as Thatcherism wasn't a neat, fully elaborated package ready for immediate use. The electorate didn't rise up in 1979 and plead for Thatcherism. However, a national crisis that had proven intractable to measures conforming with the postwar template had created an openness to reorientation. The crisis did call forth a set of policies and a style of governing that had evolved during the 1970s. A forceful personality—decisive leadership and self-assurance—helped to keep Thatcher in office for over a decade. So identified was she with the government's new direction, the political attitudes that made a variety of policies seem an integrated program, and the governing style that seemed essential to implementing the ground-breaking steps that using her name to encapsulate what was happening in British politics seemed natural. She became an "ism." Such a term is unique in British politics. How sharp a break with the post–World War II consensus, whose major elements we described earlier in this chapter, was needed for such a term to be coined?

Thatcher didn't dismantle the British welfare state. During her final election campaign in 1987, she made a point of replying to Labour's charges by asserting that the national health system was safe in Conservative hands. Spending on health as a proportion of all government spending actually *increased* by a couple of percentage points during her time in office. Furthermore, the share of spending devoted to social security jumped from somewhat more than 22 percent to nearly 30 percent.

On the other hand, Thatcher did seek to control total spending and to make government more efficient. When she entered office, public spending was 44 percent of GDP; when she left, it was down to 39 percent. During her decade in power the number of civil servants was cut by about a quarter. By constraining the growth of spending, she managed to reduce the tax burden. For example, a married man with average income paid 20 percent of his earnings in income tax in 1981–82; by 1989–90 this had declined to less than 16 percent. Thatcher's view was that if government took less from the people, individuals could decide for themselves what services and benefits to purchase.

Applying the same outlook to the total economy argued for letting the market, rather than government fiat, make the key decisions. One way to do this was to divest the government of the many enterprises it owned. While Thatcher was Prime Minister three and a half dozen enterprises, such as British Telecom and British Airways, were sold to private investors.

Thatcher didn't argue that the government could abandon its economic role entirely. In contrast to the post-war consensus, however, she gave top priority to reducing inflation, even at the cost of high unemployment. Combating inflation might well require high interest rates to encourage enterprises to become more efficient and resistant to union demands for wage increases. Here again she was willing to pay the price of business failure produced by lack of cheap financing. Unemployment rose above 3 million during the 1980s. The proportion of full-time workers whose earnings were below a decent minimal living standard increased from 28 percent of the work force when she entered office to 37 percent when she left. The number of company bankruptcies each year more than tripled while she was Prime Minister, and personal ones quadrupled.

Her willingness to let the chips fall where they may carried over into the decision-making process. Corporatism was out. The government would run its affairs; business and the unions could run theirs. Consultation with vested interests, she feared, would only weaken her Government's resolve to administer harsh, but essential, remedies. Furthermore, she would not permit vested economic interests to impede the government by vetoing her remedies. Not only would the unions not be consulted, they must be brought to heel. During her decade in office, six bills were enacted to cut the unions down to size. Constraints were placed on strikes and picketing. Membership in unions became more voluntary and formal ballots, rather than the old procedures of voting by a show of hands or by voice, were required for important decisions. Nor did she flinch from seeing that these reforms were implemented, even when the result was violent clashes between unions and the police. Such a confrontational style had been unknown in British politics for a half century.

Her leadership style within the Government was similar. Instead of seeking to evolve a broadly acceptable course of action from diverse views, she proclaimed her plans and challenged associates to disagree with her, if any dared. Although she would listen to advice on occasion, she did so only if she was certain that the source was "one of us." Those who didn't share her basic views had, by definition, nothing of interest to say and could only divert her from a single-minded pursuit of the truth.

Clearly, the template created by the Attlee Government had been discarded. But was this just a particularly wide swing of the pendulum to the right or had Thatcher advanced the ratchet? Was there, as one of the groups supporting her had named itself, "No Turning back"? As you've seen, the welfare state is the one element of the postwar consensus that Thatcher altered least. Labour might complain that more should be spent on the health service, but Thatcher hadn't cut spending. Changes to the health service were aimed at greater efficiency, at introducing an element of market discipline while keeping medical care as a governmental program. This continued to be the objective of the Conservative Government after Thatcher's fall from power. Should Labour win an election, it probably could alter such policy only at the margins. Finding funds for some major expansion of the health service, or for other welfare benefits, seems impossible short of a major spurt in economic growth.

Sale of government-owned enterprises to private investors proceeded quite far under Thatcher. Therefore, the pace might have been expected to slacken even if she had not left office. Although sales have slowed under her successor, John Major, they have not been halted. The sale of the railroads, in preparation in the early 1990s, was such a major effort that even she had left it to later. Furthermore, any change in electoral fortunes that returned Labour to power would not make a major difference here either. When Thatcher started the process of privatization, Labour asserted that it would reverse the policy as soon as it returned to power. It threatened that it might not even fully reimburse investors forced to sell their shares back to the government. Little was heard of all this by the time Thatcher left office. Labour certainly wouldn't continue privatization, but it wouldn't be able to renationalize—bring under government ownership again—much either. In part, this was a matter of money. The funds needed to reacquire ownership, even if they could be generated, would be much better spent on welfare or education. On public ownership of enterprise, Thatcher indeed advanced the ratchet.

In the sphere of economic management, Major has been just as committed as Thatcher was to low inflation. His Government has been able, in fact, to obtain a lower rate than her best effort. He has remained committed to this objective even when the level of unemployment stopped falling, reversed, and began a relentless climb toward 3 million once again. Granted, a high level of unemployment did seem to bother him more than it had her. At times Thatcher almost seemed to believe that the unemployed had only themselves to blame—if only they really tried, they could find work. Major was more sensitive; those out of work were victims, and some efforts would have to be made through programs such as job training to try to help them. Given a forced choice between low inflation and low unemployment, however, he, like her, would choose the former.

A change in control of the Government certainly would change this preference. Labour would favor low unemployment. On the other hand, that party could devise no surer recipe for electoral disaster than ignoring inflation. If a return to the double-digit rate that had been common during Labour's period in power in the 1970s seemed imminent once again, the electorate would decide that it never should have risked putting that party in charge of the economy again. The Thatcher turn of the ratchet has made normal, if not entirely tolerable, a rate of unemployment far above what the postwar concensus would have considered permissible.

As you saw in Chapter 3, links between the government and interest groups weren't eliminated during Thatcher's time in office. To that extent, an element of corporatism continued. But corporatism in the form of economic summit meetings between leading Cabinet members and leaders of business organizations and unions ended. These were not revived when Thatcher left office. She had so curtailed union power that little further action was required. A return of Labour to power wouldn't transform government-union relations. Labour might repeal a bit of the trade union legislation enacted while Thatcher was Prime Minister, but wouldn't dare to return regulations to what they had been in 1979. One of the main aims of John Smith, who became Leader after Labour's defeat in the 1992 election, was to reduce union influence in the party. He understood that appearing to be beholden to the unions was a major electoral liability for Labour. For that party to reverse all that Thatcher had done to deprive the unions of a veto over public policy would only convince the electorate that it was merely the mouthpiece of vested economic interests.

Thatcher's fall from power produced an immediate change in leadership style. Public support for such a shift had developed even before her departure. As you saw in Chapter 2, people had begun to weary of her fervent intensity. A decade of seeing opponents as fools at best and malign conspirators at worse was more than enough. In contrast to the views held in the mid-1980s, by 1989, a year before her fall, most people wanted to try to meet opponents halfway rather than to stick rigidly to their own beliefs. Major was more likely, as well, to prefer the former course. He brought the emollient to remedy her abrasive personality. Cabinet meetings became more collegial; the executive became a more collective entity. Thus, in leadership style the pendulum provides a better analogy than does the ratchet.

And yet Thatcher had so conditioned expectations that the public had difficulty in adjusting to Major's style. His government seemed dogged by several serious problems and an unending sequence of minor difficulties. He seemed indecisive. When economic strains forced Britain out of the EC Exchange Rate Mechanism in September 1992, he didn't replace the Government's main financial minister, the Chancellor of the Exchequer, only to do so nine months later. When the ousted Chancellor delivered his resignation speech in the House of Commons, he complained that under Major the Conservatives too often seemed to be in Government, but not in power. This turn of phrase was widely accepted as a telling assessment.

Gallup regularly asks people in Britain whether they are satisfied with the Prime Minister. For almost all of the first half of 1992, less than 30 percent were satisfied with Major. The same had been true for Thatcher during the first half of 1990. Even worse for him, he fell in May 1992 to only 21 percent, the lowest level of satisfaction in the history of opinion polling in Britain. Thatcher often had been unpopular, but this was because she applied harsh measures. In contrast, Major was unpopular because he seemed unwilling to deal with pressing problems. He firmly committed himself to ratifying the Maastricht Treaty, indeed, argued that he had negotiated a major victory for British interests in that treaty. When a number of Conservative

MPs opposed the treaty, he complained that his small majority in the House of Commons prevented decisive action and then lapsed into a long drawn-out process of evasive actions, minor concessions, and vacuous threats. Thatcher would have beat them around the head and got on with it.

■ ■ ■

Britain in the post-Thatcher period remains a welfare state. But it is a welfare state in which everyone is much more aware of financial constraints. Not everything desirable, whether it is preventing unemployment or providing a service, can be done. And whatever is done must be carried out with such close monitoring that those in charge often appear callous or niggardly. Government in Britain, as in other countries, continues to play an important role in the economy. The expectations of what it can accomplish, however, are more limited than in the past. Choosing one mix of policies or another produces gross differences in economic outcomes but cannot fine-tune detailed results to achieve specific goals. Ownership of major enterprises didn't give the Government the anticipated ability to manage the economy, and, in any event, the bulk of those holdings have been relinquished—permanently, in all likelihood. In place of a broad economic remit and extensive consultation—indeed, policy making—with key groups, the Government now focuses on a more narrow range of concerns and maintains more modest links with such groups.

An electoral victory for the Labour party would not transform the template. What a decade of Thatcherism did was to alter the terms of debate. Just as Bill Clinton won the Presidency by arguing that he was a new-style Democrat, the Labour party can win only by convincing the electorate that it accepts the essential features of Britain's new template, not by threatening to undo all of Maggie's work. Just as Attlee and Labour advanced the ratchet in the immediate post–World War II period, Thatcher and the Conservatives did so in the 1980s. Social democracy has been replaced by the social market. Now the pendulum can swing for some decades (assuming that it hasn't become stuck to the right of center), until changing conditions once again require a new template.

Part Three

France

Great Britain

Dunkerque

Lille

Belgium

Germany

English Channel

LeHarve Rouen

Reims

Moselle

Rhin

Metz

★ Paris

Nancy

Brest

Seine

VOSGES

Rennes

Mulhouse

Nantes

Tours

Loire Orleans

Dijon

FRANCE

Switzerland

JURA

Limoges

Clermont-
Ferrand

ALPES

Atlantic Ocean

Dordogne

Bordeaux

*MASSIF
CENTRAL*

Italy

Nice

Garonne

Montpellier

Marseille

Pau

Toulouse

Sete

PYRENEES

Perpignan

CORSICA

Spain

Mediterranean Sea

Ajaccio

The hexagon that is France

.....10

The Setting of French Politics

■ GEOPHYSICAL AND SOCIOECONOMIC DIVERSITIES

Even fewer Americans know where France is than can locate Britain. Italy's distinctive shape allows most Americans (three-quarters) to find it. France is northwest (up and to the left) of Italy. Although France has the largest area of any country in Western Europe, it is considerably smaller than Texas. Not only is the country compact, but it is not divided by any mountain barriers. Navigable rivers, an extensive network of canals, and railroads provided the country with a superb system of internal communications long before there were airplanes or major highways. On the north, west, and south, France is bordered by water, and the Alps on the southeastern border and the Pyrenees on the southern provide natural divisions between it and Switzerland, Italy, and Spain. The one break in these natural boundaries occurs in the open country of the northeast. This has not produced any problem in relations with Belgium, but relations with Germany have been another matter.

The country's geophysical configuration has helped to give the French a highly developed sense of national identity; they have never been uncertain about who they were and where "the others" began. Nonetheless, identity and ease of communication have not produced either homogeneity of customs or similarity of opinions throughout the country. Significant regional differences are common. One of the principal contrasts is between the north and the south. (Does that sound like any other country?) Some people trace this difference back to the effect of the Romans in the south contrasted with the influence of Germanic tribes in the north. Instead of contrasting France north of the Loire River (which enters the Atlantic Ocean at Nantes, located just below the peninsula jutting out into the Atlantic) with that south of it, some experts contend that the "two nations" fall on each side of a line dividing the country diagonally. Such a line would run from near Le Havre in the northwest, near where the Seine enters the English Channel, to Marseille on the Mediterranean Sea in the southeast. However the dividing line is drawn, the point is that the southwest portion is largely a rural area of conservative farmers and population decline, and the northeast section is an area of large factories, modern farms, and dynamic growth.

Another frequently cited contrast is between Paris and the provinces. The use of the word *provincial* to indicate a narrow, ignorant, and unsophisticated outlook or person derives from this contrast. Paris has played a dominant role in French history, probably even more so than London has in British history. Paris monopolizes many aspects of French society—national administration, banking, industry, and intellectual life. More than one-third of all industrial and commercial profits are earned in the Paris area, and more than half of the financial transactions of French business occur there. In several important industrial and commercial sectors of the economy, Paris employs a majority of the workers. With a population of about 10 million (around 2 million within the official city limits), Paris is the model for contemporary urban life. The next largest city, Marseille, has less than a million inhabitants. Paris seems to embody all that it means to be French. Yet it is precisely the glamour, sophistication, and drive of Paris that make it seem almost a foreign country to many French people; they would tell you that the "real" France is the country away from the capital.

The typical France is the small market town. Here the hectic, hurried pace of Paris gives way to a more deliberate, less hustled lifestyle and a more tranquil and reflective outlook. This, for many of the French, is the true spirit of their people. In all of France only a half dozen cities have more than a half million people; Germany has almost twice as many cities that size, and Britain has three times as many. Thus, well over half of the British live in cities of a half million or more, but only a third of the French do.

An important element in the provincial lifestyle is an attachment to the soil. The average French peasant's (the term usually used for farmers) particular piece of land has been in the family for generations. It is regarded not just as a piece of ground, but as a family heirloom. This strong rural family tradition has been an obstacle to improving agricultural productivity. A desire to farm in the same way as previous generations did has encouraged resistance to modern agricultural techniques.

Much has changed in the last couple of decades, however. Many of the smaller, less efficient farms have been merged into larger, more productive units. The number of farms was cut in half between 1950 and 1990. As farms were merged, many peasants left the land. In 1960 more than a fifth of the French labor force was engaged in agriculture; by the early 1990s only 5 percent was. Despite this sizable decline, the proportion of the work force engaged in agriculture in France is two to three times as great as in Britain or the United States. More so than in either of those countries, farmers continue to be an occupational group of both economic and political significance.

Despite the mergers, the average French farm contains only 70 acres, compared with 300 acres as the average size in Iowa. Nearly 40 percent of French farms are smaller than 25 acres. The typical French peasant owns only about half the amount of land required to prosper in farming. As a result, many of them are disaffected and willing to engage in rather extreme direct action, such as barricading roads or participating in violent demonstrations. Although farming is little more than a subsistence activity for many peasants, agriculture as a whole is a significant element in the French economy. Abundant arable soil, a variety of climates, and adequate rainfall support a diversified agricultural sector. France is a major source of agricultural output for the European Union (EU).

Although France has a good supply of natural resources, it long remained a nation of small farmers, artisans, and shopkeepers. When Britain initiated the Industrial Revolution, France was slow to follow. The attachment to the soil hampered change, as did a conception of manufacturing as artisanship, or handcrafting. Artisans took great pride in conceiving and creating individual products. They abhorred the idea of using machines to mass-produce exactly the same item over and over again. Quality and craftsmanship were preferred over quantity and standardization. Thus, the French were slow to adopt power-driven machinery in many industries.

Furthermore, since France had achieved a balanced and prosperous economy prior to the Industrial Revolution, people saw little reason for change. Thus, during the seventeenth and eighteenth centuries, agriculture, commerce, and handicraft production were the dominant features of economic life in France. Industrious peasants helped make the country self-sufficient. Since foreign trade was not necessary, manufacturing for export could be ignored in favor of producing a few luxury goods for the domestic elite. This balance was challenged in the nineteenth century as the Industrial Revolution moved more and more countries into mass production of standardized goods for an entire population of consumers. While other countries were making major technological advances in their economies, the French resisted.

Thus, at the start of the twentieth century, appearance belied reality. France seemed to be largely self-sufficient, a comparatively rich nation maintaining a good balance between agriculture and industry. The response to increasingly advanced competition from abroad, however, was a policy of cartels, tariffs, and subsidies, rather than improved methods of production. Despite national values that seemingly stressed individualism, the economy's basic character was corporate or collective. Cartels protected industrialists from domestic competition, and high tariffs and restrictive quotas shielded them from foreign competition. Peasants demanded subsidies so that they could afford to purchase domestically produced goods, which, because of technological backwardness, were more expensive than comparable goods being mass-produced in other industrial countries. Industrial workers pressed for wage supplements and other benefits. Even well past the end of World War II, about a third of the French national budget went for direct or indirect subsidies.

French business did not operate according to classical capitalistic principles. Most businesses were relatively small, family enterprises that aimed more at perpetuating the family name than at making profits. Cutthroat competition was frowned upon, since driving a competitor out of business ruined a family. Investing capital in a new venture was unattractive because failure would denigrate the status of the family. Profits tended to be small and were used as family income rather than reinvested. Little was spent to replace obsolete equipment. The old handcraft orientation to manufacturing encouraged limited production runs. The lack of economies of scale meant high unit costs (unit costs are reduced by making large quantities of standardized items).

The result was economic stagnation. France's gross national product was only slightly higher in 1938 than it had been just prior to World War I. The country had hardly grown at all in a quarter of a century—it had merely maintained itself as a nation of villagers in a world of cities. Unproductive practices and institutions were protected from external competition. Modern industrial methods were regarded as foreign intrusions. France had tried to freeze time, to remain aloof from the real world of the twentieth century.

The effect of industrial backwardness on the occupational structure was politically significant. Industrial workers were a smaller proportion of the work force than in other European countries, and many fewer belonged to unions. On the other hand, many of those who did join were members of the Communist-dominated CGT (French acronym for General Confederation of Labor) and were likely to use what economic muscle they had for political purposes.

Failure to embrace mass production methods resulted in a large number of small businesses—France had a greater percentage of economic units involved in distribution than did any other industrialized nation. The large number of middlemen meant small profits for each. This, combined with the high unit costs of manufacturing, produced many marginal businesses. Thus, the commercial interests were just as estranged from the twentieth century as the workers were.

Although the government enjoyed some success in strengthening the economy during the 1940s and 1950s, dramatic change occurred only with the return to power of Charles de Gaulle in 1958. Tax and investment laws were reformed, trade and distribution channels and rural public utilities were improved, and scientific research and technical education were promoted. New resources, including oil, electricity, and nuclear energy, were developed. Many enterprises merged to produce more efficient units, ones more likely to utilize modern technology. Perhaps most important, de Gaulle's Fifth Republic not only provided political stability, but also eliminated the financial uncertainty and foreign-exchange crises of the past, giving business and capital greater confidence.

By the mid-1960s industrial production was twice what it had been only a decade earlier, and ten years later it was three-fourths of the way toward doubling again. When the international economy weakened in the early 1990s, growth slowed in France, just as it did most everywhere. Even so, with the British economy in recession and the German economy laboring under the strain of trying to resuscitate that of what had been East Germany, France grew more in 1992 than did either of those two countries. Unfortunately for France, this success was not sustained. GDP declined by 0.7 percent in 1993, the first instance of negative growth in nearly two decades. Prospects for 1994 were only marginally better: growth of around 1 percent was anticipated.

At least France did not have to contend with inflation. In the early 1990s the rate typically was around 2 percent. This benefit may have been purchased, however, at the cost of unemployment, which has aroused increasing concern. Even before the end of the 1980s, unemployment in France was worse than in Britain. At the start of 1991 the number out of work began to climb relentlessly; by early 1994 the unemployment rate was more than 12 percent—around 3.3 million without jobs. The problem for government was how to stimulate growth, thereby creating new jobs, without fueling inflation. Perhaps the former finance minister who became France's new Prime Minister in 1993 could devise a solution.

Like the economy, the French population has shown a period of stagnation followed by a recent spurt of growth. In 1800 France was the most populous country in Europe, having well over twice as many people as Britain. But while other countries grew in population, France expanded little. Its population in 1940 was only a couple of million more than it had been in 1860. From 1930 to 1940 the total population (not the growth rate, but the absolute numbers) actually declined.

A major cause of this stagnation was the large number of Frenchmen killed in World War I—1.5 million. In comparison, the United States, which at the time had twice as many people as France, lost 115,000. In 1870 France had as many men of military age as did Germany, but by 1940 it had only half as many. The effects of the World War I massacre and the reaction to it help explain why French military resistance to Germany collapsed so early in World War II. Furthermore, the slaughter forced France to rely on old or second-rate leaders for much of the interwar period; many of the middle-aged men who might have led the nation were dead.

After World War II, however, the birth rate began to climb, eventually leveling off in the 1960s. With a current population of about 55 million, France is comparable in size to Britain, although still considerably smaller than Germany. The period of population growth produced a disproportionately young country—nearly a third of the people were under twenty in the 1960s.

Accommodating so many young people put a considerable strain on the educational system. Any student in France who has taken the college preparatory course in secondary school and has passed the school leaving exam is entitled to attend a university; furthermore, no tuition is charged. By the late 1960s the number of university students in the Paris area alone—more than 100,000—was greater than it had been for all of France little more than twenty years earlier. At the secondary level, raising the age at which students could leave school to sixteen compounded the problem of increasing numbers of young people. The events of May 1968 showed that young people could be a significant force in national politics. Student demonstrations for more adequate educational facilities sparked a process that ultimately led to de Gaulle's resignation as President.

Religion might appear at first glance to give considerable national unity. The overwhelming majority of the population has been baptized into the Catholic Church. Few people in France are Protestants, and even fewer are Jews. For most of the French, however, Catholicism is nominal, not practicing. They tend to be Catholics only at four points in life: birth, first communion, marriage, and death. Even more important is the longstanding French tradition of anticlericalism. The revolution that created a republic was directed against the Church as much as against the monarchy. For its part, the Church opposed republican institutions throughout the nineteenth century. Finally, in 1904, the government formally separated Church and state.

This step in no way ended the significance of religious issues in French politics, especially in matters of education. About a sixth of primary and secondary school children attend Catholic schools. At the start of the 1950s, the Church managed to obtain a law providing government subsidies for Catholic schools. Continuing opposition from secular forces modified this policy before the decade ended: Catholic schools could continue to receive subsidies only if they accepted greater governmental control. Such a school could sign an "association agreement," which obligated the government to pay teachers' salaries and the other expenses of running the school, in exchange for which the school had to comply with the regulations and curricula of the nondenominational, state-operated schools. Or a school could opt for a "limited agreement," under which the government paid only the teachers' salaries and had no influence over curricula and only some control over teachers.

Virtually all of the Catholic primary schools and most of the secondary ones signed an agreement. The primary schools tended to prefer the limited agreement, and the secondary ones opted for the association agreement. Since the limited agreements were to be for a trial period only, however, the issue still had not been resolved. At the start of the 1970s, new legislation made limited agreements with primary schools permanent, but provided that those with secondary schools would lapse by the end of the decade. At that time a Catholic secondary school had either to sign an association agreement or to become entirely financially independent.

Although the Church was forced to concede to the government some measure of control over parochial education in exchange for financial assistance, it continued to operate a sizable school system of its own. The Socialist Government of the mid-1980s wanted to integrate the Catholic schools more fully into the state system. An outpouring of dissent, including a protest march of 1.5 million people in Paris, quickly caused it to drop these plans.

Thus, religion continues to affect politics in France more than in either the United States or the United Kingdom (except for Northern Ireland). Many French people remain concerned about the role of the Church in society, especially in the educational system, because of the opportunity it provides to shape basic values, which in turn can have significant effects on political attitudes and behavior. Like many other aspects of French life, religion divides more than it unifies.

Despite a strong sense of national identity, France remains a country of considerable diversity. After stagnating for many years, France in the latter part of the twentieth century entered a period of dynamic change. This development often served to sharpen contrasts that already were present.

■ HISTORICAL BACKGROUND

France was one of the first countries in Europe to develop a sense of nationhood, symbolized by the monarchy. Unlike Britain, however, France did not steadily evolve toward stable and effective parliamentary democracy. Not only did such progress occur later in France than in Britain, but French political development often was interrupted and, at times, even reversed. Moreover, political change in France was much more likely to involve violence and to disrupt fundamental political consensus. The widely shared sense of unity as a culture, a people, did not produce agreement on political institutions. As a result, in the last two centuries the basic form or type of governmental structure has been altered more than a dozen times in France.

France of the *ancien régime* (from about 1000 to 1789) was governed by a king, who wielded his powers through secretaries of state personally selected and directed by him. They, in turn, exercised their authority through a centralized bureaucratic machine, which was several centuries in the making. The *ancien régime* culminated in the reign of King Louis XIV, who, with considerable accuracy, proclaimed, "I am the State." Following his death in 1715, the system weakened because his successors lacked the leadership to give it cohesion.

A form of representative assembly, the Estates General, developed in France in the fourteenth century—about a century later than Parliament emerged in Britain. The First Estate and the Second Estate, or the clergy and the nobility, were by far the most powerful, even though they accounted for only about 5 percent of the population. The Third Estate was something of a residual category, with the bourgeoisie (the middle class) being its most important element. Again in contrast to Britain, the Estates General proved unable to constrain the power of the monarch. The assembly's irrelevance is clear from the fact that it fell into abeyance, not even meeting from 1614 to 1789.

Any limiting of royal authority was performed by *parlements.* These bodies, which had developed during the medieval period, were initially advisory. Since royal decrees were promulgated by registering them with a *parlement,* however, these bodies could expand their influence by criticizing the decree or even refusing to register it. Strong rulers would simply override such opposition, but weaker ones were forced to comply, and so *parlements* came to be regarded as guardians of liberty.

In 1788 Louis XVI decided to suspend all *parlements* and to call a meeting of the Estates General. This was a confession of defeat, signifying the end of absolute monarchy. The privileged classes, many of which had sided with the *parlements* against the king, had not considered the possibility that the Third Estate would gain leadership of the opposition to royal authority. And the Third Estate itself failed to understand that once the genie is out of the bottle, controlling it is far from easy. Within a short time constitutional struggle evolved into civil war—with a profound social revolution in the offing.

Since the French Revolution occurred little more than a decade after the American Revolution, you might think that the two conflicts were basically similar. This is not true. The leaders of both revolutions had read the same political philosophers and used very similar universal rhetoric. The American Declaration of Independence declares that "all men . . . are endowed with certain inalienable rights" including "life, liberty, and the pursuit of happiness." The French Declaration of the Rights of Man proclaims liberty, fraternity, and equality for all. The similarities end there.

The American Revolution was a colonial war for independence; the French Revolution was a civil war. Since the American colonies had enjoyed a measure of self-government under English rule, many leaders of their revolution were part of the political elite. Furthermore, the dominant social class in the colonies maintained its position after the revolution. And although the new governmental system that ultimately emerged in America was innovative, it built on the practices and structures of English government.

The French Revolution was much more far-reaching in its changes. It brought to power not only new leaders but a new social class. The bourgeoisie replaced the aristocracy. The Revolution was directed not only against the monarchy but against the Church, regarded as one of the main defenders of the existing power structure. So pervasive was the Revolution intended to be that even the calendar was transformed. The months were given new names, and instead of using the birth of Christ as a starting point, years were numbered from the time of the Revolution. Only the Communist revolution in Russia early in the twentieth century has had anything like the same impact. Throughout Europe the hopes of people struggling against oppressive monarchical regimes were raised. The ideals of the Revolution motivated progressive political forces for at least a century and, some would say, continue to do so even today. Certainly, in France itself the Revolution was a watershed event that continues to affect attitudes toward political structures.

Unfortunately, the French Revolution, unlike the English Glorious Revolution a century earlier, failed to resolve the issue of legislative-executive relations. Consensus on basic political institutions and values was not achieved. The Revolution—its values and structures—continued to divide the French for at least two centuries, some would say even today. The Revolution disappointed many of its supporters by failing to uphold its ideals. The conflict quickly degenerated into excessive violence, such as arbitrary executions. Many of those who had been among the leaders in toppling the old regime found themselves denounced as enemies of the state because they refused to support widespread extermination of opponents. Furthermore, the Revolution failed to produce a stable political order. After having enjoyed nearly eight centuries of stability under the old regime, the French had to endure a century of political turmoil. Not until 1875, with the establishment of the Third Republic, did France again have a durable political system. Although this system was intended only as a temporary compromise, which few expected to endure long, it proved to be the most durable political system that France has had from the Revolution to the present.

To return to the Revolution, at first the revolutionaries attempted to establish a constitutional monarchy. Louis XVI was unwilling, however, to accommodate himself to reality, unlike British rulers a century earlier. His constant intrigues against the constitutional government's officials as he tried to regain unlimited power soon led to his execution and the creation of a republic. The Convention, the legislative body that was the supreme organ of government, proved too weak and inexperienced to govern. (The Estates General hadn't met for over a century and a half, so who knew anything about how to operate a parliament?) Social and political dislocation rapidly reduced France to virtual anarchy. The need for order and direction soon swung the country in the opposite direction—to executive domination. From this shambles Napoleon Bonaparte, who had played a major role in directing the Republic's armed forces against the efforts of foreign monarchies to strangle the Revolution at birth, emerged preeminent. Napoleon's boundless ego could never be satisfied with halfway measures, and he continued to enlarge his powers until in 1804 he had himself declared emperor, jettisoning the Republic for the Empire.

Although it might appear that France had come full circle and was back where it had started only a decade and a half earlier, the Empire was not a triumph of the old order. Napoleon had perverted the Revolution, but he had not destroyed it. He was not from an aristocratic background and would have had no chance of rising to power had the Revolution not occurred. Furthermore, he did not reverse all of the Revolution's institutional reforms. His reconciliation of state and Church did not return Church leaders to the positions of political dominance they had formerly held. Nor did the nobility recoup its losses. And Napoleon retained the trappings of democracy. He pretended to consult the citizens, for example, through the frequent use of plebiscites. Just as many twentieth-century communist countries call themselves people's democracies despite the fact that the people have nothing to say about their countries' operation, so did Napoleon feel obliged to give lip service to democratic values. Concentrated political power could no longer be simply asserted; it had to be rationalized with popular rhetoric. More positively, Napoleon's reform of the French bureaucracy was so thorough and effective that it provided the basic structure for the country's administration down to the closing years of the twentieth century.

Military defeat ended Napoleon's rule and brought the Bourbons (the pre-Revolutionary ruling house) back to the throne. A classic phrase says that the Bourbons had learned nothing and forgotten nothing. They governed entirely as though the Revolution had never occurred. Once again, they demonstrated their inability to adapt to changed circumstances. Their high-handed rule produced another revolution—this one more moderate—in 1830. A new king, one willing to accept the position of constitutional monarch, was placed on the throne.

By now, however, revolution had come to be seen as virtually a regular part of the political process, as acceptable as elections for gaining a change in government. Thus, in 1848 unemployment and discontent in Paris combined with conflict over extension of voting rights to topple the monarchy, and once again a republic was formed. Napoleon's nephew Louis was elected president. He quickly parodied his uncle by making himself emperor in 1852 and conned 97 percent of the electorate into approving this step in a plebiscite. (By now you may be getting a sense of *déjà vu*.)

Like his uncle's, Louis Napoleon's rule was ended by military defeat, in the Franco-Prussian War in 1870. A new Republic—the third—was proclaimed to replace the Empire. The first election for the new representative body, the National Assembly, however, gave a majority of the seats to monarchists. Reacting to this and to the humiliation of surrendering in the war, the people of Paris revolted and set up their own government, the Commune. In order to avoid harsher treatment by the victorious Germans, the rest of France—that is, the official government—had to bring Paris under control. The result was the bloodiest civil war in French history; during just the last week of fighting 20,000 people were killed. (Marxists subsequently propagated the myth that the Commune was a self-conscious proletarian uprising. They still continue to honor the Communards as class martyrs.)

Although the National Assembly's main task had been to agree to peace terms with Prussia, it continued to govern France for five years and served as a constitutional convention. So deep were its divisions, however, that ultimately the National Assembly gave up on formulating a constitution and simply passed three "organic laws" that sketched out a framework for a new system of government. Much to everyone's surprise, this temporary expedient managed to last for sixty-five years. In acquiescence, rather than with purposefulness, the French managed to end a century of systemic instability. Although the *system* proved to be stable, it fell short of being an unqualified success because its *executive* wasn't stable. Prime Ministers frequently fell from power, and the partisan composition of Cabinets often was restructured.

Early in its life, the Third Republic was threatened by a right-wing coup. Conservatives believed that a republican form of government could not provide effective national leadership, and chauvinists condemned the Republic's failure to seek revenge for the 1870 defeat by Germany. Both of these groups, along with supporters of the Church and military officers, focused their hopes in the late 1880s on General Georges Boulanger, Minister of War. By advocating revenge against Germany and wider powers for the executive, he won great popularity. With financial support from those who wished to restore the monarchy, he organized the National Party. Regarding him as a threat to democracy, supporters of the Republic planned to have him arrested for conspiring to subvert the government. He fled France (which rather jeopardized his reputation as a fearless, decisive leader), was tried in absentia, and was convicted. Two years later he committed suicide in Brussels.

Boulangism is an excellent example of the man-on-horseback syndrome that often has bedeviled French politics. When we discuss political culture in Chapter 11, we will describe more fully this phenomenon of the popular military figure whose political ambitions threaten democracy. Ironically, the ultimate effect of Boulangism was to strengthen the Third Republic. The democratic politicians demonstrated that they could be decisive and strong in a time of crisis. In the end Boulanger was revealed to be so disreputable that the royalists and conservatives were discredited.

Hardly had the Boulanger affair been settled when another *cause célèbre* polarized politics and then festered for a decade. In 1894 a Jewish captain of artillery, Alfred Dreyfus, was convicted in a secret court-martial of selling military secrets to Germany. He was sentenced to life imprisonment on Devil's Island off the northern coast of South America—the most infamous penal colony until the Gulag Archipelago. Hysterical anti-Semitism swept France. Again royalists, clericals, chauvinists, and conservatives were arrayed on one side and supporters of the Republic on the other.

After a lengthy campaign, intellectuals and republicans eventually were able to establish (in 1906) that the whole case against Dreyfus was bogus—the evidence against him had been forged, and the court-martial had been conducted in a grossly unjust fashion. He was freed, given the rank of major, and awarded the Legion of Honor, one of the highest awards for civil or military service in France. Once again, the royalists and clericals were discredited. The leaders of the Republic were strengthened by gaining greater control over the military, which had continued to be the preserve of the heavily royalist upper classes.

Thus, the Third Republic had sufficient durability to survive World War I and the economic problems that beset the world in the 1930s. In fact, had France not been defeated by Germany in World War II, the Third Republic might still be the French governmental system. Following their victory in 1940, the Germans initially occupied only the northern and western parts of France. They entrusted the rest of the country to a puppet government located in Vichy, a small town in central France northwest of Lyon. As required by the surrender terms, the French Parliament voted full power to Marshal Henri Pétain, France's most illustrious hero of World War I. Hardly dashing at eighty-four, Pétain was nonetheless another man on horseback. He issued constitutional decrees giving himself full legislative and executive powers and dismissed Parliament. He required all high officials to swear personal loyalty to him rather than to the nation or the government. Thus, the Third Republic was replaced by a dictatorship.

Following the military liberation of France, the people voted overwhelmingly for a new political system rather than a revival of the Third Republic. When the popularly elected constituent assembly submitted its proposed constitution to the electorate for approval, the nation that had consistently and frequently given virtually unanimous support to anything the two Napoleons had been pleased to propose rejected it. A revised version of the constitution subsequently was approved, but by a vote of only 9 million for to 8 million against. This narrow margin was bad enough, but what made it disastrous was that another 8 million abstained. Some said that just as in the days of Caesar, all Gaul (the Romans' name for France) was divided into three parts. Throughout the Fourth Republic (as the new system was called), the supporters of Charles de Gaulle, who adamantly opposed the constitution because of its weak executive powers, taunted supporters of the regime with the fact that their political system had the approval of only 37 percent of the populace. Crippled by such a birth defect and with de Gaulle waiting in the wings to head an alternative political system, the Fourth Republic was unlikely to enjoy a long life.

To make matters worse, the Fourth Republic increasingly came to resemble the discredited Third Republic. The same executive instability, the same governmental ineffectiveness, the same dissatisfaction were soon rampant. The average life of a Cabinet during the Fourth Republic was less than six months, even shorter than it had been in the Third. During the period from 1951 to 1958, the average length of Government crises—the time from the resignation of one Government until its successor was approved—was two and a half weeks; that is, more than half a month often passed in which no one was really running the country.

Both the Third and Fourth Republics suffered from a fractionalized party system. Not only was the country divided into a number of partisan groups, but each deeply distrusted its opponents. Conservatives believed that Socialists and Communists sought a Marxist dictatorship; the left feared that the right favored a repressive, neofascist regime. Clericals expected that if anticlericals gained power, they would persecute the Church; anticlericals anticipated that clericals would install a Jesuitical regime. Even those located close to each other on the political spectrum fought savagely. A party could gain strength only by winning supporters from its political neighbors, but one's neighbors were often viewed as traitors to the cause since they did not approve wholeheartedly of all of one's policies. The electoral system, especially when it used proportional representation during the Fourth Republic, reflected these multiple political currents in the legislature, impeding agreement on anything.

Except for the Communists, political factions in the legislature were rarely cohesive. The executive branch, which was responsible to the legislature, could seldom count on consistent support, even when it supposedly commanded a majority of the members, and thus was unable to act decisively to deal with the most pressing problems. Governments remained in office by following the most cautious course, offending no one. Social forces opposed to modernizing the economy were able to veto most attempts at reform.

In January 1958 a public opinion poll asked a sample of the population, "What would you do if there were a coup?" (The fact that such a question was even asked tells you a great deal about the state of French politics at the time.) Only 4 percent declared that they would actively oppose it, and the majority responded that they would do nothing. Not surprisingly, four months later the Fourth Republic collapsed under a virtual coup. The system might have staggered on longer, but its inability to maintain the French colonial empire proved fatal. Paradoxically, the increasing prosperity of the domestic economy from 1953 to 1957 seemed to magnify the reverses in foreign policy, which were dragging France's international status downhill. Furthermore, foreign policy and imperial commitments were consuming a disproportional amount of French material and human resources.

The issue that finally toppled the Fourth Republic was conflict in Algeria. The French settlers there, numbering at least 1.5 million, were determined to resort to violence, if necessary, to overcome the apparent helplessness of the government in Paris to contain the Muslim nationalist movement in Algeria. Many professional military men were willing to support this stance; the humiliations of defeat in Indochina and withdrawal from Suez in 1956 had made them determined to draw the line somewhere. A military coup was a serious threat.

Many people in mainland France sympathized with the Algerian settlers and the army. Others cared little one way or the other about Algeria and were equally apathetic about the political system of the Fourth Republic. The government's authority was undercut; it lacked any mandate to deal decisively with those who challenged its legitimacy. The leaders of the Fourth Republic concluded that the only way to avoid a military coup and dictatorship was to summon the country's World War II hero, General Charles de Gaulle. He became the last premier of the Fourth Republic; his price for his return was the power to rule by decree for six months and to transform the constitution. About the only difference between the dictatorship of 1940 and that of 1958 was that during the latter no German soldiers were occupying the country.

Rather than let a constituent assembly (which, no doubt, would have been as politically divided and ineffective as the legislature of the Fourth Republic had been) revise the constitution, de Gaulle gave the task to a handful of his trusted supporters. When the new constitution was submitted to the people in a referendum, the French reverted to their voting behavior under the Napoleons: 80 percent voted for it, with only 15 percent abstaining. Thus, unlike the Fourth Republic, the Fifth began life with the approval of two-thirds of the electorate, apparently vindicating the Gaullists' jeers at the Fourth's lack of legitimacy.

During the next ten years, de Gaulle dominated French politics. He extracted France from the Algerian dilemma and flexed French muscles internationally by vetoing British membership in the European Economic Community (the precursor of the EC and the EU), developing a nuclear force, and gaining a measure of

détente with the Soviet Union. Then, in May 1968, the arrest of an extremist student leader mushroomed without warning into a confrontation between the government and the students, which grew to include the workers. De Gaulle rode out this storm, but (as can be seen more clearly in retrospect) his position of unquestioned authority had been undermined.

The following April, de Gaulle called a referendum on reorganizing the government so as to strengthen regional structures and to reduce the powers of the upper chamber in the legislature. As he had become fond of doing, he proclaimed that if his proposals for reform were not approved by a substantial margin, he would resign. The technique that had worked so well in previous referenda backfired: 53 percent of those voting said no. The negative vote was not so much a rejection of the substance of the proposals as it was a rebuke to de Gaulle's high-handed style of governing. Unbending as ever, de Gaulle made good his threat and resigned as President.

■　■　■

The fact that the Fifth Republic has survived for about a quarter of a century following de Gaulle's exit from power indicates a good deal of stability. The period of fundamental political turmoil that continued for nearly two centuries appears to be over. The reason that conclusion is stated so tentatively will be clearer to you after reading the next chapter's discussion of the French search for consensus from among its competing governmental traditions.

11

The Foundations of French Politics

■ THE SEARCH FOR CONSENSUS

Because of its location, France has never enjoyed Britain's luxury of being able to choose to remain aloof from European affairs. And since geography gave the French a strong sense of appropriate national boundaries, a top priority for government had to be ensuring that these were inviolable. Power had to be concentrated in order to protect France from incursions. On the other hand, because of the sharp divisions of French society, and because those who held power were often corrupt, a concern with curtailing power also developed. You saw in Chapter 10 how France has changed socially, economically, and politically in the last four decades. Fundamental political values, however, tend to change more slowly, to lag behind other shifts. To what extent, then, have traditional French values altered as well?

As geography would lead you to expect, France has been in the European political tradition. A hierarchical social structure with less mobility than in the United States has had a significant impact on the party system and voting behavior. A strong central government has been accorded a pervasive role in social and economic affairs. The power of this government has been enhanced by the absence of autonomous subnational units of government with a broad range of significant powers—France has been a unitary, not a federal, system. Within this central government, powers were allocated to form a parliamentary system—fusion of powers rather than separation of powers.

In all these ways France and Britain share the same political tradition, one differing fundamentally from the American tradition. Nonetheless, France and Britain differ in important ways and embody contrasting mixes of the various elements of the European political tradition. We stressed in Part Two on Britain the need to distinguish between democracy and constitutionalism, two concepts first discussed in the Introduction. Until gradual electoral reform enfranchised most adults early in the twentieth century, Britain practiced constitutionalism but wasn't democratic. France provides an example of the reverse combination. Its tradition has been one of democracy without constitutionalism. The French have preferred strict majoritarian democracy. Any effort to protect minorities has been regarded as an unaccept-

able constraint on the majority and, therefore, logically (always an important consideration in France) undemocratic.

The French Revolution was a civil war, not a revolt against a foreign colonial power, as was the almost contemporaneous American Revolution. The values of the First Republic, which was created by the French Revolution, were neither widely nor rapidly embraced by the people. Many of the French associated the Republic with chaos, arbitrary imprisonment, and even execution for political beliefs. The First Republic was majoritarian democracy run wild. Although the Third Republic, founded nearly a century later, could not be characterized in this way, its republicanism seemed to be typified by weak, indecisive government. Furthermore, that Republic seemed to be, and often was, antireligious. Even people who might not want a larger role for religious values in public life might well favor an end to persecution of the Church. Many who did not want a restoration of the monarchy might still desire stronger leadership. Thus republicanism became a tradition fervently supported by many in France, but vehemently opposed by many others.

Frequent changes in regime (see Figure 11–1) at the close of the eighteenth century and in the first two-thirds of the nineteenth century gave both supporters and opponents of republicanism their turn in command of France. Fundamental change in the political system always was a live option to the French, not just grandparents' nostalgic dream of the good old days. The founding of the Third Republic, which gave France the longest period of constitutional stability that it has known, occurred not because the people united in clamoring for this system, but because of a defeat in war and an unresolved competition among rival claimants for the throne.

As a result, French politics have involved not just conflict over relatively short-range policy preferences (typical of all democratic countries) but also clashes on fundamental values. Cleavages on basics were frequently interjected into debates on immediate goals. This tended to poison the political process. Political debate took on a highly ideological tone; politics became a matter of faith rather than of effectiveness. The political stakes seemed so high that dogmatism and hostility were encouraged. The main goal was not to negotiate a compromise, but to convert benighted opponents. Distrust and suspicion flourished among political opponents because each regarded the other as seeking fundamental change in the political structure.

Such values combined with an undisciplined multiparty system and a dominant legislature to produce immobile, ineffective governing. A fractionalized, unwieldy legislature prevented decisive action, and an executive beholden to the legislature was too weak to provide leadership. A classic analysis of this situation suggested that one way of cutting through the resulting stalemate was to unify society through a movement of charismatic nationalism.[1] A leader combining personal magnetism with patriotic deeds could give the various fragments of society a temporary sense of shared purpose. Both Napoleons provide good examples of such a leader. During the Third Republic such leaders did not come to power, but Boulangism

---

[1]Gabriel Almond, "Comparative Political Systems," *Journal of Politics* 18 (August 1956), pp. 391–409.

Figure 11–1
Relative Stability
(Duration in Years) of
French Regimes from
1789 to 1994

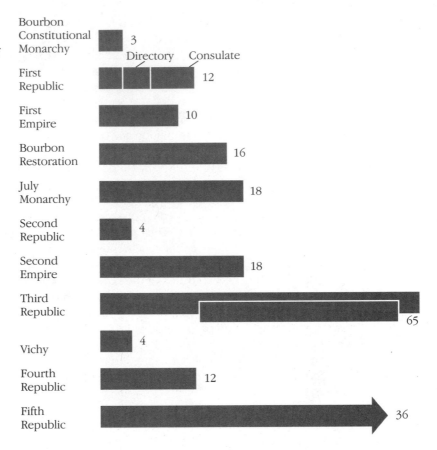

and the Presidency of MacMahon (discussed later in this chapter) seemed like this kind of threat to the republican system. Thus history gave France two competing traditions. Republicanism was preferred by supporters of democracy. They had to battle against proponents of an administrative tradition, which at times slipped into autocracy. Maintaining accountability has been a constant struggle in France.

The sixty-five years of the Third Republic did little to reconcile satisfactorily the principle of aristocratic command embodied in the administrative tradition with the principle of democratic consent at the core of republicanism. Nor was a solution worked out to the governmental counterpart of this value conflict—an equitable balance between the legislative and executive branches. A basic paradox in French political culture thwarted any resolution. Unlike Americans, French proponents of limited government didn't seek to prevent abuse by separating powers among various governmental institutions and allowing them to check and balance each other. In keeping with the French preference for majoritarian democracy, virtually all significant power was granted to the peoples' representatives in the legislature. This was accountability with a vengeance.

The problem with such a system is that a body of several hundred people, especially when it is fractionalized across a broad spectrum of political opinion, hardly is likely to be sufficiently organized to send out for coffee (or in France, wine), much less run the country decisively. Assembly government, which is what this French form of legislative dominance is known as, resulted in immobility. Thus the *system* that most French democrats preferred wound up disappointing them because it could deliver few of the social reforms that they desired. (Have you ever heard the phrase "hoist on your own petard"?) Conservative elements, who cared little that social reform was impeded, were, nonetheless, dissatisfied as well. They yearned for a strong executive, untrammeled by the legislature, to restore France to a position of international leadership and grandeur comparable to that which it had enjoyed in the days of the monarchy—a return to the administrative tradition.

So all could agree on the need for a stronger executive, whether for domestic reform or for international prominence? No, not really, because many of the progressive democrats feared that strengthening the executive would be the first step toward destroying the Republic—that it would, just as the conservatives wanted, return France to the administrative tradition. The democrats were haunted by the specter of the man on horseback (the leader who rises to power because of military exploits and whose commitment to democracy appears questionable at best). Such anxiety reveals an inconsistency in the thinking of French democrats. On the one hand, they have tended to argue that the people's will is always right. French democratic political philosophy shows little concern for minority rights, favoring instead unlimited majority rule. On the other hand, the infallible people could not be trusted to vote for a chief executive. Popular sovereignty was to be expressed solely through the legislature. Only the legislature, not even a popularly elected chief executive, was deemed the instrument of the popular will. Legislative power, therefore, should be unconstrained by any constitutional or judicial limits.

French democrats distrusted popularly elected executives because they feared such leaders would attempt to subvert the democratic system, as both Napoleons did. The people, whose will is always right, would fail to perceive the danger of a charismatic leader; they would be taken in by the glamour of a famous name and would elect a man who would destroy the Republic. Accountability had to run to the legislature, not to electorate.

Thus, French democrats traditionally preferred an executive beholden to the legislature. Only such an arrangement could ensure the survival of democracy, keeping France in the republican tradition. But they thereby not only condemned themselves to a system usually too weak to implement the reform policies they desired, but also made democracy less attractive to conservatives because of such a system's inability to enhance France's prestige and status internationally. In the name of defending republicanism, French democrats managed primarily to undercut it.

Surely the sixty-five years of the Third Republic would seem to be sufficient to lay many of these conflicts to rest. But the Vichy regime, its successor, stirred up traditional fears, causing the embers to burst into flame. True, Vichy was the progeny of military defeat. But because it provided for a strong executive and gave a prominent place to religious values, many French people were happy to support it as an improvement over the Third Republic. French democrats had fresh evidence that the battle for republicanism required eternal vigilance.

After liberation from Nazi control France did return to the republican tradition. The vulnerability of democratic institutions was demonstrated once more, however, in little more than a decade by the manner of de Gaulle's return to power in 1958. To democrats, he seemed another classic example of the man on horseback. The legitimacy of such fears appeared to be proved four years later, when de Gaulle unconstitutionally amended his own constitution to provide for direct election of the President (de Gaulle, himself, of course). Traditional republicans vigorously opposed this change, not so much because of its substance but because of what it symbolized—directly elected executives were a threat to democracy.

The ensuing third of a century, however, has not provided any additional events to arouse the anxieties of French republicans. Though perhaps a bit wary, they have come to terms with a powerful elected executive. One of the factors contributing to the failure of President Valéry Giscard d'Estaing (pronounced "jesch-car des-stang") to be reelected in 1981 may well have been the monarchical airs that he increasingly seemed to assume, yet no one regarded him or his predecessor, Georges Pompidou, as a threat to democracy. The next President, François Mitterrand, reduced some of the grandeur of the office, though he, too, at times seemed rather like an aloof constitutional monarch. Despite the complaints that he and fellow socialists had voiced about de Gaulle's constitution, he certainly did not dismantle the office in the name of a return to true republican values. Were it not for the many past examples of concerns seeming to have dissipated only to prove to have been merely dormant, one might argue that France under the Fifth Republic truly has resolved these value conflicts.

Although some progress has been made in achieving consensus on basic political values, France remains more divided than most democracies. The Fifth Republic seems to have reconciled the mainstream political right to the political and social order. As for the extreme right (which still can mobilize a not inconsiderable minority of voters), its fire is directed more at the current leaders and their policies than at the political system itself. Thus, the right end of the political spectrum no longer is a source of intransigent opposition to the Republic.

At the other end of the spectrum, the far left is as alienated as ever. On the other hand, its numbers are fewer by far than those of the extreme right. Nonetheless, much of the working class is only partially integrated into French society; many of them do not accept capitalism or the existing political institutions. On nine separate occasions from 1976 through 1980, residents of EC countries were asked by opinion pollsters to choose from among three statements: one, a revolutionary option; another, a reformist one; and another, one in favor of the status quo. The proportion of French respondents selecting the option "The entire way our society is organised must be radically changed by revolutionary action" was highest eight times (once Italy was first).[2] Although the proportion of the French favoring this option was never large—it ranged from 8 to 15 percent—it was sub-

---

[2]Norman Webb and Robert Wybrow, eds., *The Gallup Report* (London: Sphere Books, 1981), p. 84.

stantial. In Germany, in comparison, only 1–4 percent opted for revolutionary action. Furthermore, this disaffection in France was even more pronounced at the elite level. Among opinion leaders, the 10–15 percent of the population who discuss politics and try to persuade others to accept their views, about a fifth favored the revolutionary option.[3] Clearly, political conflicts in France have an intensity lacking in the United States or in Britain, even in the polarized politics of the Thatcher era.

The divided French responses are understandable in the context of the country's history. During the past two centuries, reforming French government toward greater democracy or protecting the existing democratic elements has often required armed domestic conflict. A willingness to resort ultimately to violence has seemed justifiable even to those who are politically progressive. Those who do not fully support the existing system can advocate extreme measures without being vulnerable to a charge that they are violating the country's democratic traditions. This is especially true when their past behavior suggests that their urgings are more rhetorical flourishes than serious proposals for action.

Although fundamental opposition to the system has declined, French political institutions still lack the widespread support common in other democracies. People in various countries were asked in 1984 which of a list of characteristics they regarded as their country's strong and weak points with respect to getting ready for the coming years. In Britain, the United States, and Germany, more than half said that the country's political institutions were a strength, but in France only a third thought this. Nearly half of the French (45 percent) regarded their political institutions as a weakness for the coming years.[4] Furthermore, many French people (often a majority) are not satisfied with the way democracy works in their country.

As you have seen, France has swung between decisive but undemocratic government (the man-on-horseback syndrome) and democratic but ineffective government (the executive instability of the Third and Fourth Republics). Part of the reason for this lies in contradictory French attitudes toward authority. On the one hand, many people see the need for authority to resolve conflicts; they want to avoid the unpleasantness of trying to deal with these on a face-to-face basis and do not feel able to handle such difficulties themselves. But, on the other hand, they fear the arbitrariness that often characterizes unrestrained authority. As long as the person in authority seems to be running things effectively, few will choose to rebel. But some will constantly complain about how oppressed they are, even when few specific orders have been issued to them.

Many polls have shown that satisfaction with the life they lead is less common among the French than among other Europeans. Such dissatisfaction can easily lead to questioning not only the effectiveness but also the legitimacy of the economic system, the educational system, and the political system.

France has a strong democratic tradition. Between the world wars, economic problems and political turmoil drove Germany and Italy from democratic to author-

---

[3]Ibid., p. 83.
[4]*Gallup Political Index*, Report No. 285 (May 1984), p. 39.

itarian systems, but France managed to remain a democracy. Democratic values are challenged in France, however, by a competing administrative tradition—government by centralized bureaucratic authorities, stopping just short of autocracy. The Fifth Republic originated in this tradition. The task for President Mitterrand, whose formative political years occurred during a period of democratic ascendency, was to reconcile these two traditions to produce a balanced political consensus. French democrats waited in vain during his presidency, however, for any significant enhancement of the legislature's role in policy making. On the other hand, as you'll see in Chapter 16, the tradition of centralized policy implementation was modified somewhat during Mitterrand's term in office.

Reconciling competing traditions is more difficult in France than it is in Britain because British pragmatism isn't offended by sloppy compromises. The French tend to value highly critical, analytical thinking. But the rational approach can be carried too far (imagine, college professors telling you that). A nice illustration is the difficulty the French had in deciding on the final resting place of France's unknown soldier. A location associated with the Revolution would have been offensive to those who never had accepted its transformation of the political system. As for a chapel, there was no proof that the unknown soldier was even a Christian, to say nothing of being a Catholic. In England no one considered the theological implications of burying that country's unknown soldier in Westminster Abbey. At times, a bit more pragmatism and a bit less rationality would be helpful politically in France.

Nothing that we have said should make you think that the French are not proud of their country. They are intensely loyal to the nation and its culture. The problem is that, because of their attitudes toward authority and two centuries of competing political traditions, their commitment to the political system is not as strong. Although the Fifth Republic is in the administrative, rather than the more democratic republican, tradition, it has contributed more than any other regime in two centuries to producing a long-sought consensus in support of institutions that concentrate power without complete sacrifice of accountability.

■ *THE CONSTITUTIONAL TRADITIONS OF THE REPUBLICS*

Given the great variety of governmental systems that France has had since the Revolution, to speak of a single constitutional tradition is difficult. Between the Revolution and the establishment of the Third Republic, about a dozen different constitutions were tried in France. (The durability of the principal regimes is indicated in Figure 11–1.) Even though they had relatively brief lifespans, the constitutions for these systems were elaborate and detailed. The care and precision with which a constitution is drawn up, however, implies little for the system's chances of survival. Nor does experience in drafting constitutions guarantee their practicality.

The most durable of French constitutions was that for the Third Republic. Since it and the Fourth Republic (which came increasingly to resemble it) spanned three-quarters of a century and account for nearly two-fifths of France's history since the Revolution, their basic principles deserve discussion. The discussion also will help to show you how greatly the Fifth Republic departs from earlier French republican tradition.

The three organic laws that constituted the constitution of the Third Republic were passed in 1875 (the date used in Figure 11–1 for measuring the life of the system, even though a republic was declared in 1870). They were intended as a mere stopgap, necessitated by the inability of a monarchist-dominated assembly to decide which of the two available royal families should rule France. Whenever that question was sorted out, then a "real" constitution would be created.

The Law on the Organization of the Public Powers vested legislative power in a Chamber of Deputies and a Senate, provided for a symbolic, figurehead executive (the President), made ministers (the Prime Minister and Cabinet) responsible to both houses of the legislature, and provided a procedure for amending these arrangements. The Law on the Organization of the Senate set forth in greater detail the structure and powers of that body. The Law on the Relations of the Public Powers, passed some months later, sought to clarify relations between the legislature and the executive.

These laws were no more than a framework; the actual operation of the system had to be worked out in practice. The organic laws did not limit the scope of government power, except to say that the republican form of government would not be subject to amendment. (This meant little since, as already explained, France was expected to become a monarchy again once the time was ripe, and the country was used to throwing one constitution out entirely and replacing it with another.) If they agreed, the two houses of the legislature could take whatever action they wished. No court could void as unconstitutional any law they passed. With the legislative branch having this much power, formal amendment of the constitution (the three organic laws) would hardly be necessary.

The Fourth Republic's constitution was more detailed and logically organized; it sought to remedy some of the most serious shortcomings of the Third Republic, for example, the rapid turnover of Cabinets. Spur-of-the-moment votes of confidence, which had brought down so many Governments during the Third Republic, were prohibited. A cooling-off period of twenty-four hours was required. Furthermore, only the Prime Minister was permitted to place the issue of confidence on the legislature's agenda. The Cabinet was made responsible only to the lower house of the legislature and did not have to resign unless it lost a vote of confidence by an absolute majority. As a means of keeping the Government's nominal supporters in the legislature in line, the Cabinet was empowered to call new elections whenever it wished.

The problem, however, was that this power to dissolve the legislature was virtually unusable. During the Third Republic the President had had a similar power, subject to the consent of the Senate. In 1877 President MacMahon, attempting to obtain a more conservative Government, dissolved the Chamber of Deputies and called for new elections. Since at the time the Prime Minister and the Cabinet had an effective majority in the legislature, MacMahon's action was regarded by supporters of democracy as a virtual attempt at a coup; they raised a storm of protest. As a result, dissolution came to seem so antidemocratic that it never occurred again during the rest of the Third Republic. Even during the early years of the Fourth

Republic, it seemed ruled out, despite being provided for in the constitution. When it finally was done, late in the life of the Fourth Republic, it stirred up considerable controversy. Thus, for virtually all of both republics, the executive had to try to marshal a majority in the legislature without being able to resort to threatening new elections if support was not forthcoming.

The nature of the party system made the lack of this power a serious weakness. Unlike Britain, France in the Third and Fourth Republics had several major parties as well as a number of small ones, all represented in the legislature. A Cabinet could obtain majority legislative support only by including legislators from several parties. Every Cabinet was a coalition of diverse views. Disagreement among the governing parties prevented them from implementing campaign pledges, despite having control of the executive, and prevented decisive action on any issue of importance. When something had to be done, the coalition typically broke up in disagreement and recriminations, and the Government fell.

Although Cabinets were short-lived, executive instability was not as pervasive as it seemed on the surface. Certain prominent politicians managed to retain executive positions from one Cabinet to another, despite changes in the political balance of the governing parties. This element of continuity, however, did little to remedy the Cabinet's inability to act decisively on major problems.

Prime ministers were not so much strong leaders as they were brokers seeking to formulate a compromise acceptable to all the groups represented in the Cabinet. Often one or more groups in the legislature saw more advantage in voting against the Cabinet, despite the presence of some of their members in it, than in supporting it. In this way they could avoid blame for decisions that proved to be politically unpopular. At times, groups refused to support a Cabinet to which they belonged because they anticipated gaining a larger proportion of positions in the new Cabinet that would be formed if the current one fell. The legislators could play this game of political musical chairs with impunity because they did not need to fear a dissolution of the legislature followed by elections that might cost them their seats.

The Cabinet was weakened as well by the lack of other significant powers. In contrast to British practice, the French Cabinet did not control the legislature's agenda; it could not, for example, insist that its proposals be given priority. It was at the mercy of legislative committees; Cabinet bills were buried in committee or rewritten so extensively that they resembled the original proposal only faintly. Most seriously, the Cabinet could not control government finances; the legislature could increase expenditures without providing new funds to cover the greater spending—a legislative irresponsibility prohibited by British procedures.

The Third and Fourth Republics were parliamentary systems, but they clearly differed from the British form of parliamentary government. France lacked the strong executive leadership that the British Cabinet was able to provide. To distinguish between the two countries' systems, some people have termed the French system "assembly government," indicating the predominant power of the legislature; in contrast, the label "cabinet government" indicates the key role of the executive in Britain.

The drafters of the Fifth Republic's constitution sought to redress the imbalance of power between the legislature and the executive. The legislature's role in policy making was curtailed, and its ability to vote the Cabinet out of office was circumscribed. The formerly powerless symbolic head of state (the President) was made independent of the legislature and given substantial powers, especially in times of crisis. The resultant system has been a hybrid: a parliamentary system in some respects and a presidential one in others. Which alternative prevails has tended to depend on the current political situation. A cohesive legislative majority supportive of the President makes the system more presidential; when that does not exist, the system becomes rather more parliamentary. Also relevant is whether the President or the Prime Minister is the more dominant personality.

In part to cut the legislature down to size, the Fifth Republic's constitution introduced an institution previously unknown in French government. A Constitutional Council with limited powers of judicial review, in part like those of the U.S. Supreme Court, was created. We'll discuss the Constitutional Council at length in Chapter 17. The important point to note here is that the founders of the Fifth Republic were not departing from French political traditions and seeking to implement a form of constitutionalism to protect minority rights. The aim was to constrain republicanism. True, this was a form of checks and balances, but not to protect the citizen. The legislature was to be checked to prevent it from encroaching on the executive's power.

Amending the Fifth Republic's constitution is a more formal process than altering the Third's had been. The President, the Prime Minister, or members of the legislature can propose amendments. Regardless of its source, any suggested amendment must obtain the support of a majority of each house of the legislature. The proposal then goes to a referendum for ratification. If the amendment was proposed by either the President or the Prime Minister, then the President can, if he or she so desires, call a joint meeting of the two houses of the legislature instead of holding a referendum. A three-fifths majority of those voting at the joint meeting is required to ratify the amendment.

Despite these explicit provisions, the constitution was amended in 1962 in a different fashion. Whenever de Gaulle found following the rules set forth in the constitution inconvenient, even though it had been drawn up to his specifications, he felt he had personal authority to use whatever procedures he wished. De Gaulle had his Prime Minister propose amending the constitution to provide for direct election of the President. Instead of sending this proposal to the legislature, where it probably did not have sufficient support to pass, he submitted it directly to a referendum. He deemed the popular approval it received sufficient to implement the change. Strange as it sounds, therefore, the French constitution was amended unconstitutionally.

■   ■   ■

Constitutionalism—the idea that certain rules of the game must be observed and can be altered only by special procedures—is not firmly established in France. And when procedural constraints on power are ignored, obtaining widespread consensus on new institutional arrangements is difficult and time-consuming. A system that performs well will win support during those sunny days. To survive during the rainy days that all systems encounter sooner or later, however, requires a sizable balance of legitimacy in the bank. And that is what France too often has lacked, because the values and goals of conflicting forces have seemed diametrically opposed and because rationality is valued over pragmatism. Concentrated power to strengthen the nation within and without has seemed desirable, as has constraining power to prevent its abuse. But since these principles have tended to be pursued to mutual exclusion, an effective and legitimate balance between them has been missing in the French political system.

12

Channels for Individual and Group Political Activity

■ *ELECTORAL SYSTEM TRADITIONS*

Given the many changes in the French political system, you may have a hard time believing that the French have altered their electoral system even more frequently. (Be of good cheer, we are not going to discuss all of these.) Few French electoral systems have lasted more than two elections without some significant alteration in procedures. This constant tinkering with electoral procedures has occurred not because the French were striving to satisfy some idealistic abstract conception of electoral justice, the perfect way of calling power to account, but because of partisan attempts by those in power to strengthen their own position and weaken that of their major challengers.

Following World War II, the Fourth Republic instituted an electoral system of proportional representation. We will not explain the working details of proportional representation until Chapter 21 in the part on Germany, since one of several varieties of that system currently is used there. For now, you need only know that proportional representation distributes the seats in the legislature so that each party gets approximately the same share of the total membership as it received of the popular vote—30 percent of the vote yields about a third of the seats, for example.

During the Fourth Republic, however, the parties in power fiddled with the electoral system in typical fashion so as to shortchange the Communists on the left and supporters of Charles de Gaulle on the right. This strategy succeeded in preventing two groups regarded by many as threats to democracy from gaining a majority of seats in the legislature, but it did little to strengthen people's belief in the moral virtues of democracy.

A common, but mistaken, belief is that French electoral systems usually have been some form of proportional representation. In fact, France rarely employed this system prior to World War II and never did in its pure form. For only five elections between 1945 and 1958, during the Fourth Republic, of which two were for constituent assemblies, and for only one election in the Fifth Republic, in 1986, did France use proportional representation. This needs to be stressed because some political scientists have argued that proportional representation helps to produce a multiparty system and cite France as proof of this. France had several competing parties long before it adopted proportional representation. Whatever impact proportional representation has had on French politics, it did not create the multiparty system.

When de Gaulle returned to power in 1958 with a blank check to restructure the government as he wished, he decided to abolish proportional representation and to return to a procedure known as the double ballot system, which had been typical during the Third Republic. Interestingly, the leaders of the party organized to support de Gaulle did not favor such a shift. They felt that their candidates, many of whom were amateurs new to politics, who had been swept into activism by the rhetoric of national renewal associated with de Gaulle's return, would be hard-pressed to defeat the better-known career politicians of the old parties. This possibility did not bother de Gaulle because he did not want a massive victory, even by a party organized to support him; he did not wish to be beholden to anyone. His power was to rest directly on the fervent support of the people, without any intermediary to distort his mandate to rule.

With the return to the double ballot system, the French appeared to have broken away from the practice of fiddling with the electoral system for partisan advantage. For nearly the first quarter century of the Fifth Republic, the same electoral system was maintained without fundamental change.

After de Gaulle's departure from power, change in the electoral system became possible. The Socialists—having been shut out from any share in control of the Government for the entire life of the Fifth Republic—not surprisingly wanted to abolish the double ballot system, and in the campaign for the 1981 legislative elections they pledged to reintroduce proportional representation. When they unexpectedly won a landslide victory under the double ballot system, few people believed that they would get rid of it, having found that it could be as kind to them as it had been to the right-wing parties in the past. The Socialists certainly had a number of more pressing reforms to enact.

A few years later, however, the Socialists did change the electoral system to proportional representation. This was not because they felt forced to redeem their campaign pledge or because they had the slightest idealistic concern with electoral justice. Their popularity had declined to such an extent in the public opinion polls that it appeared they might win only a tenth of the seats under the double ballot system. And a properly tailored proportional representation system offered them a chance of gaining about a quarter of the seats. So for political expediency, the electoral system was switched to proportional representation for the 1986 elections. Perhaps there is some justice in the world, for the Socialists lost these elections, and a coalition of center and right-wing parties came into power. Guess what they did. If the Socialists wanted proportional representation, then it must be bad, even though it had lost the Socialists seats. The double ballot system seemed to offer the parties that had come to power even greater strength in the legislature than they had managed to obtain under proportional representation. So the electoral system became double ballot once more, and the next election, in 1988, was held using this system. Again justice prevailed. The center-and-right coalition lost the election, and the Socialists returned to power. The Socialists apparently learned the obvious lesson: fiddling with the electoral system to gain some advantage may be more costly than leaving well enough alone. They left the double ballot system in place even when it was obvious that they were headed for a rout of landslide proportions in the 1993 elections.

■ ■ ■

In summary, then, France has used the double ballot system for all of the Fifth Republic except for the legislative elections of 1986, which took place under proportional representation. Thus, the rest of this chapter will say nothing further about proportional representation and discuss only the double ballot system.

■ ELECTORAL PRACTICES

France has four types of elections for national government institutions. General elections choose all the members of the National Assembly, the lower house of the legislature. Partial elections fill some vacancies in its membership. Indirect elections select members of the Senate, the upper house of the legislature. Popular elections choose the President. This section discusses the procedures for all these elections in that order.

National Assembly Elections

Under the double ballot system, each constituency elects a single representative. A candidate must receive more than 50 percent of the votes cast to be elected. Given the number of parties in France, this usually does not occur. The high point was in 1968, when a third of the constituencies were won on the first ballot. In 1993 less than a seventh were.

In constituencies where no candidate has received an absolute majority, another election, or second ballot, is held a week later. In this election the candidate receiving the most votes is elected, regardless of whether that number is a majority. In the interval between the two ballots, candidates may drop out as parties negotiate. Parties relatively close together on the political spectrum may want to agree on a single candidate most likely to outpoll the candidate(s) of parties further away from them. Only candidates who ran in the constituency on the first ballot may appear on the second ballot. Furthermore, unless the votes a candidate received on the first ballot account for 12.5 percent of the total electorate (not just of the votes cast), he or she is barred from the second ballot.

As a result of the regulations and political maneuvering, only two candidates run for election on the second ballot in most constituencies. More than two candidates (only three in each case) stood for election in only sixteen constituencies for the second round of ballots in 1993. If the supporters of the Government (regardless of political organization) are considered as one party and those opposed to the

Government (from whatever group) as another, then France resembles a two-party system for the second ballot. The choice for electors has been simplified and is relatively clear-cut.

To some extent, the first ballot of the French double ballot system serves a function similar to that of American primary elections in determining who the candidates will be on the decisive second ballot. On the first ballot, electors vote for the party they most prefer, regardless of its chances of winning. Such behavior involves little risk because a candidate from another party that one strongly opposes cannot get elected simply by gaining the most votes; he or she can win *only* by receiving more than half of the votes. Thus, for example, if the majority of the voters in a constituency are on the left of the political spectrum, they do not need to fear that splitting their votes among three left-wing candidates will allow a united right to win with 40 percent of the vote going to its only candidate. Having ascertained on the first ballot which left-wing candidate is the most popular, the left-wing voters can unite in support of that person on the second ballot and still win the constituency. Division on the first ballot does not cost them the seat. Alternatively, if the right-wing candidate somehow manages to obtain more than half of the votes on the first ballot, then the left would have lost the election anyway and having split its vote among several candidates again makes no difference.

You could think of the double ballot system as a step beyond public opinion polls. The first ballot ascertains exactly what each party's strength is in each constituency; there is no need to take a poll to find out. Instead of a sample of the voters telling a pollster how they think they will vote, the voters actually go to the polls and vote their preferences. Thus, the parties have fairly reliable data as they plan their best strategy for the decisive second ballot. Of course, some people may vote on the second ballot who abstained on the first, and vice versa. Furthermore, the deals that party leaders negotiate among themselves cannot be imposed on their followers. For example, a Socialist candidate may get fewer votes on the first ballot than a Communist candidate and withdraw in the latter's favor, in exchange for a Communist giving way to a Socialist in a neighboring constituency. Some of the people who voted for the Socialist on the first ballot may be so hostile to communism, however, that they will vote for a center or right-wing candidate on the second ballot.

Despite these uncertainties, the parties do tend to regard the first ballot as a chance to test their relative strengths. The parties supporting the Government in 1981, for example, spoke of having "primaries," meaning that each of them offered candidates in many constituencies on the first ballot, allowing the electorate to determine which party would provide the jointly supported candidate for the second ballot.

The French electoral system differs significantly from the American and the British, but you should not assume that the distribution of seats in the legislature is proportional to the share of the vote that each party received in the election. (Remember that the double ballot system is *not* proportional representation.) In 1958, for example, about 7 million Communist and Socialist voters elected 54 members of the National Assembly, and about 4 million voters for the Gaullist Union for the New Republic returned 212. In another election ten years later, the left-wing parties got the same share of the popular vote as the Gaullists did, but obtained less than a third as many seats.

Candidates for the National Assembly must be French citizens at least twenty-three years old. They are not required to live in the constituency where they run for election. Candidates must deposit 1,000 francs (about $175), which is forfeited by those failing to win at least 5 percent of the votes cast. Each candidate must have an alternative, usually called a *suppléant*. If someone who has been elected to the National Assembly dies or resigns (as the constitution requires if a legislator is appointed to the Cabinet), the *suppléant* serves the remainder of the term.

When a seat falls vacant and the *suppléant* cannot serve for any reason, a special election is held to fill that seat. Several such elections are usually held at the same time; these are termed partial elections. Such elections cannot be held during the last year of the National Assembly's maximum term; the seat simply remains vacant until the general election occurs.

As in Britain, the legislature's term cannot go beyond five years, but may be less than that. The National Assembly can be dissolved for new elections whenever the President chooses, but at least twelve months must pass between elections. President Mitterrand, seeking to capitalize on his victory in the election for chief executive in the spring of 1981 and gain support for his Socialist party, called for legislative elections even though the maximum term of the National Assembly still had almost two years to run. This proved to be such a successful tactic that Mitterrand tried it again after his reelection in 1988, despite the fact that the National Assembly elected in 1986 had served less than half of its maximum term. This time he enjoyed only partial success; his Socialist party did regain control of the Government, but it fell short of a majority in the National Assembly.

Also as in Britain, the official campaign period is brief, lasting only about three weeks. Of course, preparations for the campaign and political maneuvering often begin weeks or months earlier. This was not the case in 1988, however. Since the legislature had more than half of its full term left, some people assumed that Mitterrand would not seek to renew it. But less than a week after he was reelected chief executive, he dissolved the legislature. Three and a half weeks later, the first of two ballots to elect legislators was held. The National Assembly elected in 1988 completed its full term. The Socialists had become so unpopular that their only hope was to delay the election as long as possible on the off chance that conditions might improve. Therefore, everyone knew months in advance when the elections would occur in 1993.

Every candidate receiving at least 5 percent of the vote is reimbursed from public funds for the cost of posters and for printing and mailing campaign material to every voter. This subsidy is intended to cover a candidate's election expenses, but additional personal funds may be spent. Scandals about party finances produced some regulations in 1990. Candidates are prohibited from spending more than about $85,000. Individuals can contribute no more than about $4,500; businesses can give no more than about $7,500. Parties are required to publish full accounts of their finances.

Television plays an important role in the campaign. Voters regard it as the most important and useful of the various media in influencing their vote. Parties and candidates are barred from buying TV time. Broadcast time is officially allocated to parties on the basis of their strength in the legislature, and no charge is made for the time each receives. The programs the parties prepare are broadcast simultaneously on radio and television during prime time on weekdays.

Poster sites also are allocated officially. The law limits candidates to a specified number of posters, not exceeding a given size, and requires that they be placed only at designated locations. Furthermore, in the six months prior to the election, little advertising is permitted.

The government maintains a list, updated annually, of eligible voters. Women in France were denied the vote until after World War II; now suffrage is universal at age eighteen. Shortly before polling day, each voter is mailed a packet containing a number of ballots. Each candidate prints his or her own ballot, although it must conform to a standard size (approximately four by six inches). Other than the names of the candidate and the *suppléant*, what is printed on a ballot varies a good deal. Some include the name of a nationally recognized party; others do not. Some include the age and occupation of the candidate and *suppléant;* others do not. A voter either takes one of these ballots along to the polling station on election day or picks up the desired one there. The voter puts the ballot of the candidate for whom he or she wishes to vote in an envelope provided by an election official and drops the envelope in a ballot box.

French elections are held on Sundays to help produce a high turnout. During much of the Fifth Republic, turnout was around 80 percent, reaching a high point of 83 percent in 1978. In 1981, however, it dropped to only 71 percent. Increased interest in 1986 brought participation back up to about "normal." But in 1988 it plummeted—less than two-thirds of the electorate went to the polls on the first ballot. This was the worst turnout in over a century and improved only slightly (to 70 percent) on the second ballot the following Sunday. The electorate participated at about the same rate in 1993. Turnout for the first ballot was 69 percent and declined by nearly 2 percentage points for the second. Interestingly, in the last decade and a half, the only election with high turnout has been the one when proportional representation was in effect. Perhaps that means of converting the vote into legislative seats made an individual's ballot seem potentially more influential.

Some people may decide whether to vote on the basis of whether an election looks close. In the United States, TV networks have been criticized for using the results of interviews with people who already have voted to project the outcome of an election before the polls have closed in all parts of the country. The complaint is that some people will decide not to vote because one party appears to have enough votes to win. The French have tried to limit this influence on voting behavior. Since 1977, French law prohibits publishing, distributing, or commenting on the results of opinion polls within one week of an election. This doesn't mean that polling is illegal during the final week. Parties or other groups may commission polls for their own use. Should they do so, however, they may not tell the public what they find out.

Senatorial Elections

For administrative purposes, France is divided into ninety-six departments. Each department is entitled to one senator, and those with a population of more than 154,000 are allocated another senator for every additional 250,000 people or fraction thereof. Senatorial candidates must be French citizens at least thirty-five years old.

Senators are elected indirectly by an electoral college in each department. This college, which meets to cast its votes, is composed of all the department's members in the national legislature, the members of the department's council (the legislative body at that level), and representatives from the local governments in the department. The total number of people in all the electoral colleges surpasses 100,000.

The French Senate, like the U.S. Senate, is a continuing body; that is, only a third of its members come up for election at any one time. French senators, however, have nine-year terms, so the process of renewing the Senate takes longer than in the United States. In departments with fewer than five senators, the electoral college uses the double ballot system. Where more senators are to be elected, proportional representation is used. Votes are cast for slates of candidates, usually drawn up by parties. Each slate is given a number of seats comparable to its share of the vote.

Membership in the electoral colleges tends to be skewed toward small towns and rural communities. That, along with the relatively slow renewal of membership and the age requirement, has tended to make the Senate more conservative than the popularly elected National Assembly.

Presidential Elections

Initially in the Fifth Republic, the President was chosen by an electoral college very similar in composition to the ones that elect the senators. As we explained in Chapter 11, in 1962 the constitution was unconstitutionally amended to provide for direct election of the President. De Gaulle insisted on this change, in part because of attempts on his life. He felt that he had sufficient personal magnetism to make the office a strong one, but no one else did. Were he to be assassinated, his successor would be unable to prevent a return to the traditionally weak executives of the Third and Fourth Republics. But, he reasoned, a President for whom a majority of the electorate had voted directly might possess sufficient popular support to resist encroachments by the legislature. De Gaulle felt no need of a popular mandate to legitimate his rule; the mere mortals who would succeed him, however, could not hope to be effective without it.

Presidential elections are supposed to occur every seven years. In practice, they have not occurred regularly because France lacks a vice-president. If the President is incapacitated temporarily, the president of the Senate acts as President of France. If the President dies, resigns, or is incapacitated permanently, the president of the Senate also acts as President, but a Presidential election must be held within fifty days. While acting as President, the president of the Senate can utilize all the normal Presidential powers, except that of calling for a referendum.

French citizens who are at least twenty-three years old may be nominated as a candidate for President. At least 500 sponsors representing at least thirty different departments must sign the nomination papers. Only members of the national legislature and the departmental councils and mayors of towns can serve as sponsors. In addition to signing up sponsors, each nominee is required to deposit about $1,800, which is forfeited if he or she fails to win at least 5 percent of the votes cast.

These rather stringent nomination procedures have done little to curtail the number of presidential candidates. Ten contested the first ballot in 1981 and nine in 1988. Most of these, of course, are fringe candidates; six lost their deposit in 1981 and four in 1988.

The formal campaign lasts only about three weeks. Each candidate receives two hours of TV time and two hours of radio time free of charge. A candidate may use this time personally or allocate it to supporters of his or her candidacy. Billboard sites are officially allocated to the candidates, and each candidate can distribute one leaflet to every voter free of charge. Each presidential candidate is limited to spending about $22 million for the first ballot; the two who contest the second ballot may spend nearly $4 million more each. All candidates can obtain up to about $1 million from the government to help pay the expenses incurred in campaigning. Those who manage to win 5 percent of the vote receive nearly $6 million.

If some candidate receives a majority of the votes cast on the first ballot, he or she is elected. If not (and this always has proved to be the case), a second ballot is used. In contrast to the procedure for legislative elections, however, the first and second ballots in Presidential elections are two weeks apart, and only two candidates can contest the second election. Normally, of course, the two are those who were first and second on the first ballot. Should either of them choose to withdraw, however, the next highest candidate on the first ballot steps in. The procedure for presidential elections ensures that even a second ballot winner will have been elected by a majority of the vote.

In the two weeks between the first and the second ballots, both candidates have another two hours of radio time and two hours of TV time. In addition, face-to-face debates between the two candidates are watched by huge TV audiences. The one in 1988 lasted for two hours.

The first presidential election under the direct vote procedure occurred in 1965, when de Gaulle's first term expired. This was the first popular election of a French President since 1848, and interest was high: 85 percent of the electorate voted. To everyone's surprise, de Gaulle did not win a majority on the first ballot, obtaining only 44 percent of the vote. His main challenger was Mitterrand, with 32 percent. On the second ballot, however, de Gaulle won easily with 55 percent to Mitterrand's 45 percent.

The resignation of de Gaulle in 1969 forced an early election. Georges Pompidou, who had served as Prime Minister for some years before falling into disfavor with de Gaulle, polled as well on the first ballot as de Gaulle had done—winning 44 percent. Since Mitterrand chose not to run, the main challenger turned out to be Alain Poher (pronounced "poo-air"), a little-known senator who, as president of the Senate, had become acting President when de Gaulle resigned. On the second ballot, Pompidou outdid his former leader, winning with 58 percent of the vote.

The next election also occurred early, since Pompidou died after only five years in office. Once again Poher became acting President, but this time he did not contest the election. Mitterrand, back in the fray, was first with 43 percent, followed by Valéry Giscard d'Estaing with almost 33 percent. Giscard had been minister of finance and economic affairs under de Gaulle and Pompidou. On the second ballot Giscard managed to pick up enough of the votes that had gone to other right-of-center candidates on the first ballot to nose out Mitterrand with 50.8 percent of the vote. The turnout—88 percent—was the highest ever recorded.

The 1981 election provided a rematch—Mitterrand (labeled by one reporter "the most experienced loser in France") against President Giscard. Again the result was close: 28 percent for Giscard and 26 percent for Mitterrand. Giscard had lost much of the freshness that had made him an attractive candidate seven years earlier. He had become increasingly aloof and seemed to take on monarchical airs, such as making a point of having himself served first at state dinners, as the Bourbon monarchs had done. His image also had been tarnished by his acceptance of a gift of diamonds from an African head of state. Giscard eventually claimed to have sold them and given the money to charity, but this appeared to have been done only after public opinion objected to his keeping them. Finally, the Government's economic austerity measures—designed to cope with inflation—were unpopular.

The decline of 17 percentage points in Mitterrand's share would seem to suggest an even greater loss of popularity. In the previous election, however, the Communists had supported Mitterrand rather than offering a candidate of their own. In 1981 a Communist candidate obtained 15 percent of the vote. Most of these votes, along with those given to minor left-wing candidates, were likely to go to Mitterrand on the second ballot, and so the result was expected to be close once again. On the second ballot Mitterrand was victorious, receiving 52 percent of the vote.

In 1988 President Mitterrand, after coyly keeping political observers and potential candidates guessing for some time, decided to seek reelection; he announced his candidacy only a month before the first ballot. Even though Giscard had announced months earlier that he would sit out this contest, the center right of the political spectrum was divided. Prime Minister Jacques Chirac (pronounced "sher´-rock") ran, as did Raymond Barre (pronounced "bar"). Chirac, who also had been Prime Minister when Giscard was President, was mayor of Paris as well. Giscard had dismissed Chirac after two years and then selected Barre to be Prime Minister. Chirac was the leader of the Gaullist party; Barre, although associated with a centrist political grouping, did not head any party. Besides these three main candidates, the only one likely to be of any significance was Jean-Marie Le Pen, leader of the extreme right National Front. The Communists were once again offering a candidate, but he was not expected to do nearly as well as their nominee had in 1981.

Mitterrand said that he had decided to seek reelection because "I want France to be united. She will not be united if she falls into the hands of intolerant spirits . . . of clans and of factions." He pictured Chirac as trying to run the country for the benefit of wealthy vested interests. Lacking in content as such an appeal might seem to be, it probably was shrewdly chosen. Opinion polls showed that the electorate regarded Mitterrand as most likely to unite and least likely to divide the country. Chirac, on the other hand, was nicknamed the "bulldozer" and was regarded as more divisive than either Mitterrand or Barre.

Mitterrand personally wrote an extremely lengthy "letter to all the French people," which appeared in many newspapers. This rather vague, bland appeal was more a discussion of goals than a detailed policy proposal. Mitterrand favored spending more on education and modernization of industry. He proposed a new tax on the extremely wealthy to help pay for minimum wages to low-income workers. In order to preclude further disputes over government ownership of enterprises, he promised that he would not seek to renationalize the businesses that Chirac's Government had sold to private investors during its two years in office. Finally, he revealed that he favored reducing the President's term of office to five years.

Chirac for the most part campaigned on the record of his Government, citing the growth in the economy and the decline in unemployment. He argued that it was time to end "cohabitation," the term used to describe the situation of the previous two years, in which the legislature and the Presidency were controlled by different political forces. Electing him President would put the center right in charge of both. He argued that if Mitterrand were reelected, the legislature should refuse to permit him to appoint a left-of-center Prime Minister. Barre, in contrast, was willing to give the benefit of the doubt to whichever Prime Minister a reelected Mitterrand chose to install.

Chirac used a series of posters, each having the same head shot of him looking agreeably determined. At the top appeared a word, such as "Enthusiasm," which varied from poster to poster. At the bottom of each was the phrase "That's Chirac." Mitterrand's posters were remarkably similar, except that his head shot looked a bit more serious. Both candidates, in fact, had a poster saying "Courage" at the top. At the bottom of Mitterrand's posters, in keeping with the theme he had articulated, were the words "France United." Barre's posters were as stodgy as his campaign. They contained text only, no graphics, and even the printing was very plain. They tried to convince people: "To Beat Mitterrand Vote Barre, The Useful Vote." Some opinion polls suggested that, although Chirac had more support than Barre, the latter would be the stronger challenger to Mitterrand on the second ballot.

Mitterrand was well ahead on the first ballot with slightly more than a third of the vote. About the same share was split by Chirac and Barre, with the former winning 20 percent and the latter 17. Le Pen did even better than many had expected (or feared), gaining more than 14 percent of the vote. If Chirac could gain all of Barre's support plus Le Pen's, he would have just enough to win the second ballot.

Barre did tell his supporters to switch to Chirac, but the two right-wing candidates hardly buried all their differences. Barre explicitly opposed any pandering to the extreme right in an effort to gain the votes of those who had supported Le Pen, but Chirac was not so forthright. Despite Chirac's rather covert wooing of the extreme right, Le Pen was disgruntled at not receiving a request for support. He told his followers that they faced "a choice between the bad and the worse" and virtually recommended abstention. As for Barre's supporters, some of them preferred Mitterrand to Chirac. As a result of Chirac's inability to mobilize the center-right vote completely, Mitterrand won handily on the second ballot with 54 percent.

Mitterrand's prolonged, but steady, progress to the Presidency is revealed in Figure 12–1. On his first try in 1965, he led de Gaulle in only twenty-four departments. De Gaulle, in addition to having strength among the middle and upper classes, had sizable support among the working class. All of Mitterrand's twenty-

Figure 12–1
Support for
Mitterrand in
Presidential
Elections

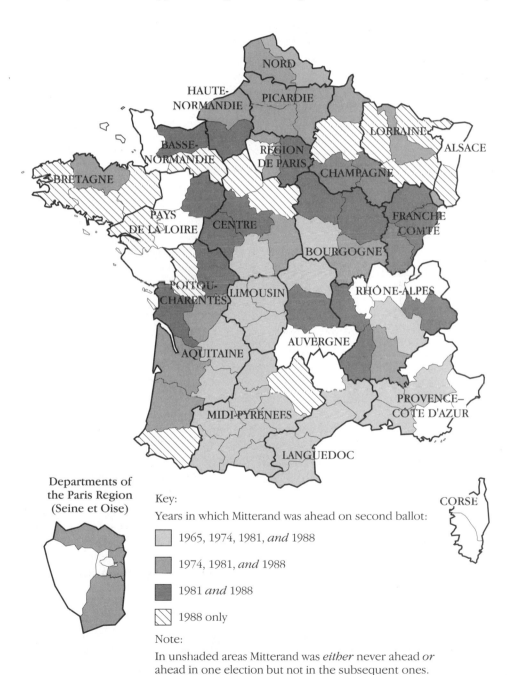

Departments of
the Paris Region
(Seine et Oise)

Key:

Years in which Mitterand was ahead on second ballot:

1965, 1974, 1981, *and* 1988

1974, 1981, *and* 1988

1981 *and* 1988

1988 only

Note:

In unshaded areas Mitterand was *either* never ahead *or* ahead in one election but not in the subsequent ones.

four departments were in the southern half of France. Although this included the area around Marseille (located on the Mediterranean in the western part of Provence–Côte d'Azur), his support tended to come from the less economically advanced sections of the country.

In 1974 Mitterrand nearly doubled his areas of strength, leading on the second ballot in forty-four departments. He had managed to expand into some of the northern industrial areas. In 1981 (his first victory) he expanded yet again. Except for Var (on the Mediterranean in Provence–Côte d'Azur), he retained all of the forty-four departments in which he had led seven years earlier and added twenty-two more, surpassing Giscard on the second ballot in sixty-five of the ninety-six departments. The new gains were mainly in areas either of Gaullist strength or where no party in the past had had a decisive lead.

Finally, in 1988 Mitterrand received the most votes on the second ballot in seventy-seven departments. He retained all but three of the departments where he had led in the 1981 election and managed to come first on the second ballot in fifteen departments where he never had done so before. In both 1981 and 1988 many of the departments where Mitterrand won the second ballot for the first time were strong Catholic areas, traditionally on the right of the political spectrum. So well had Mitterrand played the role of benign head of state, without a hint of left-wing extremism, that even these areas were willing to support him.

Turnout for presidential elections, especially on the decisive second ballot, tends to be higher than for legislative elections. The contest between two nationally known figures seems to stir more interest than does a series of contests among a number of less prominent candidates. In both 1981 and 1988, presidential and legislative elections occurred within a few weeks of each other. In both cases, turnout for the presidential elections was 10–15 percentage points higher.

▪ ▪ ▪

French elections are something of a halfway house between British and American ones. Like Britain, France does not have primary elections; the double ballot, however, does give the French voter a greater voice in candidate selection than the typical Briton has. Certainly, French electoral arrangements are quite appropriate for calling officeholders to account. The United States practiced indirect election of Senators for over half of its history, but such a system does seem rather out-of-date in the closing decade of the twentieth century. As for the office of President, the French arrangement provides for a much more direct accountability link with the voters than the American system, although the American system does work rather like direct election of the chief executive, despite the Electoral College. Whatever the differences between the three countries in detailed arrangements, the fundamental purpose of elections is equally satisfied.

▪ THE ROLE OF INTEREST GROUPS

French political philosophy, influenced by Rousseau's concept of the general will (the rather disembodied norms of society as a collectivity), regards interest groups as intruders in the relation between the citizen and the government. Thus, in France interest groups were even less likely to be regarded as a legitimate complement to electoral participation by citizens than they were in Britain.

In practice, of course, interest groups have been as active in the political process in France as they have been in other democracies. Furthermore, in a rather unexpected instance of practicality, the role of such groups was recognized formally in the constitution of the Fourth Republic, which created an economic council whose members were chosen by trade unions, business associations, and agricultural organizations. A similar institution, the Economic and Social Council (CES), was established by the constitution of the Fifth Republic. The powers of both councils were merely advisory. The CES has about 200 members, 70 percent of whom are nominated by organized interests and the rest by the Government. Although little known in France, the CES does provide an opportunity for interest groups to discover what the Government is planning, how committed to the plans it is, and how other interest groups feel about this. Thus, it formalizes consultative procedures, even if it does not have a great deal of influence.

The CES is typical of what has been termed *corporatism* (sometimes referred to as "neo-corporatism" to distinguish it from the elaborate links between government, labor, and business in Fascist Italy). You saw in the British section how part of Margaret Thatcher's break with the postwar consensus in Britain involved a rejection of corporatism in economic policy making. A government practicing corporatism seeks, by granting special favors, to get interest groups to aid it in implementing policies that could not be effectively carried out by civil servants acting alone. Although some interest groups in France do benefit from this relationship, their leaders often seem to be co-opted by the government. Whether they become more concerned with justifying governmental actions to their members than with advocating the group's interests to the government seems open to question. This apparent defection frequently has disillusioned French interest group members to the extent of alienating them from the regular political process.

A further problem is that if some interest groups are granted special access to governmental decision makers, those working in a given sector of the economy who do not belong to the favored group are denied influence in shaping public policy. Any effort to reform this situation by broadening access offends vested interests. Mitterrand's first minister of agriculture, Edith Cresson, attempted to include small, left-wing farmers' organizations (which previously had had little access) in the process of formulating agricultural policy. The large, conservative farmers' interest group that had monopolized the process was enraged. It egged on its members to stage protest demonstrations, which culminated in a mob chasing Cresson across a muddy pasture, necessitating her rescue by helicopter.

The influence of labor in France has been weakened because workers are divided among several competing and frequently mutually hostile trade union federations. The largest, the CGT, is essentially the industrial or economic arm of the Communist party, and its influence on policy has varied with the party's current political strength. Although the other union federations are also politically inclined, none is as closely related to a particular party as is the CGT. The second largest federation, the CFDT, is socialist-oriented; its main goal has been to introduce *autogestion* into French industry. This system would permit workers to elect plant managers and to formulate the production, sales, and investment plans for them to follow. The labor legislation introduced by Socialist Governments in the 1980s moved France only slightly in this direction.

Unions can, of course, influence the economy and the Government by striking. But this weapon is not very effective in France. Only one in eight French workers belongs to a union, fewer even than in the United States. As a result, unions tend to have limited funds. Prolonged strikes are unattractive. Although the one-day general work stoppages that unions have organized from time to time have received considerable press coverage and make them appear to be quite strong, in fact, they have had little impact. Toward the end of 1988, for example, the CGT encouraged strikes among various public employees, including those running the public transport system for Paris. The Government refused to cave in, the public became angry with the inconvenience, and after a couple of weeks the transport workers went back to their jobs, having gained little. Rather than demonstrating their muscle, the unions had made Prime Minister Rocard's Government appear decisive.

One of the areas in which protests may be effective is education. In 1968 student riots almost drove de Gaulle from power. One of the main concessions students won then was the right of top high-school graduates to go to whatever university they chose. Late in 1986 the Chirac Government decided to reverse this policy. No longer would these students be admitted on a first-come, first-served basis. Universities were to be permitted to impose entry conditions, which would allow them to pick and choose among applicants. Although all top students still would be guaranteed a university education, many of them would be forced to take unpopular majors in remote universities. Thousands of students rioted in the streets of Paris; about 200 students and police were injured and one student was killed. Eventually, partly because of the urging of President Mitterrand, Prime Minister Chirac withdrew the bill from the legislature and agreed that admission procedures would not be changed.

Despite such occasional evidence of success, few leaders of interest groups regard protest as an important activity for their groups. They believe that quieter methods can give their groups some influence on public policy but that relations with public officials tend to be too formal; they would prefer freer dialogue. Thus, even though the role of interest groups has progressed further toward corporatism in France than in the United States, the attitudes of most French interest group leaders are not dissimilar from those found in the more pluralistic group system of the United States.

The fractionalization of the French party system has produced a number of small, narrowly based parties that are rather difficult to distinguish from interest groups. Perhaps the best example of such an organization is the Poujadists. This movement was organized in 1953 by Pierre Poujade to defend the interests of small, marginal businesses that were being injured by economic change as France sought to modernize its economy. The most dramatic of the Poujadists' activities were their clashes with tax officials. The Poujadists objected to these officials inspecting shopkeepers' books in order to assess their taxes; they wanted the government simply to accept the shopkeepers' word, which traditionally greatly understated the amount of profit. So the Poujadists physically barred tax agents from shops and stormed tax offices. (This was a *real* taxpayers' revolt.)

At the time of the 1956 election, the Poujadists expanded their activities to offer a number of candidates for the national legislature. Thus, by one of the standard definitions of political parties (a group contesting elections), they crossed over the line from being just an interest group. Despite their electoral inexperience and short existence, they managed to poll 2.5 million votes, more than a tenth of those cast, and win fifty-two seats in the legislature. Rapidly changing economic and political conditions soon made the issue for which the Poujadists had organized less important, and the group rapidly disappeared as a political force.

Although the Poujadists as such have had no importance in the politics of the Fifth Republic, Le Pen, the extreme right-wing candidate who fared so well in the 1988 presidential election, had been a Poujadist member of the national legislature during the Fourth Republic, and much of the support he obtained in 1988 came from segments of society that had been sympathetic to the Poujadists. The key point is that in France the line between interest group and political party frequently is difficult to draw.

As we explained in Part One, governmental bodies themselves sometimes function as interest groups. Many students of American politics regard the Pentagon as a major interest group, for example. Somewhat similarly, the army in France often has exerted a major interest in the political process. The most dramatic example of its influence was the role it played in the fall of the Fourth Republic. The army reasoned that since a modernized fighting force could not cope with a guerrilla force possessing strong indigenous ties, the only way to end the conflict in Algeria was to exterminate the rebel organization by whatever means, however extreme, and replace it with a new political structure. Since, in the army's view, the nation's political leaders did not grasp the necessity of this strategy, they had to be educated.

The army was not opposed to civilian and military authorities working together but argued that, in a subversive war, the latter had to be the final judge of what policies were required. This was especially necessary in the eyes of some army officers because they believed that partisan political considerations had weakened the Government's resolve. The desire to avoid unpleasant actions was encouraging the Algerian rebels to hold out until France capitulated. Only the army, which was above political influences, could act decisively in the national interest. Elements of the army were seeking, in effect, to *be* the Government.

Although the army was instrumental in ending the Fourth Republic and bringing de Gaulle back to power, he did not implement the army's ideas—to its disillusionment and the surprise of many. When de Gaulle proposed self-determination for Algeria in 1959, a number of army officers (some retired but others still on active duty) and their sympathizers sought to prevent Algerian independence. These efforts included not only attempts to defeat the referenda held on the issue, but also open rebellion in Algeria (with the seizure of power in some areas for brief periods) and the creation of the Secret Army Organization (OAS), which aimed to overthrow de Gaulle. Despite going to the extreme of trying to assassinate de Gaulle, the dissident military officers failed to prevent Algerian independence.

Since that time the army has not seemed to play a major role in politics. On the other hand, it is interesting to note that, in contrast to Socialists in most European countries, President Mitterrand has raised no questions about nuclear weapons but has fully embraced the French independent nuclear deterrent. Nor has he curtailed

French conventional forces. In short, he has given the French military little reason to believe that elected officials are misguided or ineffective. Thus, even in the absence of a major crisis like Algeria, the military in France deserves to be recognized as a significant interest group.

■ ■ ■

Although religious groups and the military establishment are sources of important influence on policy making in both Britain and the United States, they probably have been even more significant in France. And although institutional arrangements of explicit corporatism may be more common in France, rather similar structures did exist in Britain during the 1970s, and linkages between bureaucrats and interest groups continue to be part of Britain's standard operating procedures. The role of groups in France does not differ fundamentally from that in other democracies.

.....13

Policy Alternatives

■ A MULTIPARTY SYSTEM

As you saw in Part Two on Britain, a hierarchical social structure tends to produce political parties that are more class-based than are those that operate in the United States. Continental European parties have tended to depart even further from the American experience, going beyond British parties in embodying an ideology. That is, they have derived their policies from and based their electoral appeals on references to an integrated political philosophy embodying a wide range of political, economic, and social values. This is less true in France today than it was earlier in the century. Furthermore, the extent of the emphasis on ideology varies considerably from one French party to another. Nonetheless, the lack of political consensus and the existence of sharp cleavages over basic issues such as the role of the Church have encouraged French parties to appeal to the electorate in a style that is more ideological than that of American parties.

The greater a party's emphasis on ideology, the narrower its appeal is likely to be. When a party simply stands for a particular mix of policy positions on short-range issues, people who like most of what it offers usually will be willing to accept some objectionable stands. But when the appeal is more doctrinal, support requires a greater degree of commitment, which is unlikely to be given unless the entire program is acceptable. The more ideological a party's appeal is, that is, the more a party attempts to present an integrated series of doctrines relevant to many aspects of life, the more difficult it will be for the party to secure the agreement of a large number of people.

Add to this ideological slant the tendency of French interest groups to convert themselves into parties (for example, the Poujadists discussed in Chapter 12) and the existence of a fairly rigid class structure, and you may expect the French party system to be a multiparty one. This clearly has been the case (see Figure 13–1). Since World War II, the combined share of the vote obtained by the two leading parties (ignoring electoral alliances of partisan groups) has ranged from only 40 to 60 percent. In past elections, national parties sometimes have numbered between ten and twenty, and there also have been a number of purely local or regional parties. For example, in 1978 eleven parties in addition to those already represented in the legislature qualified for free radio and TV time by running at least seventy-five candidates. The party system shows no evidence of consolidating. The average number of candidates per seat on the first ballot was 8.3 in 1988 and rose to 9.3 in 1993.

The number of parties and diverse political approaches in France is due in part to an absence of a consensus, or common understanding, concerning the basis and form of government. When political parties originated in the United States and Britain, the form of government in those two countries was not really in question. The differences that divided people into parties were primarily over the policies that government should follow. In France, on the other hand, political parties formed before there was agreement on the nature of the system of government. Differences over the question of how the state should be organized could not help but creep into party positions. Moreover, by the time the Third Republic was established, parties organized along class lines—the various socialist groupings—had appeared. And in this century the founding of the Communist party intensified the cleavage along class and ideological lines. Thus, at no time has France lacked the variety of sharp divisions that help perpetuate a multiparty system.

The governmental structures and political practices in France did little to encourage rising above these divisions. Under the system of assembly government, parties in the legislature exhibited little cohesion. Legislators could shift their votes as they pleased without reference to the partisan label under which they had been elected. Since majorities could be constructed through political maneuvering, why bother with trying to build a broad-based party combining a variety of groups? The

Figure 13–1

The Two Leading Parties' Percentage of the Vote in Legislative Elections in the Fourth and Fifth Republics

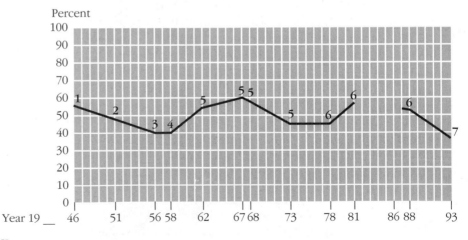

Key:
1 = Communists and Popular Republican Movement
2 = Communists and Gaullists
3 = Communists and Socialists
4 = Independents and Gaullists
5 = Gaullists and Communists
6 = Socialists and Gaullists
7 = Gaullists and Socialists

Note: Joint lists between Rally for the Republic and Union for French Democracy prevent giving a figure for 1986.

double ballot electoral system certainly did not encourage the merger of political factions into a major party since it did not penalize, as does the Anglo-American system, any failure to concentrate support. Furthermore, France, unlike the United States, had no single important national office (that is, a powerful, popularly elected chief executive), control of which could be won only by political splinters willing to coalesce into a broad, national movement.

An obvious result of a multiplicity of parties is fractionalization of the vote. The Gaullists far outstripped the success of any other political party since the end of World War II by gaining almost two-fifths of the vote in 1968, only to decline considerably in subsequent elections. In 1981 the Socialists came close to duplicating the Gaullists' 1968 achievement, but subsequently declined as well. Even the most successful parties, then, have not come close to winning a majority of the vote—to say nothing of the electorate.

This fractionalization of the electorate is reflected in the political composition of the legislature: rarely does a single party win a majority of the seats. Even during the period when de Gaulle was the dominant political force of the Fifth Republic, the party organized to support him had a majority only from 1968 to 1973. On the other side of the political spectrum, the Socialists held a majority for a similar length of time, from 1981 to 1986. Since then, no single party has controlled the legislature. Thus, for more than two-thirds of the life of the Fifth Republic, a single-party majority has been lacking.

As a result of the typical distribution of legislative strengths, the process of coalition building in France differs considerably from that in the United States. In the United States, diverse interests compete for influence within institutionalized parties prior to elections, as two broad, opposing coalitions are built up. In France, this process occurs *later* and in *another arena*. Coalitions are constructed *in the legislature* among parties *after* the election.

The multiplicity of French parties is matched by their diversity in organization and objectives. Some parties, such as the Communists, emphasize rigid adherence to elaborate doctrine; others stand for only the vaguest of principles, being little more than some leader's personal following. As for organization, some parties—for example, the Communists and, to a lesser extent, the Socialists—impose tight discipline on their members of the legislature; other political groupings allow their legislators considerable independence in voting. Some groupings in the legislature are little more than labels of convenience intended to meet the requirements for official recognition; no parties with these names exist anywhere in the country.

Another characteristic of French parties is their fluidity. New parties skyrocket into prominence, bursting on the political scene in a dazzling display of pyrotechnics, only to flicker rapidly out of sight, leaving not a trace. Such parties usually do not embody significant shifts in political opinion. Studies of French voting behavior indicate considerable stability over time, with political inclinations being passed on from one generation to the next. What changes, primarily, are the party labels. An analogy is an advertising campaign for a "new and improved" soap—the contents of the box hardly differ from what they used to be, but the box itself has been given a new appearance.

Thus, the French party system differs considerably from the British. France has had a multiplicity of parties, and many of them have not been very cohesive or tightly disciplined. The party system has served to fractionalize, rather than concentrate, power. As a result, implementation of sustained, consistent programs to deal with the country's needs has been difficult. You saw in Chapter 10 that many things have changed in the setting of French politics. Now we need to consider the crucial question of whether anything has changed in the party system. Has France moved from a fractionalized system toward one that would facilitate effective public policy making?

■ THE LEADING PARTISAN GROUPINGS

After two decades of political evolution under the Fifth Republic, four principal groups had emerged in the legislature: the Communists, the Socialists, the Giscardiens, and the Gaullists. The first two of these could be labeled the left, and the second two the right. In the 1978 legislative election, each of these four was able to gain a little more than a fifth of the vote; the remaining nearly one-fifth was fractionalized among a number of minor groups. The political fortunes of these four main groups varied considerably during the 1980s, but none of them disappeared. And only toward the end of the decade did any new group begin to mount the kind of challenge that might allow it to join the principal four (or displace one of them) as a major political force. Therefore, in discussing French parties, we will concentrate primarily on these four groups, moving across the political spectrum from left to right. The final section of this chapter will discuss the new parties that have risen to prominence in the 1990s.

Doctrines and Policies

The Communists   The French Communist Party (PCF) clings closely to basic Marxist doctrine. It has been the most hard-line Communist party operating in a Western democracy. This does not mean that it is a highly subversive, revolutionary force. The student and worker street demonstrations in 1968, for example, were organized almost totally without the help of the Communist party, which became involved only at a relatively late date and after considerable doubt and hesitation. The PCF has been extremely dogmatic in its policies and rigid in its rhetoric—none of what once was called revisionism and later was known in the Soviet Union as *perestroika* for the PCF. Its members are people who still seem to be living in the nineteenth century, who think that nothing has changed since Marx was writing in the British Museum. Furthermore, the PCF has been the Western party most loyal to Moscow, or, at least, to the Moscow of Stalin and Brezhnev.

Toward the close of the 1960s, however, the party appeared to alter its stance. In 1968 many French Communists criticized the Russian invasion of Czechoslovakia, and in 1972 the party formally condemned the political trials of the deposed Czech leaders. Although lagging far behind Communist parties elsewhere in Western Europe, the PCF ultimately seemed to come to terms with Eurocommunism. The basic thrust of this movement was that each Communist party would interpret Marx in the context of politics in its particular country, rather than being told what to do by Moscow. The significant implication was that in

Western democracies Communists would accept the democratic process and not attempt to install a dictatorship. Thus, the PCF officially dropped its goal of establishing a dictatorship of the proletariat. In 1972 the PCF agreed on a Common Program with the Socialists.

Like some "reformed" alcoholics, however, the PCF fell off the wagon. In the latter 1970s the party went back to many of its old ways. In domestic affairs it was business as usual: the PCF wanted virtually total government control of the economy, a reduction or elimination of profits, and confiscatory taxing of the rich to provide benefits for the workers. As for foreign affairs, the old pattern of loyal support of the Soviet Union combined with strong anti-American and anti-German views and condemnation of NATO returned to the fore. Unlike the Italian Communists, who condemned the Soviet Union's invasion of Afghanistan in 1979, the PCF refused to do so; in fact, its leader, Georges Marchais (pronounced "mar-shay"), defended the Russian action.

One element of the PCF's policy on defense may seem a bit surprising. The party regards France's nuclear weapons as essential to the country's security and independence. Whereas many people in the British Labour party have wished to eliminate Britain's nuclear forces unilaterally (get rid of them without demanding any similar response from other nuclear powers), the French in the PCF, a party much further to the left than is British Labour, would be horrified by any suggestion that their country should implement such a policy. (In France, virtually everyone is a Gaullist on nuclear weapons, and members of the PCF are no exception.)

What did a party like this do when communism collapsed in Eastern Europe and began to transform itself in the Soviet Union? For starters, its leader, Marchais, claimed that the PCF had been "duped" by Soviet and Eastern European Communist leaders about the achievements of communism. On television he admitted that the programs implemented in Eastern Europe had "clearly not succeeded." You can say that again, Georges!

In the 1992 election campaign the PCF took a staunch nationalistic position. It continued to inveigh against the Maastricht Treaty, which had been ratified by France the preceding year. It denounced the reforms of the EC's Common Agricultural Policy (CAP) and the tentative agreement reached between the United States and the EC in the General Agreement on Tariffs and Trade (GATT) negotiations as sellouts of the French farmers (the proletariat doesn't just work in factories). The party's position on CAP and GATT certainly wasn't unique—every party banged that drum during the campaign. The PCF also advocated controls on the export of capital in order to have more money available for domestic investment. It also wanted the standard work week to be reduced to thirty-five hours without any reduction in pay as a means of creating new jobs and lowering unemployment.

The Socialists   For much of the postwar period, the French Socialists' rhetoric was further to the left than was that of either the German Socialists or the British Labour party. Party documents often talked of class struggle and even revolution, saying that the Socialists aimed to replace capitalism, not reform it. The Common Program with the Communists in 1972 included an extensive plan for taking private enterprise into government ownership. In keeping with long tradition, the

Socialists wanted to eliminate Catholic schools so that all education would be secular. In practice, however, the Socialist party (PS) is much more social democratic than Marxist. The PS accepts the mixed economy; its main concern is to ensure that sufficient welfare programs are available, along with some redistribution of wealth to aid the lower middle class and the workers.

When the PS won majority control of the legislature in 1981, it greatly expanded government ownership; almost all private banks, steel producers, a major armaments firm, and several French multinational corporations were nationalized. Seeking to end the recession and reduce unemployment, the Socialist Government increased public spending by about 25 percent, even though this produced an unprecedented deficit. This attempt to reflate the economy produced serious problems. Although the rate of inflation was declining in the rest of the EC, it continued to grow in France. The large deficit in France's international trade forced the Government to devalue the franc three times. After about only a year in office, the Socialists had to resort to *rigueur*, or austerity measures. These measures included a four-month freeze on wages and prices. That a Socialist Government would reverse its policies in this way, despite strong dissent from the trade unions, is remarkable.

Other actions of the Socialist Government included reducing the age for retirement to sixty and raising pensions, cutting the standard work week to thirty-nine hours, requiring a fifth week of paid vacation for workers, and imposing a new tax on those having great wealth. As for social affairs, laws discriminating against homosexuals were reformed and the death penalty was abolished (France was still using the guillotine until then). The Socialist Government's policies certainly could be called liberal but were scarcely Marxist extremism.

The present Socialist party was founded by François Mitterrand, but he did not automatically control it. He typically had the support of the party's largest *current*, the term used for the three or four factions into which it was divided. Another current, one taking a social democratic position, has been led by Michel Rocard (pronounced "row-car"). Rocard, who has the image of a technocratic intellectual, incurred Mitterrand's displeasure by indicating a desire to be the Socialist candidate for President in 1981. Nonetheless, Mitterrand made him Prime Minister when the PS emerged as the largest party in the 1988 legislative elections. Whether this was in recognition of Rocard's strength within the PS or in the hope that a difficult assignment would cause him to fail is uncertain; Mitterrand is one of the most devious and inscrutable of French politicians.

Mitterrand's advanced age and poor health guaranteed that he would not run for President again in 1995. Therefore, at the start of the 1990s, the various currents in the PS were jockeying for position, each trying to get its particular leader well placed to be designated the Socialist candidate in that election. So divided was the party that it appeared that its national convention would have to adjourn its meeting in the spring of 1990 without the traditional agreed-upon policy statement. Only Mitterrand's intervention from afar—he did not attend in order to maintain the appearance of Presidential aloofness from partisan squabbles—managed to smooth over the divisiveness sufficiently to get the statement passed.

Defeat appeared so inevitable in the 1993 elections that the PS campaign was half-hearted. The party could point to accomplishments during its time in power—inflation, running at about 2 percent, was at its lowest level in thirty-six years. This did little to combat the malaise caused by unemployment running at 3 million, a tenth of the work force. The remedy that the PS proposed was job sharing. Few workers, however, were attracted by the prospect of less pay for less work. Like the other parties, the PS threatened to veto the deal that the EC and the United States had worked out in the GATT negotiations.

The Giscardiens   In his pursuit of the Presidency and eventual service in that office, Valéry Giscard d'Estaing developed a political base that came to be referred to as the Giscardiens. In recent elections and in the legislature, this group has used the label Union for French Democracy (UDF). The UDF, in contrast to the PCF and the PS, is a grouping around an individual leader, rather than a movement advocating a doctrine, and an alliance of political groups, not a single party. (That's why it was ignored for the purposes of Figure 13–1.)

The largest party within the UDF is the Republican party (PR). The PR is a descendant of an economically right-wing grouping of the Fourth and early Fifth Republics. In the 1960s the organization split, with the more liberal and pro-Gaullist faction following Giscard and becoming the PR. Although supportive of Gaullist Governments, the PR sought to maintain a separate identity. It was much more in favour of European unity than were the supporters of de Gaulle and more inclined toward a legislature sufficiently strong to avoid subservience to the executive. Giscard himself also emphasized protection of civil liberties and social reforms such as easier divorce and abortion.

The other major element within the UDF has been the Center of Social Democrats (CDS). Contrary to what the name suggests, the party has nothing to do with socialism, but is what is called Christian Democrat in other European countries. This movement emerged as a major political force in Europe following World War II. The idea was to use religious values to revitalize the Continent and prevent authoritarianism from becoming dominant again. Religious parties, primarily Catholic ones, had existed in Europe long before then, but usually had been conservative and opposed to social and economic reform. The new Christian Democrats were reformers. Although anti-Marxist and opposed to doctrines of class war, they were critical of capitalism. Although these new parties usually had a Catholic orientation, they were independent of the Church and included Protestants among their supporters.

Given the tradition of anticlericalism in France, the French manifestation of this political development did not dare call itself Christian Democrat, as occurred in Italy and Germany, but selected the label Popular Republican Movement (MRP). In one of the elections immediately after World War II, the MRP managed to win more votes than any other political party in France. Its support soon dwindled, and after various factional conflicts it was reorganized in 1976 as the CDS. Following the 1988 legislative elections, the CDS tried to distance itself from the UDF. Rather than remain part of that grouping, most of the CDS, under the leadership of Pierre

Méhaignerie, sought official recognition as a separate legislative group known as the Union of the Center (UDC). The CDS remains the French party most in favor of European unity. It also favors greater decentralization of government.

Another element, not a party, within the UDF is a group linked with Raymond Barre, former Prime Minister and candidate for President in 1988. Barre has his supporters but does not head any organized party as such. An expert in economic affairs, he favors denationalization of most government-owned enterprises, cuts in spending, and an emphasis on law and order. Differences between Barre and Giscard are due more to personal career ambitions than to substantive disagreement, although the two have been on different sides of one of the most fundamental institutional issues in French politics. In 1986 Barre opposed cohabitation, arguing that Mitterrand should resign as President if the Socialists lost the 1986 legislative elections. If the right won a majority, Barre did not want any of its leaders to accept an invitation from Mitterrand to become Prime Minister, but Giscard took the opposite view. Events developed in accord with Giscard's views; the Gaullist leader Jacques Chirac was willing to become Prime Minister, serving until the Socialists returned to power in 1988.

As we noted in discussing the Presidential elections of 1988, the two sides seemed to reverse positions. Chirac favored an end to cohabitation if Mitterrand was reelected, whereas Barre adopted the more cooperative approach. A cynic might argue that Barre was hoping to be made Prime Minister or, at least, to be given a position in a new Government. Mitterrand had seemed to suggest that, were he reelected, he would try to replace Chirac with a center-left Government, including middle-of-the-road politicians as well as Socialists. But rather than trying to find a new majority in the existing legislature, Mitterrand called for new legislative elections, and Barre did not receive a position in the new Government. Rumor says that Mitterrand did offer to make him Prime Minister, but this story seems suspect. Barre had no reason to be happy with the UDF, since the PR leader François Léotard clearly favored Chirac in the 1988 Presidential elections, even though Barre was supposed to be the UDF candidate. This was a departure from loyalty that UDF chief Giscard did nothing to correct. Thus, not surprisingly, when the UDC was organized, Barre allied himself with it.

The Gaullists   The Gaullist movement has changed its name many times since the end of World War II. The current name, the Rally for the Republic (RPR), was adopted in 1976 when Chirac reorganized the movement. The Gaullists have stood for loyalty to de Gaulle more than for particular policies. Although they agreed on the need for his leadership, they were divided on exactly what role he should play. Furthermore, although they believed that France needed a national renewal, they were vague regarding the specific goals this involved and divided on the means of achieving them. They were, however, clearly united in opposing the political system of the Fourth Republic and in desiring constitutional reform so as to strengthen the executive.

The Gaullists never called themselves a political party, claiming instead to be a movement of the people. De Gaulle had only contempt for parties, believing that their petty squabbles had made France too weak to resist German attack. Thus, more than semantics is involved when the Gaullists label themselves a "rally" or a "union."

Although the sequence of this discussion puts the Gaullists furthest to the right among the mainstream political groups, they are best characterized as nationalistic rather than conservative. In France these two positions have been distinct. Nationalists frequently have been willing for a strong executive to act to improve workers' living standards. This has been regarded as a means of cementing together the various classes of the nation and thus strengthening it. The Conservative party in Britain has a similar tradition stretching back to Disraeli in the latter part of the nineteenth century.

Thus, the Gaullists have supported some economic and social reform, such as government support for housing and social services. Unlike right-of-center parties in most democracies, they have not opposed government economic intervention and at times have even regarded it as necessary to ensure that the nation has sufficient strength to possess international influence. For Gaullists, international independence (meaning lack of dependence on the United States) has meant development of the French nuclear striking force and suspicion of the EC and NATO as possible infringements on French sovereignty. As for the political system, only a strong executive and a weak legislature could ensure the decisive action and consistent policy necessary for France to have a major role in international affairs.

The UDF and the RPR formulated a joint platform for the 1993 legislative elections. This was less of a free-market document than had been their joint appeal in the 1980s. Nonetheless, the UPF (the Union for France, as their cooperative campaign was called) did propose considerable privatization of government-owned enterprises, lower taxes, and cuts in spending to reduce the deficit. A program of job creation to deal with unemployment was promised. France's central bank was to be made independent (rather like the Federal Reserve Bank in the United States) to prevent politicians from manipulating the monetary system for electoral benefit.

The UPF agreed with the Socialist Government's *franc fort* policy, a commitment to high interest rates and a refusal to devalue the franc. This meant keeping France in the European Monetary System, despite currency turmoil in the EC. Not only did the joint program support the EC on monetary matters, but it also wanted progress on an EC defense policy. Despite this support for European integration, the UPF (especially its Gaullist wing) was not about to let anyone defend French farmers more vigorously than it did. Giscard wanted to reverse the CAP reforms that the EC had agreed to months earlier, and Chirac quite simply declared that the EC–United States GATT agreement was dead and if this position caused a crisis in the EC, so be it. The UPF believed that only through such a hard-line stance could France's rural economy be preserved.

Finally, the UPF played its law-and-order card (quite frankly little more than an apparently respectable means of being racist). The aim was to crack down on immigration. Chirac, never one to mince words, promised that when the UPF won power there would be more police to track down and expel illegal immigrants. (You should not have much difficulty in thinking of another country currently stirred up about illegal aliens.)

Although the UDF and the RPR fought the 1993 campaign together, they clearly have policy differences. To briefly summarize, the UDF is more inclined to decentralize power, whereas the RPR prefers strong central government. The UDF is economically conservative, but liberal on social reform, whereas the RPR is the reverse.
Finally, the UDF is more pro-EU than is the RPR.

Party Strengths and Supporters

Having looked at the policies that the main political forces offer to the French electorate, the appeals they make for support, we now turn to discussing the response
they receive—who favors which alternatives?

The Communists   The Communist party emerged after World War II as the
largest single party in France. Its membership expanded rapidly to over a million,
and it could count on winning more than a quarter of the popular vote in elections. Most Americans are incredulous that anyone with a free choice would *want*
to vote Communist. A number of factors explain why a sizable part of the French
electorate chooses to do so. Put simply, the French do not fear or loathe communism to the extent that Americans typically do. In part, this is because France has a
tradition of voting for the revolutionary left. Historically, the left was the defender
of the institutions of the Republic; you might say that the left occupies in France a
position similar to that of the Founding Fathers in the United States. The left also
gained popularity because those who opposed it were responsible for brutally suppressing the workers' uprisings in 1848 and 1871. As the party furthest to the left,
the PCF became the beneficiary of the leftist voting tradition. Those who wished to
demonstrate how progressive they were were likely to vote for the PCF almost
automatically.

The PCF has not just sat back, however, and let support fall into its lap; it has
labored at winning additional voters. The party devotes a great deal of time and
effort to its organizational and propaganda drives. It sponsors youth groups and
discussion and protest meetings; it issues numerous publications. Going beyond
rhetoric, it has organized cooperatives to sell goods cheaply to members and provided poor tenants with legal aid to fight landlords. As a result, the PCF could usually mobilize a substantial share of any protest vote cast by those discontented with
social and economic conditions. Such voters were not necessarily convinced that
the Communists could solve their problems; they simply wished to vote for the
most vocal opponent of the system to demonstrate how greatly dissatisfied they
were.

In addition to these strengths, the PCF had the great advantage of controlling a
large segment of the trade union movement. Many workers regarded the PCF as
the working-class party, the party that wasn't afraid to stand up for them against the
bosses. Well over a third of the manual workers and about a fifth of the white-collar
workers voted Communist.

Finally, after World War II the party seemed well placed for the future because
it was more successful than any other party in winning the support of younger voters. Given all these strengths, perhaps the most significant political development of
the Fifth Republic has been the ability of the Socialists under Mitterrand to margin-

alize the PCF. (Of course, it must be admitted that Mitterrand had a good deal of help from the PCF, whose stupidity in clinging to the same old doctrines, as discussed earlier, is a classic example of a political death wish.)

The appeal of de Gaulle's nationalism to every social class, including the workers, made some inroads into Communist support at the start of the Fifth Republic, and the change in the electoral system from proportional representation to the double ballot had an even more adverse impact on the PCF's share of the seats in the legislature. Nonetheless, the party remained a major political force until the resurgence of the Socialists under Mitterrand.

In 1981 the PCF suffered its worse legislative election result since 1936, falling to well below a fifth of the vote. Worse was yet to come, as PCF support dwindled to only a tenth of the vote in the next legislative elections. Although the party managed to stop the rot in the 1988 elections, in 1993 its share declined slightly to only 9 percent of the vote. A party that once had hundreds of members in the legislature now had only twenty-four.

The Communist party's decline has been a matter not just of the loss of fringe supporters but of serious erosion of its core clientele. Now only about a fifth of manual workers vote Communist—fewer than vote for the main parties of the right—and only about a tenth of white-collar workers do. As for the youth vote, the PCF does *least* well among those under twenty-five.

Analyzing the geographical distribution of party support is a well-established scholarly tradition in France. Just as the American South was solidly Democratic for several generations, so support for one political tradition or another (whatever its current party name might be) is entrenched in particular areas of France. A word of caution, however, about interpretation of electoral maps. Since population density varies, maps showing areas of party strength make a party appealing to the urban electorate appear weaker than it actually is in the legislature. More than a quarter of all the seats in the lower house of the French legislature, for example, are concentrated in the Paris region and the two departments to its north—Picardie and Nord. If you keep that qualification in mind, electoral maps can provide insights into the nature of party appeals.

The geographical bases of PCF strength lie around Paris (but not in the city itself) and in the northern industrial areas, as you can see from Figure 13–2. A secondary area of strength lies along the Mediterranean coast and includes the major seaport of Marseille. In central France, the PCF manages to gain better than average support in departments to the north and west of the Central Massif, despite their largely rural nature. Here the party not only gains votes from poor farmers and farm workers but is able to capitalize on a tradition of leftism.

Although the PCF had lost considerable support by the late 1980s, the locations of its strength had not shifted notably. If you were to look at maps of Communist strength in the Fourth Republic, the chief difference you would see would be many more departments where the party polled at least 15 percent. As it lost support over the years, the number of departments shaded on the maps would decline. Those departments shaded in Figure 13–2, however, would have appeared as areas of considerable strength on earlier maps as well. Whatever the flux and instability of some aspects of French government and politics, other things have altered little over the years.

Figure 13-2
Communist Strength
in Recent Elections

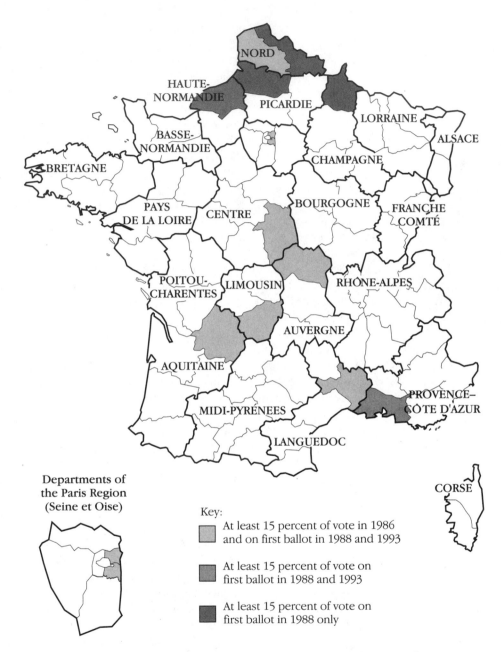

Departments of
the Paris Region
(Seine et Oise)

CORSE

Key:

☐ At least 15 percent of vote in 1986
and on first ballot in 1988 and 1993

☐ At least 15 percent of vote on
first ballot in 1988 and 1993

☐ At least 15 percent of vote on
first ballot in 1988 only

The Socialists   Immediately after World War II, the Socialists polled a quarter
of the vote. They soon declined, however, and by the close of the 1960s had only
half their former support. Although the Socialists had introduced dues-paying, card-
carrying mass party membership into French politics, their party had declined to
fewer than 80,000 members. Financial problems were so serious that the party had
difficulty maintaining an active national organization. In short, by the start of the

1970s, the Socialists appeared to be withering into irrelevancy, like other great parties of the past.

Ten years later, however, the Socialists won the second greatest triumph in French electoral history, and throughout the 1980s they were the most popular party in France. What accounted for this resurgence, which no one would have dared to predict? To a considerable extent, the answer lay in the efforts of a single person—François Mitterrand. Mitterrand, an old war-horse of French politics, had not even been a member of the Socialist party. When those who had dominated the party and run it into the ground threw in the towel, however, Mitterrand perceived an opportunity. He brought together a number of left-wing political groups to give decisive shape to a new Socialist party (PS) in 1971. His thrust was the need for unity on the left—including cooperation with the Communists—as the only means of driving de Gaulle's followers from power.

Support for the PS began to grow; perhaps its newness alone gave it some attractiveness. As Mitterrand had preached, a Common Program was agreed on between the PS and the PCF for the 1973 legislative elections. When, with the approach of the next legislative elections, the renewal of the Common Program was discussed, cooperation broke down. Mitterrand managed to pin the blame on the Communists, gambling that the PS had become sufficiently strong not to need the PCF. This tactic paid off. In 1978, for the first time since immediately after World War II, the Socialists received a greater share of the popular vote than the Communists did.

Three years later a presidential election occurred. By now Mitterrand was widely known, and, as we explained in Chapter 12, the bloom was off the Giscard Presidency. Mitterrand won, and his victory seemed to signal the end of an era. The right had controlled both the executive and legislature ever since the founding of the Fifth Republic—for more than twenty years. Sensing that France was ready for a change, Mitterrand immediately called for legislative elections. Furthermore, by surpassing the Communists in 1978, the Socialists had transformed the electoral situation. Clearly, the PS no longer was beholden to the Communists. The concern that a series of conservative Presidents had used to instill caution in the electorate had lost all validity—France *could* have reform *without* revolution. The dikes burst, and the Socialist tide surged in to inundate much of France.

The PS received 36 percent of the vote and a majority of the seats in the legislature. The surge of the party was nationwide. In 1978 the PS had won more than a quarter of the vote in only about a third of the departments. In 1981 it won more than 30 percent of the vote in *all* but a seventh of the departments and more than 35 percent in three-fifths of them. Although the Socialists lost power in 1986, two years later they were back with 35 percent of the vote, nearly as much as in their 1981 triumph.

The second term, however, proved to be a disaster. During the first few years, while Rocard served as Prime Minister, things went fairly well. Then, in 1991, Mitterrand replaced Rocard for no apparent reason other than personal animosity. Mitterrand wanted to prevent Rocard from being the only viable PS candidate for President in 1995, preferring instead Laurent Fabius, the party's secretary general, who had been Prime Minister from 1984 to 1986. Perhaps Rocard was lucky to have been removed before everything went wrong. Rising unemployment was bad enough. In addition, the Socialists were implicated in several scandals involving illegal contributions (really kickbacks for government business in some cases) from businesses. Even worse was the contamination of the blood supply with HIV virus, which resulted in several people contracting AIDS. Legal proceedings were instituted against the Government officials responsible at the time—Fabius and a few other Socialists. Although both houses of the legislature voted to remove any bar to a prosecution, the case was dismissed on a technicality. Whether the public was more outraged by the initial effort to cover up knowledge of the contamination or the subsequent escape from responsibility is hard to say, but the Socialists were discredited.

Less than a month before the election, in the midst of the campaign, Rocard in effect wrote off the PS and proclaimed the need for a "big bang" that would create a new political universe after the election. There would have to be a new center-left movement combining socialists, ecologists, and communists (led by guess who?). Furthermore, Rocard asserted that much of the PS's electoral weakness was due to Mitterrand's unpopularity. Even those inclined to accept much of his diagnosis and remedy thought that the closing stages of an election campaign were not the appropriate time for presenting them.

Little wonder that the PS was buried under an avalanche. Its support was cut in half, to only 18 percent. Given the vagaries of the French electoral system, this earned the party only fifty-three seats, less than a tenth of the National Assembly's membership and only about a fifth of what it had held prior to the election.

Historically, the Socialists were the party of the workers. But once their left wing broke away to form the Communist party after World War I, their support among voters of this class declined. As part of the governing coalition during much of the Fourth Republic, the Socialists were unable to compete effectively with the Communists for the vote of disaffected workers. With the resurgence of the PS, however, this changed. The PS has outstripped the PCF among manual workers, recently obtaining about a third of their votes. Among white-collar workers, the source of the PS's greatest support, nearly four times as many vote Socialist as vote Communist. Support for the PS is not limited to workers. About a third of those in professions or with careers as top managers vote Socialist, as do about a fifth of farmers. The PS is most popular with younger voters; about two-fifths of those under thirty-five vote for the party—far more than for any other party.

The success of the PS during the 1980s gave it a more nationwide distribution of support. Nonetheless, as Figure 13-3 indicates, the PS tended to have more areas of strength in the south than in the north. The party did not lack for supporters in the northeast and northwest, but its strength there was circumscribed by a long-standing tradition of strong Catholicism. As for the north, despite the decline of the Communists, the PCF still polled enough to keep some of these industrial areas from being major bastions of socialism. (Note that a higher level of support is required for shading in Figure 13–3 than in 13–2.) The Socialists have never done well in Paris and its environs—the Communists have support in areas around Paris and the right within the city itself. For many years the Socialists were the dominant force in the politics of the city of Marseille. But support for the Communists and,

Figure 13–3
Socialist Strength in
Elections in 1986 and
1988

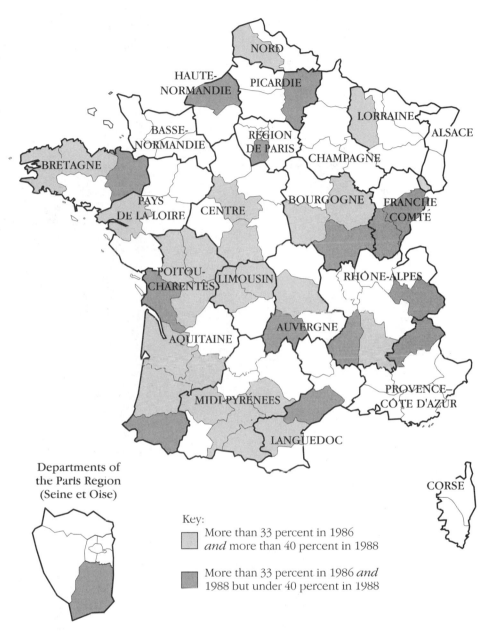

Departments of
the Paris Region
(Seine et Oise)

Key:

More than 33 percent in 1986
and more than 40 percent in 1988

More than 33 percent in 1986 *and*
1988 but under 40 percent in 1988

then, for the right-wing National Front prevented that area from being one of PS
dominance in the late 1980s.

For the most recent results, the geographical pattern remains much the same,
but the *level* is drastically different, as Figure 13–4 shows. Only seven departments
shaded for Socialist strength in Figure 13–3 are unshaded in Figure 13–4. The two
departments with the greatest strength in the earlier map missed being shaded in

Figure 13–4
Socialist Strength in
the 1993 Election

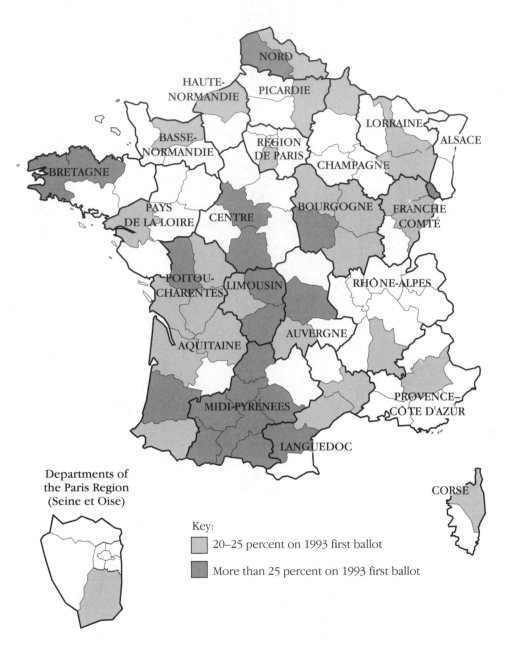

Departments of
the Paris Region
(Seine et Oise)

Key:

□ 20–25 percent on 1993 first ballot

■ More than 25 percent on 1993 first ballot

the more recent map by only 0.5 percentage points each. As for the other five departments that changed to unshaded, an average of 1.5 percentage points more Socialist support in each would have qualified them for shading.

Strictly speaking what appears in Figure 13–4 is support for the "Presidential Majority" (Nearly 90 percent of the votes cast for the Presidential Majority went to PS candidates, however, so the two maps are comparable.) For some of the instances in which a department is shaded in Figure 13–4 but not in Figure 13–3, it is because of votes for a non-Socialist ally of the PS. Northern Corsica (Corse) and three additional departments in Midi-Pyrenees represent not so much new areas of PS strength as votes for the party's splinter allies. With that qualification, the two maps suggest that the PS clientele is shrinking, rather than being transformed.

In the early 1990s the PS was back where its ancestor had been twenty years earlier—ready to be cast into the dustbin of history. Pierre Bérégovoy (pronounced "bay-ray-ga-vwah"), Prime Minister from 1992 to 1993, who had had a reputation for absolute integrity, found it all most depressing. Then shortly before the election someone leaked a story that he was being investigated for having accepted an interest-free loan of about $180,000 from a businessman later charged with insider trading and stock market fraud. Another Socialist financial scandal, said many people, just what we've come to expect from them. Although Béré, as he was called, had violated no law in accepting the loan, it looked bad. He sought support from President Mitterrand, but Mitterrand never bothered to speak out in his defense. The electoral disaster made Bérégovoy feel repudiated by his party, his mentor, and the public. So shortly after the election, he had his chauffeur drive him to a secluded spot, said that he wanted to take a stroll alone, and, when he was out of sight, shot himself. Mitterrand denounced the press for hounding an honest man to his death.

For other Socialists, presumably less depressed, it was internecine conflict as usual. Rocard got the party executive to vote Fabius out as general secretary and had himself put in charge of a major party overhaul. Clearly, he was trying to lay the groundwork for a successful run for President in 1995. Leaving the matter of personal ambition aside, Rocard does have a perceptive understanding of the basic problem facing socialism everywhere in Europe. As he has put it, "The very name of socialism was forged in a conception of the world wholly based on production and class relationships. . . . We have entered a market society where inequalities appear in many forms but where the feeling of belonging to a class, to a collective movement, is no longer perceived as reality." As you have seen, Labour's failure in Britain to perceive and adapt to these new conditions has kept the party out of office for a decade and a half. Only recently have Labour's leaders come to embrace Rocard's diagnosis. Diagnosis is only half of a solution, however; the other half is prescription. And Rocard, like British Labour, has yet to devise a convincing remedy. Mitterrand seized a moribund socialist organization in 1971 and so revitalized it in ten years that it swept to an exhilarating victory. Whether Rocard has the skill to duplicate the feat of his longtime *bête noire* will determine whether a socialist party survives in France.

The Giscardiens   As we move to the right on the political spectrum, recall that the UDF is an umbrella group, whose leading components are the PR and the CDS. Both the UDF and the PR are at least as much the creatures of Valéry Giscard d'Estaing as the PS is that of François Mitterrand. Giscard has been less successful, however, in constructing a unified major party. During his Presidency, the UDF never held a majority of the seats in the legislature; nor was it even the largest group there.

The proportional representation system used for the 1986 elections forced the right-wing parties to cooperate closely in order to have any hope of driving the Socialists from office. In about two-thirds of France's departments, the UDF and the Gaullists offered a single list of candidates (under proportional representation, a constituency elects several legislators). The switch back to the double ballot system for the 1988 elections permitted the parties greater independence. Although the UDF and the Gaullists did cooperate, especially on the second ballot, they ran competing candidates on the first ballot in virtually every department. Slightly less than a fifth of the electorate supported UDF candidates on the first ballot. When the final results were in, the PR had won about sixty seats and the CDS about fifty. Not quite another two dozen seats had gone to various minor groups within the UDF.

Cooperation between the UDF and the RPR was even closer in 1993. Joining in the Union for France (UPF), the two parties managed to agree on a single, joint candidate in about 85 percent of the constituencies. In total, the various elements in the UDF won 207 seats. In contrast to the previous election, the PR, with 104 of these seats, was far ahead of the CDS, which won 57.

Support for the UDF has been fairly diverse, since each party within the alliance has its own clientele. The PR has received votes from both the wealthy and the lower middle class. Industrialists and businesspeople (including shopkeepers), along with bankers and managers, have joined with farmers and some civil servants to back this party. The CDS has appealed primarily to the lower middle class: salaried workers, civil servants, and middle-level professionals. It also has limited support among industrial workers, attributable in part to Catholic efforts at trade union organization.

The forerunner of the PR, though not a Catholic party as such, did receive a substantial segment of the Catholic vote, and the PR has inherited some of this. Although the CDS is in the Christian Democratic tradition, the fact that it is more liberal than Catholic parties of the past has somewhat attenuated its religious support. Nonetheless, to some extent, religion is associated with voting for both the PR and the CDS. Not surprisingly Figure 13–5 shows some UDF strength in eastern and western France, traditionally heartlands of strong Catholicism.

A second area of strength for the UDF can be seen around the Central Massif, in south central France. Some of this area has personal associations with Giscard, who was reelected for a constituency in this area (the department at the top of the three shaded in Auvergne) with nearly 60 percent of the vote on the first ballot in 1988 and again with almost as large a share in 1993. Finally, an area of UDF weakness is notable: in the urban, industrial areas—the north and the Paris region—the UDF is not a significant factor.

The Gaullists   Although parties dedicated to supporting de Gaulle existed during the Fourth Republic, the current Gaullist party originated with his return to power at the start of the Fifth Republic. The party reached its peak in 1968, winning nearly two-fifths of the votes cast and three-fifths of the seats in the lower house of the legislature—a victory unprecedented in French history. With de Gaulle's withdrawal from French politics, however, the party declined.

In 1976 Jacques Chirac reorganized the movement, renaming it the Rally for the Republic (RPR). Chirac possesses boundless energy and ambition, along with a

Figure 13–5
UDF Strength in the
1988 Election

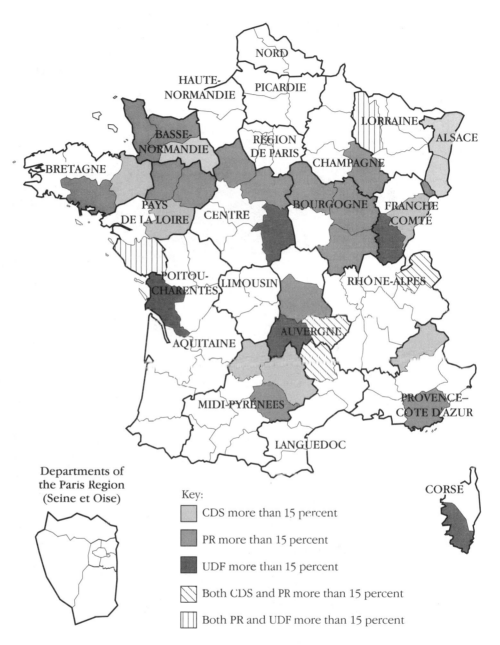

NORD

HAUTE-
NORMANDIE

PICARDIE

LORRAINE

ALSACE

BASSE-
NORMANDIE

RÉGION
DE PARIS

CHAMPAGNE

BRETAGNE

PAYS
DE LA LOIRE

CENTRE

BOURGOGNE

FRANCHE
COMTÉ

POITOU-
CHARENTES

LIMOUSIN

RHÔNE-ALPES

AQUITAINE

AUVERGNE

MIDI-PYRÉNÉES

PROVENCE–
CÔTE D'AZUR

LANGUEDOC

CORSE

Departments of
the Paris Region
(Seine et Oise)

Key:

CDS more than 15 percent

PR more than 15 percent

UDF more than 15 percent

Both CDS and PR more than 15 percent

Both PR and UDF more than 15 percent

considerable capacity to mobilize and alienate people simultaneously. He is not old enough to have been a lieutenant of de Gaulle, and many of those who did work closely with "The General" regard him as an upstart. Factional maneuverings within the RPR have been so medieval that the older generation, de Gaulle's associates, are referred to popularly as "barons." It is all rather like a big happy Carolingian royal family, each member on the lookout for the opportunity to murder the others.

Figure 13–6
RPR Strength in the
1988 Election

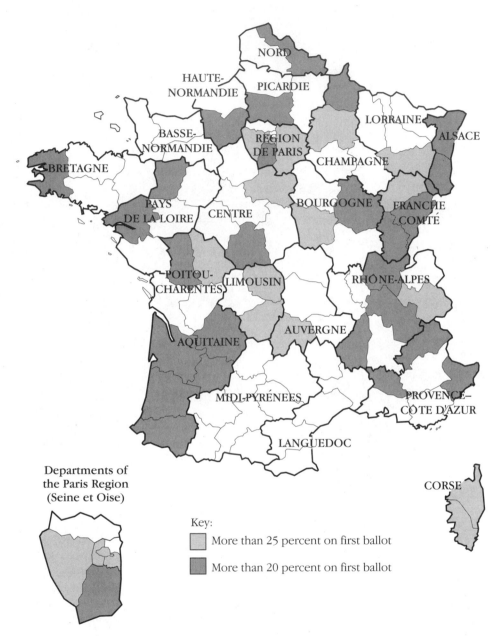

Departments of
the Paris Region
(Seine et Oise)

Key:

More than 25 percent on first ballot

More than 20 percent on first ballot

Chirac has had some success in developing the grass-roots organization of the RPR, making it a mass membership party. Many members have complained, however, about the hierarchical style of operation. In 1988 some changes were made in party organization, supposedly to increase internal democracy. As an example, more of the party's officers are elected by the members rather than appointed by the leaders.

In 1988 the RPR won about a fifth of the votes cast and obtained about a fifth of the seats in the legislature. That made it the second largest party, although it held only about half as many seats as the PS did. The RPR fared even better than the UDF did in the 1993 landslide, winning 242 seats. These two political forces each won about the same number of seats on the first ballot. The RPR, however, led in the great majority of those constituencies in which a joint candidate had not been fielded. The UDF was required by the cooperative agreement to withdraw in the RPR's favor for the second ballot. As a result, the RPR totaled about three dozen more seats than the UDF.

Support for the RPR has been concentrated among businesspeople, professionals, and farmers. In fact, it has done better among the latter than any other party. The RPR has had some working-class support, but this is relatively limited. You can see this from the geographic distribution of RPR support shown in Figure 13–6— the party does not have great strength in the northern industrial areas. This is a change from the Gaullism of the early Fifth Republic, when the movement was a national political force with substantial support in most areas and segments of society. The RPR has become less a party of the industrial north and more a party of conservative, rural France. Although the Gaullists never have been a clerical party, their emphasis on patriotic values has made them attractive to some Catholics, accounting for some strength in the east and west.

The main exception to the RPR's growing ruralism is, as Figure 13–6 reveals, its strength in the Paris region, which no doubt is related to the fact that Chirac is mayor of Paris. Chirac's legislative constituency, however, is located in south central France in the lower of the two departments that are shaded in Limousin. Like Giscard, Chirac was reelected on the first ballot in both 1988 and 1993 with around 60 percent of the vote. (It's interesting that these two rivals should represent constituencies in adjoining departments.)

Because the RPR and the UDF fielded so many joint candidates under the UPF umbrella in the 1993 election, Figure 13–7 shows the distribution of UPF support. A familiar pattern of strength in the east and west appears, along with support in some Parisian areas. Note the decreased support in the northern industrial areas and along the Mediterranean coast. What we said earlier about the pattern of support for the PCF and the PS partially explains this relative UPF weakness; further explanation is presented in the discussion of the National Front in the next section.

■ OTHER POLITICAL MOVEMENTS

After hearing about four political forces and five parties, you may feel you've had more than enough. You need to endure, however, a brief discussion of a few minor parties.

The Ecologists

France has had a Green party (*Les Verts*, meaning "The Greens") dedicated to environmental concerns for some years. Its leader is Antoine Waechter, who as a young

Figure 13–7
UPF Strength in the
1993 Election

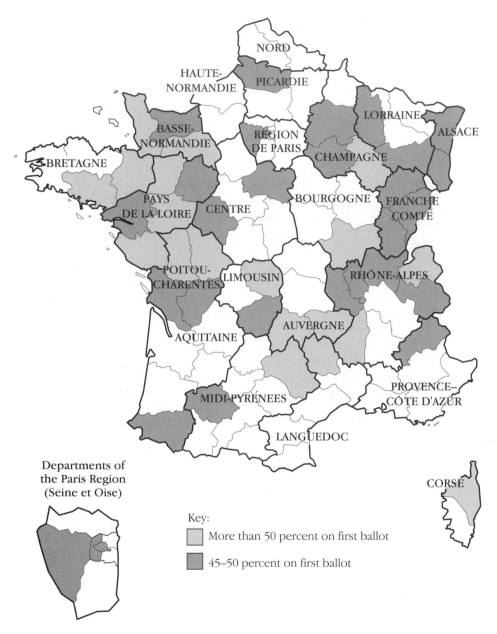

Departments of
the Paris Region
(Seine et Oise)

Key:

More than 50 percent on first ballot

45–50 percent on first ballot

man was active in the student protest demonstrations of 1968. The party has been rather far to the left on economic policy. In part because of this, President Mitterrand supported the efforts of Brice Lalonde to found another environmental-ist group. Lalonde was in the Socialist Cabinet from 1988 to 1990 but left in disgust at the Government's failure to defend the environment. Lalonde's *Génération Ecologie* (abbreviated GE and translated as "Ecology Generation") was, not to be too derogatory, a more trendy, yuppy-oriented group. As would be expected, Waechter did not take too kindly to GE, considering Lalonde an interloper.

Surprisingly, the Verts and GE managed to agree on a single, joint candidate for the great bulk of the constituencies in 1993 and on a joint program. In addition to their environmental concerns, for example, the phasing out of nuclear energy, they advocated a return to a proportional representation electoral system (whom do you suppose that would help?) and a shortening of the work week to thirty-five hours with no reduction in pay (similar to the proposal of the PCF). The Verts are more anti-nuclear and pro-conservation but less supportive of the EU than GE is.

Given the decline of the PS, the ecologists had great hopes for the 1993 elections. In the months prior to the campaign, it seemed conceivable that they would win more votes than the PS. When that outcome began to seem too optimistic, the ecologists still anticipated winning forty to fifty seats. In the end, they got absolutely none. It can't even be said that the electoral system shortchanged them since the Verts got only 4 percent of the vote and GE fractionally less.

This disappointment led to a parting of the ways. Waechter announced after the first ballot that the electoral pact was over. Each party would run separate candidates for the European Parliament elections in 1994 and for the presidential election in 1995. He declared that the results demonstrated that the two parties had different clienteles and, therefore, any further attempt at cooperation was pointless. The ecologists appear unlikely to be a leading partisan grouping any time soon.

The National Front

In the latter part of the 1980s, the growing strength of a party on the far right began to have an impact on French politics. Although the National Front (FN) had been around for some time, it gained substantial electoral support only in 1986. The FN was founded by Jean-Marie Le Pen. For a time Le Pen wore a black patch to cover an eye lost in a street fight. His estranged wife claimed that she was forced into prostitution because he failed to give her sufficient money to run their home. Whatever the truth of that, Le Pen has a charismatic speaking style, reminiscent of Mussolini (the Italian Fascist leader during World War II), able to galvanize crowds of thousands.

Le Pen holds a number of right-wing views, such as virulent anti-communism and restoration of the death penalty, but the issue he stresses most is immigration. France is estimated to have well over 3 million immigrants from North Africa (remember that Algeria used to be a French territory), who have distinctive customs and religion and a darker skin color. Advocating the repatriation of such foreigners, Le Pen argues that he is not being racist, but merely pointing out the striking coincidence that at one point there were 2 million foreign workers in the country and 2 million unemployed people. If the foreigners were sent back where they belong, all the French people looking for work could have jobs. Unless something is done, he warns, in twenty years France could become an Islamic republic. In the meantime, welfare and public housing should be provided for French people first; only after taking care of them should any assistance to foreigners be considered.

Few would say that there is anything subtle about Le Pen. One of his posters for the 1988 presidential campaign, however, provided a good example of how to get a racist message across without actually coming out and saying it. At one side the poster had a large picture of Le Pen captioned "The Outsider." A group of horses was shown racing neck and neck across the poster. Above them appeared the phrase "We'll defend our colors." Now, of course, one could say that this was simply a reference to the contrasting livery of racehorses. You would have to be pretty stupid, however, not to understand the implied reference to skin color.

So how many people in France find appeals of this sort attractive? In both the 1986 and 1988 legislative elections, a tenth of the vote went to the FN; in 1993, its support rose to more than 12 percent. In the 1988 presidential election, Le Pen himself polled over 14 percent—only 2 percentage points and three-quarters of a million votes behind a respected candidate, Raymond Barre. (Before you express too much shock over this, you should recall that in the 1968 U.S. presidential election, George Wallace managed to poll 13.5 percent of the vote with an only somewhat less blatant form of racism.)

The proportional representation electoral system used in 1986 gave the FN three dozen seats in the legislature. The double ballot system employed in 1988 reduced its number of seats to only one, even though its share of the vote remained constant. The one legislator the FN did elect was kicked out of the party a few months later for taking policy positions that Le Pen did not like (for example, advocating the extension of the minimum wage to foreign workers). Increasing its share of the vote slightly in 1993 did the FN little good; it still won no seats.

The social group most disposed to vote FN is the self-employed. In that respect, as in some others, it is the spiritual descendant of the Poujadists (discussed near the end of Chapter 12), the party in which Le Pen got his start in politics. As you can see in Figure 13–8, the FN does best along the Mediterranean coast, in the environs of Paris, and in the Catholic east. Many of the areas shaded in Figure 13–8 would have been shaded in similar maps for the 1986 and 1988 elections. What is notable about Figure 13–8, however, is the expansion of the FN's appeal. More northern industrial, central, and southwestern departments are shaded than would have been the case on maps for previous elections.

As we've noted, Le Pen has linked immigrants to unemployment. Figure 13-9, showing those areas of France with relatively large numbers of foreigners and high unemployment in the early 1990s, offers some interesting comparisons with Figure 13–8. Twenty departments in which the FN did best in 1993 are shaded in Figure 13–8. Nine of these are shaded in Figure 13–9 for high unemployment *and* a relatively large foreign population. Another eleven are shaded in that figure for a relatively large foreign population only. Thus, all but one of the FN's best departments in 1993 were ones with high unemployment and/or a relatively large foreign population. On the other hand, some areas shaded in Figure 13–9 aren't shaded in Figure 13-8. High unemployment and a relatively large foreign population created conditions in which the FN could garner support but didn't guarantee its success. Those who wanted to protest unemployment could vote for the PCF or, for that matter, for the UPF. Indeed, UPF offered what some might see as a "respectable" racist option.

What is disturbing is not so much support for the FN as the responses some mainstream politicians have made to Le Pen's rhetoric. In the runup to the 1988

Figure 13–8
Support for FN in the
1993 Election

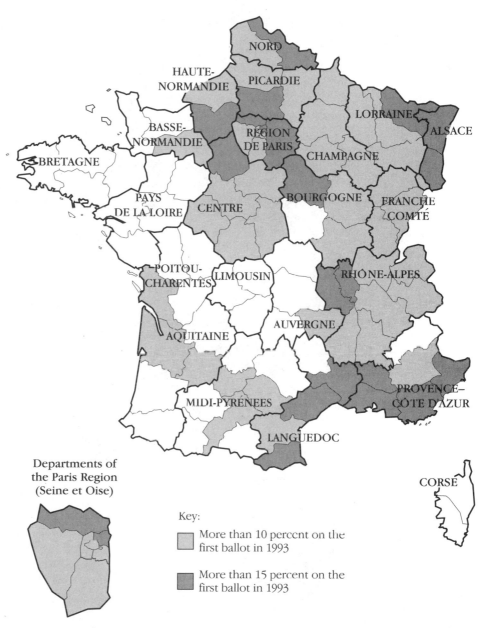

Departments of
the Paris Region
(Seine et Oise)

Key:

☐ More than 10 percent on the
first ballot in 1993

■ More than 15 percent on the
first ballot in 1993

presidential election, Chirac reversed his former support for the existing practice of paying for abortions under the government-financed medical benefits program. The reason he gave for doing so was that easily available abortions would result in population decline, which would soon make offsetting the flow of immigration from North Africa impossible. During the campaign he said in a speech in Marseille (the heart of FN territory), "I do not support racism, but I understand it." Hardly a

Figure 13–9
Unemployment and
Foreign Residents in
the Early 1990s

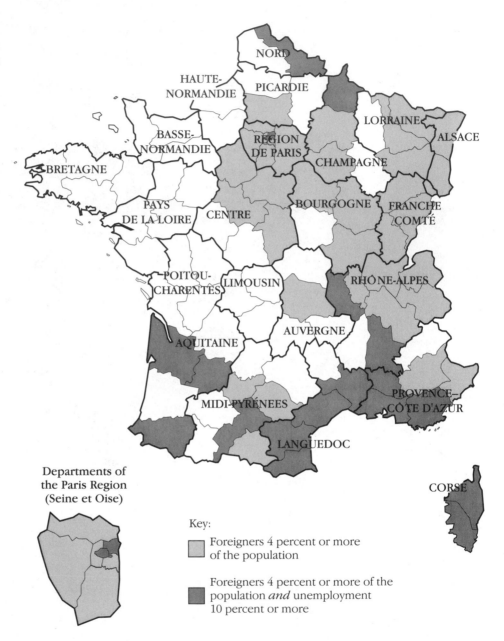

Departments of
the Paris Region
(Seine et Oise)

Key:

☐ Foreigners 4 percent or more
of the population

■ Foreigners 4 percent or more of the
population *and* unemployment
10 percent or more

ringing condemnation of prejudice. At other times he has referred to the noise and
smells of immigrants. In discussing the RPR's campaign for the 1993 elections, we
noted other comments by Chirac on law and order and immigrants.

After the first ballot in the 1988 legislative elections, the leader of the UDF in
the area around Marseille made an electoral pact with the FN. The UDF withdrew
some of its candidates in constituencies where the FN had a chance to win on the

second ballot, and the FN did the same for the UDF. The relevant national party leaders ducked any blame by saying the pact was purely a local matter. Some on the right argued that the Socialists had no right to criticize since the PS made even more of these deals with the PCF in many parts of the country.

The current electoral system will keep the FN from having any substantial voice in the legislature. If this party proves to be simply another skyrocket, as the Poujadists were, popular support will dwindle as well. So far that shows no sign of happening. Le Pen has a following, and he will continue to make the issue of immigration and color of some importance in French politics. The willingness of center and mainstream right politicians to pander to the followers of Le Pen means that the FN, with no representatives in the legislature, is having greater impact on French policy making than is the PCF, which has a couple of dozen.

■ ■ ■

We have not exhausted the list of French political groups, although we probably have exhausted you. Those we have not mentioned can be ignored. Although together they polled about an eighth of the votes cast in 1993 and won about a tenth of the seats, they are so splintered that none of them is significant.

Entering the mid-1990s, France had two parties that were each receiving about a fifth of the vote. One of these, the RPR, although divided on some issues, was in good health. The other, the PS, could not know whether, or in what form, it would survive. Another fifth of the vote was being cast for an umbrella group, the UDF, encompassing two big fish—the PR and the CDS—as well as a number of minnows. An eighth of the vote was going to the FN and a tenth to the PCF. Perhaps these two should be considered of equal strength since the PCF has legislative representation and the FN does not.

Another way of viewing the French party system is to note that no single party is able to mobilize virtually all of the left. The PS has dominated that end of the political spectrum, but the PCF and the ecologists receive appreciable support. Although the UDF occupies the center, this part of the spectrum is at best only loosely organized. As for the right, it is split between the mainstream RPR and the disreputable FN. Not even the main tendencies on the political spectrum are able to coalesce into a single party. In short, France remains a multiparty system.

Some people have argued that one of the reasons the United States has a two-party system is because of the Presidency. Since that office is the supreme prize in U.S. politics, considerable party activity is directed toward winning it. Only a broadly based national party can have any hope of success in this contest, and so American parties are forced to be coalitions of diverse, even discordant, interests, united primarily by their desire to win the ultimate victory. This quest for a winning coalition prohibits the luxury of having small, programmatic parties, each appealing to a narrow segment of the electorate.

The Presidency is the supreme prize in France as well. As will become clear in the next two chapters, the French President dominates the policy process at least as much as the U.S. President does. Yet the quest for this office seems to have had only limited impact on the French party system. Perhaps this is because the double ballot electoral system is used in French presidential elections. Each small segment of the political spectrum can offer its separate candidate on the first ballot, and then join in a broad national coalition only briefly for the second ballot.

Not all French parties are sectarian organizations of limited appeal. Both the Socialists and the Gaullists are coalitions of diverse groups and interests; in this respect, they tend to resemble U.S. parties. Yet neither has been able to encompass the full breadth of support enjoyed by U.S. parties. In France, the cleavages, doctrines, and habits of the past continue to shape the party system. Thus, political arrangements impede and constrain constitutional changes that are designed to concentrate power for effective policy making.

.....14

Legislation and Accountability

As you saw in Chapters 10 and 11, France has swung between legislative preeminence and executive dominance. That is, the country has switched from dispersed power to concentrated power (at times so concentrated as to be autocratic or tyrannical) and back again. The irony is that, although dispersed power has seemed more democratic (thus, traditional belief in France equates democracy with assembly government), it has undermined accountability. Ascertaining who was responsible for shortcomings in public policy was difficult in France. When all officeholders can pass the buck, democracy is attenuated, even if the people need not fear violations of their basic liberties and freedoms (since power is too little concentrated for that to be a danger).

De Gaulle was determined that the new system he drew up in 1958 would do something about the dispersion of power, not because he was deeply concerned about accountability or democracy, but because he wanted the government to possess sufficient power to restore French glory, to make it once again an important nation in world affairs. So how did he have the new system arranged? Before answering this question, we will give you some information about those who serve as legislators and the places where they serve. This should give you a bit of a feel for the atmosphere of the French national legislature.

■ THE CHAMBERS AND THEIR MEMBERS

The French Parliament is divided into two houses. The popularly elected National Assembly consists of 577 deputies—555 from France proper and 22 from overseas departments and territories. When proportional representation was adopted for the 1986 elections, the size of the National Assembly was increased by almost a fifth. When the Chirac Government decided to return to the double ballot system, rather than restoring the old number of constituencies, it retained the new number of deputies and drew new constituency boundaries. The upper chamber, the Senate, has 320 members, who are elected indirectly. We discussed election procedures, qualifications for office, and terms of office in Chapter 12.

The National Assembly meets in the Palais-Bourbon on the Seine, not far from the Louvre (see Figure 14–1). The original building was built in 1722 as a home for a daughter of Louis XIV. During the Revolution the palace was confiscated and served as the meeting place for the lower house of the legislature. As regimes came and went, so did control of the palace, until in 1843 the government bought the entire property. But legislative bodies met in various places until 1879, when the Chamber of Deputies (the lower house in the Third Republic) settled into the Palais-Bourbon. Except during the German occupation from 1940 to 1944, the lower house of the French Parliament has met there ever since.

The meeting chamber itself is arranged more like that of the U.S. Congress than like that of the British House of Commons. The deputies sit in a semicircle on curved benches behind desks facing the rostrum. Each row is raised slightly, as in an amphitheater. Since a large number of parties are represented, no clear-cut separation between Government and Opposition exists. Deputies sit according to political association, however, from the far left (presiding officer's left) to the extreme right.

Seating arrangements have caused some controversy at times. At the beginning of the Fifth Republic, the Gaullists favored an arrangement like that of the British House of Commons. But they were unable to win the support of any other political group for this change and were not strong enough to implement it. The other parties did concede to the Gaullists' demand to sit in the central seats, thus demonstrating to the electorate (all of whom, no doubt, were following this controversy with great interest) that they were not a reactionary party of the right.

The reduction of Communist strength in the National Assembly in the Fifth Republic has had a significant impact on the social composition of the lower house.

Figure 14–1
The Palais-Bourbon

Whereas in the Fourth Republic manual workers accounted for about an eighth of the membership, during de Gaulle's Presidency their proportion usually was less than half that large. During the 1980s, only about 3–4 percent of the deputies were manual workers. Teachers have become the largest single group in the chamber, making up about a quarter of the membership. Higher-level civil servants and managers each account for about a seventh of the members. Doctors and lawyers together comprise another seventh. Women are grossly underrepresented. During most of the 1980s, only a couple of dozen of the members of the National Assembly were female, a proportion well below 5 percent of the total membership.

The first Parliament of the Fifth Republic saw a considerable number of new faces in the lower house. Less than 30 percent of those deputies who stood for reelection were successful. Although this sizable turnover doesn't mean that most of those elected were political novices (many had been active in local politics and/or had run unsuccessfully for Parliament in earlier elections), it is evidence of the extent to which the electorate was turning its back on politicians associated with the discredited Fourth Republic. As the Fifth Republic became institutionalized, however, such a turnover didn't recur. The right-wing landslide of 1993, however, did produce a dramatic change. Just over half of the members of the newly elected National Assembly had not been members of the previous one. (Some had served in earlier legislatures and weren't complete novices.)

One characteristic of political parties' recruitment patterns that did not change with the founding of the Fifth Republic was that candidates had local government experience. As had been true in both the Third and Fourth Republics, well over a majority of the deputies—three-fourths in 1958—had been members of local government councils before being elected to the national legislature. Even more remarkable from an American perspective is the large number of national legislators who have continued to hold local government offices. Since in France nothing prohibits serving simultaneously in more than one elective office, many nationally prominent politicians serve as mayor of a town or city while also being a member of the National Assembly.

In contrast to typical practice in other countries, the two houses of the French legislature do not meet in the same building. The Senate's chamber is located some distance across Paris from the Palais-Bourbon, in the Palais-Luxembourg (see Figure 14–2). Behind the Palais-Luxembourg are attractive formal gardens, including a reflecting pool, where children sail toy boats. The Palais-Luxembourg was built early in the seventeenth century and then remodeled in a Florentine fashion for the widow of Henry IV. During the Revolution it served as a prison. Subsequently, Napoleon lived there for a short time. The Senate began meeting there in 1801 and, with some breaks in tenure, has continued to do so ever since. The seating arrangements in the Senate's meeting chamber are similar to those for the National Assembly.

In keeping with its more rural and conservative electorate, the Senate usually has contained fewer workers but more farmers than has the National Assembly. Its different electorate (discussed in Chapter 12) explains why the first Senate of the Fifth Republic, unlike the National Assembly, experienced little turnover in membership. Of those seeking reelection to the Senate at the start of the Fifth Republic,

Figure 14–2
The Palais-
Luxembourg

seven-eighths were successful. As for the few who were new to that chamber, sever-al of them were experienced national politicians seeking some political haven after having been defeated in the elections for the National Assembly, which were held earlier than those for the Senate.

■ POWERS AND PROCEDURES

Sessions and Agenda

The easiest way to control a legislature, of course, is to keep it from meeting. Given their bias against assembly government, it is not surprising that the founders of the Fifth Republic sought to do exactly that. The legislature is limited to two regular ses-sions a year, neither of which can exceed three months. A majority of the National Assembly can call for a special session, as can the Prime Minister. Such a session, however, can meet for no more than twelve days. Furthermore, in practice, the National Assembly can't be certain of getting a special session. During a period of emergency rule in 1961, President de Gaulle refused to call a special session even though a majority of the National Assembly requested one. Although his refusal clearly seemed to violate the constitution, the legislature could do nothing about it. Once again de Gaulle had demonstrated his refusal to abide by the rules—even those drawn up by his followers under his guidance—whenever doing so was inconvenient for him.

Not until 1979—twenty years into the Fifth Republic—was a special session held, when President Giscard complied with the request of a sizable majority of the National Assembly for such a meeting. The executive was subjected to strong criti-cism of its economic policies, but basically emerged unscathed. Another special ses-sion was called immediately after the Socialists' 1981 victory to begin work prompt-ly on the party's reform program. President Mitterrand called a one-day special session early in 1992 to combat the furor over permitting a Palestinian leader thought to have been involved in terrorism to enter France for medical treatment.

The constitution gives the executive considerable control over the scheduling of legislative business. To prevent the legislature from clawing back any of this power to determine the length of debate on bills, the constitution provides that the legislature's standing orders of procedure cannot become effective until they have been examined by the Constitutional Council, to be certain that they conform with the constitution.

Although the executive ultimately controls the legislature's timetable, the National Assembly does have a committee that deals with such matters. The Conference of Presidents, composed of the leaders of all recognized political groups in the chamber, the chairpersons of committees, and the six vice-presidents and the president of the chamber, sets the agenda and allots the amount of time to be spent in debating each item. Voting strength in the Conference is according to the size of recognized political groups in the chamber. Given the power of the executive in these matters, however, the Conference votes only rarely. It functions as a channel for communicating the views of the various political groups to the executive and as a means of negotiating with the executive, in hopes that occasionally the executive may be persuaded to concede a change in legislative priorities.

Officers and Political Groups

Each chamber is presided over by a president. French presiding officers remain members of their respective political parties, unlike the Speaker of the House of Commons, and do not have that Speaker's unchallenged authority. The president of the National Assembly is elected for its duration, that is, until another national legislative election is held. The president of the Senate is elected for a three-year term. A new election for the Senate's presiding officer occurs after each partial renewal of its membership.

The office of president of the National Assembly has a good deal of prestige and has been sought by nationally known politicians. For example, following the Socialists' return to power in 1988, they managed to elect Laurent Fabius, who had served as Prime Minister when they had been in power previously. The president he replaced was also a former Prime Minister and had been a candidate for President of the country some years earlier.

The president of the National Assembly is assisted in presiding over the debates and in organizing and directing the chamber's activities by the Bureau. The Bureau is composed of the six vice-presidents, twelve secretaries, and three *questeurs* (members in charge of the administrative and financial arrangements of the Assembly). These positions are distributed among the various political groups, according to their strength in the chamber.

Until 1988 a political group needed to have at least thirty adherents in the National Assembly to be formally recognized. In the 1988 elections, the Communists were reduced to only twenty-seven representatives. The Socialists agreed to reduce the minimum number in exchange for the votes of the Communists in electing Fabius president. Each formal group must draft a statement of policy, which all its adherents must sign. These statements are usually so vague as to be meaningless. The leaders of recognized groups are granted special debating privileges.

Part of the apparent confusion of the French party system stems from the fact that the formal groups in the National Assembly do not necessarily correspond to the various political parties that have been active during election campaigns. Candidates may give themselves a label on election ballots that is not the name of a party. These labels may not provide even a hint as to what recognized group a successful candidate will choose to join in the National Assembly. Parties that fought an election separately may join together to form a group in order to increase their voice in the legislative process. Alternatively, there may be a falling out between election time and legislative organization. As we discussed in Chapter 13, the Center of Social Democrats (CDS), which fought the 1988 election in association with the UDF alliance of center-right parties, decided subsequently to form a new group, the Union of the Center (UDC), in the legislature. Thus, parties may have no counterpart among the National Assembly's recognized groups, and those groups may correspond to no party organization existing outside of the legislature. (Nor do the labels for political groups in the Senate correspond exactly to those in the National Assembly.) In recent years, four to six recognized groups have been typical for the National Assembly.

Committees

The number of committees in the lower house was reduced at the start of the Fifth Republic from nineteen to only six. The aim was to avoid the time-wasting practice of submitting identical matters to several committees and, more important, to reduce the power of the committees in the legislative process. During the Fourth Republic, legislative committees were independent centers of powers, just as they are in the U.S. Congress. Their number permitted some specialization, and each committee was able to build up a fund of expertise on a specific subject. Committee chairs became virtual shadow ministers, able to keep an informed watch on and considerable control over members of the executive. In a multiparty system having no single party as the opposition, the committee system was an important element in legislative dominance of the executive.

The small number of committees in the Fifth Republic legislature forces them to be larger and less specialized. Two of the committees have about 120 members, and the other four have 60 each. Absenteeism keeps them from being entirely unwieldy; only those deputies particularly interested in the bill being discussed are likely to attend a given meeting. Even so, the larger size of the committees has made it more difficult for interest groups to gain the support needed for legislation they favor.

Special committees consisting of not more than thirty members, with no more than fifteen from any single regular committee, may be created on an ad hoc basis to deal with a specific bill. These have not been used to any great extent, however.

Only recognized political groups are entitled to seats on the committees. Although the initial allocation of places corresponds in each case to the relative strength of the group in the National Assembly, committees differ in partisan composition. The groups swap seats with each other in order to gain the greatest strength on the committees likely to deal with the subjects of special interest to them. Once the distribution of committee places is determined, each group decides which of its members will fill the seats available to it.

Typically, committees meet all day on Wednesdays and in the morning on other days. The National Assembly convenes on Tuesday, Thursday, and Friday afternoons. No quorum is required for debates, but no vote is valid unless half the members are present. If there are too few present, the vote is postponed for an hour; then the vote is valid regardless of the number participating. Deputies may speak for no more than five minutes, except in organized debates. In such debates the Conference of Presidents allocates the time available to the various recognized groups, and the groups, in turn, decide which of their members will speak for how long.

The executive's legislative business is placed on the priority order of the day, ensuring that it will be dealt with first. Following that, bills introduced by the legislators can be considered as part of the complementary order of the day, but this does not happen frequently. About seven-eighths of all legislation originates with the executive. During the Fourth Republic, about twice as much legislation was introduced by the deputies. The source of legislation in the Fifth Republic is further evidence of the extent to which the role of the legislature in France has been curtailed from what it had been. On the other hand, the situation under the Fifth Republic differs little from British practice.

Only a handful of the bills introduced by deputies are enacted. Furthermore, deputies are limited in their ability to alter the bills proposed by the executive. The executive can prevent floor discussion of any amendment to its bills that was not considered during committee stage; spur-of-the-moment amendments during floor debate are not allowed. Thus, the executive is protected from being caught off-guard by an apparently innocuous amendment that has a hidden effect.

Bills return from a committee in exactly the same form as when they were sent to it. So what is the point of the committee's consideration? The report indicates which amendments the committee favors, and thus the bill has been examined in detail. Prohibiting amendment in committee, however, strengthens the executive's hand. No longer, as was true in the Fourth Republic, does the executive have the task of trying to cobble together a series of majorities to restore to original form a bill that was mangled by committee. The burden of constructing majorities now falls on those who want to alter the executive's legislative proposals. The executive decides how votes will be taken on bills. It can limit votes to only the popular sections of a bill or even require that the bill be voted on as a whole.

Policy Role

In contrast to the constitutional documents of the Third and Fourth Republics, the constitution of the Fifth Republic spells out Parliament's powers. In all matters not mentioned, it grants the Government the power to set policy by decrees. As we have discussed in previous chapters, the basic aim of those who created the Fifth Republic was to strengthen the executive branch at the expense of the legislature.

Within the jurisdiction granted to the legislature, matters for which it is permitted to set only general principles are distinguished from those for which it can make detailed regulations. Parliament can legislate in detail on civil rights and obligations; nationality, contracts, gifts, and inheritance; crimes and criminal procedures; taxation and currency; electoral systems; public institutions; and economic plans, including nationalization and denationalization of enterprises. Parliament can establish only the policy outlines and must leave the details to the executive on general organization of national defense; education; property rights; employment, unions, and social security; and the administration of local government units. Parliament declares war and votes the budget by a special procedure for organic laws. The President alone ratifies treaties except for certain types, such as peace treaties, which must be ratified by law and, therefore, require action by Parliament. In all other matters the constitution says that the Government is free to legislate by decree.

Furthermore, under Article 38 of the constitution, the executive may ask the legislature to delegate to it for a limited time even those powers that the constitution has specifically granted to the legislature. If the legislature accedes to this request, any decrees issued by the executive—which needs only to consult with the Council of State before acting—are effective immediately. The decrees become null and void, however, unless the executive seeks the legislature's ratification within the time period specified in the request for decree powers.

While de Gaulle was President, the Government availed itself of Article 38 fairly regularly, around fifteen times over a decade, much to the anger of the left. Once he departed from office, resort to the procedure lapsed as his successors tried to demonstrate that they were less imperious. Shortly after winning power in 1981, however, the Socialists asked Parliament to authorize decree powers for three months so that the labor laws could be amended. The executive claimed that this procedure was necessary because its extensive program of reforms had created a backlog in the legislature, preventing prompt action to help the unemployed. When in 1983 the executive felt that additional austerity measures were needed, it once again resorted to Article 38. The Socialists' willingness when in power to use procedures they had opposed when out of office made them seem somewhat hypocritical.

Since the legislature's enumerated powers appear to be fairly comprehensive, limiting it to those matters may not seem to curtail its role significantly. Legislation by executive decree has long been a practice of French government. In the past, however, such *cadre* laws always were based on grants of authority to the executive from the legislature, grants that could be revoked at any time. Under the Fifth Republic that is not the case. *Most* of the executive's decree power now comes from the constitution; it is not subject to control or modification by the legislature.

Perhaps the most important political power is control over financial matters. Not surprisingly, therefore, the founders of the Fifth Republic weakened the legislature in this regard. If the legislature has not passed the budget within seventy days of receiving it from the executive, the executive can implement it by decree. Thus, the legislature retains the power to pass a budget that the executive doesn't like, but is no longer able to hold the budget up indefinitely in an effort to force concessions out of the executive. The executive doesn't need to worry about dissent in the legislature; if it can't get its budget passed, it can implement it by decree. As for the possibility that the legislature might pass a budget the executive opposes, the risks are limited because the constitution bars deputies from introducing bills that would either reduce revenues or increase expenditures.

In addition to its legislative function, Parliament is supposed to have a role in amending the constitution. As you learned in Chapter 11, this provision has been circumvented on one occasion. In this matter, as well, the legislature's power and status have been undercut.

Intralegislative Relations

In the Fourth Republic the upper chamber of the legislature was weak, in contrast to the practices that had developed during the Third Republic. The founders of the Fifth Republic deliberately sought to return in part to the old tradition. De Gaulle's supporters were uncertain that they would have sufficient electoral strength to control the lower house of the legislature but were confident that the conservative upper house would be an ally.

With only a few exceptions, the powers granted to the Senate equal those of the National Assembly. Finance bills must be submitted first to the National Assembly. The bill can be introduced in the upper house, however, should the lower one fail to act within forty days. If the two houses disagree on a bill, it dies—unless the executive intervenes by calling for a conference committee (*Commission Mixte Paritaire*, or CMP) composed of members chosen from both houses. Even if a CMP reaches a compromise acceptable to the representatives from both houses, its draft can be considered by the legislature *only* if the executive approves, and only the executive is permitted to offer any amendments to the draft. If a CMP fails to agree, then the executive can ask the National Assembly to act. In that instance the decision of the lower house is sufficient to pass the bill, regardless of any continuing opposition from the Senate.

If the Senate agreed with the executive but the National Assembly didn't, then the executive could count on the upper house to block any undesirable action by the lower house. On the other hand, if the lower house and the executive saw eye-to-eye and the Senate disagreed with them, then the executive could use the National Assembly to overcome any obstacle in the upper house. The Senate, then, was designed so that it can check the lower house (if the executive needs that) but cannot impede the executive's goals. For this arrangement to work as intended, however, the executive must be in command of the lower house. Should control of the National Assembly be tenuous, then the Senate could become, in the eyes of the executive, something of a loose cannon.

A conference committee is summoned for about a tenth of the bills. The executive has never used the option of rejecting a CMP's report. About a quarter of the time, the executive has asked the National Assembly to make the final decision, because a CMP has been unable to work out a compromise.

Contrary to their expectations, the supporters of de Gaulle were never very strong in the Senate. During the Presidencies of de Gaulle and Pompidou, the

Senate was often a sharper critic of the executive than the National Assembly was. Under Giscard this changed because his closest allies were stronger in the upper house than in the lower. Mitterrand's election as President altered the situation again. Although the senatorial elections of 1980 had made the PS the largest party in the upper house, it held little more than a fifth of the seats. The conservative majority in the upper house was not a pressing problem, since the Senate lacks the power to vote the Cabinet out of office. Nonetheless, the Senate did create some troubles for Mitterrand. Opposition in the Senate to the Socialists' nationalization bill forced this law to be enacted by vote of the National Assembly alone. To avoid another such conflict with the Senate, the executive modified its bill to decentralize French government so as to make it acceptable to the upper house.

Mitterrand and the Senate clashed in 1984 on amending the constitution. Public demonstrations had forced the Socialists to withdraw their proposals to integrate the Catholic schools more fully into the state educational system. Mitterrand sought to devise an alternative means of accomplishing this goal, to avoid losing the support of those in his party who remained fervently committed to the Socialist tradition of secular education. He proposed amending the constitution to permit referenda on what he termed basic public liberties. The Senate, fearing that Mitterrand might be able to enhance his popularity by frequent use of this power, defeated the proposal. Since the Senate's power in amending the constitution is equal to that of the National Assembly, the adverse vote killed Mitterrand's plan.

The new center-right Government formed after the 1993 elections could anticipate firm support in the Senate. The RPR was the largest party with nearly 30 percent of the seats. Adding the seats of the various center groups would give the Government a two-thirds majority. The Socialists and the Communists together held only a quarter of the seats. Nonetheless, so catastrophic had been the left's rout in the National Assembly elections that it was considerably stronger in the "conservative" upper house than in the lower house.

■ LEGISLATIVE RELATIONS WITH THE EXECUTIVE

We already have touched at various points in this chapter on executive-legislative relations. We have noted the curtailing of the legislature's sphere of competence and the complementary expanding of the executive's, the ability of the executive to play one house off against the other, and the executive's greatly enhanced control over the legislature's procedures. Despite the great contrast with legislative-executive relations in the United States, such executive domination is not unusual in a parliamentary system—provided that the executive is accountable to the legislature for the way in which the country is being run.

The essence of the parliamentary system is to provide a means of removing the executive from office—not for illegal action, but for failure to perform the job as well as the legislature prefers or to seek the goals that it wants. Note that the behavior at issue here has nothing to do with corruptness or illegality. Although the U.S. Constitution provides for impeachment of the President, this does not make the United States a parliamentary system. (Similarly, in France, the President and other members of the executive can be tried for high crimes and misdemeanors. A majority of the total membership of both the National Assembly and the Senate must vote for an indictment for a case to be tried. The case is heard in the High Court of Justice, which is composed of deputies and senators elected in equal numbers by the two houses of the legislature.)

The parliamentary system is concerned with political, not legal, shortcomings. In this sense the French President is not accountable in any way to the legislature. Were the position simply a symbolic one, similar to the British monarch, the lack of legislative control would not be important. Many republics have ceremonial executives who perform the rituals associated with hereditary rulers in constitutional monarchies. As you'll see in the next chapter, however, the French President's role and powers go well beyond that of symbolic head of state. Thus, the inability of the legislature to call the President to account undermines the basic purpose of the parliamentary system.

The Fifth Republic is virtually unique in providing for a dual *substantive* executive: both the head of state (the President) and the head of government (the Prime Minister) possess significant powers. In most parliamentary systems the latter executive is the one who exercises the important powers, and it is his or her accountability to the legislature that constitutes the heart of legislative-executive relations. Despite the new status given to the President, the Fifth Republic did not completely abandon the parliamentary system; it retains an element of fusion of powers along with separation of powers. The rest of this chapter will focus on the relations characteristic of the parliamentary form of government, those between the legislature on one hand and the Prime Minister and Cabinet on the other.

Questions

One element in the ability of a parliament to call a Cabinet to account is the power to force it to justify its actions. Questioning of Cabinet ministers in France takes a variety of forms. In the National Assembly, the Bureau (the group of presiding officers discussed previously) filters questions submitted in writing by the deputies. Half of the few it selects to place on the agenda are from deputies opposed to the Cabinet and the other half from deputies supporting it. In addition, the Bureau separates scheduled questions into those with debate and those without debate.

For questions without debate, a deputy is allowed up to two minutes to elaborate on the written form of the question. After the relevant minister replies, the deputy may comment for up to five minutes. Finally, the minister may make a rebuttal. Note that this procedure (which occurs weekly) differs somewhat from the daily question time in the British House of Commons, which we discussed in Part Two. Questions with debate present more of a contrast with British procedure because the French deputy submitting the question is allowed up to twenty minutes to discuss the minister's reply. In the French upper house the rules permit a full-fledged debate. The senator submitting the question speaks for a half-hour, followed by other senators who may speak for up to twenty minutes each. A minister then speaks at length, and, finally, the original senator responds.

Various factors attenuate the impact of questions in the French legislature. Questions occur only once a week. Initially in the National Assembly that day was Friday, when absenteeism was high. A subsequent change to Wednesday was a slight improvement. The problem that remains is delay and, thus, lack of topicality. Up to a month may pass between the time the deputy submits the question and its appearance on the National Assembly's agenda—assuming that it is selected at all. The procedure in the Senate has the potential to allow some impact, but the subsidiary position of that house in the French legislature means that what occurs there usually is accorded little importance. We commented in Part Two that question time in Britain, contrary to popular belief, is not an effective procedure for calling the executive to account. Questions, of whatever type, are even less efficient in France. Although the *form* of the parliamentary system has been retained, the *substance* of calling power to account is little served.

Varieties of Votes of Confidence

A parliament's ultimate weapon for calling an executive to account is the power to remove it from office. During the Third Republic, the Cabinet had to please both houses of the legislature, although adverse votes in the upper house came to affect the executive's survival less than did those of the lower house. Only the lower house had the power to dismiss the Cabinet in the Fourth Republic. In both Republics the executive had few weapons to defend itself. Cabinets fell not only because the legislature had voted to eject them, but even more often because the executive was unable to get the legislature's support for its program and simply threw in the towel. The Fifth Republic was deliberately designed to break free from this tradition of legislative dominance; the executive was given the means to maintain itself in office and to govern effectively.

Newly formed Cabinets in the Third and Fourth Republics had to seek legislative approval through investiture. The Prime Minister made a policy statement to the lower house of the legislature, which would then vote either to accept or to reject an executive with such goals. A simple majority in favor of rejection was sufficient to prevent the newly formed Cabinet from being maintained in office, and the search for an acceptable executive would continue. Accountability was given a very high priority; the executive could not even begin work unless its plans were acceptable to the legislature.

Article 49 of the Fifth Republic's constitution seems to provide for an investiture procedure, and the first three Cabinets did seek legislative approval at the start of their tenure in office. Then the practice changed. New Prime Ministers continued to make a speech to the National Assembly explaining what their policy goals would be, but they did not ask for any vote of approval. French Presidents appeared to be trying to demonstrate that the Cabinet was accountable to them, not to the legislature. Only two of a dozen newly formed Cabinets during most of the 1960s and the 1970s sought investiture.

The 1980s saw a return to the earlier practice. Four consecutive new Prime Ministers not only made a statement of policy to the National Assembly, but also requested its approval. Since the change occurred when a Socialist became Prime Minister for the first time in the Fifth Republic, one might conclude that the party was attempting to demonstrate that it, unlike its right-wing opponents, believed that executive accountability to the legislature was essential in a parliamentary system. The fourth in this sequence of investitures was sought, however, not by a Socialist but by Jacques Chirac of the RPR. Furthermore, when the Socialists returned to power in 1988, the new Prime Minister, Michel Rocard, did not seek an initial legislative endorsement of his plans. Nor did the two Socialists who followed him.

Thus, little more than a third of the new Cabinets of the Fifth Republic have sought investiture (nine of twenty-five through 1993). Each one that has asked for legislative approval has obtained it, although the Chirac Cabinet of 1986 received only seven more positive votes than negative ones. To the extent that investiture has fallen into abeyance, the ability of the legislature to call the executive to account has decreased.

The executive may ask the legislature to endorse its program or a general policy statement at times other than the beginning of its tenure in office. If critical rumblings become quite loud, the Cabinet may feel compelled to demonstrate that it still retains the confidence of the legislature. As with investiture, a simple majority voting against a policy statement is sufficient to drive from power any Cabinet staking its existence on such a vote. A Cabinet that seeks the legislature's support in this fashion recognizes that it is accountable to that branch of government.

During the Fifth Republic, Cabinets have sought such endorsements only rarely. On each occasion the legislature has given its support. One of Chirac's Cabinets had the closest call, winning by only thirteen votes when it sought endorsement in December 1987. More recently, Rocard sought endorsement on the use of French troops in the Gulf War in January 1991 and received overwhelming support. When farmers protested that the Government was too feeble in defending their interests in the GATT negotiations, Prime Minister Pierre Bérégovoy sought the legislature's backing in November 1992. The fifty-vote majority he obtained was comfortable, but not entirely reassuring. In sum, this procedure does contribute a bit to executive accountability, but fails to enhance greatly the legislature's ability to perform its essential parliamentary function.

In addition to seeking legislative endorsement of its general policies, the executive can request, under Article 49-3, support for a specific proposal. That is, the executive tells the legislature that a specific bill is of such crucial importance to its program that it will resign from office if the bill is not passed. In this case the procedures differ significantly from those we have described for endorsement. When the executive makes passage of *a bill* a matter of confidence, the constitution provides that legislative approval is *assumed* unless a censure motion is filed in the National Assembly within the next twenty-four hours. Filing such a motion requires the signatures of at least one tenth of the deputies in the National Assembly. If the motion is filed, a vote is delayed for forty-eight hours to give the executive time to mobilize its supporters in the legislature. When the vote is held, only the votes in favor of censure are counted. The Cabinet must resign if a majority of the *total* membership of the National Assembly has voted for censure. If the motion fails to obtain this *absolute* majority (not just the simple majority applicable in other cases discussed so far), then the bill to which the Cabinet committed itself is considered approved.

This provision can result in an extraordinary process of statutory enactment. Under the Fifth Republic a bill can become law even though *a majority* of those present have *voted against it*, because a censure motion fails unless supported by *a majority of the total membership.* In fact, a bill can become law without ever having been voted on at all— this would occur if a tenth of the deputies failed to offer a censure motion in response to the Cabinet's having made a bill a matter of confidence. The intent of this procedure is to allow the executive to get on with its program, unless the National Assembly is determined to remove the Cabinet from office.

This procedure was used over three dozen times during the first thirty years of the Fifth Republic.[1] It appeared to be falling into abeyance because it was employed only four times between 1962 and 1978. Then conflict became so sharp on government spending, taxation, and social security that the Cabinet had to resort to Article 49-3 to get its budget implemented. Within a period of a month, Communist and Socialist deputies responded with a flurry of seven motions of censure—all of which failed.

As is often the case in politics, it all depends on whose ox is being gored. When the Socialists came to power in 1981, their Cabinet used this procedure to get some controversial legislation enacted. On average they used Article 49-3 about twice a year. A shift in power in 1986 to Chirac and the RPR doubled the rate to an average of four times a year. All this was as nothing, however, compared to the use of Article 49-3 under the next Socialist Prime Minister, Michel Rocard. In just three years he utilized it twenty-eight times—three-fourths as many times as in the entire preceding thirty years of the Fifth Republic!

The reason for this dramatic increase is easily discovered. Rocard's Socialists didn't control a majority of the seats in the National Assembly. Although his use of Article 49-3 is especially frequent, Fifth Republic Cabinets, of whatever political orientation, that have had only tenuous control of the legislature have found this procedure an invaluable aid. Even Cabinets that appear to possess a working majority in the National Assembly may use the procedure to combat dissension among their regular supporters. Some deputies may be willing to vote against a bill proposed by the executive but would not be willing to eject "their" Cabinet from office and let the other parties into power. Thus, when the Cabinet stakes its life on a bill, its deputies have little recourse but to swallow it, distasteful as it may be.

When the Cabinet makes a specific bill a matter of confidence, deputies do respond with a motion of censure slightly more than half the time. Thirty-one times from 1958 to 1991, however, no such motion was submitted. That means that three and a half dozen times during the Fifth Republic a bill has become law *without a vote.* On those occasions when a vote has occurred, the Cabinet has always won.

We commented in our discussion of the role of the House of Commons that executive accountability doesn't require that a Cabinet be defeated and removed from office. Although Article 49-3 can produce a legislative process that hardly can

---

[1]Robert Elgie, "From the exception to the rule: the use of article 49-3 of the Constitution since 1958," *Modern and Contemporary France* NS1 (Number 1, 1993), pp. 17–26.

be called democratic, nonetheless, the procedure *does* make the Cabinet ultimately accountable to the legislature. On the other hand, requiring that an absolute majority be opposed, rather than just a simple one, does tend to load the dice in favor of the executive. The French Cabinet is buttressed procedurally in a way that the British Cabinet is not.

In all the procedures discussed so far, the initiative has been with the executive. The one remaining form of executive accountability to the legislature allows the latter branch to *act*, not just *react*. Whenever a tenth of the deputies so desire, they can move a motion censuring the Cabinet; they do not need to wait until the executive raises the issue of confidence. The founders of the Fifth Republic did not intend, however, to permit dissident legislators to make life unpleasant for the executive by engaging perpetually in obstructionist tactics. Therefore, if a motion of censure initiated by the deputies (as distinct from one moved in response to the Cabinet's use of Article 49-3) fails to pass, none of those deputies who signed the motion may sign another such motion for the remainder of that session of the legislature. This means, assuming that the Cabinet has majority support (more than 50 percent of the members) in the legislature, the executive will face no more than four motions of censure in any session.

Once such a motion has been submitted, the vote is delayed for forty-eight hours. Here, again, an absolute majority is required for the motion to pass. The pattern of usage resembles that for Article 49-3. During the first thirty years of the Fifth Republic, censure motions averaged fewer than two a year. The minority Socialist Governments following the 1988 elections, however, had their legislative watchdogs constantly nipping at their heels. Over the five-year period until the 1993 elections, censure motions averaged about five a year.

During the entire life of the Fifth Republic, legislators have attempted to call the Government to account and remove it from office by means of a censure motion more than sixty times. Only once have they succeeded. In 1962 the National Assembly censured the Cabinet when President de Gaulle bypassed the legislature in amending the constitution to provide for direct, popular election of the President. Obviously, the legislature was angry with the President, not the Cabinet, but it had no way to call the President to account. This illustrates quite well the problem of categorizing the French governmental system. The constitution *does* make the Cabinet responsible to the legislature—the fusion of powers which is the hallmark of the parliamentary system. The President, who possesses significant powers, is insulated, however, from legislative pique. Like his American counterpart, the French President ultimately is accountable only to the electorate. In France, this accountability is attenuated because the President serves not for four years, but for seven. Thus the French system *both* provides for and eschews accountability.

When in 1962 the National Assembly did manage to censure the Cabinet, de Gaulle sought to undercut even that one instance of accountability. Instead of telling the Cabinet to resign, he dissolved the legislature and called for new elections. Furthermore, he held a referendum to approve the proposed amendment to the constitution exactly as he had intended to do in the first place. In both the elections and on the referendum he won substantial victories. Needless to say, this out-

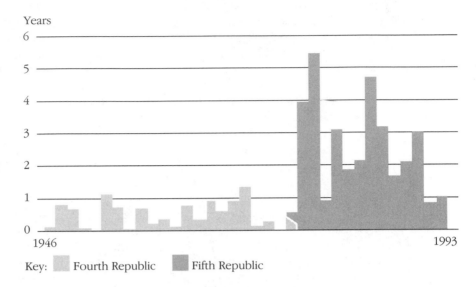

Figure 14–3
Number of Years Served in Office by Each Prime Minister, 1946–1993

Key: ▨ Fourth Republic   ▪ Fifth Republic

come didn't make motions of censure seem very attractive and may help to explain why they weren't used very often for the next quarter of a century.

On average (clearly, the instances have *not* been evenly distributed), motions of censure and votes of confidence of whatever type have occurred somewhat more frequently than three times a year. Although that hardly is frequent, the gap between one opportunity for the legislature to determine the life of the Cabinet and another is not terribly lengthy. Typically, not too much time passes without the Cabinet having to account for its actions. That the Cabinet has been rejected only once during the more than three and a half decades of the Fifth Republic, however, is remarkable. The power to harass the executive that the legislature wielded in the Third and Fourth Republics plainly has been eliminated.

Graphic evidence of the change in relations appears in Figure 14–3. In twelve years the Fourth Republic had twenty-two Prime Ministers; in its first twelve years the Fifth had only four. Even after three and a half decades it had had only thirteen. Prime Ministers in the Fourth Republic averaged only six months in office; in the Fifth they have averaged well over two and a half years. Only two Prime Ministers managed to last for more than a year during the Fourth Republic; only two have failed to last longer in the Fifth.

■ ■ ■

Can the constitutional reforms of the Fifth Republic be said to have achieved their objectives? Although they certainly have contributed to a new executive stability in France, changes in the party system have had an even greater impact. France has not moved to a party system like that of Britain in the 1950s and 1960s, but neither has it remained trapped in its system of the Third and Fourth Republics. The decline of Communist strength in the legislature and the emergence of three or four dominant political groups have greatly simplified the executive's ability to control the legislature. For most of the Fifth Republic, the Cabinet has had an assured working majority in the legislature. Had the Prime Ministers of the Third and Fourth Republics enjoyed such support in the legislature, they, too, would have headed more durable Cabinets.

Since greater stability would have occurred even in the absence of constitutional reform, the costs of that reform need to be assessed. In trying to cut the legislature down to size, in the ways explained in this chapter, what have the founders of the Fifth Republic produced? Most experts seem to agree that as far as legislating—efficient processing of proposals for laws—is concerned, the reformed legislature performs much better than its predecessors. But passing laws is not the only, or even the most significant, function of a legislature in a parliamentary system. A major task is to control the executive, to require it to give an account of the results of its program for running the country and to justify the way it administers public policy. In a larger sense, the legislature has the task of ensuring that the executive makes available sufficient information about its actions for the electorate to assess its stewardship of the country. On this score, the experts agree, the Parliament of the Fifth Republic fails to measure up well. The legislature has not been very effective in scrutinizing the actions of the executive or in calling it to account. The responsibility of the executive to the legislature has been seriously attenuated, not only because of the constraints placed on oversight of the Cabinet but also because of its lack of control over the President.

In short, despite the achievements of the Fifth Republic in concentrating power sufficiently to produce a more effective political system, the fundamental problem of French government—achieving a balanced relation between legislative and executive organs—remains unresolved. And when a system is deficient in accountability, it is not surprising that, as our discussion of political values in Chapter 12 indicated, many of its citizens are apathetic or alienated.

15

Policy-Making Structures

Many republics that used to be monarchies have dual executives—a president and a prime minister. The president functions as the ceremonial head of state (in effect, doing much of what the monarch formerly did), and the prime minister exercises real political power as the head of government. This was the arrangement in both the Third and Fourth Republics, except that the Prime Minister actually had little power because the executive branch was so dominated by the legislature.

The constitution of the Fifth Republic sought to strengthen the executive, as we saw in the previous chapter, by making the Prime Minister less beholden to the legislature. It also created a President who is independent of the legislature and possesses substantial powers, well beyond those of a ceremonial head of state. The result is a hybrid system having elements of both parliamentary and presidential systems. Chapter 14 examined the parliamentary aspects of this system: how the Cabinet and Prime Minister relate to the legislature. This chapter considers the President's role, how that office relates to the rest of the executive, and what this implies for the entire pattern of legislative-executive relations in France. What accountability exists with this further concentration of power?

■ *FORMAL POWERS AND DUTIES OF THE PRESIDENT*

The French President is designated the head of state, whereas the Prime Minister serves as head of government. This does not mean that the President is to be merely a ceremonial figure, like the British monarch. The constitution says that the President is the guarantor of national independence, of the integrity of the territory, of respect for international treaties and agreements—certainly impressive sounding responsibilities. Furthermore, the President is entrusted with the task of protecting the constitution itself, and to this end, he or she is empowered to "arbitrate" among political forces and governmental bodies to ensure the regular functioning of the state and its continuity. This responsibility is so vague that it is hard to know precisely what actions it authorizes. The first President of the Fifth Republic, for whom the office was designed, seemed to feel that this provision justified his taking whatever action he felt necessary.

The President's powers are impressive. Some of them, such as the power to pardon and to appoint people to various official posts, require the countersignature of the Prime Minister (or another relevant minister), which is typical of parliamentary systems. But the President can exercise a number of substantive powers without reference to the views of those political leaders who can be held accountable by the legislature.

The President designates the Prime Minister. Although the National Assembly can vote the Prime Minister out of office, the person the President chooses needs no legislative approval to select a Cabinet and begin governing. (As you saw in Chapter 14, the investiture procedure has fallen into desuetude.) The President may dissolve the National Assembly and call for new elections at any time. The only limits on this power are that dissolutions must be at least a year apart and the President must consult with (but doesn't have to comply with the views of) the Prime Minister and the presidents of both houses of the legislature. If the Prime Minister wishes to have new elections, however, the President can refuse the request to dissolve the National Assembly. Similarly, the Cabinet or the legislature can propose that a referendum be held on some issue, but the President can refuse to call one.

The President can ask the Constitutional Council (three of whose members, including its presiding officer, are presidential appointees) to rule on the constitutionality of bills and laws. If the Prime Minister agrees, the President can ask Parliament to reconsider a bill that it has passed. Although this step forces Parliament to take the bill through all its stages a second time, no special majority is required to enact it again. Thus, the French President, for all the powers of the office, lacks the veto power of the U.S. President.

In some matters, then, the French President can be constrained by other political institutions—something of a Gallic (not Gaullic) version of American checks and balances. In one key instance, however, that of emergency powers, no constraint exists. "When the institutions of the Republic, the independence of the nation, the integrity of its territory, or the fulfillment of its international commitments are threatened in a grave and immediate manner and the regular functioning of the constitutional governmental authorities is interrupted," says Article 16 of the constitution, "the President of the Republic shall take the measures required by these circumstances." If ever a blank check existed, this is it. The President needs only to consult the Prime Minister, the presidents of both houses of the legislature, and the Constitutional Council. Having done so, the President may rule as he or she chooses. True, the nation must be informed of what is being done, and the legislature cannot be dissolved or adjourned, but these are hardly serious limitations. The President's actions "must be prompted by the desire to ensure to the constitutional governmental authorities, in the shortest possible time, the means of fulfilling their assigned functions." Such a justification differs little from the motives expressed by military officers staging a coup in a banana republic. The constitution sets no time limit on the emergency powers; the President can continue to exercise them as long as he or she wishes.

Although the legislature is entitled to meet while emergency powers are in effect, it apparently cannot remove the Cabinet from office. Article 16 has been invoked only once—for five months in 1961. During that period no censure motions were permitted on the agenda of the National Assembly. The rationalization offered for this bar was that if the Cabinet were censured, legislative elections might be necessary to determine whether the electorate sided with the executive or the legislature. Since Article 16 prohibits dissolution of the legislature during an emergency, elections could not be held. Therefore, allowing a censure motion could create an impasse. The logic of this argument could be used to support a coup. An incipient dictator who managed to get elected President not only could take whatever actions he or she claimed some trumped-up emergency required, but, by keeping Article 16 in effect, could avoid ever calling new legislative elections.

Given the ambiguities and elasticity of the constitution, the actual operation of the Fifth Republic is of considerable importance in manifesting the complete nature of the office of President. Furthermore, remember that the office was tailor-made for its first occupant, General Charles de Gaulle. The French Presidency is shaped even more by de Gaulle than the American Presidency was by George Washington, partly because Washington served two centuries ago and de Gaulle held office only a generation ago.

■ *DE GAULLE'S IMPACT ON THE PRESIDENCY*

During the first decade of the Fifth Republic, de Gaulle so dominated France that the political system often was labeled "the de Gaulle Republic." His serving as President ensured that the office would be much more than a ceremonial post.

Although often seeking to convey the impression that he stood aloof from the partisan battles of the political arena, de Gaulle was the prime mover in the politics of the early Fifth Republic. His style of personal leadership often violated both the spirit and the letter of the constitution. Having arrogated to himself the power to interpret the meaning of "his" constitution, he avoided any serious challenge to his rule until the crisis of 1968. His high-handed behavior evoked considerable criticism, however, and caused partisan controversy—precisely the situation that the ceremonial head of state in Britain seeks to avoid at all costs.

Trying to explain how de Gaulle conceived of the office of Presidency, some students of the Fifth Republic developed the doctrine of reserve powers and open areas. According to this view, defense and foreign policy were reserved for action by the President. Domestic policy was an open area, where the entire executive could participate in the discussion of policy alternatives.

The constitution does, indeed, make the President commander of the armed forces and says that he or she "shall preside over the higher councils and committees of national defense." On the other hand, it also provides that the Prime Minister "shall be responsible for national defense." De Gaulle wasn't concerned about any confusion. Since foreign policy and defense obviously affect the entire nation, they must be my affair, he concluded, since my office has the duty to guarantee national independence, the integrity of the territory, and the continuity of the state.

As for domestic policy, de Gaulle once contemptuously dismissed these matters as "decisions concerning the price of milk." As such, they lacked the exalted importance of defense and foreign policy and, generally, were below the President's dignity. Nonetheless, should he care to intervene in such affairs, the President's views would be decisive. Quite simply, de Gaulle himself never accepted the doctrine of reserve powers and open areas. Such a doctrine was too restrictive—his authority to make policy should be unlimited.

In the exercise of emergency powers, de Gaulle insisted that he was the sole judge of the propriety of all governmental actions for the duration of an emergency. Even though a majority of the deputies, in accord with constitutional provision, requested a special session of the legislature during the time that emergency powers were in effect in 1961, he refused to permit this.

Thus, in whatever matters he considered vital, de Gaulle used the Presidency to determine official policy. At times, he would decide what steps should be taken and then simply inform the Prime Minister and the Cabinet, rather than involving them in reaching the decision. He maintained his own set of technical committees and personal advisors totally apart from the rest of the executive. If the Prime Minister made a policy statement that de Gaulle disliked, he simply contradicted him, and the Prime Minister would be forced publicly to "change his mind." Only those people of whom de Gaulle approved were appointed to the Cabinet, regardless of what the Prime Minister preferred. And when the President became dissatisfied with their work, they would have to resign, no matter what the Prime Minister thought about their service.

Through trips and declarations of policy, he became the voice of France in both foreign and domestic policy. His insistence on pomp and ceremony focused the political limelight on himself. He was able to exert personal leadership because of his success in appealing to French national pride. On matters such as the future of NATO, the development of the EEC, and relations with the Soviet Union, de Gaulle forced other countries to concede considerable weight to France's positions. Unlike the situation during the Fourth Republic, the international community could not discount French views.

Another major element in de Gaulle's success was popular support. As French rulers in the nineteenth century had, he used referenda to demonstrate that the people approved of what he was doing, thus buttressing his authority. Although the constitution gave him no power to initiate referenda, he was in fact the source of all that were held. One referendum was used to amend the constitution in a fashion not permitted. Despite the patent illegality of this action, neither the legislature nor the Constitutional Council could prevent it. Thus, the constitution was amended unconstitutionally simply because that was President de Gaulle's will.

The dominance of de Gaulle began to crumble toward the close of the 1960s. In mid-1968, student demonstrations over centralized, outmoded, and overcrowded universities soon triggered worker protests. Half of the French industrial work force went out on strike, and workers occupied hundreds of factories. We now know, from the posthumously published memoirs of Georges Pompidou (Prime Minister at the time), that for perhaps the only time in his life de Gaulle panicked. He fled Paris without leaving a forwarding address—the Prime Minister did not know where to find him. Many speculated that de Gaulle had gone to Germany to assure himself of the support of the French troops stationed there before taking a tough stance against the demonstrators. Although he indeed had gone to Germany, his purpose was to arrange to go into exile there. Only when the general in charge of the French troops there persuaded him to return to Paris did he do so.

Upon his return, he dissolved the National Assembly, calling for new elections. To the public it appeared that he had once again demonstrated decisiveness and coolness under fire. In any event, the public had become exasperated with the disorder caused by the protesters. The Prime Minister and de Gaulle managed to make the public believe that the demonstrations were all the fault of the Communists, and the Gaullists won a landslide victory.

Once again de Gaulle seemed firmly in control, but a new restiveness was developing in France. Early in 1969 he sought again to amend the constitution by means of a referendum. Once again, as he had done so often in the past, de Gaulle told the people they could do what they wished, but if they failed to approve his proposed reforms he would take his marbles and go home.

Despite this threat (some might have said inducement), the electorate rejected de Gaulle's proposals by a vote of 11.9 million against to 10.5 million in favor. He promptly declared that he was ceasing to exercise his functions as President of the Republic, despite being only about halfway through a seven-year term. He felt repudiated by the French people, and, just as he had done twenty-three years earlier when they had ignored his advice to reject the constitution for the new Fourth Republic, he turned his back on them and left them to work out their destiny for themselves. Given de Gaulle's use—indeed abuse—of referenda, it seems fitting that this is the tactic that finally brought him down. (Those who live by the sword . . . .)

The fascinating question, of course, is why did the French do it? Why, after years of supporting de Gaulle in all kinds of questionable actions, did they finally repudiate him? No one can say whether the French really did intend to cast de Gaulle aside, whether they believed he really would carry out his threat to resign if the referendum failed. Perhaps they had wearied of his high-handed style and no longer cared whether he stayed in power. If this is so, a key factor may have been that for the first time an alternative was available. When asked about the future, de Gaulle often had said, *"Après moi, le déluge"* (which translates loosely as "When I'm gone, all hell will break loose"). Until 1968 this had seemed a pretty plausible prediction.

Whatever the public might have known about de Gaulle's conduct during the 1968 demonstrations, they were aware that Prime Minister Pompidou had played an important role in containing the protests. He had demonstrated that he could act coolly and effectively. Despite the assistance that Pompidou had provided to de Gaulle in winning the 1968 legislative elections, the President had not kept him on as Prime Minister. As a result, Pompidou was not shy in making clear his interest in serving as President, should there happen to be a vacancy in that office. Thus, the French, relatively confident that disaster would not befall them for their transgression, may have decided to defy their guardian's instructions. De Gaulle had become what he never anticipated he would be—expendable.

■ THE PRESIDENCY SINCE DE GAULLE

Although de Gaulle's decade in office was the formative influence on the French Presidency, the actions of his successors and their relations with their Prime Ministers also have shaped the office. For more than two-thirds of the Fifth Republic, someone other than de Gaulle has served as President. Thus, there has been ample time to ascertain whether the form he gave to the office has been able to endure through diverse successors and their experiences.

The second President, Georges Pompidou, had only limited opportunity to put his mark on the office, since death shortened his term to only five years. Ironically, although Pompidou had been irritated by de Gaulle's treatment of him when he served as Prime Minister, he himself functioned as President much as de Gaulle had. The grandeur of the office and its dominant role in French politics were maintained or even enhanced. The photos of the first two Presidents of the Fifth Republic in Figure 15–1 seem to have been shot at one of those amusement arcades where you have your picture taken with your head thrust through a sheet of plywood painted to show a funny scene or character. The background and the body appear to be the same and only the head has changed.

When Giscard was elected to succeed Pompidou, he seemed to offer a less regal image. He stressed his relative youthfulness—not only was he the youngest major candidate, but he was considerably younger than de Gaulle or Pompidou had been—and his dynamism. His four children bicycled around France leading groups of teenagers wearing tee-shirts emblazoned with the slogan *Giscard à la barre* ("Giscard to the helm"). It was all very American and would have appalled de Gaulle.

Although Giscard was from a party on the right of the spectrum, he projected the image of a reformer. He wanted to liberalize France's abortion and divorce laws and to end the political bias of government-controlled broadcasting. To demonstrate his desire for close contacts with the people, he announced that he would accept dinner invitations from private citizens. For several years after becoming President, he actually did eat with "typical" families two or three times a year. Driving his own car, he and his wife would arrive unescorted for dinner, remaining a few hours afterward for conversation. Although his motives may well have been sincere, an idea of the general reaction to such behavior can be gleaned from the fact that Paris specialty shops began to sell plasticized aprons with a caricature of Giscard's face and the question *Devine Qui Vient Diner Ce Soir?* ("Guess Who's Coming to Dinner Tonight?").

Further undercutting Giscard's image were various "scandals," the most widely discussed of which concerned diamonds. The dictator of a former French colony in central Africa gave some diamonds to Giscard, apparently in appreciation for French military and financial aid, which helped him keep control over his country. In the United States, gifts (other than those of the most minimal value) received by the President in his official capacity must be turned over to the government. The gift is assumed to be to the office rather than to the holder of it. If the President kept the gift, it might appear that he was being bribed. Giscard did not reveal that he had received such a gift. Only some time later did a satirical French magazine

Figure 15–1
Presidents of the
Fifth Republic

Charles de Gaulle 1958–1969

Georges Pompidou 1969–1974

Valéry Giscard d'Estaing 1974–1981

François Mitterrand 1981–

break the story. Giscard first claimed that the diamonds were small and worth little. When this failed to quiet criticism, he claimed to have sold them and given the money to charity (recipients unspecified).

Giscard's graceless exit from office did little to help his image. No one knew how to handle the Presidential transition. Since de Gaulle had resigned and Pompidou had died, Giscard was the first President to serve a full term after being directly elected. Did Giscard's term expire seven years from the day of his election, or from the day that the results had been announced officially, or from the day that he took up residency in the Palais-Elysée, the President's home? Giscard broadcast a farewell to the nation seven years to the day after he had been elected, and two days later he transferred power to Mitterrand. Thus, the new President came into office only eleven days after his election, quite a contrast to the two and a half months of cooperative activities that smooth the transition from one U.S. President to another. Giscard's attitude throughout the proceedings seemed to be one of pique that the voters had dared to deprive him of a personal possession and bestow it on an interloper.

Thus, by the end of his Presidency, Giscard had become at least as aloof and regal as de Gaulle had been. During the Johnson and Nixon Administrations in the United States, many observers worried about an "imperial presidency." In France, such an executive seemed almost a matter of course. Mitterrand's Presidency has provided a good test of whether the office itself tends to produce such behavior. For the first time someone from the left of center has been in charge. Although Mitterrand had often complained about the excessive grandeur of the Presidency, he was not known as someone having the common touch. Despite his long career in politics, he is a remarkably private man. He is quiet, even taciturn. His great love of nature and the countryside causes him to spend a good deal of time in solitary pursuits, out of the public eye.

The effects of the office soon seemed to exert themselves on Mitterrand. People said that his press conferences resembled in style the legendary ones of de Gaulle: "Let me have your questions for the answers I have prepared." His behavior was sufficiently autocratic that he was nicknamed Uncle Napoleon. Conflicts within the executive would be resolved by a phone call from "The Château," as insiders mockingly referred to the Palais-Elysée (see Figure 15–2). Just as de Gaulle had done, Mitterrand came to rely on his own staff of advisors in making policy, rather than developing it in discussions with the Cabinet.

Mitterrand has proved to be a pragmatist, little committed to ideology. His socialism has been more a socialism of the heart; he has scorned the power that wealth bestows and has been committed to social equality. Given his limited knowledge of economic principles and theories, he has had little interest in economic collectivism.

Rather hawkish on defense, he has been more sympathetic to the United States and suspicious of the Soviet Union than were any of his predecessors, despite complaints about U.S. policy in Central America and his refusal to let U.S. planes fly over France on their way to bomb Libya. Mitterrand did not bring France back into full military integration within NATO, but he made France a more cooperative member of the alliance than it had been under de Gaulle. Contrary to de Gaulle's obsession

Figure 15–2
The Château

with ridding Europe of American influence, Mitterrand welcomed an American presence (although not in France) as a major contribution to European stability and French security.

Austerity measures undercut Mitterrand's early support. Midway through his first term he had become the most unpopular President in French history—only a quarter of those polled were satisfied with his performance. Subsequent improvement in the economy helped him to recover. During the 1988 presidential election campaign, he managed to project the image of a shrewd elderly uncle, which the voters found more attractive than the frenetic personal ambition of Chirac. Mitterrand won handily—the first President to be reelected under the direct popular vote system. Only a few months later, however, a French newsmagazine was complaining about his regal airs and staff of flatterers, referring to "the king and his court."

Recall that after a decade in office, de Gaulle was weakened by the riots of 1968; the following year he left office. (Recall also that Margaret Thatcher served just about the same length of time as Prime Minister of Britain.) Perhaps there is something about ten years in office for a chief executive that makes the public long for change. As Mitterrand approached his decade in the spring of 1991, the cry was heard, *"dix ans, ça suffit"* ("ten years, that's enough"). Mitterrand was not to be budged. Even though he often had talked of reducing the President's term to five years, he made clear that such a change would not apply to him. By the end of 1991, he had established a new record low for presidential unpopularity. Only 22 percent were satisfied with him, and 65 percent were dissatisfied.

Fascinatingly, a referendum almost did him in, just as it had de Gaulle. Mitterrand decided to let the public vote on the Maastricht Treaty, even though the constitution didn't require this for France to ratify the treaty. At the time it looked like a shrewd maneuver. Opinion polls showed substantial public support for the treaty, suggesting that a referendum was risk-free. But its real attraction for Mitterrand was the chance to make mischief among his opponents. As you saw in Chapter 13, the RPR has been suspicious of, if not hostile to, supranational aspects of the EC. On the other hand, the UDF, especially the CDS component, has been quite supportive of European integration. Mitterrand saw a chance to split his opponents by forcing them to campaign for and against the referendum. As a Frenchman, Mitterrand might not be familiar with the British expression "too clever by half." When the referendum was held in September 1992, a third of the voters stayed home. Worse, the treaty just squeaked through, 51 percent to 49 percent. Narrow as the margin was, Mitterrand could claim something of a personal victory since he had performed well in the debates during the referendum campaign.

Shortly before the polling day for the referendum, Mitterrand entered a hospital for surgery for prostate cancer. Upon his release, when asked whether he was thinking of resigning, he rejected the idea, saying, "I don't think that they gave me a lobotomy." Nor did they put a splint on one of his legs, but if ever there were a lame duck, it was Mitterrand—with three years still to serve.

One would be hard-pressed to find four individuals more different from each other than the men who have served as French President. As he himself would have been the first to say, there could be only one de Gaulle. But the style in which he served and the precedents he established have shaped the office perhaps even more than the constitutional arrangements have. His conceptualization of the French Presidency as an office of substantive powers, going well beyond a mere ceremonial role, has endured in the decades since he departed from the political scene. He left a heritage of power more concentrated than in any other French republic. His successors have seemed almost compelled to conform to the template he created.

■ INTRAEXECUTIVE RELATIONS

If the French Presidency were merely a ceremonial office, like the British monarchy, then its relations with the rest of the executive would be of limited interest. Since the Fifth Republic divides substantive executive power between the President, on the one hand, and the Prime Minister and the Cabinet, on the other, relations within the executive are a matter of major importance.

The Position of the Cabinet

The Cabinet (officially the Council of Ministers) is composed of the Prime Minister and an unspecified number of colleagues. Recent Cabinets have numbered close to thirty. Most of those included are ministers in charge of particular departments. The Balladur Government formed after the 1993 elections, included four ministers of state, who ranked above the others in the Cabinet. Some junior executives, known as minister delegates or secretaries of state, have been included at times. Counting all types of positions, the total number of executive leaders can run to about fifty.

Article 23 (the incompatibility rule) prohibits anyone holding one of these positions from serving in the legislature. This may be why the total number of executive positions in France is only about half as large as in Britain. If a French deputy is selected to serve in the executive, he or she must resign from the legislature. This does not prevent Cabinet members from participating in the legislature's debates; however, they no longer have a vote. In Britain, the Cabinet can count on the support of the "payroll" vote—holders of executive office number about a sixth of the House of Commons' membership—to see them through votes in the legislature. The French Cabinet lacks such aid.

The incompatibility rule is another instance of the hybrid nature of the French political system. The hallmark of a parliamentary system is the fusion of powers. Typically, this means that members of the executive not only are drawn from the legislature, but also continue to serve there while they serve in the executive. Although departing from this practice, the Fifth Republic has not swung over to the U.S. system of complete separation of powers; members of the French executive branch continue to have floor privileges in the legislature, unlike U.S. Cabinet members.

The incompatibility rule was intended to strengthen the executive. During the Third and Fourth Republics, members of the executive played musical chairs. Once a Cabinet fell, those ministers who did not manage to find a place in the subsequent one remained in the legislature waiting their turn, which probably would come about six months later, given the life of a typical Cabinet in those Republics. The fall of a Cabinet cost a minister something, but was not a major career setback. Therefore, a minister lacked incentive for making an all-out effort to marshal friends to support a challenged Cabinet.

When a Cabinet falls in the Fifth Republic, however, ministers not only are out of executive office, but also find themselves without a seat in the legislature. Increasing ministers' personal stake in a Cabinet's defeat was seen as a means of strengthening their commitment to the Cabinet. They would be more likely to try to mobilize all their friends to beat off any challenge to the Cabinet's program.

The constitution provides that the Cabinet "shall determine and direct the policy of the nation." The Cabinet can regulate by decree those matters not entrusted by the constitution to the legislature. Furthermore, the legislature can delegate areas normally within its domain to the executive for regulation by decree. When it does so, it denies itself any power to legislate on those matters.

Despite having such powers the Cabinet is not a forum for collective decision making. The Cabinet usually meets once a week for two or three hours. Much of each meeting is devoted to what elementary schools call "show and tell." Dissent is rarely permitted, and discussion occurs in name only. The meetings amount to little more than highly formal reports of important decisions that have been made elsewhere. The atmosphere of Cabinet meetings is encapsulated in the following incident. President Giscard had maneuvered his Prime Minister, Jacques Chirac, into resigning. Chirac's imminent departure was widely known. The day on which he had scheduled a public announcement happened to be the day of a Cabinet meeting. Giscard conducted the meeting as though nothing unusual were to occur. Then at the end he turned to Chirac and said, "Mr. Prime Minister, I understand you have something to tell us."

The President's Relations with the Prime Minister

As the incident just described indicates, the President—not the Prime Minister—presides over Cabinet meetings. The Prime Minister supervises the drawing up of an agenda for these meetings. This draft, however, has to be discussed with the President, who must give final approval before it is issued. Minutes of the meetings are taken by both a member of the Prime Minister's staff and one of the President's staff. The Prime Minister's office submits draft minutes to the President for approval. The minutes are confidential, and the only copy of record is kept in the presidential archives.

The President clearly can decide what the relationship with the Prime Minister will be; so far in the Fifth Republic it has been basically one of superior to subordinate, despite a good bit of variety. One of de Gaulle's early Prime Ministers, Maurice Couve de Murville, was a career diplomat who functioned as little more than the President's agent. In contrast, Pompidou did initiate some policy as Prime Minister, despite having to deal with de Gaulle as President. Giscard used his Prime Minister, Raymond Barre, as a shield. When the tough measures necessary to deal with inflation aroused public discontent, Barre had to take the blame. On the other hand, Giscard did give him a relatively free hand to formulate economic policy.

Regardless of his earlier complaints about excessive presidential power, Mitterrand showed no inclination once he was elected to the office to defer to the Prime Minister. He and his personal assistant met each Tuesday morning at breakfast with the Prime Minister and the head of the Socialist party. The point of these meetings was not so much to let the President know what was going on in the Government as it was for him to issue instructions concerning what he wanted to have done. At times Mitterrand would secretly formulate new policies of his own, informing the Prime Minister only when they were fully drafted and ready to be introduced to the legislature. Mitterrand was not content simply to direct policy; he also kept a close watch on style and procedure. At one point the Prime Minister made light of disagreements among members of the Cabinet, observing that Socialists ran a more democratic government than did parties of the right and thus tolerated contrasting views. From on high, Mitterrand issued the pronouncement that ministers could speak outside the Cabinet only if in doing so they did not undermine the Cabinet's coherence and cohesion.

From 1988 to 1991, Michel Rocard served as Prime Minister. He and Mitterrand have been longtime political rivals, heading opposed currents in the PS. As Prime Minister, Rocard clearly was more than just the President's errand boy. Yet even he didn't oppose the President's lead. For example, he gave way when Mitterrand refused to let him use Article 49-3 to enact legislation on local government taxes.

Edith Cresson, France's first female Prime Minister, followed Rocard in office and served for only ten and a half months—the shortest prime ministerial tenure of the Fifth Republic. Although she had been in politics for some time, she lacked any power base in the PS and was a Mitterrand protégé. Thus she functioned merely as Mitterrand's agent.

Cresson's successor, Pierre Bérégovoy, was a longtime Mitterrand associate, having run the President's 1988 campaign for reelection. Bérégovoy was the archetypical socialist, having been a skilled manual worker who never went to high school. That kind of background counts for something in the PS. Although Bérégovoy could count on more personal support in the PS than Cresson could, he certainly wasn't the power baron that Rocard was. Thus he had little scope for developing a policy program independent of the President's. Whatever the variations in detail for specific instances, the President remains the chief figure within the executive.

Cohabitation

The truth of the statement just made, however, was not entirely certain at two points in the Fifth Republic, one from 1986 to 1988 and the other beginning in 1993. For almost the first thirty years of the Fifth Republic's existence, the President and the legislature always coincided; that is, parties favorable to the President held a majority of the seats in the legislature. Americans have gotten used to divided control. Of the forty years from 1953 to 1993, the Republicans held the U.S. Presidency for twenty-eight. During that time they controlled the Senate for only eight years and the House of Representatives never. Republican Presidents always had to wonder whether they would be able to get Congress to approve their policies. Such a situation may be tolerable in the United States (although many reformers argue that this is the source of most of the country's governmental problems), in part because the American system has separation of powers: there is no Prime Minister; the legislature cannot vote the Cabinet out of office. Therefore, the United States doesn't have executive instability.

As you have seen, the Fifth Republic is not a pure parliamentary system in the British fashion. Nonetheless, it does have elements of a parliamentary system: part of the executive is accountable to the legislature. How can the Prime Minister please a legislature having one political orientation and a President having another? Can the President, with all the powers of the office, be an effective leader without majority support in the legislature? In short, is the Fifth Republic fundamentally unworkable when the majority of the legislature and the President are from different parties? Until this question could be answered, it was impossible to say whether the Fifth Republic would be a durable, viable system or—like its predecessors—would have to be scrapped in favor of a Sixth Republic.

Since the President's term is seven years and the legislature can serve for no more than five, the possibility that the two branches might be out of phase became a reality in 1986. Mitterrand, a Socialist, still had two years left in his term when his party lost its control of the legislature and right-wing parties won a majority of the seats. Mitterrand had been fully involved in the campaign for the legislative elections and had threatened to resign if there was a big right-wing victory. Some thought he should do so to see whether the voters would elect a right-of-center President in order to bring the two branches into political coincidence again. Mitterrand remained in office, however, and appointed the leader of the dominant right-wing party, Chirac, as Prime Minister. The Prime Minister clearly could count on the support of the legislature, but could he and the President "cohabit"?

The first conflict arose over membership in the Cabinet—Mitterrand vetoed some of Chirac's choices. The agreement that eventually was reached was that since the constitution gave the President preeminence in defense and foreign policy, Chirac would concede the final say about these two appointments to Mitterrand. Concerning other Cabinet posts, Mitterrand would have to give way if Chirac insisted. This arrangement was not a major departure from past practice. Remember that de Gaulle had a major voice in determining Cabinet appointments and that the doctrine of reserve powers and open areas had been widely discussed, if not fully accepted. The difference, of course, was that in the past such negotiations were conducted by two executives from the same party.

As for the substance of policy, an arrangement was not worked out, although conflict never got entirely out of hand. Chirac wanted to implement various economic measures by decree. Mitterrand responded that the law enabling the executive to do this must be quite precise and the subsequent decrees few in number, in order to protect the legislature's powers. He warned that he would block (refuse to sign) changes in labor legislation unless they were approved by the legislature.

Nonetheless, provisions making it easier for employers to dismiss surplus staff were enacted by decree. On the other hand, Mitterrand refused to sign decrees that would have denationalized enterprises that had been taken into government ownership prior to 1981—he regarded these takeovers as having happened sufficiently long ago that changes in their status should no longer be a matter of public debate. As a result, the Cabinet had to act in this area by passing a bill through the legislature.

Similarly, Mitterrand refused to sign decrees establishing new constituency boundaries when the Cabinet changed the electoral system from proportional representation back to the double ballot system. He argued that the legislature, not the Cabinet, should decide these. He was on particularly firm ground in this instance because the bill that had given the Cabinet power to determine the boundaries by decree had been passed after only two hours of debate—the Cabinet had simply rammed it through. Opposition from Mitterrand again forced the Cabinet to take a bill through the legislature to make changes rather than implementing them by executive fiat.

One aspect of the period of cohabitation descended almost to the comical. Neither Mitterrand nor Chirac was willing to let the other represent France abroad. They both traveled to international conferences. What the leaders of other countries made of this bicephalous delegation is hard to say.

Although the French electorate did not find the arrangement intolerable, they apparently were less willing to accept divided control than American voters are. In

1988 Mitterrand's term expired. When he was reelected, he offered an opportunity to get both branches back into sync by calling for new legislative elections. The results made it possible to appoint a Socialist in place of Chirac, even though the voters did not give the Socialists a majority of the seats. Thus, to some relief, the period of cohabitation came to an end. Although brief, it lasted long enough to demonstrate that the Fifth Republic's hybrid system is workable even under adverse circumstances that subject it to a fair amount of strain.

Another period of cohabitation began following the 1993 legislative elections. In this case, however, instead of having only a modest majority, the RPR and the UDF held well over three-quarters of the seats. Clearly, the new Prime Minister would be able to speak with an authority that Chirac had not enjoyed. Mitterrand appointed Edouard Balladur of the RPR. Balladur comes from a rich banking family. He is what is known as a technocrat, an expert (in his case, in economics) with a career in business and governmental bureaucracy. He was not a career politician; Balladur didn't enter parliament until his late fifties and had served in the legislature only a few years before becoming Prime Minister. He had been a close advisor to Pompidou both when he was President and when he served as Prime Minister.

Balladur is much more emollient than Chirac is; the second period of cohabitation promises to be much smoother than the first one was. In contrast to the previous haggling over executive appointments, Balladur submitted his list of ministers and Mitterrand accepted it, despite the fact that the nominee for minister of defense had been rejected for that post by Mitterrand in 1986. Balladur quickly established the practice of regularly consulting with Mitterrand. They agreed that foreign policy would not be a reserved presidential area (recall the earlier discussion on de Gaulle's influence on the Presidency), but a shared responsibility. In contrast to the François and Jacques show at international conferences, Balladur was willing to remain home and let Mitterrand represent France at the G7 conference in Tokyo in 1993.

Although clashes over the substance of policy could develop, major storms didn't seem to be lurking just over the horizon. Balladur's Government launched a drive for privatization of government enterprises. Such flagship operations as Air France and Renault were among the twenty-one enterprises to be sold to private investors. Mitterrand didn't attempt to raise obstacles as he had when the Chirac Government had embarked on such a program. Referring to the law authorizing the sale, he commented, "Once it has been passed I become a notary. It is my duty to sign and I sign." He contented himself simply with urging "extreme caution" about the sale of enterprises important to national security, such as an aerospace company, an aero-engine manufacturer, and an oil group.

Law and order appeared to be the main aspect of the Balladur Government's program that might cause a problem. The new Minister of Interior, Charles Pasqua, planned a strong anti-immigrant policy. When, in his capacity as head of the police, Pasqua submitted to the Cabinet a report on law and order embodying his views, Mitterrand demurred. He felt the report was biased because it failed to say anything about the three instances in the previous week in which the police had shot (needlessly, it seemed) young lawbreakers.

So "Cohabitation II" seemed to be working well. To the extent that cohabitation leaves ambiguous who really wields the ultimate power, however, it makes establishing responsibility more difficult. That is, it tends to attenuate accountability.

■ ■ ■

Although cohabitation blurs the picture somewhat, the Fifth Republic has operated more like a presidential system than like a parliamentary one. The tilting of power away from the dominant legislatures of the Third and Fourth Republics and toward the executive has strengthened the President considerably more than it has the Prime Minister and the Cabinet. Although the system has developed this way, the constitution does not require Presidential dominance. A future President might conceive of the office as simply that of ceremonial head of state and might defer to the Prime Minister and the Cabinet on policy formation. Had de Gaulle chosen to be Prime Minister, not President, back in 1958, we no doubt would be writing about the preeminence of the Prime Minister. The main advantage the President possesses in constitutional power is the ability to invoke emergency powers, but nothing compels the use of that power. The President also has some advantage in enjoying a fixed term of seven years, since the Prime Minister can be voted out of office by the legislature at any time.

Thus, the personality of officeholders has been more important than constitutional provisions. In Chapter 14 you saw that changes in the party system have contributed more to the new executive stability in France than have constitutional arrangements. This is also the case with relations within the executive—the constitution is not unimportant, but it has not been the determining factor. Those who draft constitutions can have only limited impact on their country's political development—a point of some relevance when we discuss Germany.

......16

Policy-Implementing Structures

The Third and Fourth Republics, with their tradition of assembly government, were characterized by dispersed, not concentrated, power. Paradoxically, the most notable feature of one element of those systems—the administrative structure—was centralization. This continues to characterize French bureaucracy in the Fifth Republic.

Like Britain, France is a unitary state. Therefore, you should expect the national government in both countries to be more pervasive in local affairs than is true in the American federal system. Despite this similarity in type of system, however, the two countries differ so greatly in the relevant structures that what is termed local government in Britain is more appropriately considered the lowest level of national administration in France. Much of the centralized bureaucracy created by Napoleon nearly two centuries ago still survives. Because of the weakness and instability of the political executive during the Third and Fourth Republics, the professional, career civil servants in the executive branch played an important role in French government. Precisely because the bureaucratic administration provided a source of concentrated power, offering some continuity and direction as an antidote to excessive flux and drift, it won a good bit of favor.

Paradoxically, in another aspect French public administration was loosely integrated and did disperse power. At the national level (as distinct from the national-local relation noted in the preceding paragraph), governmental departments are not as hierarchically organized as in Britain. This chapter examines these contrasting arrangements and assesses their implications for accountability.

■ STAFFING THE BUREAUCRACY

Not until the Fourth Republic did France establish a single, unified civil service system. Hiring on the basis of merit had been instituted much earlier, but each government department was basically free to recruit staff according to its own procedures. As a result, personnel entering the civil service in one ministry rarely moved to another. Civil servants developed a highly specialized knowledge of their own ministry, but lacked a broad view of the government's activities and responsibilities.

A unified recruitment system with common rules throughout the government concerning promotion and discipline was established under the Fourth Republic. Even then, however, some agencies remained outside the civil service staffing regulations. Training of personnel did become more uniform, and transferring staff from one ministry to another became easier.

To establish a common recruitment system and provide top administrators with the skills needed in their work, the National School of Administration (*École Nationale d'Administration,* or ENA) was created by executive order in 1945. The office of the Prime Minister is in charge of the ENA, and a director chosen by the Cabinet is responsible for its day-to-day operations.

The school is open to two groups of people: those with university degrees who are not yet twenty-five years old and civil servants under thirty with five years of service. Two means of entry were provided to try to "democratize" the civil service—to reduce the class bias that characterized the French bureaucracy, just as it does the British. Making young civil servants who lacked a university degree eligible for entry would permit people from lower economic and social levels to rise to positions of responsibility, if they were capable.

Admission to the ENA is highly competitive. Students must take a long and difficult series of written examinations; those for civil servants are somewhat easier. Applicants who score well on the written exams are given a series of oral ones. The exam results are used to rank the applicants, and the top 150 or so are admitted each year. Despite the intent of using promotion from within to help democratize the civil service, usually about two-thirds of those admitted to the ENA are students. Civil servants lacking a university education or an upper-class background tend not to do well on the type of exams used to determine admission.

When the Socialists came to power early in the 1980s, they made a further attempt at reform. People who "have shown their devotion to public service," for example, trade unionists, local government councilors, and members of community associations, are permitted to take a special entrance exam. Furthermore, they are guaranteed an interview with the admissions committee. Ten of the places for admission each year are reserved for those going through these procedures. Although of possible symbolic importance, this actually was a very modest reform.

The ENA training program begins with a year's internship at some important administrative agency. The duties assigned are not mere errand running, but include discretionary decision making. The internship is followed with seventeen months of study back at the school itself. For virtually all of its life, the ENA was located on a rather dingy side street. Unless you knew where to look, you could easily walk right by the brass plaque identifying the school on the pillar next to the doorway leading into the courtyard around which the classrooms were grouped. You can see the entrance in Figure 16–1.

In 1991 the Government announced that the ENA would be moved to Strasbourg in 1992. This was supposed to be part of a program of shifting government offices out of Paris and into the countryside. Remember, however, that the Prime Minister at the time, Edith Cresson, was little more than Mitterrand's agent. Neither she nor he had attended the ENA. The move may well have been motivat-

Figure 16–1
The Entrance to
the ENA

ed more by a desire to win favor with the public by attacking an elite than by a desire to decentralize the government. Jacques Chirac, an ENA graduate, announced, as mayor of Paris, that the city would purchase the ENA building so that the school could be returned to Paris when the right returned to power.

The typical ENA course is a small seminar. The ENA has no regular faculty, using instead, on a part-time basis, those holding relatively high positions in the civil service. An elaborate grading system covering all aspects of work during the program is used to rank the participants. Each year the members of the graduating class choose, in order of their rank, among the available government positions. Only the top fifteen to twenty have much hope of getting one of the "plums," a position with the *grand corps* (the elite sections of the civil service, including the Council of State, the Court of Accounts, and the Inspectorate of Finances).

Overestimating the importance of the ENA would be difficult. The reason is not the quality of its educational program. What the participants have learned no doubt helps them to function effectively as administrators. More important is the program's effect in creating a pool of recruits for top governmental positions, all of whom have had a similar socialization experience, which facilitates their interactions throughout their careers.

Although the total number of ENA graduates is not great—under 4,000—they occupy key positions not only in the bureaucracy but also in the political leadership. At one point in the mid-1970s, half the members of the Cabinet were ENA graduates. The school's alumni can be found across the political spectrum. Both Chirac (as mentioned earlier) and Giscard graduated from the ENA, as did Prime Minister Edouard Balladur, Laurent Fabius (the Socialist Prime Minister early in the 1980s), and Michel Rocard (the Socialist Prime Minister at the close of that decade). Pierre Bérégovoy, the manual worker who became Prime Minister in the early 1990s, was seen as something of an outsider, despite his long career in politics, because he hadn't been to the ENA. Although it is a bit of an exaggeration, someone coined the term *enarchy* to suggest that France is ruled by an elite produced by the ENA.

■ BUREAUCRACY'S IMPACT ON PUBLIC POLICY

National Administration

As in Britain, political leaders in France are placed in charge of the various ministries making up the administrative system. These ministries tend to be rather loosely organized. The basic unit is the bureau, headed by a chief. Related bureaus are combined in *directions* (divisions), which are headed by directors. In contrast to British ministries, however, no official comparable to a permanent secretary exists in France to coordinate the various divisions.

Thus, contrary to what some have argued, the instability of the executive was important. The rapid turnover in political ministers was dismissed as of little significance because the civil servants continued on as usual, keeping the government operating efficiently. The lack of a permanent secretary on the British model, however, made coordinating policy and maintaining continuity difficult. Given the administrative structure, policy tended to be less consistent and integrated during times of political instability.

The bureaucracy's effect on policy tended to be negative. That is, in the absence of adequate coordination, preventing something from being done is much easier than implementing a new program. The brief tenure of ministers during the Third and Fourth Republics encouraged civil servants to pay little attention to a new minister's desire for policy or procedural innovations. Civil servants could simply drag their feet for a while, and the minister who was making waves would be gone, to be replaced by a new minister who might prefer a quiet life, or at least might have other ideas. Why try to implement a minister's ideas? Especially since change always requires additional work. Ministers came, with good reason, to distrust the bureaucracy.

Had the ministries been structured as in Britain, career civil servants could have had a positive, as well as a negative, influence on policy. That situation, however, hardly would have been an improvement. A British-style administrative structure, coupled with the instability of the French Cabinet, would have made the problem of making policy makers accountable to the electorate even greater than it was during the Third and Fourth Republics.

Because of their distrust of the bureaucracy and its inadequate coordination, French ministers appoint a group of up to a dozen people who enjoy their absolute confidence and share their outlook. These groups are known as ministerial *cabinets* (pronounced "cab-in-nay"). A *cabinet* advises and assists a minister and acts as intermediary between the minister and the career civil servants. Heading such a group is the *directeur de cabinet*, a senior civil servant, usually from the *grand corps*, personally selected by the minister. The *directeur* is the functional equivalent of the British permanent secretary, supervising the operation of the ministry, in particular, coordinating the various divisions. Dealing with the political aspects of the ministry's work is the *chef de cabinet*, typically a close political friend of the minister—the British equivalent is a Parliamentary Private Secretary. The *chef* handles relations with the legislature, arrangements for political speeches, and matters of that type. Assisting the *chef* are several *attachés*. The *cabinet* also includes some technical staff, junior-level civil servants recruited from other ministries, such as Finance.

In the Third and Fourth Republics, the bulk of the members of the *cabinets* were bright young people who had just completed a university degree in law or politics. The experience they gained in a *cabinet* was a means of launching their political careers. In keeping an eye on the work of the civil servants and trying to ensure that they implemented the minister's policies, the *attachés* learned a good deal about practical government and politics and demonstrated their loyalty and usefulness to their political mentor, the minister.

In the Fifth Republic, this has changed. The overwhelming majority of the members of *cabinets* are senior civil servants. Their primary concern is not relations with the legislature, but coordination of policy with other ministries. The bureaucracy and the political executive have become more closely intermeshed. Politics has become more bureaucratized and bureaucracy more politicized. The civil servants serving in *cabinets* continue to be paid by the *corps* to which they belong, despite the fact that they are serving a political apprenticeship, rather than functioning as merit employees. The British aim of a politically neutral civil service able to serve a Government of any political hue has not been pursued in France.

A related development is the reversal in the pattern of legislative-administrative relations. Typically, in a parliamentary system, the legislature places some of its members in the executive to supervise the bureaucracy and to make certain that it is accountable. In the Fifth Republic, the executive has been "colonizing" the legislature. Political careers are less likely to develop from grass-roots electoral support to national office and more likely to progress from national administrative positions to legislative and local influence.

Balancing such concerns about French administrative practices on the positive side are gains made in integration and effectiveness. The structural reforms instituted since the end of World War II—centralized recruiting of career executives and establishment of the ENA—have helped break down excessive specialization and departmental isolation. As for intradepartmental relations, more stable Cabinets in the Fifth Republic have meant less ministerial turnover. Thus, the coordination provided by ministerial *cabinets* has been able to produce integrated, coherent policy. As you've seen in earlier chapters, changed patterns of behavior, more than structural reforms, have played a dominant role. The diffuseness of policy implementation at the national level is largely a thing of the past.

The Prefectorial System in Transition

Centralized administration has characterized national-local relations in French government for centuries. The modern system was created under Napoleon and survived largely intact, despite the many changes in constitutional structure since his fall from power. The extremely significant reforms of this system implemented during the 1980s can be understood only in the context of the arrangements that endured for nearly two centuries. Therefore, we must first describe the system as it stood.

The traditional system France is divided into regions, departments, arondissements, cantons, and communes. Although most of the thousands of communes are small towns, some of them are major cities. The key subnational unit has been the department (not to be confused with the departments or ministries making up the national government's administrative structure), of which there are ninety-six. In contrast to the position of the states under the American federal system, departments in France can be reorganized or abolished at the will of the national government. The department was created not so much as a unit of local government as an element in the centralized administration of a nationally integrated government. This was not just a matter of some subnational units of government serving as administrative agents to deliver programs established by the national government, as happens under the American federal system. In France, the relation went well beyond this to establish a direct line of administrative responsibility from the national government to the local level. Characteristic of this system was the fact that one national ministry, the Ministry of Interior, supervised implementation of all national laws throughout France. To grasp the far-ranging powers of the Minister of Interior, you must visualize central control of everything from the police to the supervision of elections.

Each department had a popularly elected council. Councils possessed some budgetary power and could pass regulations on some matters, but their powers were limited. They met for only a few days each year. Although each council selected one of its members as president, he or she was not the executive officer of the department. The actual job of running a department fell to a *préfet,* or prefect. The prefect, a national civil servant, was appointed by the Minister of Interior to maintain direct, centralized control of subnational government. The Minister could remove the prefect at will. Instructions from the Cabinet (*décrêts d'application*) and regulations formulated in the Ministry of Interior told the prefect how to run the department. Not only did the prefect prepare the budget for action by the departmental council, but the council could consider *only* those matters referred to it by the prefect. The prefect attended council meetings and, if he or she disliked the way in which the discussion was developing, could walk out, thus preventing the council from making any legally valid decisions.

Prefects kept the national government informed about what was going on in "their" departments and coordinated and supervised all governmental activity and services there. They were assisted by a staff that included experts on various services such as welfare and housing. Although sent to the department from the relevant national ministry, these experts were responsible not to their home ministry, but to the prefect.

The popularly elected councils at the commune level were also closely supervised by the prefect. If a commune council did not balance its budget, the prefect could raise taxes to do so. If a council failed to provide for services mandated by the national government, the prefect included these in the budget and raised taxes to pay for them. In most matters the councils needed the prefect's approval before final decisions could be made.

This system of controls was known as *tutelle* (tutelage) and was intended to ensure unified republicanism throughout the country. (Remember that the Revolution and the Republic were not universally accepted throughout France and only slowly won widespread approval.) If education were left to local control, for example, clerical influence might be too great in some areas. Many might not object to this but might be concerned that Communist strength in some locales would be a subversive threat if the police were not subject to national control.

Most prefects did not function as petty dictators. Those who tried to order and coerce were unlikely to be effective or to remain in their post very long. The style of the successful prefect was a combination of persuasion and manipulation. Their complex relation with the mayors is instructive.

Although a mayor is a politician, selected by the commune council from among their number, and not a career administrator, he or she had the same status at the commune level as the prefect did at the department level. That is, the mayor is the final link in the administrative chain that stretches from Paris to every locality. Commune councils, like department ones, exercise little influence. Members of commune councils tend to be locally prominent people who consider being elected a matter of social recognition, not an opportunity to formulate policy. They are quite willing to support the mayor's view and to rubber-stamp his or her objectives. This makes the commune appear united in its struggle to secure as many benefits and grants as it can from the national government.

Mayors also win deference from the commune councils because many mayors are not just local politicos, but prominent national politicians. Many members of the national legislature serve simultaneously as mayor of a commune. An American parallel would be for the mayor of Chicago to also serve as U.S. Senator from Illinois. A town's mayor might well have better access to the national government than the department prefect. In any event, mayors usually had sufficient political clout that prefects could not just order them about.

Those national legislators who were not mayors often were members of department councils. The number of *cumulards* (politicians who hold two or more elective offices simultaneously) reached its apex during the Fifth Republic in 1981. When in Paris for meetings of Parliament, these *cumulards* were likely to spend a good bit of their time lobbying ministries about the needs of their departments or communes. A sensible prefect would want the cooperation of the *cumulards* from his or her department. The political pressure they could bring to bear would buttress any efforts made by the prefect through administrative channels. Although the prefect was supposed to be the means by which the national government exerted control, in many cases he or she "went native" and became a channel for championing local interests with the national government. Playing such a role won the support of local leaders who otherwise might have caused trouble and also was likely to gain more benefits from the national government, thus making the prefect appear to be more effective. In sum, the prefects had a major role in subnational decision making, but had to be discreet in exercising their extensive powers. They also had to figure out how to balance the conflict between local demands and national constraints.

Partial reforms   In the early years of the Fifth Republic, several reforms were made to the administrative system. To facilitate cooperation among the departments and to promote the Government's plans for economic growth, twenty-two economic regions were established. A superprefect was assigned to each to coordinate economic programs in the region. In addition, prefects were given increased responsibility for management, arbitration, and coordination of economic activities at the department level.

To facilitate cooperation, constraints on intercommunal and interdepartmental communication were relaxed. In conurbations divided into several communes, establishing joint services or public works programs became easier. Thus, activities that any single unit of government had not been able to perform adequately became possible.

Special reforms were required for Paris. One of these created the Paris Area Authority to coordinate the many administrative units having to deal with a concentration of people amounting to about a fifth of the country's population. And some moves toward better land use in the urban area were taken. Just as the British had moved much of the wholesale produce and meat markets out of the business and residential areas to the less populous urban fringe, so the French shifted Les Halles, the central markets, away from the center of the city.

Although Paris had an elected council, it was governed to a considerable extent by two prefects, both responsible to the Minister of Interior. The city had no mayor, since that office had been abolished in 1871, when the Paris Commune was overthrown. The national government wanted to eliminate any possible focal point for the supposedly radical views of Parisians. In 1977 the Paris council was permitted once again to choose a mayor, and Chirac has held the position for more than a decade and a half.

The Socialists' reforms   The reforms made early in the Fifth Republic were welcome improvements of governmental efficiency, but they were not aimed at decentralizing power. Administration became more rational, but no less centralized. The reforms introduced by the Socialists during the first half of the 1980s differed fundamentally in aim. Contrary to the stereotype that socialism involves concentrating all power in the hands of the central government, the party implemented an extensive program of decentralization. This was by far its most significant action, much more far-reaching than its expansion of governmental ownership of various enterprises. Interestingly, when the Socialists lost power in 1986, their successors did return to private ownership some of the enterprises they had nationalized, but did not reverse the reform of the prefectorial system.

Why did the Socialists make decentralization such a major element in their reform program? The idea of giving people a greater say in running their lives was being discussed a good deal in the party at the time. Many Socialists were interested in, for example, work-place democracy. Probably more important than ideological considerations, however, were certain practical interests and experiences. The party had a good deal of support in a number of urban areas, so the idea of shifting some power from the national government to those had some appeal. Furthermore, both the first Socialist Prime Minister at the start of the 1980s and his Minister of Interior had served many years as mayors of big cities and presidents of department councils. They were particularly interested in expanding the responsibilities of those holding such positions.

The reforms abolished *tutelle*. Prefects, renamed commissioners of the Republic for a few years, no longer can tell a council what to do. If a council's action appears to be irregular, all that a prefect can do is appeal to a special tribunal, an administrative court that determines whether or not the action was valid. Preemptive control by an administrator has been replaced by retroactive assessment by judges. This in turn means that the criterion for evaluating actions has changed from advisability to legality.

The council, not the prefect, is now responsible for running the department. The council's chief agent in discharging this function is its president. Therefore, the executive powers formerly wielded by the prefect and the ability to control local budgets have been turned over to the council president.

The regions have become full-fledged units of government with expanded responsibilities. Representative councils, created in 1964, now are popularly elected. (The first elections were held in 1986.) Each council is to promote its region's development in economic and social affairs, health, culture, science, and environmental planning.

The new functions of the regions are simply one aspect of a shift of functions and powers from the national government to one or another subnational unit. For example, local units have been given greater power over their finances. In summary, the shift was from center to periphery and, within the periphery, from prefects to heads of councils. The prefects no longer function as political governors and are more involved in economic coordination. Although their role has been altered substantially, they have not become unimportant. They direct all of the national government's services in their area; that is, they have become the chief field administrators. That means, among other things, that they are in charge of the local police. Also, the prefect is the official spokesperson for the national government in meetings of the councils.

These reforms clearly have made France less centralized. Whereas subnational units used to be little more than elements in a national hierarchy of administration, now they can be considered relatively autonomous agencies of local government. You should not think, however, that France now differs little from the United States in relations between central and subnational governments. The United States has a federal system, and France, for all its changes, retains a unitary one. Consider, for example, education, one of the prime responsibilities of subnational government in the United States. Thousands of popularly elected local school boards throughout the United States exercise considerable power over what is taught in their schools. In France, subnational units of government are responsible for building elementary and secondary schools, for adult education, and for vocational training. The national government, however, not only provides all higher education, but also controls staffing and curriculum content for lower education.

Whereas the states have an independent existence in the United States, the Cabinet in France can dissolve any regional or departmental council that is so deadlocked politically that it cannot function. If this occurs, the president of the council becomes responsible for day-to-day affairs in the area. His or her decisions are valid, however, only if agreed to by the prefect.

How the reforms will affect the policy process will not be clear for some time. Under the old system, specialist activists sometimes managed to short-circuit the prefect by going directly to the relevant ministry in Paris to get action on a particular issue of concern to their area. Now that the prefect has become the chief field administrator, this may be less possible. This change could mean that the national government will become less responsive to local concerns.

Under the old centralized system, implementing a uniform and consistent policy throughout the country—that is, ensuring national standards—was easier than it is in the United States. On the other hand, a single standard may be too inflexible to deal with sectional diversity in France. To the degree that power has shifted away from the center in some matters, policies and practices tailored for local conditions have been facilitated. Purely local interest groups had little influence in France in the past, being filtered out of the policy process. Only groups well organized throughout the country could hope to influence national ministries. Smaller interests now may have, for better or for worse, a greater voice in policy making.

Policy making in France had been rather bureaucratized. The process was not very open and not very participatory. Furthermore, administration tended to be rather partisan—the way in which bureaucrats implemented the laws tended to be influenced by partisan considerations. Since the prefects have been removed from politics and consigned more clearly to administration, this should be less true. And insofar as local affairs are to be run by popularly elected councils, the policy process should be more open.

What is not clear, however, is whether decentralization really has democratized the system, has enhanced popular accountability. Some people fear that power has simply shifted from national bureaucrats to subnational political bosses. Will the French electorate really take an interest in the elections for and the activities of the various councils from regional on down? The reforms may prove to be of concern only for the career ambitions of the political elite and make little difference in the lives of the people. On the other hand, political bosses are responsive (something that often is not true of administrators). As anyone who has studied American politics knows, their responsiveness is the means by which political machines are perpetuated.

Despite all the uncertainties, the Socialists' reform of the prefectorial system seems to have the potential to initiate more responsive, more flexible government in France. We keep referring to paradoxes; here's another. The underlying thrust of the Fifth Republic's transformation of the French political system was in the direction of concentration of power—and this change, by and large, was not reversed when those initially hostile to it finally managed to attain power—but the reforms of the administrative structure have been in the direction of greater accountability. Despite the contrasting directions, each reform movement had in common the goal of tilting the government system back toward a more balanced arrangement after it had moved too far in a particular direction. Perhaps our comments early in this part of the book about the French concern for intellectual consistency at the expense of practicality were too harsh.

17

Judicial Structures _____

You probably found the British judicial arrangements, which we discussed in Chapter 8, somewhat different from the American ones with which you are likely to be familiar. Despite the specific contrasts, however, the two systems are essentially similar. American legal principles derive primarily from British ones, and the two countries share the common law system. France's legal system is of a different basic type—a code law system. Therefore, the material in this chapter is going to seem more unfamiliar to you than was the comparable chapter in the British part. On the other hand, when we get to the Constitutional Council later in this chapter, you will find a judicial institution closer to the American system than anything in the British system is.

As usual, our concern is whether basic rights and liberties are adequately protected, whether power is limited sufficiently to prevent most abuses, and whether some recourse is available to redress any flaws or failures. Are French procedures for settling conflicts fair?

■ *THE NATURE OF FRENCH LAW AND JUDICIAL PROCEEDINGS*

The French judicial system is based on Roman law. Because it was systematically codified during Napoleon's reign, French law is often referred to as the Napoleonic Code. As we noted earlier, common law is largely case law (judge-made), modified by legislative enactments. Roman law, in contrast, is primarily code law. Carefully written detailed statutes enable the judges in a Roman law system to turn to the legal code, the systematized collection of all of the actions of the country's legislature over the years; in contrast, judges in common law systems have to examine the decisions in previous similar cases. Interpretation of previous cases can be used to provide some flexibility in Roman law systems, but the practice is not essential. The core characteristic of common law systems is *stare decisis*, that is, using the holdings in previous cases to determine the outcome of current ones. Roman law systems do not follow the principle that precedent (the outcome of previous cases) is binding on new cases, although reference to precedent has become more common in France.

French judicial procedure also differs from that of the United States and Britain in being inquisitorial rather than accusatorial, or adversarial. The inquisitorial system emphasizes the rights of society and the need to root out crime; the accusatorial system stresses the rights of the accused and the prevention of injustice. The difference is a matter of priorities, and, in principle, one system is no more fair than the other. What matters is the actual practice.

One of the first actions of the new Balladur Government in 1993 was to give new power to the police. Everyone in France is required to carry an identity card. Previously the police had to be able to prove that a person was acting suspiciously before they could demand to see an identity card. The right complained that this requirement so constrained police that identity checks couldn't be carried out at all. Therefore, the Government introduced legislation to permit such checks "irrespective of the behavior" of an individual. Allowing the police to stop whomever they wish for whatever reason, or no reason, may help combat crime. On the other hand, many were concerned that it would encourage arbitrary harassment of innocent people—particularly immigrants. To some extent the change in procedure was yet another example of mainstream politicians trying to outdo Jean-Marie Le Pen.

A person taken into custody by the police in France may be held for twenty-four hours without any charge being brought. The public prosecutor may authorize holding the person for up to forty-eight hours, but in that case the detainee must be visited by a doctor. Once a charge is brought, the prisoner can be held in preventive custody for up to four months (even longer for repeat offenders) for crimes carrying a sentence of as little as two years. Unlike British and American law, French law does not provide for a writ of *habeas corpus* (which requires the police to release a prisoner unless good cause can be given for not doing so). Those in preventive custody, however, may apply to a judge for release and get a ruling within five days. Despite this provision, thousands of people have been jailed for some time, only to be released ultimately because the evidence against them was insufficient to warrant a trial.

Eventually the accused is brought before an examining magistrate (*juge d'instruction*), who decides whether sufficient cause exists for the case to go to trial. A judicial reform implemented in 1993 now permits someone who is arrested to get in touch with a lawyer after twenty hours of detention—*before* any questioning by the magistrate. The magistrate examines witnesses, including the arrested person (in the presence of his or her lawyer), and studies other pertinent information. Neither the accused nor his or her lawyer is present when the magistrate examines the witnesses, although a direct confrontation in court occurs fairly regularly if the case proceeds further. The defense lawyer is given access to the record the magistrate is compiling. This dossier mixes facts with rumors that might tend to incriminate the accused. It may even include a survey of the accused's past. If the magistrate decides that the evidence justifies it, the accused is committed for trial; if not, he or she goes free.

The powers and politics of the magistrates have worried French civil libertarians. Early in 1993 about a fifth of the magistrates asked the Ministry of Justice to be relieved of their investigating duties because they disliked the judicial reform bill (mentioned in the preceding paragraph.) The Socialists' normal suspicion of the magistrates was heightened in mid-1992 when a magistrate's dossier was leaked to the press. This revealed that the president of the National Assembly, Henri Emmanuelli, was being investigated for political corruption for financial irregularities during the time he served as treasurer of the PS. Since he had not been formally charged, this leak appeared to be an attempted political smear. Certainly, the incident posed the question of whether the magistrates are politicized, that is, fail to rise above partisan preferences. Before being too critical, however, you may wish to consider how some American district attorneys, perhaps the closest U.S. equivalent of the magistrates, conceive of their role and the extent to which they are involved in politics. Crusading law-and-order DAs are common in American cities and some (Mayor Giuliani of New York, for example) capitalize on the prominence they gain to seek elective office.

Trials raise additional concerns about possible unfairness. A French judge, unlike an American one, does not act as an umpire between two opposing sides. Instead the judge orchestrates the trial. He or she has the dossier from the magistrate and has formed some ideas about the case. Beginning with the accused, the judge interrogates the witnesses. The sole aim is to discover the truth. Witnesses may speak at length; no rule of evidence excludes irrelevant eloquence on their part. Lawyers do not cross-examine witnesses; they only suggest questions to the judge, who poses them as seems best. Lawyers do not sum up their side of the case in a final speech to the jury, as occurs in the United States.

The most illustrious French historical document, *The Declaration of the Rights of Man*, proclaims that the accused are innocent until proven guilty. Nonetheless, scholars disagree sharply over whether this presumption of innocence is adhered to in French courts as it is in Anglo-American ones. Some argue that being held without being charged before trial neutralizes the presumption of innocence. The procedure aims at getting a confession. The magistrate isn't too concerned about how that was obtained and tends to ignore signs that the accused has been roughed up by the police. Others agree that most defendants are convicted, but argue that the pretrial investigation is fair and often results in the charge being dropped. And some assert that the burden of proof in criminal trials falls on the prosecution.

Given this diversity of views, about all that seems safe to say is that in France being required to stand trial implies a bit more that someone has done something wrong than does an indictment in the United States. An indictment is supposed to mean only that the evidence appears to be sufficient to justify holding a trial to establish whether a crime was committed. Even under the American legal system, however, many people regard an indictment as an indicator that the accused probably has done something wrong.

Whatever occurs in practice concerning the presumption of innocence, the French and American systems do differ in their treatment of the accused in one respect. In the United States, the stress on protecting the accused from injustice means that the defendant does not have to take the witness stand to be questioned. In France, the concern to discover the truth and protect society means that the accused must stand examination. (Interestingly, Britain decided at the close of the 1980s to try a middle road. The accused does not have to take the stand for questioning, but if he or she fails to do so, the judge can comment unfavorably on this behavior to the jury. The reason for the British departure from the practice followed in the United States was the desire to have a better chance of convicting accused terrorists of the Irish Republican Army. The change in procedure was introduced first in cases involving them, but was quickly extended to all cases.)

A case in France may involve both criminal and civil proceedings. An injured party may seek damages from a person that the government is prosecuting on criminal charges. The two actions may be separate, or the injured party may join in the criminal prosecution, being represented by his or her own lawyer. Such linked proceedings can produce a curious result: a person may be ordered to pay damages for killing someone whom he or she has been acquitted of murdering.

French courts are free from many of the legal technicalities that characterize the Anglo-American system. Justice tends to be accessible because France has a large number of courts that are geographically well-distributed. Although judicial proceedings are not cheap and the wealthy are more likely to be able to avail themselves of this service, costs probably are not as great a problem in France as in Britain and the United States. Legal aid is provided without charge to those who cannot afford to hire a lawyer.

■ *ORGANIZING AND STAFFING THE COURTS*

Legal Careers

One of the differences between Roman law and common law systems is the pattern of judicial careers. In the common law system, judges are recruited from the legal profession. In the Roman law system, a person interested in the law must decide before starting a career whether to be a judge or a lawyer. French judges are civil servants and train for their work through the Ministry of Justice.

Law graduates under twenty-seven years old who have passed a competitive exam spend three years training at the National Center for Judicial Studies. The Center is intended to serve the same role for the judiciary as the ENA does for the bureaucracy, that is, to produce a pool of highly competent and respected personnel. Before completing the program at the Center, students must decide whether they wish to become a judge or a prosecutor.

The fact that both are trained at the same school may make judges feel a kinship with prosecutors that they do not feel with defense attorneys. Judges tend to show a good bit of deference to prosecutors. This, in turn, tends to give the police considerable influence in judicial proceedings, especially as their supervisor, the Minister of Interior, usually is much more powerful than the Minister of Justice.

Judges are formally appointed, not by the Minister of Justice, but by the President, acting on the basis of recommendations from the High Council of the Judiciary. The High Council is composed of the Minister of Justice and nine others appointed by the President for four-year terms. The President presides over the High Council's meetings. In the case of judges for the Court of Cassation (the highest judicial level) and the presidents of the courts of appeal, the High Council itself generates a list of potential appointees. For other judicial appointments, the

Minister of Justice proposes appointees and the High Council comments on them and sends them on to the President. The High Council also acts as a disciplinary body for judges.

Although the judiciary is supposed to be independent of the executive, in practice this is somewhat questionable. The Minister of Justice has considerable discretion in promoting judges, and those who have shown a willingness to decide cases as the government desires seem to advance in their careers more rapidly than those who ignore political pressures.

Civil and Criminal Courts

As is common in Europe, French courts are divided at the lower levels between those handling civil cases and those hearing criminal ones.

At the bottom of the civil court system are the courts of first instance (*tribunaux d'instance*). These deal with cases involving only a few hundred dollars. Since there are more than 450 of these, they are quite accessible. Each court has several judges, but each case is heard by only a single judge. The judges must reside where the court is located to ensure that they are attuned to local values.

At the next level are the nearly 200 courts of major instance (*tribunaux de grande instance*). The jurisdiction of such courts extends throughout a department, although the larger departments have more than one. The more important civil cases begin here. These courts also hear appeals from the courts of first instance and from special labor and commercial courts. Three judges preside together in the courts of major instance and decide cases by majority vote.

The lowest criminal courts are the police courts. These are as widely distributed as the civil courts of first instance. The police courts deal with petty offenses having a maximum sentence of only a couple of months in jail.

Above the police courts are the correctional courts. Here the maximum sentence can be as much as five years in prison. The judges who preside over the courts of major instance also staff the correctional courts. Like the courts of major instance, the correctional courts use a three-judge bench and a majority vote on verdicts.

Trials of the most serious criminal charges begin in the assize courts. Indictment by the court of appeal in the area or by the Court of Cassation is necessary for a trial in an assize court. Each department has an assize court, which is called into session quarterly. Three judges hear each case; the most important of these judges (called the president) comes from the court of appeal in that area. A jury of nine people is also used. Two-thirds of the twelve people (judges plus jury) must vote to convict. Decisions of the assize court are final. Even though the cases heard there are being tried for the first time, no appeal is permitted. A petition to the Court of Cassation, however, may request a review of the decision to see whether the law has been interpreted correctly.

The separate civil and criminal judicial systems are merged in the twenty-seven courts of appeal, one for each of the judicial regions into which France is divided. These courts hear appeals from the criminal courts (except the assize courts), the civil courts, and the various special courts, such as farm lease courts, labor courts, and commercial courts. Should the Court of Cassation object to the decision of a court of appeal, it can refer the case to another court of appeal for retrial. In civil cases the court of appeal reviews both matters of fact and matters of law, but in criminal cases the only question is whether the law was correctly interpreted and applied when the case was first tried.

At the top of the judicial hierarchy, handling only appeals, is the Court of Cassation. This court is divided into five civil chambers and a criminal chamber, each with a minimum of seven judges. Criminal appeals go directly to the criminal chamber. Civil cases are sent to a chamber of requests, which forwards to one of the civil chambers only those cases that it believes contain substantial grounds for reversal.

As is true of the highest American courts, the Court of Cassation does not finally dispose of a case. When an appeal is successful, that is, when the Court of Cassation reverses a lower court's decision, it sends the case back for retrial. In deciding the case anew, the lower court is to follow the reasoning of the Court of Cassation on the points of law that caused the original decision to be reversed. If the lower court fails to do this and the decision is appealed again, then the entire Court (a minimum of half of all the judges) hears the case. If the Court remains convinced that the lower court is wrong, it sends the case to another lower court at the same level with instructions for decision that must be followed. This procedure ensures that the law will be interpreted consistently throughout the country.

The President can pardon a person sentenced to capital punishment. Before doing so, however, he or she must consult with the High Council of the Judiciary. Before authorizing a reprieve (the conviction is not expunged, but the sentence is not carried out), the President may consult with the Council.

Administrative Law Courts

In addition to the regular (civil and criminal) court system, France has a fully developed system of administrative law courts. Since these courts play a major role in the French governmental system and are not very familiar to students of Anglo-American legal systems, we need to devote some attention to them. Despite our reassurances, you may feel a bit uncomfortable with the French inquisitorial system. You may prefer to put the emphasis on guarding the rights of those who are in conflict with the government. In the case of the administrative courts, the French have been more solicitous than either the Americans or the British in seeking to defend the individual from governmental abuse.

In the course of providing a public service, governmental agencies inadvertently may damage some individuals. Bureaucrats sometimes misinterpret, deliberately or accidentally, the law conferring power on them and act beyond what is authorized. An agent of the government, even when discharging duties improperly, is acting in a public capacity, not as a private citizen. To prevent the abuse of administrative power or to rectify results requires judicial action against the bureaucrat in his or her public role. For example, if a bureaucrat gets drunk some weekend and runs his car into another one, he can be tried just the same as any other citizen. But if another bureaucrat, in her capacity as an employee of a social welfare office, tells a person that he is not entitled to a social security pension when in fact he is, then special judicial procedures are needed to deal with her failure as a government employee.

The rules that apply to individuals acting in a public capacity are administrative law. Such law deals not only with the rights and liabilities of citizens in their relations with agents of the government, but also with the relations between bureaucrats and the government. The administrative law court system is intended to provide an inexpensive, accessible, and efficient means of redress for people injured by governmental action. Of fundamental importance is the fact that this system allows private citizens to sue the government without first having to obtain the government's approval to do so. The general principle in almost all governmental systems is that the government can do no wrong. Therefore, it can be subject to legal action only to the extent that it permits. Many countries, such as the United States, have authorized suits of this type against the government on a blanket basis to avoid clogging up the legislature with a multitude of ad hoc requests for permission to sue.

The French have gone beyond Britain and the United States in creating an entire court system to deal with such cases. Statutory rules and regulations comprise the backbone of this system, but French administrative law also makes considerable use of the holdings in previous cases. Thus, in this branch of the law, France follows the Anglo-American case law approach more than it does in criminal and civil proceedings.

The genesis of the administrative law courts can be traced back to the Revolution. To ensure that the courts could not thwart the Revolution, a law was passed declaring that judicial functions must be distinct from administrative ones. Subsequently, the constitution of 1791 forbade the courts from infringing upon the administrative field. The distinction was not only due to a Revolutionary desire to constrain the courts but also in keeping with French understanding of Montesquieu's doctrine of separation of powers. The undesirability of freeing government from any kind of judicial control quickly became apparent to the French. Safeguards evolved over the decades in the form of the administrative law courts. The result is a system for making the government responsible for its acts and protecting the individual from administrative abuse.

Procedure in administrative courts differs from that in regular courts. Anyone who feels wronged by administrative action files a petition indicating what was done and what remedy is desired. The court then functions like an investigating committee to ascertain the facts of the matter. The petitioner does not have to hire a lawyer; the court is duty-bound to make sure that all relevant points of law are considered. Once it has considered all the relevant information, the court announces its findings. Then, in closed session, it decides whether these facts provide a basis for voiding what the administrators have done.

An advantage of this system is that costs are quite low even if a case is lost. Those with little money are not prevented from seeking redress from maladministration. The administrative law courts have a high reputation for fairness; many people feel that justice is more likely to be done there than in the regular court system. Unfortunately, these courts have been losing another of their advantages—speedy disposition of cases. Delays of as much as two years between petition and decision are no longer uncommon.

The system's impact is limited because the courts can deal only with administrative acts, not with all governmental actions. Actions by administrative agencies may be nullified only if the agency or administrators in question were not empowered to do what they did or sought to do, if prescribed procedures were not followed, if power was abused (that is, legal acts were performed, but for purposes not contemplated by the law), or an error existed in the law. An administrative court may consider only the way in which a law was implemented, not a challenge to the validity of the law itself.

Recently, however, decisions have tended to expand the scope of review, to examine the merit of action, instead of merely technical correctness. Nonetheless, the system's ability to protect civil liberties is limited because the actions of judges and the police cannot be challenged in administrative courts. Arrests and searches, for example, are not within the administrative courts' jurisdiction.

When it is unclear whether a case should be heard in the administrative courts or in the regular courts, the question is referred to the Court of Conflicts. This Court is composed of the Minister of Justice, three members of the Court of Cassation, three members of the Council of State, and two from either of the latter two bodies. Although the Court of Conflicts usually decides only where the case should be heard, it may, in exceptional circumstances, decide the case itself.

Thirty-one administrative law courts of general jurisdiction are distributed throughout the country. Each one is staffed by a president and several councilors. A group of three hears each case. In addition to these general courts, a number of specialized courts are included in the administrative court system. Among these are the Court of Accounts, which verifies the accounts of all persons handling public funds, and the Superior Council of National Education, which deals with complaints against the school system.

At the apex of the administrative court system is the Council of State. Its nearly 200 members are divided into five sections, only one of which deals with judicial business. Although its members are appointed by the Cabinet, acting on the recommendation of the Minister of Justice, the Council of State is not the puppet of the executive. If any bias can be found in its decisions, it is in favor of the citizen.

Members of the Council of State do not serve for a specified term. They can be removed from office only for malfeasance. Typically, membership is a lifelong career, although some members may take a leave of absence to serve in the legislature or the executive branch. Most members are chosen by means of competitive examination. A predominant source of members is the ENA. To enable the Council to deal adequately with changing conditions, a small number of members are appointed for one-year terms on the basis of expertise in special subjects that have come to be of importance for the Council's work.

The Council of State hears appeals from the decisions of the various administrative law courts and also tries the more important cases for the first time. Cases are heard by five councilors. If the exercise of discretionary power is being challenged, the Council will require the ministry involved to state the reasons for its actions. The Council can call for documents and files relevant to the case. It is the final authority on whether administrators exceeded their authorized power. The aim is to preserve the scope for proper action while ensuring that the actions taken are reasonable. The balance that the Council has struck seems to have gained it the confidence of both administrators and citizens and has helped to produce responsible administrative behavior.

Considerable delay may occur before the Council of State acts on a case. Furthermore, even though it seeks to assist citizens, it cannot invalidate any law. If the proper procedures have been followed, it may not be able to give the citizen any redress, despite injury having been suffered. Because of this possibility, the French finally decided to appoint an ombudsman. This change was made reluctantly since the administrative court system should have been sufficient. Many of the other countries that had established an ombudsman did not have France's elaborate administrative law system.

The French ombudsman is known as the *Médiateur*. He or she is appointed for a nonrenewable six-year term. Complaints about administration cannot be filed directly with the *Médiateur*. Instead one must contact a member of the legislature, who will decide whether the complaint has sufficient merit to be passed on for action by the *Médiateur*. Nonetheless, it may be possible in some cases to obtain redress for grievances against administrative action without having to use the quasi-judicial procedures of the administrative courts.

As we mentioned earlier, the Council of State has four sections in addition to the one that serves as the final court for the administrative law system. These sections act in a consultative capacity to the executive on administrative matters. In some instances, the executive is required to consult with the Council—for example, on decree laws and nonlegislative decrees and before submitting a bill to the legislature. The Council also can suggest areas where legislative or administrative reforms seem desirable. Each ministry designates an official of high rank to participate in meetings of the Council when matters relevant to that ministry are being considered. Thus, each ministry can be certain the Council knows its views and that nothing that the Council proposes will catch it off-guard.

The advice of the nonjudicial sections of the Council of State does not bind the judicial section in any case that comes before it, nor does it bind the Cabinet. Nonetheless, the Council's prestige is so great that the executive branch usually complies with its views. Thus, the Council may help to check arbitrary action in its consultative capacity, as well as in its work as the highest court in the administrative law system.

■ ■ ■

The French legal system provides a number of protections for the individual. In theory, there is nothing unjust about the system; in practice, as we have seen, there are areas of legitimate concern. The balance that any judicial system must strike between authority and individual liberty is tilted more toward the former in France than it is in the United States.

■ *THE STATUS OF JUDICIAL REVIEW*

As you saw in Chapter 8, no court in Britain can declare a law unconstitutional, despite Britain's sharing the same basic legal system with the United States. Traditionally, this was true in most other European countries as well. That their courts lacked the equivalent of the American power of judicial review was not especially surprising, since most of them, like France, had code law systems. In these systems, courts cannot question the right of the legislature to enact rules on anything that it wishes.

As you know, France, unlike Britain, has had several written constitutions. Typically, however, these did not impose specific limits on what the legislature could do, and there were no subordinate units like states to which some powers were reserved. Thus, there were no limits to or allocation of powers for any court to enforce. Furthermore, the idea of judicial review stirs little enthusiasm among French democrats. They regard it as rule by judges and, thus, in conflict with the rule by legislators that they see as the essence of democratic arrangements. The Fifth Republic's constitution was not drawn up, however, to satisfy left-wing democrats. The changes it made in traditional legislative-executive relations necessitated changes in the traditional judicial role as well.

Maintaining Legislative-Executive Boundaries

As you learned in Chapter 14, the Fifth Republic's constitution departs from French tradition in specifying and, therefore, limiting the powers of the legislature. For this provision to have any meaning, some form of judicial review was necessary. Unless someone could invalidate legislation that went beyond what the constitution authorized, the legislature would continue to have a free hand. The main institution for deciding whether the legislature's actions are valid is the Constitutional Council, created at the beginning of the Fifth Republic, although the Council of State also is involved to a lesser extent.

The Constitutional Council is composed of nine people appointed for nine-year terms. Three are chosen by the President, three by the president of the National Assembly, and three by the president of the Senate. The Council has several functions. For example, it supervises elections. If the Cabinet requests, the Council decides whether the President is so incapacitated that the powers of the office should be exercised by the president of the Senate. The Council's primary duty, however, is to interpret the constitution.

As you may guess from the discussion in Chapters 14 and 15, disputes are likely to occur concerning the boundary between those matters that the executive can regulate by decree and those that can be controlled only by the legislature through enactment of a statute. To compound the confusion, the laws of the Fourth Republic, passed under a different constitutional allocation of power between the legislature and the executive, did not cease to exist simply because a new constitution went into effect. Who can alter Fourth Republic laws that remain in effect? If the subject of the law is one of those that the Fifth Republic constitution places within the legislative sphere, then a new law will have to be passed to alter the old legislation. If the subject now falls within the executive's sphere, then the change can be made simply by decree. Whether the old law belongs in one sphere or the other is up to the Council of State. As is true for the Council's other decisions, its opinion on this matter is purely advisory, although generally followed.

As for laws passed since the beginning of the Fifth Republic in 1958, responsibility for maintaining the boundary between the legislature and the executive lies with the Constitutional Council. The executive can ask the Council to rule that the subject of a law actually falls within its decree powers rather than within the legislative sphere. Should the Council agree, then the Cabinet can alter the law by decree. Alternatively, the Constitutional Council can be invoked before a law is enacted. If the executive believes that a bill being discussed in the legislature infringes on its decree powers, it can declare that bill out of order for legislative consideration. The president of whichever house of the legislature is involved must indicate whether he or she agrees with the executive's view. Should the president disagree, the matter goes to the Constitutional Council for decision.

In these circumstances the Constitutional Council is not really declaring a law unconstitutional. Instead, if it agrees with the executive, it is simply permitting the executive to alter the law without having to get an amendment through the legislature.

The constitution does not provide a procedure for the legislature to object if it feels that the executive has issued a decree in an area seeming to be within the legislative domain. As we noted in earlier chapters, the Fifth Republic was designed to tilt the power balance decisively in the executive's favor.

Voiding Laws

In certain circumstances the Constitutional Council can void a law for being unconstitutional. During the fifteen-day period between the final legislative passage of a bill and its promulgation (the official announcement that the law is in effect), the President, the Prime Minister, or the president of either house of the legislature can ask the Council to rule on the law's constitutionality. A significant constitutional amendment in 1974 extended this power to any group of sixty deputies or sixty senators. If the Council decides that the law is unconstitutional, then it is dead. If no one challenges the law during the fifteen days and it is promulgated, then it is valid regardless of whether it might seem to violate the constitution. No procedure exists for subsequently considering its validity.

Although this is a form of judicial review, it differs in several ways from procedures in the United States. First, the Constitutional Council is not the final appellate court for the regular court system, as is true of the U.S. Supreme Court. Second (a necessary outgrowth of the first difference), in France the decision on constitutionality is made in the abstract. In contrast to the American judicial process, no case or controversy exists; that is, no effort has been made to apply the law. The Constitutional Council is giving something that would in American law be called an advisory opinion. The U.S. Supreme Court refuses to do this. Its position is that only an actual legal conflict between opposed parties permits the full ramifications of the law to be ascertained; rights cannot be ascertained in the abstract.

Given the Anglo-American emphasis on the case law approach, the requirement for a case or controversy is understandable. Similarly, given the preference in France for the Roman or code law system, it is understandable that the French feel that issues of constitutionality are best decided in the abstract—when a general, rather than a specific, rule can be laid down and when the confusing facts of a particular case aren't allowed to muddle issues of basic principle. (Even U.S. lawyers have an old cliché: "hard cases make bad law.") What is less easy to understand is why the power to challenge a law's constitutionality should be reserved to the political elite and denied to the common citizen. In this regard, American citizens enjoy greater opportunity to assert their basic rights than French citizens do.

For more than a decade during the early years of the Fifth Republic, the Constitutional Council seemed little more than the executive's lapdog. A Gaullist majority on the Council supported the executive's request for rulings expanding its power at the cost of the legislature. In 1961 the Council was asked to rule on whether a motion censuring the Cabinet could be introduced while Article 16's emergency powers were in effect (an action that President de Gaulle opposed); it ducked the issue and refused to rule.

Similarly, the next year the Council avoided confrontation with the President on the issue of amending the constitution. As mentioned in Chapter 15, de Gaulle resorted to a referendum to amend the constitution so as to provide for direct election of the President, rather than following the procedures for amendment stated in the constitution. When this dispute was referred to the Council, it said that it had no jurisdiction in such matters. It held that its powers applied only to laws passed by the legislature and not to what the people might decide in a referendum. Had they decided otherwise, a major constitutional crisis would have ensued, since it is unlikely that de Gaulle would have backed down. Nonetheless, the decision demonstrated the Council's unwillingness to seek to constrain the President. What really made the Council appear spineless was the fact that it had given an advisory opinion before the referendum saying that the procedure violated the constitution.

In addition to pandering to the executive, the Council seemed irrelevant. During the first twelve years of the Fifth Republic, it was asked to rule on the constitutionality of a law on fewer than a half dozen occasions. Thus, the Council seemed little more than another inconsequential example of overkill, one of an excessive number of safeguards that de Gaulle's followers had written into the constitution to be absolutely certain that the legislature wouldn't be dominant.

The Constitutional Council's Transformed Role

In the early 1970s two important changes occurred. First, the Council seemed to acquire some backbone. (Perhaps the departure of de Gaulle made it feel less intimidated.) The Cabinet attempted to pass a bill limiting freedom of association by giving prefects the power to refuse to register (thereby denying legal recognition to) any group that the prefect *thought would engage* in illicit activities. Thus, a group could be punished not for something that it had done, but for what a government official guessed that it might do. The president of the Senate referred the bill prior to its promulgation to the Constitutional Council. Amazingly, the Council declared the bill unconstitutional. On several other occasions during the 1970s, the Council ruled all or part of a law unconstitutional. What made these actions especially significant was the second important change. The 1974 amendment allowing members of the legislature to seek a constitutional ruling from the Council greatly expanded its work load. For the rest of the 1970s, the Council averaged as many decisions on constitutionality each year as it had given in the entire fifteen-year period up until the amendment.

Many people on the left began to think that perhaps they would have to revise their views of the Constitutional Council. But when Mitterrand was elected President in 1981 and his Socialists shortly afterward won the legislative elections and formed a Cabinet, the situation was reversed. The watchdog became a roadblock.

The Socialists quickly passed an extensive program for taking private enterprises into government ownership. Opposition legislators took the bill to the Constitutional Council. The Council held that since the private owners had not been compensated fairly, the law was unconstitutional. Greatly angered, the Cabinet revised the method for calculating the compensation and passed the bill through the legislature again. Whether intimidated by the Cabinet's bluster that it had better not void this version or for other reasons, the Council accepted the second bill.

Thus, regardless of the Council's opposition, the number of workers employed in state-owned enterprises nearly doubled (although still amounting to only about a tenth of the labor force), and the percentage of industrial sales derived from state-owned enterprises increased from 16 to 29 percent. On the other hand, the Council had delayed the Cabinet's economic recovery plan and had forced it to pay about a third more in compensation. Since a couple of years later the Socialists had to implement austerity measures because the economy had failed to expand sufficiently to generate the revenues needed, this forced increase in expenditure was significant.

The nationalization conflict was just the start of perpetual conflict between the executive and the Council during the first part of the 1980s. Legislators opposed to the Socialist Government referred bills to the Council virtually as a matter of course. The number of cases on which the Council ruled more than doubled from what it had been during the 1970s. Furthermore, the Council was as likely to decide against the executive, that is, rule a bill totally or partially unconstitutional, as it was to rule in favor of it. Even these facts probably understate the influence of the Council. In some cases the Cabinet probably watered down its proposals in order to avoid having them voided by the Council. For example, it might very well have gone further than it did in transforming the prefectorial system had it not feared that the Council would rule such legislation unconstitutional.

Part of the reason the Socialists had difficulty with the Constitutional Council was that when they came to power in 1981, none of the nine Council members were from the left. Remember that the President and the presiding officers of the legislature appoint the members of the Council. No Socialist had been President to that point in the Fifth Republic, and the party had not controlled either of the houses of the legislature. After 1981, a Socialist was President of the Republic and president of the National Assembly. As the nine-year terms of Council members expired and new people were appointed, its political composition altered.

Since the Council doesn't announce its votes and doesn't issue minority opinions, the partisan dynamics of its decisions can't be examined. Changes could be expected though, when by 1986 four of the nine members had been appointed by Socialists. These appointees included the president of the Council (equivalent to Chief Justice of the U.S. Supreme Court), Robert Badinter, who had been Socialist Minister of Justice from 1981 to 1986. Badinter is an ardent civil libertarian, and one of his major reforms was the abolition of capital punishment.

The irony was that just as the balance of power on the Council was about to shift to the Socialists, the party was put out of power by the legislative elections of 1986. Nonetheless, the partisan composition of the Council had changed sufficiently that the new right-wing Cabinet could not feel assured of its support. In other words, Prime Minister Chirac had to worry not only about how to cohabit with President Mitterrand, but also about how to manage a *ménage à trois* with the President and the Constitutional Council.

Less than a year after Chirac came to power, the Council invalidated one of his Cabinet's bills. Chirac wanted to stimulate the economy by freeing business from many government regulations. He and Mitterrand had already clashed over decrees making it easier for employers to lay off workers. Now he wanted to ease regulations concerning working hours. With his usual impatience Chirac had been ramming a number of bills through the legislature with only the most cursory debate. The Constitutional Council overturned the bill on working hours on the grounds that the legislature had not been given sufficient time for adequate consideration.

The Chirac Cabinet lasted for only a couple of years. As you learned earlier, once Mitterrand won reelection in 1988, he called for legislative elections, and the Socialists returned to power. As terms on the Constitutional Council continued to expire, the point was soon reached where the majority of its members had been appointed by Socialists. Thus, by the start of the 1990s, major clashes between the executive and the Council were not a feature of French politics. Whether the return of a right-wing Government in 1993 meant that the Council would again impede executive action remained to be seen.

Whatever the outcome, the Council is a considerably different body than it was in the early years of the Fifth Republic. It hardly plays the role the Supreme Court does in the U.S. political system, but it is an important participant in the French policy-making process and introduces an element of checks and balances into the French system.

18

Contemporary Trends in French Politics: A Deluge or Just Showers?

American political parties are rudimentary organizations. Each has a national headquarters and national officers. The national organization, however, has only a modest effect on party activities throughout the country. Some have asserted that what the United States actually has is fifty-one Democratic parties and fifty-one Republican ones. Even that comment overstates American parties' level of development. Party organization is just as poorly elaborated at the state level as it is at the national level. American parties actually are conglomerations of Senator X's office, Representative Y's supporters, Mayor W's adherents, and the like. The result is not a well-integrated organization espousing an agreed-upon set of policies, but loosely linked personal machines. The Speaker of the House of Representatives in the 1980s won some fame with his dictum, "All politics is local." That is, American politics is personal.

Contrast this with the European scene, where parties have formal, dues-paying members. Local party organization is not the product of the organizational efforts of some local officeholder. Local organizations were established by the national party and are subject to its direction. The national party advocates a program, an integrated set of policy proposals deriving from an intellectual conception of government and society, and its local manifestations are required to pursue those goals as well. The party, not the individual politician, is what matters. The organization continues beyond any person's individual career.

In the United States (before people became sensitive to gender concerns), voters used to explain their behavior by saying, "I vote for the man, not the party." In Britain, a voter interviewed during an election campaign explained how he planned to vote by saying, "I'd vote for a pig, if my party put one up." How surprising, then, that American politics has not spawned a "personism." About as close as the United States has come is "Reaganomics." Although that term did encompass a rather general view about the role of government, it was little more than a convenient way to refer to a number of economic actions—not really integrated into a coherent program—being taken while Ronald Reagan was President.

How equally surprising that Britain, a country of strong, fully elaborated national parties with detailed manifestos should have experienced a "personism." Britain, after all, was the country that had so little valued "personism" and so greatly emphasized party that it was willing to eject its charismatic national leader immediately at the end of a war for survival in order to get rid of the Conservative party. Yet it also was the country whose politics revolved around Thatcherism in the 1980s. Europe has seen even more centralized and elaborated ideological parties than has Britain. Yet French politics produced a "personism" long before British politics did. For more than a quarter of a century after the fall of France to the Nazis in 1940, Charles de Gaulle, whether on stage or off, dominated French politics. A series of parties advocating his views and a distinctive prescription for constitutional reform were identified with his name. True, the typical term was Gaullist, rather than Gaullism, but the idea was the same.

France and Britain appear to have shared a political phenomenon that has not been central to American politics. What called forth both de Gaulle and Thatcher were national crises. In Britain it was an economic crisis: the growing belief that none of the political leaders preceding her had a clue about how to right the economy and get it sailing on as serenely as it had done fifteen years earlier. The worldwide Depression of the 1930s had similarly alarmed the American public and called forth Franklin Roosevelt. But the United States didn't develop "Rooseveltism," because Roosevelt lacked an integrated plan of action. What he offered was a style of government, a confident dynamism. His pragmatic approach to solving the crisis was as far as one could get from deriving complementary policies from a philosophy of government. The economy wasn't the crisis in France; that was about the only thing that did work fairly well in the Fourth Republic. The problem that had festered for years and finally came to crisis was a political system that produced decision-making stalemate, preventing any coherent, effective action.

The contrast between American and European politics in this regard is not the occurrence of a crisis, but the nature of the response to it. Although we want to emphasize this difference in the American and the European experiences, we also need to examine the contrast *within* the European experience, the extent to which Gaullism differed from Thatcherism. Margaret Thatcher came to power through the regular party and electoral procedures that existed in Britain. She worked within, was a creature of, the system. Charles de Gaulle had taken his stand outside and in opposition to the system. He obtained power through a quasi-coup because the only alternative was a true military coup.

As you saw in Chapter 9, Thatcher changed the terms of political debate in Britain. She altered the role and reduced the size of government. Her main concern, however, was policy issues; structural and constitutional questions held little interest for her. You saw in the British part that the House of Commons—the key structure in enforcing accountability—had been subject to a worrying long-term decline in effectiveness, and that political movements on the periphery were raising significant questions about excessive centralization in Britain. Thatcher's response was merely to reinforce the status quo. Although she wanted to reduce the scope of government, she vehemently opposed weak government. She wanted government to be even stronger, more centralized in those matters that were its responsibility. Only within what must be considered fringe parties—the Liberals and the nationalists—does one find any concern during the Thatcher decade with such constitutional questions as proportional representation, devolution, and a written bill of rights.

Gaullism did encompass some substantive policies. France's nuclear striking force, its balancing role between East and West in international politics, and its refusal to accept supranational development of the EEC are examples. De Gaulle's concerns, however, were much more constitutional than issue-oriented. Although something of an American analog, George Washington is a misleading comparison. The stature that Washington possessed in the last couple of decades of the eighteenth century is quite similar to that which de Gaulle enjoyed for about the same period of time in the middle of the twentieth century. Each may have been the only person capable of holding his country together at the time. Washington chose to function as a mediator, however, presiding over the constitutional debate and seeking to reconcile opposed views. He lacked a vision of his own that he sought to implement. De Gaulle most certainly did have a fully developed conception of governmental structure and was determined that he would impose this on the country. Any of the (sneer) politicians who opposed him would be stepped on like ants.

To be so personally dominant as to be able to dictate a country's constitutional structure certainly is extraordinary. The key question, however, is whether that structure will endure once you are gone. When the cement that held the stones together crumbles, will the wall tumble? In the Introduction, we discussed institutionalization—the durability of governmental structures beyond the lifetime of any individual leader. The Fifth Republic was tailor-made for de Gaulle. The problem of regimes founded on a charismatic leader is their inability to institutionalize themselves. A leader's personal magnetism may enable him or her to unify a country and direct it through a period of considerable achievements, in the process becoming an "ism." Once that leader is gone, however, much of what was accomplished is dissipated. Precisely because the people's loyalty was to the leader as an individual, rather than to the political system, commitment and dedication wane with the leader's passing. Since the charismatic leader does not need to establish new institutions to be effective, such bodies are irrelevant at best and an impediment at worst. He or she wants a free hand to govern as seems best, untrammeled by confining procedures or governmental institutions. As you have seen in this part, de Gaulle often behaved in this fashion. Thus, rule is personally based, not institutionally buttressed.

De Gaulle, despite or, perhaps, because of his ego, was not optimistic about the future of his handiwork. His well-known prediction was *"Après moi, le déluge."* He had shown France what could be done. But he despaired of having convinced his countrypeople that it had to be done. He feared that his reforms would be eroded once he no longer was present to protect them. The way in which he left power—the willingness of the voters to repudiate him in a referendum—could only have reinforced his belief that the public had not learned the essential lesson that he sought to inculcate.

That de Gaulle should have been so modest in claiming credit for his accomplishments is amazing. The Fifth Republic—the de Gaulle Republic—has become the second most durable political system that France has known since the Revolution two centuries ago. Everything about de Gaulle as a personality, about the nature of his return to power in 1958, and about his methods of governing for the subsequent decade would have justified a prediction that the Fifth Republic, like the other regimes of modern France, would have fallen by the wayside by now, replaced by a Sixth Republic or some other form. Yet it has endured for a quarter of a century beyond de Gaulle's exit from the political scene. His departure from power was *not* followed by chaos.

Not only has the Fifth Republic endured, but for about a third of its life the key governmental position has been occupied by someone from a point on the political spectrum very different from de Gaulle's, someone who before attaining power had sharply criticized de Gaulle's constitution for its break with French Republican tradition. Nonetheless, he didn't alter the system devised for de Gaulle. Furthermore, the system has managed to function more effectively, even through two periods of divided government (the legislature controlled by one partisan grouping and the President's office by another), than did the Third and Fourth Republics. Divided government has been common in recent American political experience, but was unknown in France until 1986. Until it occurred, some people speculated that it would produce tensions so great that the Fifth Republic would be torn apart. Clearly such views underestimated the extent to which the Fifth Republic had become institutionalized. Rarest of events, de Gaulle bequeathed to France a political system that, despite its personalized origin, is durable.

France has solved the problem of systemic instability. Because that solution also remedied the problem of executive instability, France no longer suffers from ineffective government. The cost, however, has been attenuated accountability. In the case of Britain, you saw that a long-term decline in the influence of the House of Commons has been arrested. Although the problem of accountability hasn't been solved in Britain, the Commons is more assertive than it was a third of a century ago. Accountability may be on the mend; at least, it is more healthy than it was. The same cannot be said in France. Cohabitation can be seen in some respects as a French version of American checks and balances. It operates within a single branch of government, however, and is an exceptional, rather than typical, form of power relations. The Constitutional Council has established some precedents for checking executive power, but its role is miniscule compared to that of the U.S. Supreme Court. The fundamental concern in France remains the legislature. De Gaulle was determined to cut an overmighty branch of government—which showed no ability for decisive action despite its dominant position—down to size. So effectively did he do so that he undermined its ability to call power to account. That fundamental reorientation at the start of the Fifth Republic has not altered over the years. Accountability may be recovering in Britain, but has yet to do so in France. Nonetheless, the Fifth Republic deserves some praise for not returning France entirely to the autocratic administrative tradition.

A final significant point is that constitutional transformation has played an essential role in establishing a durable, effective regime in France. Equally, if not more, important, however, have been a "personism" and a party system realignment (which in turn depended to a considerable extent on changes in political culture). Problems of governance are not solved merely by enacting a new constitution, a point of particular relevance to the next part of this book.

Part Four

Germany

Denmark

Baltic Sea

North Sea

Kiel •

• Rostock

• Hamburg

Bremen •

Ems

Mittelland Canal

Poland

Berlin •

• Hanover

Netherlands

Halle •

Elbe

• Dusseldorf

*THURINGIAN
FOREST*

Dresden •

ORE

Belgium

Bonn ★

Rhine

• Suhl

• Frankfurt

Czech Republic

Lux.

• Nurnberg

France

• Stuttgart

Danube

*BLACK
FOREST*

Munich •

Austria

Switzerland

.....19

The Setting of German Politics

■ *PHYSICAL CONDITIONS*

The Influence of Geography

Germany's geographic position is astride the center of the European continent. To the west lie France and the Low Countries, to the north the North Sea and Denmark, to the south Switzerland and Austria, and to the east Poland and the Czech Republic (see Figure 19–1). Covering almost 138,000 square miles, Germany is about half again as large as the United Kingdom but only about two-thirds the size of France. Germany lacks well-defined geographic frontiers except for the seacoast to the north. Most of the main rivers either rise on foreign soil or leave Germany for other countries. The Rhine, for example, originates in Switzerland and flows into the sea in the Netherlands. This fact of geography has had an immense—and mostly adverse—impact on German history. The absence of geographic barriers meant that little impeded the spread of the German language beyond the political boundaries of Germany. Germans naturally felt a kinship with people in neighboring countries who shared the German language and culture and often saw no reason why areas inhabited by such people should not be incorporated into Germany, even when the other countries did not want to relinquish those areas. Thus, at times, geography encouraged Germany in aggressive attitudes toward its neighbors.

But, equally, geography has put Germany on the receiving end of aggression. Given Germany's location, almost any European war of any importance was certain to involve German territory. Until German-speaking areas strengthened themselves by unifying late in the nineteenth century, they were the regular battleground of Europe. As you can imagine, the Germans eventually got tired of this and decided it was time to show some muscle, simply for self-protection. To some extent Germany's belligerent international attitudes in the late nineteenth century and the first half of the twentieth were the product of having been bullied by other countries for some centuries prior to that.

More positively, Germany's location made possible the development of great ports on the North Sea coast, such as Bremen and Hamburg, and of international trade. Unfortunately, even this had a negative aspect. Had Germany not been a sea-

Figure 19–1
The German
Federal System

faring nation, then the late nineteenth-century tensions with Britain over naval armaments would not have developed, and the world wars of the twentieth century might never have occurred.

The western part of Germany is rich in the natural resources essential for a modern, industrialized society. Iron and coal are plentiful, as are other important minerals. The many rivers, in addition to facilitating domestic and even international transport, have been a source of hydroelectric power. Farmland is an abundant resource as well. Although more than half of the land in the western parts of Germany is arable, the chief agricultural areas are in the east.

With a population of around 80 million, Germany is nearly as densely populated—around 580 people per square mile—as the United Kingdom. Like that country, Germany is highly urbanized, especially in the west. No single city dominates the country as London does, however. Berlin, with nearly 3.5 million, is large enough to do so, but was divided into Communist and non-Communist parts until 1990. Although the Communist part of Berlin served as the capital for East Germany, West Germany selected Bonn as its capital after World War II. Bonn, which espionage novelist John Le Carré referred to as *A Small Town in Germany*, has only about 300,000 people and had been little more than a sleepy college town (see Figure 19–2). Although it can claim fame as Beethoven's hometown, many think it has not changed much from what it was in the past. Shortly after the collapse of communism, Germany decided that it would return its capital to the unified Berlin in 1995. The cost of constructing new buildings in Berlin and moving an entire government apparatus from Bonn began to sink in, however, and so this shift now seems unlikely to occur before the turn of the millennium.

Hamburg, in the north, and Munich, in the south, are the only other cities over a million in population. Although they are major cities, they do not overshadow a number of other small ones. Two of the main industrial areas, the Ruhr (just to the north of Bonn) and the Rhine-Main (in west central Germany), are quite populous: the former has 11 million people and the latter 3 million. But both of these are conurbations (continuous urban conditions that include several separate city governments) rather than single cities. As we commented when discussing Britain, city life calls for an activist government. Dense, urban populations give rise to problems that cannot be left to benign neglect.

Figure 19–2

Marketplace in Front of Town Hall in a Small Town in Germany

Regional and Other Diversities

Since the original German unification occurred relatively late, as we will explain in the next section, a variety of Germanic customs and dialects exist. Just as in the United States, regional stereotypes are common. A south German, for example, is expected to be more emotional and fun-loving than a north German, who is regarded as more austere and sober. Unification of East and West Germany in the 1990s only adds to the contrasts.

Germany, like the United States and in contrast to both Britain and France, is a federal system. Few German states (called *Land*, singular; *Laender*, plural), however, have a long tradition. When the West German system was created after World War II, the boundaries established for the states rarely corresponded to those that had existed prior to the war. In part, the aim was to discourage strong subnational loyalties that might interfere with commitment to the new national political system. Similarly, in East Germany the traditional states were dissolved in 1952 and replaced with administrative areas. With the collapse of Communist rule, the old states were re-established, but after a hiatus of nearly forty years, they were unlikely to generate strong feelings of loyalty.

Germany's sixteen states vary considerably in size, as can be seen from Figure 19–3. Two small ones are something of a curiosity. Bremen and Hamburg are city-states; an American analogy would be if New York and Chicago were separate states. Both are dwarfed by Bavaria, whose area is nearly twice as big as the next largest state. Bavaria is not the most populous state, however. North Rhine–

Figure 19–3
Area and Population of Germany's States

A. Area

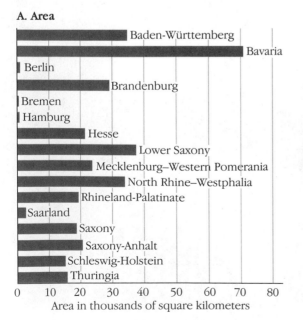

Area in thousands of square kilometers

B. Population

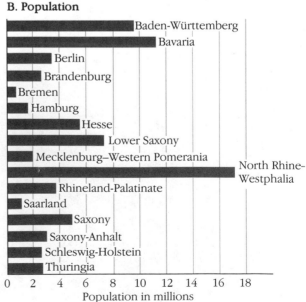

Population in millions

Westphalia, which includes the Rhine-Main area, one of the industrial conurbations mentioned earlier, is about half again as populous as Bavaria.

Prior to World War II, Protestants had outnumbered Catholics in Germany two to one. The areas that became East Germany or were given to Poland after that war were overwhelmingly Protestant. This made what became West Germany about equally divided on religious preference, with about as many Protestants as Catholics. Religious strength varied by region; Catholics were more prevalent in the south and Protestants in the north. Unification in 1990 made Germany more Protestant once again.

Although religion has some relevance to politics, it does not divide the country into hostile sects. Suspicion and dislike of other segments of society are more likely to be the product of class differences. Because of Germany's rapid transformation into a corporate industrial economy, the country has lacked a sizable entrepreneurial middle class. Thus, Germans have found it easier than Americans to believe that the economic system pits the proletariat against the capitalists and their toadies. Income distribution in West Germany was less equalized than in either Britain or Scandinavia, but more so than in France. Furthermore, educational opportunities were limited. Children from working-class families found rising to a new status or a more prestigious occupation difficult.

We have seen that some people in both Britain and France have been hostile to "immigrants." This issue has been prevalent in German politics as well. During the immediate post-World War II years, West Germany was almost inundated with a flood (about 13 million in all) of refugees from Communist countries to the east. Although most of these people were similar to the country's population in having a Germanic background, they clearly differed in feeling dispossessed and disaffected. The government sought to integrate these people into the population by means of a number of measures, only some of which were economic. A key economic measure was the "equalization of burdens" law passed in 1952.

Under this law, all Germans were required to contribute half of what they possessed for redistribution to refugees and Germans who had suffered major losses due to war damages or the currency reform, thus equalizing the burden of recovery. Certain public organizations, such as the central banks and religious and charitable institutions, were exempt. One's worth was determined according to tax liability in 1948–49. This was a relatively lean time and, thus, made the bite of the law less onerous. Also payment of the sum owed could be spread out over thirty years. These provisions made the law more tolerable, yet it remains an extraordinary example of seeking to integrate a society by making everyone responsible for the less fortunate. The fund was distributed as grants or loans for housing and furniture and pension payments.

This measure was extremely influential in preventing the huge group of refugees from becoming an ocean of malcontents, ready to be whipped into a tidal wave of dissent by some demagogue. Not only did West Germany avoid this, but by making more refugees feel at home in the Federal Republic, the country managed to channel the determination and energy of these people in ways that speeded economic reconstruction. Unfortunately, the "immigrant" issue has been handled less well subsequently.

The West German birth rate became one of the lowest in the world, thereby reducing the work force during the 1960s when industrial expansion demanded additional labor. Especially needed were people willing to perform the less desirable low-skill jobs for menial wages, which prosperity had made unattractive to Germans. Just as Britain recruited "coloureds" from the West Indies and Africa and France recruited people of Arabic background from North Africa, so West Germany welcomed the *gastarbeiter* (guest worker) from Turkey, Yugoslavia, Italy, and Greece. The number of such foreign workers rose to about 2 million, or 7 percent of the work force. They and their dependents, another 2–3 million people, brought into Germany different customs and languages, which were not especially welcomed. When the economy slowed down in the 1970s, many West Germans resented the guest workers because they regarded them as the cause of unemployment among German workers. Not only are these foreigners easily distinguishable because of skin color, customs, and language, but they also tend to be concentrated in a few areas. Foreigners made up about a tenth of the population of Hamburg, for example, at a time when unemployment there was double the national average. You can see the potential for conflict.

To make matters worse, the collapse of communism produced another flood of immigrants. Some of these people were ethnic Germans who had lived in Poland or the former Soviet Union and had been prohibited by their governments from moving. Such newcomers presented no great problem. The concern was asylum-seekers, non-German immigrants who fled their countries to escape political persecution or to find better economic conditions. More than a quarter million came to Germany in 1991 and more than 440,000 in 1992. Most prevalent among these asylum-seekers were people from the former Yugoslavia and Romania.

Extreme right-wing groups began attacking "immigrants," some of whom had lived in Germany for years. They set fire to houses and killed a number of people. Although the government did try to protect foreigners living in Germany and outlawed a small neo-Nazi group, its main efforts focused on amending the law so as to cut the stream of immigrants. Any asylum-seeker who passed through a "safe" country would be returned, since there was no danger of persecution there. If a Romanian, for example, went to Austria before coming to Germany, he would be sent back to Austria. What Austria did was of no concern to Germany. In addition, the government pursued special agreements with countries through which the major flows were coming. In effect, Germany bribed Poland to take back asylum-seekers who had passed through its territory on the way to Germany.

The ever-growing number of asylum-seekers *was* a strain, especially when the effort to revive East Germany was a drain on the German economy. Nonetheless, many Germans do not deal well with diversity. The prime minister of Bavaria said in 1993, "We are not an immigration nation. That would result in a multi-cultural society. And a multi-cultural society would be a terrible thing." Such views are enshrined in Germany's citizenship laws. Germany practices *jus sanguinis* (law of the blood) rather than *jus soli* (law of the soil). If your parents are German, you are German. But if your parents are Turks, even if they have lived in Germany for years and you are born in Germany, you don't acquire German citizenship. Only by going through a complicated procedure between the ages of 16 to 23 can you obtain it.

Immigrants, especially those easily identified by skin color, customs, and language, are likely to be a continuing issue in German politics.

The Economy

One of the keys to the growth of Germany as an international power was the country's rapid transformation in the latter half of the nineteenth century from a primarily agrarian country to a modern industrial one. Economic growth was particularly rapid after unification in 1870. German coal production jumped from about 30 million metric tons in 1871 to more than 190 million in 1914. From a low of a few hundred thousand tons in 1850, Germany's iron extraction expanded to more than 8 million tons in 1900, equaling Britain's. By World War I, German production was more than double that of Britain. At the same time, Germany became Britain's rival in merchant shipping. Germany also developed a sizable electric power industry.

By the late nineteenth century, Germany had used the advantages of its geographic setting to jump from a precapitalist economy to a mature capitalistic one with heavy corporate concentrations. Germany's rapid industrial and commercial expansion was facilitated by a banking system purposely designed to promote economic growth. The German economic empire extended far beyond the country's borders. Large enterprises evolved into cartels (monopolies), which were able to fix prices, regulate markets, and avoid competition.

Germany's position as the industrial leader of Europe was devastated by World War II, many urban, industrial areas were obliterated. West Germany recovered rapidly through hard work and determination, supplemented by American aid. In East Germany the story was different. The Soviet Union seized much of the country's assets in payment for damages it had suffered in World War II.

By 1953 West Germany had achieved an industrial output that was 59 percent larger than it had been in 1936. By 1956 its gold and dollar reserves were larger than Britain's. Its exports quadrupled between 1952 and 1961, in part because of heavy investment in the production of goods for export. In many areas West Germany's share of the world export market exceeded that of Britain or the United States. West Germany's total national income surpassed that of France in 1960. Its gross national product (GNP) rose to the third largest in the world until Japan overtook it in 1968. East Germany had been thought to have recovered rather well also. It appeared to be one of the most prosperous of the Eastern European Communist countries. When the Communists were driven from power in 1989, however, it became clear that the East German economy was in shambles.

The East German economy was based on guaranteed markets in the Soviet bloc, to which products could be sold no matter how poor the quality. The collapse of communism destroyed that market and meant that East Germany had little outlet for its products. Beyond that, trying to establish the free market of capitalism among people familiar only with the command economy of communism produced chaos. In less than a year after unification in October 1990, East German industrial production was halved. Unemployment, which had been zero under communism because everyone was guaranteed a job, even if a useless one, rocketed to 17 percent of the work force by the end of 1991.

In real terms the West German economy grew by only 3.2 percent in 1991—its lowest rate since 1987. East Germany's GNP plummeted by more than 28 percent, virtually wiping out the West German gains and giving the entire country no growth in 1991. The west was attempting to revive the economy in the east. In 1992 about $100 billion was transferred to the east for economic development. As a result of the financial strain, West Germany grew by only 0.8 percent in 1992, the worse rate in a decade. The eastern economy, however, was beginning to respond. Nonetheless, because the east has such a small portion of the total economy (only 7 percent, despite having about 20 percent of the total population), Germany's GNP grew by only 1.3 percent in 1992.

The first part of 1993 saw almost endless financial negotiations. The government met with opposition parties, employers, and the unions to hammer out a "solidarity pact," a package of tax increases, spending cuts (including cuts in unemployment benefits), and wage restraints to finance unification. Despite general agreement by all sides, conflict over the details continued. Unemployment had increased in the west to more than 7 percent and had declined only slightly in the east to under 15 percent.

The main positive economic news was that inflation was running around 4 percent. As you will see later in this chapter, inflation frightens Germans much more than unemployment does. In the mid-1990s Germans could see that unification would be quite costly. The rising prosperity of the west for most of the postwar period would not be enjoyed again for some time. Thus the country was likely to discover whether Germans have supported democracy because it brought good times or are committed to its basic principles come rain or shine.

■ HISTORICAL BACKGROUND

Despite four decades of democracy in West Germany, some people wonder whether democracy is firmly established there. The concern is not that other political traditions challenge democratic values, as in France, but that no democratic tradition exists at all in Germany. A brief historical survey will explain how democracy played so little part in German development.

During the latter part of the Middle Ages, the Holy Roman Empire (despite this name, it was basically a Germanic political system) was the leading European political structure. Its significance began to wane in the thirteenth century, and by the next century it was little more than a facade. No unified German nation existed. Any ties that Germans felt were weakened when the Reformation and the religious wars of the sixteenth century split the Protestant north from the Catholic south. Following the Thirty Years War in the seventeenth century, which devastated Germanic areas and greatly reduced the population, the Peace of Westphalia (1648) formally recognized the independence of the various German princes. Germanic areas were so fractionalized by these developments that 314 German political units, of diverse sizes, existed in 1800.

By smashing and amalgamating the smaller political units in this conglomeration, Napoleon unintentionally paved the way for German unification. Austria and

Prussia struggled to lead the process. Prussia's rulers, especially Frederick the Great (1740–1786), raised it from a weak principality to one of the strongest countries in Europe by combining ruthless military action with economic modernization. Despite their achievements, Napoleon was able to deal Prussia a disastrous defeat in 1806. Determined not to be humiliated again, Prussia swept away lingering feudal institutions, modernized the bureaucracy, and introduced military conscription. The regenerative process that would result in German unification by military prowess was under way.

The German response to the French impact on central Europe at the turn of the eighteenth century was to reduce sharply the number of German political units. At the Congress of Vienna (an international gathering of statesmen in 1814–1815 that marked the end of the Napoleonic wars and attempted to restore eighteenth-century political systems), the German Confederation, a loose combination of thirty-eight states, was established. At this point, Austria still predominated, although Prussia would eventually seize the lead.

Prussia's dominant position was of immense significance for Germany's political development. Prussia was not a liberal monarchy, but, rather, a militaristic society. Its political system was not even remotely democratic. An attempted democratic revolution in 1848 was repressed, driving many in the middle class to emigrate, especially to the United States. Unlike comparable groups in Britain, these Germans could see no hope of liberalizing the political system from within. Thus, political leadership among the middle class, which in many countries played a key role in the movement toward democracy, was weakened greatly.

Certain virtues, however, must be conceded to the Prussian system. The rulers did not live in the luxury of the French Bourbons, preferring a rather austere or Spartan existence. Administration was scrupulously honest; there was not a hint of corruption. And the system's legal codes were adhered to rigidly, which meant that arbitrary governmental action was extremely rare. Thus, for all its lack of democracy, the system was attractive to many.

The person who completed the unification efforts and was widely seen as the unifier of Germany was Otto von Bismarck (1815–1898). At the age of forty-seven, he was made minister-president of Prussia. For three decades he guided the nation's destiny, and to a large extent that of Europe as well. From the outset he made clear that he was no democrat. His method would be force, "blood and iron." In two quick wars, against Denmark in 1864 and against Austria in 1866, he established Prussia's dominance. Then, in 1867, he set up the North German Confederation, a union of twenty-two states and principalities. Unification was completed with the rapid defeat of France in 1870 and the ceding to Germany of Alsace and a part of Lorraine. In 1871 the North German Confederation was abolished, and a German empire, consisting of Prussia and the north and south German states, was proclaimed. By "blood and iron," Germany had been unified.

The Empire

Unified Germany was called the Empire or the Second Reich (the Holy Roman Empire being considered the first). The Empire lasted longer than any subsequent German political system (see Figure 19–4). Although the Empire was supposedly

Figure 19–4
Length of German
Regimes from 1871
to 1994

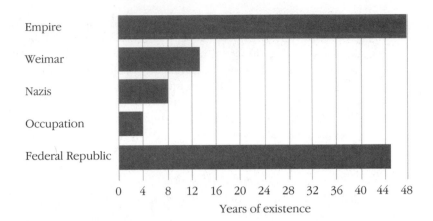

organized as a federal union of twenty-five political units, one of these—Prussia—
held the predominant position, being able to veto any amendment to the constitution. Moreover, although in theory powers not delegated to the central government
were retained by the states, in practice more and more power was transferred to
the central authorities.

Bismarck did more than unify the nation. For two decades (from 1871 to 1890)
he manipulated and guided the social forces in the Empire and made Imperial
Germany a power among the nations of Europe. In domestic policy he is best
known for his actions against, first, the Catholic Church and, then, the Social
Democrats.

The first effort, known as the *Kulturkampf* (struggle for civilization), was not so
much an antireligious campaign as it was an effort to undermine the moral and
intellectual authority of the Church. Bismarck's memories of his conflicts with
Catholic France and Catholic Austria were still fresh, and he suspected that the
political loyalties of German Catholics might lead to a possible civil war of revenge.
His expulsion of the Jesuits and confiscation of Catholic Church property contributed significantly to the formation of the Catholic Center party. When this party
became reconciled to the German Empire and when its political demands proved
to be exceedingly moderate, Bismarck repealed the anti-Catholic laws and sought
to enlist the Catholics in what he had come to regard as a more important struggle:
his campaign against the Social Democrats.

Bismarck apparently feared that the Paris Commune of 1871 could have a
German counterpart. He had the legislature enact laws prohibiting socialist groups,
suppressing any socialist newspapers and pamphlets, and barring "radical" meetings. The police supervised trade unions and expelled anyone thought to be a
socialist. The laws were so extreme and arbitrary that they threatened the liberties
of nonsocialist liberals as well.

The fact that other political groups joined with the socialists in opposing the
laws may explain why they proved only a temporary setback for the Social
Democrats, rather than destroying them as a party. In 1890 the Social Democrats
doubled their support, polling 20 percent of the popular vote. Then the new Kaiser,

Wilhelm II, determined to rule rather than be a figurehead, dismissed Bismarck from office. Although Wilhelm regarded socialists as enemies of the state, he allowed the ban on them to lapse.

Bismarck sought to forge a strong and united Germany through a balancing of social forces. Despite his hostility to the socialists, Bismarck tried to bring the working class into the grand balance of social groups through an extensive program of social legislation. This included the first system of national health insurance anywhere in the world (a good fact to recall when you hear someone damn a government-financed system of health care as socialist). With Bismarck's departure the equilibrium collapsed. Neither Kaiser Wilhelm nor his several Chancellors sought to make meaningful concessions to the middle class or to come to terms with the growing political strength of the workers. By the eve of World War I, the Social Democrats were polling over a third of the popular vote, more than twice as much as the second largest party, but the real power rested in the hands of the Kaiser.

The political system did not evolve toward full parliamentary democracy. Occasionally, some political groups were consulted about the measures that the Cabinet introduced into the Reichstag (the national legislature). But generally the Reichstag influenced public policy only slightly. It had little or no control over financial matters and could not call the Cabinet to account. The Chancellor was responsible to the Kaiser, not to the Reichstag, and the other members of the Cabinet were chosen for their administrative abilities rather than for any political support that they could muster in the Reichstag. The German Empire had the form, but not the substance, of parliamentary democracy.

At the end of September 1918, the military leaders advised the Kaiser that Germany had lost World War I. He indicated that he would accept reform of the political system. The imperial constitution was revised quickly to make the Chancellor accountable to the Reichstag and responsible for all political acts of the Kaiser. Thus, the imperial system became a parliamentary democracy. But it had no chance to evolve. When the Kaiser soon abdicated, the system collapsed.

The Weimar Republic

Germany embarked on its first real experience with democracy in January 1919, when it elected a constituent assembly to form a republic. The delegates, who included some of the leading constitutional scholars in Germany, met in the town of Weimar in what is now the state of Thuringia. The parliamentary system they drew up organized Germany as a federal system with seventeen states. Remembering Prussia's dominance of the imperial federation, the delegates made certain that it could not overshadow the other states in the new system. They also gave the central government more power than was exercised by the national government in the American system at that time.

Unfortunately, the democratic system created at Weimar, which went into effect in mid-1919, lasted less than a decade and a half (see Figure 19–4). As was true of the Third Republic of France, the Weimar Republic experienced considerable instability of the Cabinet. In fourteen years there were twenty Cabinets; these frequent changes hindered effective governmental response to the problems facing

Germany. Many Germans thought the government seemed weak and indecisive compared with what they had been used to under the Empire.

The old order was crumbling in Germany. In a country where the family traditionally had a hierarchical, even authoritarian, structure, children no longer respected their parents. The older generation was seen as having brought defeat in the war. Furthermore, because of the economic collapse of 1929, many fathers were unable to support their families. By 1932 almost one-third of the work force was unemployed.

Another pillar of the old order, the monetary system, was falling apart. After World War I, the *Deutsche Mark* (DM) had stabilized at a rate of 4.2 trillion to the dollar. This wiped out pensions and savings and hit hardest at the middle class, the segment of the population often regarded as the foundation of a democratic political system. In 1929 economic collapse made it appear to the Germans that they would suffer this financial chaos yet again. Even German postage stamps of the Weimar period reflect this fearsome runaway inflation. They were constantly being surcharged, reissued with new higher values printed over them, as the value of the mark plummeted.

Thus, to many Germans life came to appear meaningless, to be without order. Sociologists term this mental state "anomie." And they suggest that the behavior typically associated with it is to seek a savior. One searches for someone who can eliminate the aimlessness of existence by stating authoritatively rules and guides for life. No democratic politician or structure was able to satisfy this felt need.

Into this vacuum stepped an embodiment of the charismatic leader—Adolf Hitler—who spoke as one having authority. Hitler told many Germans exactly what they wished to hear at that point: that it was not their fault that they had lost the war, for the democrats, particularly the Jews, had betrayed the army. He denounced the Treaty of Versailles, hated by Germans for the harsh terms it imposed on Germany as a war settlement, and promised that he would make Germany strong enough to ignore its terms. Germans were a superior people, he proclaimed, and must be restored to their former greatness. He used the business interests' fear of communism and their hostility to the trade unions to get financial support from the pillars of society. Thus, he was able to create a political organization and make an electoral appeal that proved to be equally successful, if not more so, than those of the other parties.

The Weimar Republic never succeeded in creating a fundamental political consensus. The country was torn ideologically between the far right and the far left, each of which comprised a sizable element of the population that did not believe in a democratic system. The country was also in economic turmoil. To many Germans, the Weimar Republic became synonymous with poverty, inflation, national humiliation, and fruitless debate in the Reichstag. In his rise to power, Hitler was able to dramatize and exacerbate a pre-existing climate of fear and frustration. Existing discontents were there to be shaped into a political force by a leader and an efficient organization. These Hitler and the Nazis provided.

Given the rising tide of nationalism in Germany in reaction to the harshness of the peace treaty and the widespread economic dissatisfaction, it is not surprising that by 1930 about one-third of the electorate was voting for extremist parties.

Among these was Hitler's Nazi party, which originally attracted demobilized soldiers who could not adjust to civilian life and soon gathered a motley crew of social misfits, cranks, political adventurers, criminals, and some idealists. By 1930 it drew strong support from the lower middle class, youths, and militarists. It also won significant favor in financial and business circles. Organized along military lines, the Nazi party stirred up delirious demonstrations and carried violence into the streets and into the meetings of other parties.

In 1932 the Nazi party polled 14 million votes, leading all other parties and winning almost 40 percent of the seats in the legislature. This enabled Hitler to attain power legally. In the midst of the political, economic, and social chaos, President Hindenburg invited Hitler to form a Cabinet of "national concentration" in which the Nazis and the Nationalists would share power. At that point party strengths in the legislature were such that the only possible majority grouping had to include the Nazis. The only alternative would have been a Cabinet ruling without regard to the legislature, precisely what democrats had found objectionable in the old imperial system. The army feared that an attempt to return to those days might produce a civil war, given the potential reaction of the left end of the political spectrum. Ironically, then, Hitler was placed in charge of the government in an effort to avoid civil war and illegality.

Although Hitler appointed only three Nazis to Cabinet positions, the offices they received were key ones, which helped to solidify his control of the government. He then called for legislative elections in March 1933. These elections were only nominally democratic. The Nazis curtailed their opponents' use of the radio and the press; they suppressed the right to assemble for political meetings; they looted and destroyed the offices and organizations of other parties. As a result, they and their allies, the Nationalists, won more than half the seats in the legislature.

The Nazi Reich

On March 24, 1933, in an atmosphere of frenzy, coercion, and terror, the Enabling Act was passed, which served as the "constitution" for the Nazis' totalitarian system known as the Third Reich. This label recalled the international status and grandeur of Germany under the Empire and the Holy Roman Empire. Hitler rapidly consolidated his dictatorship. When President Hindenburg died in 1934, Hitler merged that office with the position of Chancellor, which he held. Thus, unrivaled as leader of both the government and the party, he was able to control the country.

The party dominated the government. If a government employee received conflicting instructions from a party superior and a governmental superior, the former was to be obeyed. Since the governmental bureaucracy, a very cohesive and traditional structure in Germany, was not always as responsive as Hitler wished, some functions that normally would be performed by the government were turned over to an agency of the party. An example was the creation of several party control agencies in addition to the usual police forces. These control agencies included the Gestapo (the state secret police), the SS (an elite political police organized along military lines), and the SA, or storm troopers (a paramilitary organization). Although not the most feared or the most powerful, the latter group eventually had over a million members in 1939. To some extent these organizations were intended to control each other, in addition to controlling society, thereby ensuring that no coup could topple Hitler. The rivalry among these organizations and the infighting among their leaders meant that the Nazi system, although totalitarian, was not the monolith it is sometimes portrayed as being.

Also among the party's tasks were educating the public about Hitler's values and goals and recruiting and training loyal and able followers for governmental positions. Party groups were organized for virtually every significant segment of society—for doctors, lawyers, teachers, students, women, and others. These groups served both as a means of indoctrination into party ideology and as a control mechanism in that they allowed the leaders to keep tabs on party members. The line between political and nonpolitical activity, between public and private life—usually fairly distinct in most countries—became blurred. There were party groups for sports and for art appreciation, for example. All activity was politicized. Only by controlling everything could the party be certain that no organization could possibly become an alternative focus for loyalty.

The breadth and depth of control made the system totalitarian: nothing was outside the concern of the Nazi party. Hitler sought not just to govern, but to "purify" the German people. The *Volkgeist*, the essential spirit of Germans as a historical community, was to be instilled in the entire nation. According to Nazi ideology, this mystical force would restore the Germans to their natural superiority in the world and enable the country to fulfill its destiny. This new faith was to be the sole guide for behavior for the good German. Anyone who was not a Jew, a Slav, a Gypsy, or a nonconformist and who embraced this faith and followed orders unquestioningly found that life under the new order could be pleasant. As Pastor Martin Niemoeller, who had commanded a U-boat in World War I, said many years later, "In Germany they came first for the Communists, and I didn't speak up because I wasn't a Communist. Then they came for the Jews, and I didn't speak up because I wasn't a Jew. Then they came for the trade unionists, and I didn't speak up because I wasn't a trade unionist. Then they came for the Catholics, and I didn't speak up because I was a Protestant. Then they came for me, and by that time no one was left to speak up." Niemoeller spent years in a concentration camp.

For those whom the regime saw as posing no threat or who were not bothered by injustice as long as it affected only others, the system was a relatively open one. One could travel to other countries, and tourists were welcomed to Germany. One had only to remember that first—no, sole—loyalty went to the *Führer* (leader). Neither religion nor family ties could be allowed to compete with dedication to or adoration of Hitler. When a man entered the army, he took an oath not to the political system or even to the Fatherland, as had been traditional, but to Hitler personally. As for opponents, the secret police rooted them out. Other political parties were abolished, and newspapers were shut down. Concentration camps were filled not only with non-Nazi politicians, but also with union officers, artists, religious leaders—anyone who opposed or was imagined to oppose the *Führer*.

To suggest that the early sufferings caused by the Nazis were not major would be almost obscene. They paled almost into insignificance, however, compared with what was to come. In the 1930s the deaths were numbered in the thousands; in the 1940s in the millions. Persecution of Jews—denial of employment, seizure of property, and other penalties—began almost immediately under the Third Reich. Those willing to abandon everything they possessed still had time to escape. About half of Germany's half million Jews left before World War II started. Those who remained suffered the same fate as Jews living in the areas that Germany overran during the war. Hitler's "final solution" exterminated nearly three-quarters of the Jews in these areas—a total of 6 million people, many of them children.

Germany after World War II: Fragmentation and Unification

In the end the geographical vastness of the Soviet Union and its inexhaustible supply of military personnel combined with the economic strength of the United States to defeat Nazi Germany. Portions of what had been Germany even before Hitler began his expansion were taken away. The territory that remained was divided into four occupation zones: one each for the United States, the Soviet Union, Britain, and France. Berlin, located inside the Soviet zone, was also divided into four sectors. These arrangements were intended to be transitional—to last only until an acceptable government could be established in Germany. The inability of the occupying powers to agree on the form of government, however, meant that Germany was fragmented once more.

In its zone the Soviet Union installed a communist system, which became the German Democratic Republic (*Deutsche Demokratische Republik*, or DDR). The three Western powers merged their zones into another political system, the Federal Republic of Germany. Thus, two Germanys were created. The area of the western one was somewhat more than twice as large as that of the eastern one. The difference in population was much greater. East Germany had little more than one-fourth the population of West Germany.

Under the guidance of Western occupation officials, delegates chosen by the legislatures of the states drafted a constitution. Since they hoped that the division of their nation into two separate countries would not be permanent, they called this document the Basic Law, rather than a constitution. The Basic Law provided that it would be replaced by a new constitution as soon as Germany was reunited. The launching of the Federal Republic under the Basic Law was the beginning of a second German experiment with democracy. Economic prosperity, Cabinet stability, and the decline of ideological conflict helped to establish a tradition of parliamentary democracy in West Germany.

Within a few years East Germany, under the orders of the Soviet Union, created a three-mile-wide prohibited zone all along its border with West Germany. This area included barbed wire, sentry dogs, guard towers, and so forth to deter anyone from crossing it. In Berlin—over a hundred miles from West Germany and totally surrounded by East German territory—no three-mile zone could be created because the line between East and West Berlin went through the middle of the city. This embarrassed East Germany and the Soviet Union because guards simply could not manage to catch all the daring people willing to risk their lives by fleeing to the west. Suddenly, in August 1961, East Germany built a concrete wall along the border of the two sections of Berlin. For more than a quarter of a century, the Wall divided Germans from each other, in many cases preventing relatives from any contact.

For the four decades of its existence, East Germany was integrated fully into the Soviet bloc. It belonged to Comecon (the Soviet response to the EC) and to the Warsaw Pact (the Soviet response to NATO). Ironically, given the result of World War II, just as West Germany became increasingly important in the defense of the Western alliance, so East Germany became the linchpin in the Soviet bloc—its military forces were second only to those of the Soviet Union. The East German secret police force, the Stasi, was one of the most invasive and brutal in any communist system.

Furthermore, East Germany seemed to be one of the most loyal of the Soviet Union's protegés. An uprising against the government (largely to protest bad economic conditions) did occur in 1953, but this was quickly suppressed by Soviet troops. East Germans subsequently seemed little inclined toward such "misguided" behavior. When the Czechs tried to liberalize their Communist regime in 1968, Walter Ulbricht, the East German head of state, was in the forefront of those urging the Soviet Union to suppress such dangerous behavior. Ulbricht even contributed a division of East German soldiers to the Soviet-led invasion of Czechoslovakia that August. Thirty years, almost to the day, after Hitler had seized Czechoslovakia, goose-stepping German troops once again marched into that country (yes, the East Germans continued that Nazi practice).

State control of the East German economy ensured full employment and a relatively stable cost of living. The price was an inefficient economy; a third of all East German factories operated at a loss. No one ever lost a job because no state-owned factory was allowed to go bankrupt and shut down. If some jobs were eliminated in one plant, those workers were reassigned automatically to an equivalent job in another. An extensive network of child-care institutions subsidized by the government ensured that women could work full-time outside the home.

State control of most prices and state subsidies worth about a fifth of national income helped to keep housing and food costs relatively constant. Dismayed by the shoddy quality and limited variety of consumer goods in the stores, East Germans consoled themselves that at least they did not have to worry about inflation. (This seems only a slightly better situation than that in a Woody Allen joke about the resort hotel where not only was the food bad, but the portions were small.) As late as 1989 the East German government managed to keep the price of a bread roll at five *pfennings* (about a nickel).

Although each Germany was clearly integrated into a separate economic and military bloc, in other spheres the division was less sharp. From the early 1970s East Germans were able to receive West German television and radio broadcasts without interference by government jamming. An entire generation of East German youth grew up as familiar with the musical superstars, issues, and current political-cultural trends in the West as their West German counterparts were. Undeterred by official suppression, environmental and antinuclear peace activists tried during the 1980s to launch movements in East Germany similar to those West German youth were organizing. Both Protestant and Catholic clergy, in defiance of the Stasi, allowed their churches to be used for such gatherings.

Restrictions on travel between East and West Germany were eased early in the 1970s. Many West Germans were able to visit their relatives in East Germany each year. East Germans sixty-five or older were permitted to emigrate and could retire in the West. Toward the close of the 1980s, East Germans under sixty-five could get a visa for a vacation in Western Europe. The number of members from one family who could travel together was limited, however, to discourage tourists from seeking asylum once they were outside of East Germany.

During the summer of 1989, Communist regimes in Eastern Europe began to crumble. East Germans found that they could escape their prison. Initially they would travel to Hungary, whose reformed government wouldn't prevent them from slipping into Austria (Hungary had rolled up the barbed wire that was its portion of the Iron Curtain) and the West. Later they crossed the East German border into Czechoslovakia and besieged the West German embassy in Prague with requests for permission to be admitted to West Germany. In October the East German government sealed the country's border with Czechoslovakia, the last remaining country to which East Germans could travel without a visa. Mikhail Gorbachev, the leader of the Soviet Union made clear that he wanted the East German emigration crisis ended. Unlike in East Germany in 1953, in Hungary in 1956, and in Czechoslovakia in 1968, however, this time orders were issued from Moscow that Soviet troops were to remain in their barracks in East Germany and were not to intervene in propping up the Communist regime.

East German leaders invited Gorbachev to Berlin for an elaborately orchestrated fortieth-anniversary celebration of East Germany's founding. With several hundred Western journalists in the country, the East German police had to be more restrained than usual and had to avoid brutally attacking any political protesters. The identification of Gorbachev with democratic reforms in the Soviet Union gave East German dissidents encouragement to organize protests and demonstrations throughout the country. The day after Gorbachev spoke in Berlin, 70,000 East Germans in the city of Leipzig marched in peaceful protest against the regime. The banners they carried not only attacked the regime, but also, notably, demanded the democratic reforms Gorbachev was pushing for in the Soviet Union. The Leipzig march—supported by the clergy, prominent intellectuals and artists, and even local Communist party officials—was the first instance in the more than forty-year history of East Germany that protest against the government was not put down by water cannons and club-wielding police.

The absence of repression in Leipzig encouraged a wave of antiregime marches, protests, and demonstrations in most other East German cities throughout the rest of October 1989. By the end of the month, millions of emboldened East Germans were marching daily against the regime. In Leipzig, where it had all begun, 480,000 people—over half the city's entire population—staged a protest march on November 6.

In Berlin thousands of people gathered on both sides of the wall. Some scaled it and actually danced along its top, incurring no more than a sporadic dousing with water from high-powered hoses. People began breaking off parts of the Wall with sledge hammers and pickaxes. And soldiers stood by and did nothing; some even smiled as flowers were placed in the barrels of their rifles. The East German government announced that it was abolishing travel restrictions. Suddenly a trip that had involved risking your life—and had resulted in death for many brave enough to try it—had become no more inconvenient than waiting in a traffic jam to drive into West Germany. Or you could just climb to the top of the Wall and jump ten feet into the arms of the waiting West Germans.

The East German government scrambled as best it could to retain some power. Several leadership changes, promises of free elections, and formation of a national unity government including autonomous non-Communist parties had little effect in reversing widespread contempt for the former rulers. The political repression and the low quality of life under the old regime were bad enough. What made things worse were the growing revelations that the Communist leaders had lived in luxury—elaborate country estates, expensive food, and so forth—while the rest of the population had had to stand in lines for hours to get basic foodstuffs and lived in deteriorating housing.

Many East Germans decided to go west not just for a brief visit and to purchase a few consumer goods, but to take up residence. And those most likely to take this step were better educated and possessed marketable skills—precisely the people needed for economic renewal. Even months after travel barriers came down, the flow of East Germans into West Germany continued to average 2,000 a day. The only way to stem the tide appeared to be a step literally no one had expected to see in his or her lifetime—reunification. If East Germany and West Germany were one, then East Germans would not have to move to live in a democratic system; they would not have to fear any reversal of their regime's new moderation. Furthermore, prosperous West Germany could be counted on to pour money into rebuilding the economy of what had been East Germany because it would be part of the same country.

Needless to say, many people with any sense of twentieth-century history (regardless of whether they lived in the Western or the Eastern bloc) were less than wildly enthusiastic about a reunited Germany of nearly 80 million people bestriding Europe. But to the amazement of all, the Western allies and the Soviet Union agreed early in 1990 that the two Germanys could work out domestic relations on their own, however they saw fit. Only in matters of international relations would the four victors be involved in deciding what arrangements to make.

Most Germans were joyful that prospects for a reunited nation were moving so rapidly. Nonetheless, the burden these developments placed on the Federal Republic were immense. Even with its great prosperity, could it manage to resuscitate the East German economy, and what would be the impact of doing so on the West German economy? How extensive would the changes in the constitutional structure of the Federal Republic have to be to accommodate what had been East Germany, and what would be the impact on West German politics? In addition to the domestic or internal problems, the international problem loomed large. Could the two Germanys be reunited in such a way as not to frighten the world with visions of the colossus again (to use the title of one pessimist's warning from the 1950s)?

In March 1990 East Germany held its first democratic elections in nearly sixty years—none occurred under either the Nazis or the Communists. The Communists changed their name to the Party of Democratic Socialism (PDS). This did little good. After difficult negotiations, a new, broad-based government was formed. For the first time in nearly forty-five years the Communists were out of the government. Although the new East German government had to run the country, its main task was to arrange for its demise. Everyone knew that East Germany would continue to exist only as long as was needed to work out the details of how to join it to West Germany.

The first formal step toward unification occurred on July 1, 1990, when the two Germanys began implementing an agreement on monetary, economic, and social union. For the first time since the end of World War II, both countries had the same currency. An even more elaborate treaty (running over 1,000 pages) was negotiated to merge all other aspects of the two countries. Meanwhile the four World War II victors—the United States, the Soviet Union, Britain, and France—agreed to relinquish their occupation rights. The Soviet Union agreed to withdraw all the troops it had stationed in East Germany. Thus, on October 3, 1990 a single Germany was born, fully sovereign over all its territory. Less than a year after the breaching of the Wall, nearly a half century of fragmentation had ended and Germany was again unified. Two months later national elections for this new Germany were held, and the two political systems were fully integrated.

■ ■ ■

As a Briton might say, "Piece of cake. Now comes the hard part." How does one integrate a bankrupt command economy with inadequate infrastructure such as railroads and highways and some of the worst pollution in Europe with a prosperous market economy, especially when the former's population lacks all understanding of how to operate efficiently under the rules of supply and demand? How does one integrate into a democratic system people who have lived under Communist autocracy for forty years? When East German elections were held in March and national German elections in December 1990, these were the first opportunity for all East Germans under the age of seventy-nine (!) ever to vote in free elections. Imagine living to that age and never having participated in the democratic process. How could such people comprehend the role of democratic citizen when their whole lives had been spent adhering to the role of autocratic subject? Such are the problems facing the German political system in the 1990s.

20

The Foundations of German Politics

■ *BASIC VALUES: AUTHORITARIAN OR DEMOCRATIC?*

Until the end of World War I, German political life was characterized by autocracy. The lack of progress in adopting democratic institutions contrasted sharply with the rapid strides Germany was making in industrialization. It contrasted as well with the liberal political developments occurring in other Western European countries.

The revolutionary tide that swept across Europe in the mid-nineteenth century achieved little democratic reform; its impact in Germany was even slighter than elsewhere. Politics continued along an autocratic path, especially after Bismarck came to office in Prussia in 1862. Despite denouncing parliamentary democracy, Bismarck was forced to accept a moderately free press, political parties, and a popularly elected legislature. Although the legislature was relatively powerless, its existence did provide an opportunity for the German people to learn something of the rudiments of the democratic process.

Support for parliamentary democracy was undermined, however, by a feeling that the Prussian parliament contributed nothing to German unity. It had, in fact, seemed to hamper this development—contrary to the desire of the great majority of Germans—by opposing the strengthening of the army. This was the instrument that accomplished what all the politicians' hot air had not advanced a single step: Prussian conquest had unified Germany. The lesson was clear: might makes right.

In German politics, personal morality came to be divorced from reasons of state. That is, duplicity and ruthlessness, which would not have been countenanced by political leaders in their social relations with others, were utilized by them in their political and governmental actions. Success was the only criterion for judging political actions. Power politics was the order of the day. And this approach yielded its greatest dividends when supported by a military spirit that valued order, authority, and unquestioning obedience to one's superiors.

This is not to say that the German political tradition was one of arbitrary government. Another fundamental value was legalism. Germans were firmly convinced that order required an all-encompassing set of rules. These rules were not the product of extensive popular discussion, but derived from the detailed study of experts. Since these rules were formulated by those whose knowledge and training fitted them for the task, naturally the rules should be followed. The good citizen did not seek to participate in the process of making the rules—all that was too complicated for the average person—but was concerned only to learn what the rules were so that they could be obeyed.

Given such attitudes, the democratic political process had little attraction for most Germans. The ideal was the hierarchical, orderly system of the Empire. Bureaucrats were regarded as the true superiors of society, in part because of their education and honesty and in part because the bureaucracy had historically been staffed by the nobility. As recently as 1951, almost a majority of West Germans—45 percent—told pollsters that the time of the Empire was the best period of recent German history.

A legacy of such political values did not augur well for the durability of the Weimar Republic, no matter how much its constitution impressed democratic theorists. World War I shattered Germany's autocratic system; the country's basic political values, however, were not transformed. Germany got a democratic republic primarily because the victors insisted that it must have one. And the Weimar system proved to be neither long-lived nor effective enough to encourage support for democratic values. Under Hitler, Germany reverted to a political system embodying values even more thoroughly authoritarian than those of the Empire.

Nazi Values and National Character

Nazism was more than just exaggerated nationalism or reaction to military defeat or anti-Semitism. Some of the ideas on which the movement was built went back a century or more. The myth depicted a past golden age when the German people (the mystical *Volk*) lived in harmony and happiness, partly because they were superior to other people and partly because they were close to the soil. The Industrial Revolution, with its big cities and modern lifestyle, and its financiers, who were Jews, had uprooted the *Volk* and corrupted them. Such doctrines were propagated by several generations of teachers well before the Nazis arrived on the scene.

In promising Germany a new glory and telling Germans that they were a superior people, Hitler was perpetuating a traditional belief that Germany had a destiny, a mission to advance *Kultur*. *Kultur* could be advanced, he proclaimed, only by superior races subjugating inferior ones. German scholars had long talked of the importance of a *Kulturstaat*. They believed that democratic systems, with their emphasis on equality, produced mediocrity rather than individual greatness. *Kultur* had nothing to do with the sophisticated, degenerate values of French society. It embodied instead the rough-hewn, primitive, pure mores of the *Volk*. The validity of these mores lay in their conformance to and expression of the forces of nature, the vital life forces. These subconscious, mystical forces were supposed to be felt in the blood of all those who were racially pure.

The stereotype that many Americans have of Germans is of very rational, calculating, unemotional people. They are perceived as being very methodical and disciplined. For example, a poll conducted in March 1990 found that nearly 90 percent of Americans associated the quality "disciplined" with West Germans, and more than 80 percent associated "efficient" with them. Germans themselves take this view. The same survey carried out in West Germany found that 97 percent associat-ed themselves with "efficient," and more than 80 percent with "disciplined."

The fallacy lies in believing that such stereotypes are the entire picture. German culture includes another sharply contrasting stream or theme—a wild, romantic, undisciplined strain. Hitler and the Nazis drew heavily on this lesser-known trait.

In yet another respect, Nazi ideology had roots in German thought. German political philosophy had long tended to personify the state, to accord it much greater importance than the individual. Hegel, for example, one of Germany's foremost political philosophers in the early nineteenth century, had interpreted the course of history as the progressive revelation of the *Weltgeist* (literally "world spirit"). This revelation manifested itself, he maintained, not in individuals, but in nations. And, of course, the highest revelation of the *Weltgeist* was in the Prussian state.

Because the Nazis set forth their ideas in philosophical and quasi-scientific lan-guage, their ideology gained a certain amount of acceptance in respectable academ-ic circles. The disciplined organization of the party and the political genius of Hitler were necessary, however, to produce a mass movement. Even then, Hitler might not have succeeded had it not been for a combination of circumstances (the eco-nomic crisis, the legacy of defeat, the alienation of military officers, the indebted-ness of the peasants, and the alleged threat of the Communists), which he was able to exploit to the fullest.

Since traditional German beliefs seemed to have meshed with Nazi values much more easily than they had with democratic ones, many people worried after World War II that any new political system would lack the democratic consensus needed to make it viable. The failure of democratic institutions to take root in Germany, along with the prevalence of autocratic leaders who directed the country into aggressive international policies, seemed evidence of a basic flaw in German national character.

National character is a dubious concept. True, liberal institutions emphasizing the dignity of the individual and popular control of government had not been established in Germany. Part of the reason, however, was the speed with which Germany became a major industrial nation. In Britain and other Western European countries where democracy fared better, industrialization was a more gradual process and was largely the work of private entrepreneurs, not the government or corporations. In Germany, liberal institutions had insufficient time to take root and were impeded by a statist tradition of governmental domination.

Although Germany became industrialized relatively late, it did so before sweep-ing all vestiges of feudalism aside. The aristocracy remained a power well into the nineteenth century. The bourgeoisie had made little headway in Germany and was largely excluded from public life. When change came, it was so rapid that the mid-dle class had little experience to help it in shouldering the political and social responsibilities thrust on it. The failure of democracy in Germany is far too complex an event to be satisfactorily explained by a national character argument.

Infusing Democracy after World War II

The Allied occupation authorities in the western segment of Germany partially understood the lesson of the earlier attempt after World War I to make Germany safe for democracy: "correct" constitutional arrangements are not sufficient to guarantee a democratic system. If not national character, at least basic values had to be transformed. Thus, they attempted to "denazify" and demilitarize the German people. Germans were to be acquainted fully with the horrors of the Nazi era, so that no one could claim that it was mere exaggeration or had never happened. Anyone who had been more than a nominal participant in Nazi party activities was to be removed from public office, as well as from important positions in private organizations.

These proposed programs proved impossible to implement. Examining millions of personal dossiers was a mammoth task. It quickly became apparent that every case would have to be decided on an individual basis, rather than according to a few general rules. Many of those who had been compromised proved to be indispensable in running the country. As a result, lesser offenders sometimes were penalized, and some who had been much more closely associated with the Nazis were given influential positions. Such arbitrariness called the entire program into question. Furthermore, the beginning of the Cold War made a strong West Germany seem an essential bulwark against the threat of Communism. Some thought it might be justifiable to forget about the atrocities of the past, if doing so facilitated a better defense against the dangers of the present and the future.

Nonetheless, the programs did succeed in removing a number of persons with Nazi connections from the judiciary, the communications media, the teaching profession, and the civil service. Also, many former trade union leaders were restored to their pre-Nazi positions. The educational system was revamped, and steps were taken to ensure that future German citizens were presented with a more objective and truthful account of their country's history than had been typical under either the Empire or the Weimar Republic.

In East Germany, although the Communists were authoritarians, they had no love for the Nazi system. In denouncing the Third Reich, however, they made it seem that all the Nazis had lived in what now was West Germany. The people who now made up East Germany were the "good" Germans, who hadn't been involved in any of the atrocities. To that extent they were much less willing than the West Germans to try to come to grips with their horrendous past and admit at least complicity in those events.

Figure 20–1 provides some indication of how the impact of the past on German values has changed only gradually. A decade after the Federal Republic was launched, few West Germans had pride in their political system, tending instead to see their economic system and their national character as the country's strong points. Two decades later, nearly four times as many people were proud of their political system, more than the number who cited national character as the strength. Although political pride did not reach the extraordinarily high level that it had in the United States before the disillusionments of the 1960s, the Federal Republic had managed to win over many skeptics.

Asked in 1951 when their country had been best off, virtually no West German mentioned the existing system; 45 percent said the Empire, and 42 percent the Nazi period before the war. Twenty years later an overwhelming 81 percent chose the Federal Republic, and only 5 percent each cited the Empire and the prewar Nazi regime.

Figure 20–1

Percentage of People
Feeling Pride in Each
of Three Aspects of
Their Country

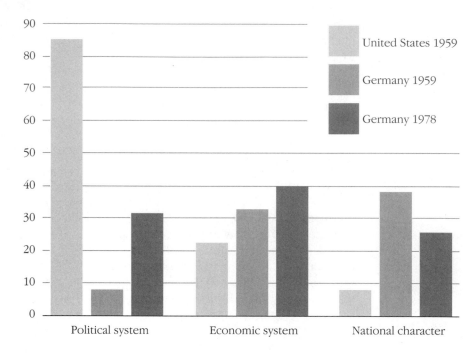

In 1950 a quarter of those polled thought it would be best for the country to have only one political party. Twenty years later only 6 percent held such antidemocratic views. In 1953 only a bare majority felt free to express political views. Less than twenty years later, 84 percent saw no reason to be careful about the opinions they expressed. Furthermore, an overwhelming majority had come to regard democracy as the best form of government.

On the other hand, views about Hitler are not reassuring. In 1955 nearly half of the respondents to a poll agreed that Hitler would have been one of Germany's greatest statesmen had World War II not occurred. Little more than a third disagreed with this idea. A decade later a majority disagreed, but the fact that a third could still hold such a view is shocking. Once another decade had gone by, only 7 percent were willing to say that they would vote for "a man like Adolf Hitler." The responses show a generational contrast: 12 percent of those over fifty said they would vote for someone like Hitler; only 5 percent of those between twenty and forty-nine would do so.

Measuring the impact of the East German system on basic political values is difficult because of the absence of reliable public opinion data for the years it existed. When the collapse of that system made polling possible, some surveys found significant contrasts between east and west. A higher proportion of *Ossis* (the term used for Easterners) than of *Wessis* (Westerners) were proud to be German—remember that the *Ossis* had been taught that Nazism wasn't their fault. As the turmoil of unification soon bore in upon the *Ossis*, however, and the *Wessis* told them how lazy and incompetent they were, this soon changed. By mid-1991 fewer than half of the *Ossis* were proud to be German, lower than for the *Wessis*. Not that the *Wessis* weren't also suffering a bout of self-esteem trauma. The proportion of them who were proud of being German dropped by 15 percentage points to around 57 percent.

A month after unification, two-fifths of *Ossis* said they were happy with democracy "as we have it in the German Federal Republic." Obviously, those responses were supported by virtually no experience. Getting acquainted with reality seemed to disillusion some. By July 1991, fewer than a third were happy with democracy.

The euphoria of unification soon withered as well. At the time of unification, *Wessis* were asked to rate *Ossis* on a scale from +5 to –5; the average was +2. Eight months later their average assessment had declined to +1.1. The *Ossis* showed the same alienation, although at a somewhat more generous level. Their initial assessment of +2.7 declined to +1.7. By July 1992, little more than a third of Germans regarded unification as a cause for celebration. Nearly half saw it as an "overwhelming cause for worry." Potentially dangerous was the fact that three-fifths of the *Wessis* said that any further calls by the government for sacrifices to remedy the problems of unification would produce "anger and refusal."

Many *Wessis* regard *Ossis* in the same way some Americans view "welfare chiselers." To these *Wessis,* the *Ossis* seem impatient, demanding to enjoy the West German standard of living immediately when (horrors!) they hadn't worked hard for it. Many *Wessis* have a well-founded concern about how much reunification will cost them (Chancellor Helmut Kohl hadn't invited them to read his lips, but he had promised that unifying Germany wouldn't require new taxes). Reviving industry in the east will cost huge sums. Little had been invested for years. All of a business's income beyond costs and wages went to the government, which owned virtually all enterprises. Those in charge of the business could not decide to plow back part of the profits to buy new equipment. Only favored industries were given funds for capital investment. Thus, much equipment was obsolete. Pollution from East German industry was the worst in Europe. Estimates of cleaning up the environment in the east ran as high as 100 billion DM (more than $65 billion). Some factories were so deficient that they would have to be torn down entirely and rebuilt from scratch.

Ossis and *Wessis* may both be German, but mutual suspicion and ill-will abound. In such circumstances, integrating the Easterners into the West German value system will be an even greater challenge. The mistake would be to expect an immediate integration. The Westerners themselves only gradually acquired democratic values. Nonetheless, as one generation of Germans replaces another, acceptance of democracy grows. A democratic value system, the absence of which helped to undermine the Weimar Republic, now exists in Germany and should help the system to endure the strains of unification.

■ CONSTITUTIONAL FRAMEWORK

The Historical Heritage

Since the constitution of the Empire remains the longest-lived of the constitutions of modern Germany, any discussion of German constitutional traditions must mention it. The system could claim some elements of democracy. All men twenty-five or older were enfranchised. Britain, long considered the model for parliamentary democracies, did not make the right to vote that extensive until 1918. Although not written into the Empire's constitution, programs such as old-age pensions and national health insurance made provision for social, as well as political, democracy.

The Empire failed to qualify as a parliamentary democracy, however, because it lacked the essential feature of such systems—an executive accountable to the legislature. The powers of the Reichstag were so insignificant that it was unable to develop into a genuine instrument of the popular will; instead, it served mainly as a debating society. The upper house, the Bundesrat, was more important. Since its members were representatives of and controlled by the governments of the various states, it functioned rather like an international conference. Prussia clearly was in command, since it had seventeen of the forty-eight members and no other state had more than six.

The Kaiser and the Chancellor wielded the executive power. Here, again, Prussia dominated. The Prussian king served as Kaiser of the Empire and the Prussian prime minister as his Chancellor. Although the Kaiser was not granted the power to veto laws passed by the legislature, almost the only ones of importance that did pass were those initiated by the Chancellor. Cabinet ministers, chosen from among top bureaucrats rather than from party or legislative leaders, served simply as assistants to the Chancellor, who could dismiss them at will.

No matter what the Reichstag did, it could not compel the Chancellor to resign. He served as long as the Kaiser wished. Bismarck's successors as Chancellor, lacking his political skills and forceful personality, did concede a greater voice in budgetary matters to the legislature. They never, however, acknowledged any accountability to the Reichstag.

Since World War I had been fought, according to the American President, to make the world safe for democracy, the victors decided that Germany must have a democratic constitution. They held a naive belief, which fit in well with traditional German legalism, that good government was purely a matter of proper institutions. See that the Germans got the "right" form of government, and the country would be democratic and unaggressive. War hysteria—"Hang the Kaiser!"—meant that the new system would have to be a republic. Constitutional experts met in the small town of Weimar to draw up an appropriate document.

The constitution for what subsequently has been known as the Weimar Republic was regarded at the time as a very progressive document, setting up perhaps the most democratic system in the world. The legislature was made up of two houses: the Reichstag, whose members were elected by universal, equal suffrage, and the Reichsrat, whose members were appointed by the governments of the member states. Since a two-thirds vote of the Reichstag could override the decisions of the upper house, the popularly elected lower house had the final say in legislative decisions.

Even more progressive was the role in the legislative process given to the public. A deadlock between the two houses of the legislature was to be resolved by a referendum. Should the legislature ever fail to respond to a popular desire for action, the public could launch legislation by means of an initiative, a novel procedure that had been pioneered at the state level in the western United States by the Progressive movement. This was intended to involve the people in the governmental process as fully as possible. In addition, an electoral system thought to be highly democratic and fair was created. It was a form of proportional representation in which the number of seats in the legislature was not predetermined. A party was to receive one seat for every 60,000 votes it obtained. Thus, all interests and opinions, however slight their following, would have a voice in the legislative process.

A new office of President was created. This official was not to serve as a mere figurehead, like the British monarch or the President of France in the Third Republic. The President of the Weimar Republic was granted considerable power, being able, among other things, to dissolve the Reichstag and dismiss the Cabinet. To ensure that the person holding the office had political clout, it was to be filled by direct, popular election. The President's most important single power was contained in Article 48. The idea was to enable the government to defend itself in a crisis by giving it emergency powers. This was a sound enough objective; any system must have some reserve powers that can be called on to see a country through extraordinary circumstances. Lincoln, for example, stretched the U.S. Constitution to its limit (some would say beyond its limit) during the Civil War. The Weimar constitution provided that when the President felt the country faced a constitutional crisis, he could permit the Cabinet to do whatever was necessary to restore order.

This may sound quite similar to what the French did years later in Article 16 of the Fifth Republic's constitution. Unlike that provision, however, Article 48 did attempt to include some safeguards to prevent abuse of the emergency powers. The grant of power to the Cabinet was to lapse as soon as the emergency was over. All actions taken under this power had to be submitted to the legislature, which could void any of them it wished. The constitution itself could not be infringed during the emergency. The effectiveness of this safeguard was compromised, however, by a provision that permitted suspending some basic rights—free speech, free assembly, and *habeas corpus*, for example—during emergencies.

Despite creating a strong President, the Weimar constitution retained the office of Chancellor as head of the government. Here, again, there are some similarities to the constitution subsequently drawn up for the Fifth Republic in France. As has been possible under the various Republics in France, the German legislature was permitted to delegate power to the Chancellor and the Cabinet. It did this during the postwar reconstruction period (1919–1923) and again during the subsequent economic depression (1930–1933). Despite such legislative abdications, the Chancellor and the Cabinet never were very strong, exactly as was true in the Third and Fourth Republics and for the same reason. All Cabinets were coalitions, usually short-lived, since the legislature was fractionalized; no single party could come even close to holding a majority of the seats.

By 1930 each of ten separate parties was able to gain more than a million votes. Proportional representation ensured that each of them, along with a number of splinter groups, was fully represented in the legislature. Fair enough, you may say, since that is what the people voted for. The result, however, was to make the legislature virtually unworkable. Lack of any cohesive majority regularly prevented passage of the Cabinet's budget. In desperation the Cabinet decided to declare that such situations were an emergency within the provisions of Article 48, and the President went along with this strategy. Frequent resort to Article 48 from 1930 on made government in the remaining years of the Weimar Republic largely a matter of rule by decree. Thus, Hitler's initial actions did not seem all that different, in form at least, from what people had become used to under a democratic system.

In seeking to explain why a system so progressive, so ideally democratic as the Weimar Republic should fail to survive, some scholars have blamed Article 48 and the proportional representation electoral system. Others regard this argument as too mechanical and deterministic, as based on the old naive view that all that matters are the formal legal structures. They note Germany's lack of a democratic tradition to support the institutions created by the constitution and cite the many economic problems that inundated the Weimar Republic.

Nonetheless, both the Western allies and the Germans themselves were influenced by the failure of the first attempt to establish democracy in Germany when the time came to draw up a new framework document after World War II. They were determined that this second attempt to create a democracy, in that part of the country that would be known as West Germany, would not repeat the errors of the past, that any possible shortcomings or loopholes of the Weimar type would be avoided. Thus, although the Western allies did attempt to eradicate authoritarian values through denazification, they retained the concern of earlier victors over Germany to devise the proper formal institutional structure.

Divergent German Systems

The post–World War II framework document for West Germany, called the Basic Law, was intended to make the Chancellor's position more secure, so that he or she could not be toppled by a temporary alliance of legislative dissidents. In keeping with German tradition, but also to avoid centralized power, West Germany was organized as a federal system. The central government was given the exclusive right to legislate in such matters as foreign affairs, citizenship, currency and coinage, railways, posts and telecommunications, and copyrights. The central government and the state governments were given concurrent powers for civil and criminal law, for laws relating to the economy, labor, agriculture, public welfare, and ocean and coastal shipping, and for "the prevention of the abuse of economic power" (antitrust actions). In other matters, notably education and cultural affairs, the states were to exercise primary responsibility. If laws passed by the central government and by any state government clashed, those of the former would prevail.

In at least two matters, taxation and education, the trend was toward strengthening the role of the central government. The states (especially the richer ones) wanted as much independence as possible in tax policy, whereas the central government wanted to equalize the distribution of major tax revenues between the more and less prosperous states. After much controversy, the central government's position finally prevailed. In 1969 the Basic Law was amended to expand the central government's financial powers, thus enabling it to redistribute tax revenues among the states. Other amendments increased the central government's responsibilities for educational planning. The aim was to make educational standards more uniform throughout the country so that people moving from one state to another would not be handicapped by varying educational requirements.

Reflecting American influence, the Basic Law provided for a Federal Constitutional Court, with power to annul acts of the legislature or the administration that violate the Basic Law. The Court is also authorized to ban unconstitutional parties, if the Cabinet recommends such action. This was done to a neo-Nazi party in 1952, to the Communist party in 1956, and to some splinter neo-Nazi groups in the early 1990s.

The Basic Law can be amended by a two-thirds vote of the members of both houses of the legislature. Some provisions, however, are unamendable. These include the organization of the country into states and certain basic democratic provisions, such as protection for fundamental civil liberties.

The most significant amendment to the Basic Law occurred two decades after the start of the Federal Republic and dealt with the touchy, and previously unresolved, issue of emergency powers. This amendment, consisting of seventeen articles, is commonly referred to as the "emergency constitution." Ten years of discussion and debate preceded its adoption. Given the experience of Weimar, West Germans obviously were wary of any provision for emergency powers. Yet they realized that a need for them can arise in any system. The concern was how to draft an amendment providing the needed powers without jeopardizing democratic rights.

The procedure agreed on was that for an emergency to exist, it must be recognized by the Bundestag (the lower house of the legislature) and then that house's decision must be approved by the Bundesrat (the upper house). In both cases a two-thirds vote is required. Furthermore, in the Bundestag this two-thirds must include at least a majority of the total number of members. If insuperable obstacles prevent the Bundestag from meeting or the situation demands immediate action, an emergency parliament (called the Joint Committee) can make the decision. Since the unification of East and West Germany, the Joint Committee is composed of forty-eight members, of whom two-thirds are Bundestag deputies and one-third are Bundesrat members (one from each of the states). The thirty-two members from the Bundestag are selected so as to represent political parties in proportion to their strength in the legislature. No member of the Cabinet may be chosen. A two-thirds vote (including at least a majority of the members) is required for the Joint Committee to decide that an emergency exists.

The emergency constitution specifies in considerable detail various procedural and substantive safeguards. Among other things, the Bundestag may not be dissolved during an emergency, and the Constitutional Court cannot be tampered with. Moreover, the Bundestag, with the approval of the Bundesrat, can repeal laws enacted by the Joint Committee (which functions as the legislature, if that body cannot convene) and can declare that an emergency has ended at any time.

Since there has been no occasion when the provisions of the emergency constitution have been put into practice, there is no way of knowing whether the safeguards are adequate. Perhaps the key point is the way in which their country's constitutional heritage has caused the West Germans to specify in extraordinary detail the procedures that are to apply in quite rare circumstances. This is evidence of a national tendency to give greater priority to legal, constitutional arrangements for protecting democracy than to basic values and beliefs.

The Basic Law does not specify a particular electoral system. The delegates who wrote it also drafted, however, electoral procedures, which became law after the occupation authorities modified them somewhat. Over the years the details of this law have been modified, but the basic form remains unchanged: a complicated form of proportional representation seeking fairness while avoiding the splintering effects of pure proportional representation. (We will explain the details of the system in Chapter 21.) Clearly, the Basic Law and related fundamental statutes have been influenced greatly by German history. West Germans feared that they would be revisited by an evil specter from the past—Adolf Hitler.

Fortunately, as you saw earlier in this chapter, considerable progress occurred in West Germany toward establishing a democratic political culture, despite the limited effectiveness of denazification. This is primarily because the system that was created worked. As we explained in Chapter 19, from the rubble of total destruction in 1945, West Germany recovered to become an economic powerhouse. Clearly, this system could deliver the goods, something few believed about the Weimar regime. And economic recovery was not the only way in which the system proved itself. As we'll discuss in subsequent chapters, impressive leadership at a formative time and a less fractionalized and more pragmatic party system were great aids to effectiveness.

When a system proves effective in many ways for more than four decades, as the West German government did, it builds up a reservoir of support on which it can draw to survive reverses. The typical German under Weimar was no more than a sunshine democrat at best. Something more than a half century later, a few showers are unlikely to dissolve German commitment to a democratic system that has become legitimated.

The DDR established in the east also had states initially. These units of government had little power, however, in keeping with the Soviet Union's preference for centralized government. Despite the East German constitution's provision that the states were the foundations of the republic, they were abolished in 1952, and the country was divided into fourteen districts, which were no more than administrative areas. Initially the East German national legislature had two houses, and the upper one represented the states. After 1952 it was vestigial, and eventually, in 1958, it was formally abolished.

Superficially the East German system resembled the British form of government. The legislature was to be supreme, just as the British Parliament is. Of course, East Germany didn't have a monarch but a President, who was elected by the lower house of the legislature and served as head of state. In 1960, upon the death of the then President, East Germany decided to change to a collective executive. A Council of State with two dozen members was created. The chair of this body, elected by the legislature, would serve as head of state. The Council of State did not correspond to the British Cabinet, however, since East Germany also had a Council of Ministers, which was more equivalent to that Cabinet and whose chair was similar to the British Prime Minister. Some changes in detailed arrangements were made through a new constitution that went into effect in 1968, but the basic nature of the system wasn't changed.

As is typical in communist systems, the formal constitutional arrangements didn't matter a great deal. Power was concentrated in the hands of Communist party leaders, and governmental organs were little more than rubber stamps for party orders. The Communist party in East Germany was known as the Socialist Unity Party (SED). The government did permit other parties to operate; for example, there was a Christian Democratic Union (CDU) and a Liberal Democratic Party (LDP). These parties had no connection with their counterparts in West Germany, however, and were permitted to operate only because they were willing to collaborate with the Communists. Any leaders of these parties who dared to criticize the government were removed from their positions.

Furthermore, elections were run in such a fashion as to ensure control of the government by the SED. East Germany established a system of "bloc politics," which combined parties with various mass organizations, such as trade unions. At election time the ballot would contain a single list of candidates, a "unity list." Each organization included in the official bloc would be allocated a certain number of seats—thus, everyone knew how many each group would "win" even before the election was held. The various organizations were permitted to select candidates for "their" seats, but the Communists could veto any they didn't like. Thus, even the "opposition" candidates would be people acceptable to the Communists. Obviously, elections offered the voters no real choice.

How were two such divergent political systems to be joined in 1990? One possibility was for representatives from East and West Germany to draft a new constitution. The Basic Law's preamble stated that its drafters had "acted on behalf of those Germans to whom participation was denied" (meaning those living in Communist East Germany). And its final article (146) declared that the "Basic Law shall cease to be in force on the day on which a constitution adopted by a free decision of the German people comes into force." But why scrap the Basic Law when it had proven to be quite effective over a period of more than four decades? Furthermore, calling a new constitutional convention would be quite time-consuming and could produce a number of divisive disputes.

Therefore, instead of a merger to form a new political system, the addition of East Germany to West Germany—rather like Alaska and Hawaii becoming the forty-ninth and fiftieth American states in 1959—seemed preferable. An alternative to Article 146 could be found elsewhere in the Basic Law. Article 23 stated that "for the time being, this Basic Law shall apply in . . ." and lists the West German states. It closed with the provision that "in other parts of Germany it shall be put into force on their accession." The fact that the Saarland had become part of West Germany in this way in 1957 provided something in the way of a precedent. Unfortunately, however, this procedure seemed to resemble what in corporate finance would be called a take-over bid. West Germany had acquired a bankrupt enterprise, which it would incorporate into its existing operation. The *Ossis* were being told, in effect, that they had nothing to offer and the *Wessis*—out of the goodness of their hearts—would bail them out.

As mentioned in the historical discussion in Chapter 19, various treaties spelled out in detail how East Germany would be incorporated into the West. Five East

German leaders were added to the West German Cabinet. The representatives from West Berlin were, for the first time, given full voting rights in the legislature and 160 new members from East Germany and East Berlin were added, bringing the Bundestag's total membership to 656. Each of the states in East Germany was given four seats in the Bundesrat. The four largest West German states each received a sixth seat. These changes enlarged the Bundesrat to 69 members. The holding of nationwide elections in December 1990 completed the unification process.

In addition to questions about constitutional structure, unification raised some other perplexing legal issues. Many East Germans feared that they might be dispossessed of their homes. Hundreds of thousands of people who had once lived in East Germany had fled to the west to avoid living under communism. Their property—homes, farms, businesses—had been seized by the government, which allocated it for the use of those who remained in East Germany. Once the Communist regime crumbled and it became clear that unification was soon to follow, some residents of East Germany began receiving letters and legal notices from West Germans saying that they would be reclaiming the property they had been forced to abandon when they fled to the west. In many cases East Germans had lived in the houses for decades.

The rules for settling such matters may be legally sound, but defy common sense. Property seized by the Nazis prior to 1945 can be claimed. Property seized by the East German government from 1949 on can be claimed. Property seized by the Soviet Union from 1945 to 1949, when it occupied part of Germany, *cannot* be claimed. Although one of West Germany's parties, the Christian Social Union of Bavaria, wants people to be allowed to claim that property as well, the unification agreement with East Germany and the World War II Allies prohibits returning the property to its former owners; all they can receive is limited compensation.

By the end of 1992, 1.1 million people had claimed 2.5 million properties in the former East Germany, but only about 15 percent of these claims had been resolved. Thus many *Ossis* must live with the terrible uncertainty of perhaps being made homeless, bad enough under any circumstances but even worse at a time of widespread unemployment. Furthermore, attracting essential investment to the former East Germany is hampered because those having capital to invest are unwilling to risk it when it is unclear who possesses a valid title to an enterprise.

On another issue, one that was social and moral, as well as legal, East German women feared that they would be *less* free after reunification. Under communism, abortion had been available on demand. Although West Germany did not prohibit abortion, the circumstances under which it could be obtained were much more restricted than in East Germany. The compromise proposed was that for a transitional period the reunited country would have two different abortion laws—one set of regulations in what had been West Germany and another in what had been East Germany. Conservative politicians in West Germany protested vigorously. They wanted to be certain that no woman from what was formerly West Germany would be able to travel to what had been East Germany to get an abortion that would be illegal where she resided. (As any American could have told them, such are the joys of federalism.) They lost the argument. The huge treaty between the two Germanys on legal details provided that both laws would remain valid through 1992 and no western woman would be prosecuted for going to an eastern locale to get an abortion. But for women living in the eastern parts of the reunited Germany that still left open the question of what the law would be in 1993. Would it be made more restrictive? Would reunification ultimately mean curtailment of a right? We'll tell you what happened when we discuss the judicial system in Chapter 26.

■ ■ ■

In short, many East Germans—for a variety of legitimate reasons—were quite anxious. How ironic that the ending of communism had made them feel insecure. Those who had criticized the old East German government certainly hadn't felt secure. On the other hand, those who had kept quiet and didn't try to think independently had enjoyed social and economic security under communism. But now they were setting forth in uncharted seas, and they were frightened. Here also the German political system faced a daunting test of its durability and effectiveness.

......21

Channels for Individual and Group Political Activity _____

■ *THE ELECTORAL SYSTEM*

When devising their electoral system, the West Germans were of two minds. On the one hand, like many other Europeans, they were attracted by proportional representation's apparent fairness. That a party's share of the seats in the legislature should correspond closely to its share of the popular vote—an outcome produced only fortuitously by the Anglo-American single-member, simple-plurality system— seems only proper. Yet the Germans were also aware that proportional representation has flaws as well as virtues. And this was not just a matter of abstract theory— the experience of Weimar seemed clear proof of proportional representation's adverse effects on the party system.

Proportional Representation with a Difference

The Germans sought a compromise, a hybrid electoral system that would yield benefits without associated costs. This is why the system we are about to explain is so complex. The Germans wanted electoral justice, but not at the cost of party fractionalization. They wanted to avoid depersonalized representation, the lack of any link between the electorate and an individual representative. And they wanted, perhaps most important, to prevent extreme, antidemocratic parties from burgeoning from splinters to major political movements.

The basic procedure Students of elections have devised several different formulas for deciding how the popular vote is to be converted into legislative seats in proportional representation systems. Some of these methods tend to favor small parties. The d'Hondt method (named after the person who devised it) used in Germany is a highest-average system, which tends to favor large parties. Each party's total vote is divided by the number of seats it already has been awarded plus one. The party with the highest average is awarded the seat for that round. This process continues round after round until all the seats have been allocated. A hypothetical case will clarify this process.

Assume that five members are to be elected and that the voters have cast their ballots as summarized in Table 21–1. In the first round, no party has any seats, so the total number of votes for each is divided by 1. Party A has the highest average (52,000) and wins a seat. Now party A's votes must be divided by 2 (1 seat won plus 1); its average becomes 26,000. This places it between parties D and E. Since no party other than A has been allocated a seat, the other parties' votes continue to be divided by 1 in next round.

Party B now has the highest average (36,000) and wins the second seat. Now its total vote, like that of party A, is divided by 2 (1 seat won plus 1); B drops to the bottom of the pack with an average of 18,000. The totals for parties C, D, E, and F, which have yet to win a seat, continue to be divided by 1.

Party C wins the third seat, and party D the fourth one. By this point the votes for parties A, B, C, and D are being divided by 2; those of parties E and F are still divided by 1, since they have yet to win a seat. Nonetheless, party A's average, 26,000, is higher than party E's, 24,000, so the fifth seat goes to party A.

All the seats have been allocated: A has received 2; B, C, and D have obtained 1 each; and neither E nor F has won any. Had there been a sixth seat to allocate, it would have gone to party E, which topped the list after five rounds were completed. Party A, whose total would be divided by 3 (2 won plus 1), would have an average of 17,333. Were more seats to be allocated, A would not get a third seat until parties E and F each received their first seat and party B got a second seat.

As this example suggests, each constituency in a proportional representation system must return several members to the legislature. Thus, the voters in a given area are not represented by a single legislator. No single representative need feel any special responsibility for a given constituency—all that a representative has to do is to keep the local party leaders happy. Doing so will help to ensure being placed near the top of the party's list of candidates for the constituency. If the party is of any significance at all, such placement virtually guarantees reelection. In short, those selected in a proportional representation system have little incentive to be responsive to their constituents.

The Anglo-American element   To offset this lack of responsiveness, the West Germans injected an element of the single-member, simple-plurality system into their electoral procedures. The unified country is divided into 328 constituencies, each of which returns one representative. The boundary lines are drawn on the

Party	Votes	Percentage of Votes
A	52,000	26
B	36,000	18
C	34,000	17
D	32,000	16
E	24,000	12
F	22,000	11
Total	200,000	

Table 21–1
Hypothetical Vote
Totals Illustrating
d'Hondt Method

basis of the number of qualified electors in each constituency, with the stipulation that no constituency's electorate may be more than one-third above or below the national average. In each constituency the candidate receiving the greatest number of votes, regardless of whether this is a majority, is elected, just as happens in the United States.

Since Germany has a multiparty system, however, most of those elected in the single-member, simple-plurality constituencies receive less than half of the votes cast, in contrast to the typical result in the United States. In 1987, for example, less than a third of the constituency winners in West Germany obtained a majority of the votes cast in their constituency. A more important contrast is that these American-style electoral procedures are used to select only half of the total membership of the lower house of the national legislature.

The proportional representation element   Each German voter gets to vote twice—once for a specific candidate to represent the local district and once for a party, from whose list of candidates the top ones will be elected to represent the entire state. Thus half of the lower house is elected from state party lists and represents an entire state, not just a single-member constituency. A sample ballot for a German election appears in Figure 21–1.

The complicated part of this system is that the votes cast on the party-list side of the ballot (the right-hand side in Figure 21–1) determine the party strengths for the *entire* membership of the legislature, not just for half of it. Even though half of the members are elected in single-member, simple-plurality constituencies, the *entire* system is proportional representation. All the votes cast for the SPD (Social Democrats) party list, for example, in all of the states are added together to produce a total national vote. This total is used to calculate how many of all the seats in the legislature are to go to the SPD.

Once all the seats in the legislature have been allocated, each party's total representation in the legislature will have been determined. Now each party's seats must be distributed among the states. That is, if the SPD has won, for example, 200 seats, how many of these are from, say, Lower Saxony? The whole process described above is repeated for each party separately, for as many rounds as it takes to assign the total number of seats to which it is entitled. Only at this point will it finally be known, for example, that the SPD is entitled to 27 seats in Hesse.

Combining both elements   Now comes the complicated part (now?!). The number of single-member seats that the SPD has won in a particular state is subtracted from the number to which the two separate proportional representation calculations have shown it is entitled to there. The difference is the number of candidates from the top of the SPD list of candidates for that state who will be declared elected, in addition to those SPD candidates who won single-member seats. Thus, if the calculations show that the SPD is entitled to 27 seats in Hesse and it has won 15 single-member seats there, then the first 12 names on its party list for Hesse will be elected. (Unless, as is permissible, some of these 12 had been candidates for a single-member constituency and were elected there. In that case they would not be counted when the top 12 were selected.)

Figure 21–1
Sample Ballot for a German National Election

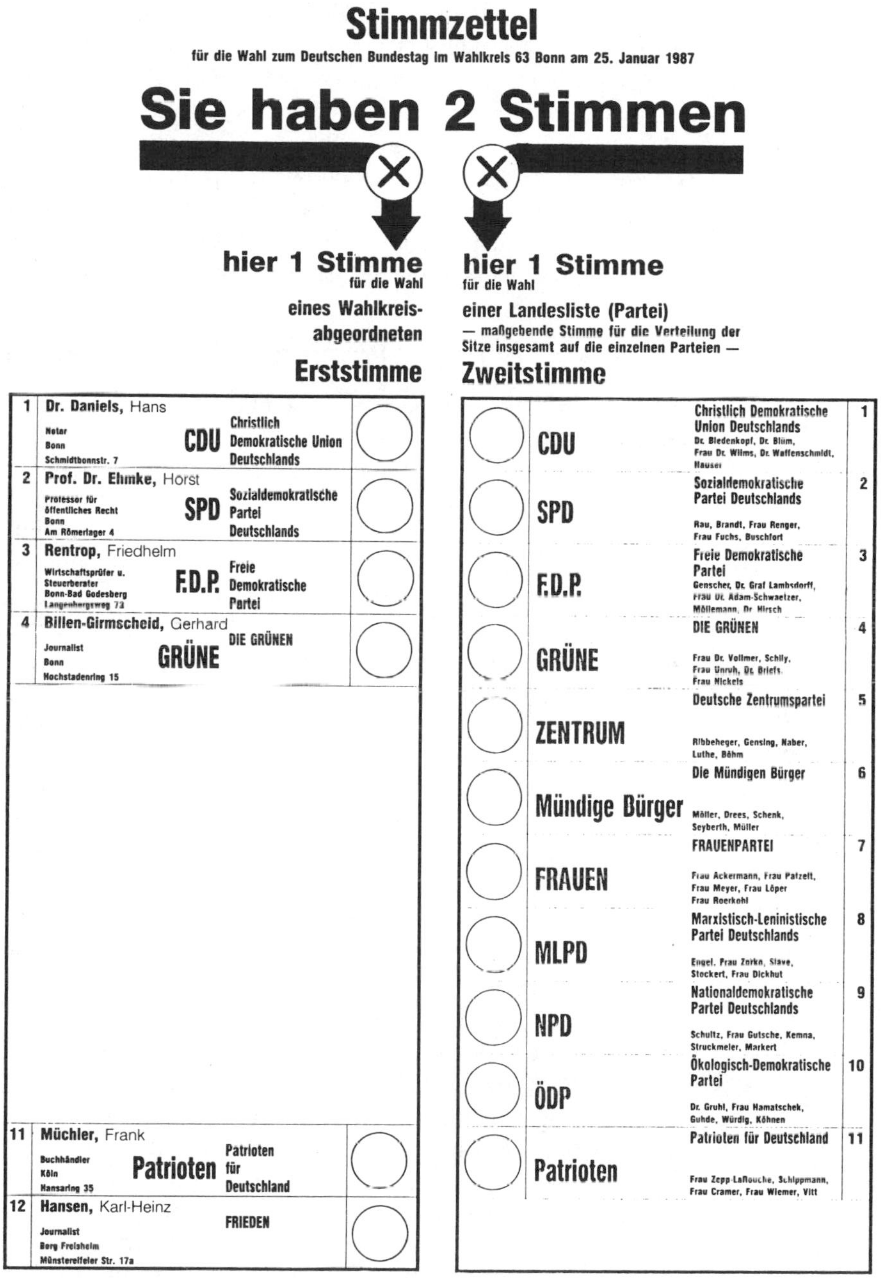

Stimmzettel

für die Wahl zum Deutschen Bundestag im Wahlkreis 63 Bonn am 25. Januar 1987

Sie haben 2 Stimmen

hier 1 Stimme für die Wahl eines Wahlkreis-abgeordneten **Erststimme**	**hier 1 Stimme** für die Wahl einer Landesliste (Partei) — maßgebende Stimme für die Verteilung der Sitze insgesamt auf die einzelnen Parteien — **Zweitstimme**

1	**Dr. Daniels,** Hans Notar Bonn Schmidtbonnstr. 7	**CDU**	Christlich Demokratische Union Deutschlands
2	**Prof. Dr. Ehmke,** Horst Professor für öffentliches Recht Bonn Am Römerlager 4	**SPD**	Sozialdemokratische Partei Deutschlands
3	**Rentrop,** Friedhelm Wirtschaftsprüfer u. Steuerberater Bonn-Bad Godesberg Langenbergsweg 73	**F.D.P.**	Freie Demokratische Partei
4	**Billen-Girmscheid,** Gerhard Journalist Bonn Hochstadenring 15	**GRÜNE**	DIE GRÜNEN
11	**Müchler,** Frank Buchhändler Köln Hansaring 35	**Patrioten**	Patrioten für Deutschland
12	**Hansen,** Karl-Heinz Journalist Burg Frelsheim Münstereifeler Str. 17a		FRIEDEN

CDU	Christlich Demokratische Union Deutschlands Dr. Biedenkopf, Dr. Blüm, Frau Dr. Wilms, Dr. Waffenschmidt, Hauser	1
SPD	Sozialdemokratische Partei Deutschlands Rau, Brandt, Frau Renger, Frau Fuchs, Buschfort	2
F.D.P.	Freie Demokratische Partei Genscher, Dr. Graf Lambsdorff, Frau Dr. Adam-Schwaetzer, Möllemann, Dr. Hirsch	3
GRÜNE	DIE GRÜNEN Frau Dr. Vollmer, Schily, Frau Unruh, Dr. Briefs, Frau Nickels	4
ZENTRUM	Deutsche Zentrumspartei Ribbeheger, Gensing, Naber, Luthe, Böhm	5
Mündige Bürger	Die Mündigen Bürger Möller, Drees, Schenk, Seyberth, Müller	6
FRAUEN	FRAUENPARTEI Frau Ackermann, Frau Patzelt, Frau Meyer, Frau Löper, Frau Roerkohl	7
MLPD	Marxistisch-Leninistische Partei Deutschlands Engel, Frau Zorka, Slave, Stockert, Frau Dickhut	8
NPD	Nationaldemokratische Partei Deutschlands Schultz, Frau Gutsche, Kemna, Struckmeier, Markert	9
ÖDP	Ökologisch-Demokratische Partei Dr. Gruhl, Frau Hamatschek, Guhde, Würdig, Köhnen	10
Patrioten	Patrioten für Deutschland Frau Zepp-LaRouche, Schippmann, Frau Cramer, Frau Wiemer, Vitt	11

Those of you who are still with us at this point and who like to stump your teachers with "what if " questions, no doubt want to ask what happens if a party wins *more* single-member seats than the total number of seats to which it is entitled in a given state. This is extremely unusual, but has occurred from time to time. The lucky party keeps the extra seats—you can hardly disqualify somebody who has been properly elected. As a result, the total number of seats in the German legislature often varies slightly from one election to the next. In 1987, for example, the Christian Democrats won 36 of Baden-Württemberg's single-member seats; the proportional representation calculations showed that the party was entitled to only 35 seats from that state given the size of its vote there. The Christian Democrats retained all 36 seats that they had won, even though none of their party-list candidates—not even the top one—was elected from that state. In the unusual circumstances of the first elections for unified Germany in 1990, such outcomes added another 6 members to the legislature, raising its total to 662.

The Effects of Hybrid Proportional Representation

This electoral system may seem strange, but it has an even more unusual aspect. Although the number of single-member seats for each state is determined before the election and although these seats represent half of the total membership of the legislature, in any given state the number of candidates elected from the party list may be greater or smaller than the number of single-member constituencies. The reason is that a state's total representation is a function of the share of the total national party vote that each of the parties receives in that state. That is, representation is affected by whether voter turnout in a state is markedly above or below the turnout nationally. In effect, abstaining is voting to reduce your state's representation in the national legislature. Relatively low turnout in the former East Germany and in Bavaria in 1990 effectively reduced their representation in the legislature by a few seats.

Voting for a minor party has the same effect. In order to avoid the splintering effects of proportional representation on the party system, the Germans have modified the electoral system to hamper minor parties. A party must win either 5 percent of the total national vote or 3 single-member constituencies to be allowed to share in the proportional allocation of seats. If a party wins 2 single-member seats and 4.9 percent of the vote nationally, it gets only the 2 seats. If it wins 3 single-member seats and 4.9 percent, it receives 32 seats (4.9 percent of 656). If it fails to win any seats, but polls 5 percent of the vote, then it gets 32 seats. Thus, at this marginal point, winning one more constituency or another 0.1 percent of the national vote is worth about two and a half dozen additional seats. In effect, the Germans were saying to minor parties that they must either have generalized support throughout the country at something more than a minimal level or have concentrated strength in some areas sufficient to outpoll the other parties. Such parties would be regarded as reasonable contenders for representation; others would be considered detrimental to the party system and, thus, not entitled to representation.

The point of this detailed discussion of the mechanics of Germany's electoral system is to clarify our earlier statement about the goals of the Bonn Republic's founders. Since the electoral system allocates to parties a share of the total seats in the legislature roughly equal to their share of the popular vote, the system can be deemed fair. Since it allows each elector to vote for a single candidate to represent the constituency, it contains an element of personal representation and concern. And insofar as it establishes a hurdle that minor parties must clear before they are represented in the legislature, it avoids the fractionalization of the party system frequently associated with proportional representation. The system is complex, but it has done a good job in achieving the conflicting goals the founders set up.

Given the way in which East Germany was amalgamated with the west, the West German electoral laws applied for the first unified elections in 1990. Remember that these regulations include a 5-percent barrier designed to eliminate splinter parties. Recall further that East Germany had little more than a fourth of the population of West Germany. Some of the small parties allied with the governing Christian Democrats in the East clearly had no hope of getting 5 percent of the total vote cast in all of Germany; they would be eliminated from the legislature. Chancellor Helmut Kohl of the Christian Democrats obviously didn't want to lose some of his allies. So the law was amended to permit small parties to form alliances with larger ones—to piggyback, in effect—thereby protecting the Christian Democrats' small eastern allies.

Parties unlikely to be able to form alliances (the former East German Communists were especially concerned that no one would care to associate with them) objected and brought suit in the Federal Constitutional Court. Late in September the Court invalidated the law. Not only did it throw out the piggyback provision; it also held that applying the 5-percent barrier to the east's small parties would be unfair and declared that provision unconstitutional as well. Thus, the Court opened the way not only for the former East German Communists to gain seats in the national legislature, but also for the extremist parties on the right, which had been shut out of the West German legislature for four decades by the 5-percent barrier. The legislature had little over two weeks to revise the law so that the elections could occur as scheduled. What it did was to divide the unified country into two distinct electoral regions. This arrangement was for the 1990 elections only. We mention it simply as another example of the complexities of putting Humpty Dumpty together again.

The German electoral system provides a unique opportunity to study the effect of candidate personality on voting, since each voter can vote twice: once for a candidate and once for a party. Some people might regard a particular candidate in a given election as especially capable and articulate, even though they do not usually support the party of that candidate. Such voters might decide to abandon their usual party loyalty and vote for such an appealing candidate. During the 1950s in the United States, many people who normally thought of themselves as Democrats nonetheless voted for the Republican presidential candidate, Eisenhower, because they agreed with millions of others, "I Like Ike." Unlike American voters, German voters do not have to choose between remaining loyal to their party and supporting an attractive candidate from another party. They can vote for such a candidate on one side of the ballot and vote for their party on the other side. Furthermore, since it is the party-list vote, and not the candidate vote, that determines partisan strength in the Bundestag, they can split their vote in this fashion without helping the opposition party at all. Their vote for the individual candidate will aid only him or her and not his or her party.

Apparently, the Germans themselves do not fully understand what is involved in the ticket splitting their electoral system permits. During the time (in the 1970s) in which the Socialists (SPD) and the Free Democrats (FDP) formed a governing coalition, the FDP appeared to be dropping dangerously near the 5-percent level. So the SPD urged its supporters to "lend" their party-list vote to the FDP to prevent it from being eliminated from the national legislature. Only later did it dawn on the SPD that since the party-list vote, not the single-member constituency vote, determines a party's strength in the legislature, "lending" votes to the FDP was reducing SPD strength.

In 1976 Chancellor Helmut Schmidt of the SPD urged Christian Democrats, FDP supporters, and undecideds to split their ticket; Schmidt encouraged voting for their party's individual candidate and "giving me your *Zweitstimme*" (party-list vote, see Figure 21–1). Schmidt did not go on to explain that, given the way the calculations are made, Christian Democrats who did this would be cutting their party's strength in the legislature and increasing that of the SPD. The request was, in fact, much less reasonable than it sounded. As Figure 21–2 shows, the SPD was still playing the *Zweitstimme* game in 1987.

When the Christian Democrats and the FDP formed the governing coalition in the 1980s, the Christian Democratic leader from Bavaria, Franz Josef Strauss, was constantly feuding with the FDP. Therefore, during the 1987 campaign, few were surprised when he said that his party did not have any votes to "lend" to the FDP. The interesting point is that he used that word, as though he would have been prepared to lend some votes if he and the FDP had gotten along better. Strauss did not oppose lending in principle, as something that would reduce his party's representation; he simply didn't want to help the FDP. In short, the idea of lending party-list votes seems firmly established in the German political mind, despite the fact that it is of questionable rationality.

Despite all the talk about lending, ticket splitting is relatively uncommon. The overwhelming majority of those who vote for a Christian Democratic or SPD candidate on the left-hand side of the ballot vote for his or her party on the right-hand side. Although most of those who vote for an FDP candidate also vote for that party on the other side of the ballot, the level of loyalty to the FDP is not as high. Looked at from the other perspective, a substantial proportion, at times a majority, of the party-list votes that the FDP receives comes from voters who voted for another party's candidate on the single-member side of the ballot. Apparently, a number of voters are willing to "lend" their party-list vote to the FDP.

Parties that concentrate their support primarily in certain areas will win most of their seats by electing representatives in the single-member constituencies. Parties with support spread fairly evenly throughout much of the country may not be suffi-

Figure 21–2
SPD Poster for the 1987 Election Campaign

ciently strong in any given area to elect individual candidates. Nonetheless, their total national vote may be substantial, in which case they would obtain a fair number of representatives in the legislature from their various party lists.

The success of Germany's two main parties during the last three decades reveals an interesting pattern, shown in Table 21–2. At the start of the 1960s, the Christian Democrats (CDU/CSU) won the bulk of their seats in the single-member constituencies, doing considerably better in this regard than did the Socialists (SPD). At the end of that decade, the pattern reversed; by 1972 it was almost exactly the opposite of what it had been ten years earlier. The SPD won the majority of its seats in the single-member constituencies, whereas the Christian Democrats got less than half of theirs in this fashion. The reversal was only temporary, however, and by the close of the 1980s the pattern had returned to almost exactly what it had been more than a quarter of a century earlier.

Although the relationship is not exact, these proportions are linked to the relative popularity of the main political forces. When the two parties are roughly equal in popular support, then the share of representation each wins in single-member constituencies is fairly similar or the SPD's share is noticeably larger. When the Christian Democrats have a substantial lead in the popular vote, they get the great bulk of their representation by winning individual constituencies and the SPD gets its through the party lists. Since the 1983 election was the worst result for the SPD in twenty years, the marked shift in the proportions for that election is not surprising. And in 1987 the party's share of the popular vote was even a bit smaller than it had been four years earlier.

In addition to the way in which the parties gain their seats, it is important to consider the impact of the electoral system on party strengths. If the lower house of the legislature had been composed of only the single-member constituency representatives in 1972, then the SPD would have dominated it by holding 61 percent of the total membership, instead of having only 46 percent, as actually was the case.[1] With an electoral system based on only single-member constituencies, the Christian Democrats in 1976 would have had 54 percent of the seats; instead, they just failed to get a majority. The electoral system permitted the SPD, in coalition with the FDP, to remain in power and prevented the Christian Democrats from returning to

Table 21–2

Percentage of Each Party's Total Representation Won in Single-Member Constituencies

	Election								
	1961	**1965**	**1969**	**1972**	**1976**	**1980**	**1983**	**1987**	**1990**
CDU/CSU	64	63	50	43	55	54	74	76	74
SPD	48	46	57	66	53	58	35	42	38

[1]These figures and the ones in the rest of this paragraph are not inconsistent with Table 21–2. A party with 100 seats might have won 50 in single-member constituencies and, thus, would have 50 percent listed in the table. But 50 seats would be less than 10 percent of the total number of single-member seats. This paragraph and the preceding one (along with the table) focus on two different aspects of party representation.

office. Without proportional representation 1983 would have been an unmitigated disaster for the SPD. It obtained only 27 percent of the single-member constituencies, but the electoral system gave it 39 percent of the legislature's seats.

Given the relative stability of public opinion, proportional representation tends to stabilize party strengths in the legislature. The SPD's share of the popular vote dropped only 3 percentage points from 1972 to 1976, and, thus, under the German electoral system, its share of the seats in the Bundestag fell by only 3 percentage points. Had only single-member districts existed, its legislative strength would have fallen by 15 percentage points, from 61 percent of the seats to 46 percent. To some extent, therefore, proportional representation makes elections a bit less of a gamble for parties.

The parties with the biggest stake in the present electoral system, however, are the third and minor parties. Even a third party as significant as the FDP would be destroyed were proportional representation abolished. In 1990 only one of its seventy-nine seats in the legislature was won in a single-member, simple-plurality constituency; all the rest were elected by means of proportional representation from the party lists. Without proportional representation, Germany would be as much of a two-party system as Britain is.

Election Practices

In addition to the 5-percent barrier, newly formed small parties face another obstacle. A party with fewer than five seats in the national legislature or in the state legislature must obtain the signatures of 0.1 percent of the eligible voters in a given state to place its party list of candidates on the ballot there. That may not sound like much of an impediment, but in the larger states it means gathering 5,000 to 10,000 signatures.

Germany does not use primary elections. An individual can run for a single-member seat by getting the signatures of 200 voters in that constituency. Nonetheless, the overwhelming majority of the candidates are not independents, but party nominees. Candidates for single-member seats are selected either by all the party members in that constituency or by a special nominating committee elected by the members. The party lists of candidates for a state are drawn up by nominating conventions in that state. National party leaders have some influence in this process, but local and state party organizations will not accept orders. Placement on the party list is crucial, since those near the top of a leading party's list are almost certain to be elected and those far down on the list have little hope. Adverse placement on the list can end a politician's career. Conversely, the German electoral system can provide candidates a safety net. About two-thirds of the Christian Democrat and SPD candidates for single-member seats are also included on the party list. Assuming they have been able to obtain a good position on the list, they can expect to be returned to the legislature even if they are defeated in the single-member vote.

National party leaders were denied the power to draw up the party lists because it was feared that this would give them too much power. The process of candidate selection has been decentralized, but it does not involve mass participation. The group making the selection often consists of only a couple of hundred people or fewer for single-member constituencies, quite small compared with the number of people making the choice in American primaries, even when turnout is low. This does not mean, however, that incumbents wishing to run again can count on automatic nomination. For single-member seats as well as for places on party lists, the nomination process increasingly produces strong factional fights, especially in the SPD.

In addition to dispensing with primary elections, the German system does not provide for by-elections or interim elections. When a member of the legislature dies or retires, he or she is replaced by the next person on his or her state's party list, regardless of whether he or she had been elected from the list or from a single-member constituency.

Candidates are not required to live in the state they represent, but most do. They must be at least eighteen years old, which is also the minimum age for voters. The government assumes the responsibility for seeing that citizens of the proper age are registered to vote. Lists of eligible voters are posted well before an election so that any errors can be corrected.

Voter turnout in West Germany was quite high. Only in the first postwar election in 1949 did it fall below 80 percent. During the 1970s it reached a high of 91 percent. In 1987 turnout remained impressive at 84 percent. In the first unified elections in 1990 it fell to 78 percent. In part this was because turnout in the former East Germany was 74.5 percent, but even in the former West Germany only 78.5 percent voted, a tie with its record low of 1949. Many voters felt that Chancellor Helmut Kohl's Christian Democrats were certain to win the election, and so they saw little reason to vote. Even the 1990 German turnout was high compared to participation rates in the United States. To encourage voting, Germany holds elections on Sunday so that going to the polls will not conflict with work for most people.

German political campaigns have tended to be long by European standards—two or three months rather than a few weeks, as in France and Britain. Elections must occur no more than sixty days after the legislature is dissolved. Since elections usually occur at regular four-year intervals (as you can see from Table 21–2), the date of an election is fairly certain, and parties can begin to campaign well before the official sixty days begin. The campaign for the 1987 election was rather abbreviated, however, because the election was held in January. The parties could do little campaigning before Christmas—one saw virtually no political posters in December—and thus the length of the campaign was rather similar to what is typical in Britain.

The Germans decided to avoid such an impediment to campaigning for the 1990 election. Rather than have the polling day exactly four years later, that is, in January 1991, the election was held a few weeks earlier in December 1990, before the Christmas holidays were in full swing.

The publicly operated TV networks give the parties free broadcast time. Two-and-a-half-minute spots after the evening news are allocated on the basis of parties' strength in the legislature. A face-to-face debate among party leaders on television has become a tradition at the end of the campaign. Although the SPD leader wanted a one-on-one confrontation with the Christian Democratic Chancellor in 1987, this was refused, and the past practice of a multisided exchange of views among all the party leaders was continued. These debates have become marathon sessions, running three or four hours. Nonetheless, they draw a huge audience.

In 1980, for the first time since 1969, the leading parties signed an agreement for a "fair" campaign. They pledged themselves "to conduct a fair and nonpolemical election campaign." Among other things, they agreed to "desist from personal disparagement or insult in any form" and "not spread any disparaging allegations about other parties." An arbitration body was created to investigate any complaints about violation of the agreement. Its powers were limited, however, simply to publicity; it could not fine or otherwise penalize violators. Some matters were referred to it, but the agreement did not seem to have any significant impact on campaign tactics. The 1987 campaign was so dull that perhaps some disparagement might have stimulated public interest.

Campaign Financing

From time to time, the parties have agreed among themselves to limit the amount spent on campaigns; no limit is imposed by law. When such agreements have not been reached, the amount spent has been enormous, even by American standards. In the 1972 campaign, for example, the leading parties spent about $90 million.

German tax law had permitted taxpayers to deduct political contributions from their taxable income. When the Federal Constitutional Court declared this law unconstitutional, party income dropped considerably. To strengthen party finances, governmental subsidies were enacted. The national government as well as other levels of government gave grants to parties. In July 1966, the Federal Constitutional Court sharply curtailed these grants. It held that government could not finance party activities designed to mold public opinion but could help only with "necessary expenses of a reasonable election campaign." Even more significant was the Court's ruling that any program of subsidies had to include even those parties not represented in the legislature. The decision was a major blow to the leading parties, especially the Christian Democrats, who had to cut back the staff at their party headquarters by 40 percent.

The Political Parties Act was passed in 1967 in an effort to respond to the Court's decision. All parties that polled 2.5 percent of the vote or more in an election would receive a set sum per vote. The Court was not satisfied; it ruled that parties getting as little as 0.5 percent of the vote must share in the subsidies. As a result of this holding, a neo-Nazi party received $400,000 from the government to help pay its campaign expenses in 1969.

Any party obtaining 0.5 percent or more of the party-list vote (right-hand side of the ballot) in any constituency in an election for the national legislature qualifies for a public subsidy. In order to qualify, independent candidates (who do not appear on any party list) must receive 10 percent of the votes cast on the left-hand side of the ballot in their constituency. The government pays 5 DM (around $3) per eligible voter into a fund. Each qualifying party receives a share proportional to its share of the party-list vote. Qualifying individual candidates are given 5 DM per vote received. The sums received under this program are quite sizable. The votes the SPD received in 1987, for example, entitled it to about $40 million. Even the neo-

Nazi party, which got only miniscule support, qualified for well over $600,000. In 1990 the total amount paid to parties by the national government was around $300 million.

These payments are called "reimbursements," but this is a misnomer. Despite the fact that the exact sum to which a party is entitled cannot be determined until after the election, advance payments can be obtained a couple of years beforehand. Furthermore, parties are entitled to the sums for which they qualify, regardless of whether they actually spent that much in running their electoral campaigns. In 1983 most of the parties made a profit of several million dollars, spending considerably less on the election than they received in subsidies. Campaign financing in Germany may be "fair," but it certainly isn't inexpensive.

■ ■ ■

Campaign finance regulations and the electoral system complement each other. The electoral system has a bias against small parties. In seeking to avoid a fractionalized party system, it constrains the efforts of minor elements of public opinion to gain a share in formulating public policy. On the other hand, those minor segments are not prevented from—indeed, are assisted in—expressing their views to the electorate. Granted, this balance was achieved through the efforts of judges and not of the politicians leading sizable parties. Nonetheless, the balancing of constraint of and support for minority views is in keeping with responsible and effective democracy. Thus, as you will see is true of Germany's governmental institutions, concentration of power has been balanced with accountability.

■ THE ROLE OF INTEREST GROUPS

As in other democracies, interest groups are very much a part of the political process in Germany. Although the public tended initially to distrust them, they developed rapidly and sought to exert their influence on political parties. The principal categories of interest groups are religious, business, and labor. Environmentalists and opponents of nuclear energy have transformed themselves into a political party: the Greens.

The Church

Although Germany does not have an established church, as Britain does, its system never separated church and state, as the U.S. system does. The state collects religious taxes and pays the clergy and church educators. In theory, each baptized German belongs to some church and is taxed for its support unless membership is officially given up.

Church groups were particularly important during the chaotic period after World War II because they were one of the few solid institutions remaining. Allied occupation authorities often asked church leaders to take posts in local government. Many who began this way became influential in party organizations, especially in the Christian Democratic party. Roman Catholic groups were so active within that party that many people feared that it would become totally Catholic. Prior to World War II, most of the religion-based parties that existed in Europe tended to be unidenominational. The Christian Democrats differed in encompassing both Protestants and Catholics, and this mix needed to be maintained if Germany were to avoid having a fractionalized party system.

During the 1960s and 1970s, however, the political activity of the Catholic Church declined, becoming virtually negligible. Therefore, events during the 1980 campaign were a surprise. Two Sundays before the election, priests read to their worshippers a pastoral letter from the bishops warning about the "dangerously high level" of the national debt and the threat of government intrusion in citizens' private lives. For the clergy to condemn easier divorce and abortion, as they had done some years earlier, was one thing; to comment on questions not related to the family or morals was another. Chancellor Helmut Schmidt of the SPD respond-ed in his usual acerbic style: "I've not heard of a theological chair of state financing and, so far as I know, there's nothing about the subject in either the Old or New Testament." The day before the letter was read, the Christian Democratic leader, Strauss, had asserted that if the SPD won the election, it would stop government collection of the church tax for the Catholic Church. Schmidt termed this "a mali-cious and unbelievable defamation" and set a deadline for a retraction by Strauss. When this was not made, the SPD labeled Strauss a "liar." So much for the agree-ment the parties had made to avoid personal disparagement and insult!

The whole affair may not have done either the Catholic Church or the Christian Democrats much good. A poll found that less than a third of Catholics agreed with the substance of the bishops' letter and only a quarter felt it was nonpartisan. The SPD won the same share of the vote in the 1980 election as it had in the previous one, and support for the Christian Democrats declined by a few percentage points.

No similar incident has occurred subsequently. Furthermore, the importance of the Church seems to be declining in general, not only in politics. The proportion of Catholics regularly attending church has declined from about half to less than a third. Thus, although the Church hardly is irrelevant to German politics, it is not a major political influence. On the other hand, when unification made the question of abortion (see the discussion toward the end of Chapter 20) a live issue once again, religious groups, especially the Catholic Church, were actively involved in lobbying for new law preserving West German practice, rather than shifting to the less restrictive East German practice.

Economic Groups

Labor's influence is exerted primarily through the German Federation of Trade Unions, which has a membership of about 8 million. The proportion of the work force unionized in Germany has always been quite high. During the late 1950s and the 1960s, however, it declined sharply in West Germany, eventually falling to under a third. Although this is somewhat below Britain, it is twice the American rate and about two and a half times that of France. Unionization varies considerably by sector of the economy. In 1990 nearly half of Germans in the western part of the country working in manufacturing belonged to unions, while only a fifth of those working in services were members.

Most trade union officials support the Social Democrats. In the immediate postwar years, union sympathy for the SPD was open. Since 1957, however, formal neutrality in politics has been the rule. German trade unions are not directly linked to the SPD the way British ones are to the Labour party.

Germany has not practiced the neo-corporatism encountered in Britain, but consultation with unions is not uncommon. When Chancellor Kohl was seeking to construct a "solidarity pact" early in 1993 to meet the financial strains of unification, support from IG Metall was deemed essential. With 4 million members this engineering workers' union is Germany's largest. Clearly, its leaders had to be involved in the negotiations. IG Metall was a crucial negotiator, also, in pay equalization. Workers in the former East Germany endure a standard of living far below that enjoyed by workers in the west. Their pay was to increase gradually until it equaled that in the west. Getting them there by the target date of 1994 would require raises of 20–30 percent in some years. Since their productivity increases were nowhere near that large and since the entire country had economic problems, this was impossible. Workers in the east, however, saw the refusal as a betrayal of what had been promised them. In the spring of 1993 the eastern part of Germany saw strikes for the first time in 60 years. After about three weeks of turmoil, IG Metall agreed to a deal in which pay equality would be delayed until 1996.

German unions have managed to build up financial resources to obtain an importance well beyond the traditional concerns of wages and working conditions. They own entirely or in part a number of businesses, including banks, cooperatives, breweries, hotels, insurance companies, and publishing houses. The fourth largest bank in Germany, for example, is owned by unions.

The most powerful organization for business interests is the Federation of German Industry (BDI). Nearly 90 percent of all industrial and commercial firms belong to it. Not surprisingly, it openly favors the Christian Democrats. At times it has promoted some business leaders for elective office. Also, a number of business firms set up sponsors' associations as means of channeling funds to the Christian Democrats and the FDP. When the tax law permitted deducting these from taxable income, many large corporations contributed to these associations. Once the Federal Constitutional Court ruled this law unconstitutional, the importance of sponsors' associations declined. Nonetheless, various trade associations continue to make some contributions to the Christian Democrats and the FDP. The Social Democrats can't expect contributions from large corporations. They have managed, however, to sell expensive advertising space in party publications to some businesses, notably breweries and department stores.

The principal voice for farmers has been the German Farmers' Association. Although it has favored the Christian Democrats, its influence was probably greatest when the SPD/FDP coalition was in power. Josef Ertl, a Bavarian farmer and conservative FDP member of the Bundestag, was appointed Minister of Food, Agriculture, and Forestry to maintain the support of the FDP's right wing. He won a considerable reputation as a champion of the farmers' interests. (Figure 21–3 shows the center spread of the FDP's 1976 campaign pamphlet, highlighting Ertl and agricultural policy.) Ertl fought tenaciously against any changes in the EC's Common Agricultural Policy (CAP) that would reduce farmers' income, even when they were desired by the German government.

Figure 21-3
FDP Pamphlet for the
1976 Campaign

Whenever the EC discusses reform of CAP or changes in policies for trading farm products with the rest of the world, German farmers are mobilized, just as you saw French farmers have been. Although the French protests frequently have become violent, the German ones have been calmer. Ah, yes, you may say, the Germans are sober, humorless people. One event from a demonstration against what farmers regarded as inadequate government defense of their interests late in 1992 will disabuse you of that stereotype. A protesting farmer held up a pole with a cabbage on its top. The sign below it read "*Dieser Kohl Ist Hohl,*" which translates literally as "This cabbage is hollow." Just a coincidence, of course, that the German Chancellor is named Helmut Kohl.

The techniques and methods of interest groups are varied (there are only so many ways to use cabbages). Since ministerial officials draft legislation, interest groups have tended to contact them more often than they do members of the legislature or government ministers. The advisory bodies of experts, which many ministries have established, facilitate such contacts. Representatives of interest groups are likely to be included in such bodies. Ministers often want some evidence as to public opinion before taking the responsibility of advocating specific legislation. Therefore, they may authorize their staff to seek interest groups' reactions to policy proposals. As a result, interest groups may well have more influence on the policy process than do members of the legislature.

Although individual legislators cannot introduce bills in the German legislature, interest groups do not ignore the legislature—they concentrate on the committees. Legislators are assigned to committees on the basis of special competence in the topic with which a committee deals. Many of these expert legislators have, or have had, some association with an interest group. In some sense, interest groups are represented on legislative committees by their own people. This provides them with an alternative channel for exerting influence on the bureaucracy, should it prove to be unresponsive.

Interest groups also seek direct links with civil servants. German law permits government employees to take leave and return subsequently to their post. Interest groups invite some bureaucrats to work for them full-time while on leave from governmental employment. One does not need much imagination to visualize the value to a group of a high-level civil servant who knows the internal workings of the regulatory process affecting that group. And when that civil servant returns to the bureaucracy at the end of a leave, he or she is hardly likely to be hostile to the group for which he or she worked.

■   ■   ■

Interest groups have an important role in German politics not only when legislation is being debated in committees, but also when new policies are being considered in ministries and when existing measures are being implemented by bureaucrats. They constitute one influential means for keeping governmental power accountable in West Germany.

......22

Policy Alternatives _____

■ *WHAT TYPE OF PARTY SYSTEM?*

Traditionally, German parties emphasized ideology and doctrine. In part this was because, as you learned in Chapter 19, the personal rule of the Kaiser and his Chancellor during the Empire permitted the parties little influence on governmental policy. Taking a moderate stand in an attempt to gain increased popular support was largely pointless; the Chancellor ran the country as he wished, regardless of party strengths in the legislature. Parties had little opportunity to try to implement their policies; therefore, they could not build up a distinctive record of accomplishments. Rigid, unrealistic doctrines and elaborate programs were about all that served to distinguish one organization from another.

The term for such political organizations is *Weltanschauung* parties (literally "world-view" parties). These parties presented all-embracing philosophical outlooks; they offered the voters not just alternative sets of policies, but a comprehensive political faith. When any new issue arose, this faith determined the party's position. Thus, policies and doctrines were to be an integrated whole, to be intellectually satisfying to the party's supporters, even if somewhat abstract and idealistic.

Weltanschauung parties tended to be totalitarian in a special sense. It is not that they were against liberty or in favor of dictatorship. Instead, they failed to recognize any distinction between public and private life; everything was the party. Such parties formed a wide variety of auxiliary groups dealing with sports, hobbies, adult education, and so forth, so that a connection between a party and its supporters could be maintained even during social and recreational time.

The effect that such an approach had on the party system is easy to understand—it helped to fractionalize it. A party that stresses ideology and doctrine is likely to have a rather narrow appeal. The more comprehensive a faith it presents, the fewer will be the number of people willing to accept all its views. And because it is a faith, not just a set of policies, that is being offered, a supporter is forced to accept everything. Only true believers are welcomed in *Weltanschauung* parties. Since each such party can accommodate only a narrow segment of the electorate, a multiplicity of them will be necessary to appeal to the entire population. Furthermore, such parties tend to instill insularity, or feelings of exclusivity, in their adherents. Politics becomes a struggle between us (who embody all that is good) and them (ill-intentioned, benighted malefactors).

During the Empire, parties ranged from the Conservative party on the right, dedicated to protecting Prussia's privileged position and the interests of the great landowners, to the Social Democrats on the left, espousing a radical reconstruction of the economic system and establishment of parliamentary democracy. During the Weimar Republic the spectrum was even broader. On the far left were the Communists, patterned after the Russian model and consistently hostile to the Republic. They held a tenth to a seventh of the seats in the legislature. On the far right was the German National People's party, a focus for reactionary opposition to the Weimar regime. It was replaced by the even more extreme Nazi party.

The largest party during the Weimar Republic, until overtaken by the Nazis in 1932, was the Social Democrats. In theory, the Social Democrats were Marxist, but in practice they were much more moderate. Most of the time they were a major part of the governing coalition. Given more time and fewer strains, an effective party system might have evolved in the Weimar Republic. Before that could happen, however, a surge of support for the Nazis transformed the political system. Once firmly in power, the Nazis outlawed all parties but their own and constructed a totalitarian one-party system.

A few months after the defeat of Nazi Germany in World War II, the Western occupation authorities began authorizing party activities on the local level in their sections of Germany, expanding this the next year to the state level. Parties suspected of Nazi leanings were prohibited. By the time the licensing procedure was abandoned (1948 in the American zone and 1950 in the British and French zones), two and a half dozen parties had been approved. Germany appeared set to resume its traditional multiparty system of doctrinaire, narrow-appeal *Weltanschauung* parties.

Indeed, in the first postwar national election in West Germany in 1949, nearly a dozen parties managed to win seats in the legislature. The fact that two parties, the Christian Democrats and the Social Democrats, together received 60 percent of the vote and two-thirds of the seats in the legislature, however, suggested that the party system had not returned to its earlier multiplicity. This development soon became a trend toward concentration of political forces. The number of parties represented in the legislature was halved in the next election. The Christian Democrats won 45 percent of the vote and half of the seats in the legislature. Then in the third election of the Federal Republic, the Christian Democrats obtained half of the popular vote, unprecedented in German history. (Remember that no party has received half of the vote in Britain's so-called two-party system since 1935.)

As the strength of the Christian Democrats grew, the Social Democrats were making steady, although less spectacular, gains. As you can see from Figure 22–1, the two parties reached a summit in 1976, when between them they captured nine-tenths of the popular vote. Only one other party, the Free Democrats, was able to elect anyone to the legislature. In the 1980s the two largest parties' share of the vote declined somewhat. The main cause was the growing strength of the Greens, an environmental, antinuclear party. Even the political turmoil of unification failed to alter the basic pattern of the party system. The two largest parties' share of the

Figure 22–1

The Two Leading Parties' Share of the Vote in Post–World War II German Elections

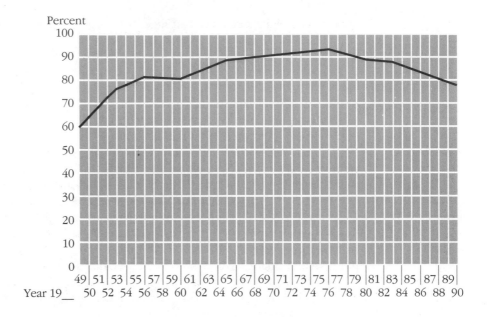

vote declined only modestly and remained well above three-fourths of the total vote.

In Part Two we discussed the extent to which Britain departs from the pure two-party system familiar to Americans. Fitting Germany into that category is even more difficult. Nonetheless, its current party configuration does differ sharply from what existed during the Empire and the Weimar Republic. What accounts for this striking change? The electoral system with its 5-percent barrier (discussed in Chapter 21) certainly has helped to curtail a multiplicity of splinter parties. Beyond this, Konrad Adenauer's long and successful tenure as Chancellor (more about this in Chapter 24) helped to win additional supporters to the Christian Democrats and enabled that party to swallow up some of the minor parties that existed at the start of the Federal Republic.

In East Germany, although the Communists allowed a few puppet groups to exist, they established a one-party system. When communism collapsed, a number of small democratic parties sprung up. These lacked the resources and expertise to survive on their own, however. Most of them had to form links with western counterparts to avoid extinction. Therefore, unification did little to fragment the German party system.

Religion and class differences ceased to stir the emotions as they formerly had, and no longer so sharply divided society. Little ground existed for exclusive, abstract visions of alternative societies. And after the Nazi regime, most Germans had had enough of ideology. *Weltanschauung* parties are a thing of the past. In West Germany the leading parties became more moderate, less dogmatic, and more willing to compromise. As a result, they succeeded more than parties during the Weimar Republic did in attracting diverse followings. The more broadly based parties are, the fewer are needed to encompass the entire electorate. The nature of political conflict changed in Germany, and this helped to reduce the traditional fractionalization of the party system. Although five political groups were represented in the national legislature following the 1990 elections, political forces were sufficiently concentrated that there was no problem in constructing a coalition that could provide decisive government. A multiparty system? Yes, but hardly a fractionalized one.

■ THE LEADING PARTIES

The oldest party in Germany, in existence for well over a century, is the Social Democratic party (SPD). During the 1930s, when the party was suppressed by the Nazis, its leaders went underground or into exile. In 1945 the party was revived and became the major opposition party. It became part of the governing coalition in 1966. Finally, from 1969 to 1982, it was the principal governing party.

In contrast, the Christian Democratic Union/Christian Social Union (CDU/CSU) is a postwar product. A Catholic Center party had been active during the Empire and Weimar, but the Christian Democrats are not direct descendants of that party. The CDU/CSU was founded to unite all Christians, since both Catholics and Protestants had suffered under the Nazis. Furthermore, both kinds of Christians opposed communism. The party's first leader, Konrad Adenauer, opposed clericalism even though he was a Catholic. When he was succeeded by a Protestant, Ludwig Erhard, the party's nondenominational image was further enhanced.

As we will clarify when we discuss party organization, the Christian Democrats are an alliance between the CSU, which operates only in Bavaria, and the CDU, which functions in the rest of the country. We will refer to the entire organization as the Christian Democrats, except in those instances when we need to distinguish between the main party and its southern affiliate.

The remaining sizable party in the legislature is also a postwar creation. The Free Democrats (FDP), like the Christian Democrats, are in some ways heir to an earlier political tradition. Nonetheless, the current party dates only from 1948, when four separate regional parties sharing similar liberal views merged to form a national political force.

Doctrines and Principles

The Socialists Although the SPD originated in the nineteenth century as a Marxist party, it had already given up some of its extreme views by the turn of the century. The party came to accept parliamentary democracy and gradual, evolutionary reform. When, after World War I, its left wing broke away to form the Communist party, it became even more moderate.

The party's transformation into a contemporary social democratic party was not completed, however, until well after World War II, largely due to the intransigence of its first postwar leader, Kurt Schumacher. Schumacher had been a socialist for too long to be willing to consider any revision of basic party doctrine. In keeping with traditional party policy, the SPD under Schumacher opposed German rearmament and membership in NATO. He scornfully referred to Adenauer as "the Chancellor of the Allies" for advocating these measures.

Schumacher's death in 1952, combined with the SPD's failure to expand its electoral support as rapidly as the CDU, encouraged a reassessment of party policy. This process culminated in a major policy revision in 1959. The new basic program of the SPD became known as the Bad Godesberg Program, after the town where the party met to approve it.[1]

The Bad Godesberg program reversed the three main policy themes or doctrines that traditionally were associated with SPD: socialism, pacifism, and anticlericalism. The aim was to project an image of a moderate, nondogmatic party. In economic matters the program avoided reference to such traditional socialist policies as total state planning or class struggle. Instead, free competition was said to be one of the "essential conditions of a social democratic economic policy." The SPD explained that it favored "a free market wherever free competition really exists." "Efficient small and medium-sized enterprises are to be strengthened to enable them to prevail in competition with large-scale enterprises." This is about as socialist as Teddy Roosevelt's trust busting was.

The traditional socialist remedy of public ownership was not ignored entirely. Where natural monopolies existed, as in the supply of electricity, public ownership would be necessary. And government-owned industries might be useful as competitors to keep private concerns from so dominating the economy as to abridge freedom. But the program went on to warn that "every concentration of economic power, even in the hands of the state, harbors dangers." Although conservatives might think that concentrated economic power would be a danger especially (rather than "even") in the hands of the state, they would agree that this represents a new attitude for socialists toward governmental economic activity.

To guard against this danger, the SPD wanted to avoid a centralized bureaucracy. A government-owned business should be run by governing boards representing workers and consumers. Government ownership was viewed as a last resort, however, which unfortunately might be required in some cases, but which the true socialist would resist with great effort. The aim should be not to abolish the capitalist system, but to correct its abuses. The party's slogan in the 1960s was innocuous: "As much competition as possible—as much planning as necessary."

Given Marx's view of religion as the opiate of the people, it is hardly surprising that socialist parties traditionally have been anticlerical. This disposition has been reinforced in Europe by the generally highly conservative social and economic stance of the Church and by its active involvement in politics. In Germany anticlerical feeling has been directed at least as much against the Lutheran Church, which as the dominant Protestant faith has almost been an established church, as against the Catholic church.

Reversing all this, the Bad Godesberg Program revealed that socialism was "rooted in Christian ethics, humanism, and classical philosophy." (Had there been many Muslims in Germany at the time, that religion probably would have been

---

[1]*Bad* is not a term of evaluation, but part of the town's name. It is pronounced "bahd."

included as a source as well.) Contrary to what some may have thought, the SPD emphasized that it "does not proclaim ultimate truths . . . out of respect for the individual's choice in these matters of conscience." And just in case someone had still not gotten the point, the program proclaimed that "freedom to preach the gospel must be protected." The party did stop short of changing its name to Christian Socialists.

Finally, the SPD changed its stance on military matters. It gave firm support to military preparations that were essential for national defense. The year after the Bad Godesberg conference, the SPD defense spokesman in the legislature carried this reversal in policy to the next stage by formally announcing the party's acceptance of German membership in NATO.

Thus, the SPD became more of a social democratic or social welfare party than a pure socialist party. It is more progressive or reformist than other parties; it favors a larger role for the government in ensuring that everyone is cared for adequately.

The Christian Democrats Although you might expect the Christian Democrats to have a religious *Weltanschauung*, the party has not developed a well thought-out and integrated program. A community of religious views does not guarantee agreement on political issues, and the Christian Democrats, in appealing to both Catholics and Protestants, lack even religious consensus. Thus, the Christian orientation of the party has amounted to little more than acceptance of the traditional views of Western civilization and vague references to the dignity of humanity and divine moral law.

Just as encompassing diverse religious views has produced a vague policy, so also has accommodating contrasting economic groups resulted in ambiguous stands. Since the party offers a political home to Christian trade unionists as well as to big industry and finance, it has been forced to favor policies attractive to both. In the immediate postwar years, the Christian Democrats advocated nationalization of basic industries, especially in industrial areas. But as the German recovery progressed, this part of the program was toned down or dropped altogether. In areas where the working-class vote was inconsequential, the party was more of an advocate of free enterprise from the beginning.

The Christian Democrats' goal was a "social-minded market economy," that is, free enterprise tempered by social conscience. In the early and mid-1960s, the party enacted laws designed to promote widespread ownership of stocks and securities, particularly among lower- and middle-income groups. Tax breaks and other inducements were offered to both employers and employees as a means of encouraging more and more people to invest in the economy.

For the first twenty years of the party's existence, one person, Konrad Adenauer, was its leader, and for fourteen of those years he also served as Chancellor of Germany. To a considerable extent he came to be the embodiment of Christian Democratic policy. Its objectives did not need to be elaborated; the party's mission was simply to maintain support for his direction of Germany's affairs (a role you have seen political groups play for Charles de Gaulle in France). A graphic example of this was the party's slogan in the 1957 election. Their posters pictured Adenauer's head along with the simple exhortation "No Experiments."

In foreign policy Adenauer sought to make Germany once again an acceptable member of the international community and an influential voice in the Western alliance. Although he negotiated with the Soviet Union, he took a hard and, some thought, excessively inflexible line on relations with Communist countries. In keeping with this tradition, the Christian Democrats were quite skeptical of *Ostpolitik* ("East politics"), a policy favoring relations with Eastern European countries launched under SPD Chancellor Willy Brandt.

The Christian Democrats also attacked the SPD in the 1976 election campaign for mismanaging the economy and running up a large budget deficit. They depicted the SPD as dangerous radicals, telling the public the choice was between "Freedom or Socialism." The SPD's response involved some (unintended?) irony; their campaign featured a virtual remake of the 1957 Adenauer poster—a poster picturing Chancellor Helmut Schmidt, who had held the office for two years and had served in several other top governmental positions, along with the caption "Experience Is What Counts." (See Figure 22–2 for SPD stickers emphasizing that Schmidt must remain Chancellor.) As for the argument that *Ostpolitik* proved the SPD was soft on communism, the SPD retorted that the Christian Democrats were warmongers. To vote for the SPD, the party said, was to "Vote for Peace."

Although foreign policy and defense were once again issues in the 1980 election, what that contest really came down to was the familiar argument that changing leaders was risky, especially given the current uncertain international situation. This traditional appeal was, even more so than usual, a personality issue because the Christian Democratic candidate for Chancellor was Franz Josef Strauss. Strauss, leader of the Bavarian CSU, had more impact on German politics since the end of World War II than any other political figure except Adenauer.

A man of great personal magnetism and high ability, Strauss also behaved erratically and frequently made serious errors of judgment. In 1962, for example, while serving as Minister of Defense, he ordered the police to raid the offices of the newsmagazine *Der Spiegel,* ostensibly to search for improperly obtained classified military information, but really to silence its criticisms of the Cabinet's defense policies. For many people this incident demonstrated Strauss's lack of commitment to democratic values.

In 1972 the legislature had to vote on treaties with the Soviet Union and Poland; these were part of the SPD's *Ostpolitik*. The leader of the CDU wanted the party to vote for ratification to demonstrate that Germany was united in trying to close the books on the past and to establish normal relations with countries that had suffered Nazi aggression in World War II. Strong opposition from Strauss, however, forced the CDU legislators to abstain on the vote.

Thus, many people, both in and outside of the CDU, felt considerable qualms about Strauss becoming Chancellor. Some felt that the party picked him to head the ticket in order to shut him up. If he actually managed to win the election, at least the party would be back in power. If he lost, then the party would no longer have to contend with his Monday morning quarterbacking of the official party leader. Strauss ran a very circumspect campaign, but polls showed that almost twice as many people wanted Schmidt to remain Chancellor as wanted Strauss in that office. Thus, he probably contributed to the Christian Democrats' defeat.

Figure 22–2
SPD Stickers from the
1976 Election
Campaign

The Free Democrats   The Free Democrats (FDP) have made the task of being distinctive yet appealing more difficult for themselves by policy shifts over the years that have blurred their image. Originally the FDP sought to appeal to those who disliked socialism but also opposed religious values in politics. It emphasized the need for political, religious, and economic freedom. By the early 1960s it was stressing the last of these the most and had moved to the right on the political spectrum. This shift halted in the mid-1960s, when the FDP withdrew from its coalition with the Christian Democrats.

During the Grand Coalition between the Christian Democrats and the SPD in the late 1960s, the FDP was the only party in the legislature that was not included in the Cabinet. As the sole opposition party, it offered energetic and constructive criticism of the Cabinet's policies. When the Grand Coalition broke up, the FDP swung even further away from the right by joining a Cabinet headed by the SPD.

That alliance endured for well over a decade. Although the FDP was clearly more middle-of-the-road than the SPD was, their policy differences were mainly matters of degree. One area of conflict concerned the role of trade unions. When legislation giving workers a voice in the management of private industry was passed, the FDP forced a concession denying union representatives complete equality with management on the directing boards.

What finally tore the coalition apart was the question of how to deal with unemployment in the early 1980s, when the rate became the worst it had been in more than three decades. The SPD wanted a large public investment program to create new jobs. The FDP wanted to stimulate the economy with tax cuts, which would require extensive reductions in spending on welfare. As a result, the FDP helped to vote the SPD out of office and went back into coalition with the Christian Democrats.

Despite a set of policy positions that are difficult to pigeonhole under a simple label and have hardly been notable for consistency over the years, the FDP has managed to map out for itself a fairly distinct identity in German politics.

Recent Politics and Policies

Early in the 1980s the SPD/FDP coalition Cabinet broke up, and Helmut Schmidt fell from office. Furthermore, dissension within the SPD over his policy on U.S. nuclear missiles in Germany so disgusted him that he refused to lead the party in the 1983 election. Unable to make the familiar argument that the voters should stick with the existing Chancellor, the SPD almost seemed to be claiming that its candidate, Hans-Jochen Vogel, was Chancellor (see Figure 22–3). The title of the campaign paper in Figure 22–3—"In the German Interest"—is noteworthy. The SPD was arguing that Germany should not be subservient to the United States and that the government should not hesitate to stand up for Germany's national interests—here was a new nationalism on the left of the political spectrum.

Although Helmut Kohl had been in office for only a half year at the time of the 1983 election, his CDU did not pass up the opportunity (as Figure 22–4 shows) to tell the voters that they now had an affable fellow as Chancellor (much nicer than that abrasive Schmidt) and should stick with him. Leader personality continued to be a factor in electoral politics.

As for the CSU, it stressed (see Figure 22–5) that thirteen years of socialism (that is, SPD Chancellors from October 1969 to October 1982) were more than enough. Clearly, demonstrators in the streets were too much for the conservative wing of the Christian Democrats; order needed to be brought back to Germany.

In the 1983 election the FDP stressed its role in the political system more than its specific policies. It warned the voters that only by electing some FDP legislators could they be certain of denying the Christian Democrats a majority and preventing Strauss from dominating the government. (Although Franz Josef was not the candidate for Chancellor this time, he was still firing off missiles—guided or not—from the forests of Bavaria.) As Figure 22-6 shows, the FDP campaigned explicitly for the

Figure 22–3
SPD Campaign
Literature from 1983

Im deutschen Interesse

Die wichtigsten Punkte aus dem Regierungsprogramm von Bundeskanzler Hans-Jochen Vogel.

Die Regierungsmannschaft von Hans-Jochen Vogel. Von links nach rechts: Hans-Jürgen Krupp, Anke Fuchs, Klaus Meyer-Abich, Egon Bahr, Volker Hauff, Horst Ehmke, Eva Rühmkorf, Willy Brandt (Parteivorsitzender), Hans-Jochen Vogel, Hans-Jürgen Wischnewski, Manfred Lahnstein, Herta Däubler-Gmelin, Jürgen Schmude, Heinz Westphal und Hans Apel.

Ein neuer Bundeskanzler: Hans-Jochen Vogel

Hans-Jochen Vogel besucht im Januar 1983 Parteichef Juri Andropow in Moskau.

Die deutschen Sozialdemokraten haben auf ihrem Wahlparteitag in Dortmund den Willen und die Bereitschaft bekundet, mit Hans-Jochen Vogel als Bundeskanzler nach der Wahl am 6. März erneut Regierungsverantwortung für die Bundesrepublik zu übernehmen. In ihrem Wahlprogramm und mit einem Sofortprogramm für die ersten 100 Tage einer sozialdemokratisch geführten Bundesregierung hat die SPD konkrete Schritte zur Überwindung der Arbeitslosigkeit, zur Wiederherstellung sozialer Gerechtigkeit, zu einschneidenden Umweltschutzmaßnahmen und zu einer sofortigen Abrüstungsinitiative angekündigt. Mit ihrem Kanzlerkandidaten Hans-Jochen Vogel kämpft die SPD um die politische Führung, weil sie überzeugt ist, daß nur eine kompetente Regierung die deutschen Interessen entschieden vertritt und das Vertrauen der Menschen besitzt, den Frieden im Innern und nach außen bewahren und sichern kann.

Hans-Jochen Vogel hat versprochen, unverzüglich nach seiner Wahl zum Bundeskanzler eine persönliche Initiative zur Förderung der Genfer Verhandlungen über die Mittelstreckenraketen mit dem Ziel zu ergreifen, daß es dort zu einer einvernehmlichen Regelung kommt, „die die Aufstellung neuer Systeme auf dem Boden der Bundesrepublik entbehrlich macht". Die SPD steht unverrückbar an der Seite ihrer westlichen Verbündeten, aber sie verwechselt Bündnistreue nicht mit Vasallentreue. Sie will im deutschen Interesse das jetzt Mögliche unternehmen, damit das Wettrüsten eingedämmt und vertragliche Regelungen gefunden werden, die den Frieden sicherer machen.

Ein Sofortprogramm für Arbeit und Beschäftigung steht an der Spitze der Vorhaben der SPD. Eine von Hans-Jochen Vogel geführte Bundesregierung wird einen nationalen Solidarpakt gegen die Arbeitslosigkeit anstreben und nach international auf den Abschluß eines

Beschäftigungspaktes dringen. Die finanziellen Lasten zur Überwindung der Arbeitslosigkeit sollen wieder gerechter verteilt werden, unter anderem durch eine Ergänzungsabgabe zur Einkommensteuer für die Besserverdienenden und durch die Beschneidung ungerechter Vorteile für Wohlhabende, die sich Steuerspar-Modelle im großen Stil leisten können.

Unter Hans-Jochen Vogel wird die Bundesregierung dafür sorgen, daß künftig wieder von sozialer Gerechtigkeit im Land gesprochen werden kann: viele von der Übergangsregierung Kohl verfügten Gesetzesänderungen werden korrigiert oder rückgängig gemacht, vor allem die Verschlechterung des sozialen Mietrechts, der Abbau der BAföG-Leistungen und die Selbstbeteiligung der Versicherten bei Krankenhausaufenthalten und Kuren. Zur Rettung des Waldes will Hans-Jochen Vogel ein Notprogramm in Angriff nehmen.

Die SPD wendet sich in diesem Wahlkampf ausdrücklich an die Frauen. „Sie

spüren", so das Wahlprogramm, „daß sie die eigentlichen Verlierer in einem CDU/CSU-Staat sein würden. Vieles würde zurückgedreht werden, was in der letzten Jahren als neue Lebenschancen für Frauen erreicht wurde."

Hans-Jochen Vogel erklärte auf dem Wahlparteitag der SPD in Dortmund, die Sozialdemokratie erstrebe die Regierungsverantwortung nicht deswegen, weil die Führer der Union für politische Verbrecher und ihre Anhänger für unanständig halte. Solche Vorwürfe, die der Generalsekretär der Union an die Adresse der SPD gerichtet hatte, seien schlimme Töne, die an eine schlimme Zeit erinnerten. Für seine Partei begründete Hans-Jochen Vogel den politischen Führungsanspruch der SPD mit den Worten: „Wir erstreben Regierungsverantwortung, weil nach unserer Überzeugung unsere Politik dem Frieden der Gerechtigkeit und der sozialen Qualität unseres Volkes besser dient als die Politik unserer Gegner. Weil unsere Politik in deutschen Interesse liegt."

Hans-Jochen Vogel besucht im Januar 1983 US-Präsident Ronald Reagan im Weißen Haus.

Geben Sie beide Stimmen der CDU und Bundeskanzler Helmut Kohl. Sprechen Sie mit Ihren Nachbarn. Überzeugen Sie Ihre Freunde. Wählen Sie am 6. März CDU.
Arbeit
Frieden
Zukunft
Miteinander schaffen wir's
CDU
sicher sozial und frei
Bundeskanzler Helmut Kohl
Dieser Kanzler schafft Vertrauen

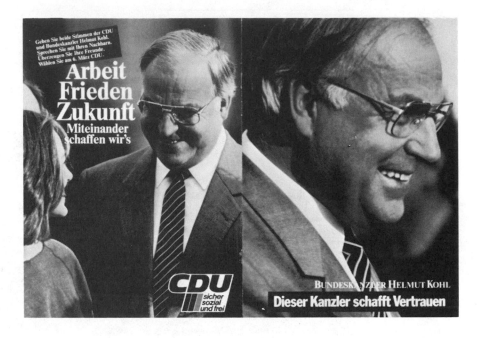

Figure 22–4
CDU Campaign Literature from 1983

electorate's "second vote" (the party-list vote), since that is the only way in which the FDP ever manages to elect any of its candidates.

Despite losing the 1983 election, the SPD failed to reverse the drift to the left that had caused Schmidt to give up its leadership. In 1986 the party's conference voted to close all nuclear power plants within a ten-year period, to negotiate with the United States for removal of its nuclear missiles sited in Germany, to work for a nuclear-free zone in Central Europe, and to restructure the military so that it had no offensive capacity. Although the party's candidate for Chancellor, Johannes Rau, was more moderate than the party itself on many issues, appealing for support simply on the basis of his personality did not prove to be a successful tactic.

The Christian Democrats' appeal in 1987 was continuity; the vacuity of their slogan, *Weiter so Deutschland* ("Keep Going On, Germany"), was not made much

Nach 13 Jahren Sozialismus
Wir sind in tiefer Sorge um unser Vaterland: Millionen Arbeitslose, geplünderte Kassen, die Wirtschaft in der Krise, der Sozialstaat in Gefahr. Die Regierungspolitik von CDU und CSU wird Deutschland wieder in Ordnung bringen. Mit Verantwortung, Tatkraft und Vernunft.
Am 6. März wird ein neuer Bundestag gewählt. Wählen Sie eine sichere Zukunft.
CSU

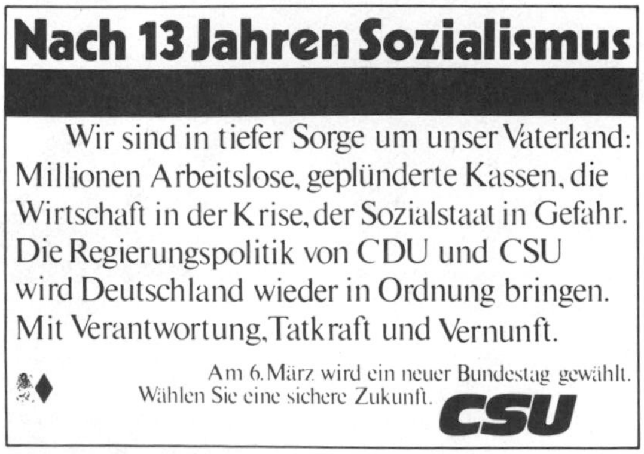

Figure 22–5
CSU Poster from the 1983 Campaign

Figure 22–6
FDP Leaflet from the
1983 Campaign

more specific by references to stable prices, secure pensions, and more jobs. Just to be certain that the voters understood the danger of any change, the Christian Democrats also used the slogan "The Future—instead of Red-Green." In other words, if the electorate voted for a coalition between the SPD and the Greens, Germany would not have a desirable future.

During the 1980s the FDP demonstrated an ability to check some of the more conservative of the Christian Democrats' proposals. It blocked making the abortion law less liberal, placing new constraints on immigration of dependents of foreign workers, and granting amnesty to people who had broken the tax law through financial contributions to parties. (Some irony in the last of these, as you will see later in this chapter.)

On other matters the FDP's success has varied. The party opposed laws branding as terrorists those who attack nuclear power facilities and punishing them with stiff prison terms. But they eventually gave in, after some years of resistance, to a law permitting instant arrest of anyone wearing a mask at a demonstration. Despite considerable internal conflict on the issue, the party did not block legislation giving immunity to former terrorists willing to testify against their colleagues. Nor did they prevent passage of a law making "advocating violence" a crime.

Perhaps the area of greatest FDP influence was foreign policy. Hans-Dietrich Genscher, longtime FDP leader and almost perpetual Foreign Minister regardless of what parties were in power, was a strong proponent of détente. He wanted Germany to accept Mikhail Gorbachev's offer of the "zero option," removal of Soviet and American missiles from Europe. Chancellor Kohl was willing to negotiate about the medium-range ones (those that could reach targets at distances of 600 to 3,000 miles) but did not want to consider removal of the short-range ones (300 to 600 miles) as Gorbachev had proposed. Eventually Kohl yielded to Genscher's

Figure 22–7
CDU Sticker from the
1990 Election
Campaign

views and agreed that Germany would be willing to accept reciprocal removal of both medium- and short-range missiles.

At the end of the 1980s the overwhelmingly dominant issue in German politics was unification of East and West Germany. Helmut Kohl, who never had been known for decisive, innovative action decided to everyone's surprise to seize an opportunity that others had not even perceived to exist. Instead of favoring a gradual merger of east and west over a period of some years, he advocated a "damn the torpedoes, full speed ahead" approach in which West Germany would absorb East Germany in a few months. At the start of December 1990, the first democratic, all-German elections in well over a half century cemented his year of triumph. A plodding, pedestrian fellow somehow had had the courage (or the recklessness) to seize the moment and surf on the wave of history. A CDU sticker from the campaign (see Figure 22–7) shows the party rejoicing (the colors of the German flag in the background) that Germans now were one people.

The leaders of West Germany's SPD, on the other hand, seemed much more cautious and wanted to proceed more slowly, working all the details out in advance rather than charging ahead on blind faith. Oskar Lafontaine, the party's candidate to replace Kohl as Chancellor, stressed that unification would cost West Germans a lot of money and was being rushed into so quickly that much needless economic dislocation would occur. He only managed to appear to be a killjoy, however, constantly carping about the costs rather than enjoying the euphoria, as Kohl was. If you're going to have a big bash, swing—plenty of time the next morning to figure out how you'll pay the bills. In his personal life Lafontaine was something of a swinger, but this only made him seem somewhat frivolous. Kohl was sufficiently stolid that he possessed the gravitas necessary to be a Chancellor.

Nonetheless, as had been true for the previous election, the SPD campaign stressed personalism (see Figure 22–8). Despite Lafontaine's doubts about the pace

Figure 22–8 SPD Poster from the 1990 Election Campaign

of unification, the SPD proclaimed that he was the man for the new epoch or era. Lafontaine's campaign went so badly that a former SPD Chancellor, Helmut Schmidt, said that Lafontaine would lose the election and deserved to do so. Immediately after the election, Willy Brandt, another former SPD Chancellor, revealed that he had considered resigning as honorary chairman of the party to protest Lafontaine's apparent hostility to unification.

The Free Democrats capitalized even more than usual on their traditional appeal as a moderating factor. They warned that too large a gratitude vote for Kohl's role in producing German unification might give the Christian Democrats more than 50 percent of the vote. This would let them form a one-party Cabinet (considering the CSU to be the same party under a different name), something that had never occurred before. Not having to satisfy the centrist FDP, the Christian Democrats would move to the right. To prevent this shift, the voters should give the FDP enough support to make it a significant voice in the governing coalition. The party even produced a leaflet devoted solely to emphasizing the importance of *Zweitstimme* (see Figure 22–9). So strenuously did the FDP push this line that Kohl finally rebuked Otto Lambsdorff, its chairman, for disloyalty.

The SPD responded with a poster urging the importance of giving it *both* votes in order to make Lafontaine Chancellor (see Figure 22–10). The FDP apparently got the best of this battle; it was the only party (other than the extremist Republicans) to gain more support on the party-list side of the ballot than on the single-member side, going from 7 percent (members) to 11 percent (party) in what had been West Germany and from 12 percent to more than 13 percent in what had been East Germany.

As we discussed in Chapter 19, immigration became a major issue in unified Germany. As one would expect the right-wing Christian Democrats saw the situation as a law-and-order issue and wanted to crack down harshly. Both the FDP (with its traditional civil libertarian doctrine) and the SPD were opposed. The SPD was particularly loathe to compromise the role that West Germany had played for forty years as a refuge for the politically oppressed seeking asylum. Although the two parties managed to moderate the Christian Democrats' proposals, in the end all parties had to agree that some tightening of Germany's liberal admission policy was needed.

Another major issue in the mid-1990s concerned Germany's international role. After World War II the victorious Allies were determined to prevent further German aggression. Although eventually both East and West Germany were permitted to have military forces, various constraints were placed on them. Some of these continue to exist (primarily as a matter of domestic law) despite the fact that unified Germany is fully sovereign. For example, no German troops are supposed to be used for active operations outside the NATO area—that is, Germany can defend itself and its allies, but it can't engage in military action outside of Europe. How does this relate to UN peace-keeping and peace-maintaining activities? Many countries have criticized Germany for failing to pull its weight in efforts to maintain world order. Many Germans believe that their constitution and laws prohibit them from an active role.

Can German troops assist humanitarian efforts in Somalia? If so, what do they do should the so-called war lords' forces shoot at them? Can German air and naval

Figure 22–9
FDP Leaflet from the
1990 Election
Campaign

forces be involved in the UN monitoring and embargo actions in the former Yugoslovia? Is this within the NATO area? The Christian Democrats have wanted to demonstrate that Germany will accept its international responsibilities. The SPD and, to some extent, the FDP have been reluctant to expand the country's military role.

Figure 22–10
SPD Poster from the 1990 Campaign

*Beide Stimmen ✗ ✗
für die SPD – damit
Oskar Lafontaine gewinnt.*

When Chancellor Kohl sent German ships to help monitor the UN trade embargo against Serbia and Montenegro in 1992, the SPD demanded a special session of the legislature to debate the action. The FDP leader and Foreign Secretary Klaus Kinkel supported action, saying that there was "no international understanding any more for a German refusal to make any formal contribution" to the UN effort. The legislature, controlled by the Christian Democrats and the FDP, duly endorsed the measure. Less than a year later, however, Kinkel was unwilling to accept automatically the presence of German air crews on AWACs monitoring planes over the former Yugoslavia. He wanted them removed until such time as the Federal Constitutional Court ruled that their presence didn't violate the constitution.

In 1991 an SPD party congress voted in favor of amending the constitution so that German troops could participate in UN peace-keeping activities. Nonetheless, when the Christian Democratic Government attempted to amend the constitution along these lines in January 1993, it failed to obtain the necessary two-thirds vote because of lack of support from the SPD.

※　※　※

Policy differences among the parties were clear and often fervently argued in the early 1990s; nonetheless, the leading parties hardly were poles apart. The electorate was not being offered a choice between Marxist socialism and laissez-faire capitalism. The policies were sufficiently similar at times that elections could be waged on leader personality and the advisability of switching horses in midstream.

Supporters and Strengths

Voting behavior　Religion and occupation influence German voting behavior considerably. In general, Catholics vote for the Christian Democrats and workers for the SPD. As we noted in discussing party doctrines, the Christian Democrats have not emphasized religious views; they certainly have not tried to present their party as a vehicle for Catholic doctrine. Nonetheless, the party does have a special appeal to Catholics, and this has been important in giving it support from diverse classes.

Religion and occupation interact in interesting ways. Two-thirds to four-fifths of Protestant workers support the SPD, but only half or less of Catholic workers do so. In fact, white-collar workers who are Protestant are much more likely to favor the SPD than are manual workers who are Catholic. On the other hand, those who are self-employed, even if Protestant, vote predominantly for the Christian Democrats. Catholics who are self-employed, naturally, are overwhelmingly committed to the Christian Democrats. As a result, the SPD is more class-based than the Christian Democrats are. In the early years of the Federal Republic, the overwhelming majority of SPD votes came from manual workers. Despite expanding its support among white-collar employees since then, the party still gets most of its votes from blue-collar workers.

Although the Christian Democrats depend most heavily on white-collar employees, their support is distributed fairly evenly among white-collar, blue-collar, and self-employed segments of the electorate. Were it not for the Catholic base, however, the Christian Democrats would have primarily middle- and upper-class support. Given the composition of Germany's population, a party with such a clientele would have little hope of ever winning an election. Clearly, religion has been a major element in the success of the Christian Democrats.

The FDP's main source of support has been the urban, Protestant middle class. To some extent its appeal has been more negative than positive. Business and professional people who feel that the Christian Democrats are too dominated by big business prefer to vote for the FDP. The party also has received support from large farmers. Over the years its strength has tended to shift from the self-employed to white-collar employees and civil servants.

Figure 22–11 provides an idea of areas of long-term party strength. (Since the eastern part of Germany has had only one free election, it is omitted.) The "city-states" of Bremen and Hamburg have been SPD strongholds. Not only do these urban, industrial states contain large numbers of workers, but relatively few Catholics live there. Germany has other industrial areas, but those are in states sufficiently large to encompass rural areas as well, so the impact of the working-class vote is diluted there. Even the Saar, although small, is not totally industrial. Furthermore, since it has the highest proportion of Catholics of any state, the limited success of the SPD there is understandable.

At the other end of the spectrum, Baden-Württemberg, Rhineland-Palatinate, and Bavaria have substantial Catholic populations, and relatively large segments of their work forces engaged in agriculture, which helps explain their continuous support for Christian Democrats. About half of the population of North Rhine–Westphalia is Catholic, but this state is a highly urbanized, industrial area. Thus, it has been about as likely to favor the SPD as the CDU.

Few Catholics live in Schleswig-Holstein, but it is primarily an agricultural state and, thus, not likely to support the SPD. In both Hesse and Lower Saxony, the proportion of Catholics is well below the national average. Hesse has rather more of its work force in industry than does Lower Saxony, and this contributes to the former's usually being in the SPD column.

Figure 22–11
Major Party Victories
in National Elections

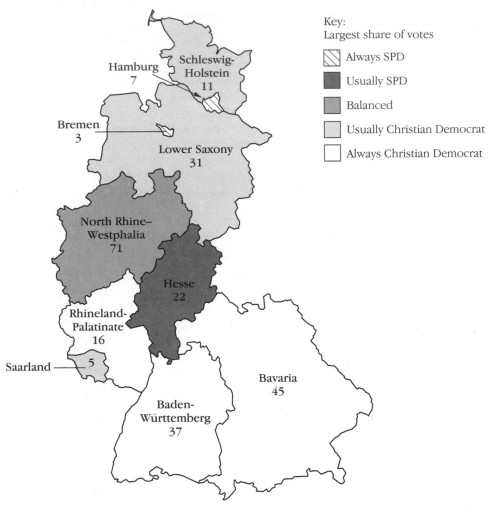

Key:
Largest share of votes

- Always SPD
- Usually SPD
- Balanced
- Usually Christian Democrat
- Always Christian Democrat

The SPD sought to appeal to the interests of left-of-center white-collar workers in 1983 in an effort to contain the growing appeal of the Greens. The attempt proved to be counterproductive, costing the SPD the support of substantial numbers of skilled manual workers who had voted for it in the past. Such workers, rather conservative in some ways, did not appreciate the SPD's apparent approval of protest demonstrations and weakened support for the Western alliance. (The Democratic party in the United States has faced the same problem in trying to maintain the support of its traditional working-class clientele in presidential elections.) The SPD lost some 2 million voters to the Christian Democrats, while winning only about 150,000 away from them. Furthermore, the policy shift failed to prevent losses to the Greens, since about three-quarters of a million former SPD votes went in that direction.

Most of the voter shifts in 1987 tended to cancel each other out. The SPD, for example, lost about as many former supporters to the Christian Democrats as it gained from them. The smaller parties were the main beneficiaries of switches, and their gains were modest. Transfers between the Christian Democrats and the FDP netted the latter something more than three-quarters of a million votes. The FDP gained on balance about half that much in switches with the SPD.

The ebb and flow of party support   For the first two decades of the Federal Republic, the Christian Democrats were dominant, constantly controlling the Government. Although, as Table 22–1 shows, the Christian Democrats won only eight seats more than the SPD did in the first election, they formed the Cabinet. In the next two elections the Christian Democrats gained considerable ground, mainly at the expense of minor parties, which fell by the wayside. The vagueness of their doctrines and the appeal of Adenauer's strong leadership enabled the Christian Democrats to construct a broad coalition of diverse supporters. This culminated in the party's winning half of the popular vote in 1957, an event unique in German political history.

During the 1960s the party slipped back a bit, and toward the close of the decade had to share governing power with its chief rival, the SPD, in the Grand Coalition. Worse was yet to come, because the Christian Democrats had to watch the SPD govern the country from 1969 to 1982 in coalition with the FDP. When the FDP switched sides again in 1982, the Christian Democrats were able to return to power and run the country for the rest of the 1980s.

The postwar division of Germany into two countries initially hurt the SPD. What became East Germany included many areas that were formerly SPD strong-holds. Had East Germany been part of the Federal Republic, the SPD almost cer-tainly would have been the largest party at the start. Had the Soviet Union not objected to considering West Berlin a part of West Germany, the SPD would, in any event, have been the strongest party in the legislature in 1949, since the delegation from West Berlin was overwhelmingly Socialist.

Subsequently, the SPD failed to grow as fast as the Christian Democrats did and appeared to be condemned forever to the role of opposition party. The mood of futility pervading the party helped the efforts of those wanting to revise its doc-trines. Since all else had failed to bring success, why not try the change of image entailed in the Bad Godesberg Program? A major change in a party's fortunes is unlikely to be caused by a single factor. Nonetheless, in the ten years prior to the Bad Godesberg Program, the SPD vote had increased by only 3 percentage points (as Table 22–1 shows), whereas in the decade following the program's approval in 1959, it saw a gain of 11 percentage points. Early in the 1970s the SPD even man-aged to win more of the popular vote than the Christian Democrats did.

Since that high-water mark, it has been all downhill for the SPD; it slipped back to where it was immediately after the Bad Godesberg Program. The party was seri-ously hurt by the challenge of the Greens. Not only did former SPD voters desert it for the Greens, but it dithered over how to respond to this threat. Some wanted to move to the left and adopt positions on nuclear power, nuclear weapons, and the environment that were virtually the same as those of the Greens. Others feared that this would undo all that the Bad Godesberg Program accomplished and once again consign the party perpetually to opposition status. In the meantime, an indistinct image gave the SPD the worse of all worlds.

Table 22–1
National Election Results in the West German Republic

	CDU/CSU		SPD		FDP		Greens		Others	
	Percentage of Vote	Number of Seats	Percentage of Vote	Number of Seats	Percentage of Vote	Number of Seats	Percentage of Vote	Number of Seats	Percentage of Vote	Number of Seats
1949	31	139	29	131	12	52	—	—	28	80
1953	45	243	29	151	10	48	—	—	17	45
1957	50	270	32	169	8	41	—	—	10	17
1961	45	242	36	190	13	67	—	—	6	0
1965	48	245	39	202	10	49	—	—	4	0
1969	46	242	43	224	6	30	—	—	5	0
1972	45	225	46	230	8	41	—	—	1	0
1976	49	243	43	214	8	39	—	—	1	0
1980	45	226	43	218	11	53	2	0	1	0
1983	49	244	38	193	7	34	6	27	1	0
1987	44	223	37	186	9	46	8	42	2	0

The FDP also suffered from self-inflicted wounds. Many of its supporters were alienated by its shift of support from the SPD to the Christian Democrats, especially since the FDP had pledged during the 1980 election campaign that it would remain in coalition with the former for the entire four-year period between elections. In the next election following the coalition switch, the FDP lost about a third of its support and suffered its second-worst result in the entire history of the Federal Republic.

Since the electorate's memory tends to be rather short, the FDP was able to recoup some of its losses in the 1987 election. The death of Franz Josef Strauss in October 1988, however, posed a potential threat to the FDP. For years the FDP had appealed for the *Zweitstimme* of CDU voters who did not want their party to be dominated by the right-wing bombastic CSU leader. With Strauss gone, what bogeyman would the FDP be able to use in its appeal for support?

The FDP, aided by the German electoral system, has managed to make the most of fairly modest support. This party usually fails to get a tenth of the popular vote; the Liberals in Britain at times have won twice as large a share. Yet not only does the FDP receive much greater representation in the legislature than the Liberals do, it also often holds three or four seats in the Cabinet. Nor are these minor positions, since they have included the foreign, justice, and economic ministries. Even more startling is the fact that during the West German Republic, the FDP was in power more than any other party. It was out of office for only eight years during more than four decades. The Christian Democrats were out of office for a period of thirteen years. As for the SPD, its time in office has been only half as long as that of FDP.

Table 22–2 provides the results of the 1990 election. Perhaps what is most remarkable is how small the changes are. The combined CDU and CSU vote was exactly the same as it had been in West Germany in 1987 (look back at Table 22–1). The FDP vote is only 2 percentage points higher. The SPD share is only 3 percentage points lower. Although only a small shift, this was somewhat surprising. Back in Weimar Germany, the east had been an SPD stronghold. Perhaps that was too long ago to have any relevance to current politics. An even more likely reason for the poor SPD showing in the east was Kohl's ability to portray himself as the enthusias-

Table 22–2

Results of the First National Election for the Unified Germany

	Percentage of Vote			
	East	West	Total	Number of Seats
CDU	43	35	37	268
CSU	—	9	7	51
SPD	24	36	34	239
FDP	13	11	11	79
Greens (West)	—	5	4	0
Greens (East)	6	—	1	8
PDS	10	—	2	17
Republicans	1	2	2	0
Others	3	2	2	0

tic proponent of German unity. As we have mentioned, the SPD seemed more concerned about the problems that would have to be solved. Thus the party's vote held up well in the west, but lack of support in the east made its share of the total vote the worst in more than thirty years.

Party finances   In 1990 (an election year) the SPD and the CDU had approximately equal incomes, both somewhat more than $200 million. The income of the CDU's Bavarian associate, the CSU, was somewhat more than a quarter of this amount, giving the Christian Democrats as a group considerably more income than the Socialists. Although the FDP operates throughout the country, its income was a bit less than that of the CSU, which is confined only to Bavaria.

As we explained in Chapter 21, the German government makes substantial payments to parties, ostensibly to cover the costs of election campaigns, but in fact as a subsidy for regular operations. In 1990 two-fifths of the CDU's income came from this grant, about a quarter from membership fees, and a fifth from donations. The government grant was nearly as large a share of the SPD's income, but because of that party's stress on dues-paying members, membership fees equaled the subsidy. Half of the FDP's income came from the government grant, with a quarter deriving from donations. The leading source of income for the CSU was donations—two-fifths of its income, a larger share by far than that for any other party. The government grant was a slightly smaller source of CSU income than were donations. Each party has its own distinctive pattern of income.

In addition to the "reimbursement of campaign costs," parties receive another subsidy to help finance their operations. Each year the government pays each party a sum that is calculated from number of members, membership fees, donations, and number of votes received. In 1992 the Federal Constitutional Court declared this subsidy unconstitutional (another example of the Court's importance). Fortunately for the parties this particular subsidy accounted for less than 3 percent of their incomes. The Court also voided a 6-percent bonus on the flat per vote campaign cost reimbursement, which had been enacted for parties winning 2 percent of vote.

Parties must report any donation of more than about $12,000 and publish their financial accounts. For several years substantial tax relief could be obtained by donating to parties. The Federal Constitutional Court ruled that relief was too great and must be cut back. As a result, only gifts of up to about $36,000 can be deducted from income tax. Although the Court has complained that even this is too high, it has not required a change.

A loophole in the campaign contributions law involves nonprofit research foundations. Some of these foundations are legitimate scholarly organizations. Others, unfortunately, have been established by the parties (the CDU, for example, has the Konrad Adenauer Foundation) as a means of dodging the tax law. A business firm may commission a foundation to write a research report or provide some consulting service. Some allege that a portion of the income generated in this way actually is passed on by the foundation to its parent party. Even if that does not occur, the foundation is able to finance any work that it does for the party from the income that it receives from business clients.

Despite substantial government subsidies to parties, illicit funding was the biggest, longest-running scandal during the West German Republic. The most prominent incident was the "Flick affair." In 1975 the Flick industrial conglomerate wanted tax concessions on the income it received from selling its holdings in Daimler-Benz. Tax law provided that if it invested the money in operations "particularly beneficial for the national economy," it would not have to pay any tax on the sale. Flick wanted a ruling that its investments, some of which were in other businesses that it owned, met the criterion. Flick got what it wanted. Then in 1983, after two years of investigation, the public prosecutor revealed that he suspected Otto Lambsdorff, the FDP Economics Minister, of having received from Flick a gift for his party of nearly $50,000. The gift just might have helped encourage Lambsdorff to support the tax ruling that Flick had sought. Several months later Lambsdorff resigned from the Cabinet because formal charges were filed and he would have to stand trial.

The trial dragged on for months. Eventually the chief charge of bribery by Flick to obtain a tax concession was dropped for lack of evidence. Lambsdorff was fined about $100,000, however, on a related charge that, while treasurer for a state branch of the FDP, he helped firms evade taxes by contributing to the party through nonprofit front organizations. Note that the issue was party, not personal, corruption. Lambsdorff himself did not get any money out of all these shady dealings. His principal defense was a rationalization familiar to most teenagers: everyone else was doing it. This was true enough, but the court was unwilling to accept it as an excuse.

The Lambsdorff saga was not an isolated instance. Rumors circulated, for example, that Helmut Kohl was able to become leader of the Christian Democrats because Flick, in effect, bought the resignation of his predecessor. A legislative committee decided that it had better look into party financing. It questioned leaders from all parties except the Greens, who, naturally, loved every minute of it. They escaped simply because they had not yet been formed when all this was alleged to have happened.

Kohl's testimony was not very enlightening; he seemed to suffer from some curious lapses of memory. He did admit asking Flick for donations for the CDU, but denied that he had ever promised tax concessions in return. Public prosecutors investigated his testimony for many months, looking not only for corrupt action but also for possible perjury in the testimony. In the end the matter was dropped without any charges being made.

Party Organization and Power Structure

The Socialists Although highly centralized and hierarchically structured, the SPD, having developed as a traditional working-class party, also emphasizes mass membership—that is, dues-paying, card-carrying adherents rather than just verbal or electoral supporters. The SPD has seen itself more as a movement of the working class than as a political party. It has actively sought a large membership and has maintained that the rank-and-file members are to participate fully in making party decisions. The number of party members varied a good bit during the West German Republic. During the 1970s the SPD reached a high point of about a million.

In contrast to the arrangements during the Empire and the Weimar Republic, the SPD is no longer connected officially with the trade unions. Trade union officials decided after World War II that the only way to get a united union movement was to break with tradition and avoid any link with a party. In that way both Christian Democratic and Socialist trade union leaders could belong to the same union organization. Nonetheless, most trade union officials have actively assisted the SPD. This was one of the reasons why trade unionists who weren't socialists formed a Federation of Christian Trade Unions in 1955. Despite this breaking away of some of its members, the German Federation of Trade Unions remains formally unconnected with the SPD.

Every year the SPD convenes a large gathering of party members. This convention can act on party rules and policy. But perhaps its most important function is to elect the party executive. The executive is responsible for "the control of the party," conducting the party's business, and guiding "the fundamental attitude of the party organs." Since the executive meets only once a month, the day-to-day operations of the party are directed by the Managing Committee, composed of the national chairperson, the deputy chairperson, and four or five paid party officials. Although intended to function primarily as an administrative body, the Managing Committee, in practice, exerts considerable influence on party policy.

Much of the stress the SPD has put on intraparty democracy has been more talk than action. The leadership has tended to dominate party elections, perpetuate itself in power, and control the policy-making process. In fact, a classic study of party organization, which concluded that all parties are oligarchies, drew most of its evidence from the operation of the SPD early in the twentieth century.

During the 1970s, changes in party composition began to alter the power structure. In the 1950s two-thirds of the SPD's members were working class, and nine out of ten had only a primary education. Twenty years later only two-fifths were blue-collar employees and half were white-collar employees, who often were considerably better educated. In addition, substantial numbers of young people were joining the party. These young people and the middle-class members wanted to participate fully in running the party. Furthermore, many of them tended to be further to the left than the traditional working-class members were.

The Helmut Schmidt leadership group found that it was unable to set the party's policy on nuclear weapons. This repudiation was a major factor in Schmidt's refusal to continue as party leader. With Schmidt's departure early in the 1980s, the most influential figure in the party was Willy Brandt, who had been Chancellor before Schmidt. Brandt wanted to open the party to those on the left who might otherwise become active in the Greens. His positions on defense, nuclear power, and other issues were to the left of Schmidt's. Furthermore, he seemed to be more favorable to rank-and-file participation in party decision making.

When Brandt resigned as chairman in 1987, the SPD lacked a dominant successor and has been running through leaders at an alarming rate. Johannes Rau, the party's candidate for Chancellor in 1987, was not interested in succeeding Brandt. Following the SPD's defeat in the 1987 election, he simply went back to being head of the state government in North Rhine–Westphalia. The party turned to Hans-Jochen Vogel, its candidate for Chancellor in 1983 and leader in the legislature. Vogel was from Bavaria, but had nothing of the stereotypical fun-loving southern German about him. He was a workaholic whose manner earned him the nickname of "Headmaster." He was hardly the traditional SPD leader, since he was not from a working-class background (he was the son of a university professor) and was a Catholic.

Since Vogel was little more than an interim choice, the rising leader of the party appeared to be Oskar Lafontaine, who led the SPD in the Saar. Lafontaine often had criticized SPD leaders for being too conservative, especially on defense policy. His left-wing image was blurred, however, by his proposal that new jobs should be created by getting workers to voluntarily agree to work fewer hours each week. This suggestion was hardly likely to win support from the trade unions. Nonetheless, he was designated the SPD's candidate for Chancellor for the 1990 election. He managed to fight the election despite having been attacked at a public meeting by a woman with a knife. Although seriously injured, he recovered quickly.

Following the SPD's 1990 election defeat Vogel retired. Lafontaine, irritated by criticism from past leaders Brandt and Schmidt about the way he had led the election campaign, refused to be considered for the post of national chairperson. This probably was just as well since a year and a half later he had to defend himself against charges that he had accepted a pension (at age forty-two) after having served as mayor of Saarbrücken while he was simultaneously receiving a salary as a member of the Saar's cabinet. The party instead selected Björn Engholm, Prime Minister of the small northern state of Schleswig Holstein.

Engholm failed to last sufficiently to lead the party into even one election campaign. Less than a year after the Lafontaine "scandal," he was implicated in a very complex shady affair that had been the source of rumors for years. Engholm admitted that he had lied to a parliamentary commission investigating the details (including the death of one of the principal figures in a bathtub in a foreign hotel) of a possible smear attempt against him in one of Schleswig-Holstein's state election campaigns. So he resigned. (Are you familiar with the word "disarray"?)

Therefore, in mid-1993 the party turned to Rudolf Scharping, prime minister of Rhineland-Palatinate (the SPD seems to have established a pattern of calling people up to the majors from triple A). For the first time ever, this supposedly democratic party decided to let the members get involved (figuring, perhaps, that they could do no worse than the party elite had in selecting leaders). The members were allowed to vote for their preference *before* the executive nominated anyone. Nearly three-fifths of the party's 870,000 members participated, with two-fifths voting for Scharping and a third for the prime minister of another state. The executive then nominated Scharping as its choice for national party chairperson, and the selection was confirmed at an emergency party congress. Thus, Scharping would seek to depose Kohl as Chancellor in 1994.

The Christian Democrats   The Christian Democrats lack a tradition of mass membership. During their initial period in power—the first two decades of West Germany's existence—they resembled American parties. The party's organization did little more than loosely group the various state Christian Democratic parties, which were themselves little more than electoral machines with little membership activity.

Once it fell from power, however, the CDU transformed itself into a mass membership party. Although it never quite managed to reach as high a point as the SPD did, the CDU had three-quarters of a million members in 1984. By the 1990s it had declined to about two-thirds of a million. As a result of this shift in party type, CDU organization at the grass-roots level became about as active and effective as that of the SPD. Despite these changes, the Christian Democratic leaders did not encounter the same demands for member participation in policy making as have been voiced in the SPD.

The most significant aspect of the Christian Democrats' organization relates to the link between the Bavarian segment and the rest. In Bavaria the Christian Democrats are called the Christian Social Union (CSU), which is legally a separate party organization. In the proportional representation calculations required to award seats in the legislature following German elections, the votes that the CSU receives are not added to those cast for the CDU to make a total of Christian Democratic support as the basis on which seats are allocated.

Although the votes for them are counted separately in elections, the two organizations have more in common than just the word "Christian" in their names. The CDU does not run any candidates in Bavaria, and the CSU contests elections only there, leaving the rest of Germany to the CDU. The legislators elected by the CDU and by the CSU work closely together in the national legislature, yet the CSU legislators frequently caucus separately from the CDU ones. The CSU has its own party officers. Despite the existence of two separate organizations, it was the CSU's leader, Strauss, who was the candidate for Chancellor for the entire Christian Democratic organization in 1980.

The size of Bavaria and the extent of CSU domination there gave Strauss a strong power base. In 1987, for example, the CSU won 55 percent of the vote in Bavaria. The best CDU performance, in Baden-Württemberg, was only 47 percent. The CSU usually provided more than a fifth of the Christian Democratic strength in the legislature. Although it offered candidates only in Bavaria, it usually won more of the total national vote than did the FDP, which contested elections throughout West Germany. A side effect of German unification was to dilute somewhat the relative strength of the CSU. In the 1990 election the FDP's share of the vote was half again as large as that of the CSU, and the CSU seats in the legislature comprised only about a sixth of the total Christian Democratic representation.

Although Strauss was often able to get his way, Kohl managed, once he became Chancellor, to deny Strauss the only Cabinet positions of interest to him—Foreign Affairs, Economics, and Defense. Strauss remained in Bavaria, occasionally emerging from the forest to growl. Kohl must have been somewhat relieved when Strauss died late in 1988. Theo Waigel, leader of the CSU in the legislature, was chosen as the new party chair. Although as Finance Minister, Waigel is an important politician, he lacks the power base in Bavaria that Strauss had. When the position of prime minister of Bavaria was open in 1993, Waigel indicated that he would like to leave national politics to run his state's government. The Bavarian CSU, however, preferred another leader, making Waigel appear repudiated.

The Free Democrats   The FDP has been dominated by a small group of leaders; however, at times these leaders have lost important votes at party conferences. From the mid-1970s to the early 1990s, the party's most prominent leader was Hans-Dietrich Genscher. His decision to switch from a coalition with the SPD to one with the Christian Democrats in the early 1980s cost him support within the party. Although he continued on as Foreign Secretary and Vice-Chancellor in the coalition Cabinet, he was forced to resign as party chair sooner than he had intended.

Since then the FDP has had as much leadership instability as the SPD. Genscher's successor as chair served for only a few years with little distinction. He departed for a position with the Commission of the EC and ceased to be active in domestic politics. The contest to select a new chair proved interesting. The winner was Otto Lambsdorff (yes, the one who was involved in the Flick scandal). He was chosen by only two dozen votes over a former party treasurer and junior minister in the coalition Cabinet, who happened to be a woman. Lambsdorff and Genscher were the two leaders featured in the FDP's 1990 election campaign material.

When Genscher retired from the Cabinet in 1992, his successor as Vice-Chancellor looked set to become the FDP leader. Less than a year later, he had to resign, however, admitting that he had used his office to help a relative's business. A few months later the FDP chose as the replacement for Lambsdorff as chairperson, Klaus Kinkel, the Foreign Minister and Vice-Chancellor. Kinkel certainly is sufficiently prominent, but since he joined the FDP only two years earlier, the party appeared to be saying that none of its long-term adherents had any leadership ability.

■ OTHER PARTIES

Although several other parties in addition to the three or four (depending on how you count the CDU/CSU) that we have discussed won seats in the legislature in the first few elections, by the start of the 1960s they were unable to win even one, as Table 22–1 shows. Despite not being represented in the national legislature, extreme right-wing parties frequently have caused concern. Various neo-Nazi parties existed in West Germany. One of them was banned by the Federal Constitutional Court in 1952. The most successful was the National Democratic party (NPD), which during the 1960s managed to elect representatives to legislatures in most of the states. The 5-percent barrier of the national electoral law kept the NPD out of the national legislature. What limited support the party had collapsed rapidly in the 1970s. In 1987 the NPD received fewer than a quarter of a million votes, less than 1 percent of the votes cast.

Toward the close of the 1980s, a new party called the Republicans appeared on the far right of the spectrum. Although its policies were highly xenophobic, its leaders denied any Nazi sentiments. They claimed merely to be good nationalists, standing up for German interests in the world. They saw no reason why more than a generation after World War II, Germans should have to continue to apologize. Why should Germany be treated as a second-rate power and have to defer to others because of the distant past? In the 1990 national elections the Republicans received only 2 percent of the vote and were kept out of the legislature by the 5-percent hurdle. Some worried that that barrier would prove insufficient in the 1994 elections. In a state election in Baden-Württemberg in 1992 the Republicans won more than a tenth of the vote, more than the Greens and twice what the FDP received. They seemed to appeal both to those who were nostalgic for the past and to those too young to have experienced it first-hand. The Republicans polled best among those eighteen to twenty-four and those over sixty.

Another party with views similar to the Republicans is the German Peoples' Union (DVU). It also has enjoyed some success at the state level. In Bremen in 1991 it doubled its share of the vote, going from 3 to 6 percent. The next year it also polled 6 percent in Schleswig-Holstein, more than the FDP did there.

Just as with the National Front in France, such parties can have an impact even if they fail to gain seats in the legislature. The support that the Republicans appeared to be gaining in local elections and in opinion polls almost certainly had an effect on Chancellor Kohl. He was reluctant to guarantee that a unified Germany would renounce all claim to a change in the border between the former East Germany and Poland. Ostensibly he was trying to defend Germany from Polish claims for reparations for the devastation the Nazis had wrought in that country during World War II. Kohl wanted a deal—a guarantee of the existing Polish-German border in exchange for dropping claims. In hedging on the border question, however, Kohl was trying to show that he would stand up for German interests. Clearly his aim was to convince disgruntled Christian Democratic supporters not to defect to the Republicans. Only when his equivocation was widely denounced in Europe and the United States did he finally give way and support a border guarantee.

At the other end of the spectrum are two parties that have managed to gain representation in the legislature. In West Germany a Communist party polled 6 percent of the vote and received fifteen seats in the first national election. In the next election its share fell to only 2 percent, and it won no seats. In 1956 the Federal Constitutional Court, in accordance with the Basic Law's prohibition of antidemocratic parties, banned it. About a decade later another Communist party was organized. No legal action was taken against it. By the end of the 1980s its support, always miniscule, had dwindled away to nothing.

In East Germany until the latter part of 1989, the Communist party, of course, was the dominant party. When communism collapsed, the old Communist party (trying on sheep's clothing), renamed itself the Party of Democratic Socialism (PDS). In the 1990 elections the PDS polled only 2 percent of the total vote. That should have kept it out of the legislature. The Federal Constitutional Court had ruled, however (as we mentioned in Chapter 21), that for this one election the two former Germanys had to be treated as separate electoral units. The PDS had polled a tenth of the vote in the former East Germany—twice the 5-percent hurdle—and thus qualified for seventeen seats in the legislature.

Prospects look bleak for the PDS. A constant flow of revelations about the atrocities of the Stasi (the secret police) and its network of informers during the East German regime hardly can attract voters. Even more damaging is the discovery that as the old Communist system was crumbling, the party had smuggled huge sums of money out of the country into foreign bank accounts. Furthermore, in 1994 east and west will be fully integrated in a single electoral system. The PDS will have to win 5 percent of the *total* vote to obtain any seats. Almost certainly the provision included in the electoral laws to eliminate splinter parties will put the PDS out of the national legislature.

Not as far to the left as the Communists are the Greens. In West Germany the party gained prominence in the 1980s, electing members to the national legislature for the first time in 1983. At times the Greens seemed to go out of their way to shock the sensibilities of conservative Germans: wearing casual clothes, long hair, and beads in the national legislative chamber and putting pots of flowers on their desks there. For all this apparent frivolity, the Greens presented a serious political alternative on two main issues. As the name suggests, the party grew out of the environmental movement. The energy crisis initially made nuclear power seem an effective solution. Concerns about the safety of nuclear power plants and the disposal of the waste products of such operations soon caused second thoughts. The SPD was sharply divided on this issue and as a result tended to straddle the fence. The Christian Democrats asserted categorically that nuclear energy was justifiable and necessary. The FDP took a similar stand. The Greens declared that all nuclear power plants should be closed down immediately. Related to this position was their belief that economic growth at the highest possible level of output was not desirable. Concern for the ecology may well mean slower, even zero, economic growth.

The other main theme of the Greens' policy was pacifism. Not only did they want all U.S. missiles to be removed from West Germany, they wanted all NATO troops to be withdrawn. Germany should withdraw from NATO and unilaterally disarm. As for NATO itself, it was deemed incompatible with the maintenance of peace and should be abolished.

A less prominent theme of the Greens was a stress on direct democracy. They believed that social change often requires nonparliamentary action, such as demonstrations, as well as passage of laws. They wanted a binding referendum established as a means to direct democracy. In keeping with a desire to reduce central authority and facilitate untrammeled individual self-fulfillment, the Greens were actively involved in the campaign to thwart the 1987 census. The police raided the party's headquarters in Bonn to seize leaflets calling for a boycott of the census. And twenty-two of its members in the legislature were fined more than $5,000 each for standing outside the parliament building holding up anticensus posters.

The Greens were more seriously committed than any other party to expanding opportunities for political service to women. About three-fifths of the candidates the Greens elected to the Bundestag in 1987 were women. At one point all of the party's parliamentary leaders were women.

Not only did the Greens stake out a distinctive position for themselves, but the fact that they were on the fringe of the political spectrum rather than in the center affected the nature of party competition in Germany. The move of the SPD toward the left was largely in response to a fear that it might lose many of its supporters to the Greens. Thus, the Greens played a role in sharpening the contrasts among Germany's parties.

The Greens were rather loosely organized. Although the party had very few members, it was determined that they, not the leaders, should run affairs. To keep their leaders cut down to size, the Greens required their representatives in the legislature to donate to the party about three-fourths of their salary and most of their tax-free expense allowance. Even more important was the party's rotation principle. Greens elected to the legislature were not permitted by the party to serve a full term. After two years a legislator had to relinquish the seat to a party-designated replacement. Only a 70-percent vote from a legislator's local Green party could grant an exception. This principle caused a great deal of internal conflict and finally was abandoned.

This dispute was fairly typical of the split within the party between the "realists" and the "fundamentalists." The former wanted the Greens to function like other parties: try to elect members to national and state legislatures, form coalitions with other parties, accept some distasteful measures as a trade-off for managing to enact some of the party's policies. The "Fundis" denounced such tactics and accused those favoring them of an elitist thirst for the trappings of office. They wished to demonstrate their moral purity by rejecting any compromise. Demonstrations in the streets, they believed, are more effective than electoral politics.

In the 1990 election the party discovered the truth of Kermit the Frog's lament, "It's not that easy being green." The Greens were wiped out in what had been West Germany. Although they had cleared the 5-percent barrier there in both 1983 and 1987, in 1990 they failed to do so. Green *candidates* in the west did surpass 5 percent, receiving a combined 5.4 percent of the vote. In the *party-list* voting, however, the Greens managed only 4.7 percent. An additional 110,000 votes would have meant about twenty-five seats in the Bundestag. The Greens had been even more skeptical about the rush to unification than the SPD had been and thus incurred even more voter enmity. The continuing battles between the "Realos" and the "Fundis" also hurt, especially as the latter seemed to be triumphing in the months prior to the election and swinging the Greens even further to the left.

In what had been East Germany the indigenous Greens cooperated with Alliance '90, a loose grouping of grass-roots movements that had sprung up to help drive the Communists from power. This joint group did manage to surpass the 5-percent hurdle in the eastern electoral region. As a result, all eight seats won by Greens in the 1990 election were from the former East Germany (see Table 22–2). A few months after the election the Greens in the west split. The "Fundis" left to form a new party called the Ecological Left/Alternate List. A year and a half later the remaining Greens in the west combined with those in the east and Alliance '90. Only such a grouping could have any hope of surmounting the 5-percent hurdle and avoiding the likely fate of the PDS.

▪ ▪ ▪

Although East and West Germany were unified into a single political system, the 1990 election results suggested that two separate party systems still existed. In the west both the SPD and the CDU received slightly more than a third of the vote. Both the FDP and the CSU won about a tenth. The result was a balanced party system with two closely competitive major parties and two equally significant minor ones. In the east, however, the CDU clearly predominated, with more than two-fifths of the vote to less than a quarter for the SPD. The Free Democrats were stronger in the east than in the west, with more than an eighth of the vote. Finally, the PDS was of some importance, with a tenth. The next election not only will help to produce a national party system, but also seems likely (because the special rules for 1990 will be abolished) to repeat the trend toward concentration seen in the early years of West Germany's existence.

Depending on whether the CSU is counted, Germany is likely to have a three- or four-party system, with two parties predominating. In numbers alone, this clearly differs from the system of the Weimar Republic. Furthermore, in contrast to Weimar, the parties in the legislature make neither narrow sectional appeals nor dogmatic ideological ones. Only at the fringes of the political spectrum does anything like a *Weltanschauung* party exist. The robust democracy of Germany is in large measure due to an effective party system. The system does not impede the effective concentration of power, but is also sufficiently vital and offers a breadth of choice that facilitates accountability.

23

The Legislative System

■ THE COMPOSITION OF THE HOUSES OF PARLIAMENT

The Bundestag

Like most other countries, Germany has a bicameral legislature. The lower house, the Bundestag, is composed of 656 members, elected by the procedure discussed in Chapter 21. Their term of office is four years, unless the Bundestag is dissolved early, which has occurred only in 1972 and 1983.

German law permits civil servants to take a leave of absence from a post in the bureaucracy to serve in an elective office and then return to the administrative position without any loss of status. In fact, only recently did the Federal Constitutional Court bar civil servants from continuing to draw a civil service salary while serving in the legislature. So you should not be surprised to learn that about a third of the members of the Bundestag are civil servants. That figure is a bit misleading since it includes teachers and professors, who have civil service status. Teachers at all levels are the largest single occupational group—a sixth of the total membership. Nearly as numerous are lawyers. Next, somewhat less prevalent, are the self-employed. Farmers account for about a third of this group. Other sizable occupational groups are managers from private industry and officials from organizations such as parties and trade unions. Only a handful of members are manual workers.

Although a woman served as the presiding officer of the Bundestag in the mid-1970s and again at the start of the 1990s, women continue to be grossly underrepresented. The 1987 election returned a record number of women (81), but they still made up only a sixth of the total membership of the Bundestag. The first unified elections in 1990 saw a major increase. Now more than a fifth of the Bundestag members (136) are women.

The educational level of members has risen over the years. Formerly only about half had university degrees; now about three-fourths do. Furthermore, another sixth have had other higher education. In addition, the parties differ less in this regard than they used to. Christian Democrats and Free Democrats used to be much more likely to have university degrees than SPD members. Now the proportion of SPD members with degrees equals or surpasses that of the Christian

Democrats and the FDP. On the other hand, more SPD members than Christian Democrats have only an elementary education. The average age of Bundestag members has not varied much over the years, ranging from a high of fifty-three in the late 1960s to a low of under forty-seven in the mid-1970s.

Salaries of Bundestag members have been generous. Until the mid-1970s, when the Federal Constitutional Court ruled to the contrary, the salary was tax-exempt. To compensate members for this change, the salary was almost doubled to about $70,000. They also receive a tax-exempt expense allowance, funds to hire part-time clerical or research assistance, and free travel.

The Bundesrat

The upper house, the Bundesrat, provides a federal component in the legislature, as does the Senate in the United States. In implementing the federal principle, Germany has gone beyond the United States. For the first century and a quarter of the U.S. system, Senators represented the states more than the people living within their boundaries, because they were chosen by the state legislatures. Since 1913, however, Senators have been elected by the people of the states they represent. Thus, in the twentieth century, Senators do not represent the constituent governmental units in the U.S. federal system. In Germany members of the Bundesrat represent the state governments because they are chosen by the executive branch of those governments. In the United States a comparable practice would be for the governor of a state, in consultation with executive colleagues, to appoint the two U.S. Senators from that state. The German practice ensures that the views of state governments are considered in the national legislative process. States' opinions, if not states' rights, have been carried a step further in Germany than in the original U.S. Constitution.

Bundesrat members are usually members of the Cabinet of their state government, and thus they play both a national and subnational role. A seat in the Bundesrat has no set term; its members serve as long as their various state governments send them to the national legislature. Each state has from three to six members, depending on its population. Total membership is sixty-nine, smaller than the U.S. Senate. Seating is alphabetical by state delegation. The Bundesrat's presiding officer, its president, is elected annually. The position is rotated among the states. (The Bundesrat can be seen in session in Figure 23–1.)

The political composition of the Bundesrat depends on the partisan situation in the states. When the Christian Democrats control a state government, for example, they naturally send Christian Democrats to the Bundesrat. The deputies from each state vote as a bloc, as instructed by their state's Cabinet. Since the Bundesrat has an important role in the national legislative process, national parties must take a special interest in the strength of their various state branches.

As a result, election campaigns in the states are frequently dominated by national issues, rather than turning on controversies of special interest to the people living in the area where the election is being held. Thus, paradoxically, making the Bundesrat a more federal body than the U.S. Senate has resulted in nationalizing politics—that is, reducing the importance of purely regional and local political

questions. The composition of the Bundesrat also lends itself to divided political control, a point we'll examine in some detail at the end of this chapter.

■ *ORGANIZATIONAL STRUCTURE*

The physical arrangement of the Bundestag chamber has caused some controversy. You might consider this a trivial matter, but remember that when Britain rebuilt the House of Commons chamber, which had been destroyed during World War II, Winston Churchill stressed the great influence that the size and shape of the meeting room would have on legislative role and procedure. For the first several years of its existence, the Bundestag met in what had been a lecture hall. Since Berlin had always been Germany's capital, no governmental buildings existed in Bonn, the new center of West German government. The Bundestag had to use facilities that had belonged to a teachers' college. The Cabinet sat on a raised platform at the front of the hall. Bundestag members wishing to speak had to go to a rostrum at the front of the chamber.

Such arrangements did not produce stimulating debates, any more than they do in the U.S. House of Representatives, not known for the cut and thrust of its members' remarks. Early in the 1960s the Bundestag considered trying to inject some life and relevance into its proceedings by becoming like the British House of Commons. The proposal was to remodel the chamber to have the governing party sit on one side and the opposition parties on the other—just as in the Commons. This would have been a major change, since no German legislative chamber had ever been so arranged. Perhaps this explains why opinion on the proposal was so closely divided. In the end detailed plans were left to be determined later, as the intended expansion of parliamentary facilities progressed. A sizable new building was constructed, but it contained only offices for Bundestag members. The Bundestag chamber was remodeled, but only slightly; the arrangements did not break with tradition (see Figure 23–2).

Figure 23-2
The Bundestag
in Session

At the front of the chamber to the presiding officer's left were long desks where the Chancellor and the Cabinet sit. Originally these seats were raised above floor level. Subsequently, as a symbolic gesture, they were lowered to the same level as the members' seats so that the executive would not seem to be looking down on the legislature. To the presiding officer's right were another series of long desks, where members of the upper house were permitted to sit as observers during the debates.

The Bundestag members sat at desks arranged in a fan shape, in keeping with German tradition and like the U.S. Congress. Although the term *Hinterbankler* (equivalent to the British "backbencher") is used in Germany, it is misleading. Apart from the first row of seats, which are reserved for legislative leaders so that they have easy access to the rostrum, seating arrangements are not related to status. The Christian Democrats assigned their seats based on what state the members represented, the SPD did so alphabetically, and the FDP drew lots. Even these assignments were flexible. Most of the time, many seats were vacant because members were absent. So those attending sat wherever they wished. As the subject being debated changed, the people occupying the front row also changed, so that those most expert on the current topic could be close to the rostrum.

In 1986 the West German Bundestag moved to a converted waterworks building temporarily so that their chamber could be remodeled. When the unified Bundestag sought to return to the refurbished chamber in 1993, it was enraged to find that its expensive, high-tech voice amplification system didn't work. The extensive use of glass panels for the chamber's walls (to show how open the legislative process was) made the acoustics so lively that no one could hear what a speaker was saying unless everyone else was totally silent (not even a whisper to a fellow member). As a result, the Bundestag had to remain in the waterworks until 1994.

Compounding the problem was the narrowness of the majority—eighteen votes—that in 1991 had supported moving the Bundestag to Berlin in 1995 as part of a shift in capitals from West Germany's Bonn to the traditional German capital. A year after this vote, the Cabinet decided that half of the government's executive departments would move to Berlin—but no date for this transfer was set. The more Germans looked at the expense of constructing and refurbishing government build-

ings in Berlin and at the serious economic problems and costs involved in unification, the more the date for the transfer of the capital to Berlin receded into the
future. The latest plans call for the Bundestag to be in Berlin by 2000 and the
Bundesrat to stay in Bonn.

The presiding officer of the Bundestag, the president, is elected by the members in a secret ballot. The position almost always has been held by a Christian
Democrat. Only from 1972 to 1976 was the president a member of the SPD, and
that person was doubly unique as the first woman to hold the office. The president,
like the Speaker of the House in the United States but in contrast to British practice,
does not separate himself or herself entirely from party activity. The president is
responsible for maintaining order and protecting the rights and prerogatives of
Bundestag members. He or she can exclude unruly members from sessions for up
to thirty days. Assisting the president are four vice-presidents and a number of
recording secretaries, also elected by the Bundestag from among its members.

The president, Rita Süssmuth, was involved in some controversy in the early
1990s. As explained in Chapter 20, one of the problems of unification was reconciling the contrasting abortion laws of the east and west. The Christian Democratic
Government proposed in 1992 that the western provisions should prevail. The
unborn should be protected and abortion would be permissible only if a doctor
approved on specifically cited physiological or psychological grounds. Although
Süssmuth was a CDU legislator, she broke with her party to support an amendment
offered by the SPD and the FDP that would make abortion more easily obtainable.
This amendment, which permitted abortion during the first twelve weeks of preg-
nancy provided only that the woman had been counseled three days before the
procedure, was passed. The amended bill was enacted. (As mentioned earlier, we'll
tell you in Chapter 26 what the Court did with this legislation.)

The Fraktion

The key organizational element of the Bundestag is the *Fraktion* (party group). All
those elected under a given party label combine to form a *Fraktion*. The
Bundestag's standing orders set 5 percent of its total membership, currently, about
two and a half dozen, as the minimum for forming a *Fraktion*. This rule was important during the first decade of the West German Republic, when a number of splinter groups held seats in the Bundestag. Subsequently, the parties managing to be
represented in the Bundestag had no trouble in qualifying, although the Greens
just barely did so from 1983 to 1987.

As you saw in Chapter 22, in the unified 1990 elections the renamed Communist
party from the east won some seats in the Bundestag. These were too few, however,
for the PDS to qualify as a *Fraktion*. Nor were the few seats won by the Greens from
the east sufficient. So only four *Fraktionen* (plural of *Fraktion*)—the CDU, the CSU,
the SPD, and the FDP—were recognized. Should some right-wing party such as the
Republicans or the DVU manage to gain representation in the 1994 elections, they
almost certainly would have too few seats for official recognition.

Only *Fraktionen* are entitled to committee assignments and permitted to
introduce legislation. Furthermore, debate time is allocated to *Fraktionen* on the
basis of their relative strengths in the Bundestag. Thus, an independent legislator or

a splinter party with only a handful of representatives is frozen out of much of the legislative process. The Germans wanted to be certain to avoid the fractionalizing of the legislature that weakened the Weimar Republic.

Each *Fraktion* decides how to allocate to its members the committee posts allotted to it. It also determines how the debate time granted to it is to be divided up among its members. Even though Article 38 of the Basic Law says that representatives are "not bound by orders and instructions and are subject only to their conscience," the *Fraktionen* clearly are in charge, and representatives can play a part in Bundestag activities only by accepting their discipline.

Committees

An important center of power in the German legislature is the Council of Elders, a type of steering committee. A permanent body of twenty-eight members, it is composed of the Bundestag president (who chairs it), the vice-presidents, and representatives designated by each *Fraktion* in proportion to its strength in the Bundestag. The Council meets weekly to set the agenda for the Bundestag and determine the time to be allowed for debate on each subject. It also appoints the presiding officer of each legislative committee. The Bundestag could override the Council's decisions, but rarely does so.

The Bundestag has about two dozen permanent committees, the majority of which are specialist or subject-matter committees. The number of members serving on a committee ranges from thirteen to thirty-seven, with each *Fraktion* represented according to its Bundestag strength. Committee heads are not necessarily from the largest party or even the governing coalition; the presiding positions are distributed among the parties according to strength in the Bundestag.

Although the Greens served on committees and even chaired some before unification, a controversy arose concerning their allocation on one committee. When they first entered the Bundestag in 1983, they were barred from serving on the committee that oversaw financing of the intelligence services because it was felt they could not be trusted to keep confidential the information to which they would have access. The issue was taken to the Federal Constitutional Court, which ruled against the Greens. Following the 1987 election, the Bundestag voted to maintain this bar.

Most of the Bundestag's significant legislative work occurs in its committees, as is also true of the Bundesrat. It has only about a dozen of them, each state being represented on every one. They are intended to relieve the full house from having to consider the details of legislation. Although the committees have powers of administrative surveillance, they function mainly to scrutinize proposed legislation and revise it as necessary. Rhetorical debate and partisan dogmatism are relatively rare. No public record of committee votes is kept, which helps to avoid rigid partisan positions and facilitates compromise.

The emphasis in committee proceedings is on acquiring expert knowledge in order to construct "correct" laws. Committees are empowered to summon Cabinet ministers for questioning, as well as to call expert witnesses to testify about proposed bills. Committees frequently invite civil servants from a relevant department and representatives of the states and from the Bundesrat to provide advice.

Few subcommittees are created, but from time to time special committees are established to deal with some specific issue likely to be of only temporary importance. The special committee may be charged with gathering information or revising a particular bill. Investigatory committees can be established to look into matters of malfeasance or improprieties in government. Neither of these two types of committees has been as important as the permanent legislative committees.

Since so much of the work is entrusted to the committees, the Bundestag spends less time in regular session than most legislative bodies do. Furthermore, the first two days of business each week typically are left open for various party meetings. The Bundestag has averaged only about sixty meetings a year, many of which last for less than a full day. In a typical year the Bundestag will sit for little more than 300 hours, not much more than a quarter of the time the U.S. Senate devotes to full sessions. Nonetheless, for better or for worse, the Bundestag has no difficulty in churning out new legislation: 350 to 500 bills are passed in a typical year.

■ POWERS AND PROCEDURES

The power to make policies is divided between the German central government and the governments of the states. The Basic Law specifies that in some matters the central government has exclusive jurisdiction and in others authority is concurrent between both levels. The central government has exclusive power (Article 73) in such matters as foreign affairs, citizenship, freedom of movement (passports, immigration), fiscal regulations (currency, coinage), customs and tariffs, postal service and telecommunications, railroads and air traffic, industrial property rights (patents), and relations between national and state police. In areas of exclusive national power, the states can legislate only if, and insofar as, they are expressly empowered by the central government to do so.

The Basic Law (Article 74) lists many areas of concurrent powers, matters concerning which the states can legislate as long as the central government has not done so. The central government is somewhat limited by the stipulation that it should legislate only if a national policy is needed because the states are unable to deal effectively with the matter or because the action taken by some state is injurious to the interests of other states or the nation as a whole.

Finally, Article 75 lists several matters for which the central government may issue general directives, but must leave detailed regulation to the states. Provisions in other articles round out the division of powers between the central government and the states. Significantly, education and cultural affairs are left primarily to the states.

Law-Making Procedure

Bills may be initiated by the legislature or by the Cabinet. Legislative bills may start in either house; Cabinet bills must begin in the Bundesrat, which sends them on to the Bundestag via the Cabinet. In this way the Bundestag receives the views of the Bundesrat (that is, of the executive branches of the state governments) on the

Figure 23–3

German Legislative
Procedure

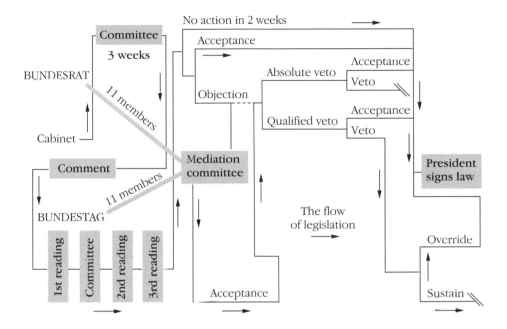

Cabinet's proposals, as well as the Cabinet's reaction to these views. Bills originated by Bundesrat must go through the Cabinet, which must attach a statement of its views, before reaching the Bundestag.

The process of passing a bill from this point on can be followed in Figure 23–3. The diagram assumes that the bill is being proposed by the Cabinet, since that is by far the most common situation. You should start on the left with the Cabinet and trace the solid line in the direction indicated by arrows. You will see what happens to a bill, depending on what each of the legislative chambers does, and this, in turn, will help to clarify their relative power.

The Cabinet introduces the bill in the Bundesrat, which considers it in a committee and within three weeks sends it back to the Cabinet along with its views. The Cabinet adds its comments on the Bundesrat's position and sends the bill to the Bundestag.

Like many legislatures, the Bundestag considers a bill on three readings. Germany follows the American, rather than the British, practice of sending a bill to committee after the first reading, instead of after the second. In the Bundestag, however, first reading can involve a short debate in which the parties state their general views on the proposed legislation.

Committees devote a great deal of time to considering a bill. Six months to a year or more may elapse before the bill returns to the Bundestag. Although the coalition in control of the Government has a majority on each committee, it normally does not force its proposals through. Some points will be conceded to opponents in an effort to get agreement. The German Cabinet is much more likely to compromise during the committee stage than is the British Cabinet. At times the committee stage may be the stage on which factional conflicts within the Cabinet are fought out. Should the Cabinet have eliminated some portion of a bill that a minister favored, he or she may try to get allies on the Bundestag committee to restore that provision.

When the bill returns from committee, it is accompanied by a detailed report, usually written by the committee's staff, which explains the need for the bill, the main points discussed by the committee, the views of both its majority and minority, and why changes (if any) needed to be made in the bill that was originally proposed. Since this report has the aura of having been written by those who are experts in the substance of the bill and in legal drafting, it carries considerable weight with the Bundestag's members.

Second reading provides an opportunity to discuss the detailed provisions of the bill and to consider amendments, although the general principles of the bill may be debated as well. Discussion on third reading is confined largely to general debate of the main features of the bill, although amendments are in order if supported by at least fifteen deputies. In urgent circumstances all three readings of a bill can take place in a single day, provided that the members agree unanimously.

Rules prevent filibustering during debates. On the motion of thirty members, closure can be voted on, and debate is ended if a majority votes to do so. The main speaker from each *Fraktion* is limited to no more than forty-five minutes; additional speakers from that *Fraktion* may not exceed fifteen minutes. Curtailing lengthy debate has not, however, been a problem for the Bundestag. Many bills are passed without any discussion, and most members never speak at all. This is not quite as bad as it may sound, if you recall how much work is done in committee to get the bill into acceptable shape.

Voting in the Bundestag is by a show of hands or by standing. In case of doubt, a division—similar to British practice—in which members file through doors past counting clerks is employed. If at least fifty members request it in advance, a roll-call vote is taken.

Once bills have passed the Bundestag, they go back to the Bundesrat (we're at the upper center of Figure 23–3). Most bills are sent to a committee. When it reports, the entire chamber decides what action to take in a single reading. Voting is by roll call of the states. A state may not split its delegation of three to six votes; all of them must be cast the same way. If the Bundesrat approves the bill or fails to act within two weeks, the bill goes to the President of the Republic for signature.

Should the Bundesrat oppose a bill, however, the process is complicated. When the Bundesrat and the Bundestag disagree, the Mediation Committee seeks a solution. Unlike conference committees in the U.S. Congress, which are set up for particular bills as the need arises, the Mediation Committee is permanent. It is composed of eleven members from each house of the legislature. In contrast to procedures within the Bundesrat itself, Bundesrat members serving on the Mediation Committee are not bound by instructions from their states' Cabinets on how to vote. Except for Cabinet ministers, no one other than Committee members may attend its meetings unless it decides otherwise. In order to provide continuity, the standing orders permit no more than four changes of membership during the life of a single Bundestag.

In the overwhelming majority of cases, the Committee manages to work out an acceptable compromise. Therefore, Figure 23–3 shows the Bundestag accepting the Mediation Committee report, the usual situation. Having been passed by the Bundestag, the bill returns to the Bundesrat. Now, as you can see, two possibilities exist because the Bundesrat has two types of vetos.

In matters affecting the interests of the states, the Bundesrat's approval is required for a bill to become law; without it the bill dies. An example of such a bill is one providing, as frequently is the case in Germany, that a portion of the revenue raised by a tax is to go directly to the states. Bills on administrative matters affecting the states are also subject to absolute veto. Since most national laws in Germany are implemented by the states, a large number of bills are of this type. In all, somewhat more than half of all the bills considered by the legislature are subject to the absolute veto of the Bundesrat, that is, must have its approval to become law.

On all other bills—those not involving the interests of the states—Bundesrat approval is not required. If the upper house opposes a bill, the Bundestag can override it and pass the bill anyway. In these cases the Bundesrat has only a qualified veto. Here again two possibilities exist (not separately distinguished in Figure 23-3). If the Bundesrat has rejected the bill by a simple majority, a majority in favor of it in the Bundestag is sufficient to override. But if the Bundesrat voted against the bill by a two-thirds margin or greater, then the Bundestag must vote for it by at least a two-thirds margin.

The Bundesrat's Significant Role

When the Bundesrat may impose a qualified veto, it may, and usually does, call on the Mediation Committee rather than vote against the bill. (It could, however, simply vote against the bill. That is why Figure 23–3 shows a dotted line by the word "Objection"; the part of the process involving the loop through the Mediation Committee does not always occur.) When the Bundesrat may impose an absolute veto, then the Cabinet or the Bundestag, as well, can invoke the Committee. Either way, the arrangement worked out by the Mediation Committee usually includes a good deal of what the Bundesrat wanted.

Recall also that the Cabinet's legislative proposals must go to the Bundesrat for comment before they are introduced into the Bundestag. This means that the Cabinet typically consults with the Bundesrat when bills are being drafted in order to avoid adverse comments on them from the upper house. In addition, the Basic Law requires that the Cabinet keep the Bundesrat informed about its conduct of affairs. To comply, the Ministry of Bundesrat and Laender Affairs was created. About once a week, the head of that ministry meets top administrators from the states to bring them up-to-date on Cabinet policy. Since this minister also attends most Bundesrat meetings, he or she can inform colleagues in the Cabinet on the views of the states. Given the various ways in which the Bundesrat can influence the Cabinet, it hardly is surprising that the upper house initiates few bills.

The Bundesrat is one of the world's strongest upper houses. It (which is to say the states' Cabinets) frequently has played an important role in the policy process. State elections are held at various times, none of them coinciding with national legislative elections. During the latter years of the SPD/FDP coalition, the Christian Democrats won control of enough states to obtain a majority in the Bundesrat, even though the SPD and the FDP controlled the Bundestag. In 1982 the Christian

Democratic–dominated upper house defeated part of the SPD/FDP coalition Cabinet's plan to alleviate unemployment through a job-creation program financed by a 1-percentage-point increase in the value-added tax (VAT). The Cabinet agreed not to try to reverse this defeat, if the Bundesrat would accept, which it did, a program of grants to firms for investment in new plants and equipment, which would provide new jobs.

With the return to power of the Christian Democrats early in the 1980s, the partisan composition of the Bundesrat once again reflected that of the lower house and the Cabinet. Toward the latter part of the decade, however, the Christian Democrats began to lose ground in some states. Every state election became an important matter for the national governing coalition. The swing eventually occurred at a crucial time. In the spring of 1990, the SPD managed to win an election in a state previously controlled by the Christian Democrats. Therefore, that state's five Bundesrat votes shifted, giving the Christian Democrats only eighteen seats in the upper house to the SPD's twenty-three. This meant that Chancellor Kohl's Government would not control the upper house when it voted on the treaty for currency, economic, and social union between east and west. Since the SPD had criticized the treaty for failing to provide adequately for East Germans' social security, for the adjustment by their small businesses to a free market economy, and for environmental protection (East German industries under communism had been notorious polluters), it could decide to block ratification. On the other hand, the SPD would not want to appear to impede the dream—reunification—long desired by virtually all Germans.

Eventually the SPD decided that, despite its reservations, the treaty had to be supported. The party did not fully endorse the treaty, however, for it instructed its representatives in both the Bundestag and the Bundesrat to vote however they wished when the treaty came up for ratification. Since the Christian Democratic Government controlled the Bundestag, Kohl had to focus the bulk of his efforts for treaty ratification on the Bundesrat. Once again, the upper house had a major role in the West German policy-making process.

Unification again gave the Christian Democrats a majority in the Bundesrat. In the first unified elections for the Bundestag, the Christian Democrats easily emerged as the leading party in the lower house, and so all branches of the government were in partisan synch. A few months later, however, the SPD won the state election in Rhineland-Palatinate to gain a clear majority (thirty-seven) of the seats in the Bundesrat. The Christian Democrats controlled states totaling only twenty-eight seats in the upper house. (Berlin's four seats couldn't be placed in either party's column because there a grand coalition of the SPD and the CDU was in power.) The result was a number of clashes between the Cabinet and the Bundesrat.

In June 1991 the Bundesrat blocked the Government's proposal for heavier penalties for exporting illegal weapons to such countries as Iraq. Although the SPD, in control of the Bundesrat, also opposed such sales, it objected to the Government's plan to allow customs officials to tap telephones. The Bundesrat also rejected the Government's tax increase package to finance the costs of unification. It forced the Government to offer an alternative package that retained business taxes that were to have been abolished in the initial plan. On the other hand, desperate conditions in the east meant that party discipline had its limits. Yet another tax package designed to benefit the east was expected to be thwarted in the Bundesrat. But Brandenburg, the only state in the former East Germany controlled by the SPD, broke with the national party to vote with the Christian Democrats, and the Government's package squeaked through.

Perhaps an even more important effect of divided partisan control of the legislature concerned constitutional amendment. As we discussed in Chapter 22, a major controversy in German politics in the 1990s concerned the country's international military role. Some experts argued that Germany could not participate fully in UN peace-keeping activities unless the constitution were amended to eliminate constraints that had been included as part of the World War II settlement imposed by the victorious Allies. Although the SPD is not opposed to such UN activities, its antimilitarism makes it very cautious about any changes of this type in the constitution. Its strength in the Bundesrat means that without its consent Chancellor Kohl can do little to enable Germany to perform what he feels is its international duty.

Another international issue that highlights the significance of the Bundesrat is European union. Britain is not the only country in which questions are being raised about whether any further steps toward greater integration involve an unacceptable loss of sovereignty. The German states have been concerned that their strong position within the German federal system may be undercut by a shift of decision making on key issues to Brussels (the location of executive headquarters of the EU). As a result, the states negotiated with the Government a constitutional revision that would give them, by means of a vote in the Bundesrat, a check on any further shift in power to the EU. In addition, the states also demanded that the Government pay more attention to their views on day-to-day German input to EU decision making. The result was a European Union committee in the Bundesrat that the Government must consult prior to negotiations in Brussels. Clearly, the Bundesrat, as an upper legislative house, is more comparable to the U.S. Senate than to either the British House of Lords or the French Senate. Both Germany and the United States, as federal systems in contrast to the unitary systems of Britain and France, need to represent in the policy-making process interests based on territorial contrasts. Both have devised a means of doing so in an upper legislative house.

■ ■ ■

Traditionally, Germans have tended to regard the legislative process as an activity that brings legal expertise to bear on a proposed statute so that it will be properly worded. Extensive discussion of the general principles at the heart of the bill by those lacking legal knowledge has not been regarded as useful. You will have noticed at several points in this chapter's discussion that this preoccupation with legal expertise in the legislative process continued into contemporary German government. It is as though Germans regard legislating as a legal, rather than a political, activity.

Add to this attitude the fact that various deals or compromises typically have been worked out among the concerned interests during the committee stage of a bill, and you can understand why extensive discussion of bills on the floor of the

Bundestag has seemed superfluous to German legislators. As you saw in the British part of this book, if you consider only changes in the provisions of a bill, then floor debate is superfluous in the House of Commons also. Bills rarely are modified in any significant way because of what is said in the debates. What the British understand, however, and the Germans have not fully grasped, is the importance of debate and discussion in the legislature as a means to legitimate governmental policy output. People are much more willing to accept distasteful rules and regulations if they feel that the various alternatives have been considered fully and that the particular point of view they favor has had a chance to be heard. Related to this legitimating function of the legislature is its educative function. Through debates on the principles of legislative proposals, a parliament has the opportunity to air the leading views on the public issues of the day. Even limited reports in popular newspapers of such debates help to educate and inform the citizens. The Bundestag, however, apparently regards performance of this function as either unnecessary or unimportant. To this extent, the German policy-making process retains something of an elitist orientation.

The Bundestag lacks a core of assertive members who recognize that their chief task is to explain to citizens the values and constraints that shape the setting of public priorities, thereby laying the foundations for future support for policies. Many energetic members spend much time on committee work and in trying to compete with the bureaucrats in mastering statutory details. Such activity is not to be deplored, but its price often is inadequate debate on the central issues of the policy. The German legislature does what it does well, but it leaves undone some functions of considerable importance for legislatures in democratic systems.

......24

Policy-Making Structures

Germany follows the traditional parliamentary pattern of having a dual executive, that is, both a head of state and a head of Government. The head of state, whose position is largely ceremonial, is known as the President. The head of Government, the equivalent of a prime minister, is called the Chancellor.

■ *THE ROLE OF THE PRESIDENT*

Although the President was popularly elected during the Weimar Republic, this is no longer the case. The change was intended to help restrict the President to a ceremonial role; a head of state not popularly elected cannot claim to embody the popular will as fully as does the legislature. The Weimar experience with a popularly elected head of state possessing fairly extensive powers had not been very satisfactory. Although the drafters of West Germany's Basic Law recognized a need to restructure the office, they did not want to eliminate it entirely. They saw some merit in providing for a nonpolitical official who could symbolize the nation and discharge ceremonial duties, while another official who had emerged from the interplay of political forces would be responsible for directing policy making.

The President is chosen by a body known as the Federal Assembly, which is composed of the members of the Bundestag plus an equal number of persons chosen through proportional representation by the legislatures of the states. Unlike the American Electoral College, the Federal Assembly actually does meet as a group to cast ballots for President. But neither debate nor campaign speeches are allowed.

Any German who is at least forty years old and qualified to vote is eligible for the office of President. On the first and, if necessary, second ballots, an absolute majority of the votes is required to be elected. If no one manages to win, then a third ballot is held on which a plurality is sufficient. Thus, elections cannot drag on interminably.

Only once in the nine presidential elections of the West German Republic was a third ballot necessary and from 1974 on a single ballot was sufficient. Presidents serve a five-year term and can be reelected once. Both of the first two Presidents were reelected (each getting their second term on the first ballot), but the next three served only a single term. Then the last President elected before unification was reelected for a second term.

The FDP, the Christian Democrats, and the SPD all supplied a President at one time or another. The latter party did least well—one single-term President. Furthermore, the party affiliations of that President, Gustav Heinemann, were a bit unorthodox. Originally a member of the CDU, he had resigned to oppose that party's policy of rearming Germany. For a time he headed a somewhat neutralist splinter group before joining the SPD.

On a couple of occasions, most recently from 1979 to the end of 1982, control of the executive has been divided, with the President being from a party that was not part of the governing coalition. This has produced no difficulties; the Germans do not even have a word for what the French call "cohabitation." Of course, as you saw in this book's part on France, the French President is considerably more than a ceremonial head of state.

The President can be impeached for "willful violation of the Basic Law or any other Federal law." A vote by one-fourth of either house of the legislature is sufficient to introduce the motion for impeachment. A two-thirds vote is required, however, for the matter to proceed to a trial. Were that to occur, the case would be heard before the Federal Constitutional Court; it would decide whether the President was guilty and, therefore, to be removed from office.

Germany lacks a vice-president. If the office of President falls vacant, the president of the Bundesrat serves the remainder of the term. That person also performs many of the President's functions when the head of state is out of the country or incapacitated by illness.

As can be seen from Figure 24–1, German Presidents have lived in splendor comparable to that of the French and American Presidents. The Villa Hammerschmidt was built as a private residence in 1863. Around the turn of the century it was owned by a wealthy industrialist. It was acquired as a presidential residence in 1950, a few months after the West German Republic was launched in Bonn in the fall of 1949. In the mid-1990s, the President's office and residence moved to Berlin.

Despite the impressiveness of Villa Hammerschmidt, the German President lacks the powers wielded by either the French or American counterpart. The President cannot dismiss the Chancellor or authorize the use of any emergency powers. All of the President's official acts, except for nomination of the Chancellor, must be countersigned by the Chancellor or another appropriate minister. Despite such constraints, the President possesses some discretion of action; to some extent the powers of the office are ambiguous.

Following each election for the Bundestag, the President proposes to it a possible Chancellor. If one party clearly predominates in the legislature, the President will have little alternative but to select its leader. The more concentrated party system in West Germany reduced the President's influence in these matters more than any change in constitutional provisions.

If the Bundestag accepts the President's nominee by an absolute majority of its vote, then that person becomes Chancellor. If the Bundestag's response is not that

Figure 24–1

The Building and Gardens of the Villa Hammerschmidt

wholehearted, if, for example, it favors the President's nominee by only a plurality, then a complex procedure is initiated. The Bundestag may then elect anyone of its choosing, provided that it does so by an absolute majority. But perhaps the legislature is so divided that it cannot attain even that. If it deadlocks for as long as two weeks, then it can choose a Chancellor by a plurality. If events took this course, however, the President could either accept the Bundestag's choice for Chancellor or call for a new election of the Bundestag.

The point of these provisions is to prevent the President from forcing a Chancellor on an unwilling Bundestag. On the other hand, to be effective a Chancellor needs fairly broad legislative support. If this appears not to be the case, if only a plurality, not an absolute majority, of the Bundestag backs the Chancellor, then the President can decide whether the electorate should be consulted.

These elaborate procedures—drafted before anyone could foresee the shape that the party system of the West German Republic would take—never were necessary. The President's nominee always received an absolute majority. On the first occasion, in 1949, however, the vote was close. Konrad Adenauer had not a single vote to spare, even when three ballots were counted that had his name on them rather than aye, which was the proper vote on the motion of whether he should become Chancellor.

Among the ambiguities concerning the President's powers is the question of a veto. Although the Basic Law does not provide for such a power, it does say that the

President must sign laws before they go into effect. The drafters intended for the signature to be automatic, no more than formal evidence that the law had been passed. The first President, Theodor Heuss, withheld his signature on occasion. He questioned, for example, whether a tax law that had been passed only by the Bundestag needed the Bundesrat's approval as well. When the Federal Constitutional Court ruled that passage by both houses was necessary, Heuss refused to sign the bill, and it never went into effect. This may not be exactly a veto, but the effect on the legislation was the same.

Although the point at issue was one of correct constitutional procedures, an issue of substance was involved as well. The Cabinet and a majority of the Bundestag had favored the tax law on its merits. In blocking it, the President was becoming involved in politics. To the extent that this occurs, the President is less able to discharge the ceremonial role, which requires that the holder of the office appear above politics so as not to alienate the supporters of any party. A ceremonial leader must be a symbol of national *unity*. (You might want to review the role of the British monarch, discussed at the start of Chapter 6.)

Heuss's action proved not to be an isolated incident. Subsequently, when it was unclear whether the Bundesrat could apply a qualified or an absolute veto, the Cabinet looked to the President for some decision. The precedent established was that the President will sign a bill opposed by the Bundesrat only when convinced that Bundesrat approval is not required—that for legislation of that type it does not have the option of absolute veto. Although this is an important area of discretion for the President, it may make the power of the office sound greater than it is. In some sense the President's signature on the law is no more than an advisory opinion, indicating the President's belief that Bundesrat approval was unnecessary. The signature does not settle the matter legally. Should the law be challenged in the Federal Constitutional Court, the Court may rule that the law is invalid because Bundesrat approval was needed, despite the fact that the President's signature indicated a contrary opinion. Clearly, the President's discretion is limited; the power to withhold a signature should not be equated with the American President's veto power.

Perhaps the most impressive of all the West German Presidents was the final one, Richard von Weizsäcker. His election in 1984 was notable for several reasons. This was the first time a change of Presidents had occurred without a change in the party controlling the office. More important, von Weizsäcker received 832 votes, over 300 more than were needed to win, a record victory for a President's first term. Although he had been an active Christian Democratic politician, having served, for example, as mayor of West Berlin, even many SPD electors voted for him.

Von Weizsäcker was from the liberal wing of his party and was able to speak for the country in a way that Christian Democratic Chancellor Helmut Kohl often failed to do. At times, in an effort to put the past behind the country, Kohl seemed to dismiss or belittle the atrocities of the Nazi period. In contrast, von Weizsäcker frequently called on Germans to show by their devotion to humanitarian, democratic values that they had turned their backs on the past. A man of rather patrician appearance, he managed to give the office dignity without seeming aloof.

So admirably did he perform the role of President that when his first term expired, he was reelected with ease for a second term. Not for a quarter of a century had a President been reelected. Furthermore, the 881 votes that he received constituted the highest total ever won by a candidate. (Since the Federal Assembly was somewhat smaller in the early years of the West German system, von Weizsäcker's share of the total vote was the second highest on record.) No candidate even stood against him in the election, so that those who did not favor him (about 140) either abstained or voted against him.

Basically, the President's influence, like that of the British monarch, depends on his or her personal characteristics and current political circumstances. Heuss said that the President "may not . . . take part in the practical decisions of day-to-day politics, but he is permitted to help in improving the atmosphere and facilitating the putting into effect of certain quite simple, reasonable, and generally accepted points of view." Although that doubtless was a correct summary, von Weizsäcker didn't feel that refraining from day-to-day politics meant that he had to shun controversy. The partisan political maneuverings that followed unification distressed him. Although he knew that such a step would be unpopular, he favored additional taxes to help bail out the former East Germany. When politicians tried to avoid this necessity, he attacked the leaders of the parties as "power crazy" in a June 1992 speech. Clearly, this ceremonial head of state can be more involved in politics than the British monarch can. The Chancellor, however, like the British Prime Minister, does not have to accept the advice of the head of state; the Chancellor, not the President, is the key maker of policy.

▪ CHANCELLOR DEMOCRACY

Power shifted from the Council of Ministers to the President as France moved from the Third and Fourth Republics to the Fifth. Similarly, in Germany the distribution of power within the executive branch differs from what existed under Weimar. The shift, however, has been in a different direction—from the President to the Chancellor. As we noted in Chapter 15, the power shift in France was not just due to an altering of the constitution, but also owed a great deal to the personality of the first President of the Fifth Republic. In West Germany, as well, the personality of the first Chancellor, in combination with changes in the constitutional structure, altered the role and status of that office.

We have already explained the process by which the Chancellor is chosen, but an interesting historical sidelight should be noted. Although West Berlin participated fully in electing the West German President, the votes of its delegates to the Bundestag did not count in selecting the West German Chancellor. Had this not been the case, the history of the Federal Republic might have taken a very different course. Counting the delegates from West Berlin in 1949, when the Bundestag first met, would have made the SPD, not the Christian Democrats, the largest party. The SPD would have had first opportunity to form a coalition and, had it managed to do so, the Christian Democrats' domination of the first two decades of the West German Republic's politics would not have occurred.

The Basic Law required the Chancellor to appoint a deputy. For the first two decades of the West German Republic, this person was a mere figurehead. A domineering person such as Chancellor Konrad Adenauer shared responsibility with no one. When the Grand Coalition between the Christian Democrats and the SPD was formed in 1966, however, Willy Brandt, the SPD leader, was made deputy. The significance the position attained then was reinforced when the Grand Coalition was followed by the SPD/FDP coalition: the FDP leader was made deputy. The position came to be known as Vice-Chancellor. Hans-Dietrich Genscher, leader of the FDP, held the office, along with the position of Foreign Minister for nearly two decades. Thus, the office was significant for political, more than constitutional, reasons.

The Chancellor selects the Cabinet members, whose formal appointments are signed by the President. Members of the Cabinet may be, and usually are, members of the Bundestag. Cabinets have varied from fifteen to twenty members. The President may offer advice to the Chancellor on these appointments, but, as the first Chancellor made clear, it can be ignored easily.

The Cabinet or its ministers may issue decrees having the force of law, but only when authorized by statutes already in effect, which the decrees must cite. Moreover, this decree power may not be used by the central government to avoid the constitutional requirement of Bundesrat approval for certain types of legislation. In such matters, the central government's decrees require the Bundesrat's approval. As we explained in Chapter 20, the Basic Law was amended in the late 1960s to give the Cabinet power during emergencies to deal with transportation and communication, supplies of food, water, fuel, and industrial materials, and the labor market.

The German Cabinet is intended to be a very formal body and has elaborate operating rules. These specify the number of ministers needed for a quorum and require formal votes to reach decisions. When the Cabinet is divided, the majority rules, except in some key instances. On financial matters, for example, the Chancellor and the Finance Minister are allowed to have their way, even if the rest of the Cabinet is opposed. All this differs considerably from the practice in Britain, where the Cabinet is governed by informal procedures that have grown up over the years, rather than by written rules, and where the Prime Minister normally ascertains the sense of the meeting by going around the table to "collect the voices," rather than by calling for a formal vote.

Adenauer's Formative Impact

Despite the German Cabinet's elaborate rules for joint decision making, collective responsibility for policy has been limited. The Basic Law makes the Chancellor alone, not the entire Cabinet, responsible to the Bundestag. Furthermore, Article 65 says that the Chancellor "determines, and is responsible for, general policy." Adenauer interpreted this provision to mean that he did not need to consult the Cabinet in making policy. He regarded the Cabinet as a board of experts whose role was to assist him only on his request. Should he so desire, he might consult them for information on which to base *his* decisions. This might not be necessary, however, since he established a system of research committees reporting to him alone. When he presented his proposals to the Cabinet, he had independent, expert opinion to fend off any objection from his ostensible colleagues. Although he utilized his ministers at times, his personal research network tended to make him more knowledgeable than the rest of the Cabinet, thereby reducing the ministers' authority.

Adenauer did not hesitate to criticize his Cabinet colleagues publicly when he disagreed with the positions they had taken in speeches. On the other hand, he was reluctant to dismiss ministers who were loyal to him personally, even if they were ineffective. He tended to relate to his Cabinet in much the same way as a U.S. President does. Again, this contrasts sharply with British practice (at least until Margaret Thatcher), in which the Prime Minister, although *primus,* still remains *inter pares*. This contrast is the more remarkable because Germany, like Britain, is a parliamentary, not a presidential, system.

Of further aid to Adenauer in dominating the Cabinet was the Federal Chancellery, provided for by the Cabinet's standing orders. The Chancellery staff, numbering about 500, is the German equivalent of the Executive Office of the President in the United States. The head of Chancellery performs many of the functions that in the United States are the responsibility of the President's chief of staff. The Chancellery's administrative staff performs two types of functions. It issues in the Chancellor's name relevant instructions to all ministries and thus deals with many important matters before they ever reach the Cabinet. And it coordinates policy by settling disputes among ministries. Only those disputes that it cannot resolve go to the Cabinet for settlement.

Originally, the Chancellery's work was directed by a personal appointee of the Chancellor who was known as a state secretary. During the Adenauer period this state secretary was, in a sense, second in command and more powerful than anyone in Adenauer's Cabinet. In 1984 Chancellor Kohl created a new position, head of the Chancellery, to which he appointed, not a bureaucrat, but a politician, who was also given a seat in the Cabinet. This new arrangement curtailed the power of the state secretary and was intended to ensure that someone fully attuned to political and electoral considerations was in charge. It also allowed the Chancellor to gain the full benefit of the Chancellery staff.

The Chancellery is located in the building that looks like three E's in the lower right-hand corner in Figure 24–2. (The low, white buildings in the center of the picture are the permanent meeting chambers for the Bundestag and the Bundesrat. Connected to this building is the original legislative office building, and the nearby high rise is the more recently constructed one.)

Figure 24–2
Governmental
Complex, Bonn

After serving as Chancellor for the first fourteen years of the West German Republic, Adenauer resigned in 1963 at the age of eighty-seven. So dominant had he been, so restricted was the role of the Cabinet, that Germany's system was labeled "Chancellor democracy," just as the Fifth Republic sometimes has been referred to as the "de Gaulle Republic." Despite its autocratic features, Chancellor democracy had its merits. Adenauer faced the problem of holding a number of diverse elements together in the CDU. By mediating among them, he prevented any one group from dominating the party, which would have narrowed its appeal and had unfortunate effects on the development of the German party system.

Although Adenauer fully exploited the opportunities that the Basic Law offered to enhance his powers, he did not go as far as de Gaulle did during the Fifth Republic in stretching the constitution to, or even beyond, its limits. Adenauer's handling of foreign affairs was skilled; he made himself virtually the sole voice of Germany in the eyes of the world. Even his opponents had to admit that he won considerable international status and prestige for Germany by knowing when to be patient and when to be tenacious. In pursuit of the German national interest, he was imaginative, flexible, and statesmanlike.

Most important, by providing a stable and effective government, Adenauer demonstrated that democracy and authority are not mutually exclusive. Thus, he contributed significantly to German acceptance of democracy, a major achievement in a nation lacking a democratic tradition. The West German Republic's rapid economic recovery and general prosperity after World War II, so sharply in contrast to the ruinous inflation and eventual economic collapse of the Weimar regime, seemed due to his capable rule. Strong leadership, decisive policies, economic well-being—all of these gave Germans reason to believe that democracy could work. Paradoxically, had his political style been more democratic, his historical contribution to German democracy would not have been as great. Clearly, he possessed the attributes appropriate to the times.

Chancellors since Adenauer

The Christian Democrats remained in power for some years after Adenauer retired; although his successors as Chancellor were not ineffectual, none was the dominant leader he had been. When the 1969 election brought the SPD to power in coalition with the FDP, Germans wondered what sort of Chancellor a Social Democrat would try to be. Willy Brandt, the new Chancellor, preferred to reach decisions more collectively than had Adenauer. Nonetheless, his prominence in German politics was such that no one considered him a weak Chancellor. His authority was enhanced considerably when he was awarded the Nobel Peace Prize in 1971 in recognition of his efforts to improve Germany's relations with the Soviet Union and Eastern Europe through policies known as *Ostpolitik*.

With Brandt's successor, Helmut Schmidt, Germany seemed to have come full circle back to the Adenauer style. Schmidt, who served as Chancellor from 1974 to 1982, had a reputation for bluntly speaking his mind, regardless of the consequences, and for pursuing his own goals without consulting others much. His detractors called him *Schmidt-Schnauze*, meaning "big-mouth Schmidt," or "Schmidt, the lip." Whereas Brandt tried to modify positions so that others would find them acceptable, Schmidt was more likely to strike out on his own, expecting others to follow along because of the obvious intellectual soundness of his view. Since Schmidt could remain in office, however, only with the support of the FDP, he had to compromise at times and pay some attention to the views expressed in the Cabinet. Not infrequently, Schmidt had to employ de Gaulle's tactic of threatening to resign unless his colleagues went along with his views.

When the Christian Democrats returned to power late in 1982, their new Chancellor presented a marked contrast to both Schmidt and Adenauer. Helmut Kohl seems to bumble along from one mishap to another, exerting little leadership. Critics have referred to him as *Kanzel Tunix*, or "Chancellor Do-Nothing." He dislikes disagreement among his Cabinet colleagues but, instead of deciding which course the government should pursue, simply shouts at them to agree among themselves. His leadership style has been labeled the "anaconda approach." He smothers opposition and difficulties with slow, sustained pressure—it is procrastination carried to a high art.

Kohl's image makes it difficult for some people to take him seriously. He is a huge, almost hulking, man. But instead of being intimidating, he has a folksy demeanor. Were it not for the fact that he has been little concerned about environmental issues, he could almost be nicknamed the "Jolly Green Giant." Unlike some of his predecessors as Chancellor, he is not an intellectual and knows little about economic matters. He unquestionably supports traditional values, such as the family and hard work.

Compounding his problems is a tendency to put his foot in his mouth. During the 1987 election campaign, he asserted that East Germany operated concentration camps and indirectly compared Mikhail Gorbachev, the Soviet leader, to Josef Goebbels, the Nazi head of propaganda. Another notable gaffe was his commenting in 1990 that the border between Poland and Germany could not be settled until after East and West Germany reunited. As a result, the Poles and many others became fearful that a reunified Germany might seek to reclaim territory that had been part of that country prior to World War II. Kohl eventually had to support a formal declaration guaranteeing the inviolability of the Polish border. Even passage of this declaration by the Bundestag, however, could not eradicate all the concern that his rather insensitive comments had roused.

Whatever his flaws, Kohl did manage to get to the top of the German political system and to keep himself there. Despite being the butt of snide remarks and outright criticism from the CSU leader Strauss, Kohl usually managed to keep Franz Josef in his place. Although Kohl's response to inquiries about possible scandals involving tax breaks and political contributions was less than impressive, he emerged unscathed, if not exactly vindicated. Anybody able to coordinate a bifurcated party with an assertive coalition partner for the better part of a decade and win three national elections must be doing something right. Either Kohl is extraordinarily lucky or he is considerably more skilled than he is generally credited with being.

Kohl's handling of reunification seems to warrant the more positive assessment of his abilities. In contrast to his typical procrastination when confronting tough problems, he quickly decided that full steam ahead was the best course. While others talked of years to realize the merger of the East and West German political systems, Kohl talked of months. In his visits to East Germany in the spring of 1990, he was hailed by ecstatic crowds as virtually the father of the nation. Although he had not worked out the details of unification, his rhetorical generalities were what many wanted to hear, especially since his few specific promises tended to be generous, if ill-considered. The more practical comments from SPD leaders seemed like foot dragging.

As a traditionalist, Kohl could be expected to be a fervent proponent of unification. His innate views were significantly reinforced by personal political calculations. Kohl's apparent strategy was to get the detailed process of reunification well underway prior to the 1990 West German elections. Doing so, he hoped, would so impress West German voters that they would keep the Christian Democrats in office. Shortly after that electoral triumph, new elections could be held throughout Germany for the merged political system. Again the electorate would credit him with this achievement, and he would become the first Chancellor of the new, unified Germany. Not a bad way to cap a political career. As it happened, unification moved so fast that no West German elections were held in 1990; instead the elections were the first for the newly unified Germany. Given the costs and problems of unification, however, being the architect of the new Germany has not proven to be the unalloyed joy that Kohl anticipated.

■ LEGISLATIVE-EXECUTIVE RELATIONS

Legislative leadership is in the Cabinet's hands. About four-fifths of all bills are initiated by the Cabinet. In the early years of the West German Republic, many bills were introduced by the legislature. Since such bills have been much less likely to pass than those introduced by the Cabinet, their number has declined considerably. Cabinet-sponsored legislation also has the advantage of having been drafted by civil servants with detailed legal training; such services are not available to the Bundestag.

In contrast to the U.S. Congress, all members of a party in the Bundestag tend to vote together as a group, but party unity in Germany has not reached the level of cohesion attained in Britain in the 1950s. The period from 1976 to 1980 is particularly interesting because the SPD/FDP Cabinet had only ten seats more than the Christian Democratic opposition did; a defection of only a few representatives from the Cabinet parties could kill bills that the parties' leaders wished to enact. In fact, a handful of left-wing SPD representatives did not hesitate to vote against Cabinet legislation or abstain. As a result, some Cabinet bills squeaked through by only one or two votes, and some were defeated. For example, left-wing SPD representatives were able to kill a bill they felt established too stringent requirements for conscientious objectors.

Such legislative behavior is nothing out of the ordinary in the United States. Until relatively recently, however, it was unheard of in Britain. Thus, the German legislature plays a larger role in the policy-making process than does the British Parliament, both in its voting power and in its thorough examination of bills in committee. One indication of the limits of such activity, however, is the provision in the

Basic Law that the Bundestag may not increase expenditures or taxes beyond what the Cabinet wants. Such a constraint is a key feature of parliamentary systems. Such control over finances has long been exercised by the British Cabinet and was obtained by the French Council of Ministers as France shifted from assembly government to a more balanced parliamentary system.

Calling the Executive to Account

Performing the legislative function is important, but the primary role of the legislature in a parliamentary system is to call the executive to account. As you learned in Chapter 23, the Bundestag does not perform this function at all well in debates on the floor. What about other procedures, particularly those intrinsic to the parliamentary system, as distinct from the separation-of-powers system, for ensuring that the executive power does not go unchecked?

Members of the Bundestag can question ministers at the start of each meeting of that chamber (remember, however, that the Bundestag meets only two or three days a week). Questions need be submitted only three days in advance, and members are limited to three in any week. Supplementary inquiries, however, are in order during the question time. Unfortunately, questions cannot be directed to the Chancellor.

Bundestag procedure provides for a "topical hour." If thirty members so request, the Cabinet must make a statement to the Bundestag on a specific subject. If only fifteen make such a request, the Bundestag votes to see whether a majority favors it. Statements are scheduled immediately after the question period. An hour-long debate, during which each speaker is limited to five minutes, follows a statement.

Furthermore, during regular debates a Bundestag member who disagrees with what a minister is saying to the chamber can be recognized immediately and can take up to twenty minutes explaining why he or she differs. Should a *Fraktion* or any group of twenty-six Bundestag members request it, the chamber's presiding officer can grant "short-talk time," during which those interested in the subject can speak for five minutes each.

Despite such provisions, Bundestag sessions have little give and take between the legislature and the executive. Members continue to complain that ministers make statements to the press and television before informing the Bundestag. Means are still being sought to make more effective the procedures through which ministers have to defend and justify their policies.

Although statements and questions are important elements in calling the executive to account, the distinctive feature of a parliamentary system is the legislature's ability to remove the executive from office for political, as distinct from illicit, actions. This power takes two forms: one for dealing with individual members of the executive, and the other for the executive as a group. These correspond to the doctrines of individual ministerial responsibility and collective responsibility. The former is concerned with shortcomings in administration of existing programs, and the latter relates to questionable policies and goals.

Although the doctrine of individual ministerial responsibility is not as fully elaborated or as well-established in Germany as it is in Britain, instances of this kind of accountability have occurred. A minister of the interior resigned, for example, because of complaints about his ineffectiveness in dealing with domestic terrorists. He accepted responsibility for the failure of the police to respond quickly enough to a tip that might have saved the life of an industrialist who had been kidnapped by terrorists and, eventually, was killed. He also accepted blame for the border police's practice of keeping a list of people who entered Germany carrying copies of left-wing publications.

An even better example of such accountability involved the resignation of a minister of defense. He discovered that military counterintelligence had bugged more telephones than he had stated during a Bundestag debate. Thus, not only had an organization under his direction acted improperly, but he himself had been guilty, admittedly inadvertently, of misinforming the Bundestag. "To protect the armed forces from any harm that might befall them in consequence of political disputes about the incident," he accepted responsibility. Whether a British minister would have adhered so faithfully to the doctrine and resigned in similar circumstances is dubious.

Another instance, however, not only shows that the executive may ignore the doctrine, but also reveals a good deal about Kohl's style of governing. Another defense minister dismissed a German general who was serving as one of NATO's deputy commanders. Information from counterintelligence indicated that the general was a homosexual and possibly a security risk. Eventually this proved to be a matter of mistaken identity. But in the meantime the minister had made incorrect statements and had to admit that he had acted on the basis of unverifiable information. The general was reinstated. Kohl was angry that this debacle made his government look incompetent. Unfortunately for him, not only had he been well informed by the defense minister from the start, but he had not asked a single question about the matter. Kohl rejected the minister's offer to resign. He said that admitting mistakes and apologizing was sufficient. Thus, although accountability was upheld, the penalty for bad administration was hardly harsh.

Yet another defense minister resigned in 1992 for maladministration. The Bundestag had voted an embargo on arms shipments to Turkey because of that country's treatment of its Kurdish minority. The defense minister, nonetheless, permitted a previously scheduled delivery of tanks to occur. When this information leaked out, he gave up his office.

Responsibility for police misdeeds was accepted by the interior minister in July 1993. An elaborately organized stake-out managed to apprehend a highly sought-after terrorist at a small town railway station. So far so good. But the terrorist was shot dead. Not so good. Even worse, the rumors were that a police officer had fired point blank when the terrorist already was in custody and unarmed. Even though the matter was only at the rumor stage, the minister accepted blame and resigned. Although some suggested that the minister had been on the verge of retiring from politics in any event, the way in which he departed did uphold the principle that executive leaders are responsible for misconduct engaged in by their subordinates.

Collective responsibility requires balancing conflicting objectives. On the one hand, the legislature must have the ultimate weapon to dismiss the executive from office to ensure accountability for failed policies and programs. On the other hand, if the legislature is able to eject the executive too easily, then decisive leadership becomes impossible and the government ineffective. The latter situation—executive instability—was regarded as one of the defects of the Weimar Republic. The drafters of the Basic Law, therefore, sought to devise procedures that would more firmly entrench the Chancellor but would not move away from the parliamentary system toward a separation-of-powers system.

The Constructive Vote of No Confidence

The underlying idea of a constructive vote of no confidence is to prevent a negative majority, of, say, the extreme left and the extreme right, from voting the executive out of office, when all they can agree on is their dislike of the existing Cabinet. Therefore, a Chancellor defeated in the Bundestag—even by an absolute majority—is not required to resign. The only way that the Bundestag can force a Chancellor out is to elect a successor by an absolute majority. This forces the executive's opponents to agree on what they want in place of the existing Cabinet before getting rid of it.

Not until April 1972—nearly a quarter of a century into the West German Republic—did a Bundestag attempt to pass a constructive vote of no confidence. Some FDP representatives had defected from the SPD/FDP governing coalition, so the Christian Democrats thought they might be able to oust the SPD Chancellor Brandt. Since the vote was taken by secret ballot rather than by roll call, the Christian Democrats hoped that even more FDP members might defect. But the total for the Christian Democratic leader who was intended to replace Brandt as Chancellor fell two votes short. (Rumors, never substantiated, said that a couple of waverers had been paid not to vote for Brandt's replacement.)

A decade later the Christian Democrats tried again. In 1982 the entire FDP pulled out of the coalition with the SPD. That seemed to make the result of the vote a foregone conclusion, but the outcome was rather close. Since the Bundestag had 497 members, Kohl needed at least 249 votes to replace Schmidt as Chancellor. The vote was 256 for Kohl and 235 for Schmidt, with 4 abstentions. Had all of the FDP members voted solidly with all of the Christian Democrats, Kohl would have had 279 votes. It appears that only 30 FDP members voted for Kohl. The 4 abstainers probably were FDP members. The party's remaining 19 members apparently voted for Schmidt, since his party could have mustered only 216 by itself (2 of its members were ill and unable to participate in the vote). However divided the FDP was over the wisdom of shifting its support from one large party to the other, the constructive vote of no confidence had carried. For the first time in the history of the Federal Republic, a Chancellor had been removed from office by the Bundestag.

These two instances, one successful and one not, are the only times in some four decades that the procedures for a constructive vote of no confidence have been employed.

The other side of the accountability coin is the Chancellor's ability to try to mobilize support for some action by making it an issue of confidence. When this happens, forty-eight hours must elapse before a vote is taken, just as is true for a constructive vote of no confidence. Chancellors have called for such expressions of confidence from the Bundestag on only three occasions, and only one of these was truly for the purpose of mobilizing support. In 1982 Chancellor Schmidt asked for a vote of confidence in support of his policies for combating unemployment. He was trying to whip wavering FDP members into line and did secure a 269 to 226 vote in his favor. But before the year was out, the FDP had withdrawn from the coalition, and the bulk of its representatives had supported the Christian Democrats in the constructive vote of no confidence described above.

The Basic Law provides that if the Chancellor asks for a vote of confidence and fails to obtain an absolute majority, the Chancellor may request the President to dissolve the Bundestag and call an election. This is the only circumstance in which an election can be called before the Bundestag has served its full term. This is why German elections tend to occur regularly at four-year intervals, even though the country has a parliamentary system. (Recall the irregular pattern of British elections.) Unlike the British Prime Minister, the German Chancellor is not free to schedule elections according to when opinion polls indicate that the governing parties have high levels of support among the electorate.

Despite the clear language of the Basic Law that failure to obtain an absolute majority is sufficient to permit a request for elections, the prevailing interpretation has come to be that a Chancellor must actually be defeated in a vote of confidence in order to be allowed to ask the President to dissolve the Bundestag. Although, as we have already explained, the Christian Democrats failed in their attempt to oust Brandt in 1972, the FDP defections did mean that the Cabinet no longer had a majority in the Bundestag. Brandt decided to seek a vote of confidence, deliberately intending to lose, which would entitle him to ask for elections. The danger in this strategy was that the Christian Democrats might elect someone Chancellor before the President had responded to Brandt's request to dissolve the Bundestag; if so, they would gain control of the government. Nonetheless, the SPD risked that action. The party instructed some of its representatives to abstain to ensure that Brandt would be defeated. The Christian Democrats did not attempt to elect one of their members Chancellor before the President could dissolve the Bundestag. Thus, elections were held, and the sixth Bundestag lasted only a little over three years.

After Kohl became Chancellor, the question of premature elections came up again. He wanted popular approval of the actions his Cabinet had been taking since ousting Schmidt. Although the Bundestag had served little more than half its term, Kohl decided that he wanted elections. So in December 1982, for only the third time in the Federal Republic's history, a Chancellor called for a vote of confidence. As Brandt had done a decade earlier, Kohl arranged to lose—the vote was 8 for, 218 against, and 248 abstaining—and asked for elections.

If you have been reading carefully, you will have noticed that we said the Chancellor may request the President to dissolve the Bundestag and call an election. The Basic Law says that the President may do this; it doesn't say that he must. This is another of those ambiguities concerning the President's powers, like the requirement of signing laws.

President Karl Carstens had some doubts about the propriety of what Chancellor Kohl had done (despite the fact that they were from the same party). Brandt's action in 1972 had seemed justifiable because a vote on the budget, always a key element in any Cabinet's program, had produced a tie—247 for and 247 against. Since it was not clear whether Brandt's Cabinet could control the legislature to pass essential bills, elections to resolve a possible stalemate appeared to be in order. In 1982, however, Kohl's Cabinet clearly did control the Bundestag, and his contrived defeat on the motion of confidence was not aimed at resolving a potential deadlock between executive and legislative branches, but solely at calling elections at the time of his preference. Carstens consulted with the leaders of all the parties and, having established that they all favored early elections, did grant Kohl's request to dissolve the Bundestag. Nonetheless, this procedure clearly demonstrated that the President believed he had discretionary power in this matter. In Britain the monarch would have granted a similar request automatically without consulting anyone. British constitutional practice doesn't permit the head of state such discretionary power.

Carstens's decision did not dispose of the issue; four members of the Bundestag took the question to the Federal Constitution Court. In mid-February 1983, as the election campaign was moving into its final stages, the Court dismissed the suit by a vote of six to two. The majority argued, a bit sophistically, that, although deliberately losing a vote was improper, dissent within the FDP was such that the Cabinet could not tell whether its control of the Bundestag was firm. Therefore, Kohl's maneuver was acceptable, and the elections were legal. Whatever the legal merits of the decision, a contrary ruling   which would have called off the elections—would have made the government look ludicrous to the people.

When East Germany collapsed, Kohl argued that the rapid deterioration of its economy required unifying the two Germanys no later than mid-October 1990, holding all-German elections at that time. Since the previous West German elections had been held in January 1987, however, elections weren't due again until early 1991. Given the criticism that he had received for manipulating the election date in 1983 and the uncertainty of how the Federal Constitutional Court might rule on another such maneuver, Kohl was unwilling to instruct his party in the Bundestag to vote against him so that he could lose a vote of confidence. Instead, he asked the SPD to agree to a constitutional amendment that would permit early elections. It refused. As a result, the first unified elections occurred in December, a couple of months *after* formal unification on October 3, 1990. (The shift of a few weeks—from just after Christmas, which would have been exactly four years after the previous elections, to just a few weeks before Christmas—presented no legal problems.) Without going into the details, suffice it to say that this scheduling problem complicated the unification process.

Although the constructive vote of no confidence is intended to insulate the Chancellor and, thereby, ensure Cabinet stability, constitutional provisions—contrary to typical German belief—can't provide absolutely certain results. In 1966 the SPD and the FDP carried a motion in the Bundestag calling on Chancellor Erhard to ask for a vote of confidence. They knew that he would lose such a vote, since the withdrawal of the FDP from the coalition with the Christian Democrats (seems like those folks are always deserting somebody, doesn't it?) meant that he no longer had a majority in the Bundestag. Once Erhard lost the vote, the SPD and the FDP would demand new Bundestag elections, which they expected to win.

Erhard refused to play this game and ignored their motion. Unfortunately for him, however, the Christian Democrats no longer wanted him as Chancellor either. They met and chose a successor. Erhard had no choice but to resign. The Grand

Coalition between the Christian Democrats and the SPD came into office. (So much for the FDP.) Thus, the Chancellor and the political composition of the Cabinet changed by procedures not provided for in the Basic Law.

Even though the procedures for a vote of confidence have been used only three times and those for a constructive vote of no confidence only twice, these provisions have not been unimportant. The entrenched position of the Chancellor has facilitated flexibility in party discipline in the Bundestag. Bills that the Cabinet did not favor have been passed without the Cabinet falling, as might well have occurred under the British parliamentary system. The German system makes quite clear that confidence in the Cabinet and passage of legislation are two separate matters, a distinction the British lost sight of in the 1950s and have begun to recognize again only recently.

The Basic Law does not provide for a motion of censure (legislative initiative), as distinct from a vote of confidence (executive initiative). Nonetheless, in 1977 the Christian Democrats introduced in the Bundestag the first such motion in the history of the Federal Republic. They did not seek a vote on a motion of confidence because they did not believe that they had any chance of defeating Chancellor Schmidt on such a vote. They hoped, however, that a motion of censure could attract a sufficient number of votes from the FDP and from dissident SPD members to pass. This would have embarrassed Schmidt and, perhaps, made him more willing to respond to Christian Democratic views on policies. Whether (as seems unlikely) the Christian Democrats had correctly assessed Schmidt will never be known; the maneuver failed, and the motion was defeated. But note that even had it passed, Schmidt would have continued to serve as Chancellor. Thus, the Basic Law has entrenched the Chancellor well beyond arrangements in the Weimar Republic.

The Legislative Emergency

Little purpose would be served if a Cabinet remained in office while all of its bills were being defeated in the legislature. The Germans have devised a procedure to entrench the Chancellor, but it does nothing to assist in getting the executive's legislative program enacted. If the Bundestag no longer supported the Chancellor but could not agree on a successor, and the Chancellor felt that the political situation made calling an election undesirable, the result would be deadlock. If the Chancellor eventually resigned in frustration, the whole purpose of the constructive vote of no confidence (executive stability) would have been defeated. Yet another special arrangement was needed.

Therefore, Article 81 of the Basic Law provides for a "legislative emergency." (Do not confuse this with the emergency powers given to the Cabinet by the constitutional amendments of the late 1960s, which we discussed earlier.) You can best understand the procedures involved by tracing each line in Figure 24–3 from left to right to ascertain the various outcomes, depending on the choices made.

As you have already learned, if the Cabinet is defeated on a vote in the Bundestag, the Bundestag may select a new Chancellor by an absolute majority. (The line for this action goes up at the left-hand side of the figure and then along the top.) Alternatively, the Cabinet may ask for a vote of confidence on the bill. If it

Figure 24–3
German
Legislative-
Emergency
Procedure

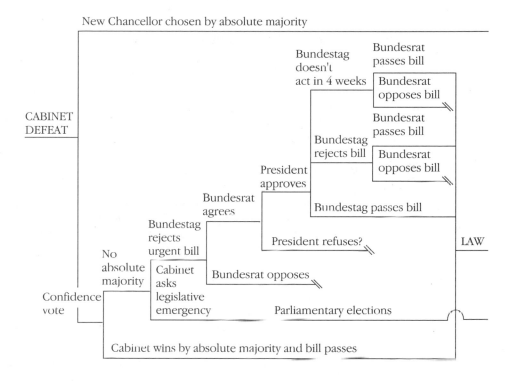

wins an absolute majority, the bill passes the Bundestag and (assuming approval by the Bundesrat) becomes law. Should the Cabinet fail to receive an absolute majority in the vote of confidence, then it may ask for elections. Should it choose not to do so, then Article 81's legislative-emergency provisions become operative.

The Cabinet labels the bill "urgent" in a last attempt to persuade the Bundestag to pass it. If the Bundestag votes against the bill anyway, then the Cabinet may ask the President to declare a legislative emergency. To do so, however requires the Bundesrat's support. Whether the President has any discretion in dealing with the request is another of those ambiguities concerning the powers of the head of state to which we've often referred in this chapter. By saying that the President may declare a legislative emergency, the Basic Law seems to imply that the request could be rejected.

If the President declares a legislative emergency, this allows an obstructionist Bundestag to be bypassed in the legislative process. Any bill that it rejects or fails to act on within four weeks can become law anyway, if the Bundesrat approves it. This means that thirty-five people, a majority of the Bundesrat, can enact a law. The legislative emergency remains in effect for six months unless the Bundestag elects a new Chancellor.

To prevent the abuse of this procedure, the Basic Law provides that another emergency cannot be declared until after legislative elections. Article 81 is intended to be simply a temporary aid; if it fails to solve existing problems in a few months, the voters must be asked to sort matters out between the Chancellor and the

Bundestag. As a further safeguard, the Basic Law cannot be amended, repealed, or suspended during the legislative emergency.

This procedure seems almost painfully convoluted. You need to understand it, however, as part of an attempt to correct the deficiencies of the Weimar Republic so that democracy could survive in Germany. The search for executive stability required some procedure like the constructive vote of no confidence. Since that in turn created a possibility of deadlock, a way out—Article 81—was necessary.

This is a perfect example of what it means to respond legalistically to pressing problems. The drafters of the Basic Law, operating in the context of German political culture, believed that a viable democracy could be produced if the governing law—the constitution—were drawn up properly and contained all the right provisions. Few understood that maintenance of democracy is a political process more than a constitutional or legal one. And this is why Article 81, which was not invoked during the West German Republic's four decades, is likely to remain equally vestigial in the unified Germany.

The important change from the Weimar to the West German Republic was in the party system. The fact that two moderate, near-majority parties emerged meant that the circumstances for which Article 81 was drawn up were unlikely to arise. Deadlocks such as it envisioned might occur in fractionalized party systems (like that of the Weimar Republic), but not in the focused system that developed in the West German Republic, especially given the tradition of strong party discipline and cohesive voting in the legislature. And as you saw in Chapter 23, the first elections in the unified Germany did little to fractionalize the party system that had developed in West Germany.

▪ ▪ ▪

Like France, Germany seems to have solved the traditional European political problem of executive instability without departing from a democratic framework. Interestingly, the two neighbors have achieved this result by contrasting means. France has strengthened that part of the executive that is not responsible to the legislature, whereas Germany has entrenched the part that is. That is, accountability of concentrated power has been given higher priority in Germany than in France. Furthermore, the legislature has not been curtailed as much in Germany as in France. Despite the Adenauer tradition, German Cabinets have had to make concessions at times, have had to seek consensus in support of their programs. Where political development in the two countries has been similar is that change in the party system has been at least as important as institutional reform in explaining the success in dealing with longstanding defects in the political process.

25

Policy-Implementing Structures

Increasing governmental activity in economic and social areas has made administration more vast and complicated in virtually every country. Even apart from this trend, however, administration has long been a significant element in the German political system. The Germans very early established a systematically organized civil service as one of the twin pillars on which the state rested (the other was the army). Administration in Germany differs from that in Britain and France because Germany is a federal system and vests some significant powers in the states.

■ STAFFING AND ORGANIZING THE BUREAUCRACY

The German civil service in the nineteenth century earned the reputation of being competent, incorruptible, and objective. Since recruitment was based on expert training and knowledge and since higher education was generally unavailable to the lower classes, positions in the higher civil service tended to be filled by the sons of the upper classes. Furthermore, civil servants who expressed liberal or democratic views endangered their positions. Consequently, the civil service developed into a conservative, class-based system. But precisely because of their prestigious background, civil servants were looked up to by the general population. The high-level civil servant seemed to typify all that was best in German national character. Added to this was the orderliness of the bureaucratic machinery itself, another quality attractive to most Germans. Thus, in general, the Germans were willing to allow bureaucrats to exercise a great deal of power.

Despite the high esteem civil servants traditionally enjoyed, Germany was the first country in which the government accepted responsibility for wrongful acts by officials while performing their official duties. Part of the reason may have been that state ownership of enterprises occurred earlier in Prussia than in most other countries. The present constitution acknowledges this legal responsibility and authorizes administrative courts, similar to those in France, to deal with such cases.

During the Weimar Republic an attempt was made to liberalize recruitment into the civil service, resulting in some decline in quality. In the Nazi period, civil servants whose loyalty to the new order was questionable were removed, and recruits were vetted carefully. Quality declined still further. Once World War II was over, denazifying and rebuilding the civil service became a major task in West Germany. After the first few postwar years, the general quality and competence of the service improved.

German bureaucracy has been criticized for being unimaginative, authoritarian, and enslaved by routine and rules—charges that do not sound much different from what one hears in most countries about government employees. Traditionally, however, Germans differed from Americans in their views of civil servants. In the United States most people tend to regard the bureaucrat as aloof and to see the politician as the defender of their interests. For Germans the politician was seen as remote and the bureaucrat as sympathetic to the average person's problems. Public opinion in the West German Republic moved, however, in the direction of American beliefs. Germans came to expect more responsive government. The citizen's willingness to challenge the traditionally sacrosanct position of the civil service is one more bit of evidence attesting to the health of contemporary German democracy.

The Current Structure

Bureaucrats in Germany are divided into three basic groups: the higher service, the intermediate service, and the ordinary service. To qualify for the first of these, a person must have a university education and pass an initial exam. Then he or she serves at a lower rank for three years before being eligible to take another exam, which must be passed to enter the higher service. A post in the intermediate service requires a secondary education and three years of probationary service followed by passing of an exam. For the ordinary service, an elementary education, along with a period of apprenticeship, is sufficient to obtain a permanent appointment.

Traditionally, legal training was required of those entering the higher service. Now degrees in economics or political science also are acceptable. Although most recruits are still the sons of either the wealthy or civil servants, the class composition of the bureaucracy has broadened somewhat. The problem is that internal promotion from lower to higher groups is uncommon. Entry into the higher service normally is directly at that level. Only those with the proper education (and the German educational system tends to be biased toward the upper classes) can secure the top positions.

German ministries are headed by political appointees and staffed by permanent civil servants. The political minister in charge usually appoints one state secretary, although some departments have two. The state secretary is the equivalent of the British permanent secretary of a department. Although state secretaries are usually promoted from the ranks of the higher civil service, the Chancellor is permitted to appoint a few without restriction.

The Federal Personnel Committee regulates conditions of employment and appointment for the civil service. Its members are chosen from various branches of the bureaucracy. The civil servants' trade union nominates some of the members. Working closely with the Committee are similar organizations in the states. Special councils exist to deal with grievances. Although civil servants may belong to trade unions, they have no right to strike.

Every political system must decide what level of political activity is appropriate for government employees. The constraints imposed and the reasons for them vary considerably from one country to another. In the United States civil servants' political activity is limited to protect them from venal politicians, who otherwise would force civil servants, by the threat of loss of their jobs, to contribute time and money to the politicians' reelection campaigns. The British, as you saw in Part Two, also constrain bureaucrats' political activity, but not because they fear abuse by politicians. Their concern is the possibility that civil servants who disliked the politicians' party might sabotage its policies. British civil servants are required to be neutral politically so that they can be trusted to serve whatever party currently is in power.

Continental European systems follow another pattern for yet other reasons. In those countries civil servants are commonly believed to be better educated and more intelligent than politicians and, therefore, naturally should run the country. German civil servants are permitted, indeed, almost encouraged, to be active in politics, even as candidates for national office. They may pursue a political career without having to resign from their administrative position. If they are elected to the Bundestag, they simply take a leave of absence. After a period of legislative service, they are reinstated in the civil service. Constraints on seeking local or state elective offices are even more minimal. Since civil servants turned politicians are quite likely to return to the bureaucracy, they tend to maintain their links with colleagues continuing to hold administrative posts.

In the early years of the West German Republic, the boundary between politician and civil servant was further blurred by some ministers' practice of sending bureaucrats to address the Bundestag in their place or to respond for them during the question period. Administrators were brought into executive decision making so extensively that at times they were instructed to sign unpopular regulations, thus allowing politicians to avoid seeming responsible for them. Such deliberately fostered confusion undermined accountability.

Partly as a result of the negotiations that produced the Grand Coalition, the situation was improved. A new post of parliamentary state secretary was created in the larger ministries. Those appointed to this office had to be members of the Bundestag. Their role was similar to that of junior ministers in Britain. By standing in for ministers during question time, for example, they strengthened the concept of the political executive's accountability to the legislature. This reform also helped career civil servants to become more like permanent secretaries in Britain by sparing them from having to be involved visibly in partisan politics.

The Extremists' Decree

Orthodox political activity by German civil servants supporting mainstream parties may be permitted or even encouraged, but those holding less acceptable political views encounter a very different situation. In 1972 the West German government and the heads of the states agreed on a standard procedure to keep extremists out of government jobs. Some might approve of that goal, but the way in which it was pursued stirred controversy.

The Extremists' Decree established a national office, the Office for Protection of the Constitution, to screen applicants for government jobs. State governments would inquire of the Office whether its files had information on the political activities of people who had applied for civil service positions. The stringency with which the decree was implemented varied from one state to another, with states controlled by the Christian Democrats tending to be most zealous. Bavaria, home of the CSU, averaged nearly 25,000 inquiries a year during the 1970s.

The type of information gathered and the conclusions drawn from it often were highly questionable. Applicants for teaching positions in one state were questioned because they rented rooms in the same house as a Communist. Elsewhere applicants for government jobs were questioned for having stood on a left-wing ticket in university student elections, for having handed out political leaflets, and for signing a candidate's nomination papers. After a person was interviewed about what the authorities regarded as questionable activity, months would pass before any notice was received of whether government employment would be permitted. Because the range of occupations considered to be civil service jobs is considerably broader in Germany than in the United States, a large number of people were affected by the Extremists' Decree. Not only were teachers subject to the procedure, but also people such as railway and postal employees. (Do you really care whether the person driving the train on which you are riding is a Communist?)

Only a few hundred people actually were denied employment under this screening program, and even fewer were dismissed from jobs they already held. Nonetheless, the thought of a government agency keeping extensive files on citizens' political activities (most of which were obviously innocuous) is disquieting. Injustices clearly were done. The teachers' union complained about arbitrary administration of the decree. Late in the 1980s the International Labor Organization said that the procedure was discriminatory and violated one of its conventions on rights of public employees.

By that time the issue had become almost moot. Part of the reason the decree had been issued was that the SPD was trying to defend itself from Christian Democratic attacks of being soft on communism. Eventually, however, the excesses of the procedure forced the SPD to admit that it had overreacted. States controlled by the SPD began to indicate that they no longer would routinely refer applications for government employment to the Office for Protection of the Constitution. Finally, even a CDU-controlled state adopted such a policy. When the program was in full swing, however, it had a negative effect on free discussion, especially among young people, in particular those at the universities. In the eyes of many future opinion leaders, the democratic state lost a good deal of legitimacy from such illiberal actions.

The rights of government "employees" of another type have been better protected. When the West German army was established, the post of defense commissioner was created. The Bundestag elects a commissioner to investigate all complaints about possible violations of the basic rights of soldiers or of the principles of internal leadership in the military forces. The commissioner, who has access to pertinent papers and other necessary information, is intended to serve as a watchdog, guarding against the development of antidemocratic sentiments in the military. On several occasions the commissioner has alerted the Bundestag to practices that needed to be eliminated.

■ THE ROLE OF THE STATES IN NATIONAL ADMINISTRATION

As you have seen, civil servants in Germany are found in a broad range of occupations. Teacher, railway conductor, meter reader—all of these are considered employees and, therefore, representatives of the state. Even more significant, instead of being way off somewhere in the capital city, most administrators are nearby and in regular contact with the people.

Unlike France and Britain, Germany is a federal system. Federalism not only divides powers between the central and constituent units of government, but also prohibits either of the two levels from altering this division without the assent of the other. As we mentioned in Chapter 23, some powers belong exclusively to the German central government. Residual, or reserve, powers are retained by the states. These are relatively few, and the most important concern education and cultural affairs. The great bulk of governmental powers are concurrent; that is, either the central or the state governments can legislate on these matters. Should their regulations conflict, then the central government's laws take precedence.

Although the states can levy some taxes, they have little significant financial resources of their own. As we mentioned in Chapter 20, a tax equalization system was established in 1969. The central government enacts tax legislation and raises the bulk of public finances. These monies then are divided between the central government and the states. Finally, yet another allocation is made among the states to help ensure that even the poorest states can operate essential programs at acceptable standards. The costs of unification imposed considerable strains on the German economy and required extensive negotiations throughout the system on a program of action. The poorer states in the western part of Germany were concerned that burgeoning aid to the east would sharply reduce their funds. Negotiations focused on the VAT, since it offered the greatest flexibility for change. The package finally agreed on early in 1993 shifted the allocation of VAT revenues from 63 percent to the central government and 37 percent to the state governments to 56 percent and 44 percent, respectively.

A couple of examples illustrate the important policy decisions that can be made at the state level. Immediately after World War II the state government of Bavaria took into government ownership a number of private enterprises in order to be able to coordinate recovery efforts. Among these were energy holdings. As a result Bavaria was able to develop a sizable nuclear energy program and obtain an inexpensive source of energy that bolstered its prosperity for many years. By the 1990s the availability of cheap energy from other sources made energy holdings by the government less crucial. Furthermore, economic problems gave new urgency to the hunt for monetary resources. To avoid increasing taxes or borrowing funds, the Bavarian government announced that it would sell to private investors over $1 billion worth of the enterprises it owned. Interestingly, in light of the controversies you have seen in France and Britain about such action, the SPD indicated that it would not oppose privatization.

In the former East Germany a special agency has been created by the German central government to dispose of the huge number of enterprises that the Communist government had owned. Since these had belonged to the central government, the states themselves have nothing to sell. They have had to be creative in seeking to raise additional funds. The government of the state of Mecklenburg–Western Pomerania, for example, has announced that it will welcome foreign *private* investment in water and sewage utilities and in the housing and tourist industries. That is, a British company, for example, could be providing water for a profit in part of eastern Germany.

Such instances help to refute the position sometimes argued that the central government is granted such broad powers that Germany is little more than a quasi-federal system. Furthermore, evaluating German federalism solely on the basis of the constitutional allocation of power is misleading. The German states play a much more significant role in administering laws passed by the central government than do the states in the United States. And administrators in the states enjoy a fair amount of discretion in implementing these laws. The law, after all, is not so much how the statute reads on the books, but what the actual practice of implementing and enforcing it is. The administrative role of the German states is sufficiently significant to offset any skewed allocation of power; this is the sphere of activity that gives vitality to federalism in Germany.

Most civil servants are employed by a state or local government, not the central government. Not counting defense, railways, and the post office, the central government employs only about a tenth of all civil servants in Germany. About a third work for local government, with more than half being employed by the states.

Ministries of the German central government have little administrative machinery of their own. Ministry staffs number only about 100,000, of which about a tenth are in the higher service. The central ministries have an important role in coordinating administration, but the implementing of laws is left to the bureaucracy of the states. This is more than traditional practice; the constitution requires it. The states "execute the federal laws as matters of their own concern insofar as this Basic Law does not otherwise provide or permit." The central ministries devote attention primarily to drafting uniform legislation and seeing that administrative practices of the states conform with statutes and the Basic Law. The central offices of a ministry are usually rather small. Many of the relatively limited number of staff that a ministry does employ will be stationed in supervisory offices in the major German cities.

You will recall from Chapter 23 that members of the Bundesrat serve in both legislative (central) and executive (state) branches of government. They participate in the legislative process at the central level, while also exercising executive authority in their respective states. Given the structure of German bureaucracy, they oversee implementation of not only the laws passed by their state legislature, but also those passed by the central legislature. Thus, they are responsible for administering laws that they themselves have helped to pass or, alternatively, have voted unsuccessfully to defeat.

Stressing the importance of the states in administering the law should help to allay concern about excessive centralization, but what about excessive diversity? How can any national standards be established if state governments of contrasting views have to be relied on to implement national policy? How can conflict between national and state goals be resolved? (Think about how naive the central government of the United States would have been to have left the racial integration of the public schools in the hands of the relevant state officials in many Southern states.)

The German central government can send its agents to investigate the quality of state administration. If deficiencies are found, the central government can demand improvement and compliance. Doing so, however, requires the consent of the Bundesrat. Similarly, the central government is empowered to issue administrative regulations that are binding on state administrators. This also requires Bundesrat approval, which means that at least half of the state governments must agree. Thus, recalcitrant states can be required to comply with national policy, but only when half of their counterparts support the policy. Given the ample opportunity for input from the states into the legislative process of the national government, as discussed in Chapter 23, conflict over administrative matters rarely comes to this point. Thus, when both administrative and legislative responsibilities are considered, Germany seems to have struck a viable balance between unity and diversity. Excessive centralization has been avoided, but not at the cost of impeding effective action on public problems.

26

The Judicial Structure

The German judicial system follows a pattern typical on the Continent, a pattern you have already seen in France. The law is code law rather than case law, although precedent has become increasingly important in Germany. The judiciary tends to be more closely identified with the state than in either Britain or the United States. Anglo-American courts are expected to protect the individual from harmful public or private action. In Germany, as in other countries on the Continent, the courts tend to be seen instead as dispensers of justice, ensuring that justice is done from the standpoint of society as a whole, with less concern about the individual's welfare. Finally, as we discussed in Part Three, court procedure under the Roman law system differs from Anglo-American practices.

■ JUDGES AND COURT ORGANIZATION

Although Germany did not become a democratic state until after World War I, the German courts gained considerable independence as early as the first quarter of the nineteenth century. Offsetting this was the fact that judges were drawn from the conservative strata of society, since judicial positions were open only to university graduates (typically those with law degrees). As a result, the German judiciary was of little help in protecting the Weimar Republic from Nazi violations of law and order and seemed only too willing to enforce the Nazis' regulations once they had attained power. Such attitudes were a cause for concern when the West German Republic was being established, but few charges were subsequently heard about lingering extreme-right sympathies of judges.

Judges are recruited from among those law school graduates who decide not to be attorneys. After spending three or four years in probationary and preparatory service, the recruits take an examination. At both the national and the state level, ministers of justice, assisted by nominating committees chosen by the legislatures, make the appointments. Thus, being a judge is a career that one chooses early in life, rather than coming to it at middle age after years of private law practice, as is the pattern in the United States. Judges do not have a set term—they hold their positions unless they are found to have engaged in misconduct. They are supervised by the Ministry of Justice, but can be removed only by their fellow judges through procedures regulated by law.

As in France, judges in Germany dominate court proceedings. In contrast to the American idea of providing a fair forum in which contending parties can fight out their differences, judicial proceedings in Germany are aimed at ascertaining the truth. The rules of evidence are relatively flexible; whether evidence is admitted or excluded turns not so much on fairness to the case being argued as on whether the evidence advances the search for truth.

Pretrial investigations are common. During this period an accused person is seldom released on bail, although the detention is reviewed periodically. Defendants who ultimately are acquitted may seek indemnification for their pretrial detention.

A system of financial aid seeks to make justice available to everyone, regardless of personal finances. Based on one's monthly income, one may be able to take a case to court without having to pay for a lawyer—public funds foot the bill. Assistance also is provided so that low-income citizens can obtain legal advice, regardless of whether they pursue a case in court.

Although Germany is a federal system, its state and national court systems do not parallel and partially overlap each other, as is true in the United States. There is a single integrated system of regular courts. The three lower levels of this system are all state courts. These courts try cases under national laws as well as under state laws. In other words, just as the national government uses state bureaucrats to administer national law, it uses state judges to adjudicate national law. As a result, virtually all cases in Germany start in a state court.

This arrangement raises the same question we addressed in Chapter 25: how can any uniform national policy be implemented when there is such provision for diversity? First, the top-level courts are agencies of the national government. Beyond that, all courts are regulated by national codes, both as to procedure and as to the bulk of the substantive law that they apply. Moreover, all legal judgments and instruments (documents) are applicable throughout the country. This helps to produce greater uniformity in the law throughout the country than is true in the United States.

At the bottom of the judicial hierarchy are the local courts. In smaller locales a single judge hears all types of small civil suits and minor criminal actions. In larger towns the local court is likely to be divided into specialized sections, each presided over by a different judge. Whatever the arrangement, a judge is assisted by two lay assessors; for some criminal matters, a second judge is added. The lay assessors are chosen by lot from lists of local inhabitants, but an American-type jury is not used.

Above the local courts are the district, or provincial, courts. These have both original and appellate jurisdiction; that is, some cases begin at this level, and others are appealed from the local courts. District courts are divided into various sections. One civil section deals with appeals, and another with cases being heard for the first time because they were too serious to start in the local courts. On the criminal side there are two appeals sections (little chamber and big chamber) and two original jurisdiction sections (big chamber and assize court). The assize court tries the serious cases, such as murder. Except for the little chamber, which has one judge and two lay assessors, each of the district courts is presided over by three judges. In both of the big chambers, two lay assessors assist the judges. The assize court uses a six-member jury, which votes jointly with the three judges. Although the majority rules in deciding the disposition of the case, the judges tend to exercise a dominant influence.

The superior courts are divided into a civil and a criminal section. The civil section, presided over by three judges, reviews the judgments of district courts and may alter them. The criminal section at this level is also divided into a little chamber and a big chamber; the former has three judges and the latter five. Neither chamber tries cases. The judges simply consider disputed points of law. Should their decision necessitate a retrial, they order a lower court to conduct it.

Decisions of the superior courts may be appealed to the Federal High Court, which has approximately 100 judges. The Minister of Justice, in association with legal officials from the states and an equal number of members from the Bundestag, selects them. The Court is divided into a number of sections, some for criminal cases and some for civil; each section is presided over by five judges. Most of the Court's work is appeals; it must review all cases submitted to it. Its major function is to ensure uniformity of legal interpretation throughout the states. In addition, the Court has original jurisdiction over some crimes, for example, treason. Even though such cases will have been tried only once, the Federal High Court is the court of last resort, unless a constitutional issue is raised. Only in that instance can there be an appeal to the Federal Constitutional Court (discussed in the next section).

As in France, the government in Germany accepts liability for the wrongful acts of its officials while performing their official duties. Unlike the French practice, claims against individual officials, as well as salary disputes and other pecuniary claims of civil servants, all go to the ordinary courts in Germany. Judgments, however, are directed against the state and not against the offending officials.

The separate administrative courts that exist in Germany are reserved for claims against public agencies and conflicts among them. The German administrative court system is extremely elaborate and complex. Special courts concentrate on such matters as labor relations, commercial disputes, tax questions, and social security cases. Because of the large number of pension cases, Germany has forty-nine social welfare courts organized at three levels. Tax courts exist at two levels: at the regional level there are eleven to hear cases originally, and at the national level there is the Federal Financial Court for appeals.

Perhaps the most important elements in this system are the general-purpose administrative courts. These are intended to protect citizens against government officials who the citizens feel are infringing on their rights by arbitrary or unfair action or by refusing to act. The system consists of thirty-one administrative courts, ten superior administrative courts for appeals, and the Federal Administrative Court to hear cases involving the constitution.

A citizen with a complaint appeals first to the agency responsible for the action or inaction. If the response is not satisfactory and fails to settle the matter, then he or she may go to an administrative court. At neither the original nor the appellate level is a lawyer needed; the citizen can argue his or her own case. Only in the Federal Administrative Court must lawyers be used.

Since at times citizens may learn about administrative actions only when it is too late for satisfactory redress, government agencies must warn citizens. That is, whenever some intended action might infringe on citizen rights, the agency planning to act must tell the citizens of this and point out that they have a right to protest. Failure of the agency to do so can be sufficient grounds for an administrative court to void governmental action.

The matters dealt with by the administrative courts do not involve abstract rights or fundamental civil liberties so much as they concern people's day-to-day relations with the government. Whether somebody gets a liquor license or a building permit is not a basic question of democracy. Yet such matters are important to the individuals involved, and fair treatment by the government is a right. The administrative court system helps Germans fight the government on a more equal basis and defend themselves from arbitrary action.

■ BASIC RIGHTS AND THE CONSTITUTIONAL COURT

Remembering what had happened to their basic rights under the Nazis, the Germans were anxious to provide all possible legal safeguards against losing them again. The first section of the Basic Law, consisting of nineteen articles, deals in detail with the people's rights. The Basic Law declares that the "dignity of man is inviolable" and that it is the "duty of all state authority" to "respect and protect it." The enumerated basic rights are said to "bind the legislature, the executive and the judiciary."

Elsewhere the Basic Law forbids extraordinary courts, double jeopardy, and retroactive laws. The right of *habeas corpus* is also preserved; the police may not hold a person longer than the end of the day following arrest unless he or she is charged with a crime. The judge's decision in a *habeas corpus* proceeding is subject to appeal to higher courts. Also, provision is made against mental and physical ill treatment of detained persons. And due process and the equal protection of the laws are declared to be part of the constitutional order.

On the other hand, aware that both the Nazis and the Communists used fundamental rights during the Weimar Republic to subvert democracy and destroy those rights, the framers of the Basic Law sought to shield the political system from abuse of freedom. The goal was to strike a balance between liberty and license. Article 9 prohibits associations whose aims and activities violate criminal laws or are directed against the constitutional order. Article 18 provides that "whoever abuses freedom of expression of opinion, in particular freedom of the press, freedom of teaching, freedom of assembly, freedom of association, the secrecy of mail, posts and telecommunications, the right of property, or the right of asylum, in order to attack the free democratic basic order, forfeits these basic rights."

To defend basic liberties and determine how far they may be employed without subverting the system that guarantees them, the Germans readily gave in to American insistence on judicial review, despite lacking any tradition of such power for their courts. On the other hand, despite the arbitrary actions of the Nazi regime, German political culture long has valued the supremacy of the law. That value foundation could be built on when the Basic Law established a Federal

Constitutional Court and when the states created similar courts to consider the validity of state legislation.

The Federal Constitutional Court is empowered to rule on petitions by the Cabinet or the Bundestag that a political party be banned because it seeks to overthrow the established democratic order. This power has been used to outlaw various neo-Nazi and Communist groups over the years. The Court also has ruled, however, that a person cannot be punished for membership in or service to a banned party at the time before it was declared illegal.

The Court consists of two panels of eight judges each. To be eligible for appointment, one must be at least forty and of proven legal ability. One need not have had a career as a judge; a legal degree is sufficient. Judges have been the most common appointees to the Court but comprise fewer than half of the appointees. Civil servants, professors, and lawyers are the other principal groups from which members of the Court are recruited.

The Minister of Justice maintains a list of potential nominees. Included are the top judges, along with others suggested by the Cabinet, state executives, or a party in the Bundestag. As vacancies occur on the Court—the judges serve for twelve years and cannot be reappointed—the Bundesrat and the Bundestag alternate in selecting a replacement from the list of nominees. In the Bundestag the decision is made by a twelve-member committee having the same partisan composition as the chamber itself. Eight votes are required to appoint a judge. Given its smaller size, the Bundesrat as a whole makes the choice. A two-thirds vote is required.

The appointment procedure provides another interesting contrast between German and American federalism. The state governments are involved in the process well beyond the role of the states in the United States. They can suggest nominees and half the time, through their representatives in the Bundesrat, actually appoint the judges on the Court. As is true of the U.S. Supreme Court, one of the duties of the Federal Constitutional Court is to settle disputes between the central and state governments. The states have an opportunity to defend what they conceive to be their vital interests in these conflicts by selecting judges sympathetic to states' rights. This is not to suggest that Federal Constitutional Court judges are biased. But, obviously, the way in which one judge interprets and applies a constitution differs from how another does so—some are strict constructionists and others are more liberal. The German states, because of their role in the selection process, have less reason than American states do to regard the country's highest court as a hostile agency of another level of government. The Federal Constitutional Court seems more like an impartial arbiter.

One panel, or senate, of the Court deals with questions of violation of civil liberties and constitutional rights; the other hears all the other types of cases. Examples of these are conflicts between two or more states or between a state and the central government. Even though the first senate deals with only one type of case, it has had the heavier work load.

The Court has three types of jurisdiction: concrete jurisdiction, abstract jurisdiction, and constitutional complaint. Under concrete jurisdiction the Court considers an actual case that raises a question of constitutionality. This is what the U.S. Supreme Court does. If a case in the regular court system involves a claim that the

Basic Law has been violated, then the case goes to the Federal Constitutional Court. (If it is claimed that a state constitution has been violated, then the case goes to the constitutional court of that state.)

Under abstract jurisdiction the Court can rule on a constitutional question when no actual case has been presented to it. As we noted in the discussion of the form of judicial review practiced in France, this kind of jurisdiction has been rejected by the U.S. Supreme Court. In Germany the Cabinet, a state cabinet, or one-third of the total membership of the Bundestag can request that the Court rule on the constitutional validity of a law before it is implemented or, if it is already in effect, before any case questioning it has arisen. Our comments in Chapter 17 on the appropriateness of this procedure in a code law system are relevant here as well. Unfortunately, whichever party is in opposition in the Bundestag has tended to use the Court's abstract jurisdiction as a partisan maneuver. When legislation passes that a party strongly opposes, it seeks to thwart the majority by displacing the political conflict into the legal arena and asking the Court to invalidate the law. German experience with abstract jurisdiction suggests that the U.S. Supreme Court made a wise decision in forgoing such rulings.

Constitutional complaint is similar to abstract jurisdiction, but broader in scope. Anyone in Germany can challenge any law on the grounds that it infringes rights guaranteed by the Basic Law. There are no court costs for this procedure; the challenger does not even need to hire a lawyer. In Germany when someone says "I'll fight it all the way to the Supreme Court," it is not the idle threat it often is in the United States.

Constitutional complaints account for the great bulk of the matters brought to the Federal Constitutional Court. Thousands are filed every year. When a complaint is made, the law in question is suspended and not enforced until the Court disposes of the matter. Given the Germans' litigious nature, the procedure would get totally out of hand unless some limits were imposed. Typically, a case based on constitutional complaint must go through the regular court system before getting to the Court. Furthermore, a screening committee of the Court can reject a case. The committee does not examine the evidence, but simply checks whether due process was observed and whether the decision of a lower court conformed with constitutional principles. About 98 percent of the constitutional complaints are not heard by the Court, having been rejected for lack of legal merit.

Despite the effort to make the work load of constitutional complaints manageable, the Court still gets cases that by any reasonable standards would seem to be ruled out by the principle *de minimis non curat lex* ("the law is not concerned with trifles"). For example, a man fined $20 for riding his bicycle through a pedestrian zone complained to the Court on the grounds that not all available witnesses had been called to testify. (As a result, the Court raised the limit for the complaints that it would accept to those involving a fine of $30 or more.) A pet owner complained that his constitutional rights had been violated when the city of Hamburg doubled the annual tax on dogs to $90. Some people think the Court gets so many complaints because lawyers collect $190 for filing them, regardless of their merits.

About 1.5 percent of all the complaints filed have resulted in the overturning of a law, regulation, or previous court decision. To that extent, rights that would have been infringed in some way have been protected. And some of the cases have been far from trivial. In 1983, on the complaint of two lawyers, the Court prohibited the national census only two weeks before it was to have been taken. The Court agreed with their contention that insufficient safeguards had been provided to prevent data abuse. The danger was that individual rights to privacy could be violated because the census form was so constructed that each person providing data could be specifically identified. A census was eventually conducted with a revised form in 1987, seventeen years after the last previous census.

At various points in the preceding chapters, we have noted important decisions of the Court, so we don't need to examine a long list of cases here. A couple of additional significant decisions, however, deserve mention. In 1983 Kohl's Cabinet had carried a so-called forced loan through the legislature. Single taxpayers earning more than about $16,000 and couples earning more than about $32,000 were required to pay a surtax of 5 percent on the tax due the government through 1985. This sum would be repaid to them in 1990 without interest. The aim was to raise funds for a program of housing construction intended to stimulate the economy. The Court ruled that no constitutional basis for such a surtax existed. The government was forced to stop collecting the surtax and to reimburse taxpayers for the more than $600 million it had already collected. Clearly, the Court was unwilling to authorize governmental action simply on the basis of a laudatory goal.

Some of you may have been waiting in suspense for us to fulfill the promise made in previous chapters to tell what the Court did on abortion. The problem, you recall, was caused by unification—Germany needed a law to replace the stringent West German and permissive East German ones. Of course, matters could have been left as they were. In the United States the Supreme Court simply tells a state if it has gone too far in prohibiting abortion; it does not impose precisely the same regulations everywhere. As a result abortions are more easily obtained in some states than in others. And, yes, if you want an abortion, you can travel from one part of the United States to another in search of the least restrictive regulations. That is the whole point of federalism: a country with a great deal of diversity doesn't try to formulate common policy on all matters; it leaves some issues or some parts of some issues to local preferences. Although Germany is a federal system, such legal diversity doesn't sit well with German political culture. The law, you recall, is supposed to be the product of legal expertise, not a matter of politics. Therefore, it should be the same everywhere. That is why, for example, that all of a state's votes in the Bundesrat must be cast as a single block. It is inconceivable to Germans that a state could have more than a single political will. So a common, national abortion policy it would be.

We saw in Chapter 23 that the efforts of the Christian Democratic Government to obtain stringent regulation were defeated, in part because some of its party colleagues broke ranks to vote with the opposition. In August 1992, therefore, 247 Christian Democratic members of the Bundestag (about three-quarters of the total Christian Democratic representation) sought an injunction. The Federal Constitutional Court ordered that the law could not go into effect until its constitutionality was determined. In May 1993 the Court ruled by a vote of six to two that both the permissive former East German law and the new law enacted by the unified German legislature were unconstitutional. Furthermore, no state funding could be provided for women seeking abortion. The only positive aspect for pro-choice advocates was the Court's ruling that abortion was not criminal. Presumably neither the doctor performing an abortion nor the woman obtaining one would be prosecuted. Although not criminal, abortion can be regulated. An emergency abortion to save a woman's life would appear to be one of the few instances in which it would be acceptable. Poor women, in particular, would have considerable difficulty finding anyone to perform an abortion under proper medical procedures. Consider that in 1991 in the former East Germany there had been 32 abortions for every 100 live births. It had turned out just as many in East Germany had feared. In this one area, East German women had less freedom after unification than they had had before.

You will recall our mentioning in Chapter 22 the issue of the international use of German troops. In 1993 the Federal Constitutional Court declined to issue an injunction to bar German service in UN actions related to the former Yugoslavia. In a separate case it ruled that German forces weren't prevented by the constitution from participating in the humanitarian aid efforts in Somalia. Given the volatile nature of events in these two areas, further litigation seemed likely. Clearly, the Federal Constitutional Court will continue to have a significant voice in German policy making.

▪ ▪ ▪

Defense of rights and liberties cannot be left solely to the courts; parties have an important role to play as well. At times those controlling the government, in their efforts to strike a balance between liberty and license, seem to have gone too far in trying to defend against those who might subvert liberty. The Extremists' Decree discussed in Chapter 25 is one such instance. Another is the Kohl Cabinet's measure against protesters. Reacting to peace and antimissile demonstrators, the Cabinet sought a change in the law to permit arrest of passive onlookers at demonstrations who failed to disperse when told to do so by the police. This change not only would have curtailed the right to move about in public, but also would have abridged freedom of assembly. The FDP did manage to get added to the law a provision that anyone arrested for failing to disperse could avoid conviction by proving that he or she had been trying to calm the demonstrators. Although this made the law a bit less harsh, it also shifted the burden of proof from the government to the individual, who had to prove that he or she was exempt from the penalty, rather than the government's having to prove that the individual should be subject to it.

Clearly, a constitutional court cannot always guarantee that liberties will be protected. But it can play a major role in educating the public to the importance of basic freedoms and in providing them with a means of defense when the government goes too far in trying to control those it fears might be a threat to liberty. It can contribute significantly to establishing a tradition of liberal democracy and a conviction that citizens are entitled to exercise their basic rights. To secure these goals, the Federal Constitutional Court is willing to listen—even to citizens who want to complain about the doubling of a dog license fee.

27

Contemporary Trends in German Politics: Der Führer, der Alte, und der Tunix

Of the three countries we have examined so far, the one that faced the greatest challenges after World War II was Germany. Britain had to endure a period of austerity, rationing, and controls. By the mid-1950s, however, prosperity had returned and Britons soon could be told that they never had it so good. France had to repress memories not only of defeat by Germany, but also of collaboration with the occupiers. Once the facts of some heroic harassment of the Nazis had been transformed into the myth of The Resistance, the French could enjoy an economic boom just as did the British. Both countries did go through a few rough years, but this was as nothing compared to Germany. So total was the destruction in Germany that the period sometimes is referred to as "ground zero." The Germans truly had to start from scratch. As a result, they had no choice but to install the most modern equipment and employ the most up-to-date productive methods. These, along with American aid and German hard work, soon made the country an economic powerhouse.

Perhaps there is a simile here for governmental affairs. Given its centuries-old parliamentary traditions, Britain saw no need for reform. France needed to return to the republican tradition as part of the effort to obliterate the shame and sorrow of Vichy's collaboration. In both countries, so far as the governmental structures were concerned, it was a return to business as usual. In Germany, however, the Third Reich had been repudiated, and the Weimar Republic was seen as a grievous failure; there was nothing to which to return. Germany had to start from scratch politically as well as economically.

And yet, Germany did not really start from scratch politically, any more than it did economically. The Germans had the productive skills and experiences that enabled them to resuscitate the economy. They also had certain political traditions and values. This political culture, along with the restraints imposed by the Western Allies, produced what became the West German Republic, which four decades later absorbed the East German system to become the current Germany. Taking account of all these factors—diverse views among the Allies, political culture, recent historical experience—resulted in a system more complex and intricate than that of either

France or Britain. Underlying the process was the traditional German belief that what really matters is the legal structure. If only they could get that right, they would avoid the errors of the past.

As German democracy approaches its half century, the Germans might say, "You see how correct we were? We did get it right this time and look at what we have accomplished." Such an argument, however, is much too simple. You have seen in Britain and France, as well as in Germany, how crucial the party system is to the operation of any governmental structure. If the Weimar Republic's party system had continued in West Germany after World War II, all bets for four decades of success would have been off. The party system, in turn, certainly is affected by electoral arrangements, which may not be spelled out in a country's framework document, but which are sufficiently basic to be considered constitutional. Think where the German FDP would be likely to be under the British electoral system and where the British Liberal Democrats would be under the German electoral system—how different the party system of each country would be in that case. Important as the electoral laws are, however, party systems are most fundamentally shaped by the behavior and values of the electorate. Yes, the 5-percent barrier helped to keep extremist parties out of the West German Bundestag. But the unwillingness of the electorate to vote for extremists in anything more than derisory numbers did even more.

Nor can constitutional arrangements be the primary explanation for a system's success or failure because they don't take account of leadership. When the British system began to run into serious problems in the later 1960s and on into the 1970s, few people suggested that constitutional reform was the solution. The remedy the public clearly preferred was a new-style leader. Thus in the 1980s Britain had a decade of Thatcherism. Some of the changes she brought did alter the *nature* of British politics; she did not, however, change the *structure* of the British political system. The most that can be said is that her period in office stimulated more debate about the British constitution than had occurred for about three-quarters of a century. Whether this will result in some constitutional change remains to be seen. (Molasses flows more rapidly in January than governmental reform moves in Britain.)

France, given its many constitutions during the last two centuries, always has been more willing than Britain to inject constitutional issues into political debate. Furthermore, after World War II France ran into fundamental problems sooner than Britain did. At home France experienced what Americans would call gridlock, and this produced setbacks abroad that many French people felt dishonored and disgraced their nation. Thus, twenty years before Britain felt compelled to do so, France sought a new-style leader. Even though this resulted in a fundamental constitutional change, the resulting constitution was tailor-made for the leader and was little more than a means of cloaking whatever actions he wished to take with some vestment of legitimacy.

This is not to dismiss constitutions as trivial; they do matter. The ability of Charles de Gaulle's successors to operate "his" constitution effectively is evidence that the institutional arrangements have validity beyond his mere whim. And yet it was de Gaulle's near decade in power that demonstrated how the constitution was to operate. He established, for example, a template for the role of the President to which his diverse successors have seemed compelled to conform.

So both Britain and France, two countries of markedly different histories and political cultures, have felt the need in the post–World War II period for "personalism." The solution to fundamental problems was Thatcherism and Gaullism—political leadership. What, then, of Germany? The Germans found themselves in the late 1940s in far worse circumstances than those of France a decade later or of Britain two decades after that. And yet apparently in this branch of the European experience, the choice was a new legal structure, entrusting to a constitutional document the hope for salvation.

Ponder Germany's uniquely difficult circumstances. Americans can refer to President Clinton as their leader, Britons can call John Major theirs. Do you realize that a German can't say something like that? The German word for leader is *führer*—a taboo word if there ever was one. To term someone a leader in Germany is tantamount to saying that he or she is like Adolf Hitler! That is enough to put anyone off "personalism."

In German politics there is no term comparable to Gaullism and Thatcherism. And yet even Germany had its crucial leader. Just as much as de Gaulle was the father of the Fifth Republic, so Konrad Adenauer was the father of the West German Republic. If de Gaulle was the only person who could have held his country together at a time of crisis, so Adenauer provided precisely the type of leadership needed in postwar Germany. Just as de Gaulle was able to employ his personal magnetism to institutionalize reforms (despite his despairing of having done so), so Adenauer's style of leadership was needed to establish the new West German system.

Adenauer had been an active politician during the Weimar Republic. Given the authoritarian hiatus of the Third Reich, he was already in his early seventies when he became West Germany's first Chancellor. Since it was at this age that he achieved prominence, it is impossible to visualize Adenauer as a young man. He seems almost to have been born at age sixty-five. Germans nicknamed him *der Alte*—"the old guy." Both Thatcher and de Gaulle had about a decade in power to impress their values on their country's political system. Adenauer served as Chancellor for fourteen years. And those years would have to be regarded as even more formative for Germany than de Gaulle's decade was for France.

In Chapter 24 we summarized Adenauer's service as Chancellor with a comment that also could be applied to Thatcher and de Gaulle. All three demonstrated that democracy and strong, decisive leadership were not at odds with each other. True, all of them were opinionated, arrogant, and dogmatic—not the sort of people with whom you'd care to go out for pizza. Despite such traits they rarely rode roughshod over democracy—they were democratic leaders, not dictators.

Although most British peacetime leaders have been emollient, the country has known dynamic, even charismatic leaders. Thus few people in Britain were likely to equate democracy with weak leaders. To that extent, perhaps, Thatcher's historical stature is not quite as great as that of the other two—in Britain the question of democratic leadership lacked the same pressing urgency it possessed in France and Germany. In France from the latter part of the nineteenth century on through the first decade after World War II, democracy seemed to entail weak executive leadership. In Germany that decade and a half of the Weimar Republic between the two world wars seemed to teach the same unpalatable lesson. Thus de Gaulle and Adenauer had to not only deal with the pressing problems of their time, but also refute the received wisdom of the political culture. They, much more than Thatcher, were compelled to produce a value shift if their efforts were to be successful. And while de Gaulle would have had a harder time impeded by the constitutional structure of the Fourth Republic and Adenauer by the arrangements of the Weimar Republic, still their precedent-setting actions were more crucial than the inherent logic and rhetorical beauty of their countries' new constitutions in firmly establishing stable, effective government.

Thatcher, de Gaulle, Adenauer three decisive leaders, even though Germany's interwar experience precluded the latter from being known as an "ism." This may suggest that the only good leader is a dynamic one. Our final words on Adenauer in Chapter 24, however, were "he possessed the attributes appropriate to the times." Effective leadership is a function of prevailing conditions. Which takes us from *der Alte* to *der Tunix*—"the do-nothing," that is, Helmut Kohl.

Physically they are so different that it is hard to think of British Prime Minister John Major and German Chancellor Helmut Kohl as similar. After a decade of Thatcher's nannying, the British public seemed to welcome the respite of relaxing a bit with the bland Major. In Germany after eight years of Helmut Schmidt, a Chancellor very much in the Adenauer tradition, people seemed happy to drift awhile with the other Helmut. And that is what they did for seven years, but, then, the world intruded—communism collapsed. And good old do-nothing was suddenly rowing furiously, instead of going with the flow.

As a result, in October 1990 Kohl attained what had always remained only a dream for Adenauer; he became the first Chancellor of a unified Germany and, two months later, was confirmed in that position by the voters. If Adenauer was the father of the West German Republic, Kohl was the father of the unified Germany. It was on all counts a stunning development. And yet by departing from his normal style of leadership, he perhaps had brought himself to grief. The sad reality for Kohl was that he had had his moment; from that point on, the only way to go was downhill, as the bills for unification began to flow in. When he made his first visit to the former East Germany only a few months following his electoral triumph in December 1990, he was booed and pelted with eggs. In the same city only a year earlier a crowd of 130,000 had wildly cheered him. In mid-1993 he felt compelled to admit that he had underestimated both the cost of rebuilding the former East Germany and the time it would take to give its population a standard of living matching that in the west. He may well have harbored second thoughts about the supposed virtues of decisive leadership. Nonetheless, only in the long run will observers be able to assess whether *carpe diem* ("seize the day") was the right strategy. Perhaps history will conclude that the one time the do nothing decided to do something, he did select the right moment.

That comment contains an implicit assumption that should be made explicit. When in 1990 the cry *Deutschland, Einig Vaterland* ("Germany, a united fatherland") was heard in the streets of East German cities, many Poles, Russians, Britons, French, and other Europeans must have thought "Here we go again!" The nationalistic fervor involved in such chants seemed not too far removed from *Deutschland, Deutschland Uber Alles* ("Germany, Germany above everything"). A third of Americans polled in the spring of 1990 said they feared that a reunified Germany could become a danger to peace in Europe.

Every country has to live with its past—the American treatment of the indigenous North American population is nothing of which to be proud, for example, nor is the herding of Asian-Americans into internment camps during World War II. But the point eventually comes when the children should no longer have to answer for the sins of the fathers. Those who ran the Nazi state are mostly in their eighties or older, if still alive. Only those Germans at least fifty years old had even been born when Hitler committed suicide. German genes do not carry some character flaw that is passed on from generation to generation. Nazi rule of Germany was appalling, but its causes lie in the context of the history and traditions of the times.

No people can break totally with the past and have a completely new beginning. You have seen at various points in this part of the book that West German government and politics have been shaped by German political tradition. The influence of history is even more obvious; the West Germans have made strenuous efforts to ensure that the nightmare does not happen again. Perhaps because of their past they are more conscious than the citizens of many other countries of potential threats to freedom and the need to defend liberty. They have constructed and established a remarkably successful political system. The democratic traditions that they lacked in the past have now been built. The cliché is true: Bonn is not Weimar. Even more important, although not a catch-phrase, Bonn is not Berlin. In the last decade of the twentieth century, World War II finally came to an end. The new unified Germany that was able to emerge was not the old Germany refurbished but instead a democratic country of pragmatic politics.

Nonetheless, Germany faced a daunting task. Giving the former East Germany a sound economy and an enhanced standard of living was important and would be difficult. But another transformation was even more important and likely to be more difficult. When the West German Republic was created in 1949, a major obstacle to its success was that the people had had no experience with democracy for more than a decade and a half. Quite simply, many of them just didn't know how to operate a democracy, how citizens in such a system should behave. Coupling East Germany with West Germany requires integrating some 17 million people having no democratic experience for well over a half century. When free elections were held in 1990, only those East Germans seventy-eight years old or over were old enough to have participated in the last election of the Weimar Republic. All younger East Germans had never known an open election campaign with truly competitive parties. How long will educating East Germans into the role of the democratic citizen require?

The ultimate goal is to produce rain-or-shine loyalists, citizens who remain steadfastly committed to the system even during those times when it fails to do a very good job of delivering material benefits. A realist must admit, however, that in the early stages of the journey toward that goal, cost-benefit pragmatists are considerably more prevalent. That certainly is the lesson of why Bonn was not Weimar. The Federal Republic worked; the Weimar Republic didn't. Once the West German system had delivered the economic goods for some years, many Germans were willing to stick with it through some hard times.

Unfortunately, the initial East German experience in the unified Germany is different. Communism was an oppressive system, the quality of life was depressing. And yet prices were kept low, everyone had a job, and the necessities of life were available. All this has changed since unification. Prices have soared, a third of the work force is unemployed or on short hours, and a *Wessi* may appear at any time to dispossess you of your home. How long can former East Germans bear these strains before questioning whether the democratic system is all that desirable? How much belt tightening will the West Germans bear in order to help people whom many of them regard as lazy chiselers whining for a handout? Fully realizing the German dream of a single fatherland will show just how prevalent rain-or-shine democrats are in Germany. The outcome turns not so much on the soundness of German constitutional arrangements as on whether *der Tunix* has another surprising burst of action in his repertoire or whether Germany needs a new version of *der Alte*. To speculate that the third option—*der Führer*—still is available is much too pessimistic and a gratuitous insult to all that West Germany achieved in four decades of democratic development.

..... Part Five

Russia and Central Eurasia

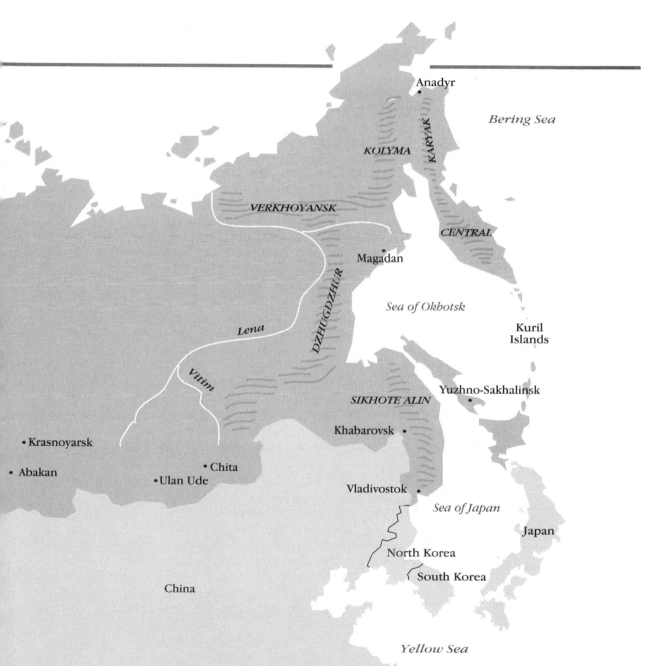

Anadyr

Bering Sea

KOLYMA

KARYAK

VERKHOYANSK

CENTRAL

Magadan

Lena

DZHUGDZHUR

Sea of Okhotsk

Kuril
Islands

Vitim

Yuzhno-Sakhalinsk

SIKHOTE ALIN

Krasnoyarsk

Khabarovsk

Abakan

Chita

Ulan Ude

Vladivostok

Sea of Japan

Japan

North Korea

South Korea

China

Yellow Sea

·····28

Mikhail Gorbachev and the Reform of the Soviet Union, 1985–1990

In 1990 the Soviet system had existed for nearly three-quarters of a century—nearly twice as long as the West German Republic and more than twice as long as the French Fifth Republic. Not only had the Soviet Union managed to become one of the world's two most powerful countries, but it maintained effective centralized control over the world's largest modern empire, one of the major empires in all of history. How ironic and unexpected that this part of the book must concentrate primarily on the tasks of nation building and regime transformation—currently the major political developments in the area where the Soviet system existed.

The reasons for this extraordinary change in fortune can best be understood by examining the careers of two Soviet political leaders: Mikhail Gorbachev and Boris Yeltsin. The first chapter in this part focuses on the former and the second on the latter.

■ THE SOVIET UNION

The Union of Soviet Socialist Republics (commonly abbreviated as Soviet Union or USSR) was the largest country in the world by area, with 22.4 million square kilometers (8.5 million square miles), constituting about one-sixth of the world's inhabited land surface. After China and India, it was the third largest country in the world by population, with 286 million people. After the United States, Japan, and Germany, it was the fourth wealthiest economy in the world in terms of gross national product.

From Russian monarchs and intelligentsia in the nineteenth century to Communist ideologues in the twentieth, both rulers and reformers had been alike in one respect. They had consistently touted the political system that they used to govern this immense landed area as something unique—the model and political salvation for the rest of humanity. Neither Russian monarchs nor Soviet leaders ever welcomed having their political system judged by the rest of humanity in terms of the standards applied to other, more "normal" countries.

Since 1917, when the Soviet Union was founded, Soviet rulers based their legitimacy on a Communist ideology that repudiated the democratic values and institutions that had evolved in countries such as the United States, Britain, and France. Soviet rulers denied that Western democracies were "democratic." For Soviet rulers, Western democracies were actually dictatorships, controlled behind the scenes by those who owned all of the wealth in those societies and who were able through their economic dominance and political power to enslave the rest of the citizenry.

Soviet rulers saw as their mission the liberation of the world through policies facilitating the eventual end of the economic system called capitalism. Adherents of Soviet ideology also ruled many other Communist states and led a global network of Communist parties that collectively made up the world Communist movement. With their allies in the world Communist movement, Soviet rulers supported efforts to replace Western democracies with political systems similar to their own, seeing this almost as an overriding moral obligation to the rest of humanity.

The creed of the Communist ideology presumed that all other political systems eventually would come to resemble the authoritarian system in the Soviet Union. For decades Soviet rulers viewed their system as the most advanced form of truly democratic political rule. Their goal was to achieve, through their political system, a stage of humanitarian utopia and material abundance for themselves and the rest of the world—called Communism. Soviet rulers predicted that the rest of the world eventually would adopt their form of political rule and evolve toward Communism, but not through Soviet military conquest. Universal forces and processes that predetermine human history would naturally impel political transformation and revolution within all countries.

Soviet rulers believed that those universal forces and processes accounted for the emergence of the Soviet Union out of the pre-Soviet Russian empire in 1917. These forces would inevitably occur in all countries, because of internal changes and conflicts unavoidable in each of them. Eventually, all the world would become politically similar to the Soviet Union and would achieve utopian Communism, although the timing of such change would vary because of differences in initial levels of social, economic, and political development.

On a military level, the Soviet Union and the United States, its major adversary among Western democracies, were the only two global superpowers. Both countries had a nuclear military capability that could destroy the world and a conventional military capability that could launch a world war or intervene in any region at will. During the four decades after the end of World War II, the Soviet Commmunist empire extended itself by subordinating the Eastern European Communist states of East Germany, Poland, Czechoslovakia, Hungary, Bulgaria, and Romania (and at one time the Communist states of Yugoslavia, Albania, and China, before they openly rejected Soviet leadership of the world Communist movement).

The armed forces of these six Eastern European Communist states, supplemented by more than 4 million Soviet troops, were unified under Soviet military command through the Warsaw Pact. Supported by Communist states, outside the European continent (Cuba, Vietnam, Mongolia, and North Korea), the Warsaw Pact represented a major threat to the democratic countries of the West. These Western countries unified their military forces in the North Atlantic Treaty Organization (NATO), under the leadership of the United States.

Any attempt by the peoples and governments in these six Eastern European Communist states to repudiate Communism, establish Western-style democracies, or declare their independence from the Soviet empire was met by brutal military suppression. Soviet rulers ordered invasions to crush the anti-Communist revolution in Hungary in October–November 1956 and the democratic reformist Communist government in Czechoslovakia in August 1968. As Hungary and Czechoslovakia graphically showed, Soviet rulers tolerated the independence and sovereignty of Eastern European countries only so far as they retained a Communist political system and membership in the Soviet-led Warsaw Pact. Economic liberalization and political reforms in any of these countries would be accepted only if they did not culminate in the end of rule by their Communist parties and control through censorship and the secret police. Anything beyond these limits threatened the entire Soviet Communist empire, because it might inspire similar reform movements and leaders in the other remaining countries and undermine the very ideological legitimacy of the Communist political systems.

Even the Eastern European countries of the Soviet empire, however, were less tightly controlled than were the more than a hundred ethnic nationalities that lived within Soviet boundaries. Nominally, the Soviet Union was a federation based on the principle of ethnic self-determination. The country was divided into fifteen union republics, whose boundaries and names corresponded to the dominant ethnic nationality historically residing in each. Within five of these union republics were a number of smaller autonomous ethnic enclaves (republics, provinces, territories, and districts), named after the minority nationality residing in each.

The appearance of tolerance for ethnic self-determination differed from the reality of Soviet policy and practices over seven decades. Ethnic nationalities were in effect colonized. Officials dispatched from the central government in Moscow maintained political control and contained any expression of ethnic cultural identity that might threaten the unified Soviet Communist state. Union republics and ethnic enclaves were allowed to instruct their children and to publish in their own languages, but only if they simultaneously encouraged the mastery of Russian as the universal language of discourse in the Soviet Union. Republics and enclaves were granted some marginal autonomy in self-administration through leaders recruited from their ethnic nationalities, but all of these leaders were members of the Communist party and were ultimately bound to follow policies and orders emanating from the central party bureaucracy and the state ministries controlled by the party in Moscow.

Since their inception, the republics and enclaves were nothing more than a short-term political concession. Soviet long-term policy intended to make the more than one hundred nationalities think and act as one "Soviet nation" of men and women. This unification was to be achieved through modernization of their societies to a high stage of urbanization, industrialization, and education and through socialization of their citizens into Soviet values, beliefs, and identities that would supersede those of their ethnic nationalities. As the Soviet Union modernized and progressed toward the goal of utopian Communism, self-identification by ethnic nationality was supposed to disappear gradually from the consciousness of all. Although administered as a federation, the Soviet Union was really an empire, whose rulers measured stability by their containment of ethnic identity and gauged progress by the eventual elimination of ethnic diversity.

Within no other nation has politics been fought for seven decades over such high stakes and aroused both fear and hope in so many other countries. Politics in the Soviet Union often seemed the stuff of high drama, consciously played out by its rulers before a world audience and typifying the twentieth-century excesses of conflict, change, terror, and repression. Soviet politics was the Bolshevik Revolution of 1917 and the Civil War of 1917–1920, resulting in the deaths of millions. It was the millions of Soviet citizens systematically murdered by the Soviet secret police, starved to death during forced agricultural collectivization, sent to forced collective labor camps in remote regions of Siberia, or deported as entire ethnic nations during the reign of Joseph Stalin from 1928 to 1953. It was the generations of Soviet youth indoctrinated in school and Communist youth groups and the generations of Soviet adults mobilized into forms of political participation controlled in every aspect by the Communist party bureaucracy.

Many outsiders, although repulsed by the incomparable tyranny of Soviet rulers, equally associated Soviet politics with the utopian idealism and indomitable spirit of its people. Soviet politics was the millions inspired—like American pioneers in the nineteenth century—by a visionary belief in a future worldwide utopia to volunteer to build industries, lay railroads, drain swamps, and found cities in the country's most desolate locales. In the last two decades of the 1970s and 1980s, Soviet political dissidents such as Andrei Sakharov achieved world reknown for their courageous defiance of the Soviet secret police and for their unshaken dedication to bringing about democratic reforms in the system.

Ironically, it proved to be neither Sakharov nor the Soviet political dissidents who came to symbolize the idealism and high drama of Soviet politics worldwide from 1985 to 1991. It was the bold if flawed political leader of the Soviet Communist system itself, Mikhail Gorbachev. Gorbachev's ability to focus awareness on his attempts to transform the Soviet Communist system into a Western-style democracy made himself and his reforms the world's most significant unfolding news story during those years. Within half a decade, this huge powerful country disintegrated into turmoil as a result of reforms initiated by Gorbachev—the most unlikely of innovators.

■ THE RISE OF MIKHAIL GORBACHEV

Mikhail Gorbachev's background, outlook, and personality gave few hints marking him as different from typical career Communist party functionaries or anticipating his profound impact on the Soviet Union. Gorbachev was born in 1931 to a peasant family on a collective farm in the grain-growing territory of Stavropol in the northern Caucasus of the Russian republic. Growing up after World War II, he in many ways was a product of the contradictions in the Soviet Communist system—a system that over decades provided unique opportunities for social advancement to those born in very humble and poor backgrounds, but at a price of total conformity and complete subservience to the will of its rulers. Conformity was enforced through a life-long pattern of political socialization controlled at all levels by the Communist party. Any deviancy was deterred by the pervasive fear of the secret police, whose agents intimidated citizens into reporting on their neighbors, friends, and relatives. Including agents, collaborators, and informers, the secret police apparatus very probably involved as much as one-fifth of the entire Soviet adult population as late as the 1980s.

As a product of political socialization, Gorbachev first gained national prominence as a teenager in 1946. He was featured on the front page of the national party newspaper *Pravda* and given an award as a hero of Communist labor in one of the numerous campaigns orchestrated by the leadership to induce behaviors supportive of the system. The award specifically singled out the teenager for his efforts with his father in sowing a record amount of grain on the collective farm. An excellent student and also someone who had been singled out as a role model for Soviet youth, Gorbachev received a scholarship to attend the Soviet Union's most prestigious university, Moscow State University, from which he graduated with a law degree in 1955.

Gorbachev did not have to look any farther than his own grandfather to see both the opportunities and problems of the Soviet system. Although from poor origins, his grandfather had led the drive to form the collective farm in the early 1930s and had served as its first chairman or leader. Ironically, Gorbachev's grandfather also exposed the young Gorbachev to the politically repressive side of the Soviet system. His grandfather was arrested by the secret police and spent time in a corrective labor camp in 1937–1938 for allegedly deviant political actions and statements. In 1990, Gorbachev confessed how profoundly he had been affected by the arrest. It epitomized for him the coercive and irrational nature of Soviet reality so contradictory to the professed ideals of Communism. It motivated him to change things, if ever given the opportunity and a position of authority.

Joining the Communist party in 1955, Gorbachev was much influenced by the winds of change and idealism affecting the entire Soviet generation that grew up in the 1950s. The leader of the Soviet Union from 1957 to 1964 was Nikita Khrushchev. Khrushchev launched a program of reforms premised on repudiating the most repressive aspects of the system, opening up opportunities to participate for millions of Soviet citizens, democratizing Communist rule, and diverting economic resources from the military to the agricultural and consumer sectors. A populist as much as a Communist, Khrushchev identified himself as the champion of the people against the Soviet political establishment. Khrushchev promised the Soviet people that his reforms would allow them to realize the material abundance and humanitarian political state of Communism by the 1970s.

Khrushchev was ousted from power in 1964, but he had inspired an entire generation of young party leaders such as Gorbachev. After 1985, Gorbachev frequently referred to himself as a "child of the Khrushchev generation" in explaining the origins of his own motivation and idealism. Those he recruited to Moscow to launch his own reforms in 1985 were in many cases party officials and liberal intellectuals who were products of the Khrushchev era in Soviet politics and were being given a second chance to change things.

On the surface, Gorbachev as a young man seemed very much like typical future party officials. Only his degree in law from the most prestigious of Soviet universities marked him as somewhat different. In Gorbachev's generation, most future party officials were typically mediocre students with degrees in agriculture or engineering earned through correspondence schools or evening divisions of higher educational institutes. At Moscow State University, Gorbachev became active in *Komsomol* (the Communist-controlled youth organization for those between fifteen and twenty-seven) and rose to become a leader of that organization at the university.

After graduating, Gorbachev returned to his native territory to pursue a full-time political career, receiving a graduate degree in agronomy in the late 1950s and advancing to the leadership of the Stavropol *Komsomol*. With a degree in agronomy and origins on a local collective farm, Gorbachev was able to project himself as an agricultural specialist particularly suited for leadership positions in the Communist party that oversaw and controlled the entire government of Stavropol. In 1962, he undertook party work full-time, holding a series of positions that eventually led to his becoming in effect the head of the entire territory in 1970 as the first secretary of the Stavropol Communist party committee.

His return to Moscow and even higher political offices occurred quite fortuitously, but seemed at the time to stamp Gorbachev even more as a typical party official willing to ingratiate himself with powerful political mentors in order to advance his career. Fyodor Kulakov, a full member of the Politburo and the Central Committee secretary responsible for agriculture, died suddenly in 1978 of a reported heart attack (but rumored suicide).[1] Western observers of the Soviet Union had long identified Kulakov as a young protégé being groomed as the most likely successor to General Secretary Leonid Brezhnev, the leader of the Soviet Union since 1965. Kulakov had preceded Gorbachev as first secretary of the Stavropol Communist party. Brezhnev apparently assumed that Gorbachev would therefore be the logical choice to succeed Kulakov and a safe one to preserve the number of pro-Brezhnev supporters in the central Communist leadership.

Brezhnev miscalculated. In the 1970s Gorbachev already had become friends with a principal rival of Brezhnev in the central leadership, Yurii Andropov, who was head of the KGB (Committee of State Security, the secret police) until 1982 and a full Politburo member since 1973. Gorbachev had first come to the attention of the central leaders such as Andropov (who also by chance had been born and raised until his late teens in Stavropol) when they had spent their summer vacations at the nearby coastal resorts on the Black Sea in the 1970s. Gorbachev took advantage of the leaders' presence to impress them with his attributes as someone who could get things done but who could still be confided in as "one of the boys." He continued the pattern after coming to Moscow in 1978, befriending even the most notori-

---

[1]The nature and powers of the Soviet Communist party's Politburo, Central Committee, and Secretariat until 1990 are discussed in Chapter 32.

ous hard-line conservatives among the central party leaders, such as Mikhail Suslov, and using his ties with Andropov to advance his own career.

Gorbachev's election to full membership in the Politburo in October 1980 allowed Andropov to counter the influence of the pro-Brezhnev faction in the central leadership. For Andropov, Gorbachev's likely attraction was his personal honesty and idealism. Since he began his political career in the mid-1950s, Gorbachev's record had been unblemished. However politically ambitious he was, in none of the positions that he had held since beginning his political career could he be accused of having used office primarily for personal material gain. Gorbachev remained very much a true believer in the values and beliefs of Communist ideology, despite his awareness of how so much of Soviet reality completely contradicted them.

Among the central leaders, Andropov was the sole political puritan and true believer. As the head of the KGB from 1967 until 1982, Andropov more than anyone else knew from KGB grass-roots reports and surveillance from around the country the scale of widespread political corruption, which was eroding the fabric of Soviet society and was seemingly encouraged by the central Brezhnev leadership over the previous two decades. For Andropov, the costs of the corruption were measurable by the billions looted from the state treasury, by the decline in economic growth, and by the cynicism and disillusionment of the Soviet public.

When Brezhnev died in November 1982, the conflict over succession pitted the Andropov faction against the Brezhnev faction and various combinations of reformists against conservatives within the central leadership of the Party Politburo and Central Committee. Andropov's ascendancy to General Secretary found policy shifting to a distinctly reformist direction. Former cronies of Brezhnev were arrested on corruption charges. Andropov became more direct in criticizing the country's mounting economic failures and in advocating decentralization of the state-run nationalized economy.

Andropov's ascendancy was cut short by his death due to a terminal illness in February 1984. During his last year as General Secretary, Andropov entrusted responsibility for personnel decisions and other matters to his protégé Gorbachev. With Andropov's death, Gorbachev inherited the mantle of leadership, instead of the Andropov faction.

Konstantin Chernenko, a Brezhnev protégé, was elected to succeed Andropov, but, through a compromise, Gorbachev was made the unofficial "Second Secretary" with authority to chair sessions of the Politburo in Chernenko's absence and oversee personnel changes at the highest ranks of the party and the government. Chernenko's only lasting mark was his attempt to stall the campaign launched by Andropov against corruption among the elite, in order to protect the Brezhnev faction in the central leadership. Chernenko's death due to a terminal illness within about a year, in March 1985, left three potential successors within the Politburo: Viktor Grishin, Moscow first party secretary; Grigorii Romanov, a former Leningrad first party secretary and Central Committee secretary responsible for the military and the police since 1983; and Gorbachev.

Grishin was already seventy-one years old, and the likelihood of a third septuagenarian General Secretary dying suddenly in office disqualified him in the eyes of a majority of the members of the Central Committee, who were entrusted with the authority to elect the new General Secretary. Romanov was approximately the same age as Gorbachev, but was disliked and distrusted by many as a cold technocrat. Both Grishin and Romanov suffered from reputations for tolerating excessive personal corruption. Grishin had headed the Moscow city party since 1970 only because of Brezhnev. Grishin had become notorious nationally for the way he ruled the city through a corrupt circle of party cronies, almost like the godfather of an organized Mafia family. Romanov was known for the wedding party that he had staged for his daughter when he headed the party organization in Leningrad, at which priceless tsarist crystal from the Hermitage museum was used and broken.

Despite Chenenko's stalling action in 1984–1985, the issue of elite corruption that had reached epidemic proportions under Brezhnev would not go away. In 1983, Nikolai Shchelokov, a longtime friend of Brezhnev's and the Minister of Internal Affairs responsible for overseeing the police nationally, committed suicide prior to being tried for accepting millions of rubles in payoffs. By 1985, a massive cotton-growing extortion ring organized by top party and state officials in Uzbekistan was uncovered, and trials in that Central Asian republic were implicating several close former associates of Brezhnev. To restore the image of the party, the Central Committee had to elect as its head someone with an untarnished reputation for honesty, like Gorbachev.

Thus Gorbachev was elected General Secretary on March 11, 1985 basically to restore the image of the party in the eyes of a public increasingly cynical after the arrest and trial of many of Brezhnev's closest political associates and even relatives. Even so, Gorbachev was elected by a very slim majority and only because he received the personal endorsement before the Central Committee of another leader of the Brezhnev "old guard"—Andrei Gromyko, Minister of Foreign Affairs since 1957 and a full Politburo member since 1973. At the time, almost all Western analysts underestimated Gorbachev and discounted his election as politics as usual in the Kremlin. They assumed that he might push for more reformist policies and continue the anti-corruption campaign initiated by Andropov and tabled by Chernenko, but they also assumed that he was a typical party official and loyal product of the system. His party background, they thought, would automatically incline him to defend the Communist party autocracy and its monopoly of power. Like Brezhnev in 1978, Western analysts misjudged Gorbachev.

Gorbachev moved quickly to initiate massive personnel changes at all levels of the central leadership of the party and the national government. By the time the Central Committee plenum ended on June 26, 1987, Gorbachev had consolidated his grip on power at the center by recruiting an overwhelming majority of like-minded supporters into the party's Politburo and Secretariat and the government's Council of Ministers (the Soviet equivalent of a national Cabinet). Gorbachev swept from office the aged and now thoroughly discredited Brezhnev-era elite, such as Viktor Grishin, who were tainted by the corruption, scandals, and major economic failures openly publicized in the Soviet media since 1982 and blamed on the previous two decades of party leadership. The Brezhnev elite had constituted the majority of conservatives in the central leadership and for the past two decades had resisted almost all but token and limited reforms. With their removal, Gorbachev changed the tenor of the debate over the necessity for reform and over the kinds of real changes required.

Gorbachev was not content simply to alter the composition of the ruling establishment. Whether political calculations led him to disguise his true intentions until he had consolidated his authority or the gravity of the national economic crisis pushed him, Gorbachev definitely changed politically within two years after he took office. At the beginning of 1986, addressing the national Party Congress in February, Gorbachev mouthed clichés critical of the corruption and political shortcomings in the Soviet system. These did not differ sharply from those that an Andropov or even a younger Brezhnev in the early 1970s might have sounded at previous party congresses. In April of 1986, when the Chernobyl nuclear power plant outside Kiev almost melted down, Gorbachev followed the Soviet Communist leaders' usual policy of refusing to admit major problems or guilt to the non-Communist world. During the first two weeks after the Chernobyl reactor exploded, Gorbachev went along with the official cover-up, denying any major catastrophe until the spread of nuclear clouds and the magnitude of the threat to all of Europe forced him to be more candid. After his original hesitancy over Chernobyl, and clearly after August 1986, Gorbachev changed.

By 1991, Gorbachev had surprised the analysts. The Russian terms *demokratizatsiya* (democratization), *glasnost* (public openness), and *perestroika* (restructuring), which Gorbachev coined to characterize his integrated program of reform in the Soviet Union, had entered the universal lexicon and become so familiar that they seldom require translation or explanation anywhere in the world. The next sections examine the evolution of these reforms, summarized in Table 28–1.

■ *ECONOMIC REFORMS*

Bluntly characterizing the Soviet economy as nothing less than a "mess" (*rasstroika*), Gorbachev openly ridiculed it for having failed to grow at all during the past two decades except for the annual 1–1.5 percent increase from the domestic sale of vodka and the export of Soviet arms and oil. Even oil revenue had been artificially boosted by the jump in world prices caused by the OPEC cartel beginning in 1973. By the spring of 1987, Gorbachev warned his audiences that unless radical economic reforms were instituted, the Soviet Union was on a path of economic decline that would revert the country to Third-World status by the beginning of the next century. The country was in an economic crisis threatening its very survival.

The Soviet Union had fallen decades behind the West in productivity and real output. Gorbachev advocated fundamental changes to reduce the level of military spending and to accelerate the pace of investments in industry to make the civilian sector competitive. He proposed a radical decentralization of control and management of the economy to the local level of factories and plants. With decentralization, factory and plant managers were elected by their employees beginning in 1987. Employee councils were invested with the authority to make many of the decisions that for decades had been arbitrarily decreed by central planners and ministers in Moscow and perfunctorily carried out by their subordinate managers. By 1989 Gorbachev even came around to supporting limited forms of private and cooperatively owned retail stores and services (the Soviet consumer sector had been owned and regulated entirely by the government since the 1930s).

Table 28–1
Gorbachev and the
Reform of the Soviet
Union, 1985–1990

March 1985 Mikhail Gorbachev succeeds Konstantin Chernenko as Communist Party General Secretary.

April 1985 Plenum of Communist Party Central Committee endorses Gorbachev's reform program of economy and society by processes of perestroika and glasnost.

July 1985 Eduard Shevardnadze becomes USSR Foreign Minister.

February 1986 Gorbachev calls for drastic reform of Soviet economy.

January 1987 Communist Party Central Committee approves Gorbachev's reforms to democratize the Party and government, including contested local elections in spring of 1987.

January 1988 Industrial enterprise law goes into effect, decentralizing control of industry to the level of factories and instituting the election of industrial and commercial managers by their employees.

June–July 1988 At 19th Communist Party Conference, Gorbachev gains support for presidential system, new national parliament, and greatly empowered legislatures at all jurisdictional levels.

November 1988 Amendment to Soviet Constitution abolishes old national legislature, which is replaced with a Congress of People's Deputies and a smaller, full-time legislature, the Supreme Soviet.

January 1989 Economic law allowing private enterprise in small commercial enterprises and services goes into effect.

March 1989 First relatively free elections since 1917 are held nationwide for contested seats of Soviet national parliament. Candidates of anti-Communist popular fronts defeat many party officials in Moscow, Leningrad, and other locales.

May 1989 Gorbachev is elected Chair of Supreme Soviet by Congress of People's Deputies.

May–July 1989 Lithuania, Latvia, and Estonia declare state sovereignty of their republics.

February 1990 Communist Party Central Committee approves ending party's constitutional monopoly on political power, which had been in effect over the previous seven decades.

March 1990 Pro-democracy candidates of anti-Communist popular fronts win many seats in contested free elections to republic parliaments and local councils.

March 1990 Congress ends constitutional ban on political parties other than Communist Party, institutes office of Soviet President, and elects Gorbachev as President.

May–December 1990 Russia, Ukraine, and other ten republics declare their own state sovereignty.

July 1990 Supreme Soviet passes law guaranteeing freedom of all media and ending censorship; Gorbachev issues Presidential decree ending Communist Party control of media.

October 1990 Gorbachev awarded Nobel Peace Prize.

Some of these reforms and proposals had been anticipated to various degrees by the experiments and policy rethinking begun during Andropov's reign as General Secretary in 1982–1983, but they went far beyond Andropov's efforts. The reforms challenged longstanding Communist party dogma on the economy, which opposed any form of private property as the foundation of hated Western capitalism. They also threatened the prerogatives of the most powerful sectors of the national political establishment in the military, central planning agencies, and ministries. And Gorbachev went even further.

By *perestroika*, Gorbachev intended to achieve personal economic freedom and choice in a country whose party-state bureauracy had owned, managed, and regulated almost every facet of its nationalized economy since 1928. The ownership and management of the economy were gradually to be devolved from the state to a private sector. Although some state-owned industries would be retained, an increasing share of the economy would be transferred over to a private sector. The Soviet economy would come to resemble the mixed (state and private) capitalist economies of Britain, France, and Germany.

The private sector would be made up of worker-owned cooperatives, family farms, and individually owned commercial, trade, and industrial enterprises—all financed by private Soviet banks and Western investors and competing for their share of the market against each other and a much smaller state-owned sector. No longer would the state completely monopolize the economy. An unregulated free market, with competition driven by supply and demand, would make all of the billions of economic decisions affecting prices, wages, and products.

The responsiblity to nurture and support this mixed state-private economy was to be increasingly devolved from the central government in Moscow to the union-republic governments and to the many thousands of local provincial and city administrations in each of the republics.The union-republic and local governments would be forced to account directly for their economic policies to the public and to the private sector.

■ POLITICAL AND SOCIAL REFORMS

By 1987, Gorbachev was arguing that even decentralization of the economy and private-cooperative ownership in the consumer sector were insufficient to arrest the critical downward slide of the Soviet economy. He bluntly attributed the country's economic problems and backwardness to the very nature of its authoritarian political system. At a Central Committee party plenum at the end of January 1987, Gorbachev cited the lack of democracy in the Soviet Union as the single major problem confronting the country. As a first step toward reform, the Central Committee approved Gorbachev's proposal to institute as an experiment contested elections in the spring of 1987 for deputies' seats on various local councils.

By the end of 1987, Gorbachev was contending that restructuring the economy by itself would never succeed without a comprehensive "social revolution" against the authoritarian Communist system. The most carefully crafted economic reforms would be doomed to failure, he argued, unless they were underwritten by equivalent changes in motivations, values, norms, and attitudes, as well as changes in the governing processes binding leaders and followers at all levels of political life. Economic revitalization could only flourish through the activation of what Gorbachev termed the "human factor," which he equated with the degree of personal commitment, enthusiasm, initiative, trust, and responsibility within Soviet society.

Gorbachev and his close personal advisors argued that such values could only arise from a social revolution against the Soviet system. They could only evolve in a political atmosphere with democratic norms and expectations for both leaders and followers throughout Soviet society, from workplace to governing institutions. In Gorbachev's vision, the rigid centralized management of the economy through all-powerful and nonaccountable ministries and bureaucracies was only the symptom of the real problem. The economy was but a reflection of the core attributes and authority relationships prevalent throughout the Soviet political culture and social institutions. Democratic changes were absolutely essential to spark and unleash the qualities required to revitalize the economy, such as trust, initiative, and assertiveness; also essential was the sharing of power by leaders and followers. Democracy was the "human factor" that could save the Soviet Union and ensure the implementation of Gorbachev's large-scale economic reforms. Gorbachev anticipated that these domestic changes would generate a renewed sense of national loyalty and identification with the Soviet Union and an enhanced legitimacy for a democratically reborn Communist system. To his conservative critics, Gorbachev responded with the Russian phrase *inogo ne dano* ("there is no alternative").

Democratization to Gorbachev meant reducing the monopoly over political power held by the Communist party as an institution. The legislatures (soviets, or councils) whose members would be chosen by the public through contested elections were to be invested with the ultimate authority. Newly empowered, the legislatures and their new chief executives were to assume the primary role of making decisions and carrying out policies in all Soviet jurisdictions. Both the legislative and executive branches would be democratically elected and ultimately accountable for their actions to the Soviet public.

Since the origins of the Soviet state, the Communist party through its central political organs and leadership had completely monopolized the legislative function. Formal legislatures for decades had meekly and unanimously voted to approve all the policies of the party. The reason was that the deputies to all legislatures, from local village councils to the national parliament, were elected from districts in which they were the only candidate to appear on the ballot. Although local Communist party officials did the recruiting, Moscow set national and local quotas for deputies by gender, ethnicity, age, profession, and other demographic characteristics to create a false image of the legislatures as being representative of a cross-section of Soviet society. The chief executives—called prime ministers at the national and union-republic levels and chairs of the executive committees at provincial, city, and district levels—were only nominally elected by their legislatures. In reality, they were designated and removed by higher levels of the party bureaucracy and obligated to implement party priorities and policies in their jurisdictions.

In March 1989, Gorbachev instituted—for the first time in Soviet history—relatively free contested elections to a portion of seats in the new national parliament called the All-Union Congress of People's Deputies. In early 1990, he allowed even freer competitive elections for the fifteen union-republic parliaments and for the several thousands of local provincial, city, and district councils. The 1990 elections resulted in the defeat of several entrenched Communist officials by reform candidates, voted into office by a public making use of their first opportunity to express themselves democratically.

Gorbachev also loosened censorship and national controls over the media and arts through *glasnost*. He had originally intended only to mobilize the liberated media and intellectual community against his political opponents and against the corruption and dictatorial abuse rampant in the system. But the mobilization soon exceeded both his expectations and his desires. From 1986 through 1991, the Soviet Union witnessed a flowering of free speech and assembly unknown under Communism and an emerging civic activism challenging all aspects of the Communist system.

A democratic spirit animated unprecedented and scathingly frank discussions in the media of almost every formerly sacrosanct institution and political truism. Soviet readers and TV viewers began to learn about the widespread prevalence of prostitution, drug addiction, and homelessness. The forced collectivization of agriculture in the 1930s, the persecution of ethnic minorities, the nonaccountable power of the Communist party and its officials, censorship, the Soviet invasion of Czechoslovakia in 1968, the Soviet occupation of Afghanistan since 1979, and the Soviet official cover-up of the Chernobyl nuclear accident were all aired in the media and subjected to wide-ranging criticism and debate.

The long silenced and intimidated majority of Soviet writers, film-makers, and other artists rebelled against the state. Since the 1930s all art forms were regulated by the dictates of the party bureaucracy and the Ministry of Culture; union guilds controlled by the party determined who could earn a living in particular fields. The majority openly rebelled at congresses of their union guilds in 1986–1989, ousting the conservative party overlords of their associations, who had suffocated artistic life for decades. The prevailing tone at these congresses encouraged secret balloting and competitive elections for leadership positions on the union guilds' governing boards and condemned any form of state censorship of the arts.

Dissidents who previously had been unable to publish, direct, or paint because their art was deemed contradictory to the norms of "socialist realism" prescribed by the guilds' overlords became the elected national leaders of the arts. Even the state monopoly over artists through required membership in artistic associations soon ended. By 1989, independent cooperatives of film-makers, theater companies, and writers had formed throughout the country, an outgrowth of these rebellions within the official union guilds. Soviet intellectuals were free to create their own film companies, select their own publications, scripts, and plays, and share the profits among themselves.

The pervasive regulation of personal behavior by the state also was being rolled back. With fewer prohibitions or restrictions, Soviet citizens were being encouraged for the first time in seven decades to speak and act freely—to criticize public policies and to organize to demand changes from their elected officials. For Gorbachev, in a new democratic Soviet Union, the guiding principle would be "Everything is permitted, unless it is prohibited by law." Public debate no longer would be confined to those areas outside of the "forbidden zones" defined arbitrarily by party censors. Gorbachev contrasted this new model of the appropriate relationship between the state and society with the completely opposite guiding principle of the authoritarian Communist system until 1985: "Everything was prohibited, unless it was permitted by party-state officials." In July 1990, Gorbachev, acting as President of the country, issued a decree ending party control of all media. At the same time the Supreme Soviet passed a national law guaranteeing the freedom of all media from any form of censorship.

However reluctantly, Gorbachev was forced to concede a real devolution of his own authority and the power of the central government in Moscow to control events in the fifteen union republics making up the Soviet Union. The March 1990 elections for the fifteen republic parliaments and the many thousands of provincial, city, and district councils had dramatically reduced the central government's power. Public pressure and demonstrations over the months prior to those elections forced the Congress of People's Deputies (of which almost 90 percent were Communist party deputies) to repeal the constitutional statute that had sanctified the Communist party as the only legal political party in the country. Gorbachev, who chaired the parliament, had initially opposed repeal of the statute, but he had been forced to concede to the public demonstrations that were by-products of the greater freedoms of speech and assembly unleashed by him since 1987.

Figure 28–1
More Than 200,000 Muscovites Protest against the Communist Party and for Democracy and the "Democratic Platform," July 1990

Source: Mike Urban

By 1990, a number of political parties had formed throughout the Soviet Union. Representing a broad spectrum of political ideologies, the parties began to attract followers and form caucuses to formalize their policies, which were increasingly in conflict with the much more limited market and democratic reforms of Gorbachev. The new parties' growing influence was daily evident in the Supreme Soviet, the fifteen union-republic legislatures, and the many local councils. On the grass-roots level, the newly emergent parties began to recruit members, organize, and raise money for pending future elections.

In some republics, such as Lithuania, Latvia, and Estonia, a majority of the seats to the republic legislatures were won by members of popular fronts dedicated to gaining the independence of their republics from the Soviet Union. In all republics, large blocs of anti-Communist nationalists and democrats won seats in the republic legislatures and the local councils. From May through December 1990, all of the republic legislatures passed resolutions declaring themselves sovereign jursidictions independent of the central government in Moscow.

In several instances, republic and local party establishments were traumatized by the results of the 1990 elections. Former political prisoners and dissidents were elected parliamentary deputies, defeating the local party bosses. Along with liberal intellectuals, they headed anti-Communist democratic caucuses on the republic and local levels. Nationalists, former dissidents, intellectuals, and reform Communists were forming political alliances and gaining national visibility and legitimacy as a counterelite capable of challenging the political rule of the Communist establishment. At least formally, the monolithic single-party autocracy based on Communist ideology that had legitimated the existence of the Soviet Union and had completely monopolized political power for seven decades had ended.

Attempting to ride the crest of a wave of revolution against the Communist system that he had intended only to reform, Gorbachev revised his goals in response to the newly empowered Soviet public. He spoke of his intent to base the legitimacy of a new democratic Soviet system on the supremacy of a "rule of law" and a constitution binding on both leaders and citizens. The Soviet government was to become a "legal state" guaranteeing democratic procedures.

Legislatures, with freely elected representatives, would be the most authoritative governmental institution. Respect for democratic freedoms and norms in the "legal state" was to be enforced through an independent judiciary. Judges would be bound solely by the constitution in ruling on the propriety of actions by state officials. Such due process rights as the presumption of innocence, trial by jury, and impartial judges—denigrated for seven decades by Communist ideologues as the political hypocrisy of Western democracies—were to be instituted to allow all Soviet citizens real equality before the law.

To guard against the concentration of political power and dictatorship by any political party or individual, Gorbachev promised that the Soviet state would be reconstituted to ensure a separation of powers and a system of checks and balances among the three branches of government in all jurisdictions. The executive branch of the national government was enhanced through a new national office of President, combining the powers of head of state and chief executive under an amendment to the Soviet Constitution adopted by the national parliament in March 1990.[2] The President was to be elected directly by all Soviet voters in a contested election every five years. As a one-time exception, Gorbachev was indirectly elected to be the first President by the parliament.

The significance of the presidency was that powers traditionally associated with the nongovernmental office of General Secretary of the Communist party were to be assumed by a national official elected by all of the Soviet people. Unlike the General Secretary, the President would be politically accountable to the Soviet public, indirectly through the independent and freely elected national parliament and directly every five years through national voting for the office. Even though Gorbachev retained his position as General Secretary, he governed throughout the remainder of 1990 and into 1991 as President, delegating most of his party responsibilities to a deputy General Secretary.

As an institution, the Communist party was breaking apart. Hundreds of thousands of party members had resigned, many of them joining the new reformist political parties, political movements, popular fronts, and interest groups that by 1991 already comprised some 60,000 so-called informals throughout the Soviet Union. The Communist party, nationally and within several union republics, was splintering into factions. On the democratic left, party factions such as the Democratic Platform advocated further diminution of the party's dictatorial monopoly of power in Soviet society. In the Baltic republics of Estonia and Lithuania, the democratic factions assumed leadership, declared the autonomy of their branches from Moscow, and openly joined governing alliances with the local popular fronts that were advocating independence from the Soviet Union. On the anti-democratic right, party factions wanted a return to the single-party dictatorship and repudiated all of Gorbachev's reforms. In the Russian republic, radical nationalists and anti-reform Communists founded their own Russian Communist Party to promote these views and to counter democratic factions among Russian Communists.

With the emergence of political pluralism and a civil society independent of the state, leaders no longer could brutally repress any public disagreement with their policies and justify their actions by the paranoid view that dissent was equivalent to treason and the paranoid reasoning that "he who is not with us is against us." In the new Soviet Union, leaders were to accept conflict and competition as the expected normal conditions in a democracy guided by an inclusive axiom for bargaining and

---

[2]The powers of the Soviet President relative to the executive and legislative branches in 1990–1991 somewhat paralleled those of the French President. Under the constitutional amendment, the Soviet President appointed individuals to the top executive and judicial positions, including that equivalent to the French Prime Minister (called Chairman of the Soviet Council of Ministers). All the positions were subject to confirmation votes by first the Supreme Soviet and then the Congress of People's Deputies. Like the French President, the Soviet President had the power to dissolve the Supreme Soviet and to dismiss the Prime Minister and other officials. In the pre-1990 government the presidency of the Soviet Union was a ceremonial position called Chairman of the Presidium of the Supreme Soviet. It was periodically held by the party General Secretary, but its powers were limited to signing legislation and treaties and formally representing the country at state functions.

compromise: "He who is not against us is with us." By 1990, universal democratic principles, values, and beliefs found in the writings of classical theorists such as John Locke, James Madison, and Thomas Jefferson were increasingly cited as the source for the model of political reform intended by Gorbachev for the Soviet Union. The same classical democratic theory, and the Western democracies founded on its postulates, had been repudiated by Soviet Communist leaders until 1985 as contradictory to human nature and to the allegedly predetermined universal processes that would lead the rest of the world to accept communism.

■ FOREIGN POLICY

Gorbachev's impact was immediately apparent internationally. His open endorsement of Western democratic values in the Soviet Union unintentionally encouraged nationalist and anti-Communist movements to arise in other countries. In 1989–1990 the Communist regimes in Poland, Hungary, East Germany, Czechoslovakia, Romania, and Albania were overthrown, despite the Soviet Union's political-military domination of Eastern Europe over the previous five decades.

The critical factor in these revolutions was Gorbachev, along with his Foreign Minister, Eduard Shevardnadze. In early 1989, Gorbachev had mistakenly assumed that the Communist regimes in the Eastern European countries could be reformed in the same way as he was attempting to institute changes in the Soviet Union. Once the popular revolutions in these countries arose, however, Gorbachev backed off from supporting the Communists in power against their own peoples. In contrast to the previous forty-four years of the Soviet Eastern European empire, the Communist leaders in these countries could no longer rely on Soviet military intervention or even Soviet political support to crush dissent by their own citizens. The Soviet troops stationed in East Germany, Poland, and Hungary were kept in their barracks under orders from Gorbachev in 1989 and were not, as would have been predicted based on past responses of Soviet leaders, mobilized against the anti-Communist demonstrations.

Gorbachev can be partially credited for these anti-Communist revolutions. They derived from his overall attempt to foster a new international climate of non-belligerency, nonmilitarism, mutual trust, arms reduction, and joint cooperation. Under this new climate, Gorbachev and Shevardnadze intended to redirect the efforts of the international community to solve global problems such as population growth, environmental pollution, and hunger.

The change internationally was also necessitated by a basic reality constantly emphasized by Gorbachev. The backwardness and stagnancy of the Soviet economy were the result of the excessive level of spending on the military—over half of the Soviet government's budget for decades. For Gorbachev, the military sector had come to dominate the government and monopolize the Soviet economy because of false dogmatic assumptions derived from the Communist ideology. This ideology presumed that a hostile capitalistic West threatened the Soviet Union and had to be deterred militarily until the processes of transformation led to the demise of the West and the rise of systems identical with Soviet Communism. Justified by a creed of liberating the world from capitalism, military expansion had ruined the Soviet economy.

The military expansion created its own self-fulfilling prophecy. Fearing the very worst from such a heavily armed Soviet Union, the Western democracies had spent ever larger sums for their own military defense and formed a number of anti-Communist alliances ringing the Soviet Union to protect themselves from the Soviet threat. In the process, an open-ended arms race between the Soviet Union and the United States over the decades since 1945 had debilitated the economies of both superpowers, leaving both them and the rest of the world even less secure.

To revive the economy, Gorbachev repudiated those assumptions and the liberation credo of the Communist ideology that had locked the Soviet Union into decades of excessive military spending and worldwide military involvement. Gorbachev committed himself to cutting Soviet military expenditures drastically and pulling back the Soviet military presence overseas. To achieve these goals, he launched a series of diplomatic overtures to the West that, along with his acceptance of the anti-Communist revolutions in Eastern Europe, he called "new political thinking" in international affairs. He withdrew Soviet troops from Afghanistan in 1988 and began the rapid withdrawal of Soviet troops from the now independent countries of Eastern Europe in 1990–1991. Crowned by treaties reducing nuclear and conventional arms with the United States, Gorbachev's efforts effectively ended the Cold War.

Gorbachev brought the Soviet Union into a new era of international relations, even allying the Soviet Union with the United States and other Western countries in

Figure 28–2
Gorbachev Acknowledging Crowd of Well-Wishers at Stanford University, June 1990

Source: The Stanford Daily

the UN operation that forced Iraq to withdraw from Kuwait in 1991. Cooperation with Western democratic governments, previously viewed as the major adversaries of Soviet Communism, had become a cornerstone of Soviet foreign policy by 1990. The West's form of democratic government—denigrated for decades by Soviet ideologues as a transitory state eventually to be replaced by systems similar to Soviet Communism—by 1990 had become the standard toward which the Soviet Union under Gorbachev was headed.

■ ■ ■

Gorbachev received *Time* magazine's accolade as "Person of the Decade" in 1989 and was awarded the Nobel Peace Prize for 1990. By 1990, he was rated among the most popular and respected world leaders in public opinion polls in several Western democracies, even surpassing the positive ratings of domestic elected leaders in some countries, such as West Germany. He was surrounded by crowds of surging well-wishers and lauded universally wherever he traveled in the West. Someone who as a teenager had aspirations to become a professional actor, Gorbachev had reached a level of adoration and uncritical worldwide fame, rivaled only by that of the rock star Michael Jackson and dubbed by Western pundits "Gorbymania."

Thus, after seven decades of increasing incompetence and corruption, the process of reform was initiated from *within* the party by one of its own progeny. Having launched reform, Gorbachev soon lost the ability to control—or even direct—it. Although his period of leadership was immensely significant, it proved to be short-lived, as we will explain in the next chapter on the unraveling of his leadership.

29

Boris Yeltsin and the Fall of the Soviet Union, 1991

Dear fellow countrymen, compatriots. Due to the situation which has evolved as a direct result of the formation of the Commonwealth of Independent States, I hereby discontinue my activities at the post of President of the Union of Soviet Socialist Republics. . . . I wish everyone all the best.

Mikhail Gorbachev
December 25, 1991

■ *THE RISE OF BORIS YELTSIN*

One of the like-minded supporters recruited by Mikhail Gorbachev after he had been elected to head the Communist party in 1985 came to haunt him politically and became his principal rival and nemesis by 1989. This was Boris Yeltsin.

Yeltsin, a native of the Russian province of Sverdlovsk in the Ural Mountains, was born in February 1931, only one month before Gorbachev. Growing up in the decades of the 1930s and 1940s like Gorbachev, Yeltsin was both a product of that era in Soviet history and almost an ideal model of the party leaders who emerged from poor working-class origins. Born to a poor peasant family in a rural village, Yeltsin was brought up with seven other members of his family in a one-room apartment in the industrial city of Perm. Yeltsin's father had taken his family and parents from the village to flee the forced collectivization of agriculture instituted throughout the Soviet Union in the 1930s and had sought work as an industrial laborer in a potash plant of Perm.

Boris Yeltsin went on to graduate from the Urals Polytechnic Institute in civil engineering in 1955, the same year in which Gorbachev graduated in law from Moscow State University. Yeltsin spent his first year after graduating apprenticing as a construction worker and learning first-hand the twelve different trades, from bricklayer to plasterer, that he would have to supervise as the foreman of a construction brigade. By 1969, Yeltsin had risen to become the manager of the largest housing-construction complex in the city of Sverdlovsk, after a string of lower

Figure 29–1

Boris Yeltsin

Source: RFE/RL Research Institute Photo

administrative positions overseeing construction in boroughs of the city. (See Table 29–1 for a synopsis of Yeltsin's career.)

Unlike Gorbachev, Yeltsin gravitated to the Communist party and to a political career relatively late in life. Yeltsin did not join the party until 1961, and then reluctantly, in order to qualify for an administrative leadership position for a construction brigade in Sverdlovsk. Yeltsin was not renowned in the province as a rising and ambitious politician, but as the star player on volleyball teams of the Institute and later the city.

Only in 1969 did Yeltsin begin his rapid rise to head the Communist party in the province. He was conscripted to become head of the construction department of the party in 1969 and was promoted to oversee all construction and industrial policies in 1975. When the first secretary of the Sverdlovsk party, Yakov Ryabov, was promoted to Moscow to become a secretary in the Central Committee, he recommended Yeltsin to succeed him. Recall that Gorbachev became head of the Stavropol party under somewhat similar circumstances in 1970, when Fyodor Kulakov lobbied in Moscow to have his personal protégé elected to the post.

Before Gorbachev was promoted to Moscow to succeed Kulakov, he and Yeltsin had become acquainted around 1976, and subsequently bartered goods in short supply between their provinces. But their political paths seemed to diverge after that. By March 1985, Gorbachev had catapulted politically from overseeing a backward Russian agricultural territory to leading the entire Soviet Union. Even though by April 1985, Yeltsin was the leader of the third-largest provincial party organization in the Russian Republic (in a locale that was a major industrial-military center of the country), he was still just one of about 150 provincial and territorial

Table 29–1

Career of Boris
Yeltsin

1931 Born in Sverdlovsk, Russia

1955 Graduated in construction engineering from Urals Polytechnic Institute, Sverdlovsk

1955–1963 Foreman and then head of construction administration, city of Sverdlovsk

1961–1990 Member, Communist party of the Soviet Union

1963–1968 Chief engineer and then head of housing construction combine, Sverdlovsk

1968–1975 Head of construction department, Sverdlovsk Communist party

1975–1976 Secretary for industry-construction, Sverdlovsk Communist party

1976–1985 First secretary, Sverdlovsk Communist party

1985 Head of department and then secretary for construction, Communist party Central Committee, Moscow

1985–1987 First secretary, Moscow Communist party

1986–1988 Candidate member, Politburo, Communist party Central Committee

1987–1988 Forced to resign from Politburo and as First secretary of Moscow Communist party

1987–1989 First deputy chair, Soviet Union State Committee for Construction

1989–1991 Deputy, national Congress of People's Deputies and Supreme Soviet

1990–1991 Deputy, Russian republic's Congress of People's Deputies and Supreme Soviet

1990 Resigns from Communist party

1990–1991 Chair, Supreme Soviet of Russian republic

1991– President, Russian Federation

party bosses throughout the country who were subordinate to the dictates of the supreme leader Gorbachev.

While heading the Russian province of Sverdlovsk, Yeltsin developed a reputation as an uncorruptible, pragmatic, and innovative manager. He fitted the mold of the new kind of party official around which Gorbachev intended to build his power base in Moscow. As the leader of Sverdlovsk, Yeltsin had never been the aloof and autocratic local official so prevalent throughout the country. During his tenure, he had publicly disdained the special privileges and isolated lifestyle of local party officials, used local transportation to experience the life of ordinary commuters in Sverdlovsk, and through his accessibility and visibility projected the image of a populist rather than a Communist.

Many in Sverdlovsk could still recall Yeltsin as the star volleyball player from the 1950s. His friends knew him as someone who, from childhood, had always been something of a rebel against authority figures and expected norms of conformity. As a fifth-grader, he had organized and led a rebellion of his classmates against an overbearing teacher. He later lost two fingers of his left hand attempting to disarm a stolen hand grenade.

Yeltsin's popularity as the hometown boy was to benefit him consistently in Sverdlovsk. Voters in the province elected him to the Russian Congress of People's Deputies in March 1990 with over 80 percent of the vote. When Yeltsin won the Russian Presidency against five other candidates on June 12, 1991, the same high percentage in his native province was his widest margin of victory in all of the eighty-nine Russian locales. Two years later, on April 24, 1993, when Russian voters were asked to vote in a referendum on Yeltsin's performance as President, the 85 percent in Sverdlovsk expressing support for him was the highest percentage he won in any of the Russian locales. In return, after he was elected President of Russia in June 1991, Yeltsin recruited some of the most important leaders for his presidential staff and his government cabinet from those former party-state officials with whom he had worked during the 1970s and early 1980s in Sverdlovsk.

In April 1985, because of Yeltsin's reputation for forthright honesty and his record managing a major industrial center, Gorbachev recruited him to Moscow and made him one of his Central Committee party secretaries overseeing the reform of the Soviet economy. By the end of 1985, Gorbachev had Viktor Grishin removed as the head of the Moscow Communist party and replaced by Yeltsin, with a mandate to clean up Moscow. As the head of the Moscow party, Yeltsin was supposed to purge Grishin's corrupt political cronies and initiate changes in the Soviet capital to make it a model for the rest of the country.

Yeltsin's initial falling out with Gorbachev resulted from his taking this mandate too literally. Yeltsin purged almost the entire party and city bureaucracy in Moscow, arrested the corrupt retail managers of the Grishin mafia, encouraged farmers to bring their products for sale in open-air markets, and staged uncensored cultural festivals for artists and musicians. By riding the trams and appearing unannounced to check on shortages at stores, Yeltsin struck Muscovites as a new sort of accessible and accountable leader. By the summer of 1987, Yeltsin began to decry the entire system of elite privileges and political nonaccountability of Communist party officials throughout the Soviet Union as the root cause of such unsavory local phenomena as the Grishin mafia.

Gorbachev's political strategy was premised on introducing changes so cautiously that they would not startle or openly threaten his opponents in the central leadership until it was too late for them to resist. Gorbachev did not wish to give them a pretext for organizing against change and against himself. He erred in considering Yeltsin a team player. Yeltsin erred in believing that Gorbachev intended to carry out a revolution against the entire Communist system. By the fall of 1987, Yeltsin had become the pretext that aroused Gorbachev's conservative opponents in the party leadership during what conventionally came to be known as the "Yeltsin affair."

At a session of the Politburo in October 1987, Yeltsin castigated Gorbachev for his willingness to compromise with those in the central leadership still defending corrupt party officials. Yeltsin specifically singled out Gorbachev's erstwhile ally in the Politburo and the Secretariat, the unofficial "Second Secretary" Yegor Ligachev. Yeltsin ended his verbal attack by threatening to resign both from the Politburo and from his position as head of the Moscow party, essentially in order to embarrass Gorbachev publicly and to force him into siding with Yeltsin. Yeltsin thought that he was going to help Gorbachev realize his true democratic nature. Yeltsin assumed that his staged showdown at the Politburo would pressure Gorbachev into removing Ligachev and other transitory allies and push for even greater democratic reforms and real political change to free Soviet society from party rule.

Instead, Gorbachev sided with Ligachev and forced Yeltsin over the next two months to step down from both positions. Gorbachev literally had Yeltsin dragged from his hospital bed and taken by ambulance to attend the city party meeting at which he was savaged by speakers and voted out as head. Those criticizing him at the meeting included some whom Yeltsin had recruited to work with him in cleaning up Moscow politically from 1985 to 1987 and some of Grishin's former corrupt political cronies whom Yeltsin had only recently fired or had brought criminal charges against.

Gorbachev still needed people like Yeltsin as a counterweight with which to threaten his die-hard opponents in the central leadership. As long as even more radical people like Yeltsin were around to point to, Gorbachev could retain support among the party leaders for his reforms by implying that he would resign if the majority failed to go along. If Gorbachev resigned, they would have to deal with the even more radical politicians waiting in the wings, such as Yeltsin.

The circumstances under which Yeltsin had been forced out—after berating the endemic corruption of the Communist party system at a Politburo meeting—made him something of a political cult hero among students, academics, and liberal young party members. Students at Moscow State University had attempted in December 1987 to collect signatures for a petition asking that Yeltsin be retained as Moscow party head. By 1988 lapel buttons with a photograph of Yeltsin had become a form of political protest against the Communist system. And Yeltsin was a highly sought-after speaker for local groups of university faculty, students, and other young liberals, even audiences of party members. These were groups whose enthusiasm and support for his reforms Gorbachev vitally needed to retain. Thus, because of Yeltsin's political value to Gorbachev, his visibility around Moscow was maintained, if only in a secondary ministerial capacity as the deputy head of the Soviet state construction committee during 1988 and early 1989.

Yeltsin's ouster from the central party leadership ultimately proved to be Gorbachev's, and not his, political undoing. From 1989 to 1991, Yeltsin became Gorbachev's chief national rival. When Gorbachev allowed contested free elections for a portion of the seats in the national parliament in 1989, Yeltsin defeated Gorbachev's candidate for deputy, representing the entire city of Moscow in the new parliament, receiving 90 percent of the Muscovites' votes. Yeltsin was once again nationally prominent. In May 1990, he was elected chair of the Russian republic's legislature. In July 1990, he lambasted Gorbachev and the conservatives on the floor of the twenty-eighth National Congress of the Communist party, dramatically resigning from the party and walking out of the hall before a national TV audience.

Yeltsin also enhanced his democratic aura and popularity by openly supporting declarations of political sovereignty by all of the newly elected republic governments in the summer and fall of 1990 and by encouraging bilateral treaties between Russia and each of them. The treaties laid the foundation for direct cooperation

Figure 29–2

Supporters of Boris Yeltsin Cheer as His Greeting to the Rally against the Communist Party is Read, July 1990

Source: Mike Urban

among the republic governments, which by 1991 were increasingly independent of and directly defiant of the central Soviet government in Moscow.

■ *THE DECLINE OF GORBACHEV AND SOVIET COMMUNISM*

Despite international acclaim, Gorbachev's popularity and support within the Soviet Union had plummeted by the beginning of 1991. The Gorbachev who only three years before had been enthusiastically embraced by millions of Soviet citizens for his promise to reform the Communist autocracy now had become widely seen as the major obstacle to any real, meaningful change. Gorbachev's public image had degraded to that of someone who no longer could authoritatively govern and who had lost both his commitment to reform and his political nerve.

In the fall of 1990, Gorbachev undercut his own economic advisors and their program to implement privatization of the economy over stages of 500 days by speaking against them and the program when it was introduced in the Soviet national legislature. His presidential decrees on reform were systematically ignored or blocked by the Soviet bureaucracy. He was politically embarrassed by party officials who still censored the media and by secret police agents who harassed the leaders of the new political parties and intimidated the public. He was berated by military officers during his speech at their convention in November 1990. In December 1990, he appointed mediocrities and hard-liners as Vice-President, Prime Minister, minister of the national police, and head of the state radio-television committee. Instead of selecting the most progressive and democratically committed national politicians, he passed over them or even forced them to resign from their offices. Many suspected that Gorbachev had sold out to those die-hard conservatives who were opposed to everything for which he had stood since coming to power in March 1985.

Since the fall of 1990, rumors from highly reliable sources had warned of an imminent coup against Gorbachev by his hard-line opponents in the Communist party, the armed forces, and the KGB. Gorbachev's closest political ally—his Foreign Minister since 1985, Eduard Shevardnadze—resigned December 20 on the floor of the Soviet parliament, delivering a dramatic speech in which he warned Gorbachev of a pending coup. Shevardnadze openly broke with Gorbachev because of the latter's apparent abandonment of his own liberal reform program and his willingness to surround himself with the very individuals likely to plot such a coup.

Shevardnadze's warning seemed especially prophetic as 1991 began. KGB troops along with the elite OMON (Russian acronym for "Special Designation Militia Attachments") of the Soviet internal police surrounded the main press building in the capital of Latvia on January 3 and the main television building in the capital of Lithuania on January 13. On January 20, they stormed the headquarters of the Latvian republic's Ministry of Internal Affairs (police). Eighteen civilians were killed by the Soviet troops during their taking of the Lithuanian television building and the Latvian police center. Lithuanian nationalists formed a human barricade around the Lithuanian parliament building to prevent its seizure by the Soviet troops.

The actions by the Soviet troops challenged the authority of the anti-Soviet and anti-Communist leaders in Lithuania and Latvia, who had come to power in the 1990 parliamentary elections. The Baltic popular fronts in Latvia, Lithuania and Estonia had become powerful political movements, demanding the political sovereignty of their republics and their eventual independence from the Soviet Union as separate countries. The leadership and the majority of Communist and non-Communist deputies in their parliaments were closely tied to the popular fronts and were committed to gaining independence. Defying the wishes of Moscow, the Baltic republics' prime ministers, with the approval of their parliaments, had appointed their own pro-independence officials to head their respective internal police forces. The print and electronic media in all three republics had been in effect free of any censorship over the past two years. Thus, the buildings attacked and seized by the Soviet troops had come to symbolize the emerging demand for independence from Soviet Communism.

Gorbachev had not known beforehand about the military actions in January 1991. He later disavowed them, but it was several months before the troops were actually withdrawn from the three buildings. More importantly, Gorbachev's own words and actions throughout 1989 and 1990 had created the climate of hostility under which his nominal subordinates had acted. Since 1989, Gorbachev had consistently ridiculed the popular fronts in all three Baltic republics.

In April 1990, Gorbachev steamrolled through the national parliament a law making it virtually impossible for any republic to secede from the Soviet Union. The law implied that Soviet military force would be used to prevent secession, if republic governments failed to comply with cumbersome procedures requiring two-thirds majorities in several referenda and a six-year waiting period. Periodically during the spring and summer of 1990, Gorbachev even resorted to imposing an economic embargo on Lithuania and threatening one against Latvia and Estonia to pressure their leaders and parliaments into suspending their declarations of independence.

Whatever Gorbachev's personal culpability, the military actions in January 1991 were clearly intended to be provocative. Those opposed to the breakup of the Soviet Union and to the anti-Communist revolution sweeping through several republics wanted the Baltic leaders to call out their own militias to defend their civilian populations against the Soviet troops. If they had, it would have provided a pretext to send in additional forces. Gorbachev as President then would have been forced into declaring emergency martial law to restore "order."

Under emergency martial law, Lithuania's and Latvia's parliaments would have been dissolved, their government leaders arrested, their nationalist popular fronts banned, and their free media shut down. Power would have been given to so-called national salvation fronts made up of collaborationists recruited from pro-Moscow Lithuanian and Latvian Communist party officials. The political crackdown would have created a precedent for carrying out similar actions and installing national salvation fronts in several other republics with popular fronts.

The Lithuanian and Latvian leadership refused to take the bait. Instead, in February and March 1991, the voters in Estonia, Latvia, and Lithuania all approved by overwhelming majorities nonbinding plebiscites in favor of their independence from the Soviet Union. Gorbachev denounced the plebiscites as anticonstitutional and a direct violation of the law on secession that he had pushed through the national parliament in 1990. Throughout the rest of the Soviet Union, many leaders elected to republic and local governments on a pro-reform platform in 1990 rallied to the defense of the Lithuanian and Latvian governments. To counter Gorbachev's embargo, they arranged to have special truck convoys and trains with supplies sent to relieve the besieged Baltic republics. Several republic and local legislatures passed resolutions supporting the governments of Lithuania and Latvia and denouncing the action authorized by the central government in Moscow.

Since his election as chair of the Russian republic's Supreme Soviet in May 1990, Boris Yeltsin had emerged as the leading national reformer among these new republic and local officials. In a national TV broadcast in February 1991, Yeltsin openly called for the resignation of President Gorbachev. He held Gorbachev at least indirectly responsible for the attacks in the Baltic republics—because of Gorbachev's abandonment of reform policies since the fall of 1990 and his appointment of the military and police officials who had sanctioned the attack.

At the same time, Gorbachev's reluctance to follow through on the attacks in Latvia and Lithuania estranged him politically and completely from the other side—the die-hard anti-reformists and pro-Unionists within the Communist party leadership, the secret police, the military, and the national parliament. Collectively, they condemned Gorbachev for his alleged cowardice in not imposing martial law in the Baltic republics in the first place and for not clamping down with force on Yeltsin and other defiant reformist politicians and movements in several other republics, provinces, and cities. Not least, they blamed him for sponsorship of economic, democratic, and foreign policy reforms over the previous five years, which had created the very conditions that were rapidly leading to the collapse of the Communist system and the dismemberment of the Soviet Union. During the first eight months of 1991, Gorbachev was continually challenged at plenary sessions of the national party's Central Committee with motions repudiating all of his reform policies and asking for his resignation as head of the party. The die-hard conservative element of the press joined the chorus by accusing Gorbachev of being an advocate of Western capitalism and implying that he was a paid secret agent of the CIA.

In the national parliament (Congress), 450 of the 2,250 deputies formed the largest caucus in 1990 and called themselves the "Union" (*Soyuz*). The conservative military officers who constituted the caucus leaders consistently berated Gorbachev and his former foreign minister Shevardnadze in floor debates for their "failures" in foreign policy. The caucus blamed Gorbachev and Shevardnadze for having "lost Eastern Europe" through their policies that had encouraged the anti-Communist revolutions in these countries, forced the Soviet military withdrawal from the region, dissolved the Warsaw Pact, and now threatened the very unity of the Soviet Union. The Union caucus also condemned Gorbachev and Shevardnadze for their unilateral disarmament of the country through the 1990–1991 agreements with the United States, which had drastically reduced Soviet conventional and nuclear arsenals.

The Union caucus came very close to charging Gorbachev and Shevardnadze with treason for their repudiation of Communist dogma in foreign policy and their abandonment of Communist allies around the world. For the caucus, Gorbachev's and Shevardnadze's close cooperation with Western countries and almost informal alliance with the United States on a number of international issues betrayed Communist morality and proved their unprincipled cowardice. The caucus was particularly outraged by Gorbachev's and Shevardnadze's support of the UN operation that ousted the long-time Soviet ally Saddam Hussein from Kuwait in February–March 1991. Shevardnadze's dramatic resignation as foreign minister on December 20 came at the height of caucus criticisms of himself and Gorbachev for the Soviet support of Operation Desert Storm, which was led by U.S. troops.

In the Russian parliament, by March 1991 conservative military and party deputies attempted to heat up the political confrontation between Gorbachev and Yeltsin and to force Gorbachev into completely abandoning the reformists. They introduced a resolution calling for the impeachment of Yeltsin as Russian chair, accusing him of undermining constitutional order by having appealed for Gorbachev's resignation as Soviet President. Street demonstrations and rallies for Yeltsin and for Gorbachev raged throughout the major cities of the Soviet Union in the winter and early spring of 1991.

The pro-Yeltsin coal miners in Western Siberia and other areas of the Soviet Union went out on general strike in March and April, demanding both Gorbachev's resignation and the dissolution of the national parliament. The majority of the national parliament now opposed Gorbachev—both the Union caucus on the right and the minority of real pro-reform deputies on the democratic left. Disillusioned by Gorbachev's vacillation over the pace and direction of reforms since 1989, the pro-reform deputies had long since given up on Gorbachev and had joined Yeltsin and others in calling for a dissolution of their own body and the creation of a new democratic Soviet state in the form of a loose confederation of independent union republics.

In a last-ditch attempt to salvage his authority, Gorbachev arranged for a national referendum on March 17, in which a majority of the Soviet population affirmatively responded to an ambiguous question as to whether they wanted the Soviet Union to be retained as a single country. In a countermove, Yeltsin had the Russian parliament include a second referendum question on the same ballot in the Russian republic, asking for the approval of voters there to amend the Russian constitution and allow for a directly elected President as chief executive and head of state of the republic. A much larger percentage of Russian voters responded affirmatively to this question than to Gorbachev's one asking their opinion on the Soviet Union. Three months later, on June 12, Yeltsin was elected the first President of Russia for a five-year term; he won out over five other candidates with 57 percent of the vote. (This was the first time in over a thousand years of Russian history that the people had chosen the chief executive!)

By the first week of April, the conflict between Gorbachev and Yeltsin reached a crisis. Many feared an open clash between Gorbachev's and Yeltsin's supporters in the streets of Moscow, which might result in Gorbachev's imposing emergency rule. Emergency rule decreed by Gorbachev would have been ignored if not countermanded by Yeltsin as the chief executive of the Russian republic. A worse-case scenario foresaw Soviet troops being called out by Gorbachev to enforce emergency rule and confronting Russian republic troops and police authorized by Yeltsin to disarm Gorbachev's troops and void the order of emergency rule. The only winners in that scenario would have been the die-hard opponents of both Gorbachev and Yeltsin.

Backing away from the abyss that emergency rule and a likely civil war would create, Gorbachev finally seemed to have reconciled himself to granting real autonomy to the fifteen union republics. At a week-long meeting with the leaders of nine of the republics in a suburb of Moscow called Novo-Ogarevo, Gorbachev conceded the necessity of drafting a new union treaty to redefine the relative powers and authority structure for the national and republic governments. The principles for a draft treaty were signed on April 23 at Novo-Ogarevo by Gorbachev and nine republic leaders, including Yeltsin for Russia.

The principles envisaged granting extensive autonomy to the republic governments under the specific terms of a draft treaty to be negotiated throughout the subsequent four months of late spring and early summer. The Soviet Union would be retained as a country but politically transformed into almost a confederation. The powers of the central government would be limited to monetary, defense, and foreign policy for the Union as a whole. With these exceptions, almost all sovereign authority would be delegated to the republic governments, including the right to make their own foreign policy and establish diplomatic missions with other countries independent of actions by the central government. Gorbachev and the nine republic leaders pledged they would adopt a new democratic constitution and call new elections for a national parliament and the office of Soviet President soon after ratification of the treaty.

Gorbachev and the nine republic leaders were to sign the treaty on August 20, and it would have gone into effect once it had subsequently been ratified by both the national parliament and the parliaments of the nine republics. The other six republics would have been allowed to join later or effectively to secede from the Union by not signing the treaty. To symbolize the repudiation of the Communist past, associated with the word "Socialist," the new name of the country as a confederation was to be Union of Soviet Sovereign Republics—whose abbreviations conveniently retain the same letters in the Cyrillic alphabet (SSSR) and English (USSR).

Twenty-four hours before Gorbachev was to return from vacation to oversee the signing, he was placed under house arrest at the orders of the so-called Emergency Committee, which attempted to overthrow the central government in a coup and assume the power to institute martial law. The leaders of the coup were the head of the KGB and the very same Vice-President, Prime Minister, and minister of internal affairs whom Gorbachev had appointed contrary to the advice of Shevardnadze and others only nine months before.

The coup failed within three days, because Soviet society and all political institutions had become bitterly divided between supporters and opponents of Gorbachev's liberal democratic reforms. The coup leaders could not even get the elite KGB Alpha force or the armed military divisions in Moscow to assault the Russian parliament building in which Yeltsin defied them on August 19 and 20. Officers of the KGB unit and the military divisions openly supported Yeltsin, smuggled arms into the parliament building, and refused to obey the orders of the coup leaders. The same pattern held in other parts of the Soviet Union. Local KGB and military garrisons were so divided that the orders of the coup leaders in Moscow to impose emergency rule were frequently ignored or countermanded by pro-Yeltsin factions.

Gorbachev returned to Moscow as the President of the Soviet Union on the evening of August 21, but it was a much different country politically than when he had left the week before on vacation. The foiled coup attempt and its consequences had fundamentally transformed the nature of power and totally discredited the remaining vestiges of central governmental authority identified with his office.

The individual who had emerged by August 21 as the most powerful official was Boris Yeltsin. Yeltsin's new national power derived not just from his position as President of the Russian republic but from his courageous opposition to the coup. It had been Yeltsin who led the public opposition from the Russian parliament building in Moscow. Gorbachev's popularity and authority, already waning over the previous two years because of his unwillingness to accelerate the pace of democratic and economic reforms, declined even further with the failed coup.

It soon became evident that Yeltsin, not Gorbachev, now held the real power and final authority to authorize decisions and carry out policies nationally. Days after August 21, Yeltsin issued a decree banning the Communist party in Russia, and his action was quickly copied by the governments in other union republics, which banned or outlawed the Communist party in their own jurisdictions. Gorbachev, who until August 19 had insisted that the party could be democratically reformed under his leadership and could still rule an integrated Soviet Union, resigned as

General Secretary. By the end of August, the three Baltic republics declared their independence and seceded from the Soviet Union, with President Yeltsin's blessing. The change from Gorbachev, who had even resorted to economic embargos in 1990 to pressure the Baltic governments into suspending their declarations of independence, could not have been any clearer.

Within three months of the attempted coup, the national executive branch of the Soviet government was dissolved. Its authority was transferred to an interim council of the heads of those republics that still intended to sign a new treaty and become members of a new confederation. The Congress of the Soviet Union, created at Gorbachev's initiative less than three years before, was disbanded. Its 2,250 deputies were promised three years' salary, which they would have received if they had completed their parliamentary term, as a kind of severance pay and incentive to accept the parliament's complete dissolution.

The parliament had been dominated by those who had openly opposed democratic reforms and Yeltsin in 1990–1991. Anatolii Lukyanov, the chair of the standing legislature called the Supreme Soviet and a close ally of Gorbachev, had been originally appointed to the position by Gorbachev in March 1990, when Gorbachev was elected President by the parliament, and had to give up the position. By the end of August 1991, Lukyanov was in prison, arrested for having allegedly masterminded the abortive coup along with Vice-President Gennadii Yanaev, Prime Minister Valentin Pavlov, KGB Chief Vladimir Kryuchkov, and Defense Minister Dmitrii Yazov.

If he had emerged as the *de facto* national leader, Yeltsin intended to hold the country together with a new union treaty that would have granted Russia, under his leadership, a predominant economic and political role. On December 1, however, the voters of Ukraine, the second-largest union republic, voted overwhelmingly to secede from the Soviet Union, approving by a large majority of over 90 percent a national referendum declaring their republic an independent country. They also elected as their President Leonid Kravchuk, by a majority of 62 percent. Kravchuk, a career functionary in the Ukrainian Communist party and Second Secretary of the Ukrainian Central Committee in early 1990, had increasingly distanced himself from orthodox Communist thinking since June 1990, when he was elected chair of the Ukrainian parliament. Kravchuk's election as President was widely credited to his supporting Ukrainian sovereignty since 1990, his identification with Ukrainian nationalism, and his enthusiastic endorsement of the Ukrainian referendum on independence before December 1.

With Ukraine no longer part of the Soviet Union, Yeltsin conceded to the inevitable. After the Ukrainian referendum, he hastily arranged for a meeting of himself, Ukrainian president Kravchuk, and Stanislau Shushkevich, the chair of the Belorussian parliament. Not a career politician, Shushkevich was a nuclear physicist. He had been elected chair a month after the abortive August coup and the banning of the Communist party in Belorussia. Conspicuously absent from the meeting was Gorbachev, who was still attempting to gain the support of Yeltsin and other republic leaders for a new union treaty based on the Novo-Ogarevo principles to preserve the Soviet Union as a confederation. Back in Moscow, he learned of the Belovezhskii accord from news reports.

■ THE FALL OF THE SOVIET UNION

Within little more than four months after the aborted coup, the Soviet Union ceased to exist as a country. The climax came in December 1991, in the suburban estate of Belovezhskii outside Minsk, the capital of the union republic of Belorussia. Yeltsin, Shushkevich, and Kravchuk signed on December 8 an agreement that sealed the fate of the Soviet Union. In the Belovezhskii accord, they declared the independence of their republics, with a combined 210 million people, from the Soviet Union and resolved that the Soviet Union no longer existed as a geopolitical entity. Within the next week, the nine remaining republics of the Soviet Union were to follow their initiative, declaring their own independence as countries. The other three former republics of the Soviet Union—Latvia, Lithuania, and Estonia—hadn't even waited for December; they had been recognized internationally as countries since September. Even before the Belovezhskii accord, their republic parliaments had already passed laws renouncing all past treaties and constitutions of the Soviet Union and nullifying the enforcement of Soviet laws on their territories.

Shushkevich, Kravchuk, and Yeltsin intentionally chose the capital of Belorussia as the site for signing their declaration of independence from the Soviet Union. Belorussia (renamed the Republic of Belarus on September 19, 1991 by a vote of the Belorussian parliament) was the smallest of the three former union republics, with slightly more than 10 million people. The three leaders intended to send a signal by choosing the capital of Belorussia for the signing of the accord. They also designated Minsk the center for the Commonwealth of Independent States, the international organization they formed to coordinate political, economic, and military affairs among the nation-states that were seceding from the Soviet Union. An independent Russian Federation would far surpass in size and population all of the other fourteen countries combined. The choice of Minsk rather than Moscow signaled a new beginning, allaying any fear in the other republics that they would secede from the Soviet Union only to be dominated by an independent Russia.

If the choice of Minsk was to assure the other fourteen republics about Russia's role in a post-Soviet Commonwealth, a certain irony existed. Twice before, Belorussia had been the site of dramatic turning points in the history of the Soviet Union, affecting the entire course of history in the twentieth century. Yeltsin, Kravchuk, and Shushkevich must have reflected on the irony, the passage of time, and the political circumstances of the past three years that led them to Belovezhskii.

From Brest-Litovsk to Belovezhskii

The first historical turning point occurred only a few hundred kilometers west of Minsk in March 1918. The founders of the Soviet Union had seized power in a coup five months before and were already embroiled in a civil war. They sent emissaries to negotiate a treaty with the German high command of the Second Reich under Kaiser Wilhelm. Both sides had gathered to end a war between Russia and Germany that since 1914 had cost the lives of over 2 million soldiers of the Russian empire. The treaty was to ensure the withdrawal of several hundred thousand German troops occupying the western regions of the Russian empire. Germany had effectively won the war.

The Russian army was in retreat and disarray, no longer willing to defend a political system that had ceased to exist. Vladimir Lenin, the leader of the Bolshevik faction of the Russian Social Democratic Labor party (later renamed the Communist party), had appointed emissaries to negotiate for the new state that he had named the Soviet Russian Socialist Republic. Naming the political system was an act of faith, for Lenin and his supporters had effective control only of Petrograd, the capital of the former empire, and some outlying provinces and isolated cities in the central region near Moscow. Lenin had proclaimed a new state and presumed the right to negotiate with the Germans as the sovereign government only by virtue of having overthrown the Provisional Government of Russia on November 7, 1917.

The Provisional Government itself had only been in power for nine months following the forced abdication in February 1917 of Tsar Nicholas II, the ruler of the Russian empire. A series of monarchs descended from the dynastic Romanov family had reigned over this empire for 300 years. With Nicholas's abdication, the empire and any form of centralized rule had collapsed. Lenin and the Bolsheviks had taken advantage of the political vacuum to seize power and declare themselves the new central government.

Named after the Belorussian-Polish town on Russia's western border where negotiations were held, the Brest-Litovsk Treaty was a calculated gamble for Lenin and the other Bolshevik leaders. They conceded defeat in the name of Russia to Germany. Under terms of the treaty, Lenin's emissaries ceded large western territories of the former empire, which were granted their freedom to pursue their own political and national self-determination. Lenin's signing of the treaty outraged the governments of Britain and France. Both of those countries had been allied with the Russian empire against Germany since 1914 and feared defeat if the German troops on the eastern front were redeployed to fight on the western front in Belgium and France. Anxious to make sure that any government that succeeded the tsar would keep Russia in the war and hold down German troops on the eastern front, Britain and France sent military forces to intervene in Russia in 1917. After March 1918, those forces supported anyone opposed to Lenin and his government, because it had pulled Russia out of the war.

Yet the gamble of Brest-Litovsk ultimately proved successful for Lenin and the Bolsheviks. The treaty ended Russia's state of war with Germany, removed German troops from Russian soil, and in the process legitimated Lenin and the rest of the Bolshevik leadership as the rulers of the political system that was the successor to the former empire. The treaty won them the gratitude of a war-weary population and projected them as the alleged national saviors of a country threatened with potential annihilation by the German army. As a result, they were able to mobilize enough soldiers, peasants, and workers into their Communist Red Army over the next three years of the Civil War (from 1918 to 1920) to defeat the forces of those who had opposed their seizure of power in November 1917 and their claim to have founded a new political system. It was Brest-Litovsk that gave Lenin and the Bolsheviks the legitimacy, opportunity, and support that allowed them to triumph militarily and politically by 1921.

Without the Brest-Litovsk Treaty as a turning point, the history of the twentieth century probably would have been quite different. The Communists under Lenin would have lost the ensuing Civil War against their opponents. The Soviet Union, which for the subsequent seven decades came to represent the principal ideological and military threat to Western democracies, would never have even come into existence. Many of the estimated 20 million citizens of the Soviet Union who died in the 1930s and 1940s through starvation and systematic political terrorism at the hands of the secret police might have lived. The home-grown versions of Communist revolutions and regimes in other countries such as China, which systematically terrorized and murdered millions of their own citizens in the subsequent decades of the twentieth century, also may never have occurred.

From Barbarossa to Belovezhskii

The Minsk region was also the site of a second historical turning point in the evolution of the Soviet Union—one that almost led to the complete physical destruction of the country and the annihilation of a significant percentage of its population. Belorussia was one of the front-line areas captured in the first three weeks after the German forces of Adolf Hitler invaded the Soviet Union on June 22, 1941, under the military code name of Operation Barbarossa.

Joseph Stalin, the Soviet leader at the time, had made a calculated gamble with the Germany of Hitler. On August 31, 1939, Stalin signed a nonaggression pact with Hitler that allowed Hitler to invade Poland and begin World War II, without fear of having to fight a two-front war against Britain and France in the west and a Soviet Union allied with them in the east. Stalin had assumed that the pact and the extensive Soviet economic support given to Hitler to launch his invasion of France and the rest of Western Europe in 1940 would allay Hitler's aggressive designs against Communism and the Soviet Union. An unofficial ally of Hitler's for 22 months, Stalin had also benefited from secret agreements with Hitler that allowed the Soviet Union to redraw its western boundaries, forcibly incorporating the eastern one-third of Poland and the formerly independent countries of Lithuania, Latvia, and Estonia. These were some of the same areas of the former Russian empire to which Lenin had been forced to grant independence under pressure from Germany at Brest-Litovsk in March 1918.

Minsk and Belorussia were only the first front-line regions to suffer from Stalin's misjudgment. Stalin's misreading of Hitler resulted in Nazi Germany's occupying all of the western one-third of the Soviet Union until mid-1943 and almost 27 million Soviet military and civilian deaths before the Soviet Union, allied with the United States, Britain, and France, eventually defeated Germany in May 1945. Those killed constituted over 13.5 percent of the entire Soviet population (the estimated 1939 population of what then made up the country plus the populations of the regions and countries that had been forcibly annexed to the Soviet Union through Stalin's agreements with Hitler). Over 250,000 ethnic Belorussians were among the total of 8.7 million killed in the Soviet military.

The defeat of Hitler quickly ushered in the Cold War between the Soviet Union and the United States. This coincided with the political-military domination of Eastern Europe as a Soviet empire for 44 years, until a wave of revolutions swept the Soviet-imposed Communist systems from power in the tumultuous fall and winter of 1989–1990. The collapse of the Soviet Communist empire in Eastern Europe in 1989 had accelerated the revolutionary waves of nationalist discontent and political rebellion in the ethnic republics in the Soviet Union. The reform politicians Yeltsin and Kravchuk and the nuclear physicist Shushkevich were all by-products of the revolutionary stirrings in their own republics.

Thus the Belovezhskii accord reversed the consequences of World War II and ended the Stalinist legacy of that war. The three Baltic states that had been forcibly annexed by the Soviet Union and had declared their independence after the abortive August coup were now assured that they would no longer be threatened by the Soviet Union. The regions of pre–World War II Poland, Czechoslovakia, and Romania absorbed by Stalin into the Soviet Union in 1945 regained their independence—as the western regions in the new countries of Belarus and Ukraine.

■ A NEW BEGINNING

On December 17, 1991, Yeltsin and Gorbachev met and signed a communique agreeing that the Soviet Union would formally cease to exist as of midnight December 31. On December 25, 1991, at 7:32 p.m., President Gorbachev spoke over national television from a studio in Moscow to announce both his resignation and the formal demise of the country. Before he even completed his speech, the red flag with its hammer and sickle emblematic of the former Soviet Union had been lowered from its mast over the Kremlin in Moscow, where all of the central governmental offices had resided since 1922. The red flag was replaced by the tricolored white, blue, and red flag of the newly independent country, the Russian Federation, whose capital is Moscow and whose central governmental offices are located in the Kremlin.

Within a few days, Boris Yeltsin, the President of the Russian Federation, had moved into the offices of Gorbachev, the ex-President of a former country and now just a private citizen of Russia. The TV studio from which Gorbachev gave his address became the property of the Russian state television and radio committee before the end of the year. On December 30, leaders of the other republics that had declared their independence from the Soviet Union after the Belovezhskii accord met with the leaders of Belarus, Ukraine, and Russia in Alma-Ata, the capital of Kazakhstan, to sign a collective declaration ending the Soviet Union. New Year's Eve 1991 found the populations of the former Soviet Union welcoming 1992 as citizens of fifteen newly independent countries constituting a region of the world known as Russia and Central Eurasia.

Eleven of those countries formed a new transitory interstate relationship as the Commonwealth of Independent States (*Sodruzhestvo Nezavisimikh Gosudarstv*). (The acronym in Russian for the Commonwealth is roughly pronounced "sneg"— the same as the Russian word for snow.) In the Russian Federation, the fourteen countries that used to constitute the union republics other than Russia are now termed colloquially the "near abroad" (*blizhnee zarubezh'e*). From 1992 on, all references to the Soviet Union by their media have been preceded by the adjective "former" (*byvshii*), as though "former" had been part of the official name of the country.

Since 1992, what is "in" societally for the fifteen countries are Western institutions such as parliamentary democracies and free-enterprise market economies, Western values such as the primacy of the individual before the state, and Western culture such as Dixieland jazz and MTV rock videos. What is "out" societally are former Soviet institutions such as the Communist party and the nationalized economy, regimentation of individuals by censorship and the secret police, and the classical music and other traditional art forms funded and supported by the Soviet state through union guilds. "Politically correct" are references to the history, ethnic heritage, and personages that predate the Soviet Union. "Politically incorrect" are positive retrospective assessments of anything that was accomplished or anyone that was politically prominent under Soviet rule.

Those who were born and raised in the former Soviet Union must be struck by the astounding changes in their lives and the ironic contrasts in their societies. Citizens no longer fear the dreaded KGB or imprisonment for their political beliefs. They do fear becoming innocent victims of shootouts on the streets between rival gangs of organized criminals fighting for control of the drug trade, prostitution, and other rackets. The international Communist movement led by Moscow no longer exists. In its place is an international criminal cartel with Russian-organized crime families run by their godfathers in Moscow and operating widely throughout Western Europe and even in the United States. Hundreds of thousands of private business establishments have formed since 1991. Many owners of these private businesses now actively seek government intrusion by the local

Figure 29–3
Street Band in Moscow in July 1990 Spontaneously Breaking into Their Rendition of "When the Saints Go Marchin' In"

Source: Mike Urban

police, in order to protect themselves from extortion and threats by the organized criminal gangs.

The media no longer are censored or told what they can present by Communist political authorities. At the same time almost all printed media cannot publish profitably because of skyrocketing costs due to hyperinflation, and the two most successful weekly publications sold on the streets in Moscow are a hard-core pornographic magazine and a newspaper that runs advertisements for massage parlors and female models. Citizens no longer are prohibited from traveling anywhere they want, passports are easily obtainable, and millions in Russia and Central Eurasia are leaving their countries every year. However, citizens visiting other countries in Russia and Central Eurasia now must have visas. Many of those seen in the railroad stations and airports and on the roads with their suitcases are fleeing civil wars and separatist movements that have sprung up almost everywhere in Russia and Central Eurasia since 1991.

Thousands of place names for factories, farms, buildings, streets, institutions, and cities have been changed—especially those that had been renamed for Soviet Communist leaders in the 1920s and 1930s. Leningrad, the second-largest city in the former Soviet Union, which was named for Lenin after his death in 1924, has reverted to St. Petersburg, as it had been known from its founding in 1721. Sverdlovsk and Kuibyshev, the fifth- and sixth-largest cities in Russia, which had been named for two prominent Communists from the first decade of Soviet rule, have reverted to Yekaterinburg and Samara, which they had been called since the eighteenth century. Gorkii, the third-largest city of Russia, which had been renamed for a favorite writer of Communist culture, became once again Nizhnii Novgorod, which it had been known as from its founding in 1221 until 1936. Frunze, the capital of Kyrgyzstan, which had been named for the leader of the Communist military force that crushed the Muslim independence movement in the 1920s, became Bishkek, a Turkic name commemorating the region's ethnic-cultural origins before it had been militarily conquered by the Russian tsars.

Thus, with a New Year's Eve celebration and not a violent political revolution, a country expired that had profoundly influenced world events in the twentieth century. With new terms, new values, new realities, and new fears, a political system was expunged that had epitomized the very worst excesses in human civilization. The changing of place names back to their pre-1917 ones blotted out reminders of the Communist autocracy that had ruled for the past seven decades.

The Soviet Union was founded on an ideology that presumed that objective social forces—not individuals—made history. The end of the Soviet Union proved just the opposite. The history of 1985–1991 in many ways was the story of two Russians, Mikhail Gorbachev and Boris Yeltsin, who had many things in common but transformed the world because of their different personalities and acts.

30

The Setting of Russian and Central Eurasian Politics

The fifteen countries of the former Soviet Union form a land mass known to geographers as Central Eurasia. The largest is a country that by amendment of its Constitution is officially named Russian Federation–Russia, which is often shortened to either the Russian Federation or Russia.[1] Although Russia is really one country *within* Central Eurasia, the misnomer "Russia and Central Eurasia" has been widely used worldwide since 1991 and will be adopted as our term for all fifteen post-Soviet countries. This name retains a sense of the geographic and historic commonality linking the fifteen countries while singling out Russia's immense size within this overall land mass spanning the European and Asian continents (see Figure 30–1).

Alternative commonly used terms for the post-Soviet countries are Former Soviet Union (FSU) and the Commonwealth of Independent States (CIS). The problem with FSU is its negative ambiguity, linking countries only by what they are not (and easily confused by students in the United States with the abbreviation for Florida State University). FSU is also considered somewhat demeaning by leaders and intellectuals in these countries. An analogy would be if countries such as Poland and Czechoslovakia that were incorporated by Hitler into the German Empire in 1939–1944 were still termed the "Former Third Reich."[2]

---

[1] In the Russian language, the name of the country is *Rossiiskaya Federatsiya–Rossiya. Rossiiskaya* and *Rossiya* are words for "Russian" and "Russia" in a geographic sense. They connote citizenship of the country not based solely on any specific ethnic nationality. In contrast, the adjective-noun in the Russian language, *Russkii* ("Russian"), denotes exclusively only those who are Russian by ethnic nationality.

[2] Equally demeaning is Newly Independent Countries (NIC). The citizens and governments of post–1991 Lithuania, Latvia, and Estonia adamantly reject the adjective "new" in referring to their countries, which they consider to be the same as those first constituted in 1919. They view the fifty-one years of their incorporation into the Soviet Union, from 1940 through August 1991, as a foreign military occupation. NIC is also ambiguous because several newly independent countries that were not part of the Soviet Union have formed in Central and Eastern Europe, such as Slovakia, Slovenia, Croatia, Bosnia-Herzegovina, and Macedonia..

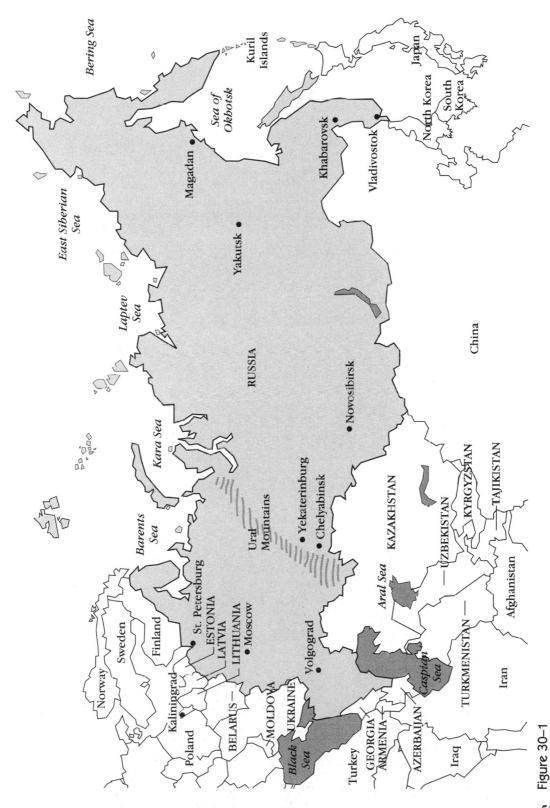

Figure 30–1
Russia and Central Eurasia

■ THE COMMONWEALTH OF INDEPENDENT STATES

The Commonwealth of Independent States is a more positive and accurate term, but the brief history of the CIS doesn't warrant complete confidence in its future. At its outset in December 1991, the Commonwealth was only a transitional arrangement made among the fifteen countries to resolve numerous issues, such as the debt each country should assume or the military arsenal and economic assets each should receive as its share of the former Soviet Union. Ukrainian President Leonid Kravchuk characterized the CIS as nothing more than a "civilized divorce" among the fifteen countries to preclude total chaos with the demise of the Soviet Union, and he termed Ukraine's membership in it only temporary.

Russian President Boris Yeltsin and Kazakhstani President Nursultan Nazarbayev had a different perspective of the CIS, visualizing it as a means of preserving the economic and military integration of the former Soviet Union, but on the basis of equality and democratic negotiations among the fifteen countries. Yet even Yeltsin and Nazarbayev have conceded that the CIS was never intended to replace the Soviet Union. The primary concern for all of the fifteen countries has been to establish and to preserve their newly won independent statehood.

A "Civilized Divorce"

Depending on how membership is defined, only nine, ten, or eleven of the former Soviet republics belong to the CIS. Moldovan President Mircea Snegur signed the treaty establishing the CIS in December 1991, but the Moldovan parliament has never even discussed ratifying the treaty and will probably never formalize the country's membership. A majority of the Moldovan parliament and Snegur, reflecting public opinion in their country, fear the CIS as a new "center" under which Russia will again dominate all of the other countries of the former Soviet Union. Ayaz Mutalibov, the President of Azerbaijan at the time of independence, also signed the treaty in December 1991, at the same time as his own cabinet members in Baku were unanimously voting against joining the CIS. Since 1991, Azerbaijan has had two other presidents, and both have denounced the CIS as either a worthless international organization or one threatening Azerbaijan's independence because of Russia's predominant influence in it. In October 1992, the Azerbaijani parliament unanimously voted against ratification of the CIS treaty signed by Mutalibov in 1991.

Never ratifying the treaty or formally becoming members of the CIS has not prevented the political leaders of Moldova and Azerbaijan from participating in CIS sessions since 1991 and even signing agreements, when they have deemed their action to be in the national interests of their countries. Moldova has enthusiastically supported various agreements of the CIS to reintegrate the economies of Russia and Central Eurasia, primarily because Moldova is one of the poorest and least developed of the post-Soviet countries. The various interstate committees of foreign and defense ministers under the CIS have provided the Azerbaijani government an important forum for meeting and negotiating with their counterparts in the Armenian government. Since 1992, Azerbaijan has been engaged in an unde-clared war with Armenia over the disputed Armenian ethnic enclave of Nagorno-Karabakh located inside the borders of Azerbaijan.

The four former Soviet republics that never signed the Commonwealth treaty in the first place are Georgia, Lithuania, Latvia, and Estonia. Georgian political lead-ers have expressed an interest in joining the CIS, but political instability in the coun-try since independence has precluded making such a commitment. Zviad Gamsakhurdia, an anti-Communist and anti-Soviet Georgian nationalist was elected President of the country in the fall of 1990, but soon turned into a dictator and was overthrown in a coup orchestrated by his own defense minister and former closest political advisors in December 1991. He was replaced by Eduard Shevardnadze, the former Foreign Minister, close friend, and advisor of Gorbachev. Shevardnadze has been prevented from joining the CIS by increasing tensions between Georgia and Russia over the support of Russian troops for the breakaway separatist movement of a Muslim ethnic minority in Georgia called Abkhazians.

The three Baltic states never indicated any interest in joining the CIS. The gov-ernments of Lithuania, Latvia, and Estonia have persistently stated that the CIS, by the very nature of things, would be dominated by Russia. And these governments are in conflict with the Russian government over the several thousand former Soviet troops, which became part of the Russian national army after 1991, that still remain in their countries.

Yet Georgia, Lithuania, Latvia, and Estonia have attended and participated as observers in various committees and international conferences organized under the auspices of the CIS to resolve problems from the demise of the Soviet Union. Excluding them and including Moldova and Azerbaijan, the eleven countries of the CIS have a combined population of 278 million people across a territory of 22.2 mil-lion square kilometers. They account for 95 percent of the population and almost 99 percent of the territory of the former Soviet Union.

Ukraine, the second largest member of the CIS, has been an extremely reluc-tant member from the outset. President Kravchuk and a large majority in the Ukrainian parliament, representing a wide spectrum of political views, have consis-tently voiced their opposition to strengthening the central organs of the CIS in Minsk. They want the CIS to dissolve entirely, once circumstances stabilize suffi-ciently. Kravchuk and Ukrainian public opinion have strongly favored close eco-nomic integration of the countries, similar to when they were part of a unified country, but only as long as that integration doesn't threaten to revive the central political authority of a Soviet Union under another name.

Among the eleven countries, Russia and Kazakhstan have been the most enthu-siastic advocates of a stronger Commonwealth with empowered international organs. Their vision in many ways resembles the confederal arrangement and new union treaty negotiated by the nine republics with Gorbachev in the summer of 1991. Recall that that treaty was never signed because of the complete collapse of the central government and the declarations of independence by all fifteen republics after the abortive August 1991 coup, followed by the formal dissolution of the Soviet Union in December.

The remaining countries fall between Ukraine and the Russia and Kazkahstan pair in their level of enthusiasm for the CIS. Belarus has been very interested in forming a joint military security arrangement with Russia. Six countries (Russia, Belarus, Kazakhstan, Armenia, Kyrgyzstan, and Tajikistan) elect deputies from their national parliaments to participate in the CIS Interparliamentary Assembly, but the Assembly meets only infrequently and has no political authority to pass legislation or to undertake any other measures in any way binding on the participating countries. Unlike the European Parliament, the Assembly has deputies that have not been elected by the populations of their countries. The sole function of the Assembly is the exchange of information among the deputies.

Decisions of the eleven countries in the Commonwealth are made unanimously by consensus at periodic summits of their heads of state. The decisions, as treaties or executive agreements, are then subject to ratification by the countries' individual parliaments, but their governments can still selectively interpret or not even enforce individual provisions. Participation in the periodic summit sessions is strictly voluntary. There is no obligation to attend, participate, or vote for the treaties and executive agreements. There are also no sanctions for noncompliance if countries fail to implement or enforce agreements signed by their chief executives and ratified by their parliaments. Given the fluid domestic political circumstances in some of these countries, their chief executives can only participate in CIS sessions as nonvoting observers. Otherwise, they would be politically attacked by radical nationalist opponents in their own countries. These nationalists view the CIS as nothing more than a furtive attempt by Russia and Kazakhstan to resurrect the former Soviet Union and see the signing of any agreements under the auspices of the CIS as a betrayal of their national independence.

A "divorce" from the Soviet Union it might have been, but the CIS has been anything but "civilized." Many of the smaller countries, insecure in their new independence, still particularly fear Russia. All of the countries to one degree or another resent the fact that the Russian government arbitrarily claimed ownership and jurisdiction over the lion's share of the Soviet Union's economic and military assets, which were on its huge territory. The Russian government has balked at dividing up these assets more equitably with the other fourteen countries. The other fourteen governments have protested that they deserve proportionate shares, because until December 1991 they had collectively, as the peoples of the Soviet Union, produced the assets. The Russian government has countered that for decades the former Russian republic and its 150 million people had essentially subsidized the economies of the other fourteen republics, and thus Russia deserves a larger share of the former Soviet assets as its compensation. Even if fear and resentment of Russia were not present, relations among the CIS members would be tense because of numerous outbreaks of violence within and along their borders since 1991.

Fear and resentment of Russia, along with political strife, have spilled over into the CIS summit sessions of heads of state. And the same kinds of restraints against any kind of collegiality have limited the effectiveness of the various ancillary coordinating bodies of the CIS, made up of the countries' prime ministers and ministers for defense, foreign policy, finance, environment, police, and security. Despite all these tensions, the CIS bodies and the CIS heads of state have made more than 200 nonbinding decisions since 1991, concerning division of debts and property of the former Soviet Union, dismantling of nuclear warheads, coordination of monetary and fiscal policies, and combating of international crime syndicates.

Armed Forces

The joint military command of the CIS created in December 1991 never became more than a building housing offices in Moscow—it had no armed force. At the time the joint command was formed, it was still assumed that the independent countries would rationally prefer to retain some kind of unified armed force, but under the control of all fifteen countries through the joint CIS command. By early 1992, Ukraine, Russia, and some of the other countries had already taken steps to create separate national armed forces, claiming sovereignty and control of the former Soviet armed forces on their territories, along with those forces' armaments, ships, and so on. In essence, the former Soviet armed forces were "republicanized." The largest segment of the former Soviet armed forces—some 2.5 million of the more than 4 million military personnel—and a disproportionate share of the Soviet navy and air force became the armed forces of the Russian Federation.

The half-million Soviet troops that had been stationed in Ukraine in December 1991 became the Ukrainian armed forces by their officers' and troops' merely swearing an oath of allegiance to Ukraine. A majority decided to remain in Ukraine even though many had been born and raised outside that country and could claim citizenship in another of the newly formed countries. The Ukrainian government simply outbid the troops' native countries. The Ukrainian government in early 1992 promised the troops higher military salaries, housing for themselves and their dependents, and better retirement benefits than the other governments did. Most of the former Soviet troops adopted Ukrainian citizenship and remained in Ukraine. A minority of them have retained their formal citizenship in their native countries while serving as the equivalent of full-time mercenaries in the Ukrainian armed forces. As a consequence, a majority of the officers in the Ukrainian army are not ethnic Ukrainians, and a minority are not even citizens of Ukraine.

In Turkmenistan and Tajikistan, countries too poor to finance entirely their own independent national armed forces, the governments have signed agreements with the Russian government. Under the terms of the agreements, the governments allow the permanent deployment on their territories of Russian troops—paid, maintained, and commanded by the Russian government. In actuality, these Russian troops were the former Soviet troops stationed in Turkmenistan and Tajikistan before both countries declared their independence in December 1991.

The commander-in-chief of the joint military command of the CIS was Yevgenii Shaposhnikov, who had been the last Soviet defense minister appointed after the abortive August coup in 1991. Without an army, navy, or air force, Shaposhnikov essentially carried out three roles in his position. Probably the most important was that, as commander-in-chief, he was authorized by the eleven CIS countries to have ultimate control, along with Boris Yeltsin as Russian President, over all of the strategic nuclear missiles of the Soviet arsenal. Shaposhnikov and Yeltsin jointly had access to the secret codes to arm the warheads and to push the button launching any of the missiles. This joint authority of Shaposhnikov and Yeltsin was instituted for the benefit of the United States and the rest of the world, worried that the dissolution of the Soviet Union left no one directly accountable for the nuclear arsenal among the four successor states of Russia, Ukraine, Kazakhstan, and Belarus. These four countries inherited all of the Soviet strategic arsenal by virtue of the missiles being located on their territory or under the command of units they declared to be their share of the former Soviet armed forces. The joint control by Shaposhnikov and Yeltsin was intended to allay the fear that any of the missiles could fall into the hands of a fanatical military officer or politician in one of the four states. Such an officer or politician might start an intercontinental nuclear war or sell Soviet missiles on the black market to someone like Saddam Hussein without anyone having the authority to countermand the sale. In March 1992, the four countries agreed eventually to transfer all of the strategic missiles to Russia. Later the Ukrainian government repudiated this agreement and declared itself a nuclear state based on its assumed ownership of those missiles. By April 1994, the government of Kazakhstan had still failed to comply fully.

Shaposhnikov served two other political roles as head of the joint CIS military command. He attempted to mediate conflicts over the division of the military inventory from the Soviet armed forces and the many other problems arising in 1992 and 1993 among the separate armed forces of the eleven countries. These countries' defense ministers met under the auspices of Shaposhnikov at sessions chaired by him. At various times in 1992 and 1993, Shaposhnikov also attempted to create an international CIS peace-keeping force composed of troops from the various national armies (principally those of Russia) that would be "loaned" to his command for assignments in areas of civil violence in Russia and Central Eurasia. Command of these troops by their own governments would have exposed the governments to charges of supporting one or the other faction in these civil wars.

The attempt to create CIS peace-keeping forces failed. The Russian defense ministry in particular objected to having Russian troops placed under the command of an international body and sent to carry out policies that could be contrary to Russian national interests. Under the international peace-keeping proposals of Shaposhnikov, the Russian government would have been responsible for supplying most of the troops and paying for them during their peace-keeping duties. In reality, since 1991 any peace-keeping forces dispatched to quell civil violence have been mostly Russian troops, but their presence has been due to bilateral agreements between the host countries and the Russian government.

By June 1993, disagreements over Shaposhnikov's attempt to create a CIS peace-keeping force, over the reluctance of Ukraine and Kazakhstan to transfer all of their strategic missiles to Russian territory, and over the division of the Black Sea fleet between Ukraine and Russia had reached a critical stage. By consensus, the defense ministers of the CIS countries voted to abolish the joint military command and Shaposhnikov's office. As an indication of how politically informal the CIS remains, the heads of state did not even bother meeting to approve this decision by their defense ministers. In June 1993, Shaposhnikov was appointed by President Yeltsin to head Russia's Security Council, overseeing the Ministries of Defense, Security, and Internal Affairs in the executive branch.

■ *REINTEGRATION AND NEW ALLIANCES*

Despite the lack of accomplishments by the CIS in its first two years, a number of nongovernmental organizations that use the designation "Commonwealth" have arisen to coordinate efforts internationally among the fifteen countries. There are Commonwealth labor union federations, Commonwealth commercial banks, a Commonwealth alliance of the managers of large defense plants, a Commonwealth committee of mayors of large cities, and Commonwealth environmental and other interest groups. These voluntary international organizations formed out of necessity because of the void left by the sudden demise of the Soviet Union. Nominally international in membership and scope, they conduct their sessions in Russian, the language of the common country to which all of them belonged until December 1991.

By 1993 these alliances came to reflect a broader integrative movement on the state level in Russia and Central Eurasia. This movement wanted to transform the Commonwealth into an international confederation akin in its powers and authority to the European Community (EC) in Western Europe. Some of the CIS countries were openly advocating abolishing the CIS and replacing it with a new economic-political international organization that all fifteen former Soviet republics would voluntarily join. Other member countries have pushed for strengthening the CIS organs in Minsk to integrate military, economic, and political affairs among the eleven current members.

Indeed, seven of the ten CIS heads of state agreed in January 1993 to support a new draft Commonwealth charter and to urge ratification of the new charter by their respective national parliaments. Under the terms of the new charter, the CIS would create permanent empowered organs in Minsk and otherwise require all member countries to act under the auspices and authority of a Commonwealth bank, Commonwealth court, and other Commonwealth institutions. The Commonwealth bank would integrate monetary policies around a common currency (most likely the Russian ruble), and the court, modeled after the International Court at The Hague in the Netherlands, would adjudicate interstate and interethnic disputes among countries in Russia and Central Eurasia. A coordinating council of full-time administrators appointed by each of the member countries would be similar in its composition and powers to the EC's European Commission in Brussels.

The heads of state of Ukraine, Turkmenistan, and Moldova did not sign the draft charter. Even those who did, such as the heads of state of Uzbekistan and Tajikistan, signed only with the stipulation that they would not be bound to comply with certain sections of it—especially the section requiring all CIS members to conform to universal standards of human rights. The governments of Uzbekistan, Tajikistan, and Turkmenistan have been the most dictatorial of the regimes in the fifteen countries since 1991, suppressing their political opponents, reimposing censorship, and reinstituting police states. Under the provisions of the draft charter, all CIS countries are obligated to ratify it no later than December 1994. Any country failing to ratify presumably will be dropped from membership in the CIS after that date, although Ukraine, Turkmenistan, and Moldova could remain affiliated with the Commonwealth in the status of associate member.

Whatever the future of the CIS, the fifteen countries were beginning to reintegrate on their own through a number of bilateral and multilateral treaties and organizations. Outside of their membership in the CIS, several of the states have formed economic, political, and military alliances and common economic markets both among themselves and with neighboring countries in Europe, the Middle East, and Asia. These alternative alliances and economic unions have evolved as the fifteen countries have confronted the daunting task of formulating their own foreign policies based on their distinct national interests and identities. The fifteen have been most immediately influenced by their geographic locales and by their common ethnic-cultural ties to neighboring non-Commonwealth countries. In many cases, those ties predated the Soviet Union and even the Russian Empire.

The predominant religions of the fifteen countries, summarized in Table 30–1, have been a major consideration in their search for national identities. For example, the Central Asian Muslim states of Kazakhstan, Turkmenistan, Uzbekistan, Kyrgyzstan, and Tajikistan formed an economic common market and political alliance in January 1993. These five countries individually have also signed numerous bilateral treaties and economic agreements with several of the Muslim states in the Middle East, especially with Turkey.

The Central Asian region and all of the Middle East, with the exception of the independent Persian empire (modern Iran), were once bound together as vassal jurisdictions of the Ottoman Turkish Empire. The Ottoman Turkish Empire and the Russian tsarist empire had been at war with each other for a total of fifty years from the beginning of the fifteenth century until the Russian monarchy collapsed in February 1917. Allied with Germany and the Austro-Hungarian Empire in World

Table 30–1

Major Religions of the Countries of Russia and Central Eurasia

Country	Major Religions
Russia	Russian Orthodox
Ukraine	Ukrainian Orthodox, Ukrainian Catholic (Uniate)
Belarus	Belarusian Orthodox, Roman Catholic
Moldova	Christian Orthodox
Estonia	Lutheran, Russian Orthodox
Latvia	Lutheran, Roman Catholic, Russian Orthodox
Lithuania	Roman Catholic
Armenia	Armenian Orthodox
Azerbaijan	Shiite Islam, Sunni Islam
Georgia	Georgian Orthodox
Kazakhstan	Sunni Islam, Russian Orthodox, Roman Catholic, Baptist
Kyrgystan	Sunni Islam, Russian Orthodox
Tajikistan	Sunni Islam, Ismailism
Turkmenistan	Sunni Islam
Uzbekistan	Sunni Islam

War I, the Ottoman Turkish Empire was dissolved in 1919 after its defeat in the war. Modern Turkey was formed out of part of the Empire's former territory.

By religion, language, and culture, the Central Asian states are reidentifying themselves as Muslim and Turkic. Muslim Azerbaijan in the Transcaucasian region has intensified its economic and political ties with Turkey but also with Iran, directly bordering it on its south. Both ethnic and economic considerations have motivated the Azerbaijani government into forging closer bonds with Iran. In Iran's northern border area with Azerbaijan resides an enclave of ethnic Azeri, the same ethnic nationality that makes up over 80 percent of Azerbaijan's population (Azerbaijan means "Land of the Azeri"). Iran, Azerbaijan, Turkmenistan, and Kazakhstan would be the natural members of a Caspian Sea trading alliance and common market—a community advocated by the Iranian government.

Christian Armenia, at war with Azerbaijan since 1991, has resisted the attempts of Turkey on its southern border to mediate the conflict between the two countries. The reason is the memory of Armenian treatment under the Turks before the Soviet era. In 1915–1916, when the majority of Armenians lived within the Ottoman Turkish Empire, over a million were murdered by Turkish soldiers in the first recorded case of genocide in this century. Indeed, to counter pressures of the Islamic Middle East to their south, Armenia and Georgia have regravitated since 1991 into a close economic and military bilateral relationship with Russia. The irony is that until 1917 the former Russian empire had a similar protectorate relationship with both Armenians and Georgians living in the Transcaucasian region because of the threat posed to them by the Ottoman Turkish Empire.

Ukraine has actively sought cooperation with its western neighbors: Poland, Hungary, the Czech Republic, and Slovakia. The latter four countries have formed the Visegrad economic and political community since 1991. The Visegrad community is an attempt by these countries to create a Central European common market and coordinate military and diplomatic policies as a counterweight to Germany in the west and Russia in the east. Although all five ultimately would prefer becoming full members of the EU (and the Czech Republic, Hungary, and Poland have been granted an associate affiliation with the EU since 1992), the Visegrad community is likely to endure for the foreseeable future. Ukraine is likely to be the fifth member sometime in 1994; its government officials have pursued Visegrad membership as an alternative to their remaining in the CIS, in which they fear domination by the much larger Russia.

Ukraine's membership in a common economic union with its western neighbors would formalize on an interstate basis the economic integration of western Ukrainian provinces with Hungary, Poland, and Slovakia since 1991. There are large numbers of ethnic Hungarians, Poles, and Slovaks who are citizens of the western provinces of Ukraine. Since independence, unable to find work in Ukraine, many Ukrainians have been working full-time in factories and small businesses across the border in Hungary, Poland, and Slovakia on permanent resident visas. Given the highly devalued Ukrainian currency, whatever salaries they earn in Polish and Hungarian currencies are worth several times that in Ukrainian currency when they return to their homes in Ukraine. So much higher is the equivalent value of the Slovak currency in terms of the Ukrainian one that Slovaks in the eastern part of

Slovakia cross the border solely to shop in western Ukraine. Conversely, private Polish and Hungarian entrepreneurs have opened a number of factories and stores in western Ukraine to take advantage of a Ukrainian labor force willing to work for much lower wages than their Polish and Hungarian counterparts, the favorable exchange rates of their native currencies relative to the Ukrainian one, and a lucrative Ukrainian consumer market of more than 50 million people.

Although Ukrainians are closely linked to Russians by language and ethnicity, all five Visegrad countries are tied by a common religious bond. Poland, Hungary, the Czech Republic, and Slovakia are predominantly Roman Catholic. In Ukraine, the eastern half of the country is predominantly Orthodox with all parishes linked to the autonomous Ukrainian Orthodox Church hierarchy in Kiev, but the western half of the country is mostly Ukrainian Greek Catholic (Uniate). Ukrainian Greek Catholics follow the doctrines and teachings of Catholicism and are subordinate to the Pope in Rome, but their religious services and practices are similar to those of the Ukrainian Orthodox Church.

The Ukrainian Greek Catholic Church was banned by Stalin at the end of World War II for allegedly fostering anti-Soviet Ukrainian nationalism. Ukrainians covertly practiced the religion, but the ban was never officially revoked until 1989. The ban only reinforced a link in Ukrainian national identity with Greek Catholicism. In the intervening five decades, Ukrainian Catholic parishes and other property had been taken over by the Ukrainian Orthodox Church. Since 1989, conflicts have simmered throughout communities in western Ukraine between congregations of the two faiths, each claiming ownership of the same churches and buildings. The pursuit of a union with other Roman Catholic countries to the west is a way for the Ukrainian government to escape being nationally identified as the "Little Brother" of Orthodox Slavic Russia to the east.

The priority of the three Baltic states has been to create an economic common market and trading alliance with other countries of the northern Baltic region, such as Poland and Germany—in essence, a modern version of the Hanseatic League that linked the city-states of the Baltic in the sixteenth century. Tied by history, language, religions, and ethnicity to the peoples of Scandinavia, the three Baltic states have also identified Finland, Sweden, Norway, and Denmark as their closest natural allies by culture and geography. These seven countries would be the most logical members of a proposed Nordic or Baltic confederation integrating their economies and foreign policies.

■ REGIONAL CONTRASTS

Kazakhstan and Central Asia

Among the countries of the former Soviet Union, next to Russia, Kazakhstan is the most richly endowed. Among the fifteen countries, only Russia and Kazakhstan possess the natural resources and agricultural potential to make themselves self-sufficient and economically viable. After Russia and Saudi Arabia, Kazakhstan has the largest untapped reserves of oil and gas in the world, 25 billion barrels of recoverable oil reserves (equivalent to those of the United States), and the ability to produce as many as 1.6 million barrels of oil a day within the next two decades. On its territory is 90 percent of the former Soviet Union's chrome, 60 percent of its silver, 20 percent of its coal, 50 percent of its tungsten and lead, 40 percent of its zinc and copper, 25 percent of its bauxite, and significant deposits of its titanium, magnesium, and uranium.

The uranium gives Kazakhstan a unique political and economic leverage among Russia and the Central Eurasian countries. The Kazakhstan government has assumed control over a portion of the formerly Soviet nuclear missiles stationed on its territory, and only Russia and Kazakhstan have the uranium sufficient to maintain themselves as nuclear military powers. The countries other than Russia are dependent on Kazakhstan for their energy needs because of Kazakhstan's uranium, oil, and gas. Those countries use nuclear-powered reactors to generate a significant portion of their electricity for industrial and commercial use. Lacking the hard currency of American dollars or German marks to buy uranium on the world market, they have to buy it for rubles from either Kazakhstan or Russia to keep their reactors operational.

Cotton is a staple crop in Kazakhstan, as in the other Central Asian countries. However, Kazakhstan avoided becoming a monoculture cotton-growing region, whereas Turkmenistan, Uzbekistan, Kyrgyzstan, and Tajikistan relied only on cotton and thus depleted the land and water, leaving them agriculturally underdeveloped at independence. In its western regions, Kazakhstan has rich black-earth soil, which was first extensively developed for grain and livestock production in the 1950s under the so-called Virgin Lands program. This program, almost the prototype of economic reform under Nikita Khrushchev, the leader of the Soviet Union from 1957–1964, proved a failure. The haste to achieve results immediately depleted top soil and caused vast erosion. Since 1965, however, more cautious long-term development of agriculture in Kazakhstan has protected the top soil and transformed the region into a reliable source of food. Kazakhstan now produces a third of the grain of the former Soviet Union and has the resources both to feed its population and to export agricultural products.

Agriculture remains the basis of the economy in the other four Central Asian states. In Uzbekistan, approximately 50 percent of the work force are employed in agriculture, compared with 55 percent for Tajikistan, 53.4 percent for Turkmenistan, and 44.6 percent for Kyrgyzstan. In contrast to Kazakhstan, however, these four suffer from a greater shortage of land and water and share more traditional values and a rural outlook. Over the past hundred years, their populations increased over 1000 percent, but the amount of irrigated land increased only 150 percent. Kazakhstan has a much greater capacity than the other countries to integrate its population into a modern economy. Kazakhstan's 17 million citizens distributed across a land equal in size to India include a plurality of ethnic Kazakhs, who since the 1950s were educated and employed in both agriculture and industry, working alongside the large communities of ethnic Russians, Ukrainians, and Germans.

Uzbekistan, Turkmenistan, Tajikistan, and Kyrgyzstan lack the capacity to modernize economically their largely rural and overpopulated societies. Whatever industrialization occurred in the four had been heavily dependent on investments from Moscow and a guaranteed market for the sale of cotton. The demise of the

Soviet Union ended the decades of economic subsidies that minimally sustained industrial expansion, leaving these countries' underdeveloped industries on the verge of complete collapse. The textile factories in Russia that had bought most of their cotton almost halved their production because of problems arising with the imposition of custom duties, tariffs, and the like among countries formerly constituting one economy. The only state of the four that has any natural resource convertible into foreign trade and domestic industrialization is Turkmenistan, with large reserves of natural gas. Turkmenistan sells its gas to Western Europe and is continuing to expand its gas production through joint investment projects with its southern neighbor Iran.

Competition over a dwindling number of jobs in agriculture and in the underdeveloped industrial sector of the four countries has led to a number of localized acts of violence between ethnic natives in their villages and cities. The shortage of water and irrigated land in the rural areas has only exacerbated tensions. Conflicts over water rights had already sparked interrepublic and interethnic conflicts along the borders of the four from 1989–1991, even before the demise of the Soviet Union. Since 1991, conflict has continued to flare between ethnic Uzbeks and ethnic Tajiks, who have fought each other in the provinces bordering Uzbekistan and Tajikistan over water and pasture land for their herds that used to roam freely back and forth over the border.

Ethnic and racial animosities among the four Central Asian nationalities have been contributing factors to the violence. Tajiks, Turkmen, and Kirghiz all resent and fear domination by ethnic Uzbeks, who constitute the largest ethnic nationality in the region—with more than double the number of the other three combined. Uzbek settlements and businesses in Tajikistan, Turkmenistan, and Kyrgyzstan increasingly have been targeted by rioting ethnic majorities in all three countries since 1989.

Ethnic minorities from the Caucasian region have also been victimized by racially motivated violence in Central Asia since 1989. The bitter tragedy is that some have lived in Central Asia for decades and others have come seeking political asylum from civil unrest in the Caucasus. In 1989, Meshketian Turks were murdered during two weeks of rioting by roving mobs of Uzbeks, who claimed the Meshketians were taking jobs away from them and gouging them in overpriced cooperative restaurants. The Meshketians are Muslims who lived for centuries in Georgia. They were one of several ethnic nationalities deported to Central Asia from their traditional homelands in 1941 and 1944 by Stalin as punishment for their alleged collaboration with Nazi Germany. Since the outbreak of war between Armenia and Azerbaijan in 1988–1989, Armenians seeking temporary asylum in Uzbekistan have been attacked by mobs of Uzbeks who accuse the Armenians of taking housing from them.

Russian Siberia

Two-thirds of Russia and Central Eurasia and one-half of the Russian Federation lie east of the Urals in an area bordered by the Arctic Ocean to the north and by China to the south. This area is termed Siberia. Siberia has a notorious association with political tyranny; it is widely perceived as a frozen wasteland where the imprisonment, exile, and forced labor of millions of political prisoners occurred in first the Russian Empire and later the Soviet Union. Yet Siberia, both historically and culturally, also has a positive connotation especially for ethnic Russians—one of idealism, selfless cooperation with others in overcoming nature, and individual opportunity. In Russian political culture, Siberia has been viewed as a universal allegory for the ability of human beings to reach almost a spiritual state by challenging and mastering the most difficult conditions. As a cultural-spiritual symbol, Siberia continued to evoke passions and stir political conflicts throughout the twentieth century.

Conservative Russian nationalists, who were patronized by a certain faction of the Communist leadership in the former Soviet Union and whose views have been embraced by nationalistic political parties in independent Russia since 1991, consider Siberia even more of a political allegory for twentieth-century Russia. For them, it epitomizes the innocence of the past, communion with God and nature, selfless sharing with others, anti-materialism, and democratic purity of the "Russian soul," which was supposedly desecrated by the Communist autocracy after 1917. Conservative Russian nationalists therefore oppose any political leaders they consider to be like those of the Communist autocracy, who undertook materialistic actions that spoiled the pristine Siberian landscape in the false pursuit of industrialization.

The march of the Russian Empire eastward to Siberia began in the sixteenth century, when trappers, explorers, and merchants settled in this desolate and sparsely populated region. In the eighteenth and nineteenth centuries, the Russian Empire expanded eastward to the Pacific. With only the narrow Bering Strait, about fifty miles wide, separating Siberia from Alaska, the empire even crossed the Pacific, claiming Alaska as a possession before selling it to the United States and founding Russian colonies along the coast of North America as far south as northern California. Russian settlers in Siberia during this period shared the idealism, frontier ethic, and pioneer romanticism of their American counterparts who were participating in the westward expansion to California.

The resurgence of separatism throughout the states of the former Soviet Union has produced a counterpart within Siberia. A number of the regions and territories of Siberia that have always considered themselves as much Asian as European have joined together to form a common political and economic union called the Siberian Agreement. Political officials in these regions and territories resent what they feel have been decades of economic exploitation and indifference by European Russia and officials in Moscow.

These Siberian officials have been supported by several owners of newly privatized coal, diamond, gas, and oil industries in Siberia. The owners resent being forced to pay excessive taxes to Moscow with little return being made to the region. The leaders and owners have been widely supported by the Siberian public. For decades, Siberians suffered the lowest standard of living in the Soviet Union, the lowest life expectancy, and the worst health conditions, due to the widespread pollution of the region. In opinion surveys, the public attributes these problems to the fact that decisions affecting Siberia were made by insensitive and politically unaccountable bureaucrats in Moscow, several thousand kilometers to the west.

Evoking a sense of a common Siberian nationhood and depending on widespread support from the private sector and the public, political leaders intend to transform the cooperative Siberian Agreement into something akin to an autonomous Siberian republic within Russia. In such an autonomous republic, elected officials and a parliament would assume the right to establish direct economic and foreign ties with other Asian countries, such as China, Japan, and Korea. The Siberian government and parliament would determine its own fiscal and monetary policies, independent of Moscow, and cooperate in renewing a region devastated by environmental pollution. Any revenues from the direct sale of Siberia's vast store of natural resources by local governments or the private sector would remain entirely within Siberia and not be transferred to Moscow. So dependent is the national Russian economy on Siberia that, were it ever actually to secede, Russia as a country would cease to exist economically.

For the most part, Russia and Central Eurasia have a cold climate, attributable more to their continental position, away from the moderating effect of oceans, than to the northerly latitude. Even with their 26,000 miles of coastline, Russia and Central Eurasia are largely landlocked except for the Arctic. All seas and rivers are frozen at least part of the year. The great rivers flow either to landlocked seas or, in Siberia, north into the frozen Arctic Ocean.

In the 1970s, a project was begun to rechannel the entire Ob River of Siberia southward through a 1,500-mile concrete canal, in order to raise the level of the Aral Sea and irrigate cotton-growing regions of Central Asia. The project was abandoned in 1986, because of its cost, infeasibility, likely destructive impact on the entire ecosystem of the Arctic tundra and Western Siberia, and political opposition from environmentalists and conservative Russian nationalists. Prior to its abandonment, the project pitted political supporters among scientists and party-state officials in Central Asia against those in Western Siberia.

For alleviating the shortage of water and irrigated land in the Central Asian states, the only potential source is the great Siberian rivers. If the Central Asian states attempt to revive the Siberian river-diversion project on an interstate basis, differences between them and the regions allied in the Siberian Agreement are likely to spark a major international conflict before the end of this century.

.....31

Geography, History, and Peoples of Russia and Central Eurasia

■ *GEOGRAPHY AND POPULATION*

Russia and Central Eurasia encompass all of the land between the Black and Baltic Seas in the west and the Okhotsk and Bering Seas of the Pacific Ocean in the east. The Soviet Union was the largest country in the world; its territories inherited by Russia and Central Eurasia constitute about one-sixth of the world's inhabited land surface and a land mass as large as the United States, Canada, and Mexico combined. Russia and Central Eurasia span eleven time zones (nine time zones within the Russian Federation alone), extending over 6,000 miles. Russia and Central Eurasia border or lie close to almost all of the countries in Central and Eastern Europe, Asia, and the Middle East. Thus, the area directly or indirectly affected by Russia and Central Eurasia accounts for 2–3 billion of the world's 5.5 billion in population.

Most of Russia and Central Eurasia lies north of the fiftieth parallel (that is, north of the United States). The northernmost 15 percent of Russia is located within the Arctic Circle, but the most southerly parts of Central Eurasia reach below the fortieth parallel and include arid desert regions in Turkmenistan, Kyrgystan, Uzbekistan, and Tajikistan, which are contiguous to Iran, Afghanistan, and China. The three countries Georgia, Armenia, and Azerbaijan, in the Caucasian mountains between the Black and Caspian Seas, border the northern tier of the Middle East, which includes the countries of Turkey, Iran, and Iraq.

As their legacy from the former Soviet Union, Russia and Central Eurasia are conditioned by their geography and population. Political and ethnic conflict and change seemed to be more intense and fought on a grander scale in the former Soviet Union than in any other country. These conflicts have not stopped with the break-up of the Soviet Union.

As Table 31–1 shows, Russia and Central Eurasia include countries that are markedly different in size and population. On one extreme are the Russian Federation, Kazakhstan, and Ukraine. Russia remains the single biggest country in the world, accounting for three-fourths of the former Soviet Union in its area of

Table 31–1

Area and Population
of the Countries of
Russia and Central
Eurasia, 1991

Country (Capital)	Area (thousands of square kilometers)	Population (millions)
Russia (Moscow)	17,075	148.5
Ukraine (Kiev)	604	52.0
Belarus (Minsk)	208	10.3
Moldova (Chisinau)*	34	4.4
Estonia (Tallinn)	45	1.6
Latvia (Riga)	65	2.7
Lithuania (Vilnius)	65	3.7
Armenia (Yerevan)	30	3.4
Azerbaijan (Baku)	87	7.1
Georgia (Tbilisi)	70	5.5
Kazakhstan (Almaty)‡	2,717	16.8
Kyrgyzstan (Bishkek)‡‡	199	4.4
Tajikistan (Dushanbe)	143	5.4
Turkmenistan (Ashgabat)§	488	3.7
Uzbekistan (Tashkent)	447	20.7
Former Soviet Union (Moscow)	22,400	286.7**

* Formerly Kishinev when Moldova was the Moldavian Soviet Socialist Republic of the
former Soviet Union (until December 1991)
‡Formerly Alma-Ata when Kazakhstan was the Kazakh Soviet Socialist Republic
‡‡Formerly Frunze when Kyrgyzstan was the Kirghiz Soviet Socialist Republic
§Formerly Ashkhabad when Turkmenistan was the Turkmen Soviet Socialist Republic
** Population figure for Soviet Union is from 1989.

17.1 million square kilometers. Russia's population of almost 150 million people is the largest in Europe, almost double that of Germany, the second most populous European country with 80 million.

Kazakhstan, from the Caspian Sea at its west to its extended border with China in Northwest Asia, covers 2.7 million square kilometers, only slightly smaller than India. Its total population of 17 million, however, is less than 2 percent of India's approximately 880 million. Ukraine is almost exactly equivalent in population and size to France, with 52 million people residing in an area of 604,000 square kilometers.

At the opposite extreme among the countries of Russia and Central Eurasia are those that are more similar to the Netherlands, Belgium, and Luxembourg in the northern tier of Western Europe. Armenia, Moldova, Latvia, Lithuania, and Estonia have populations ranging from 1.6 million to 4.4 million, residing in territories from 30,000 to 65,000 square kilometers.

All of the former Soviet republics experienced dramatic social change during the Soviet era. At the time of the Russian Revolution in 1917, less than 20 percent of their populations lived in urban areas. As recently as 1959, the Soviet Union was still a predominantly rural society, with over half of the population (52 percent) living in rural areas. Over a very short period, the Soviet Union became one of the most highly urbanized societies in the world, with two-thirds of its entire population living in areas classified by the 1989 census as urban. The urban population grew by 38 percent in just three decades. The shift was not limited to those areas already highly urbanized in 1959. In 1959 only four of the republics had more than half of their populations living in urban areas, but by 1989 the number had increased to ten republics. The most highly urbanized post-Soviet countries are Russia, Lithuania, Latvia, and Estonia, with 70–75 percent of their populations in urban areas. The least urbanized are Kyrgyzstan and Tajikistan in Central Asia, with 60–70 percent of their populations still living in rural areas in 1989.

By 1989 15 percent of all Soviet people—or 43 million—lived in twenty-three cities with populations above 1 million. This number represented an increase of 12 percent over the comparable proportion of the Soviet population residing in cities of the same size at the time of the 1979 census. An additional thirty-four Soviet cities boasted populations between 500,000 and 1 million. Moscow, with 9 million, was the largest city of the former Soviet Union, but large cities had formed in all of the republics. By 1989, the Uzbek capital of Tashkent had over 2 million, the Ukrainian capital of Kiev 2.6 million, the Azerbaijan capital of Baku 1.8 million, the Georgian capital of Tbilisi 1.3 million, and the Armenian capital of Yerevan 1.2 million.

At the time of the 1917 Revolution, over 70 percent of the population in the Russian Empire was still illiterate. From the 1950s on, the Soviet Union became one of the most highly literate countries in the world. Literacy rates, like urbanization, dramatically increased over just three decades. By 1989 more than one out of every ten Soviet adults had achieved a higher education, tripling the level in 1959. The extremes among the fifteen countries vary from Armenia and Georgia, with 13–16 percent of their populations having some higher education, to Tajikistan and Turkmenistan, with 7–8 percent.

▪ GEOGRAPHY AND POLITICS

Russia and Central Eurasia experience climatic extremes, ranging from the frigid temperatures of the Arctic to the intense heat of the deserts in Kazakhstan and the four other Central Asian countries, with some areas having moderate to semitropical climates. The only attribute that all areas share is their relative unsuitability for agriculture. Summers are brief; frosts occur late in the spring and early in the autumn. Conditions are not favorable for the planting of winter wheat or rye because of the intense cold and snow cover. Moreover, the quality of many of the soils is poor, and irrigation possibilities are limited.

Because of the unreliability of rainfall, even the more favored areas experience great uncertainty. The two principal agricultural regions of the former Soviet Union—Ukraine and Kazakhstan—are located far apart, and frequently one will experience sufficient rainfall while the other suffers drought. Rainfall for both areas depends on the atmospheric location of a countercyclical high-pressure system, which may absorb moisture from one region and produce more than adequate rainfall over the other.

From the Arctic Circle southward, there are five zones in Russia and Central Eurasia—each with a characteristic soil and vegetation. The tundra of the far north, where the subsoil is perpetually frozen, does not provide much opportunity for development. Gradually, it merges into the taiga, or forest zone, which covers nearly half of the total area of the fifteen countries (mostly along the northern half of Russia). The taiga is the largest forested area in the world and contains a mixture of trees. South of the forest zone is the steppe region, extending from the western borders all the way to the Altai Mountains in the east. This area, on the whole, has rich soil but often lacks ample rainfall. The semidesert/desert zone lie partly in southeast European Russia and in areas of the five Central Asian countries. The smallest, as well as the most southern, of the five zones is the subtropical zone. It covers about 190,000 square miles along the Black Sea coast and the Caspian Sea coast, the Ukrainian Crimean peninsula, southern Georgia, Armenia, Azerbaijan, and the Pamir Mountains of Kyrgyzstan and Tajikistan. Vegetation in the seacoast areas is extremely thick because of the humus soil and heavy rainfall.

The differences in climate and resources have been one source of conflict in Russia and Central Asia. Turkmenistan, Uzbekistan, Kyrgyzstan, and Tajikistan, with their mild winters and hot summers, were sometimes called the Imperial Valley during the Soviet era. Cotton remains the principal crop grown in these four countries, and, even prior to 1917, the Russian Empire was heavily dependent on the exports of cotton from this region of Central Asia and of wheat from Ukraine to finance loans from foreign banks and generate economic growth. During the last two decades of the Soviet era, cotton growing in these four republics figured in one way or another in several political controversies and well-publicized scandals. The officials and citizens in the four republics bitterly and openly objected to what they perceived as economically discriminatory policies by the Soviet national government, forcing them to limit economic growth and development in their region by concentrating almost solely on the raising of cotton. Under pressure to meet unreasonable quotas for cotton output, the officials in the four republics often resorted unsuccessfully to lobbying the national government for higher cotton prices, increased investments in water and irrigation facilities, or new industries to diversify their economy.

In the 1970s and 1980s, several Central Asian officials—including two successive heads of the Communist party of Uzbekistan—were implicated through judicial investigations as the ringleaders of major crime syndicates in the region. The syndicates had bribed numerous officials to falsify figures on cotton production and sales to state purchasing agencies. The syndicates embezzled hundreds of millions of rubles from republic officials responsible for cotton production, and their network of conspiracy and cover-up extended as far as highly placed officials of the Soviet government in Moscow—including Yurii Churbanov, the Deputy Minister of Internal Affairs and son-in-law of Leonid Brezhnev. The national Soviet media also disclosed that the syndicates engaged in even more lucrative illicit activities, growing opium poppies for heroin and cocaine (distributed by Soviet organized crime) on fields allegedly set aside for cotton.[1]

By 1989, nationalist movements and popular fronts advocating greater autonomy for the Central Asian regions had arisen, motivated primarily by their resentment over the longstanding colonial status of their republics as cotton-growing plantations for Moscow. A major ecological catastrophe and human tragedy in the region stemming from Moscow's policy increased the fervor of these movements and fronts. The pressure to raise cotton production at any cost had resulted in the diversion of so much water for irrigation from the Amu Darya and Syr Darya rivers (the two main rivers flowing into the Aral Sea) that the Aral Sea, the major source of water for the Central Asian ecosystem, was irreversibly drying up. Toxic chemicals from agricultural fertilizers had run off into the dried basin of the sea and entered the groundwater and food chain of the region. In certain districts bordering the Aral Sea, the toxic chemicals in water and food resulted in an infant mortality rate exceeding one out of every ten births.

The tragedy of the Aral Sea as a legacy of the Soviet era stands in marked contrast to the potential value of the natural resources of Russia and Central Eurasia. In natural resources, the former Soviet Union was perhaps the richest nation in the world. Within its borders were all of the raw materials needed to be completely self-sufficient. With the demise of the Soviet Union, the greatest proportion of its raw materials and the extensive grid of railroads and pipelines to transport them were inherited by the Russian government within its territory. The Urals in Russia have a variety of minerals; Ukraine has extensive deposits of coal and iron ore in its southeast Donbass region; and the mountains of Central Asia and the Russian Far East have many rare metals, including uranium. The eastern half of Russia that is in Siberia has iron ore reserves projected to be greater than those of the United States, Britain, and France combined. The wide belt of taiga across the northern latitudes of Russia contains more than one-third of all the forests in the world.

Natural gas fields in Russian Siberia are alleged to be the largest in the world. In the early 1980s the former Soviet Union became the principal source of gas for the national gas companies of France and West Germany. Most of the Soviet gas fields were inherited by Russia, which continues to be paid for the sale of gas to France and unified Germany. The new post-Soviet politics, however, threaten to impede or even stop entirely the flow of gas. The pipelines cross the territory of Ukraine. The Ukrainian government has threatened to nationalize the pipelines or shut them off when various political squabbles, such as that over ownership of the Black Sea fleet ported in the Ukrainian Crimean peninsula, have arisen between it and the Russian government of President Yeltsin.

---

[1]The syndicates were only the most notorious of many disclosures of elite corruption publicized in the Soviet media in 1984 and 1985. The publicity indirectly pressured a majority of the Central Committee to elect as General Secretary someone untainted by any allegations of personal impropriety in his past—Gorbachev. Thus, ironically, the mistreatment of Central Asia over decades came back to haunt the Soviet rulers. The individual elected to head the Communist system and the one person more than anyone else responsible for the demise of the Soviet Union came to hold his position of authority in 1985 in large part because of political repercussions from the Central Asian cotton-syndicate scandal.

The former Soviet Union was the single largest oil producer in the world, pumping almost 12 million barrels a day throughout most of the 1980s and possessing unproven oil reserves several times larger than those of Saudi Arabia. The former Soviet Union was also a leader in the use of nuclear energy. The nuclear power stations in post-Soviet Russia alone have a capacity to generate the equivalent of 19 million kilowatts of electricity, and before the collapse of the Soviet Union Russia was scheduled to expand its nuclear-generated electrical capacity by an additional 60 million kilowatts.

After the Chernobyl nuclear accident in 1986, anti-nuclear groups were among the most visible and successful political springboards from which broader anti-Communist and anti-Soviet popular fronts and organizations emerged in several of the former Soviet republics. Conspicuously targeted by these groups in their demonstrations as defending unsafe nuclear power were the Communist party leaders. Being anti-nuclear in 1988–1989 became synonymous with being anti-Soviet, anti-Communist, and pro-democratic. Since the end of the Soviet Union in 1991, however, the positions have reversed. Those favoring the expansion of nuclear power as a necessary and cheap source of energy are the chief executives of the governments and the most democratically oriented political parties and parliamentary leaders in several of the new countries. Without nuclear power, they fear that their national economies will entirely collapse, their national independence will be undermined, and their national democracies will be replaced by dictatorships. Many of those leading the opposition to nuclear power are die-hard former Communist officials and others who want a return to a unified Soviet state and a quasi-Communist autocracy. Lacking any other political base, they have used the anti-nuclear fears of the public to organize groups and demonstrations against local power plants. Government ministers—some of whom led demonstrations against nuclear power plants and Soviet Communist rule in 1988 and 1989—have found themselves in a position of having to defend nuclear energy against the die-hard Communist supporters. At the same time, Green political parties—unquestionably supportive of both independence and democracy but also anti-nuclear—further muddy the political waters. In Ukraine, the home of the Chernobyl reactor and the anti-nuclear movement, since 1991 Green World (*Zelenyi zvit*) has been the second-largest political party and has consistently been rated the first or second most popular in national polls of Ukrainians asked which party they would support in any future parliamentary election.

Although rivers remain the most important commercial arteries for the countries of Russia and Central Eurasia, an extensive network of railroads also exists. The railroads in the Russian Federation alone make up the world's single largest national transportation system, with an operating length of 87,500 kilometers, of which some 38,000 kilometers have been electrified. Russia's railroads ship more freight, carry more passengers, and have more electrified lines than those of any other country in the world. All the railroads of the other fourteen countries remain interconnected to this immense Russian railroad system.

A key geographical feature of Russia is the immense Russian Plain. Across this plain flow a number of great rivers, which have been important arteries of transport, commerce, and conquest. There are more than 180,000 miles of navigable rivers, although winter freezing prevents year-round use. Low watersheds and short portages between the rivers made it difficult to connect them with canals. The construction of such canals became an accomplishment celebrated by the Soviet media and leadership after 1917. Their construction was heralded as proof of the political commitment of the Soviet people, loyal and dedicated to building the new economy and Communism. In reality, as was well-known for decades in the West but only disclosed openly in the Soviet media since 1988, many of the canals built in the 1930s and 1940s were constructed by the slave labor of prisoners in Soviet corrective-labor penal camps. Hundreds of thousands of these prisoners died from brutal mistreatment by their secret-police overseers and from severe cold and hunger.

The Volga is the largest river in Europe and Russia's most important. In the former Soviet Union, the Volga carried half of the country's river freight, dropping less than 305 meters over 3,700 kilometers before emptying into the Caspian Sea. By the end of the Soviet era, the mighty Volga had been badly polluted, its many varieties of fish had been killed off, and its water level had fallen several meters. For decades Soviet officials had encouraged the construction of unregulated petrochemical and military industries along the banks of the Volga, which dumped their toxic wastes into the river and spewed toxic gases into the atmosphere. The water level of the Volga fell because, without any consideration of its wider impact, the river's water was diverted to supply hydroelectric dams and irrigation canals. The cumulative impact of decades of indifference has left its toll. Parallel to the state of the Aral Sea basin, the Volga river basin has been so badly polluted that it threatens the entire ecosystem of southern Russia, southwest Kazakhstan, and the other countries bordering the Caspian Sea. To put the problem of the Volga basin in perspective, consider that the Volga region, which extends eastward to the Urals mountain range, constitutes the geopolitical core of Russia. Approximately one-third of Russia's 148 million people live in this region. Solving the immense ecological problems of such regions as the Volga and Aral Sea basins has been complicated a hundredfold by the demise of the Soviet Union. Now, a number of independent countries have to coordinate their clean-up efforts through treaties within the CIS. As we have already emphasized, the Commonwealth has no enforcement or policing mechanisms with respect to its members.

■ THE IMPERIAL LEGACY

From the western border across to the Urals (a low, eroded mountain chain marking the division between the European and Asian continents), the terrain of Russia is relatively flat, with few natural barriers except for swampy marshland. The flat topography of this area made it an inviting avenue by which to invade the Russian Empire and the Soviet Union during the last two centuries—and the invitation was accepted by Napoleon Bonaparte of France in 1812, Kaiser Wilhelm of Germany in 1914–1917, and Adolf Hitler of Germany in 1941–1944. Western historians long speculated that the flatness of the Russian Plain affected the nation's political culture. Because of the flat, exposed topography, both Russian and later Soviet rulers had a heightened sense of vulnerability—bordering on political paranoia—about the western borders. They constantly feared that the Eastern European countries along their western boundary would be used as staging areas for invasions by dominant military powers. The long exposed borders of Russia and Central Eurasia in the south and east fronted major powers such as Iran, Japan, and China and only compounded this fear.

Domination, military aggression against these neighbors, and even annexation to preserve "safe borders" often were the responses, creating a self-fulfilling prophecy by generating even greater mistrust and hostility in those neighboring countries. The Soviet military invasion of Afghanistan in 1979 was only the most recent manifestation of this syndrome. The stated Soviet justification at the time was a fear that Afghanistan was about to be taken over by China and the United States in collusion with Iran and Pakistan. The paranoid sensitivity induced by the long borders and flat Russian Plain in the past continues to influence the conduct of foreign policy by the government of the Russian Federation toward the fourteen former Soviet republics now constituting Russia's "near abroad."

With the exception of the formerly Japanese Kuril Islands in the southeast and the eastern sections of Poland, Czechoslovakia, and Romania that were annexed to the Soviet Union at the end of World War II (and remain as the western parts of Belarus and Ukraine), the borders of Russia and Central Eurasia closely parallel those of the pre-1917 Russian Empire. The empire began expanding in the sixteenth century through both voluntary assimilation of bordering ethnic-religious groups and forced incorporation and military conquest.

The Ukrainian region became part of the Russian Empire in 1654, as a consequence of a revolt led by the Ukrainian Cossack leader Bogdan Khmelnitskii against the continued control of this region by the Roman Catholic Lithuanian-Polish kingdom. Over the previous two centuries, a sense of self-identity as a Ukrainian nation had developed among the people in this region. This sense of Ukrainian nationhood derived from the evolution of a distinct Ukrainian language (a hybrid of Russian and Polish), the conversion of the people to the Orthodox Church with its distinct Slavonic language and worship practices, and local communal self-government practiced by bands of Cossack warriors. By uniting with the Orthodox Russian Empire, the Ukrainian nation hoped to gain protection from both the Roman Catholic Lithuanian-Poles in the west and the Muslim Ottoman Turkish Empire in the south. By the middle of the seventeenth century, the Turkish Empire had already conquered the Balkan Peninsula and was militarily threatening all of Central and Eastern Europe and the Black Sea region.

The Transcaucasian region encompassing post-Soviet Christian Armenia and Muslim Azerbaijan was annexed in the 1820s from the Ottoman Turkish Empire. By the nineteenth century, that empire had become administratively overextended and militarily weak compared to the Russian Empire with its larger army. Christian Georgia in the Transcaucasian region had been incorporated from the Turkish Empire in 1783 as a Russian protectorate. The Baltic states of Lithuania and Latvia were incorporated into the Russian Empire in the eighteenth century, after the collapse of the Lithuanian-Polish state. The third Baltic state, Estonia, was annexed by the Russian Empire in 1721 from the Swedish kingdom. In the west, areas that were historically Polish were made part of Russia when the territory comprising the Polish kingdom was divided up among Prussia, Russia, and the Austro-Hungarian Empire at the end of the eighteenth century. Belarus had been the eastern part of the Polish kingdom before its annexation by Russia.

Jews became part of the Russian Empire with the dismemberment of Poland. Since the thirteenth century, Jews had been persecuted and outlawed in many Western European countries, and many had fled to Poland. An enlightened Polish ruling class held out its country as a political-religious sanctuary for Jews and other outcast minorities of Europe. Jews, among other groups, were encouraged to settle in Poland if they promised to homestead wilderness areas for agriculture. When Poland was dismembered, it had the largest Jewish population in the world, and many of these Jews suddenly found themselves subjects of the Russian tsar.

To preserve the perceived legitimacy of Russian autocracy as the defender of Christian civilization, the tsars denied Jews any rights of citizenship. Jews were prohibited from owning and farming land and were restricted to ghetto settlements set apart from the surrounding Slavic and Baltic ethnic nationalities in a western strip of the Russian Empire designated as the "Jewish Pale." The degree of anti-Semitism of state policies varied somewhat during the last 125 years of the Russian autocracy. Tsars were more or less intolerant toward Jews, depending on the general political climate in the empire. The degree of intolerance also depended on the extent of social unrest in the empire, since tsars often used Jews as a convenient scapegoat and encouraged pogroms by rampaging mobs in order to divert these mobs from expressing their discontent against the autocracy itself. By the beginning of the twentieth century, the tsarist solution to the "Jewish problem" was to make life so miserable for Jews that many would leave the country. Between 1890 and 1910, over 2 million Jews were forced to emigrate under threat of forced exile to Siberia, conscription into the Russian army, starvation, or death.

The post-Soviet Central Asian countries of Kazakhstan, Turkmenistan, Uzbekistan, Kyrgystan, and Tajikistan were originally Turkic Muslim vassal jurisdictions, which were annexed by the Russian Empire through military conquest over two decades from the 1850s through the 1870s. The American Civil War of 1861–1865 indirectly precipitated this military conquest. The Russian textile industry was dependent on cotton from the American South. With those supplies of cotton cut off by the Civil War, the tsars decided to complete their conquest of Central Asia and transform the region into a more reliable domestic source of cotton.

Kazakhstan was originally a khanate that separated from the Mongolian empire in the sixteenth century. The Mongolian empire had ruled all of Russia from the thirteenth century until it was conquered by the emerging Russian Empire centered in Moscow in the late sixteenth century. The Kazakh khanate was formally incorporated into the Russian Empire by the mid-1850s, following two centuries of encroachment by Russian trappers, soldiers, and settlers. The Kazakhs had asked the Russians to protect them from others in the region who militarily threatened them. The Far East region along the southeast Pacific coast was annexed following the defeat of the Chinese empire by Russia in a border war in the 1870s.

■ ETHNIC NATIONALITIES

The last Soviet census in 1989 showed over a hundred distinct ethnic nationalities. The fifty-nine ethnic nationalities with at least 30,000 self-identified members in the 1989 census are listed in Table 31-2 in order of descending size.

Ethnic nationalities are distinguished based on objective differences of language, race, religion, history, and culture, which always characterized the peoples within the Russian Empire and later the Soviet Union. One's opportunities were clearly affected by one's ethnic nationality. From the age of sixteen, all Soviet citizens had their ethnic nationality listed on their internal passports. Throughout their adult lives, Soviet citizens filled out forms that included categories requiring them to cite their ethnic nationality.

Self-identification in terms of a specific ethnic nationality was something of a subjective political choice on the part of Soviet citizens. Self-identification as Estonian or Tatar didn't necessarily mean fluency in the language of that ethnic group. No tests on language or history were given by authorities to validate the ethnic identification noted on an internal passport or stated to the census taker. Offspring of mixed marriages had to choose between their parents' nationalities when receiving their internal passports at age sixteen.

Western and Soviet demographers speculated that shifts in the ethnic balance by 1989 were partly attributable to the greater democratic tolerance under Gorbachev since 1985. As late as the 1979 census, members of ethnic minorities that had been persecuted in the past who felt too threatened to assert their true nationality answered "Russian." More politically assertive and less fearful by 1989, these people re-identified themselves ethnically in terms of one of the non-Russian ethnic minorities. Thus, the breakdown of ethnic composition in Table 31–2 records both objective demographic shifts in the former Soviet Union and subjective changes by those who were making an explicit political statement in responding to questions concerning their nationality.

With the demise of the Soviet Union, one-fifth of its population found themselves residing in countries other than those nominally associated with their self-designated ethnic nationality. This included over 17 percent of the 145 million ethnic Russians. Ethnic Russians in 1993, as Figure 31–1 shows, constituted a significant minority—between 20 and 40 percent—in Ukraine, Estonia, Latvia, Kazakhstan, and Kyrgyzstan, and approximately 10–20 percent in the rest of the countries, except Armenia and Azerbaijan. The most ethnically homogeneous post-Soviet countries, with 80 percent or more of the population identifying themselves with the same label, are Russia, Lithuania, Armenia, and Azerbaijan. In contrast, Latvians make up only a slight majority in their own country. The 40 percent of ethnic Kazakhs are a plurality in Kazakhstan, but an absolute minority compared to the combined Russians, Germans, and Ukrainians.

The mix of ethnic nationalities residing in each country and competing for jobs and other status symbols exploded politically even before the end of the Soviet Union. Sensitivity over becoming a minority in their own republic and losing their jobs to non-Kazakhs led to several days of rioting by Kazakhs in the Kazakhstan capital of Alma-Ata in December 1986, when a non-Kazakh was made head of the Kazakhstan Communist party by Gorbachev to eliminate the decades of corruption condoned by his Kazakh predecessor.

Table 31–2 also reveals one major source of the escalating violence and conflict in Russia and Central Eurasia since 1991—changes in ethnic composition.[2] Ethnic

---

[2] See Chapter 33 of this part of the book.

Table 31-2
Ethnic Composition of the Population of the Soviet Union in 1970, 1979, and 1989*

Nationality	Number of Persons of Given Nationality			Percentage Increase or Decrease	
	1970	1979	1989	1970–1979	1979–1989
Total Population of Soviet Union	241,720,134	262,084,654	285,688,965	8.4	9.0
Russians	129,015,140	137,397,089	145,071,550	6.5	5.6
Ukrainians	40,753,246	42,347,387	44,135,989	3.9	4.2
Uzbeks[M]	9,195,093	12,455,978	16,686,240	35.5	34.0
Belorussians	9,051,755	9,462,715	10,030,441	4.5	6.0
Kazakhs[M]	5,298,818	6,556,442	8,137,878	23.7	24.1
Azerbaijanis[M]	4,379,937	5,477,330	6,791,106	25.1	24.0
Tatars[M]	5,930,670	6,185,196	6,645,588	4.3	7.4
Armenians	3,559,151	4,151,241	4,627,227	16.6	11.5
Tadzhiks[M]	2,135,883	2,897,697	4,216,693	35.7	45.5
Georgians	3,245,300	3,570,504	3,983,115	10.0	11.6
Moldavians	2,697,994	2,968,224	3,355,240	10.0	13.0
Lithuanians	2,664,944	2,850,905	3,068,296	7.0	7.6
Turkmen[M]	1,525,284	2,027,913	2,718,297	33.0	34.0
Kirghiz[M]	1,452,222	1,906,271	2,530,998	31.3	32.8
Peoples of Dagestan[M]	1,364,649	1,656,676	2,072,071	21.4	25.1
Germans	1,846,317	1,936,214	2,035,807	4.9	5.1
Chuvash	1,694,351	1,751,366	1,839,228	3.4	5.0
Latvians	1,429,844	1,439,037	1,459,156	0.6	1.4
Bashkirs[M]	1,239,681	1,371,452	1,449,462	10.6	5.7
Jews	2,150,707	1,810,876	1,449,117	−15.8	−20.0
Mordvins	1,262,670	1,191,765	1,153,516	−5.6	−3.2
Poles	1,167,523	1,150,991	1,126,137	−1.4	−2.2
Estonians	1,007,356	1,019,851	1,027,255	1.2	0.7
Chechens[M]	612,674	755,782	958,309	23.4	26.8
Udmurts	704,328	713,696	746,562	1.3	4.6
Maris	598,628	621,961	670,277	3.9	7.8
Ossetians	488,039	541,893	597,802	11.0	10.3
Komi and Komi-Permyak	475,345	477,468	497,081	0.4	4.1
Koreans	357,507	388,928	437,335	8.8	12.4
Karakalpaks[M]	236,009	303,324	423,436	28.5	39.6
Buryats	314,671	352,646	421,682	12.1	19.6
Kabardians[M]	279,928	321,719	394,651	14.9	22.7
Yakuts	296,244	328,018	382,255	10.7	16.5
Bulgarians	351,168	361,082	378,790	2.8	4.9
Greeks	336,869	343,809	357,975	2.1	4.1
Crimean Tatars[M]	N.A.	132,272	268,739	—	103.2
Uigurs[M]	173,276	210,612	262,199	21.5	24.5
Gypsies	175,355	209,159	261,956	19.3	25.2
Ingush[M]	157,605	186,198	237,577	18.1	27.6
Turks[M]	79,000	92,689	207,369	17.3	123.7
Tuvins	139,388	166,082	206,924	19.2	24.6
Peoples of the North, Siberia, Far East	152,626	158,324	197,345	3.7	24.6
Gagauz	155,606	173,179	197,164	10.6	13.8
Kalmyks	137,194	146,631	174,528	6.9	19.0
Hungarians	165,451	170,553	171,941	2.5	0.8
Karachai[M]	112,741	131,074	156,140	16.3	19.1
Kurds[M]	88,930	115,858	152,952	30.3	32.0
Romanians	119,292	128,792	145,918	8.0	13.3
Karelians	146,081	138,429	131,357	−5.2	−5.1
Adygei[M]	99,855	108,711	124,941	8.9	14.9
Abkhaz	83,240	90,915	102,938	9.2	13.2
Balkars[M]	59,501	66,334	88,771	11.5	33.8
Khakass	66,725	70,776	81,428	6.1	15.1
Altais	55,812	60,015	71,317	7.5	18.8
Dungans[M]	38,644	51,694	69,686	33.8	34.8
Finns	84,750	77,079	67,318	−9.1	−12.7
Cherkess[M]	39,785	46,470	52,356	16.8	12.7
Iranians[M]	27,501	31,313	40,510	13.9	29.4
Abazi[M]	25,448	29,497	33,801	15.9	14.6
Others	293,403	198,552	307,228	−32.3	54.7

* Nationalities are listed in descending order by size in 1989.   M = traditionally Muslim

Sources: Itogi Vsesoyuznoi perepisi naseleniya 1970 goda, Vol. IV, Moscow, 1973, pp. 9–11; Natsional'nyi sostav naseleniya, Cbast' II, Moscow, "Informatsionno-izdatel'sky tsentr," 1989, pp. 3–5, as retabulated in Ann Sheehy, "Ethnic Muslims Account for Half of Soviet Population Increase," Report on the USSR, Vol. 2, No. 3 (January 19, 1990), pp. 15–18.

Figure 31–1

Ethnic Compostion (as Percentages) of Countries of Russia and Central Eurasia, 1993

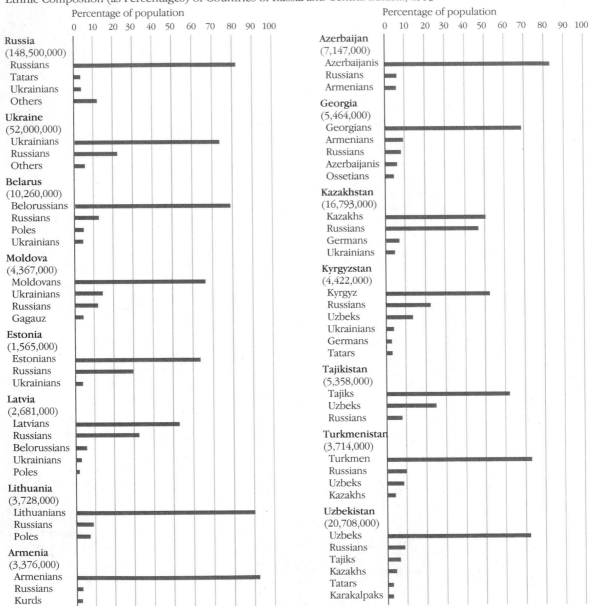

Russians constituted only a little more than half of the entire population of the Soviet Union at that time. The other Slavic and Baltic ethnic nationalities— Ukrainians, Belorussians, Latvians, Lithuanians, and Estonians—remained stable in numbers or even decreased in growth rate compared to the previous intercensal period. In contrast, in the 1989 census the combined Muslim ethnic nationalities accounted for half of the increase in the entire Soviet population since 1979.

Population increases among some of the largest Muslim groups—Uzbeks, Tadzhiks, Turkmen, and Kirghiz—were consistently one-third or more in each of the last two intercensal periods.

To a great extent, variation in reproductive rates among different ethnic nationalities accounted for the shift in the Soviet ethnic composition. Families with five to ten children are not uncommon among almost all Muslim nationalities in Russia and Central Eurasia. Slavic and Baltic nationalities on average have much smaller families, with one or two children. There are several reasons for this variation: culture, the support of the extended family in Muslim societies in raising children, the fact that more than 90 percent of all Slavic and Baltic women work full-time at jobs outside the home, and the large number of Slavic and Baltic women who have completed some higher education.

No less politically significant were the dramatic changes in the mass media—especially in the exposure of the Soviet public to television. From 1960 to 1986 the proportion of the Soviet public viewing television daily jumped from 5 to 93 percent. By 1989, an increasing number of Soviet homes were being fitted with satellite dishes and were receiving uncensored Western news and entertainment shows. Soviet reformers under Gorbachev were especially sensitive to television's impact on the public's awareness of issues and problems. Television was considered one of the factors essential to developing a greater political sophistication and knowledge of the world in the Soviet people, making them more receptive to assuming the burdens and responsibilities of the participatory political culture desired by the reformers. With the gradual elimination of state censorship and the growing sophistication of television journalism, by 1990 the national Soviet audience was exposed to extensive live coverage on television of ethnic unrest and challenges to authoritarian Communist rule by national popular fronts in several republics.

■ ■ ■

In summary, the Soviet Union by 1989 had become a much different country from what it had been as recently as three decades before. On a comparative basis, the 1989 census recorded that the balance of power in Soviet society was clearly shifting away from the ethnic nationalities that had traditionally dominated the Russian Empire and the Soviet Union. All this was occurring in a society that had experienced dramatic increases in the rate of urbanization, educational levels, and television viewing. The Soviet Union was approaching a crossroads of social change, which would be as destabilizing as the political changes under Gorbachev proved to be.

■ NAGORNO-KARABAKH

Clashes between the growing numbers of Muslims and non-Muslims did not even await the end of the Soviet Union. The most serious encounter arose between Muslim Azeris and Christian Armenians over the province of Nagorno-Karabakh within Azerbaijan. This province's population had a majority of ethnic Armenians, and the area was almost religiously sacrosanct to both Azeris and Armenians for hundreds of years.

Figure 31–2
Nagorno-Karabakh

Nagorno-Karabakh (see Figure 31–2) typifies the historical compromises and patchwork ethnicity of political subdivisions within the former Soviet Union that have continued to haunt the countries of Russia and Central Eurasia. Under the Soviet era, ethnic nationalities too small to merit union-republic status were given some lesser degree of autonomy and rights through the establishment of titled "autonomous" republics, territories, or provinces within one of the union republics. Tension and political conflict between these ethnic minorities and the dominant ethnic majority of the union republic were still heated but were kept below the boiling point during the Soviet era by the rigid authoritarian restrictions placed on any form of political expression by the KGB, the Soviet armed forces, and the Communist party.

After 1985, with Gorbachev's reforms, ethnic minorities were freer to express their political demands and grievances. They increasingly criticized policies and practices of the dominant nationality in each republic, which they had long considered to be discriminatory but did not feel free to so categorize openly. The latent tension and conflict between these ethnic minorities and the dominant nationalities that had been unnaturally bottled up for seven decades exploded into open communal warfare in certain locales.

Nagorno-Karabakh is an autonomous province of Azerbaijan because a majority of its local population are Armenians who historically resided in this region. It was included within Azerbaijan rather than within neighboring Armenia by an arbitrary decision made in 1922, which satisfied the claims of the Azeris, rather than those of the Armenians, for control of the province. Armenians within Nagorno-Karabakh and within Armenia were never reconciled to this compromise and always wanted to incorporate the province back into Armenia. As a precedent, they pointed to the example of Nakhichevan (see Figure 31–2), an ethnic enclave of Azeris inside the boundaries of Armenia near its southern border with Iran, which had been an administrative province of Azerbaijan since 1922.

In 1988, Armenians in Nagorno-Karabakh, who had always felt persecuted by the Azeris in the republic government, formed a political organization in alliance with their ethnic cohorts in neighboring Armenia to push for real political autonomy of their province or its incorporation into Armenia. This demand soon sparked the long-smoldering hatred between the two ethnic-religious communities. Roving mobs of Azeris indiscriminately murdered any Armenians they found on the streets of cities in Azerbaijan, and open warfare broke out between Armenian and Azeri villages throughout Nagorno-Karabakh. Within Azerbaijan, opposition to incorporating the province into Armenia formed around fears that Azeris living there would then become helpless victims of persecution and atrocities sanctioned by the Armenian government. Public opinion within Azerbaijan resented a perceived pro-Armenian bias of reporting in the Moscow and Western media about the conflict over Nagorno-Karabakh. Radical Azeris contended that the biased reporting reflected Western prejudice against Muslims. The indiscriminate attacks on Armenians in Azerbaijan crystallized nationalism within Armenia around memories of the genocide perpetrated against Armenians by Muslim Turks in 1915–1916.

Geography has reinforced Armenian nationalism because of the republic's vulnerability and isolation. Armenia is a very small mountainous region, surrounded on its southern and western borders by Iran and Turkey. Ethnically, Azeris are both Turkic and Iranian, and in 1990 Azerbaijani militants, opposed to any negotiation with Armenia over Nagorno-Karabakh, marched with pictures of the Iranian leader Ayatollah Khomeini. They advocated the unification of the Azeris in northern Iran into an Islamic Greater Azerbaijan Republic modeled after the Iranian Islamic Republic to the south. The Greater Azerbaijan Republic would encompass the entire southern Caucasus, effectively eliminating Christian Armenia as a political entity.

Tens of thousands of Armenians who had long worked and lived in Azerbaijan fled discrimination and attacks by Azeris and emigrated to Armenia, and an even greater number of Azeris had to flee from Armenia to Azerbaijan for similar reasons. The flow of refugees between the two republics only exacerbated the deteriorating economic situation in both on the eve of the Soviet collapse. In Azerbaijan, unemployed Azeris already exceeded a half million. The imposition by gangs of Azeris of a rail and road embargo on any freight passing to Armenia crippled the Armenian economy, already suffering from a devastating earthquake in December 1988. In retaliation, the Armenian government sanctioned a rail embargo on any freight going into the Azeri province of Nakhichevan inside Armenia's borders. The Azeris in Nakhichevan responded by tearing down the fences separating their province from Iran and by encouraging Iranian Azeris to join them in "liberating" all of the southern Caucasus from the Armenians.

Gorbachev tried to stem the wave of interethnic violence in 1989 by transferring control of Nagorno-Karabakh to a commission attached to the national government in Moscow. The transfer implied that at some time in the future the Soviet government would declare the province an autonomous republic and an administrative subdivision of Armenia. The change further galvanized the Azerbaijani Popular Front. Through demonstrations and a general strike in Baku, the front forced the republic's Communist leadership into siding with their militant stance against the province's independence from Azerbaijan. In January 1990, gangs of Azeris indiscriminately killed any ethnic Armenians whom they could find in the capital of Baku. The pogrom was finally halted by the Soviet military, which used the pretext of restoring order to kill several dozen Azeris and to arrest the leaders of the Azerbaijani Popular Front.

By November 1990, the national Supreme Soviet restored control over Nagorno-Karabakh to the government of the Azerbaijan republic under a new Communist leadership. The Supreme Soviet acted to end the blockade of Armenia and to placate an Azerbaijani government increasingly unable to control events in its own republic. The March 1990 parliamentary election in the republic had found both Communist and non-Communist candidates running on a platform against independence for Karabakh and condemning the Soviet military attacks against Azeris in January. A majority of the republic's parliament supported the continuing blockade of Armenia by the Azerbaijani Popular Front.

The action of the national Supreme Soviet failed to appease an increasing number of Azerbaijani parliamentary deputies, who were calling for secession of their republic from the Soviet Union. It also polarized a majority of Armenians, who felt betrayed by Moscow's reversal in restoring control of the province to Azerbaijan. In March 1990, the Armenian Popular Front campaigned effectively on the issue of Nagorno-Karabakh, winning a sizable bloc of seats in the Armenian parliament and electing a non-Communist university professor of languages and leader of the popular front, Levon Ter-Petrosyan, to be the chair of the Armenian Supreme Soviet.

By the end of 1990, the Armenian parliament and Ter-Petrosyan were united in demanding Armenian sovereignty over Nagorno-Karabakh. So embittered were they by Moscow's reversal in November 1990 that by early 1991 they advocated complete independence of the republic from the Soviet Union. Before August 1991, only Armenia, Azerbaijan, Georgia, and the three Baltic republics had gone as far as demanding, through their parliaments and chief executives, secession from the Soviet Union as independent countries.

Since 1991, paramilitary forces of Armenia and Azerbaijan have fought pitched battles over the contested province. Divisions of the Azerbaijani national army have openly supported the Azeri paramilitary forces in launching attacks on Armenians. In turn, the Armenian paramilitary forces have been openly armed by the Armenian defense ministry. Recruits for the Armenian forces include ethnic Russians and other non-Muslims from outside Armenia who have come to fight because they consider the conflict equivalent to a Holy War between Christianity and Islam. By the summer of 1993, Armenian paramilitary forces had captured most of Nagorno-Karabakh. Despite condemnation by the United Nations and numerous international human rights organizations, they proceeded to engage in a form of "ethnic cleansing" of Azeris from surrounding villages and threatened to take over other neighboring provinces in Azerbaijan.

The loss of Nagorno-Karabakh reverberated politically throughout Azerbaijan. The defense minister marched on Baku, the capital, forced the democratically elected president of the country to step down, and had himself elected prime minister by the rump parliament, which hadn't fled the capital. The president elected by that rump parliament was the former head of the Nakhichevan province, who previously had been the head of the Azerbaijani KGB and Communist party from the 1960s until 1981.

Political System of the Soviet Communist Autocracy, 1917–1990

As the fifteen countries of Russia and Central Eurasia confront a difficult political future, they can find few past precedents for democratic rule. The Communist system described in this chapter totally monopolized power and every facet of political, economic, social, and cultural life in the Soviet Union for almost three-quarters of a century until 1991.

■ NATURE OF THE PRE-SOVIET RUSSIAN AUTOCRACY

Neither the Soviet Communist system nor its political tyranny was accidental. Each arose indigenously—out of the failures and authoritarian style of political rule of the Russian autocracy, which had governed the country for centuries until 1917.

Russia always seemed something of an anomaly in European history—a society, culture, and political system untouched by the winds of change that altered the context of European civilization over centuries. It has often been pointed out that Russia's vastness, coupled with the building of the Russian state largely in isolation from the West, resulted in a physical and psychological separation from the influences that in Western Europe served to do away with, or at least to modify, political autocracy.

The influences of the Renaissance, the Reformation, and the Counter-Reformation did not penetrate Russia. Western liberal democratic ideas of the seventeenth and eighteenth centuries did not make any significant inroads in Russia until the nineteenth century, and then in a limited and perverted form that was reinterpreted in distinctively non-Western and Russian ways. Until 1861, over 80 percent of the population in the Russian empire was in effect enslaved as serfs to the nobility on manorial estates. From the *Oprichina* of Ivan IV in the sixteenth century to the *Okhrana* of Nicholas II as the very last tsar in the twentieth century, the autocracy relied on secret police to maintain its rule.

Isolation from the West, however, was only one factor. In the historical evolution of Western Europe, political pluralism and the concept of the nation-state as something more than simply the absolute sovereign (or monarch) evolved under feudalism, when the aristocracy succeeded in forcing political concessions and power sharing on the monarch (for example, in England with Magna Carta and the Parliament). In its classic European form, feudalism established a series of binding contractual rights and obligations between the ruling sovereign and the aristocracy. The aristocracy had an independent and distinct corporate identity as an estate of the Crown. In Britain, like other Western European countries, the Crown was always considered to be more than the monarch.

In the eighteenth and nineteenth centuries, the emerging middle class in Western Europe reaffirmed the reality of pluralism and the concept that the nation-state was independent of the ruling sovereign by gaining an autonomous corporate identity and authority in representative institutions. In the nineteenth and twentieth centuries, members of the industrial working class became partners in the nation-state. They formed trade unions and political parties, and they obtained a share of political power through voting and self-governing institutions.

In contrast, even on the very eve of the 1917 Revolution, the Russian autocracy remained basically adamant against devolving power to any political institutions that could limit or channel its monolithic authority. The tsar (caesar) of the Russian autocracy was more than just the absolute and unquestioned ruling sovereign of the Russian state. The tsar was the state—the almost mystical "little father" (*tsar-bartiushka*, as he was affectionately called in colloquial Russian) of all people in society and the sole proprietor of the land. From the tsar, all legitimate authority and rights ultimately emanated.

Tsars based their legitimacy on the principle of divine right long after the West had rejected this concept. The three pinnacles, or fundamental values, of the autocratic system were orthodoxy, autocracy, and nationality. They were actually promulgated as a state doctrine termed "official nationality" during the reign of Nicholas I (1825–1855). Official nationality presumed that, through the person of the tsar (or tsarina), autocratic rule allowed the fullest expression of God's will on earth and sanctified God's annointment of the Russian Orthodox Church as Russia's unique contribution to world civilization and salvation. Through autocratic rule, the state alone could defend and preserve Russian nationality—equated with the Slavic peoples and culture of Eastern Europe—against the threats of Turks, Germans, the Austro-Hungarian Empire, and other non-Slavic states.

From the seventeenth century until the twentieth century, the Russian autocracy assumed what was almost an embattled messianic role of saving world civilization against the onslaught of what it considered the debased religions and political systems of Western Europe. These debased religions and political systems were symptomatic of a decline of the West, against which the absolute Russian autocracy alone would stand firm for all of Christendom. Simultaneously head of state and of the Russian Orthodox Church, the tsar as absolute sovereign was justified in defending the Orthodox religion as the last true Christian faith on earth against the false misrepresentations of Christianity in Roman Catholicism and Protestantism.

The absolute decision-making power of the tsar was idealized as the most truly humane form of governance. The *tsar-bartiushka* was alleged to have a one-to-one personal relationship and mystical involvement with all the people of the country—

a moral bond allowing no intermediary institutions or groups to stand in the way of the tsar's advocacy and defense of the true interests of all of his people. The tsarist system was also extremely statist; that is, the state and the institutions of the state—especially the imperial army—through which the tsar implemented his policies as the defender of all the people were to be valued and revered for their own sake. After all, they were instruments and extensions of the very person of the absolute sovereign and thus must have an unquestioned authority that merited unquestioning obedience.

By the eighteenth and nineteenth centuries, the constitutional monarchies and parliamentary democracies in Western Europe were seen by Russian autocrats as political violations of God's will. They were based on a pluralism of political parties and conflicting interests. Pluralism interfered with and violated the direct moral bond that must be preserved between the supreme sovereign and the people. For tsarist defenders, the Western European monarchies and democracies were political blasphemies only to be expected from cultures founded on false Christian faiths. As the bastion of absolute monarchy in Europe, the Russian autocracy had to be defended at all costs to keep the tide of these political blasphemies from sweeping over the rest of Christian civilization and ushering in the decline of the West.

The Russian autocracy has often been described as "Oriental" or "Asiatic" because the tsar ruled with unlimited religious-moral authority—not unlike traditional Japanese and Chinese emperors or Middle Eastern kings and sultans. The Russian autocracy never really evolved into a true feudal system, in that the Russian aristocracy possessed no corporate identity or rights apart from those bestowed and then capriciously withdrawn by the patrimonial state centered entirely on the tsar. From the time of Peter the Great in the eighteenth century, the aristocracy were ennobled only to the extent of reaching certain grades in a Table of Ranks, by which all positions in Russian society were ranked. Service to the state determined nobility, but the tsar's disfavor could strip one of both position and noble status.

Institutions that ostensibly might have forced the autocracy to yield some of its power were created—for example, *Zemsky Sobor* (landed assembly), the Senate, the State Council, *zemstva* (local elected councils in the provinces after the 1860s), and, from 1905 to 1917, even an elected *Duma* (parliament). Yet by 1917, none of these political institutions had succeeded in challenging the inherent patrimonial nature of the state. None really held power comparable to that granted by or wrested from monarchs in the historical evolution of Western Europe from feudalism to modern nation-states.

Russian civil society under the tsars was just as restrained. Trade unions and political parties were banned until 1906. A social upheaval in 1905 following Russia's defeat by Japan forced Tsar Nicholas II to lift the ban. A free press existed only for spurts between the 1860s and 1917, subject to the arbitrary reimposition of censorship by the tsars. From the eighteenth century, the Russian Orthodox Church servilely obeyed the tsar as its head and, in return for its special privileged status in society, sanctified the autocracy.

In the sixteenth century, Ivan IV, the first tsar, had proclaimed, "Rulers of Russia have not been accountable to anyone, but have been free to reward or chastise their subjects."[1] Four centuries later, confronting widespread challenge to the autocracy and forced to concede the creation of an elected parliament and formation of political parties, Nicholas II, the last tsar, still insisted, "The Supreme, Autocratic Power belongs to the All-Russian Emperor," and "Obedience to his authority, not only for wrath but also for conscience sake, is ordained by God Himself."[2] On the very eve of its collapse, the Russian autocracy resembled a fifteenth-century absolute monarchy propelled through a time warp, as if the intervening 500 years of political development in Western civilization had never occurred.

■ ORIGINS OF SOVIET COMMUNISM

The Russian autocracy that disintegrated by February 1917 was the unwitting victim of political crises caused by the sudden and late modernization of Russian society by its own rulers. In essence, rapid modernization overwhelmed the autocratic system. It broke down traditional Russian society and increased the level of tension, anxiety, and conflict among ethnic groups and social classes in the still pre-modern transitional society. As a consequence, those groups were demanding opportunities for political participation, equality, and social justice. By its very nature, the Russian autocracy seemed unwilling or unable to satisfy these demands. It proved incapable of reforming itself quickly enough and was too inconsistent in its policies to transform Russia politically. The ethnic and social groups distrusted the commitment of the Russian autocracy to effect new political institutions and a new basis of self-governance and citizen participation.

Russia's military defeats in World War I proved to be the "triggering event" for the Russian Revolution. The critical weaknesses of the political system were exposed under the duress of war and economic collapse, and any remaining vestiges of political support for the autocracy were dissipated by February 1917. By October 1917 a temporary vacuum of political authority existed—between the abolition of the autocracy in February and the incomplete attempts to form a new political system by the Provisional Government. The Communists under Vladimir Lenin took advantage of this vacuum to seize power and overthrow the Provisional Government in a coup on November 7. Lenin and the Communists eventually prevailed over opposing political forces and armies in the ensuing Civil War of 1918–1920 and consolidated their control of the country by 1921.

The Leninist Legacy

Lenin remained the unquestioned leader of the new Soviet Communist system and the Soviet state until his death in January 1924. His supreme authority derived from his charisma and the deference shown him by other top party leaders, with whom he had been associated in exile and in the political underground as leader of the Bolshevik faction of the Russian Social Democratic Labor party prior to the October

---

[1]B. H. Sumner, *Survey of Russian History* (London: Duckworth, 1944), p. 67.
[2]Ibid., p. 68.

Revolution of 1917. Lenin never held the formal position of leader of the Communist party (as the Bolsheviks renamed their party), but subsequently the most powerful Soviet leaders from Stalin to Gorbachev would assume the title of General Secretary (renamed First Secretary from 1953 through 1965) of the party's Central Committee. Lenin held the position of Chairman of the Council of People's Commissars, at that time comparable to being prime minister. The Council of People's Commissars was the name for the national executive branch of the government until 1946; from then until the demise of the Soviet Union, it was known as the Council of Ministers.

In the initial years of Lenin's rule, some party members believed that a certain amount of opposition within the party should be allowed. In 1920 a group calling itself the Democratic Centralists appeared at the Ninth Party Congress and, among other things, accused the Leninist party leadership of being a "small handful of party oligarchs" who were exiling other party members only because of their "deviant views." Simultaneously, rank-and-file unrest evolved into the so-called Workers' Opposition, which demanded that industry be controlled and managed by the workers through their autonomous trade unions.

The problem was Lenin, never renowned for his tolerance. His utter rejection of compromise and his equating of disobedience in party ranks with treason had long left little room in the party for those who would not unquestioningly accept his direction of its course. Acting like a traditional Russian tsar, Lenin transferred to remote regions of the country or expelled from the party individuals who disagreed with him. He used the armed forces to crush those on the political left who challenged Communist rule as undemocratic, such as the Red Navy sailors on the Baltic island fortress of Kronstadt in March 1921. They had been supporters of the Bolsheviks during the Civil War but were demanding civil liberties and the end of the single-party dictatorship already evident under Lenin.

During the Civil War, Lenin had created the *Cheka* (acronym for Extraordinary Commission for Combating Counter-Revolution and Sabotage)—the Soviet secret police that in subsequent decades would become the OGPU (Unified State Political Administration), the NKVD (People's Comissariat of Internal Affairs), the MGB (Ministry of State Security), and finally the KGB (Committee of State Security). Although the Cheka initially was intended to be an ad hoc instrument to guard against the revival of the old order, Lenin personally signed orders instructing the Cheka to murder priests, peasants, or anyone whom he viewed as a threat to himself or to the regime. Most importantly, Lenin kept the Cheka in existence after the war. Force and terror—exigencies created by the circumstances of a civil war—became the operational attributes of the regime after 1920.

The Civil War only brought out the deeply ingrained authoritarian personality of Lenin. From his experience and rationalizations during the Civil War, Lenin emerged convinced of a continuing threat posed by internal counter-revolution. In 1918, he had formed an alliance to fight the White Army with "left" Socialist Revolutionaries and Mensheviks. By 1921, he was finding pretexts to outlaw these and all other political parties. Lenin's response to the challenge of the Democratic Centralists and the Workers' Opposition inside his own party was just as consistently "Leninist." At the same time as he ordered troops to crush the democratic revolt of the sailors at Kronstadt, he got the Tenth Party Congress, convening in 1921, to declare these and similar groups dissolved and to prohibit the formation of groups critical of the general line adopted by the party's ruling organs. Moreover, he insisted on a proviso, kept secret for a time, which in effect forbade agitation against the party line even by its leading officials.

The Civil War also reinforced an obsessive paranoia about outside intervention within Lenin, which was characteristic of all subsequent Soviet Communist leaders until Gorbachev. During the Civil War, in 1918, four countries allied against Germany—France, Britain, Japan, and the United States—had dispatched some troops to Russia. Originally the troops were sent with the intent of preventing any post-tsarist Russian government from signing a separate peace with Germany by which German troops could be redeployed from the Russian front to the western front against the allied armies in Belgium and France. Lenin defied these governments and, as many would contend, gave himself the opportunity of winning the Civil War by signing the Brest-Litovsk Treaty with Germany in March 1918.

The reason for the allied troops presence soon changed—they supported the White Army in the Civil War to try to prevent Lenin and the Communists from coming to power. The troops remained in Russia until 1920, even after World War I ended with the surrender of Germany in November 1918, because their governments feared that a new Soviet Communist regime would threaten peace, the stability of state boundaries, and the postwar international system forged through the Treaty of Versailles and the newly established League of Nations. Leaders in Lenin's government, such as Leon Trotsky, were openly predicting that a victory for the Communists in the Civil War would spark worldwide revolutions inspired by the Russian example, overthrowing Western governments to form new regimes allied with the Soviet state.

Lenin's political legacy for Soviet Communism survived his own passing in 1924. His suppression of all formal means of conflict within the party in 1921 inevitably led to differences over power and policy in the subsequent six decades being resolved clandestinely by intrigue, force, and violence. All Soviet leaders until Gorbachev were instinctively paranoid and rationalized repression within their society as a necessity dictated by internal and external threats to their system of governance. From Lenin, it became axiomatic for Soviet rulers to reason that "he who is not with us is against us."

Lenin was authoritarian and paranoid, but he was also a cunning politician, able to compromise his own principles when circumstances required. The new Soviet rulers confronted immense challenges once they had prevailed over the White Army and the foreign interventionist forces in 1921. They had won the Civil War, but now had to win over the hearts and minds of millions of citizens of the former Russian Empire. The people had just suffered through eight continuous years of war and deprivation. Millions had died, and society had been reduced to almost a primitive state of nature. Crops had not been harvested for several years, the Russian industries created by the last three tsars had been destroyed, disease was rampant, and starvation in the countryside and cities had reached epidemic proportions in many locales, leading some to resort to cannibalism out of desperation. Popular discontent with the new regime was widespread, and the factions within the Communist party and the Kronstadt sailors were only manifestations of the broad distrust of the regime that pervaded the country.

At this critical juncture, Lenin took what he termed two steps backward ideologically in order to advance one step forward in generating public support and legitimacy for the new Soviet state. At the Tenth Party Congress in 1921, Lenin instituted a policy that over the next seven years ostensibly refuted Communist dogma that equated private property under capitalism with the exploitation and enslavement of the working class in the West. To win the public over to the new Soviet state, Lenin had to get the national economy operational. Lenin's solution was to allow private enterprise and free commerce in the Soviet Union under a program called the New Economic Policy (NEP).

Under the NEP, farmers were allowed to own their land subject only to taxes in kind and sales of their crops almost solely to the state grain monopoly. Private businesses and industries were allowed to form, as long as they did not hire more than the prescribed number of workers considered by the state to be "capitalist exploitation." The major sectors of the economy, such as banking, energy, and the railroads—termed the socialist "commanding heights"—were all nationalized under Communist control in the name of the working class. The underlying premise of the NEP was that the state would over time buy up and nationalize all of the profitable businesses of the private sector and encourage the absorption of most private farms by collectives, jointly owned by all of their members.

The NEP was to last only until 1928, but it had both an immediate and long-term political impact. After Lenin died in 1924, the political conflict over his succession overlapped with the major policy dispute raging between radicals and pragmatists throughout Soviet society. The dispute was essentially over the desirability and necessity of the NEP as economic policy. On one side were radicals, who considered the NEP a betrayal of Communist dogma and feared that private farmers and businesspeople would only take advantage of their economic wealth and freedom to organize and overthrow the Communist regime. On the other side were pragmatists, who viewed the NEP as the only effective means of building up the Soviet economy over decades. For the pragmatists, socialism with the complete nationalization of industry and collective farms had to await a stage when the private sector had produced a relatively prosperous economy.

The long-term impact of the NEP was symbolic. It was the only time in Soviet history until Gorbachev that private enterprise was allowed. After 1928, for fifty years the only exception was the farmers' markets, in which products raised on the small personal plots of collective farmers could be sold, as a supplement to the distribution of most agricultural products through state-owned stores. After 1987, Gorbachev consistently cited the unfulfilled promise of the NEP as his goal and his ideological belief that socialism would be compatible with diverse forms of economic ownership other than state ownership. For Gorbachev, the NEP had been Lenin's real legacy, wrongly aborted in 1928, despite support for its continuation voiced by such high-ranking party officials of that time as Nikolai Bukharin.

The Rise of Stalin

In his position as General Secretary of the party under Lenin, Joseph Stalin laid the basis for his consolidation of power. This consolidation proceeded slowly. For a time, while Lenin lay dying and for two or three years thereafter, power seemed to be shared by a triumvirate composed of Stalin, Lev Kamenev, and Grigorii Zinoviev, who had banded together to keep Leon Trotsky from succeeding Lenin.

Both Zinoviev and Kamenev were jealous of Trotsky, who seemed in 1921–1924 to be the most talented individual within the leadership and the most likely to succeed Lenin. Trotsky was a dynamic, charismatic speaker. As People's Commissar of War during the Civil War, he had almost single-handedly organized the Red Army and more than anyone else had been responsible for its eventual victory over the White Army and thus the survival of the new Communist regime. Other party leaders feared that Trotsky would use his military connections to stage a coup, and they accused him of being a potential "Bonaparte."

Trotsky and Stalin had been bitter rivals for Lenin's favor since the Civil War. By 1921 the rivalry had heated up. Trotsky openly criticized Stalin for having ordered unnecessary and excessively brutal military force to suppress Georgian nationalists. He also blamed Stalin and his administrative leadership of the party bureaucracy for the growing dictatorial nature ("bureaucratization") of the new Communist regime. In a letter written on his deathbed but never published, Lenin shared Trotsky's view of Stalin and recommended Stalin's removal from key party posts. Stalin encouraged the jealousy of Zinoviev and Kamenev to isolate Trotsky and prevent him from succeeding Lenin. In response, Stalin's two temporary political allies demanded firm action against Trotsky as a "factionalist." Meanwhile, Stalin appeared to be moderate and restrained.

Gradually, Trotsky was isolated from power within the top leadership and moved from one position to another, until he was sent into Siberian exile and eventually banished from the Soviet Union in 1928. Trotsky's oratorical skills, charisma, revolutionary passion, and intelligence made him the darling of non-Soviet European Communists, but he was much less popular in his native country among the new generation of party members and officials recruited during the 1920s. They were predominantly lower-class and relatively uneducated Russian nationalists, who closely identified Communism with the building of a new society and with their own social advancement and empowerment. Stalin appealed to them with his patriotic call to build "socialism in one country."

Trotsky's eloquence, intellect, and knowledge of Marxism had as little appeal to these young anti-intellectual Russian nationalists as his Jewish origins did. Moreover, Trotsky disputed the likelihood that socialism could be created in the underdeveloped economy of the Soviet Union before socialist revolutions occurred in the more advanced industrialized countries of Western Europe. Trotsky supported continuation of Lenin's NEP, until capitalism had been overthrown in Western Europe and European industrial working-class proletarian states could help finance economic expansion in the Soviet Union.

A memo written by Trotsky in late 1923, but only released from previously closed party archives in 1990, reveals that he could easily have succeeded Lenin.[3] Trotsky turned down an offer by Lenin in 1923 to become deputy chairman of the Council of People's Commissars. As deputy chairman, Trotsky would have been the

---

[3]V. I. Danilov, "We Are Beginning to Get to Know Trotsky," *Ekonomika i organizatsiya promyshlennogo proizvodstva,* Vol. 21, No. 1 (January 1990), pp. 47–62.

undisputed successor to Lenin as head of the government in January 1924. In the memo Trotsky rejected Lenin's offer and the future leadership of the Soviet Union, because he feared that his Jewish origins would only further inflame anti-Communist attitudes as a result of anti-Semitism among several Western governments and many Soviet ethnic nationalities. This was also the reason he did not move against Stalin in 1924, when the reading of Lenin's deathbed letter at the annual party congress would have ended Stalin's career.

In the meantime, differences between Stalin and his two temporary political allies had been developing. Kamenev and Zinoviev assumed that, with Trotsky out of the way, one of them would be the logical choice to succeed Lenin. They—and everyone else—underestimated Stalin. Stalin prepared for a showdown by building a loyal following of party officials throughout the Soviet Union; his followers increasingly controlled the delegations to the annual congresses in Moscow. He also allied temporarily with the moderates Nikolai Bukharin, Aleksei Rybov, and Mikhail Tomsky, who feared that Kamenev and Zinoviev would attempt to accelerate the pace of state-run industrialization and force collectivization of agriculture. Step by step, Stalin isolated Kamenev and Zinoviev to such an extent that they abjectly confessed their policy errors and promised to abide by party discipline. They were expelled from their positions and from the party. They were later readmitted, but had been thoroughly discredited by their open admission of having acted against party unity.

Once the so-called Left Deviationists (Kamenev and Zinoviev) and their advocacy of forced industrialization and collectivization had been discredited, Stalin adopted their policy views as his own. Now these views were projected to be the correct party line. In 1928 Stalin initiated his own revolution against Soviet society by forcing millions of farmers to give up their private farms and join state and collective ones and by nationalizing the private industry and commerce that had been allowed from 1921 under Lenin's NEP. Stalin used the pretext that Soviet private farmers were deliberately hoarding their grain from market to wait for higher prices. Stalin charged the farmers with a conspiracy to starve the new Soviet state in hopes of aiding an alleged pending military invasion of the country by the capitalist countries of Poland and Japan.

Stalin's temporary allies Bukharin, Rykov, and Tomsky were denounced as "anti-party rightists" and accused of plotting as a faction to unite with the remnants of the former Trotsky-Zinoviev-Kamenev faction. Under Stalin's attacks, Bukharin, Tomsky, and Rykov capitulated, confessed their sins, and asked to be permitted to join the new party consensus in fighting all factions or deviations against the general line. They were soon removed from the important positions they held.

Political Terrorism under Stalin

Throughout the subsequent decades, Stalin consolidated his absolute power as he and his political lieutenants repeatedly declared that the need to purge the party and impose uniformity in policy views only increased as the Soviet system moved further toward Communism. Political power, they asserted, tended to attract opportunists, many of whom were able to conceal their real motives. Moreover, the Western bourgeoisie (the capitalist ruling class) would never accept defeat and would resort to all sorts of vicious means in an effort to undermine the building of socialism as the first stage toward Communism in the Soviet Union. Opportunists in the party would become convenient tools for the class enemy from the West. Therefore, said the Stalinists, the party had to be eternally vigilant against the "wrecking" activities of these elements within Soviet society.

By the mid-1930s these rationalizations led to the extermination of the Bolsheviks and to mass terror. A revealing speech concerning the Great Purge was made by the later party leader Nikita Khrushchev to a closed session of the Twentieth Party Congress in February 1956. His "Secret Speech" was published for the first time in the Soviet Union in 1989, but it was well-known for decades elsewhere because copies had been leaked to Western journalists by foreign Communists in attendance at the Congress. Although questions remained, Khrushchev's speech provided many previously unknown details. During the remaining years of his leadership, Khrushchev often used the theme of the Great Purge and references to those implicated in Stalin's so-called cult of personality and still in power in the Soviet Union to denounce "Stalinism" as a tyrannical aberration of Communist ideology.

The Great Purge ostensibly had its origins as a reaction to the assassination in December 1934 of Sergei Kirov, leader of the Leningrad party and potential rival of Stalin. At the Seventeenth Party Congress in 1934, concern among some delegations over the pace of the economic changes instituted by Stalin and over the millions who were dying allegedly led to a minor revolt against him. These delegations were reported either to have abstained or to have voted for Kirov rather than Stalin as the new party leader. Stalin was supported for reelection by the overwhelming majority of party delegates, but the rumored revolt against him only adds to the still murky circumstances surrounding Kirov's assassination. Conventional wisdom in the Soviet Union and in the West holds that the assassin was directly aided by Stalin's secret police and that Stalin himself ordered the execution. In any case, hundreds of thousands of party officials and members and millions of innocent Soviet citizens were arrested, tried, and often summarily executed by special boards of the secret police operating in the "emergency" situation created by the alleged challenge to Communist rule from those who had supposedly plotted Kirov's assassination.

After 1985, with Gorbachev's *glasnost*, archeologists, public activists, and even construction crews unearthed the corpses of tens of thousands of Soviet citizens buried in the 1930s in anonymous mass graves, or killing fields, hidden for decades in ravines or forests on the outskirts of Soviet cities. Citizens condemned as "enemies of the people" by the secret police's special boards were marched in large groups to these areas, systematically shot to death hour after hour by firing squads, and then dumped into mass graves covered by lime and dirt. Kuropaty in the suburbs of Minsk was the first and most notorious of these killing fields uncovered and widely reported by the Soviet liberal media in 1988. By 1993 ten other gravesites of this kind had been unearthed, raising estimates of the number executed just in these locales to hundreds of thousands.

Stalin's nationwide political hysteria and witchhunt presumed that a conspiracy against the Soviet Union had been hatched by such disparate individuals as Trotsky, Bukharin, Hitler, and British prime ministers. Trotsky, in exile and without any influence in the Soviet Union since the late 1920s, was assassinated in Mexico in

1940 by an agent of Stalin's secret police who had infiltrated his personal entourage. Kamenev, Zinoviev, Bukharin, Rykov, and countless others were prosecuted and sentenced to death in major show-trials in 1937 as alleged agents of this international conspiracy, which supposedly was plotting to overthrow the Communist system and had assassinated Kirov.

Many who escaped execution were sent to Siberian corrective-labor camps, from which fewer ever returned. Expulsions from the party were launched on a grand scale throughout the late 1930s. One-fifth of the entire membership was expelled, and 90 percent of the elite establishment elected to the party's Central Committee in 1934 had been murdered or had disappeared forever into labor camps by the time the next Central Committee was elected in 1939. The Great Purge devoured many officers of the Soviet armed forces, from the top marshals and generals to those at the rank of lieutenant. Estimates vary, but as many as 50 percent of all Soviet officers were probably arrested and sent to labor camps. Some were only released immediately before or following Hitler's invasion of the Soviet Union in June 1941. Even top officials of the secret police were not immune. The heads of the NKVD and their subordinates were purged and executed between 1935 and 1938 for not being vigilant enough in unmasking even more millions of alleged "wreckers" and "enemies of the people."

The wave of arrests and murders subsided to a degree in 1939–1941 but resumed in the last eight years of Stalin's life. Millions of Soviet citizens were terrorized, and many were imprisoned in Siberian labor camps after 1945 (and the war had already cost 27 million Soviet lives). There were new ideological formulas and rationales for the purges and terror. Deteriorating Soviet-American relations after World War II and the beginnings of the Cold War provided the general pretext for imposing rigid controls on Soviet society and for denouncing many as agents of Western imperialism. From 1945 to 1948, the mass campaign to purge Soviet society of Western influences was characterized as *Zhdanovshchina* after Yurii Zhdanov, Stalin's lieutenant and Party Secretary, who orchestrated the policy before his own mysterious death. Following Zhdanov's death in 1949, thousands of party officials in Leningrad and their families were rounded up and murdered for allegedly taking part in the "Leningrad affair" directed against Stalin and Communist rule. This Leningrad purge was a secret until Nikita Khrushchev disclosed it before the party congress in 1961. Mikhail Suslov, who remained among the top party leaders until his death in January 1982 (Yurii Andropov replaced him as Party Secretary), orchestrated the Leningrad purge under the orders of Stalin.

In 1952–1953 politically orchestrated hysteria surrounded a purported "Doctor's Plot" by a number of Jewish doctors to poison the entire party leadership. Anyone with a Jewish background was automatically assumed to be part of this conspiracy and persecuted. Had Stalin lived past March 1953, he might have used the pretext to arrest and execute all of his political lieutenants as clandestine co-conspirators. He also might have ordered the deportation of all Soviet Jews to Eastern Siberia in boxcars, which would have meant the deaths of several millions during their passage. In 1941 and 1944, Stalin had ordered the forced deportation of entire ethnic nations, such as the Volga Germans and the Crimean Tatars, for alleged collaboration with Nazi Germany, resulting in the deaths of over half in transit to remote areas of Siberia.

Hundreds of thousands of Soviet prisoners of war, who had been captured and brutalized by the Nazis, were welcomed back after 1945 by being sent to corrective-labor camps in Siberia as suspected enemy agents. Soviet children were encouraged through Communist-controlled youth groups and the Soviet media to denounce their parents to the secret police for deviant political beliefs. Pavel Morozov, who had denounced his parents to the police in the 1930s, was propagandized as a national role model; his picture was displayed in the buildings where the youth groups met. When individuals were denounced by their neighbors as "enemies of the state," not only were the individuals themselves sent to Siberian camps but their entire families were fired from their jobs, expelled from school, banished from their apartments, and even arrested. Their crime was not having reported their parent, spouse, or sibling to the secret police.

Anyone whose views deviated even slightly from official Stalinist policy or anyone whose apartment or job was merely desired by a neighbor were subject to being anonymously denounced, charged, and imprisoned under Article 58 of the criminal code as a "counter-revolutionary" and "traitor to the state." Under Stalinist jurisprudence, confessions in the court by those accused under Article 58 were considered sufficient proof to merit convictions. Needless to say, the secret police extracted confessions by beatings and torture and by threats against members of their families.

■ POLITICAL CONFLICT FROM KHRUSHCHEV THROUGH BREZHNEV

After Stalin's death in 1953, the situation normalized somewhat. Even under Stalin, the terrorism and the murder of millions of Soviet citizens and many party officials had muted but didn't halt internal leadership conflicts. Stalin himself encouraged these in a Machiavellian fashion to keep his political lieutenants preoccupied with fighting among themselves for his favor.

Boundaries of Elite Conflict

From 1953 through 1985, the changing top leadership of the party was divided between those supporting and those opposing various degrees of economic and political reform to correct the worst problems and forms of political tyranny inherited from the Stalinist era. Despite official claims of collegial decision making and policies unanimously endorsed by the top party leaders, conflict did rage for these three decades between "reformists" and "conservatives" over a wide range of domestic and foreign policy issues and priorities.[4]

For decades skillful Western Kremlinologists detected the lines of factional conflict and the shifts in power based on arcane clues in the censored Soviet media and rumors from Soviet informers.[5] Who was standing next to whom among the leaders

---

[4]Stephen F. Cohen, *Rethinking the Soviet Experience: Politics and History since 1917* (New York: Oxford University Press, 1985), pp. 128–157.

[5]Carl A. Linden, *Khrushchev and the Soviet Leadership, 1957–1964* (Baltimore: Johns Hopkins Press, 1966); Michel Tatu, *Power in the Kremlin: From Khrushchev to Kosygin* (New York: Viking, 1970), and Dusko Doder, *Shadows and Whispers: Power Politics inside the Kremlin from Brezhnev to Gorbachev* (New York: Penguin, 1988).

on the reviewing stand in Moscow during Soviet parades? Who spoke after whom at party congresses? How many lines did different top leaders receive in official biographies of deputies to the national Supreme Soviet? Who failed to show up at airports to welcome back top leaders from foreign trips? Who was asked to deliver the annual keynote speeches for major national Communist events (Lenin's birthday or the anniversary of the 1917 Revolution)? Who subtly departed from the exact wording of party documents in defending supposedly unanimous decisions of the leadership? Who omitted phrases of obsequious praise for the top party leader? Whose identifiable political clients were suddenly demoted or promoted?

Western Kremlinologists assumed that the total secrecy surrounding the lives of leaders and their decision making hid conflict and that different leaders were deliberately conveying hints to mobilize support among their erstwhile followers at lower echelons of the party, the government, the military, and the secret police. Because of the required party unity and the prohibition on factions since 1921, even a marginal departure from complete and absolute uniformity among the leadership could be categorized by the Russian phrase *Ne sluchaino!* ("It is not accidental!"). Since Stalin, the reality of Soviet politics had been typified by the Leninist axiom *Kto kogo?* ("Who will prevail over whom?").

At times, policy differences were used by contending factions merely to mask their own political ambitions. The policy differences were exaggerated to discredit the opposition and advance individuals' claims to supreme political authority within the party and the country. Individuals were demoted and ousted from power or promoted to the highest echelons depending on their ability to form political alliances and outmaneuver their political opponents. The top Soviet leaders were those able to position their political clients and supporters in key offices and institutions of the party, the military, the secret police, and the government.

More than just the accumulation of political power and the support of loyalists ultimately determined who would be chosen by the elite establishment as the top party leader. Leadership performance and an identifiable policy program became increasingly important. The top party leader arose and survived because he was able to project himself as the most effective problem-solver to his "constituents" in the elite establishment. In a clear change from the time of Lenin and Stalin, the supreme leader was he whose speeches and policy initiatives were best able to maintain his image of being an unthreatening consensus builder—that is, a middle-of-the-road moderate on the contentious issues separating conservatives and reformists among the political elite.[6]

Khrushchev and Brezhnev as Leaders

It is clear in retrospect that the ouster of Nikita Khrushchev as head of the party and of the government in October 1964 was essentially a vote of no confidence in his leadership from the Soviet elite establishment. His ouster resulted from mounting opposition to his political reforms among conservatives within the top ruling organs of the party. They felt that his attacks on Stalin, his attempts to rejuvenate

---

[6]George W. Breslauer, *Khrushchev and Brezhnev as Leaders: Building Authority in Soviet Politics* (London: Allen & Unwin, 1982).

the party, and his anti-military and pro-consumer policies had gone too far. Khrushchev's attacks on Stalin and disclosures about the decades of tyranny under his rule were undermining the authority of the ruling party. His intent to rejuvenate the party by promoting a new leadership stratum of younger and more highly educated officials personally threatened conservatives with a loss of their own power or even their offices. His policies to reallocate funds from the military to the consumer and agricultural sectors would reverse four decades in which the military-industrial sector and the conservatives heading those state ministries had come to monopolize the Soviet economy and real political power.

Consensus among conservatives and reformists formed around a perception that Khrushchev's policy initiatives and leadership style had failed to enhance the country's influence internationally or to resolve the country's many economic and social problems. The Soviet Union was humiliated in the Cuban missile crisis in 1962, when Soviet ships had to pull back from the American quarantine of Cuba and not follow through on Khrushchev's threat to install medium-range nuclear missiles there. Khrushchev's boisterous claim that Soviet agriculture would outproduce the United States by 1970 was deflated when a dust bowl resulted from his pet project to grow grain in the Virgin Lands. The Soviet government was forced to buy wheat from the West in 1963.

These and other policy failures seemed a dismal record for Khrushchev by 1964. Conservatives and reformists plotted to remove him in a coup. If nothing else, they were concerned that he was acting so arbitrarily, without consultation or consensus building within the elite establishment, that he was threatening to break the one unwritten commandment by which all Soviet elites had abided since 1953: no one should be allowed to accumulate so much power within the leadership that he could terrorize and murder the other members of the elite establishment at will, as Stalin had done from 1935 until his death in 1953.

Leonid Brezhnev, a Khrushchev political protégé from 1957 to 1964, ruled as head of the party from 1965 until his death in November 1982, because he was a consensus builder.[7] He was able to placate the contending factions within the top political leadership, including the conservative faction led by Mikhail Suslov in the party bureaucracy and the opposing reformists headed by Aleksei Kosygin, the head of the government. Yet even Brezhnev had to contend with opposition from neo-Stalinist conservatives and from his own military establishment to his policy of détente and arms control with the United States in the early 1970s.[8] Regional political conflicts, such as those over cotton growing in Central Asia and the diversion of northern Siberian rivers, discussed in Chapter 31, originated during the Brezhnev era. The various party-state officials representing the different regions of the country were in conflict with each other and attempted to gain endorsement of their positions among top party echelons in Moscow.[9]

---

[7]Timothy J. Colton, *The Dilemma of Reform in the Soviet Union* (New York: Council on Foreign Relations, 1986).

[8]Raymond L. Garthoff, *Détente and Confrontation: American-Soviet Relations from Nixon to Reagan* (Washington, D.C.: Brookings Institution, 1985).

[9]Han-ku Chung, *Interest Representation in Soviet Policymaking* (Boulder, Co.: Westview Press, 1987).

At times political conflict in the Soviet Union tended to resemble a Hollywood gangster movie. As an example, published accounts in the Soviet Union have revealed the circumstances surrounding the showdown between Lavrenti Beria, the head of the secret police, and the other top Soviet leaders in the summer of 1953, following Stalin's death.[10] Beria was about to arrest and execute the other top Soviet leaders. Instead, they secretly plotted against him and arranged to convene a special surprise cabinet meeting in the Kremlin. When Beria arrived at the meeting, Khrushchev, who had his own hidden pistol, offered a resolution condemning Beria. Before Beria could pull his own pistol out of his briefcase, Khrushchev grabbed the briefcase and pushed a secret button, calling in bodyguards to arrest Beria. After a peremptory closed trial, Beria was later executed by a firing squad in a Kremlin courtyard. In early 1957, widely circulated rumors in Moscow reported that Khrushchev's political opponents in the leadership had put out a contract on his life and almost succeeded in murdering him.

Even by the early 1980s, when purged party leaders could expect at worst to receive lifelong pensions in retirement, fairly solid circumstantial evidence suggested that the party leader of the Belorussian republic had been murdered in a contrived automobile accident arranged by his political opponents in Moscow and Minsk.[11] A leading official of the KGB and brother-in-law of Leonid Brezhnev committed suicide in 1982 rather than allow further investigation and disclosure of a scandal involving diamond smuggling by the adulterous lover of Brezhnev's daughter.[12] (A liberal democracy the Soviet Communist system was not, but Soviet politics could never have been accused of being boring.)

■ ORGANIZATION AND FUNCTIONS OF THE COMMUNIST PARTY

Despite factional conflicts and policy differences, until 1985 no one within the leadership of the Communist party ever questioned the right and authority of the party to govern the Soviet Union. Reformists differed from conservatives only over the degree to which the system could be democratized, the state-run economy be decentralized, or funds be reallocated from heavy industry and the military to consumer-agricultural sectors without undermining the single-party autocracy. As an institution, the Communist party almost without challenge dominated every aspect of Soviet politics and society for seven decades.

Levels of Authoritarianism

The top officials of the Communist party in the ruling Politburo made all national policy decisions—unaccountable to anyone other than the few hundred members

---

[10]Fyodor Burlatsky, "Khrushchev—Brushstrokes in a Political Portrait," *Literaturnaya gazeta*, February 24, 1988, p. 14 [translated in *Current Digest of the Soviet Press*, Vol. 40, No. 9 (March 30, 1988), pp. 1–6].
[11]Amy W. Knight, "Pyotr Masherov and the Soviet Leadership: A Study in Kremlinology," *Survey*, Vol. 26, No. 4 (Winter 1982), pp. 151–168.
[12]Zhores Medvedev, *Andropov* (London: Basil Blackwell, 1983), pp. 93–98; and Doder, *Shadows and Whispers*, pp. 53–72.

of the elite establishment. The Soviet elite establishment was composed of the party's All-Union Central Committee, which nominally elected the entire Politburo once every five years and could vote to remove any Politburo members in the interim. Some debate but eventual unanimous approval could be expected when the Central Committee convened periodically (three or four times annually) in Moscow to authorize the Politburo's policy decisions collectively in Committee plenums (plenary sessions).

Central Committee members were not entirely powerless or insulated from the ongoing factional and policy conflicts raging within the Politburo. In July 1957 they were drawn into the conflict between Khrushchev and the majority of the Presidium (as the Politburo was temporarily renamed from 1953 until 1966), who were plotting to remove Khrushchev from power by having the Central Committee vote him out of his office and renounce his reformist policies. Instead, through his control of the central patronage powers of the party bureaucracy, Khrushchev had stacked the Central Committee with his own supporters. He arranged a special unannounced plenum of the Central Committee, which ousted the members of the Presidium majority as an alleged "anti-party group" and replaced them with pro-Khrushchev allies.

Unknown to the Presidium majority, the Central Committee had been secretly flown to Moscow on transports arranged by Defense Minister Yurii Zhukov. Within a few months, Zhukov, perhaps the most popular Soviet military leader from World War II, himself was dropped from the Presidium and removed as Defense Minister by Khrushchev. Khrushchev feared that Zhukov's demand for greater autonomy of the armed forces as a political payoff for helping him could ultimately weaken party control of the Soviet military.

In October 1964 the tables were turned on Khrushchev. With the support of the Soviet military and the KGB, the Central Committee was secretly convened by his fair-weather allies within the Presidium in order to oust him. He was forced to accept as a *fait accompli* the arranged coup and to submit his resignation under the pretext of "failing health."

Brezhnev survived numerous plots among those in the Politburo who were opposed to his middle-of-the-road conservatism or were ambitious to assume leadership of the party. Prime Minister Aleksei Kosygin (until his death in 1980) consistently represented the reformists and Mikhail Suslov the conservatives who forced Brezhnev to compromise his policies from both sides of the spectrum. When Brezhnev suffered a major heart attack in 1974, Aleksandr Shelepin, the youngest and most ambitious of the conservative Politburo members, unsuccessfully plotted to force Brezhnev's retirement, before Brezhnev countered by removing him from the Politburo. To deter these political threats, Brezhnev allowed the other Politburo and Central Committee members and their lower-ranking political cronies almost lifelong tenure in their positions and carte blanche to loot and plunder the Soviet treasury for their own benefit.

Central Committee members were never elected by individual merit or by some public mandate. They were elected because of their loyalty to some political faction in the Politburo and because of the administrative positions they held in the Soviet bureaucracy. They received their seats on the Central Committee primarily ex officio; that is, they headed major posts at the republic and provincial levels, held the top positions within the government and ministries, led the armed forces or KGB, chaired the various unions of artists and intellectuals, or ran other principal power bases (the Communist-controlled youth federation, or *Komsomol*, the Communist-controlled All-Union Council of Trade Unions, and so on).

This pattern of an interlocking oligarchy in the ruling party organs was replicated at lower administrative and jurisdictional levels throughout Soviet society. Fourteen of the union republics had their own Communist party organization that was subordinate to the all-union party bureaucracy in Moscow. The exception was Russia, which was directly run by the all-union bureaucracy in Moscow until a separate Russian Communist party was formed in June 1990. The fourteen republic Politburos made all policy decisions for their jurisdictions, accountable only to their respective republic Central Committees. The republic Central Committees nominally elected their respective Politburos, and their members comprised the key party, government, intellectual, defense, secret police, and other leadership positions within each republic. In each of the approximately 150 provinces and territories, a corresponding bureau of the party made all policy decisions and was nominally elected by and subject to the approval of an elite establishment consisting of the members of the provincial or territorial committee. Below this level, urban and district-borough (*rayon*) bureaus were nominally elected by and accountable to the urban and district-borough committees within their respective jurisdictions.

Unlike the Soviet state with its nominal federal structure, the Soviet Communist party was a tightly unified national organization based on "democratic centralism." In theory, all administrative levels of the party's ruling organs from dis-

Figure 32–1

Central Committee Building of the Ukrainian Communist Party, Largest Union-Republic Branch of the Soviet Communist Party, in Kiev

tricts to republics were supposed to be accountable simultaneously to the party members who elected them through delegates and to the party officials who oversaw them at the next highest link in the chain of command of the party hierarchy. That is, republic party organs and officials were suppposed to be accountable simultaneously to all of the party members in that republic and to the all-union governing organs of the party; provincial-territorial party organs and officials were accountable to all provincial and territorial party members and to the republic governing organs of the party; and urban-district party organs and officials were accountable to all urban and district party members and to the provincial and territorial governing organs of the party.

In theory, democratic centralism meant that party members and ruling organs could debate policy issues until a formal decision had been made by higher party-elected organs, but the party was obligated to implement a decision nationally once it had been made by the upper ruling organs. In turn, party members were supposed to be recruited from a cross-section of the Soviet public. Therefore, democratic centralism in theory presumed that each level of the party's ruling organs would at least indirectly reflect the demographics of the population within its administrative jurisdiction.

Thousands of full-time functionaries (*apparatchiki*) in the party bureaucracy throughout the Soviet Union oversaw the implementation of policy decisions made by party bureaus and committees. They continuously intervened in or overruled actions by factories, farms, universities, and other institutions or officials. On the all-union, republic, and provincial-territorial levels, the party bureaucrats were collectively titled the Secretariat. As individual party secretaries, they were elected by their respective committees, and they in turn oversaw thousands of appointed instructors, who were assigned to various functional and economic departments of the party bureaucracy at each jurisdictional level. In most cases, the party secretaries were also elected full or nonvoting members of their respective Politburos or bureaus. The head of the Central Committee Secretariat and in effect leader of the party had always been since Stalin the General Secretary (First Secretary from 1953 to 1965), a position to which Gorbachev became the last individual ever elected on March 11, 1985. All full-time party functionaries at all levels of the party bureaucracy were invested with primary responsibility to oversee the party's personnel policy and to enforce party policies throughout Soviet society.

Over many decades party functionaries directly or indirectly dictated the selection and removal of personnel in tens of thousands of leadership positions throughout Soviet society—from school principals, heads of collective farms, factory managers, local party secretaries, and university rectors to heads of government ministries, trade unions, youth groups, provincial party organizations, and the armed forces. Each administrative level of the party bureaucracy had its own patronage list of positions under its jurisdiction; it had final authority to approve those nominally elected or appointed to those positions by their own constituents. These patronage lists comprised the party's *nomenklatura* powers to oversee the entire function of leadership recruitment for every segment and level of Soviet society and politics.

Thus, any real accountability of party bureaus to even their committees was attenuated. Democratic centralism had atrophied over decades to a point where party officials automatically deferred to the wishes of their superiors in the party hierarchy and showed little tolerance to challenges of their authority by rank-and-file party members—much less by average citizens who didn't belong to the party. Members of party committees, from the All-Union Central Committee to provincial-territorial and urban-district committees, held their ex-officio seats only because they had been authorized and approved by the party bureaucracy, which in turn was directly responsible to the party bureau at each jurisdictional level. The bureaus had to gain approval for their policy decisions only from individuals on the party committees, whom they had directly or indirectly selected. This circularity of political power meant that the party bureaus chose those to whom they were nominally supposed to be accountable.

Every few years each territorial level of the party gathered together in congresses or report-election conferences. Every five years an all-union party congress was convened in Moscow, at which approximately 5,000 delegates nominally elected the Central Committee from a single list of uncontested candidates, drawn up by the party bureaucracy in response to shifting factional alliances among the Politburo members. The 5,000 delegates were selected from uncontested lists drawn up by republic and provincial-territorial party officials, who themselves were appointed by the party bureaucracy in Moscow and who owed their positions to their support of various factional alliances within the Politburo.

As the highest and most authoritative elected organ of the party, the Central Committee acted in the name of the entire party during the five-year interim between congresses. At the congresses, delegates would hear and discuss reports of the Central Committee on actions undertaken to realize goals of the preceding congress. At the end of a congress, the delegates voted (unanimously) on resolutions approving the work of the Central Committee over the preceding five years and outlining goals to be carried out before the next congress. A congress concluded with the election (unanimously) of a new Central Committee, which in turn would elect (unanimously) a new Politburo and Secretariat. The Politburo in the last few years of the system convened almost weekly in Moscow to make policy decisions that were debated and formally approved by the Central Committee, when it convened three to five times annually in Moscow in its plenary sessions. The same pattern was followed at the republic level with congresses once every five years and at the local level with report-election conferences twice every five years, as well as for the elections of their respective committees and bureaus.

The number of seats and positions on the All-Union Politburo never followed an exact formula. From 1964 until 1990, there had been as few as ten and as many as sixteen full (voting) members on the Politburo, and an additional five to ten individuals participated in the weekly sessions as candidate members without the right to vote (as Yeltsin did from 1985 to 1987). The General Secretary of the Central Committee and the Prime Minister (head of the government) were always full Politburo members. With the exception of these two, the positions accorded full or candidate membership status varied widely over the decades from Stalin's death to the breakup of the Soviet Union.

At various times, the Defense Minister, the Chairman of the KGB, and the Minister of Foreign Affairs were elected full Politburo members. They won election because of their personal closeness to the current General Secretary (last evidenced by Gorbachev's recruitment of Foreign Minister Shevardnadze to the Politburo in 1985), or because the General Secretary made an implicit political deal to win the support of their respective ministries for his foreign policy by giving them a seat and vote on the Politburo. First party secretaries of the cities of Moscow and Leningrad and of the Ukrainian republic were typically full or candidate Politburo members, by virtue of their leading the three largest party organizations in the country (recall that Russia did not have its own separate party organization until 1990).

When Brezhnev was General Secretary, the first party secretaries of several non-Slavic republics held full and candidate Politburo seats. Personal friendship with Brezhnev, who valued his lifelong political cronies, figured as importantly in their selection as any attempt to establish an ethnic balance through a quota of non-Slavic seats on the Politburo. Several of the same non-Slavic party chieftains, such as the heads of the Uzbek and Georgian branches of the Communist party, were also among the most corrupt officials in the country and ran their republics almost as fiefdoms.

A very small number of women—not more than 2–3 percent—were ever elected to the Central Committee. Even fewer women were elected to party leadership positions at any level above that of the district, despite the fact that women constituted over 30 percent of all members of the national party during the last two decades of the Soviet system. Only two women in Soviet history were ever elected full members of the Politburo. The first, Yelena Furtseva, who served from 1957 to 1964, was widely rumored at the time to have been Nikita Khrushchev's mistress and was forced out for alleged corruption after his ouster. The second woman, Galina Semenova, served from 1990 to 1991, and was elected at a time when the party had ceased to monopolize power in the Soviet Union as a consequence of the anti-Communist revolution spreading throughout the society.

Party Control of Soviet Society

The party bureaucracy controlled thought and expression at every level of Soviet society. Over 400,000 primary party organizations, directly accountable to higher levels of the party bureaucracy and the only political organizations allowed until March 1990, were established in almost every Soviet factory, farm, university, government office, research institute, library, public organization, and apartment complex. At its peak, before hundreds of·thousands of party members resigned beginning in 1989, approximately 19 million Soviet adults belonged to the Communist party. Party members were assigned responsibility for implementing the party line through these primary organizations at work and at home.

Patronage choices for leadership positions made at higher levels of the party bureaucracy were almost automatically implemented. Because the primary party organizations were the only legally sanctioned political group in each constituency and work place, they alone could caucus to nominate the single candidate "recommended" by the higher party bureaucracy. In almost all cases, membership in the Communist party was a requirement for holding a leadership position. Conventional wisdom propagated by the party was that only the very best citizens were party members. Therefore, they merited being chosen as leaders, because they had proven themselves and their devotion to Communist principles through their tenure in the party. There was little mention of the fact that many people joined the party essentially because membership was both expected and required to qualify for job promotions or leadership positions.

Millions of party members (over 200,000 in the city of Moscow alone) oversaw the ongoing "mobilization of the masses" as paid or volunteer agitators and propagandists. They orchestrated the incessant electoral campaigns in which the name of the single, party-authorized candidate for a deputy seat in the local council or republic or national legislature would appear on the ballot. Quotas based on age, gender, social class, and other characteristics were formulated in Moscow and in the republics to ensure that the demographic composition of the more than 2 million deputies serving in the various councils and legislatures throughout the country closely paralleled that within Soviet society as a whole. Candidates for deputy were recruited by local party organizations in compliance with their specific quota-based instructions.

In collusion with trade union and youth leaders appointed by the party bureaucracy, the agitators and propagandists delivered lectures during lunch hours to dozing and politically apathetic workers. In classrooms at schools, they compelled millions of students to sit through stultifying recitations of Communist ideology. They expected adults living in apartment complexes to attend the lectures and participate in the activities sponsored by party agitation centers in each complex. This charade performed by agitators and propagandists and dutifully endured by millions of Soviet citizens over decades contributed to the schizophrenic personality so characteristic of communist systems like that of the Soviet Union. People would meekly listen to and mouth the expected falsehoods in public, although neither

Figure 32-2
Communist Party Agitation Center (*Agitpunkt*) in Moscow Apartment Complex

they nor most of the agitators and propagandists believed any of it. At home around the kitchen table with their trusted friends, they would speak openly and freely, as they really felt. Widespread cynicism about politics and all politicians—a historic Russian cultural attitude—became even more deeply embedded within Soviet society as a consequence. Ironically, it was Gorbachev and his idealism that broke this cynicism in 1985–1990, and the result was a public nationally politicized against Communism and the Soviet state.

Until 1985, Soviet leaders resorted to the relentless intimidation of the population to induce participation in a wide array of political activities, all carefully regulated by organizations and subordinates directly accountable to the party. All were justified as a means to educate the "new Soviet man and woman," to prepare them to assume direct self-governance upon the eventual withering away of the state under a future Communism. From early childhood, Soviet youth were drilled by their teachers to consider themselves members of collectives and to act accordingly. They were taught the necessity of participating in youth groups organized by local

Figure 32–3
Communist-Run
Youth Center in Kiev
for "Young Pioneers"
(Ages 11–15)

party officials and of accepting hierarchical discipline passively, as a norm throughout their lives. As adults, they were forced to participate in elections, in which 99 percent of the registered population meekly showed up at the polling places to vote for the uncontested candidates listed on the ballot. As workers and citizens, millions of Soviet people were compelled to participate in factory and neighborhood committees, also carefully organized and monitored under local party officials. These and the many other forms of compulsory political participation and indoctrination to which the Soviet public was subjected until 1985 were all morally justified by party leaders as a "school of Communism." At any time, as many as 35–40 million Soviet adults were involved in one or another form of party-controlled political participation.

Political dissent against state policies and leaders and any attempts by individuals to participate in outlets other than those prescribed and regulated by the party were ruthlessly crushed by the KGB. Just as the tsars for centuries equated pluralism with anti-Orthodoxy, dissent and individualism were castigated as deviancy from the overriding higher morality of unifying Soviet society into one social class, thinking and acting in unison. Political pluralism, in which diverse parties and groups could express their own demands and attempt to shape public policies, was ridiculed as reactionary and immoral. Over decades Soviet leaders judged their success in mobilizing millions of Soviet citizens into the staged forms of political participation by the standards of collective participation, passive indifference, and conformity in accepting state policies and authority—not individual free will, active enthusiasm, and real citizen influence over public policies and state officials.

Under its patronage powers, the party bureaucracy appointed the leaders of all media, whose principal obligation since Lenin had been to serve the party in mobilizing public opinion and encouraging compliance with policy decisions. The party bureaucracy also oversaw the selection of leaders for all organizations and union guilds of the intelligentsia and verified their compliance with a bureaucratically defined image of "socialist realism"—that is, the glorification in their literary or artistic works of the alleged accomplishments of the Soviet Union under the leadership of the party. Political posters displayed everywhere—at work, in school, and on the streets of Soviet cities—encouraged the public to think and act in terms of the goals adopted at the most recent party congress. These posters celebrated the alleged virtues of the communist system or the accomplishments of the current Soviet leaders (see Figures 32–4, and 32–5).

The party bureaucracy maintained its unchallenged political authority through its instruments of control: the KGB, the courts, and the state censorship agency. The KGB directly served the party in crushing any dissent or challenge to the single-party autocracy and in maintaining a general aura of fear and intimidation. As previously mentioned, the KGB apparatus, including agents, informers, and collaborators, probably amounted to as many as one-fifth of the Soviet adult population as late as the 1980s.

Judges in the Soviet legal system were all party members. They were obliged to follow the party line more than the law in their courts, and they were frequently pressured to render verdicts desired by local party officials. Local party officials controlled the housing and automobiles dispensed to all judges in their jurisdictions.

Figure 32–4

Political Displays in Kiev in 1976, Honoring (top) Soviet Workers and the Party's Five-Year Plan and (bottom) Model Communist Workers

Judges were elected periodically by the public under the usual Soviet electoral process: for each judicial position only one name appeared on the ballot, and the individuals were all carefully screened and approved beforehand by the local party organization.

The state censorship agency was called *Glavlit* (Administration to Safeguard State Secrets in the Press). For seven decades *Glavlit's* authorization was required to print anything from matchbooks and stamps to books and newspapers. Adhering to the vagaries of policy and leadership changes in the party, the state censors oversaw the rewriting of history. They did not permit any discussion of embarrassing problems or challenges to the current party leadership and forbade any written accounts of many Soviet realities. The realities that could not be discussed or mentioned publicly included the party's patronage powers over all leadership positions in Soviet society and the very existence of a state censorship agency regulating all printing and publishing. Any attempt to publish without the authorization of the state censorship agency or any attempt to disseminate ideas contrary to party policy

Figure 32–5

Political Display in Moscow in 1976, Glorifying Soviet Leader Leonid Brezhnev

or criticism of high party officials was punishable under criminal statutes as "anti-Soviet agitation and propaganda" and "slander of the Soviet system." Party-appointed judges convicted all those so accused. The convicted were subject to lengthy sentences in corrective-labor camps.

Prosecution of political dissidents under these neo-Stalinist criminal statutes declined by the 1980s. Soviet leaders became increasingly sensitive to criticisms of this policy leveled by international human rights organizations and by the Western democracies with which those leaders wanted to negotiate long-term arms control and trade agreements. To defuse the criticisms, political dissidents were typically charged and sentenced for less controversial criminal acts such as resisting arrest or violating public order. Some were jailed for vagrancy (in Soviet criminal parlance "parasitism") and for being without any visible means of support, after the KGB arranged to have them fired from their jobs and pressured all other state employers not to hire them.

Several political dissidents were committed to psychiatric hospitals for "treatment" of their alleged paranoid antisocial behavior. Soviet misuse of psychiatry to drug and incarcerate political dissidents backfired, however. The Soviet leaders were universally condemned by medical associations throughout the Western world for Gestapo-like medical torture. As a consequence, the Soviet Union was ousted from the World Psychiatric Association during the 1980s and was only readmitted right before the country collapsed in 1991.

To divide the dissident movement, the KGB selectively persecuted only certain dissidents, in order to sow mistrust among the others that those not persecuted were KGB informers or collaborators. Especially troublesome dissidents were attacked and beaten on the streets by unknown "hooligans" or were murdered by unknown assailants, all of whom the regular Soviet police were somehow never able to identify and arrest. To weaken the dissident movement further and to deflect international criticism, the most prominent and influential dissident leaders, such as Aleksandr Solzhenitsyn and Andrei Sakharov, were either deported or exiled to remote areas of the country.

The statutes making unspecified anti-Soviet viewpoints illegal never deterred clandestine policy debate within the elite establishment. Nor did those statutes discourage Soviet academics and others from expressing their conflicting views on problems and attempting to influence decision making through articles in newspapers and journals. Depending on the reformist or conservative orientation of the editors and their affiliation with one or another political institution, Soviet newspapers and journals took subtly different positions on a wide range of policy issues. Those affiliated with the armed forces could be expected to advocate pro-military positions. Those published by the trade unions assumed a more pro-worker slant. Those identified with the government emphasized approaches to economic reform that would reduce the intrusion of the party in decisions made by factory managers. Those published by the Communist party exaggerated the alleged positive role of the party in resolving any problems.

Censorship limited but never eliminated conflict over policy. There was a certain degree of political pluralism among institutional interests. The top party leaders made the final policy decisions, but institutional interests attempted to affect the drafting of administrative rules and regulations to bias implementation of policies in ways beneficial to them. Nevertheless, the statutes on "anti-Soviet agitation and propaganda" and "slander of the Soviet system" continued to have a chilling effect on civil society, stifling any truly uninhibited public debate and expression of public opinion. The statutes were finally removed from the criminal code in 1989 by initiative of the first quasi-democratically elected national legislature under Gorbachev. The same legislature passed a law in July 1990 guaranteeing freedom of the press and prohibiting any form of state censorship.

▪   ▪   ▪

The Communist system politically integrated Soviet society through the cooptation of millions of citizens into membership in the Communist party. The party defined the norms and values for society as "Communist morality" through its domination of the media, the arts, and the schools. It determined the kinds of political behavior and participation tolerated through a network of hundreds of thousands of party primary organizations and other auxiliary grass-roots organizations run by the party at work, school, and home. It anesthetized civil society through fear and indoctrination, elevated public lying and informing on one's family and neighbors to socially accepted norms, and brutalized millions over generations—all in the name of "building Communism." Through its control over their leaders and policies, it in effect ran the government, the armed forces, the economy, and every private institution in Soviet society. This all-encompassing monopoly of political power had dramatically crumbled by 1991, as described in the first two chapters of this part of the book. Yet the sudden disintegration of the Communist system, which so monpolized power and control for seven decades, has left an even greater than normal vacuum for the fifteen countries that are attempting to create their own civil societies as new nations and their own political structures as fledging democracies.

......33

Russia and Central Eurasia in Crisis and Conflict

Gorbachev's failure to transform the Soviet Union after its breakup into fifteen different countries has drastically complicated any possibility for stability and peace in Central and Eastern Europe, Asia, and the Middle East. All fifteen have seemingly repudiated the past Communist ideology and the Soviet state, all base their legitimacy at least nominally on Western democratic principles and forms of governance, but all equally confront almost insuperable problems in nation building. Witches could not have concocted a more fatal political brew of problems for new countries and fledgling democratic governments. So high is the probability of their not resolving their problems that the fifteen are likely to prove as destabilizing for the world over the next two decades as the former Soviet Union had been over the previous seven.

■ *PROBLEMS OF NATION BUILDING*

The first task of each of the fifteen independent countries is to create a sense of nationhood and loyalty among its citizens. Most of these peoples have little sense of nationhood—their ancestors conceived of themselves as members of the Russian Empire since the eighteenth century and as members of the Soviet Union since 1922. Even the Russian Federation has never existed as such. Since the seventeenth century, ethnic Russians and the other ethnic nationalities of the Federation have always lived and conceived of themselves as citizens of a unified monarchy or Communist state that encompassed most of the territories and peoples now constituting the other fourteen countries. Russia is as much a new country without any historical precedent as the others.

The only countries that have had any sense of nationhood in the past are the three Baltic states, the three Caucasian states, and Ukraine. Lithuania, Latvia, and Estonia were independent as countries for the two decades between the world wars before their reannexation by Stalin in 1940. Georgia, Armenia, Azerbaijan, and Ukraine formed briefly after the end of the Russian monarchy in 1917 and the subsequent collapse of any central authority during the Russian Civil War of 1918–1920. Then the three Caucasian states and Ukraine were reincorporated as territories of the new Soviet Union by military conquest by the Communist Red Army.

Even these exceptions provide questionable historical precedents. All were independent at least half a century ago, at a time when they were primarily underdeveloped agricultural societies with large pockets of illiteracy. The Soviet era economically and socially transformed them, as it did all of the fifteen countries. Although called parliamentary democracies from 1919 to 1940, the Baltic states were actually right-wing governments based on nationalistic ideologies and social policies that discriminated against those who were not Lithuanian, Latvian, or Estonian. The ephemeral Caucasian republics of Georgia, Armenia, and Azerbaijan fell by 1920, in part because of emerging conflicts among Communist factions in their leaderships and among the various Christian and Muslim ethnic nationalities under their nominal jurisdictions. The Communist Red Army successfully reannexed Ukraine because the actions of the independent Ukrainian Rada in Kiev (as the government was called) had alienated many non-Ukrainians under its jurisdiction.

The only other time Ukraine was even nominally independent from Soviet control occurred during the German occupation of 1941–1943, when a minority of ethnic Ukrainians collaborated with the Nazis in murdering millions of ethnic non-Ukrainians. Stefan Bandera, a Ukrainian, led a division of the German army against the Soviet Union, allegedly because the Nazis had promised to grant Ukraine independence. He is revered as one of the great Ukrainian national heroes by radical ethnic Ukrainian nationalists since 1991. Although a minority, these radical nationalists dress in neo-Nazi military uniforms, are virulently anti-Russian and anti-Semitic, and have taken over leadership of some local branches of the Ukrainian popular front called Rukh. (These radicals are only a fringe group within Rukh, which is the largest and most popular national political organization in Ukraine.) Some of the radical nationalists have formed a so-called National Front, patterned after the similarly named racist political movement in France. Their ideology decries the presence of so many non-Ukrainians among the citizens of the country as a threat to Ukrainian nationhood.

The ethnic composition of Ukraine is 73 percent ethnic Ukrainians, 22 percent ethnic Russians, and less than 1 percent ethnic Jews. As a consequence, the memory of the purges earlier in this century continues to inhibit complete trust and confidence in the new Ukrainian government among the 12 million Russians, Jews, and other non-Ukrainian minorities who are citizens of the country.

A second major task for the fifteen countries is to generate political legitimacy for democratic institutions and values. Culturally and institutionally, these societies were based on autocracy—first of the Russian Empire and then of Soviet Communism. Except for the qualified allowance of a national elected assembly called the Duma by the last Russian tsar from 1906 to 1917, both the Russian imperial and Soviet Communist autocracies forbade competitive elections and representative governments. Over three centuries, these autocracies were indistinguishable in their denigration of democratic values. They viewed free speech, assembly, and association and the principle of accountable political leaders as alien Western concepts inappropriate to the allegedly higher moral bond linking the rulers and the ruled in their countries.

The third task, finding the proper amount of authority, is perhaps the greatest common political problem for all fifteen countries. Democracy represents a fine balance between accountability and the concentration of authority in national political institutions. Too much authority can lead to a breakdown of any real accountability and to authoritarianism, as manifested to an extreme by the former Soviet Union. At the opposite extreme, too much accountability of a national government undermines its ability to govern. At a minimum, excess accountability leads to the political gridlock experienced by the German Weimar Republic in the 1920s and the French Fourth Republic in the 1950s and invites the intercession of those who would create autocracies to restore effective political authority. At a maximum, when national governments are too weak to make and enforce decisions, they may lose control entirely, collapsing into civil war and political anarchy. This problem of balancing authority and accountability has been compounded by the fifteen countries' near economic collapse, which has undermined public support for almost any form of national government.

The trend in the fifteen countries since 1991 has been to the extremes, rather than a middle course. Many of the countries have very weak national governments unable to govern. Political power and authority have devolved by default to the localities. Situations bordering on civil war, the dismemberment of the countries, and political anarchy have become commonplace. In all the fifteen have arisen political movements and politicians on both the extreme nationalistic right and the communist left that are committed to restoring central governmental authority by ending democratic freedoms and banning political parties and representative legislatures. They want to institute autocratic systems not unlike that of the former Soviet Union. The reversion to authoritarianism is justified on the basis of ideologies that combine both extremes and contend that internal and external enemies of the majority ethnic nationality are conspiring to undermine the national government and to resurrect the former unified Soviet state.

The reversion had already occurred by 1993 in Azerbaijan, Uzbekistan, Turkmenistan, and Tajikistan. All four countries are led by former high-ranking Communist officials from the Soviet era. They repress all political opposition, rule through a newly constituted national party, propagate their own personality cult, censor the media, and intimidate the public through secret police under the pretext of a nationalistic ideology. In Azerbaijan, Prime Minister Surat Guseinov is a former defense minister who marched on the capital of Baku in June 1993 and forced the democratically elected President from office. The newly elected President Geidar Aliyev was the head of the Azerbaijan KGB and Communist party until 1981 and was notorious for his reign of brutality and corruption. Aliyev was brought to Moscow in 1981 as the Soviet Union's first Deputy Prime Minister, but he was ousted from this position in January 1987 by Gorbachev, who was completing his purge of the many corrupt Brezhnevite holdovers among the top party-state officials.

By 1993 the only country of the five independent ones in the Muslim region of Central Asia not governed by a former high-ranking Communist official was Kyrgyzstan. Its President, Askar Akayev, who is a physicist, has gone further in attempting to create a Western democracy and free-market economy than almost any other leader in Russia and Central Eurasia. At the same time, Kyrgyzstan is one of the least politically stable countries among the five in Central Asia. It is the poorest country of the region, with very little irrigated land and very little water. The majority of the population are ethnic Kirghiz, who have the lowest per capita income and the lowest standard of living of any of the five principal ethnic nationalities of Central Asia. The ethnic Kirghiz have not even benefited from Akayev's economic reforms. The most fertile lands in rural Kyrgyzstan and the newly privatized industries in its cities have been taken over for the most part by ethnic Russians and nationalities other than Kirghiz.

■ ECONOMIC PROBLEMS

The countries of Russia and Central Eurasia must effectively transform their economies into modern and productive free-market ones in order to provide real jobs and an improvement in the standard of living for enough of their citizens and thus to retain a minimal level of national loyalty, democratic political legitimacy, support, and trust for their fledgling democracies. To bring about this transformation, they must dismantle an economic system that since the late 1920s had been owned, run, and controlled in all facets as a so-called command economy by the central government ministries in Moscow, under the leadership of the Communist party.

The legacy of the command economy will be a formidable one to overcome. It includes the most environmentally polluted cities and industries in the world and a national economy geared until 1991 to produce over two-thirds of its industrial output in the form of military hardware for the Soviet armed force. The fifteen countries are saddled with a technological base at least twenty years behind that of Western industrialized countries and incentives that over decades discouraged industrial managers from innovating. Finally, the fifteen have been left with national treasuries heavily in debt to Western creditors and with government budget deficits running at 20–30 percent of their entire gross domestic products.

In its last decade, the Soviet economy had failed to grow except for domestic sales of vodka and the export of Soviet arms and oil. A major reason for the stagnant economic growth was that Soviet labor productivity was well below that of all Western industrial democracies. In an economy that was already technologically backward, Soviet workers were provided with very few real material or psychological incentives to work hard. For decades Soviet citizens had suffered from the very low priority in national economic plans and spending assigned to them by the central party leadership. They were indifferently cared for by an antiquated and underfunded health care system, ill-fed, poorly housed, and inadequately clothed. Post-Soviet workers in the fifteen countries have to be convinced that conditions and opportunities have fundamentally improved. They must be reeducated to assume the responsibility to work, as they are no longer assured of a job under the free labor market of capitalism.

No less an obstacle to acceptance of a free-market economy is the cultural and psychological one. The new countries must fundamentally change the attitudes and behaviors of their citizens. Beginning with the Industrial Revolution in the middle of the nineteenth century, people in the Russian Empire have always worked and consumed in a state-regulated economy. Except for brief periods at the beginning of this century and in 1921–1927 during the NEP, the population has never experienced or known free enterprise, private property, markets, or unemployment. For generations, traditional Russian culture and Soviet ideology denigrated the accumulation of wealth and the inequalities of income and status in Western societies as immoral. Western entrepreneurs were labeled "money-grubbers," who exploited their fellow human beings. Anyone wealthier or better-off was resented and hated in Soviet society.

In post-Soviet economies, a small (5–10 percent of the population) but important entrepreneurial class of private farmers and business owners has emerged. Some have even become instant billionaires. These entrepreneurs have played a pivotal role in instituting profit and competition in an unregulated market economy but have been only partially accepted and understood by the post-Soviet publics. There is still a widespread perception, evidenced in public opinion polls, that all private entrepreneurs are criminals. There is still a nostalgia, especially among the older generations, for the predictability of the Soviet command economy, which despite its inefficiencies and shortages guaranteed them jobs and a relatively consistent if very low standard of living.

In the post-Soviet era, all fifteen countries are freeing prices and privatizing their economies. The transition to a complete free-enterprise capitalist economy will be very painful and may take several decades. In the short term, many were descending into a seemingly bottomless economic depression. Output in the fifteen countries during their first year of independence in 1992 declined by 18.5 percent, and during the first half of 1993 economic output in almost all of their industrial sectors continued to fall at a rate of 15–20 percent below the depression levels of 1992. All of the states were broke to some degree; for example, the Russian national government's budget deficit in 1992 amounted to 22.5 percent of gross domestic product.

With the freeing of prices from state regulation, hyperinflation soared to 1,200 percent in 1992, and actually surpassed 2,000 percent in Russia. That is, what had cost 100 rubles the year before now cost 1,200 rubles in fourteen countries and 2,000 rubles in Russia. These increases even understate the real potential inflation rate if all prices were freed of state regulation. Throughout the summer of 1993, energy prices for most fossil fuels and electricity were still controlled at below their true market values by the national governments. In addition, the inflation rate in 1992 was an average based on all consumer and industrial goods. The prices for dairy and meat products soared to 3,000–4,000 percent of times their 1991 levels.

Wages have increased several-fold since 1991, but still lag well behind the rate of inflation, which in Russia only began to "stabilize" at a monthly increase of 25 percent during the first half of 1993. Even before 1991, average Soviet consumers had to spend over half of their wages on food. Their only compensation had been the provision of low state-regulated rents for apartments and free medical care under the nationalized economy. With the transition to a market economy, the governments have privatized housing. They have also cut back drastically the level of financial support for state-run medical facilities, which before 1991 was only 1–2 percent of the Soviet national budget. To stay ahead of inflation, many doctors and other medical personnel have been quitting their positions in government clinics to set up their own private practices.

As late as 1990, the exchange rate between the ruble and the dollar had been artificially pegged by the Soviet government at 1.25 dollars for every ruble. After eighteen months of independence in Russia and Central Eurasia, 1 dollar was trading at an official exchange rate of approximately 1,000 rubles (and even higher on the unofficial black market on the streets). With hyperinflation, governments have been forced to print and issue ever higher denominations of their currencies to keep up. Despite printing notes with a face value of 5,000 rubles to replace 500-ruble notes issued the previous year, and despite running printing presses around the clock, Russia was experiencing periodic shortages of available currency by 1993, as were others of the fifteen countries. Banks at times lack enough currency in even the new higher denominations for companies to pay their workers. To keep up with hyperinflation, some commercial banks were charging interest rates of 60 percent or more for loans.

Economic collapse and hyperinflation have reduced as many as half of the fifteen countries' populations to a standard of living below the poverty line. Pensioners, invalids, and anyone else on a fixed income have been particularly impoverished, despite monthly cost-of-living adjustments to their benefits approved by their governments. The only solution has been to get additional loans and credits of hard currency from various international lending agencies. The problem is that the fifteen governments must comply with the terms of those agencies. These agencies have mandated that the fifteen governments impose stringent anti-inflationary policies to stabilize the exchange rates of their currencies. To comply, the fifteen governments have to cut their spending, reduce their budget deficits, end subsidies to the many remaining unprofitable state-owned industries, limit the amount of money printed, and tighten credit.

In essence, the governments are being forced to undertake measures that can only result in widespread unemployment. In the short run the real cost of compliance is further immiseration of their populations and even greater political instability. A desperate population is more likely to turn in increasing numbers to populist demagogues and movements that promise an end to the economic plight by reimposing a Soviet-style command economy and by suspending democratic institutions and processes. Opinion polls in many of the countries have confirmed that only two years after the first glow of independence, an increasing number of their citizens have become disillusioned with all political authorities. The private sector has expanded several-fold since independence, but the people see their own daily lives becoming worse. They blame the political parties, the haggling of elected officials, and the slowness of democratic processes and institutions. The populists and demagogues offer simple explanations: they blame the economic problems on conspiracies and minorities in their societies.

The other alternative for Russia and Central Eurasia is to revive the common market and ties among themselves that existed before December 1991. All of the fifteen countries have industries that are almost totally reliant on some of the others for supplies and for markets for their finished products. The breakup of the Soviet

Union has meant that industries in one country cannot depend on their normal and often only suppliers and customers without having to pay customs duties and to negotiate the bureaucratic labyrinth of government regulations of another country. Hyperinflation has made the ruble worthless as a currency of exchange, but all of the governments lack sufficient supplies of convertible international hard currency such as U.S. dollars or German marks. The governments consequently have imposed export requirements on their own industries; critical economic goods sold to other countries of Russia and Central Eurasia must be paid for in hard currency.

One country's requirement of hard-currency payments for exports only invites retaliation by the other countries. For example, Russia, which has most of the gas and oil reserves from the former Soviet Union, imposed hard-currency requirements for sales of its energy supplies to the other countries. By the summer of 1993 this had resulted in an economic war of words and threats of retaliation against Russia. The Ukrainian government threatened to close down the gas pipelines that cross its territory to supply France and Germany with gas from Russian West Siberian fields.

The breakup of the former Soviet Union also left all of the printing presses for the ruble inside the Russian Federation. All the other countries to some extent still exchange in rubles and are thus dependent on economic policies emanating from Moscow. The amount of rubles printed has been dictated not only by Russian fiscal considerations but, even more, by political considerations and the balance between various pro- and anti-Yeltsin political factions in the Russian parliament. Anti-Yeltsin factions have opposed his attempt to slow down the rate of inflation as his first economic priority. When these factions have temporarily prevailed, they have been able to institute policies leading to the easing of credit and to authorization from the Central Bank of Russia to print more money. The additional money only skyrocketed the hyperinflation.

The political consequence was to embitter interstate relations. Denunciations of Russian economic imperialism were increasingly heard in the capitals of the other fourteen countries during the first two years of independence. By 1993, some of the countries had printed and issued their own currencies in an attempt to insulate themselves from the ruble and Moscow, to assert their own national economic independence, and to qualify for their own loans from international lending agencies. The result at best was marginal. None of these currencies was exchangeable in international money markets, as none of the countries has sufficient gold or hard-currency reserves to back up the value of its currency. The only currency still widely accepted and exchanged for these countries' national currencies by their own banks and citizens is the ruble. As the amount of rubles emitted ultimately depends on actions and decisions in Moscow, Russia continues indirectly to set the value of the other countries' currencies, despite their attempt to free their economies from Moscow's dictate.

A real concern of these countries' industries is that their governments may require them to conduct their business, so vitally dependent on suppliers and markets in the other former Soviet countries, solely in their national currencies. The economic result would be an inability to import or export and complete collapse of the economies. The political consequence would be that Russia, with its immense economic resources and size, would be even more dominant.

In Ukraine, for example, the newly issued national currency, called the karbanovets, is worthless and threatening to undermine trade with Russia, on which the Ukrainian economy remains heavily dependent. The karbanovets had fallen to an exchange rate of 3,000 to every U.S. dollar by April 1993. With the accumulation of hard currency by Ukrainians on commercial trips to Eastern Europe, U.S. dollars became almost the only currency acceptable in the Ukrainian capital of Kiev to buy real estate or anything from televisions and refrigerators to vacuum cleaners and puppies. Ukrainians paid at their jobs in karbanovtsy earn a minimum monthly salary that is equivalent to $1.50 at the exchange rate used in Kiev and sufficient perhaps to buy a flea collar. If they exchange their karbanovtsy for Russian rubles, they have to do so at an official rate set by the Ukrainian National Bank of 3 karbanovtsy per Russian ruble, even though the Russian State Bank has set the rate at 4.5 karbanovtsy per Russian ruble. The Ukrainian Bank has inflated the exchange value of the karbanovets to counter the excessive amount of rubles emitted by the Russian Central Bank. Ukrainian industries required to deal in their native currency thus lose 50 percent of the value of their goods every time they sell to Russian industries using rubles (that being the difference between the exchange rate of karbanovtsy and rubles in Ukraine and Russia).

The problem is likely to be aggravated, because an increasing number of Russian industries have been reluctant to accept payment from Ukrainian industries in anything but U.S. dollars—which Ukrainian industries would have to acquire by exchanging 3,000 of their worthless karbanovtsy for each dollar. As a result, in Ukraine and the other countries that have converted to an independent national currency, industries are left to buy and sell using the only universally accepted currency of any stable value—U.S. dollars. Without dollars, they have to barter their goods, a manner of exchange typical of pre-industrialized feudal societies and economies.

■ ETHNIC NATIONALITIES AND POLITICAL INTEGRATION

To stabilize their political systems, governments in Russia and Central Eurasia must develop public acceptance and support for the newly established representative institutions and trust in the fairness of elected officials to make and carry out policies responsive to public demands. The problem is that the new governments and officials must act in societies bitterly divided into religious and ethnic groups. The diversity of religions and ethnic nationalities in all of the countries, as discussed in Chapters 30 and 31, provides a very weak basis for forming a consensual national identity. The collapse of the centralized Soviet economy and the desperate economic plight in all of Russia and Central Eurasia have only encouraged the worst aspects of a political culture grounded in intolerance, bigotry, and tribalism.

Many of the ethnic and religious groups suspect each other of manipulating government and its policies merely to discriminate. All have been socialized over decades of the Russian empire and the Soviet Communist state into a political culture intolerant of pluralism, distrustful of all governments and political authorities, highly susceptible to paranoid delusions about conspiracies, and supportive of persecuting anyone who differs from themselves. Most often, outbreaks of violence have started from the rivalry between ethnic-religious groups over the limited economic resources and opportunities. Civil unrest has quickly escalated into outright civil war. Very quickly, a pattern has developed. Persecuted and oppressed ethnic-religious groups rebel and declare their independence, only becoming in turn the persecutor and oppressor of some even more vulnerable ethnic-religious minority residing nearby.

Part of the blame for the escalating ethnic-religious violence in the fifteen countries lies with the ideologies of several of the political movements that were responsible for successfully winning independence from the Soviet Union. Openly anti-Communist and anti-Soviet, these movements were more nationalistic than democratic in their composition and appeal. Almost all of them were supported in the national election of 1989 and the republic-local elections of 1990 by voters who constituted the largest ethnic group in their republics. Candidates selected by the independence movements were primarily members of the ethnic majority. Their campaigns targeted both Moscow and other ethnic-religious groups who competed with the majority in each republic. However valid the charges of discrimination and persecution, they transformed the movements into organizations less committed to democratic principles than to self-determination and statehood for the predominant ethnic majority.

For example, in Georgia in 1990, the leading independence movement for ethnic Georgians used its control of the electoral commission to make it impossible for the largest non-Georgian ethnic minorities in the republic—Abkhazians and Ossetians—to vote for their candidates to the republic parliament. Abkhazians are a small Muslim minority in the northwestern part of Georgia bordering Russia (see Figure 33–1). A minority even within their own token ethnic enclave, Abkhazians historically relied on the Russian monarchy or the Soviet Union to protect themselves against Christian Georgians. In turn, Georgians, who constitute an overwhelming majority in the Abkhaz region, fear that independence for Abkhazia would result in their persecution by a local Abkhaz government in reprisal for the decades of discrimination against Abkhazians by the central Georgian government.

Approximately 160,000 Ossetians historically have resided in the northeastern part of Georgia. Ethnically, they are the same as the 350,000 Ossetians who constitute an ethnic enclave across the border in Russia, although the Georgian Ossetians are primarily Christian and the Russian Ossetians are primarily Muslim. Ossetians on both sides of the border have always advocated unification of the two ethnic enclaves into a single Ossetia. Ethnic Georgians have opposed this demand for the very same reasons that they have resisted greater autonomy for the Abkhaz ethnic enclave. It would dismember Georgia and make the majority of ethnic Georgians living in the Ossetian region subject to reprisals and persecution by Ossetians.[1]

---

[1]The most infamous Ossetian in this century was Joseph Stalin, whose mother was Ossetian and whose father was ethnic Georgian. In the region of Georgia bordering Azerbaijan, there are also approximately 300,000 ethnic Azeri, who since 1989 have demanded greater autonomy from Tbilisi and potentially incorporation into Azerbaijan.

Figure 33–1
Chechnya and
Ingushetia (Russia)
and Abkhaz and
South Ossetian
Regions (Georgia)

On April 9, 1989, the Georgian national independence movement arose in response to the murder of several ethnic Georgians by Soviet OMON and army troops in the Georgian capital of Tbilisi. The troops had been called out to put down a peaceful demonstration by ethnic Georgians against the Soviet government's granting independent republic status to the Abkhaz ethnic enclave. The troops killed innocent ethnic Georgians with poison gases and shovels in their own capital. As a backlash to this action, the Georgian national movement won an overwhelming majority of seats to the Georgian parliament in the fall of 1990. Zviad Gamsakhurdia, a leader of the movement and a former political prisoner, was elected President of the republic. Two years after the incident that had sparked the birth of the Georgian movement, on April 9, 1991, the government and parliament of Georgia declared the republic's independence from the Soviet Union .

The independence movements of the ethnic majorities in other republics also considered the 1990 election a mandate for their own independence and their own cause against that of other minorities in their republics. Anyone who belonged to an ethnic minority was suspected—in many cases quite validly—of harboring pro-Union sentiments and of being most likely to be recruited into groups that were secretly working with die-hard conservatives of the party, the KGB, and the military in Moscow to prevent independence for the ethnic majority and the republic.

Indeed, the Abkhazians and Ossetians had been denied the right to vote for their candidates to the Georgian parliament in 1990 because the prospective candidates all favored retention of the Soviet Union as one country. By 1990, popular fronts of the Abkhazians and Ossetians had arisen favoring independence of their regions from Georgia or incorporation into Russia to protect themselves from ethnic Georgians. Clashes of local Abkhazians and Ossetians with the majority Georgians had become commonplace by 1989. The reason that so many local candidates among the Abkhazians and Ossetians opposed Georgian independence was a fear of subsequent oppression, borne out by the very actions of the electoral commission in denying these minorities the right to vote. They feared that a Georgian independence movement in power in the capital of Tbilisi and declaring independence from the Soviet Union would mercilessly suppress Abkhazians and Ossetians, and it did.

The nationalistic tenor of the independence movements has fostered an array of political parties on the right in the post-Soviet era. These advocate various degrees of political exclusion of those who make up the ethnic, language, and religious minorities in the fifteen post-Soviet countries. The prevalence of nationalism is only reinforced by the ethnic backgrounds of a significant majority of the political leaders in these countries' executive branches and national parliaments. The majority ethnic group predominates in both branches of government. This has created an impression that ethnicity—more than competence, values, or positions on issues—is a prerequisite to hold public office. Not surprisingly, ethnic minorities in each country have been willing to believe those among them who claim that the national government doesn't really represent them, that they can't trust any publicly elected officials, and that all government policies are formed to benefit the majority ethnic group.

Ethnic minorities in Estonia and Latvia have been particularly aggrieved by the passage of laws that require minimum proficiency in the language of the ethnic majority to obtain the rights of citizenship. These laws exclude minority groups from voting, holding political office, or even remaining with visas in the countries. The same residency and citizenship laws grant automatic citizenship to anyone able to claim descendency from the majority ethnic group, even those who are natives or naturalized citizens of countries outside the former Soviet Union. The governments of these countries rationalized passage of such laws under pressure from Estonian and Latvian nationalists to rectify what they contend were decades of injustice under Soviet rule. Policies enacted in Moscow artificially flooded their republics with hundreds of thousands of ethnic Russians and Ukrainians to staff industrial enterprises or military garrisons. The proportion of ethnic Estonians and Latvians in the countries' total populations declined as a consequence. Since independence, many Russians, Ukrainians, and other ethnic minorities feel they are hated and treated almost as colonialists of the former Soviet era by the majority of Latvians and Estonians. Two years after independence, many remained in a limbo status of statelessness in Latvia and Estonia.

The end of the Soviet Union left 25 million ethnic Russians and 5 million others of indigenous nationalities of Russia living outside the Russian Federation. In most of the new countries of Central Eurasia, the national governments have gone out of their way to make these ethnic Russians and other ethnic minorities feel welcome, granting them full citizenship rights equal to those of ethnic majority residents and doing everything they could to prevent the emigration of these minorities. The reason is that these ethnic minorities represent a larger than proportionate share of the most highly educated professionals in these countries. Their loss would be a calamitous "brain drain," crippling any possible economic revival in these countries and frightening away Western investors who would see signs of political instability in any such emigration.

However, because these Russians and other ethnic minorities constitute the most highly educated and successful strata of these countries, they have become natural targets for radical nationalists among the ethnic majority communities. For these radical nationalists, the ethnic minorities in their midst mock their independence and ethnic sovereignty. The wealth and higher social status of the ethnic minorities are resented as an unnatural legacy of the Soviet period, symbolizing the decades of discrimination against the local ethnic majority practiced by Moscow. The discrimination had been condoned by local Communist officials as subservient agents in the effective colonization of their own peoples. Radical nationalists contend that a disproportionate number of outsiders hold the best professional and managerial positions only because they were recruited by Moscow during the Soviet era when educational opportunities and social mobility for the local ethnic majority received little priority.

Contributing to the legacy of mistrust and hatred among ethnic groups in several of the countries are radical nationalists among the ethnic minorities. Prior to December 1991, several organized movements of ethnic minorities actively campaigned in favor of retaining a unified Soviet Union. Some openly conspired with local Communist, KGB, OMON, and Soviet military officials to subvert and repress the popular fronts of the ethnic majorities, who were advocating independence of their republics from the Soviet Union. For example, radical ethnic Russian nationalists were to have been included in the leadership of the so-called national salvation fronts that would have been imposed under martial law in Lithuania and Latvia had the popular front governments in those republics attempted to resist the provocations of the KGB and OMON troops in seizing their parliament and press buildings in December 1990 and January 1991.

Given the polarization of conflict in several countries since 1991, radical nationalists of ethnic minority communities have emerged as elected local political officials. They have won many offices by their pledge to resist the discriminatory policies of the national governments, which they contend are controlled by radical nationalists of the ethnic majority. They have urged resorting to violence if necessary, and even secession of their locales from the country.

From a military standpoint, the incompleteness of the Soviet Union's dissolution in 1991 has further fueled tension between the majority and minority groups in many regions. Several armies of the former Soviet Union remain permanently deployed on the territories of all three Baltic states, Moldova, Armenia, Georgia, and all of the countries of Central Asia. These former Soviet armies are not part of the national armies of these countries, but have been formally incorporated into the armed forces of the Russian Federation under the command of the Russian Defense Minister, subordinate to President Boris Yeltsin as commander-in-chief. For a number of reasons, these armies have not been redeployed back into the Russian Federation. Financially, the Russian government lacks the funds to provide the soldiers with civilian jobs and housing if they were repatriated. Politically, President Yeltsin has been continually attacked by leaders across the Russian political spectrum—from ultranationalists and die-hard Communists on the right to democratic liberals on the left—for failing to protect the large communities of ethnic Russians living outside the Russian Federation. Were he to withdraw these Russian troops, he would stand accused of exposing the Russian expatriate communities to physical violence and genocide by the ethnic majorities in these areas.

Militarily, the Russian government and high military command have been attempting to pressure the governments in these countries to sign joint security agreements allowing the integration of their national armies with the Russian army units located inside their borders. The Russian troops have been the principal bargaining leverage of the Russian government for forcing these governments to come around to its position. Both the Russian government and Russian defense officials fear that removing the Russian troops could completely destabilize the countries forming the southern border of the Russian Federation, extending from the Balkans to Transcaucasia and Central Asia. These countries have faced uncontrollable civil wars since the breakup of the Soviet Union.

Countries such as Turkey, Iran, and Afghanistan have threatened to intervene in these civil wars, both to defend those whom they consider compatriots and to promote their own geopolitical interests. The Russian government and defense officials see joint national and Russian armies as a necessary peace-keeping force to quell the civil wars and restore stability in an area directly vital to Russia's national interest and territorial integrity. The alternative would be the dismemberment of these bordering countries and their incorporation as territories of Turkey, Iran, and Afghanistan. The latter two countries are led by Islamic fundamentalist regimes bent on conquering most of Central Eurasia.

However reasonable the retention of Russian troops in the other countries may seem in Moscow, it is seen quite differently in those countries. Their governments have been confronted since 1991 with outbreaks of separatist movements and bloody inter-ethnic civil wars. The armies of the Russian Federation still deployed in their countries are blamed by these governments for siding with or even arming the separatist movements and instigating the civil wars. Radical nationalists in these countries as much as accuse the Russian government of sponsoring a "Serbian Yugoslav" solution. That is, Moscow is believed to have adopted a policy like that of the Serbian government under Slobodan Milosevic in the former Yugoslavia, covertly arming and supporting Serbian ethnic minorities in Croatia and Bosnia-Herzegovina to overthrow their respective governments and to establish a Greater Serbia through the "ethnic cleansing" of non-Serbian locales.

Both rightly and wrongly, the Russian government has been widely suspected of encouraging its deployed army to intervene in civil wars in the other post-Soviet countries in order to protect the Russian ethnic communities and ultimately to establish a peace beneficial to Russia's national interests and Moscow's definition of "stability." The fear is that this definition of "stability" would include Moscow's dictating foreign policy to these countries. If necessary, Russia might intervene militarily under the presumption that the countries fall under Russia's natural geographical sphere of influence.

Even when the national leaders of these countries have not suspected Russia of ulterior motives in retaining the troops on their territory, not seeking their removal discredits these leaders politically. Their own radical nationalists, bent on finding an excuse to oust them, accuse the leaders of selling out national sovereignty by their willingness to allow the Russian armies to remain. In this highly charged atmosphere, standing up to Moscow becomes almost a political litmus test of patriotism for a country's leadership.

■ *CIVIL WARS AND POLITICAL REFUGEES*

Caught in the middle, hundreds of thousands have fled to the countries of their ethnic origin since the breakup of the Soviet Union in 1991. Russia has been the country of first choice for those fleeing from the wars between Azerbaijan and Armenia, between Georgia and the separatist Abkhazians and Ossetians, and between Moldova and the ethnic Russian Dniester republic. By June 1993, approximately 2 million "forced migrants" (officially citizens of Russia) and "refugees" (noncitizens of Russia) had fled to Russia. This total excluded countless others who had simply never been registered by Russian migration officials. The refugees and forced migrants included ethnic Russians, Armenians, Ossetians, and Meshketians seeking asylum from persecution, the interethnic conflicts, and civil wars.

The largest wave of refugees and forced migrants has been produced by the civil war in Tajikistan since 1992. Of the 380,000 Russian-speaking Slavs who lived there before the outbreak of the civil war, 300,000 had already left by April 1993. Over 50,000 ethnic Tajiks were killed, and more than a half million were forced to flee their villages during the first year of the civil war. The Tajik civil war pits the northern half of the country against the southern half because of fundamental ethnic, religious, tribal, and political differences. The northern half of Tajikistan is populated by ethnic Turks and Sunni Muslims. They adhere to a secular Tajik nationalism and are led by former republic Communist party leaders who over decades recruited most of the Tajik political elites from their native villages in the northern province of Leninabad bordering Uzbekistan (see Figure 33–2). Southern Tajikistan in the Pamir mountains is populated by those who speak Farsi (Iranian) and follow the Ismaili religion, an offshoot of Shiite Islam. The southerners resent the decades of political domination by northerners in the central Tajik government.

Ideologically, the southerners are a mix of anti-Communist democrats, anti-Sunni Shiite Muslims, and Islamic fundamentalists. They have been armed by various ethnic groups across the border in northern Afghanistan, who have also sent some of their soldiers to fight alongside the southern Tajiks. Many southern Tajiks and northern Afghans are related to each other by ethnicity and extended family ties. The northern Afghans include many who fought against the Soviet military occupation of Afghanistan in 1979–1988 and are led by those committed to spreading their Islamic liberation movement throughout Central Asia. Stinger missiles and other military weapons that the United States had supplied in 1985–1988 to all of the groups fighting the Soviet army in Afghanistan have been smuggled across the border to the southern Tajiks.[2]

---

[2]In turn, the northerners who control the Tajik government in Dushanbe are armed and supported militarily by the governments of Russia and Uzbekistan, whose troops have been deployed in Tajikistan allegedly for peace-keeping reasons but have primarily fought the southerners. The Russian government fears the collapse of its southern borders and the spread of an Islamic war to Russia if the southerners should prevail in the Tajik civil war. The Uzbek government, led by like-minded former Communists, wants to dominate Central Asia and sees the Tajik nationalist movement among southerners as the major threat to Uzbek ethnic domination.

Figure 33–2
Tajikistan

Surveys have revealed that as many as one-third of all ethnic Russians in Moldova and Tajikistan and one-seventh of all ethnic Russians in Armenia and Georgia intend to resettle in Russia to escape the violence in these newly independent countries. As many as 6 million refugees and forced migrants are predicted to enter Russia before the end of the century, as a result of the further escalation of civil wars in the countries along its southern borders. Even within the Russian Federation, tens of thousands of ethnic Russians had become forced migrants by 1993, fleeing ethnic enclaves controlled by non-Russians, which had declared their sovereignty as republics independent of Moscow.

The total of 6 million only accounts for refugees and forced migrants in Russia. It doesn't include the many millions in the other fourteen countries who have already fled or will be forced to seek asylum to escape civil unrest and outright civil wars. Before the collapse of the Soviet Union, the violence between Armenians and Azerbaijanis had already forced hundreds of thousands of ethnic Azeris to leave Armenia and resettle in Azerbaijan, and an equivalent number of ethnic Armenians to leave Azerbaijan and resettle in Armenia. With the collapse of the Soviet Union and an even nominal authority to separate the two sides, the ethnic violence escalated into an undeclared war between Armenia and Azerbaijan. By September 1993, more than 10 percent of the entire population of Azerbaijan had become forced migrants, fleeing the paramilitary Armenian forces that had captured Nagorno-Karabakh and the surrounding regions of the republic.

In Georgia, the ethnic minorities of Abkhazians and Ossetians are not the only ones who have been forced to seek asylum from the Georgian military. In southwest Georgia, supporters of Zviad Gamsakhurdia, the elected President turned dictator of Georgia who was ousted by a coup in December 1991, have formed paramilitary groups to overthrow the central Georgian government in Tbilisi and return

Gamsakhurdia to power. Ethnic Georgians living in villages have been forced to flee across the border to Armenia to escape the fighting between these paramilitary forces and troops dispatched by the Georgian government to put down the rebellion. They have been less than welcome as political refugees in Armenia. Despite their common Christian religion, ethnic Georgians are disliked by ethnic Armenians, who negatively stereotype Georgians as thiefs and swindlers. Armenians also still resent the decades before 1917 when Georgian landowners persecuted Armenian serfs and Georgian mobs attacked innocent Armenian villages in pogroms.

Returning to Russia or other countries has been a traumatic experience for those repatriated. Many have been denied the residency permits required to apply for jobs, housing, and social security benefits in their new communities and have been reduced to living in squalid camps on the outskirts of towns. In Russia, forced migrants who are citizens of Russia but are ethnically Caucasian or Asian have often been attacked by roving gangs of ethnic Russians, inspired by neo-fascist nationalist movements that identify all non-whites as the "enemy" of a racially homogenous Russian state.

Even white ethnic Russians have not been immune from persecution and physical violence in areas of the country to which they have been forced to flee. Local natives of the communities to which they have relocated perceive them not as fellow citizens and members of a common ethnic group, but as "foreigners." With national and local economies near complete collapse since 1991, the natives resent having to compete with the new arrivals for scarce jobs and consider special government subsidies for the refugees discriminatory when funding for public housing and welfare for poor natives has been severely cut back. By 1993, outbreaks of intracommunal violence among ethnic Russians and other nationalities were becoming almost as commonplace in the locales to which the repatriated groups had returned as in the regions they had fled in the first place.

POLITICAL DISINTEGRATION

Ethnic Separatism

In several regions of the post-Soviet countries, weak central governments command little national loyalty and confront separatist movements of ethnic minorities who consider the governments to be nothing but a political arm of the ethnic majority. Some minorities have formed breakaway republics, especially in locales endowed with rich natural resources. These minorities have declared their right to national self-determination and claimed legitimate sovereignty over their territories, based on their historic residence in these locales since the Russian Empire. Nineteen locales within what is now the Russian Federation were accorded token status as autonomous ethnic republics, regions, or territories during the Soviet era. Since 1991, all nineteen have reconstituted themselves as sovereign independent ethnic republics of Russia. They have been joined by an additional eleven nations that since declared their own sovereignty over districts or entire provinces and territories of Russia. The thirty so-called autonomies contain 26 million of Russia's almost 150 million people.

Some of the autonomies, such as the republic of Tatarstan, 500 miles east of Moscow on the left bank of the Volga, have adopted all the trappings of independent statehood. Tatarstan was one of the last khanates of the Mongolian Tatar empire, which was conquered by the Russian tsar in 1542. Since 1991, the independent republic of Tatarstan has its own constitution, parliament, flag, anthem, army, police, and even license plates. Tatarstan and other autonomous republics base their relations with the national government in Moscow on treaties, similar to those signed between two independent countries, even though the autonomies remain nominally parts of Russia.

In Tatarstan, ethnic Tatars descended from those of the sixteenth century make up 48 percent of the population of 3.7 million; they also comprise one-third of all Tatars throughout the Russian Federation. Yet, in eighteen of the thirty autonomies, ethnic Russians constitute a majority, ranging from 50 to 83 percent of the local populations. The ethnic nations after which the autonomies are named make up 40–75 percent of the local populations in only twelve autonomies. In but six of the thirty—Dagestan, Chechnya, Kabardino-Balkaria, North Ossetia, Tuva, and Chuvashia—does the nation claiming sovereignty in the autonomy constitute a majority of the local population and the autonomy contain the majority of all those who belong to that ethnic nation throughout Russia.

The original motive for the autonomous republics to declare sovereignty in 1992 was the fear of domination by ethnic Russians after the demise of the Soviet Union. Since 1992, the autonomous movement has snowballed. The local ethnic Russian population in these areas has supported the movements, out of a common desire to control local resources and to keep the revenues. Otherwise, the local governments would have to send a large portion of any locally collected taxes to Moscow and would be legally bound to form economic ties with foreign investors that are consistent with the laws and regulations set down by the Russian national government. At the same time, by remaining nominally part of Russia, all of the autonomies receive the subsidies and credits distributed to all eighty-nine administrative jurisdictions under programs of the Russian national government.

In an autonomous republic such as Tatarstan, the local government negotiates by protocols of its treaties with the Russian national government how much of its local taxes are sent to Moscow. In 1992, the total amounted to 93 million rubles, 10 percent of all local revenue. In return, Tatarstan received in 1992 a total of 38 billion rubles in equivalent credits and subsidies from programs of the Russian national government.

For the fifty-nine non-autonomous Russian provinces and territories, Russian national tax laws apply. The Sverdlovsk province, with 4.7 million people, had to send to Moscow over 60 percent of its local revenue in 1992, amounting to 95.5 billion rubles. Sverdlovsk received as credits and subsidies from Russian national programs 29.7 billion rubles, almost 9 billion less than independent Tatarstan. The non-autonomous provinces and territories such as Sverdlovsk also must comply with the national rules and laws affecting foreign investment and trade.

Two glaring examples of how the economic motive inspired the wave of local separatism in Russia are the republic of Yakutia (Sakha) and the republics of Yamalo-Nenets and Khanty-Mansi inside the Tyumen province. The Yakut constitute only 33 percent of the population in their republic, but Yakutia is the richest source of gold and diamonds in Russian Eastern Siberia. Following its declaration of sovereignty, the republic government of Yakutia has sent very little of any locally collected taxes to Moscow but has retained a sizable cut of the revenue from the worldwide sale of its diamonds and gold. The Russian province of Tyumen has oil reserves equivalent to those of Kuwait. The two ethnic groups, the Yamalo-Nenets and Khanty-Mansi, declared their autonomy essentially to keep the revenue from the oil fields that are licensed to foreign companies in their particular districts; these groups constitute only 6 percent and 1 percent of the populations of their respective districts.

The phenomenon of ethnic separatism has not been limited to Russia. In Ukraine, the Crimean peninsula has been reconstituted as an autonomous Crimean republic, since a majority of the population voted to change the status of the peninsula in a local referendum in January 1991. The autonomous status is justified on the basis of population and history. Ethnic Russians make up a majority of Crimea's population, and the peninsula had been an autonomous subdivision of Russia until 1946 and a directly administered province of Russia until 1954, when it was incorporated into the Ukrainian republic. Under terms of a treaty with the Ukrainian government, the Crimean republic government keeps most of the revenue earned locally from agriculture and tourism. Tourists flock to the resorts along the Black Sea, which have been taken over as the property of the Crimean republic government. Crimea has been granted autonomous status by the Ukrainian government even though Ukraine remains a unitary state since independence. All of the other twenty-four provincial jurisdictions making up Ukraine are taxed and administered directly by the national Ukrainian government in Kiev. Unhappy with even this status, a minority of radical Russian nationalists within Crimea have been pushing through a local referendum to have the republic declared a state totally independent of Ukraine.

In Russia, the grants of autonomy to various ethnic enclaves at least are consistent with the federal system of government in that country. Even the non-autonomous provinces and territories within Russia have been accorded some degree of sovereignty as political jurisdictions independent of the national government in Moscow, similar to states in the United States or *Laender* in Germany. All the Russian jurisdictions, both autonomous and non-autonomous, have reserved powers, independent of the federal government, to tax and govern their locales. During the Soviet era, federalism in Russia was a sham. The heads of the local Communist parties appointed by Moscow in effect ruled all jurisdictions as a de facto unitary republic. Since 1990, however, the sovereignty of all jurisdictions has been affirmed by laws on local self-government adopted in the Russian national parliament and by a federal treaty approved after independence in March 1992.

In Crimea, an additional complication is that a second ethnic group has returned, staking its own claim to an autonomous area within the peninsula. Descended from the Mongolian Tatars who conquered the ancient Russian feudal state of Kievan Rus in the thirteenth century, Crimean Tatars had lived continuously in the peninsula for over 700 years until their entire nation was deported by Stalin to remote areas of Siberia and Central Asia in 1944 for alleged collaboration with the

Germans. Under Gorbachev, the Soviet national government had begun measures to repatriate the 2–3 million Crimean Tatars to their native homeland, and over 200,000 had already returned by 1989.

The end of the Soviet Union and the assertion of Crimean autonomy by the local ethnic Russian majority changed all of that. Even though the national Ukrainian government continues to support some kind of autonomous jurisdiction for the peninsula, it remains powerless to contravene the Crimean republic government. Since 1991, the Crimean government has blocked all attempts by returning Tatars to form their own autonomous district. Local Crimean courts have denied the claims of the Tatars for the return of lands in the peninsula that they had inhabited for centuries before their 1944 deportation. Many returning Tatars have been forced to live in makeshift refugee camps, and some have become victims of racially motivated clashes between themselves and local ethnic Russians. Some Crimean Tatars attribute their problem to the fact that Nikolai Bagrov, the head of state of the Crimean republic, was formerly the Crimean Communist party first secretary, and Leonid Kravchuk, the President of Ukraine, was formerly the second secretary of the Ukrainian Communist party.[3]

The Governments' Dilemmas

The central governments in Russia, Ukraine, and the other thirteen countries face almost insoluble political dilemmas in dealing with the centrifugal force of ethnic separatism in the post-Soviet era. If central governments grant autonomy to certain areas, along with special tax and other financial concessions, they only stir resentment and a tidal wave of claims from all of the other administrative subdivisions of their countries. Even if the majority of the population in a subdivision belongs to the same ethnic majority as is governing the country nationally, the people resent having to pay taxes and give up ownership of their natural resources only because they had not been politically bold enough to blackmail the national government with threats of secession, as the ethnic minorities did. Thus, following the precedent of Crimea, provinces in the Donbass coal-mining regions of eastern Ukraine, where 50–60 percent of the population is ethnic Ukrainians, have declared their intent to reconstitute themselves as the autonomous Don Republic.

In Russia, some of the claims to sovereignty in locales inhabited solely by ethnic Russians have bordered on the absurd. In 1993, the government in the province of Arkhangelsk in northwest Russia was scouring the local archives to find proof for its claim to be reconstituted as the autonomous Pomory Republic. The right to local self-determination in this case is based on the presumed unique commonality of Arkhangelsk citizens as an ethnic minority, the Pomory. The Pomory are allegedly seafarers that inhabited the shores of the nearby White Sea for centuries, directly descended from those who founded Novgorod in the ninth centu-

---

[3]Conflict among the ethnic Russians and Tatars in Crimea and the Ukrainian government intensified after the direct election of Yurii Meshkov as Crimean president in January 1994. Meshkov leads a political party whose goal is to have the entire Crimean peninsula reincorporated into Russia.

ry. If its demand for sovereignty as an ethnic entity were accepted, the provincial government could claim ownership of the entire local fishing fleet and its catch. Many of those running the local government are former Communist party officials who ruled Arkhangelsk at the end of the Soviet era. Catching the separatist fever, the provincial governments of Sverdlovsk and a number of other non-autonomous Russian provinces also declared themselves autonomous republics of Russia by the late summer of 1993, using similarly dubious claims of uniqueness in their historic origins.

The lost revenue from the ethnic entities and the many non-ethnic subdivisions only compounds the national economic problems of the central governments of Ukraine and Russia. Western lending agencies have insisted that a reduction of their government budget deficits is an absolute precondition for new loans or even a rescheduling of interest payments on those loans they assumed as their share of the foreign debt owed by the former Soviet Union. Without a phased reduction of budget deficits, there will be no foreign loans. Without foreign loans, the central governments cannot fund programs for housing and jobs and stem the growing impoverishment among many of their citizens. Their only alternative has been to slow down privatization of the economy and appropriate for government programs more of their worthless national currencies. In the process, the governments exacerbate hyperinflation, further devalue their currencies, increase the number of poor in their countries, and stir a new wave of demands at the local level for autonomy.

Because of their retreat from privatization of their economies, the national governments undermine the already marginal level of support and loyalty for their fledgling democracies. Dwindling national support politically benefits only populist and nationalist demagogues, allied with former Communist officials in attempts to bring down the national governments and force restoration of the command economy and autocratic political rule associated with the former Soviet Union. The rising political power of demagogues and Communists only frightens additional locales into declaring their sovereignty if not their complete independence.

Political concessions to ethnic-religious groups may only intensify conflict within the republics. Other ethnic minorities, outnumbered and fearing the group that has become an independent republic, resort to the same political ploy. They declare their own sovereignty and demand that the central government recognize them as a territorial entity separate from the republic dominated by the rival group. Such attempts to break away then arouse open conflicts and communal violence between two or three minorities. Each selectively recalls the past injustices committed against them by the other. Each lays claim to ownership of the natural resources and land in terms of historic rights derived from the time before the area had been incorporated into the Russian Empire.

For example, Moscow's recognition of ethnic Chechen sovereignty over the republic of Chechnya in 1992 spurred the other local ethnic nationality, the Ingush, to declare a republic of Ingushetia separate from Chechnya (see Figure 33–1). Ethnic Chechen constitute almost 60 percent of the local population; ethnic Ingush, only 13 percent. Both are Muslim ethnic minorities and suffered terrible persecution and deportation as entire nations during the Stalin era; they coexisted in a single ethnic enclave called Chechno-Ingushetia for several decades from the

1950s. Since 1992, Chechen and Ingush have been warring with each other over control of the territory, taking time out only to fight Russian national army units sent to quell the local civil unrest.

A second complication has been the conflict between the Ingush and the third local ethnic nationality, the Ossetians. Since 1991, an increasing number of Ossetians have fled across the border from Georgia to both Ingushetia and the neighboring republic of North Ossetia. The separatist South Ossetian republic has been under seige by a Georgian government that refuses to grant it autonomy. Ethnic Ingush fear that the Ossetian refugees will strengthen the North Ossetian republic, which will claim territory of Ingushetia. The Ingush also suspect that the Chechen have encouraged the flight of Ossetians across the border to force the Ingush into conceding sovereignty to Chechnya.

In many instances, those leading a movement for independence of a republic or for sovereignty of an allegedly persecuted minority inside a republic are former military officers or, like Nikolai Bagrov in Crimea, former local Communist officials. Bagrov has disavowed his Communist past, but others who govern ethnic republics in Russia since 1991 have been openly supported by national leaders of political parties and movements on the extreme anti-democratic right. The extreme right opposes the Russian national government of President Yeltsin and has supplied some of the local separatist republics with stolen military arms and secret funds. The implication is that local separatist leaders will return the favor and support future national campaigns of these parties and movements. The ties of both Chechen and Ingush political leadership to extremists on the political right have been widely publicized and documented by the Russian national media since 1992.

On the other hand, just because the extreme right supports some of these separatist movements, staunch defenders of the Russian government tend to condemn *all* demands for autonomy by ethnic minorities. They assume all such demands are part of a conspiratorial plot to bring down the government and to restore Communist rule. In Ukraine, radical Ukrainian nationalists have continually pressured the Ukrainian government to revoke its grant of republic autonomy to Crimea.

If the governments refuse to grant autonomy to the ethnic republics and send military units to reimpose central control, they open themselves to being denounced by Western governments. They lose vital international credibility in their attempts to project themselves as legitimate governments and to distinguish themselves from the former Soviet Communist state in its autocratic rule and brutal mistreatment of ethnic minorities. Even when able to refute charges from the West of persecuting their own ethnic minorities, the governments discredit their countries as potentially stable and safe climates for Western investors by resorting to military force. By not sending in military units to reimpose control, the central governments open themselves to political attacks by their own radical nationalists in their parliaments and public media. The radical nationalists charge the central governments with caving in to ethnic minorities and condoning the dismemberment of the country. Parties on the extreme political right join in the condemnation, even though they have secretly armed and funded some of the separatist movements.

In the end, military forces sent by the central governments have exacerbated intercommunal violence among the disparate ethnic groups in the breakaway republics, sometimes leading to the full-scale civil war that the governments had used political diplomacy and concessions to prevent in the first place. Civil war in Georgia in 1993 directly resulted from the unsuccessful decision of the Georgian government to crush by military force the autonomous movements of the non-Georgian Abkhazians and Ossetians. The civil war even threatened to escalate into war with Russia, because local units of the Russian army stationed along Georgia's border with Russia were accused by the Georgian government of supporting and protecting the Abkhazians and Ossetians.

■ ■ ■

Since 1991, weak national governments, economic depression and hyperinflation, and ethnic-religious conflicts have led to the outbreak of secessionist movements, intercommunal violence, civil wars, and even wars between countries in Russia and Central Eurasia. Tens of thousands have been killed, and hundreds of thousands have been forced to flee the fighting as refugees. By 1993, there were an estimated 125 different ethnic disputes, of which 25 were armed conflicts. Soviet Communism has been replaced—not by liberal democracy but by an ideology of rampant ethnic tribalism. The end of the Soviet empire has resulted not so much in fifteen newly independent countries as in a state of political chaos.

The two case studies in Chapter 34 discuss two of the locales that have been beset with political instability and civil unrest since 1991 and are liable to become causes of international conflicts before the end of this century. In Kaliningrad, a Russian province is moving to reconstitute itself as an autonomous republic. In Moldova, the central government confronts secessionist movements of both ethnic Russians and ethnic Turks.

Political Instability and Civil Unrest: Kaliningrad and Moldova ▬▬▬▬▬▬▬

During the Soviet era, the past was something rewritten by Soviet historians and interpreted by Communist ideologues to suit the current party leaders. The rewritten past included that of many regions along the western border of the former Soviet Union, which were incorporated into the country through Stalin's secret protocol with Hitler in 1939 or because of the presence of Soviet troops on their territory at the end of World War II. Official histories dismissed the pre-Soviet history of these regions as a backwardness that had been overcome under the allegedly more civilized Soviet system. Soviet ideologues only cited the diversity of ethnic-religious nationalities residing in the western regions in order to emphasize the rates of intermarriage among them and other signs proving the success of Soviet policies in assimilating all peoples as one nation.

Since 1991, the disintegration of central political authority in Russia and Central Eurasia has exposed the falsehoods of those Soviet historians and Communist ideologues. Decades of Soviet political socialization did little to sever the outlook and identity of these regions and areas from their pre-Soviet cultural and historical pasts. Decades of Soviet policies to encourage assimilation created few lasting bonds of commonality and friendship among the diverse ethnic-religious nationalities.

In the post-Soviet era, reassertions of past cultural identities and conflicts among ethnic-religious nationalities have created a potential arc of crisis. The arc of crisis extends all along the western border of the former Soviet Union from the Baltic to the Black Seas and threatens to precipitate wars involving a number of countries near these regions. German Kaliningrad and Romanian Moldova, discussed in this chapter, are two of the most troublesome locales in this arc of crisis.

■ *KALININGRAD AND BALTIC SEPARATISM*

The only ice-free ports in the Soviet Union were Vladivostok, kept open year-round by ice-breakers; Murmansk, warmed by an underwater Gulf Stream current from the Atlantic Ocean; and the Baltic port of Baltiisk in the Russian province of

Figure 34–1
The Russian Province
of Kaliningrad

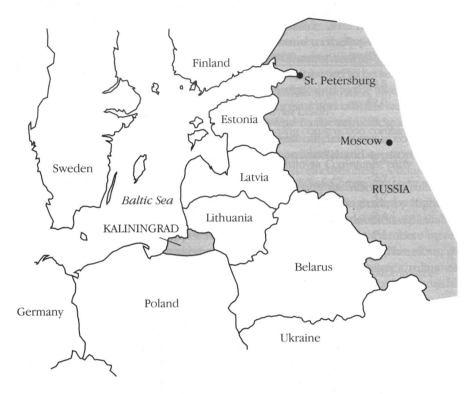

Kaliningrad.[1] Baltiisk and the city-province of Kaliningrad represent only one of the many geographical, historical, and political ambiguities arising from the dissolution of the Soviet Union. As you can tell from the map in Figure 34–1, Kaliningrad, though politically a territorial subdivision of Russia, is separated geographically from Russia by three hundred kilometers and the independent countries of Belarus, Latvia, and Lithuania. Kaliningrad is an enclave within the borders of Lithuania along its western Baltic coast. Adding to the province's ambiguous status is that historically and culturally it is much more German than Russian.

The city and province of Kaliningrad were actually the former east Prussian city called Konigsberg and its surrounding countryside. A border region between modern-day Lithuania and Poland, Konigsberg had been settled in the thirteenth century by crusaders of the Teutonic Order sent by the Pope to claim the region in the name of Catholicism from the "heathen Prussians." After murdering most of the indigenous population, the order founded monasteries and colonized the territory with German, Austrian, and Saxon agricultural settlers. As capital of the Baltic trading alliance called the Hanseatic League in the fifteenth and sixteenth centuries, this

---

[1]For information on the Russian province of Kaliningrad since 1991, Amos Elon, "The Nowhere City," *New York Review of Books,* vol. 40, no. 9 (May 13, 1993), pp. 28–33; and Magdalene Hoff and Heinz Timmermann, "Kaliningrad: Russia's Future Gateway to Europe?" *RFE/RL Research Report,* vol. 2, no. 36 (September 10, 1993), pp. 37–43.

Protestant German region became a vassal state of the Catholic Polish kingdom in 1640, until it was annexed into Prussia with the dismemberment of Poland in the 1770s.

Konigsberg was steeped in Prussian-German culture and German history. The local university founded by the German settlers became renowned as the place where the German philosopher Immanuel Kant taught and wrote in the eighteenth century and where some of the most well-known proponents of "pan-Germanism" emerged in the nineteenth century. Literally "City of Kings," Konigsberg was the site where Prussian rulers traditionally were crowned and the location of the military garrison where generations of Prussian officers were trained. The pan-Germanists provided the ideological rationale for German nationalism and the integration of all ethnic Germans in one country by 1871 in the Second German Reich.

With the defeat of Nazi Germany, the region and its important port facility on the Baltic were annexed by the Soviet Union as a subdivision of the Russian republic under terms of the Potsdam Agreement between the Soviet Union, the United States, and Britain in July 1945. The western two-thirds of Prussia became part of Poland under the same agreement, compensating Poland for the loss of its eastern one-third to the Soviet Union (postwar western Ukraine and western Belorussia). Renamed for Mikhail Kalinin, the individual who was the nominal head of state under Stalin during World War II, Kaliningrad was systematically de-Germanized under Soviet rule. Traditional German-Prussian buildings were razed, streets and villages were all renamed in Russian, ethnic German farmers were either deported or imprisoned, and privately owned German farms and estates were collectivized.

Baltiisk became the home port for the Baltic Fleet of the Soviet Navy. The economy of Kaliningrad over the four decades following 1945 was transformed into a virtual military garrison, with the deployment of a large contingent of Soviet troops and arms. The entire city and province became a closed security zone, in which all foreigners were forbidden. A vast network of highways and railroads, originally built to serve the Soviet military and fleet, linked the province's Baltic fishing and maritime fleets to the rest of the country. The fishing fleet became a major source of food for the Soviet Union; the province provided 10 percent of all fish and fish products consumed in the Russian republic alone. Connected by rail and highway to the rest of the country, the maritime fleet made the Kaliningrad ports major transit areas for Soviet trade with the rest of the world. In addition, Kaliningrad contains 90 percent of the world's amber reserves.

Given its military and commercial value, Kaliningrad was claimed by the Russian government in December 1991, based on its former inclusion in the Russian republic. Geographically, the 15,000 square kilometers of the province and its port of Baltiisk lie inside Lithuania, and, as we have pointed out, for centuries the land had been part of eastern Prussia.

The future of the province remains uncertain. Kaliningrad has been actively courted by a number of international corporations from Germany, Poland, and Finland since 1991. They see great potential in the region as an equivalent to Singapore or Hong Kong for Europe—a major center of commerce, trade, and banking linking Western Europe, Russia, and the Baltic region. With its network of railroads, the reconstruction of the highway across Poland joining it to Berlin, and the refitting of its military airfields for commercial airliners, the region could also be the center of a major European tourist area. Before the Soviet era, Konigsberg had been renowned as one of the most fashionable summertime sea resorts along the Baltic for the German aristocracy.

The political leaders of the local Kaliningrad government have attempted to leverage this outside interest in their province to gain greater economic and political autonomy from the central Russian government in Moscow. Like the leaders of the movement to reconstitute Siberia as an autonomous republic, the Kaliningrad leaders contend that its unique geographical-historical situation warrants reconstituting Kaliningrad as an autonomous Baltic republic of Russia. As an autonomous republic, Kaliningrad would be granted the right to form its own economic relations with other countries and foreign corporations, independent of the national government in Moscow, and to keep most of the revenue from tourism and from selling fish and other products in Russia and other countries.

Even before the demise of the Soviet Union, the city government of Kaliningrad had been lobbying the Soviet and Russian governments in 1990 to create a special status for the city and province. The March 1990 election resulted in a political split between the two jurisdictions of Kaliningrad. The provincial council and officials were predominantly anti-reform, tied to the party establishment, military, and KGB. The city council and officials were predominantly pro-reform, tied to the maritime and fishing fleets and related industries.

The city council and its chair lobbied Moscow to end Kaliningrad's closed security status and to make the entire province a free-enterprise zone and tourist-commercial center for all of Europe (especially Germany). In turn, the provincial council and officials lobbied their own supporters in the Soviet Ministry of Defense and Committee of State Security to retain the province's closed status. They claimed that the closed status was necessitated by the province's strategic significance as the port for the Soviet Baltic Fleet and by its many military installations. Throughout 1990 and 1991, both sides engaged in a form of political warfare, countermanding each other's authority. In one highly celebrated incident, a tourist ship from West Germany invited by the city government to launch Western investment and tourism was refused the right to dock in Kaliningrad at the very last moment by orders of the local military and KGB overseeing the port facilities.

Since 1991, the city and province of Kaliningrad have been open to outsiders, but their status has become the source of conflict among neighboring countries. In Lithuania, radical nationalists favor annexing the province under the pretext that Kaliningrad (termed "little Lithuania") rightfully belongs to Lithuania since it was part of the former Lithuanian-Polish kingdom in the seventeenth century. The Lithuanian government also fears the military threat posed by the increasing number of Russian troops redeployed to Kaliningrad from Germany and Poland since 1991. The Yeltsin government took over all of the Soviet troops located in those two countries and, under treaties signed by Gorbachev in 1990 and 1991, assumed the obligation to remove them from Germany and Poland by 1994.

The problem is that the Russian government lacks the money to build housing and facilities for these 100,000–200,000 troops in Russia. The West German government agreed in 1990 to pay for and build housing for the redeployed Soviet troops but proceeded to construct most of the housing in what became the independent countries of Belarus, Ukraine, and Moldova in December 1991. As a stop-gap measure, the Russian government has been forced to temporarily redeploy the troops to the overcrowded barracks in Kaliningrad. This build-up of a Russian military presence inside Lithuanian borders has only served to antagonize the Lithuanian government. As relations between Lithuania and Russia have remained uncertain, rail traffic from Russia across Lithuania to Kaliningrad has been somewhat politicized. Railroad ties and equipment on the Kaliningrad lines have been repaired very slowly by Lithuanian railroad crews, and Russian passengers journeying by train to Kaliningrad have been harassed by Lithuanian border police and customs officials.

In addition, Polish defense officials have charged Russia with duplicity in failing to comply with the spirit of the 1990 agreement by merely moving its troops across the border to Kaliningrad, where they continue to pose a threat to Poland's independence. Given the historic enmity between Poles and Lithuanians (same religion—Roman Catholic—but different language and ethnicity), the annexation of Kaliningrad by Lithuania would be likely to be viewed by the government of Poland as a direct threat and could spark a conflict between Poland and Lithuania. Radical Polish nationalists already claim that Kaliningrad historically was part of Poland and should be annexed by their country, following the precedent set when the other two-thirds of former Prussia became part of Poland under the Potsdam Agreement of 1945. Not to be outdone, radical Russian nationalists consider retention of the province almost a matter of Russian patriotism and would view any concession by President Yeltsin on Russia's sovereignty over the province as something equivalent to treason.

No matter whether Kaliningrad wins greater independence from Moscow as an autonomous republic or resists Lithuanian or Polish annexation, the province will probably find itself becoming a de facto state of Germany before the end of the century. So many German tourists are visiting the province, so many Germans related to those who lived in Konigsberg before the war intend to repatriate, and so many German tourist agencies and corporations are opening up outlets in the capital that Kaliningrad is already reverting to its pre–World War II ethnic and political origins. What Germany lost through the Potsdam Agreement is being bought back by German businesses with the privatization of the Kaliningrad economy in the 1990s. Since 1991, unemployed former KGB and Soviet military officers originally sent to Kaliningrad in the 1980s to protect the Soviet Union against an invasion by NATO from the West are competing for positions as managers of local German companies and banks and even as translators and tour guides for Germans and other foreigners on vacation in the province.

Kaliningrad residents assume that a Yeltsin government desperate for hard currency will eventually have to sell the entire region back to Germany, using the precedent of Tsar Alexander II's sale of Alaska to the United States in 1872. By 1993, 75 percent of students at the Kaliningrad university were enrolling in German language courses, and a survey of public opinion in Kaliningrad found a majority favoring renaming the city and province Konigsberg. A local joke circulating in Kaliningrad about the uncertain future of the province says that "optimists" should learn German, "pessimists" should learn Polish, and "realists" should learn how to shoot a Kalashnikov submachine gun.

▪ *MOLDOVA AND SECESSIONIST MOVEMENTS*

In Moldova, a breakaway group of Russian settlers led by former hard-line opponents of both Gorbachev and Yeltsin in 1987–1991 have declared the independent "Dniester Moldovan Soviet Socialist Republic."[2] They have assumed control over a territory constituting 10 percent of Moldova's area and containing 16 percent of its population. Their capital city of Tiraspol lies along the banks of the Dniester River, which forms Moldova's eastern border with Ukraine (see Figure 34–2).

The group first proclaimed this territory an autonomous jurisdiction of the former Moldavia in September 1990, in order to prevent the Moldavian popular front from gaining the independence of the union republic from the Soviet Union as an integrated territory. A bloc of deputies elected to the Moldavian parliament in March 1990 identified themselves with the pro-independence position of the popular front. Following the abortive August coup of 1991, a majority of the parliament voted on August 27 to declare the independence of the republic from the Soviet Union. On the other hand, in a referendum only days before the breakup of the Soviet Union in December 1991, a majority of the Russian settlers in the Dniester region voted to retain the unified Soviet Union.

In August 1992, the Russian settlers formally declared their independence as a country and even laid claim to the entire Transdniester region on both banks of the Dniester River. The Republican Guards formed by the settlers have consistently prevailed in numerous military clashes with armed forces sent by the Moldovan national government to suppress the secessionist movement and to protect the many non-Russians living in the region. Just one clash between the two sides in June 1992 cost approximately 1,000 lives, and 100,000 were evicted from their homes.

The settlers have justified their secessionist republic because of allegedly anti-Russian policies and discrimination against ethnic Russians by the newly independent Moldovan government. In reality, the Russian settlers represent only 30 percent of Moldova's total Russian population and only 25 percent of the population living on the east bank of the Dniester; ethnic Moldovans and Ukrainians on the east bank form 40 percent and 28 percent, respectively, of the total local population. On the national level, in Moldovan public opinion polls even before December 1991, a majority of all ethnic Slavs (Russians, Ukrainians, and Bulgarians) supported the breakup of the Soviet Union and a newly independent non-Communist Moldova.

A majority of those in the national parliament and government in Chisinau are Moldovan by ethnic origin, but ethnic Slavs and other non-Moldovan ethnic nationalities comprise a sizable number of the deputies in the parliament. All the major ethnic nationalities hold ministerial positions in the government of "national consensus" under President Mircea Snegur. Some of the newly formed national political parties have actively recruited their members and leaders from a broad cross-section of all ethnic nationalities. On the local level, the national government has devolved cultural-political autonomy to the various non-Moldovan ethnic nationalities to administer

---

[2]For information on the civil unrest in Moldova since 1991, Vladimir Socor, "Moldova's 'Dniester' Ulcer," *RFE/RL Research Report,* vol. 2, no. 1 (January 1, 1993), pp. 12–16; and "Russia's Army in Moldova: There to Stay?" *RFE/RL Research Report,* vol. 2, no. 25 (June 18, 1993), pp. 42–49.

Figure 34–2

Moldova and the
Dniester Republic

their own school districts and other areas of governance. The national government has encouraged ethnic tolerance since 1991 by funding schools and publishing houses in languages other than Moldovan, the official language of the country.

Citizenship with full and equal rights was granted to anyone residing in Moldova at the time of independence, irrespective of ethnic nationality. The Moldovan government even signed bilateral treaties with Israel, Bulgaria, Ukraine, and Turkey, committing itself to comply with U.N. policies on universal human rights in its treatment of the Jewish, Bulgarian, Ukrainian, and Turkic communities in Moldova. Under these treaties, the four countries are bound to reciprocate in guaranteeing universal human rights for the Moldovans among their citizens.

However baseless the claims of discrimination by the Russian settlers in the Dniester republic, the settlers have been armed, trained, abetted, and led by the Fourteenth Russian army deployed on the Dniester's east bank. The Fourteenth army is an elite mobile force of some 8,000 soldiers trained to fight in the mountainous regions of the northern Balkans and originally stationed to repulse the first wave of an American-led NATO invasion. Most of its career officers and reenlisted noncommissioned officers are seasoned veterans of the Soviet military contingent that fought in Afghanistan in 1979–1988.

The Fourteenth army had been a garrison directly subordinate to the Odessa military district headquartered across the border in the Ukrainian republic, but was essentially orphaned when the Soviet Union collapsed in December 1991. Like most of the half million Soviet troops in Ukraine after independence, the Odessa military district and its troops swore an oath of allegiance to Ukraine and enlisted in the newly formed Ukrainian army, essentially because the Ukrainian government was willing to offer them much higher salaries and benefits than the Russian government. The one exception was the Fourteenth army. Stationed inside of independent Moldova, it became a detachment of the newly formed Russian armed forces in early 1992 under the command of the Russian Defense Minister.

These troops have not been redeployed inside Russia for the same reason the Russian government has failed to resettle the several hundreds of thousands of other nominal Russian armed forces still stationed in countries of Central Eurasia. The Russian government lacks the funds to provide them and their dependents with jobs and housing if they were redeployed or completely disbanded. As we pointed out in Chapter 33, Russia is already being inundated by a wave of what could be as many as 6 million refugees fleeing civil conflicts along its southern border and lacks the resources to care for them, let alone more from the disbanding of Russian armed forces throughout the former Soviet republics.

In addition, the Russian government has pressured the Moldovan government to join it and governments of other former Soviet republics in a joint military security force under the Commonwealth of Independent States. As part of such a CIS joint force, the Fourteenth army and its military arsenal would already be strategically positioned to defend the borders of Russia and the other Commonwealth countries from any spillover of conflicts such as that in the former Yugoslavia. The Fourteenth army is Russia's bargaining leverage to pressure Moldova to join the CIS security force. Aleksandr Lebedev, the commander of the Fourteenth army, was a protégé of Pavel Grachev, the Russian Defense Minister, when both led Soviet paratroopers in Afghanistan.

The Fourteenth army is supposed to be neutral politically and bound by the Russian-Moldovan treaty not to intervene in the internal affairs of its temporary host country. In reality, the leaders of the Fourteenth army encouraged the Dniester settlers to declare independence from the government of Moldavia right after the abortive August coup in 1991, even before the breakup of the Soviet Union. The commander of the Fourteenth army has denounced the Moldovan government as "fascist" and has openly advocated restoration of the former Soviet Union, as have the political leaders of the Dniester republic. Soviet symbols are still displayed and Soviet Communist holidays are still celebrated by both the Fourteenth army and the Dniester republic. The leaders of the Dniester republic want their country to be annexed by Russia in the hopes that, along with the other fourteen countries, it would eventually join a reconstituted unified Soviet state. The republic finances itself through its local economy, subsidies from the Russian government in Moscow, and contributions from radical Russian nationalists and Communists in Russia and other countries who are opposed to democratic government and the breakup of the Soviet Union.

The Republican Guards are closely integrated with the allegedly neutral Fourteenth army. The Fourteenth army conducts some of its military exercises jointly with the Republican Guards and loans tanks, missiles, and armored personnel carriers to the Guards. Many officers in the Guards are active or retired officers of the Fourteenth army, who are paid as members of the Guards in addition to salaries or pensions they receive from the Russian Defense Ministry. As a consequence, the Fourteenth army has become probably the highest-paid quasi-mercenary unit in the entire Russian armed forces. The Fourteenth army and the Republican Guards even share the same pool of new recruits—unemployed teenagers in Moldova who are attracted by the salaries, housing, and other opportunities for enlistees in the Fourteenth army. Thus, the Fourteenth army, as a detachment of the Russian government, illegally draws most of its new recruits from foreign nationals, citizens of Moldova.

There are so many unemployed local teenagers because the Moldovan government has to spend its limited resources for an army to put down the secessionist movement, because a third of Moldova's industry is located in the Dniester republic, and because the continuing civil war has discouraged any outside Western investment or development of the Moldovan economy. The dilemma for the Russian government in Moscow is that disbanding the Fourteenth army and completely disowning any responsibility for it would only result in its officers and NCOs becoming full-time paid mercenaries in the Republican Guards. Only as long as Russia maintains command can it hold the Fourteenth army even nominally accountable.

Political factors further limit the options of the Russian government under President Yeltsin. The alleged persecution of the 25 million ethnic Russians living outside Russia is a highly volatile issue, potentially damaging politically to the pro-democratic forces represented by Yeltsin. Russian nationalists have consistently accused Yeltsin of abandoning their compatriots, and die-hard Communists have joined them in blaming Yeltsin for having dissolved the Soviet Union and creating the very problem of displaced ethnic Russians in the first place. The Russian national parliament (Supreme Soviet) has passed resolutions of support for the independent Dniester republic since 1991. Even centrist and liberal democratic newspapers and politicians in Russia, who otherwise politically support Yeltsin, have embraced the cause of the Russian settlers under their general concern over human rights' abuses against ethnic Russians in Central Eurasia.

Even disbanding the Fourteenth army would not necessarily cripple the Dniester republic. The Republican Guards have recruited a number of soldiers of fortune to serve under their command. These soldiers of fortune include thousands of Russian Cossacks, former KGB and OMON troops, and unemployed former Soviet soldiers. Many of the former KGB and OMON troops were those who transferred from the Baltic region after having led the bloody assaults on Latvians and Lithuanians in early 1991. The Cossacks and former Soviet soldiers include many who served in Afghanistan and a number who belong to radical Russian nationalist parties and movements that are opposed to the democratic governments in Russia and neighboring Ukraine. A Russian military division sent to the area in 1992 by President Yeltsin as a peace-keeping force to end the civil war at the request of the Moldovan President Snegur has actually wound up funneling arms to the Republican Guards and otherwise covertly supporting the secessionist movement.

Dniester is only the most visible of the conflicts threatening to escalate into a full-scale civil war in Moldova. Moldova is also populated by the Gagauz (ethnically Turkic, traditionally Russian Orthodox in religion), who even before the end of the Soviet Union were advocating cultural-political autonomy for the southeast regions of the Moldavian republic, where they predominate. The Moldovan government has been more than willing to devolve extensive autonomy to the Gagauz. However, complete independence for the Dniester Russian settlers automatically would translate into a similar demand from the Gagauz. A radical nationalist wing of the Gagauz—as pro-Communist and pro-Soviet as the Russian settlers in Dniester—wants complete independent statehood as the "Gagauz Soviet Socialist Republic" and has pressured the more pragmatic local Gagauz political leaders to assume a rigid, uncompromising stance with the central Moldovan government in Chisinau.

Caught in the middle of the two secessionist movements are hundreds of thousands of Bulgarians, Ukrainians, Jews, and Gypsies. In the Gagauz autonomous republic, gangs calling themselves the Gagauz Republican Guard, under the radical nationalist wing of the Gagauz movement, brutalize villages populated by Bulgarians. These attacks on ethnic Bulgarians have politically embarrassed the democratic government of Bulgaria, already condemned by its own radical Bulgarian nationalists for its tolerance of the large minority of Bulgarian Turks, who are citizens of Bulgaria but ethnically related to the Turkic Gagauz. The influx of ethnic Ukrainians into refugee camps in Odessa to escape the civil war across the border has aroused an equivalent political firestorm among radical Ukrainian nationalists. They are convinced that a conspiracy of ethnic Russians in Ukraine and Moldova, secretly orchestrated by the Russian government, intends to overthrow Ukraine and to reunite the country with Russia. If not resolved peacefully soon, this civil unrest has a high potential for spreading into a full-scale regional war involving four countries: Moldova, Romania, Ukraine, and Russia.

Culturally and linguistically, Moldovans are ethnic Romanians. Indeed, the Moldavian popular front in 1989–1991 was led by intellectuals and literary figures who mobilized public support for the cause of independence by claiming decades of Soviet discrimination against their Romanian ethnicity. A particular target was the forced Russification of the Moldovan language since 1945. Under Soviet rule, the Moldovan language had to be written and taught in the same Cyrillic script used for Russian. The Romanian language from which Moldovan derives is based on the Latin script and alphabet, like English, French, German, and most other European languages. Very soon after independence, the written Moldovan language was purged of Cyrillic and returned to its Latin base. This change was seized on by the Russian settlers as proof of discrimination against ethnic Russians, justifying their declaration of independence from the country. The written alphabet has sparked centuries of conflict in this region of the world.[3]

Although the Moldovan government has attempted since 1991 to create a sense of national citizenship independent of ethnicity, Romania remains the core of Moldovan national identity. Before it became a union republic of the Soviet Union in 1945, Moldova for centuries had been part of Romania—first as a Romanian principality in the Ottoman Turkish Empire until 1812, then as Romanian provinces in the Russian Empire until 1917, and finally as the eastern provinces of Romania until 1944. The one exception was the Dniester's east bank, which was annexed by the Soviet Union as an autonomous Moldavian republic of the Ukraine in 1924. The rest of eastern Romania was annexed by the Soviet Union after World War II and integrated with the Moldavian enclave inside Ukraine to become the Moldavian union republic. (Actually, Moldavia had been annexed by Stalin in 1939–1941 under terms of the previously mentioned secret protocol that he signed with Adolf Hitler in September 1939.)

---

[3]In the former Yugoslavia, for example, Serbs are primarily Greek Orthodox and Croats Roman Catholic, but the two groups are ethnically indistinguishable and speak the same language. A major distinction between them is that Serbs write in Cyrillic and Croats in Latin script.

Given Moldova's history and cultural identity as Romania, radical nationalists in both Romania and Moldova have been advocating a so-called Greater Romania to be created by reannexation of Moldova by Romania. They consider the Gagauz and especially the Dniester secessionists as major obstacles to realizing Greater Romania and have urged Romanian military intervention on the side of the Moldovan government to crush both the Gagauz and the Dniester Russians. Mircea Druc, the leader of the post-independence popular front in Moldova, was the Prime Minister in 1990–1991 but was forced to resign precisely because of his ultranationalist views advocating the incorporation of Moldova into Romania.

Druc and a minority of pro-Romanian deputies in the Moldovan national parliament have blocked any attempts to ratify the country's limited and conditional membership in the Commonwealth of Independent States, to adopt a new constitution, or to dissolve the parliament and elect a new parliament through a multiparty election. The reason why they have been able to do this is that any action by the Moldovan parliament requires an absolute majority of all its deputies, including absentees. The deputies representing the Dniester region have boycotted the parliament since 1991, and their absence has allowed the votes by the minority of pro-Romanian deputies to be sufficient to preclude any majority.

Druc and the popular front maintain close ties with the political parties and movements of Romanian radical nationalists in Bucharest, the capital of Romania. The pro-Romanian minority is opposed by President Mircea Snegur, an overwhelming majority of deputies in the Moldovan parliament, the non-Moldovan ethnic minorities, and even a majority of the Moldovan ethnic community, who identify themselves more as citizens of a newly independent country than as just ethnic Romanians. The majority of both Moldovans and non-Moldovans would resist any Romanian military intervention, however well-intentioned, as an invasion of their country. Druc and the pro-Romanians have condemned Snegur and the majority of the Moldovan parliament as "Communists," who in opposing Moldova's annexation by Romania, advocating Moldova's membership in the CIS, and negotiating over autonomy with the Dniester and Gagauz political leaders are allegedly selling out the country's sovereignty and subordinating Moldova once more to domination by Moscow.

In Moscow and Kiev, radical Russian and Ukrainian nationalists would condemn any Romanian military intervention and view it as a direct threat to their national interest and the lives of tens of thousands of their fellow compatriots in Moldava. The Ukrainian government has long suspected Moscow of promoting the separatist Dniester republic to destabilize Ukraine's western regions and to eventually pressure Ukraine back into a political union with Russia. The western half of the Ukrainian province of Odessa, which borders Moldova along the Black Sea, was a region of Romania called Bessarabia and Northern Bukovina before 1945. All western Ukrainian regions were formerly part of Poland, Czechoslovakia, or Romania, ceded to Stalin by Hitler and reincorporated by the Soviet army in 1944–1945. Since independence, the Ukrainian government, to preserve its territorial integrity, has been put in the unique position of having to defend implicitly the Hitler-Stalin secret protocol of 1939.

Radical nationalists in Romania and Moldava claim "Bessarabia and Northern Bukovina" also should be reincorporated into Greater Romania. Thus, any

Ukrainian government would find it difficult not to send its troops into Moldova to fight the Romanian army, to defend the Black Sea region of Ukraine, and to deter Russian military intervention. The Russian army would be sent to protect the ethnic Russians against the Romanians on one side and the Ukrainians on the other side.

Any confrontation between Ukraine and Russia would be further complicated by the questionable loyalty of many Ukrainian officers, a majority of whom are ethnic Russians. Conflicts already have broken out on ships and in army units of the Ukrainian armed forces between ethnic Ukrainians and Russians. Clashes among units of the Russian army led by different ethnic nationalities would be likely, as would ethnic Russians in both the Ukrainian and Russian armies joining to fight alongside the Fourteenth army and the Republican Guards.

A four-sided war in which Romanian, Moldovan, Russian, and Ukrainian troops would fight each other—and in which two of the combatants (Russia and Ukraine) would have military arsenals with nuclear weapons—is not outside the realm of possibility before the end of this decade. A fifth potential combatant that would find it difficult to remain neutral is Turkey. As ethnic Turks, the Gagauz are viewed sympathetically as compatriots by the government of Turkey, itself under pressure by radical Turkish nationalists to protect expatriate Turkish communities in the surrounding Black Sea region. Turkey lacks the nuclear weapons of Russia and Ukraine but, as a member of NATO since its founding, it has been armed and trained in conventional warfare by the United States, which has treaty obligations to defend Turkey. Emissaries of the United States, other NATO countries, the Conference on Security and Cooperation in Europe in Prague, and the United Nations have all attempted to broker some peaceful resolution of the secessionist conflicts in Moldova, but their efforts may prove to be as ineffective as their attempts to stop the civil war, carnage, and dismemberment of Bosnia-Herzegovina in the nearby southern Balkan peninsula.

■   ■   ■

Kaliningrad and Moldova illustrate the great uncertainty and instability of politics in the post-Soviet era, but this era also has been one of forming new policy-making structures. Since 1991, all countries in Russia and Central Eurasia have founded new national governments. In many cases, they have modeled their national legislative and executive branches after the parliamentary democracies in Britain, France, and Germany.

There has been a conscious effort to make these new democracies work. Substantive and procedural limitations on the powers of governments have become more widely accepted. Constitutional means to make elected chief executives accountable have been created. Norms of bargaining and compromise between the legislative and executive branches have evolved through trial and error. Political pluralism has emerged, with a number of political parties in most countries that span the spectrum of political viewpoints in those societies and are actively involved in policy making through caucuses and factions in their national legislatures. These efforts to institute new governments founded on liberal democratic principles and a multiparty system will be the central theme of the final two chapters in this part of the book.

35

Policy-Making Structures and Policy Alternatives in Russia

> The President publishes decrees, as if there is no Supreme Soviet, while the
> Supreme Soviet suspends the decrees, as if there was no President.
>
> *Oleg Poptsov, Director*
> *Russian State Television*
> *August 11, 1993*

Strong national governments like those in Britain, France, and Germany are defined by their ability to resolve most political conflicts peacefully. Their policy-making structures provide a constitutional setting in which contending sides bargain and compromise on differences, based on an overriding acceptance of procedures and norms of conduct and grounded in a rule of law. Weak national governments are defined by their general inability to command authority over their populations and to govern effectively. Lacking political legitimacy, their officials and legislatures confront a very low level of public support, trust, and confidence in the fairness of their decision making and their conflict resolution.

Weak national governments vastly increase the potential for widespread violence in their societies. The potential magnifies if the countries also lack effective political parties. Effective political parties generate public participation in the political process, shape public debate over alternative policy decisions, elect leaders committed to different policies, and make ruling governments continuously accountable for their actions. In the political vacuum left by weak national governments and weak political parties, politics becomes a sharp clash among single-issue groups, where parties don't moderate conflict by amalgamating demands. This unremitting struggle for power assumes dimensions of political anarchy. Physical force becomes an accepted means for settling differences and determining the outcome of political conflicts. In Russia and Central Eurasia since 1991, politics all too often has seemed a reversion to the "nasty and brutish" state of nature about which philosophers such as Hobbes have warned since the seventeenth century.

This reversion has occurred despite the stated intent of the national leaders in many of these countries to institutionalize Western democracies based on elections, representative governments, free civil societies, and political pluralism. Reality in the post-Soviet transition period has differed greatly from intent. An open-ended struggle for power constantly threatens to overwhelm governments and escalate into full-scale civil wars. Political pluralism among contending groups is polarizing society and making several countries ungovernable, especially since these lack any basis in their political cultures for parties and for the norms of bargaining and compromise inherent in democracies. Respect for a rule of law and constitutional procedures only marginally deters their national leaders, who frequently resort to authoritarian actions and justify them as necessary to restore order.

Previous chapters focused on the economic and societal factors accounting for these new countries' political weakness. This chapter examines the accomplishments and setbacks of the Russian Federation in attempting to establish effective government and democracy in this early stage of transition.

■ THE BATTLE FOR MOSCOW

Of the fifteen countries, Russia has most reflected the contradictions between intent and reality in attempting to lay the foundations for an effective national government based on democratic principles. Anyone who needed any reminder of the "nasty and brutish" undercurrent of all politics had to look no further than the events that unfolded on the streets of Moscow on October 3 and 4, 1993. On those two days, the television cameras of the CNN bureau on the roof of the U.S. Embassy in Moscow allowed the world to witness a violent attack on the Russian national parliament building (nicknamed the "White House") by Russian paratroopers and elite militia units loyal to President Yeltsin. The successful storming of the parliament building by pro-Yeltsin forces was the most violent political clash in Moscow since the Russian Revolution of 1917. Approximately 150 died, almost 1,000 were wounded, and almost 2,000 were arrested and jailed.

Among the most prominent of those jailed in the notorious Lefortovo prison were the leaders of what Yeltsin termed the "Fascist-Communist rebellion" against democracy, who had holed themselves up in the White House over the previous two weeks. The leaders of the rebellion were the chair of the Russian parliament, Ruslan Khasbulatov, and the Vice-President of the country, Aleksandr Rutskoi (see Figures 35–1 and 35–2). The storming of the White House climaxed two weeks of political standoff between Yeltsin and his adversaries, who were for the most part the radical anti-democratic Russian nationalists and Communists among the deputies of the parliament under the leadership of Khasbulatov and Rutskoi. They and several hundred supporters, armed with Kalashnikov submachine guns and other arms, had barricaded themselves in the parliament building to defend what they claimed was the core of Russian democracy against Yeltsin's attempt to impose his personal dictatorship.

The political standoff had begun on September 21, when Yeltsin had issued a presidential decree abolishing the national parliament and calling for elections to a new parliament on December 11 and 12. Yeltsin had issued his call for elections even though the powers of parliament, the basis for electing its deputies, and even

Figure 35–1
Ruslan Khasbulatov

Source. RFE/RL Research Institute Photo

Figure 35–2
Aleksandr Rutskoi

Source: RFE/RL Research Institute Photo

the names of its two chambers had yet to be finalized. Yeltsin was acting under the presidential emergency powers of the Russian Constitution, which he had just completely repudiated and under which the parliament—just abolished by him—had been democratically elected in March 1990.

Around 100 of the 250 Supreme Soviet deputies, soon joined by their supporters among the larger body of 1,033 deputies of the parent Russian Congress, from which they had been chosen, defied Yeltsin's decree and refused to vacate the parliament building. On September 22, they impeached Yeltsin and removed him as Russian President. The deputies acted under the standing Russian Constitution, ratified during the Soviet era in 1978 in the former Russian Republic and significantly amended since 1990 by the Russian Congress. Under amendments to the constitution since 1990, supreme political authority was vested in the Russian Congress and its subordinate body, the Supreme Soviet, as the permanent legislature.

That supreme authority included the right of the Congress to amend the constitution, to impeach and remove the President for anti-constitutional actions, and to ratify any new constitution. The standing constitution had just recently been amended by the Russian Congress at its session in late March 1993, after Yeltsin had withdrawn an earlier presidential declaration of emergency rule and a threat to disband the parliament. Under the March amendment to the constitution, suspension of the parliament by the President had been made an impeachable offense, calling for a vote by the Congress to remove the President for action contrary to the constitution. Acting under their constitutional authority, the rump Congress elected Aleksandr Rutskoi as President of the country on the evening of September 22.

Over the next ten days, Russia had two competing Presidents, as the Russian nationalists and Communists with their armed supporters barricaded inside the White House defied President Yeltsin in his official executive offices inside the Kremlin. Each side played a deliberately calculated game to mobilize their supporters and to intimidate the other into conceding. The telephones, water, heat, and electricity of the White House were shut off. Pro-Yeltsin militia effectively imprisoned those inside the White House by laying barbed wire around the entrances of the building and posting guards to prevent anyone from entering. The militia fought off those attempting to breach the cordon around the building and join the defenders inside with additional arms.

The Khasbulatov-Rutskoi rump parliament issued appeals to the Russian armed forces, urging them to rebel against Yeltsin and come to Moscow to defend the White House. Pavel Grachev, the Russian Defense Minister and a Yeltsin ally, declared that the Russian armed forces were to remain neutral in the conflict. Viktor Chernomyrdin, the Prime Minister, his Council of Ministers (the Russian equivalent of the British Cabinet), and other ministerial heads all remained loyal to Yeltsin. In response, the rump parliament selected their own Defense Minister, Interior Minister, and Security Minister. To counter Yeltsin's appeal for elections to a new parliament, the Khasbulatov-Rutskoi rump parliament passed their own resolution, calling for simultaneous parliamentary and presidential elections on December 12. Yeltsin rejected their appeal, but he conceded to schedule a national presidential election on June 12, 1994, two years before his five-year term of office as President would have ended by law under the article of the Russian Constitution just abrogated by him. Yeltsin gave those inside the White House until Monday, October 4, to give up their arms, and he threatened to use military force to disarm them if they failed to comply with his orders.

The leaders inside the White House no longer recognized Yeltsin as President. They defied the ultimatum and instead reissued their call for Russian military units to join them in Moscow in their defense of Russian democracy. By September 30, Patriarch Alexei, the head of the Russian Orthodox Church in Moscow, had been called in to act as an intermediary between the two sides and to reach a peaceful resolution of the conflict that threatened to become full-scale civil war throughout Russia. The negotiations broke down a day later, on October 1. Those inside the parliament building refused to surrender their arms without any promise of political concessions by Yeltsin in return.

On October 3, from the balcony of the White House, "President" Rutskoi addressed an afternoon crowd of his supporters, who had gathered despite the armed pro-Yeltsin militia surrounding the building. Several groups of his supporters had fought pitched battles on the streets surrounding the parliament building and were intoxicated from having overwhelmed heavily armed militia, who had futilely attempted to stop the thousands with batons, tear gas, and rubber bullets. Rutskoi called on the crowd to storm Ostankino, the state-run television and radio center in northern Moscow, as well as the Moscow mayor's offices across the street. Throughout the crisis, broadcasts by Ostankino had slanted coverage in favor of Yeltsin and excluded all but highly negative references to those inside the White House. Mayor Luzhkov of Moscow had openly sided with Yeltsin since the onset of the crisis on September 21 and had given direct orders to city departments to turn off the White House's telephones, water, heat, and electricity. Rutskoi ended his speech to the crowd by urging the pro-Yeltsin militia to join the crowd and himself before it was too late and they found themselves on the losing side of this rebellion.

That evening the crowd overwhelmed the lightly defended Ostankino and the mayor's office. Sixty-two were killed and about 400 wounded in the assault on the communications building alone. The four television channels broadcasting out of Ostankino were shut off by pro-Yeltsin officials to prevent the rebels from using them. National television broadcasts for the next twenty-four hours resumed from another communications center in Moscow. Yeltsin spoke to the nation the next morning, promising that the "armed putsch in Moscow will be crushed."

Yeltsin's address came within two hours after the paratroopers and elite militia troops launched their counteroffensive assault on the parliament building. The assault began after a 7 A.M. deadline that had been given to Khasbulatov, Rutskoi, and their several hundred followers to surrender their weapons and themselves for having instigated the actions against the communications center and mayor's offices. In the late afternoon of October 4, with the bottom floors of the parliament building taken by the pro-Yeltsin assault forces after bloody fighting, Khasbulatov, Rutskoi, and their remaining followers surrendered under a white flag.

The so-called Battle for Moscow that raged on October 3–4 was rife with ironies. Only a little more than two years before, on August 19–21, 1991, it had been Yeltsin with his closest political allies, the very same Ruslan Khasbulatov and Aleksandr Rutskoi, who had barricaded themselves inside the White House with smuggled arms, defying the attempted imposition of martial law by the Emergency Committee. The Emergency Committee had just arrested Gorbachev and declared Yeltsin and his political supporters rebels.

Khasbulatov had been hand-picked by Yeltsin to succeed him as chair of the Russian Supreme Soviet when Yeltsin was elected Russian President on June 12, 1991. Rutskoi, a highly popular general from the war in Afghanistan, had been selected by Yeltsin to run as his vice-presidential candidate in that election. Yeltsin and Rutskoi had been elected as chief executives of Russia directly by over 57 percent of the Russian voters. Rutskoi and Khasbulatov headed up the delegation entrusted by Yeltsin to fly on the afternoon of August 21 to Crimea, where Gorbachev had been placed under house arrest. Gorbachev returned to Moscow that evening with them, following the surrender and arrest of the coup's plotters.

In August 1991, CNN cameras had transmitted live around the world the scene of Yeltsin standing on a tank sent by the Emergency Committee to seize the White House and calling on the tank commander to join him and the democratic forces inside the parliament fighting against the attempted coup. Two years later, CNN cameras transmitted images of the same tanks lobbing shells into the parliament building under the orders of Yeltsin. The White House that Yeltsin almost personally had transformed into a national symbol of the new emerging democracy and defiance of Communism lay in rubble, following his banning of the national parliament and imposition of the same kind of emergency rule that he had bravely resisted when it had been imposed by the Emergency Committee.

Among the units that stormed the parliament building on October 4, 1993 was the Alpha Group. The Alpha Group was the former KGB special unit whose leaders had refused to obey the orders of the Emergency Committee to storm the White House on August 20, 1991. That refusal had proven to be among the most critical turning points, undermining the committee's authority and eventually leading to the crumbling of the attempted coup by the next day.

After the 1993 battle for Moscow, Yeltsin, acting under his extended emergency rule, banned a number of journals and newspapers, reimposed partial censorship over all other media, and outlawed a number of political parties. He dissolved by decree all city and district councils throughout the country and ordered all regional and territorial councils to disband and hold elections for new local legislatures no later than the spring of 1994. The new local legislatures were to be greatly limited in their powers relative to regional-territorial administrative heads appointed by and solely accountable to the President. Yeltsin also forced Valerii Zorkin to resign as chair of the Constitutional Court and suspended the powers of the Court for having ruled unconstitutional his decree dissolving the Russian parliament on September 21. These were some of the very same steps that the coup-plotters of the Emergency Committee had begun to institute two years earlier on August 19–20, 1991, before they were overthrown in large part because of Yeltsin's mobilization of the nation against them from inside the White House.

In certain ways, Yeltsin was continuing a longstanding Russian tradition. Respect for the rule of law and the political authority of an independently elected national parliament had never been hallmarks of any of the highest Russian executives throughout the twentieth century. The first and only nationally elected parliament under Russian tsardom—the Duma forced on Nicholas II by mass public uprisings in 1905—had been arbitrarily dissolved in 1907 by Petr Stolypin, the Russian Prime Minister, because the deputies of the Duma had rejected the right of Tsar Nicholas to appoint and remove the prime minister and the cabinet solely on his own. Until the end of tsardom in February 1917, the later Dumas were allowed by Nicholas to convene and vote on policies only because they conceded to the tsar's final authority over them. The end of tsardom found little change. The second democratically elected national body—the Constituent Assembly elected in December 1917—was locked out of its building and banned by Lenin in January 1918, one day after it convened to write a new democratic constitution for a post-tsarist Russia that would have prevented Lenin and the Bolsheviks from consolidating their control of power after their November coup. The third democratically elected national legislature—the All-Union Congress of People's Deputies instituted in 1989—was in effect dissolved in November 1991 after the abortive August coup, when Yeltsin and other union-republic leaders moved to dismember the entire Soviet Union.

■ FOUNDATIONS OF RUSSIAN DEMOCRACY

Although the Battle for Moscow graphically underscored the fragility of national governmental institutions in Russia and Central Eurasia, those events contrasted with another irrefutable political trend evident since 1991. Foundations of a Russian democracy were evolving on several institutional levels. The principles of democratic constitutionalism had been embodied in a new court, and the Russian parliament had begun to assume an authority and features similar to those of Western parliaments. Factions and coalitions had become influential in shaping legislation in the Russian parliament, and some major political parties with national membership and local branches had formed.

The Constitutional Court

The most unprecedented policy-making structure to emerge after 1991 was the Russian Constitutional Court. The Court was the first independent court in Russia since the Russian Revolution. It was set up under a law of the Russian Congress passed in October 1991 at the direct urging of President Yeltsin himself. The Court was to institutionalize the principles of constitutionalism and the supremacy of the rule of law in post-Communist democratic Russia. It was authorized to render final authoritative rulings on the constitutionality of any laws and decrees passed or issued by governmental bodies or any actions undertaken by government officials. Forbidden only from considering and ruling on cases involving "political questions," the Court was supposed to be entirely impartial and nonpartisan in its decisions, bound only by the Russian Constitution. Despite the intent to make the Court impartial and nonpartisan, the thirteen judges were all to be nominated by committees, commissions, or political factions of the Russian Supreme Soviet before being approved by a vote of the entire larger parliament, the Russian Congress.

Any laws passed by the national parliament and the actions of any government official—including the President of Russia—were potentially subject to being reviewed and overruled as unconstitutional under the Court's statutory powers. The Court's docket also included criminal and civil cases appealed from lower courts. Like the French Constitutional Council, the Court accepted and ruled on petitions from specific high-ranking government officials authorized to seek a constitutional ruling on laws or decrees that had just been passed or issued. Those authorized to seek rulings from the Court included the Russian President, the Chair of the Supreme Soviet, and the Procurator General (the highest judicial officer in the Russian government nominated by the President and confirmed by the parliament).

Within its first two years, the Court had reviewed almost 2,000 complaints involving the constitutionality of specific laws, decrees, or actions and had shown a willingness to challenge political authority in its defense of the rule of law. The Court had overruled laws passed by the Russian parliament and had even vacated as unconstitutional several of President Yeltsin's most controversial decrees and actions. As a result, there was growing public acceptance, evident in public opinion polls, of the principles of constitutionalism and the supremacy of the rule of law as embodied by the Court. Over the past thousand years of Russian history, rulers had acted arbitrarily and dictatorially, without any concern for the legality of their actions. The post-Soviet Russian public was much less willing to accept similar behavior from its officials and legislators, even when elections made them accountable.

The Constitutional Court had been headed since its inception by Valerii Zorkin, a reform-minded jurist and former professor of constitutional law. Zorkin had been nominated by a faction of reform Communists in the parliament that was led by Aleksandr Rutskoi in 1990–1991, before his election as Russian Vice-President. By 1992 Zorkin had made his own impact on the Russian public. Zorkin was constantly giving interviews to the Russian media and commenting on almost any controversy or issue arising on the national political scene. The problem was that his high national political profile at times flouted the canons of judicial impartiality. Zorkin was not reluctant to offer his opinions on the constitutionality of laws passed by the Congress or actions of Yeltsin, even *before* the Court had convened to deliberate and rule on these issues. Zorkin's alleged personal friendship with Khasbulatov and Rutskoi and his siding with them against Yeltsin raised further public doubts about his ability to make unbiased rulings.

By June 1993, Zorkin had alienated himself from six other judges on the Court, including its deputy chair, Nikolai Vitruk. They denounced Zorkin and called for his resignation. They charged him with politicizing the Court and undermining its authority as an independent and impartial defender of the Constitution through his frequent public pronouncements on the constitutionality of laws and actions before they were reviewed by the Court itself.

Despite the controversy over Zorkin's judicial misconduct, the first two years of the Court had been unprecedented. Principles of constitutionalism had been institutionalized in a court with an authority unknown in either Russian or Soviet history. The Constitutional Court was a new beginning, but it also showed that a court by itself cannot found a country governed by law. It will be decades before a real acceptance and understanding of the rule of law by Russian citizens, elected officials, and even judges will justify terming Russia a law-governed country.

Legislative-Executive Relations

The first two years of Russian independence witnessed the first steps toward parliamentary democracy. The Russian parliament, which as recently as 1989 had been merely a rubber stamp for the Communist party, was beginning to assume an authority and independence relative to the executive branch not unlike those of parliaments in Western European democracies.

Legislation was changed at times by the Supreme Soviet to preclude a threatened veto by President Yeltsin. Yeltsin appointed the Prime Minister, but reforms introduced by the executive into parliament were altered to meet criticisms raised in committee hearings and before passage as laws. Bills became laws following preliminary approval by Supreme Soviet commmittees and commissions, a debate and vote by each chamber (the Council of the Republic and Council of Nationalities), and a final debate and vote by the two chambers in joint sessions. The parent Russian Congress convened periodically both to approve the general course of policies being instituted by Yeltsin and the government and to ratify international agreements. Set times in all daily Supreme Soviet sessions were available for speeches by any deputy critical of the government; that is, the parliament was learning the norms and procedures of holding the ruling government continuously accountable. Legislative oversight of the executive branch was evolving through a pattern of committee hearings in which bills were amended, prospective ministers were grilled, and cabinet members were expected to testify about their executive agencies.

Certain committees in the Supreme Soviet had become political stepping stones for emerging nationally prominent politicians. One of these was Sergei Shakhrai, who had chaired the Committee for Legislation and had, in effect, drafted and shepherded through the Supreme Soviet almost all of the liberal reform bills passed in 1990–1991. The bills were written by Shakhrai, a former professor of law at Moscow State University, along with the liberal jurists-deputies on his committee and consultants on leave from various academic think tanks in Moscow. Recognizing Shakhrai's legal skills and political acumen, Yeltsin appointed him State Counselor on Legal Policy in 1991. In this position, Shakhrai was Yeltsin's major legal advisor and the one who drafted Yeltsin's presidential decrees during the time when the Congress had conceded to Yeltsin the right to legislate on a wide range of issues solely by decree. As State Counselor, Shakhrai also represented Yeltsin in the hearings before the Constitutional Court on the legality of Yeltsin's 1991 decree banning the Communist party and nationalizing all of its property. In 1992, Yeltsin promoted Shakhrai to Deputy Prime Minister and assigned him responsibility for a wide range of difficult policy areas such as nationalities and supervision of the Ministries of Security, Internal Affairs, and Justice.

Born in 1956, Shakhrai received his doctorate in law in 1982 from Moscow State University, writing his dissertation on interethnic relations in the Soviet Union. From his early committee position in the parliament, Shakhrai shot to national prominence in only four years, generally ranked in public opinion polls as one of the most popular and promising post-Communist democratic politicians in Russia. The youthful Shakhrai was widely considered by 1993 to be one of the early frontrunners among contenders for the office of Russian President in 1996, if Yeltsin abided by his 1992 promise not to seek another term as President.

By 1993 Shakhrai's most likely opponents among liberals in a future presidential race were Gavriil Popov, Anatolii Sobchak, and Grigorii Yavlinskii. Popov was a former professor of economics at Moscow State University who was mayor of Moscow in 1991–1992. Sobchak was a former professor of law at Leningrad State

University who was mayor of St. Petersburg in 1991–1993. Popov and Sobchak helped found the Movement for Democratic Reforms in 1991, a liberal reform party whose Russian branch Popov headed after resigning as mayor of Moscow. Yavlinskii was a professor of economics, nationally renowned for having drafted in 1990 a program termed "500 days," which was to institute a market economy in the Soviet Union gradually over two years. Gorbachev had originally endorsed Yavlinskii's economic reform program before disassociating himself from it as too "radical" in the fall of 1990. Yavlinskii remained active outside of the national Russian government after 1991, heading an economic policy research center in Moscow and advising local governments in Russia on market reforms. Shakhrai, Popov, Sobchak, and Yavlinskii represented a new post-Communist generation of politicians in their forties who were untainted by any past association with or leadership positions in the Soviet autocracy. The ascendancy of any of them to the Russian presidency promised to institutionalize the office and advance the process of democratization.

Yeltsin had been elected president in June 1991 as a Russian nationalist and populist against the Soviet Communist system. A majority of Russian voters had endorsed creating an office of President of the republic on March 17, 1991. Gorbachev had actually instigated the March referendum, asking voters throughout the Soviet Union whether they approved the country's continuance. Gorbachev intended to use the mandate of public support to undermine those such as Yeltsin who were in leadership positions of the union republics and were demanding sovereign independence from the central Soviet state. The question about creating the office of Russian President was tacked onto the Russian version of Gorbachev's national referendum by then parliamentary chair Yeltsin in order to enhance his own authority by contesting Gorbachev and achieving greater autonomy for Russia. After a majority of Russian voters approved creation of the office in the nonbinding referendum, the Russian Congress amended the republic's constitution to carry out that mandate. On June 12, 1991, Yeltsin won the first direct election to an office created especially to allow him to challenge Gorbachev and the remaining vestiges of the central Soviet state and Communist autocracy.

In certain ways, Yeltsin's election was similar to the election of 1958 in France, when the French people brought back to power their national hero, Charles de Gaulle. De Gaulle assumed the office of French President in the Fifth Republic, which was specifically created for him to save France from dictatorship. De Gaulle's successors as French President democratized and institutionalized the office, with the presidency becoming disassociated from the emergency situation in which it had been created for one individual. By 1993 democratic liberals in Russia anticipated a similar change. They hoped the continuation of the Russian presidency after Yeltsin, with the office held by another liberal, would institutionalize and depersonalize the office in a constitutional framework of government, based on a strong but not autocratic chief executive and an influential and not subservient parliament.

Parliamentary Factions and Coalitions

Deputies within the Russian parliament had organized themselves and exerted a growing influence over national legislation. Within the first two years of Russian independence, at least fourteen different party caucuses or factions had formed in the Russian Congress and Supreme Soviet. This was both a surprising and democratically positive development. None of the deputies elected in March 1990 had been affiliated with any party other than the Communist party when they ran. Recall that the constitutional ban on parties had not been lifted until March 1990. Before the March 1990 election, branches of various voters' clubs, anti-Communist political movements, and quasi-parties were able to distribute fliers to voters, endorsing their preferences for seats in the republic and local parliaments. Even in 1993, very few Russian parliamentary deputies were openly affiliated with one of the many political parties active throughout Russia.

Nonetheless, political and ideological differences over the timing and comprehensiveness of the reforms required to privatize the Russian economy and over the direction of Russian foreign policy had led to clusterings of deputies, groups who tended to side and to vote with each other fairly consistently. By 1993, these clusters had developed a distinct organizational character and leadership. The factions and coalitions attempted to impose discipline over their members on votes in the Congress and Supreme Soviet, to bargain over pending votes with each other, and in many ways to conduct themselves like deputy groups in Western European parliaments such as those of France and Germany.

The leading factions in the Russian Supreme Soviet and Congress varied in membership, policy concerns, and ideology. The largest was the Agrarian Union, composed of 158 deputies representing primarily rural districts and provinces and led in the parliament by the director of a state farm. Its members were unified in opposing hasty full-scale privatization of agriculture in Russia and in supporting retention of the collective and state farms inherited from the Soviet era. Another 54 deputies formed the Industrial Union, consisting mostly of managers of state factories and plants. Led by the head of a paper mill, the Industrial Union was critical of any precipitate move by the Yeltsin government to denationalize all of the remaining state-owned economy. On the democratic left were two prominent factions: the 75 deputies of Democratic Russia and the 36 deputies of the Radical Democrats. Liberal intellectuals from the large Russian cities, such as Moscow and St. Petersburg, made up the core of these two factions. Since 1990, these two factions had constituted the most solid bloc of support in the Russian parliament for Yeltsin and his reforms to transform Russia into a Western democracy and market economy.

By 1992 the various factions in the parliament had further coalesced into three distinct coalitions, spanning the Russian political spectrum. On the democratic left, Democratic Russia, Radical Democrats, and other liberal reformers had reconstituted themselves in December 1991 as the Coalition for Reform, with 222 deputies. They were unequivocally supportive of Yeltsin's economic reforms and his advocacy of a Russian foreign policy oriented primarily toward alliances and ties with Western democracies.

In the ideological center were the 209 deputies of the Democratic Center and the 163 deputies of the Creative Forces. They supported the general direction of Yeltsin's reforms to privatize the economy based on free markets but opposed him on specifics. They also insisted on retaining a core state-owned industrial sector for several decades. On foreign policy, the centrist blocs advocated a more balanced orientation of the Russian government toward both the Western democracies and the "near abroad," or the former Soviet republics bordering Russia.

The extreme right and left of the political spectrum combined to form the Russian Unity bloc, consisting of 375 deputies. These were allied solely by their almost complete opposition to Yeltsin's domestic and foreign policies. This opposition was their only rationale for cooperating, since their numbers included such diverse factions as the Agrarian Union, Native Land (consisting of die-hard Russian nationalists and monarchists), and Communists of Russia (die-hard Communists). Russian Unity particularly opposed privatization of the economy and advocated a more militaristic foreign policy to defend Russian national interests and ethnic Russians in the "near abroad." In attempting to maintain cohesion in a bloc spanning such diverse factions, deputies in Russian Unity were compelled to vote unanimously and illogically for resolutions calling for the restoration of both the former Soviet Union and the former Russian monarchy and affirming the principles of both socialism and the Russian Orthodox Church.

To some extent, the diverse views and positions of the fourteen parliamentary factions reflected those of many political organizations, social strata, occupational groups, and others in Russian society. The one glaring omission was any specific faction to advocate the interests of the 10–15 percent of Russians employed in private industry, farming, and commerce by 1993. The private sector was represented nationally by an interest group called the Union of Entrepreneurs and Leaseholders, which claimed to have some 10 million members in fifty-seven administrative jurisdictions of the country by the fall of 1993, including owners and employees in private businesses, farms, and commercial outlets.

The private economic sector only emerged in Russia after the 1990 election of the parliament, and few owners of private businesses or farmers had even run for seats in the parliament. As a consequence, private entrepreneurs concerned over the rates of federal taxation on businesses, private farmers concerned by the government laws on buying and selling farmland, and even kiosk owners on the streets of Moscow, who wanted government programs to aid self-employed merchants, had to depend on the parliamentary factions of reform intellectuals to express their views. These factions consistently sponsored bills to liberalize the Russian economy. The Union of Entrepreneurs and Leaseholders formed their own political party called Democratic Initiative. Yet, like most political parties in Russia, they could claim no actual members among the deputies of the Russian parliament, which had been elected when the article of the Soviet constitution banning all parties other than the Communist party had only just been removed.

Political Parties

Political parties and movements in Russian society at large closely paralleled the diversity and configurations in the Russian parliament. Even though no national parliamentary elections had been held since 1991, numerous political parties had formed, dissolved, and mutated into new coalition parties.

By 1993 the three largest national political parties in Russia were Civic Union, the Russian Communist Party, and Democratic Russia. Civic Union is a coalition of parties, parliamentary factions, and interest groups that are in the center-right of the Russian political spectrum by philosophy and policy views. The Russian Communist Party is the largest of several socialist and social-democratic parties defined as the far left of the political spectrum. Democratic Russia is a coalition of parties and movements conventionally termed the moderate democratic left of the political spectrum.

The overlap between parties in parliament and society is best exemplified in the person of Vice-President Aleksandr Rutskoi, who was strongly supported by centrist factions and coalitions in the parliament and by his own national political party, the Free Russian People's Party. Rutskoi was both the founder and national leader of the Free Russian People's Party, which by 1993 claimed to have approximately 100,000 members in Russia. Rutskoi, whose public approval ratings in polls rivaled those of Yeltsin by 1992, is a charismatic and ambitious populist politician. Although almost twenty years younger than Yeltsin, Rutskoi in many aspects of his quick-tempered personality and emotional idealism is very much like Yeltsin.

Yeltsin selected the Afghan war hero Rutskoi as his running mate in June 1991 to shore up his electoral support among Russian nationalists, but the similarity of their personalities was also widely considered at the time to have been a critical factor in Yeltsin's choice. Until their political falling-out in late 1992, Yeltsin and Rutskoi were presumed to have gotten along quite well with each other and to hold similar positions on most issues. (Recall that a similar compatibility of goals and personalities was widely presumed to have been true of Yeltsin and Gorbachev when Gorbachev recruited Yeltsin to Moscow in April 1985 and later assigned him to the key position of head of the Moscow Communist party.)

By 1992, Rutskoi began to distance himself from Yeltsin on both policies and on the issue of a future constitution. In June 1992, as the leader of the Free Russian People's Party, Rutskoi allied his party with three other parties—the Democratic Party of Russia, the All-Russian Renewal Union, and the New Generation–New Policy faction of the Russian parliament—to form the Civic Union. The fifth organizer and financial backer of the Civic Union was the most powerful interest group in Russia, called the Russian Union of Industrialists and Entrepreneurs, which had been organized primarily by managers of state-owned defense factories and had ties to similar unions of industrialists organized in Ukraine and other countries of the "near abroad". (For example, Leonid Kuchma, appointed Ukrainian Prime Minister in the fall of 1992, was a member of the Ukrainian union of industrialists and a plant manager of the factory that manufactured most of the strategic missiles.)

The leaders and founders of the Civic Union characterized their coalition as centrist and a loyal opposition to the policies and supporters of President Yeltsin on the moderate democratic left. The leaders and parties allied as the Civic Union opposed any precipitate changes to denationalize all of Russian industry under the reforms sponsored by President Yeltsin and Yegor Gaidar, whom Yeltsin had appointed acting Prime Minister in April 1992. Gaidar was attempting to privatize the entire Russian economy and to institute full-scale market reforms as quickly and as comprehensively as possible. The leaders of the Civic Union preferred a mixed nationalized-private economy, one in which the government continued to subsidize key sectors such as defense. They argued that the state-owned and subsidized defense sector still produced arms in great demand on the world market and was a critical means for the Russian government to earn hard currency for its debt repayment to the West and to reduce its balance-of-trade deficit. Elements within Civic Union affiliated with New Generation–New Policy also advocated retention of government funding for social welfare programs for all Russians, many of which were likely to be cut by the Yeltsin-Gaidar government due to a lack of funds. The programs would be eliminated to satisfy international lending agencies' demands that the Russian government reduce its budget deficit, thus sufficiently stabilizing the value of the ruble to qualify for the rescheduling of international debt and for additional new loans.

By December 1992, those who identified with the more moderate economic reforms advocated by Rutskoi and the other leaders of the Civic Union were influential enough to force Yeltsin into removing Gaidar as Prime Minister. An act of parliament stripped Yeltsin of his emergency powers to appoint an acting Prime Minister without the approval of the parliament. Yeltsin then nominated Viktor Chernomyrdin, closely tied to the state-owned industries and the moderate economic policies of the Civic Union, to become Prime Minister. Even though Chernomyrdin retained several of the reformers from Gaidar's cabinet, his selection by Yeltsin and approval by the Russian parliament seemed to signal the emerging political influence of the Civic Union, and indirectly Rutskoi, at the national level.

By 1993 the Civic Union had organized branches throughout Russia and was generally considered to be one of only three political organizations capable of running nationwide candidates in future elections and having membership and financial backing sufficient to mount national campaigns and to be termed real political parties. The other two were the Russian Communist Party and Democratic Russia.

The Russian Communist Party was re-legalized following a verdict of the Constitutional Court in November 1992. The verdict affirmed Yeltsin's nationalization of Communist party property and his outlawing of the party's national political organs in 1991 as an organized criminal syndicate, but it ruled unconstitutional his banning of the party as a voluntary organization and his prohibition of membership in it. The purported 600,000 members of the Russian Communist Party made it the single largest party in Russia in 1993. Russian Communists had good reason to believe that their candidates, in alliance with those of other socialist and social-democratic parties, could seriously compete for seats to the Russian parliament and local Russian offices in future elections. They had been buoyed by the results in national parliamentary elections in Lithuania in December 1992 and in Poland in September 1993. The former Communist parties in these countries, renamed as parties of the democratic left, had won a majority of seats to their parliaments and had become the ruling governments. Results in a few local Russian elections held in April and May 1993 only further confirmed the Communists' revived political respectability and influence. In openly contested and democratic elections, the voters in certain rural Russian locales had elected former Communist officials as heads of their provinces—in certain cases choosing them over wealthy local private businesspeople on the same ballot. The former Communist officials won because they promised to slow down the pace at which the local economies were being privatized and to increase spending for social welfare programs.

Democratic Russia was the amorphous mass movement that arose in early 1990 to sponsor anti-Communist reform candidates for republic and local offices in Russia. Since then it has generally supported Yeltsin and his more radical economic and political reforms and claims more than 200,000 members in branches through-out the country. The original founders of the movement were the leaders of the so-called Interregional Group, the coalition of the most liberal reformers in the nation-al Soviet parliament of 1989–1990. They and similar liberals in Communist research institutes split from Gorbachev because of his unwillingness to push economic and political reforms more rapidly and coherently. The problem with Democratic Russia is that it is not a true political party but a hodgepodge of voters' clubs, foundations, and publishing houses. It remains extremely questionable how many of its more than 200,000 nominally enrolled members would actively campaign for candidates in any future election solely because they had been endorsed by Democratic Russia. Financially, Democratic Russia, like many parties and movements in Russia, lacks the funds to sustain local organizations or pay staff. The movement has been very dependent on the funds donated to it by one of its original co-founders, the Russian international chess champion Garry Kasparov.

Democratic Russia, like all other Russian political parties, also confronts a major hurdle in the psychology of the Russian public. The Russian public tends to link any political party and its organizational activities with the despised former Communist party. All political parties are considered guilty by association by Russian voters, who lump their attempts to win office and mobilize citizen involvement with those of the former Communist party.

When Democratic Russia arose in 1990, it was unified by the enthusiastic oppo-sition of its leaders and volunteers to Communism and an authoritarian Soviet state. With the demise of both of these, the movement's unity and sense of purpose quickly dissipated into mean-spirited rivalries, petty ideological disputes, and per-sonal jealousies. Since 1991, Democratic Russia has been plagued with leadership conflicts that have resulted in its most prominent national figures disowning the movement and taking their own followers to form small splinter parties. For exam-ple, Gavriil Popov and Anatolii Sobchak, two of Democratic Russia's original co-founders, broke from the movement in June 1991 to found the Movement for Democratic Reforms, which by 1993 had emerged as a principal rival of Democratic Russia on the moderate democratic left of the Russian political spectrum.

One of the parties that allied to form the Civic Union in June 1992 was the Democratic Party of Russia, led by Nikolai Travkin. Travkin had been one of the co-founders of Democratic Russia in 1990, but quit in the fall of 1991 and formed his own political party, primarily because he felt the other leaders of the movement were jealous of him and his ambitions to run for Russian President in a future elec-tion. Democratic Russia wound up endorsing Yeltsin as President in June 1991, although Yeltsin himself is not a member of that or any other political party.

Travkin's party is purported to have 60,000 members, but many of the other splinter parties that have broken off from the larger political groups are nothing more than extensions of their politically ambitious leaders. In 1993 many could probably have held their annual party conferences in a Moscow phone booth. The high point for many was when their leaders were interviewed on Russian national television and radio for the first and last time, right after the parties had been formed and a few weeks before they quickly dissolved. Russians, who normally sus-pect all political parties, were hardly gaining any positive images to counter that suspicion from the transparent efforts of national politicians to form parties only to advance their own careers and to enhance their own power.

■ CRISIS OF RUSSIAN DEMOCRACY

The open violence on October 3 and 4, 1993 culminated months of a growing constitutional crisis between the executive and legislative branches. The crisis stemmed from the normal difficulties of transforming a parliament and presidency that originated under the authoritarian system of Soviet Communism into effective democratic institutions.

The difficulties escalated into a crisis because of the backgrounds and personalities of the political antagonists. After 1991, Yeltsin and many deputies in the parliament continued to reflect in their outlooks and behaviors the worst attributes of intolerance and ideological rigidity of Communist political culture. That culture tended to reduce all politics to a conflict between good and evil. It attributed all problems to consciously organized conspiracies and assumed that lurking behind the scenes were malign forces, against which extremism and violence were morally justified. Typified by the aphorism "He who is not with us is against us," the enemy mentality of Communist culture rejected appeals to reason, pragmatism, and tolerance as "intrigues" of those conspiratorial forces attempting to disarm or weaken their opponents.

Constitutional Crisis

The focus of the conflict in late 1992 was the kind of government to be embodied in a new post-Soviet Russian constitution. Yeltsin insisted that any new constitution would have to embody the principles of a strong presidential form of government, patterned in many ways after the French Fifth Republic. A majority of the Russian parliament insisted on their own draft of a new constitution, written by a commission nominally chaired by Yeltsin. Yeltsin had boycotted all sessions of the drafting commission, which had been established under his and the parliament's authority, because he rejected the draft version that was endorsed after more than a year of deliberation by a majority of the commission members. The draft constitution preferred by the parliamentary commission embodied principles of checks and balances and a separation of powers between the executive, legislative, and judicial branches, modeled after the U.S. Constitution.

Yeltsin's draft constitution had been written by his legal advisor, Sergei Shakhrai. Shakhrai's draft would have made the President the supreme political authority of the government. The President would appoint the Prime Minister, cabinet members, and many high judicial offices, subject to confirmation by the upper chamber (Federation Council) of the parliament (Federal Assembly), composed of deputies representing the eighty-nine administrative jurisdictions of the country. Under Yeltsin's proposed constitution, if the Federation Council rejected the President's nominee for Prime Minister, the President could dissolve the entire parliament and call for new elections. The President could also dissolve parliament if a "political impasse" between the President and parliament had arisen. The

President could suspend any legislation as being contrary to the Constitution, pending a final decision on a law's constitutionality by the Constitutional Court. Only the President and the ruling government under his authority—not the parliament—would be empowered to oversee foreign policy and propose bills involving taxation or expenditures.

A majority of the Russian parliament supported the draft adopted by its own commission. The terms of this draft provided for both a strong President as chief executive and a strong two-chambered parliament, still called the Supreme Soviet. Policy making and the dissolution of the parliament would have been prerogatives of the legislators themselves. The relative powers and rights of the two chambers of the Supreme Soviet would have been equal and separate from those of the President. The President would have primacy in the conduct of foreign and defense policy, and the parliament would control all matters involving taxation and economic expenditures. The commission's draft provided for a presidential veto over bills passed by the parliament, with the parliament having the power to override any veto on a second vote. The President would nominate cabinet members and federal judges, subject to their confirmation by both chambers of the Supreme Soviet. In the draft constitutions of both Yeltsin and the commission, the parliament and the President would be checked by an independent judiciary, capped by a reconstituted Constitutional Court with the authority to rule on the constitutionality of any actions by the other two branches of government.

The crisis escalated in the months preceding the Battle of Moscow. Under the standing Russian constitution, only the Russian Congress had the authority to ratify any new constitution or to designate alternative means to ratify it. In early 1993, Yeltsin and the parliament both threatened to go to the Russian voters through binding referenda, asking them to approve the principles and means of ratification for their respective drafts. Yeltsin wanted the Russian voters to approve a means to ratify a future constitution by national referendum, after it had been adopted by a nationally elected constituent assembly.

Yeltsin's political quandary was that, under the standing Russian constitution, only the Congress had the authority to initiate a national binding referendum. A majority of the parliament refused to approve a referendum on the constitution favored by Yeltsin and on a future means of ratifying any constitution that would have excluded them. Yeltsin remained so popular nationally that passage of such a referendum was almost assured. Even pro-Yeltsin legislators feared that direct ratification of Yeltsin's constitution by national referendum would have created the potential for his becoming a dictator.

In his spare time, Yeltsin may have been reading biographies of Charles de Gaulle, recounting that President's unconstitutional amendment of the French Constitution in 1962, bypassing the French parliament. Like de Gaulle, Yeltsin threatened to ignore the constitutional power of the Russian Congress and to hold a national referendum on his own under his presumed authority as President. The Russian Congress countered in December 1992 by voting to eliminate the special powers granted to Yeltsin in November 1991 to legislate a certain range of reforms by presidential decree and to appoint an acting Prime Minister and other top cabinet officers without the confirmation of the Supreme Soviet. The parliament only conceded to negotiate with Yeltsin on the language of specific questions on constitutional principles to be included in a referendum. The negotiations broke off by early March 1993, with both sides denouncing each other in the Russian media for having deliberately sabotaged them.

Yeltsin responded on March 20 with a TV address to the nation, declaring a state of presidential emergency rule to break the constitutional impasse. With the standing Russian constitution temporarily suspended by emergency rule, he intended to bypass the parliament and hold a national referendum on his draft constitution and a means other than the Russian Congress to ratify it. The declaration of emergency rule was quickly ruled unconstitutional by the Constitutional Court, and Yeltsin complied by rescinding it. He had already been under pressure to rescind it from some Western governments, concerned with the anti-democratic implications of his action.

The end of March found Yeltsin and the parliament still locked in a political standoff that had almost completely immobilized the national government. Each side continually threatened to depose each other; countermanding presidential decrees and parliamentary resolutions were issued to the executive departments and ministries in Moscow. Since the end of 1992, Khasbulatov had begun to organize and arm a special parliamentary militia to defend the White House against police and soldiers under the command of Yeltsin's Interior and Defense Ministers.

The crisis in Moscow had even spread to the Russian provinces and republics. Yeltsin and his parliamentary opposition attempted to outbid each other in courting political support among local officials. Both Yeltsin and the opposition promised grants of additional economic and political autonomy to the eighty-nine administrative jurisdictions and a dominant political role for them in any future parliament, if they would only throw their support behind one or the other draft constitution. Both Yeltsin and the opposition promised that the eighty-nine administrative jurisdictions would constitute the upper chamber of the national parliament. Each locale would elect two representatives to the upper chamber. Under Yeltsin's draft constitution, the upper chamber (Federation Council), not the lower chamber (called the State Duma), which would be elected by districts of equal population from throughout Russia, would have the power to approve the Prime Minister and cabinet.

As a consequence of the constitutional crisis, ethnic groups and others became further polarized as they were enticed to side with Yeltsin or the parliament. The promises of increased autonomy only encouraged those in the ethnic republics and rich economic regions who were pushing for complete independence of their jurisdictions from Russia. A weak Russian national government, divided between its President and parliament, was in effect mortgaging to the locales what little political authority it still had. In the process, Yeltsin and the parliamentary opposition were transforming Russia into a de facto confederation, if not unintentionally abetting its complete dismemberment.

Referendum of April 25, 1993

Yeltsin and the parliament eventually compromised in endorsing a binding referendum to be held April 25. The Russian voters were asked to vote on four questions, none of which had any bearing on the principles of a new constitution or the means to ratify it. The first two questions asked whether they approved Yeltsin's presidency and the course of policies instituted by him since 1991; the third and fourth whether they considered it necessary to call new presidential and parliamentary elections before those were required to be held in 1996 and 1995, respectively. Pro-Yeltsin volunteers canvassed neighborhoods the weeks before the referendum with placards urging Russians to vote "da, da, nyet, da" (yes, yes, no, yes) on the four referendum questions. Pro-Khasbulatov volunteers had their own placards, urging Russians to vote "nyet, nyet, da, nyet."

In November 1991, Yeltsin and the Russian Congress had agreed to suspend all national and local elections until December 1992. In December 1992, both sides approved extension of the moratorium on elections through 1993. It was feared that national and local elections would unduly politicize and divide the Russian public, delaying enactment of critical reforms required to prevent the entire collapse of the national economy. Under the 1991 moratorium, Yeltsin had been authorized by the Congress to appoint the chief administrators (called "heads") of all the fifty-eight nonautonomous administrative provinces and territories of the country. When Yeltsin threatened in March 1993 to declare emergency rule, the Congress revoked his power to appoint the heads of the administrative subdivisions and authorized their direct election. A few of the provinces that were politically allied with the Congress against Yeltsin took advantage of Congress's action and directly elected their local heads in April 1993. As we noted earlier, most of these were former Communist party leaders of these regions.

Given the continuing moratorium on any national elections, the April referendum was the first time Russians had been able to vote since their country's independence. Early forecasts had predicted that many Russians would boycott the referendum, turned off to politics in general by the endless bickering between Yeltsin and the parliament and by the drastic deterioration in their living conditions since

Table 35–1

Results of All-Russian Referendum of April 25, 1993

Subject of Referendum Question	Percentage of			
	All Registered Voters Who Voted	Those Voting Who Voted "Yes"	Those Voting Who Voted "No"	All Registered Voters Who Voted "Yes"
Confidence in President Yeltsin	64.18	58.67	39.20	37.65
Approval of Yeltsin's Socioeconomic Policy	64.08	53.05	44.56	33.99
Early Election of Russian President	64.08	49.49	30.21	31.71
Early Election of Russian Parliament	64.14	67.17	19.30	43.08

1991. On the contrary, 64 percent of all registered Russian voters showed up to vote in the first national election held since Yeltsin was chosen as Russian President on June 12, 1991, under the old Soviet state.

The results of the referendum are summarized in Table 35–1. Almost 59 percent approved Yeltsin's presidency—2 percent more than had voted for him as President. A surprising 53 percent voted in favor of his socioeconomic policy, despite hyperinflation having reduced the standard of living of as many as half of all Russians below the poverty line since 1991. Slightly less than a majority saw a necessity to call an early election for Russian president, but the largest majority on any of the four questions was the 67 percent who voted to dissolve the national parliament with new elections. Only 19 percent voted against holding early parliamentary elections, and the remaining 13 percent essentially abstained, either leaving their ballot blank or marking both "yes" and "no" on question four.

Since it had been a binding referendum, the Russian parliament should have been required to dissolve, but it was saved by a ruling of the Constitutional Court prior to April 25. The Court had ruled that an absolute majority of all registered Russian voters would have to approve the parliament's dissolution for the referendum to be considered constitutionally binding. The approximately 46 million voters advocating the dissolution of the parliament comprised only 43 percent of the more than 107 million registered voters in the country.

Polarization of Leadership

The constitutional crisis between Yeltsin and the parliament had been brewing since the collapse of the Soviet Union in December 1991. Yeltsin and those he had appointed to head the executive ministries of the government, under special emergency decree powers granted to him by the parliament in November 1991, had begun to institute radical and complete privatization of the Russian economy. With the exception of the 300–400 pro-Yeltsin deputies allied in the Coalition for Reform, the majority of the parliament opposed not the direction and goals of Yeltsin's government, but the speed at which it was attempting to make the changes in view of the negative consequences for many Russians.

A compromise could have been reached between the pro-Yeltsin deputies and the approximately 400 centrists to continue the reforms at a less rapid pace, but the remaining 400 deputies on the extreme political right (Russian nationalists) and the extreme political left (die-hard Communists) opposed any market reform and advocated restoration of a unified Soviet Union. Throughout 1992 and 1993, the differences between the radical reformists and the centrists hardened. As a result, the extremists were able to swing enough centrists to their side to pass key votes, reversing economic measures of the Yeltsin government and reducing Yeltsin's personal authority. The economic collapse of the country and the growing breakdown of central authority in many of its regions and republics fueled a sense of crisis in Moscow, which was favorable to the emerging extremist-centrist majority in the parliament.

With the two sides growing farther apart throughout 1992, Ruslan Khasbulatov increasingly distanced himself from Yeltsin and Yegor Gaidar, Yeltsin's acting Prime Minister. Khasbulatov's differences with Yeltsin were over both policy and power.

Khasbulatov, like the majority of the parliament, opposed the pace of economic reform by the Yeltsin-Gaidar government. On the issue of power, Khasbulatov began to defend his position as chair of the Russian parliament and the independent authority of the parliament for the same reason that had led Yeltsin himself as chair of the parliament in 1990–1991 to defy President Gorbachev and the central Soviet government. Yeltsin had defended the parliament against the encroachment of power by the executive branch of government personified by President Gorbachev. Two years later, Khasbulatov was defending the same parliament against the Russian President Yeltsin.

By early 1993, Rutskoi was widely assumed to be the most likely candidate to be nominated by the Civic Union to run against Yeltsin in the presidential election scheduled for June 1996. On March 20, 1993, Rutskoi denounced Yeltsin's threatened imposition of emergency rule to force his referendum to a vote by the Russian public. By May 1993, Rutskoi openly allied with Khasbulatov and the Russian parliament in opposing Yeltsin, who was pressuring the parliament to dissolve and call new elections following the overwhelming vote in favor of this alternative by Russian voters in the April referendum. By September, Yeltsin had taken away Rutskoi's personal automobile, guards, and other perquisites of his office as Vice-President, had put an armed guard around his office to prevent him from entering, and had issued a presidential decree—lacking any legal or constitutional force—removing him from office.

With the refusal of the parliament to dissolve itself after the referendum, the 300–400 pro-Yeltsin deputies stopped participating in sessions of the Congress and the Supreme Soviet. As a result of this boycott, the remaining deputies were even more dominated by the extremist Russian nationalists and Communists, who wanted to force an open political confrontation with Yeltsin and a struggle in the streets of Moscow. Both out of political necessity and because of their complete estrangement from Yeltsin, Khasbulatov and Rutskoi were forced to tie their political futures even more tightly to the more hard-line deputies in the parliament.

The hard-line deputies in turn were being egged on to take even more extremist actions by their violent followers in political organizations such as Working Moscow and the National Salvation Front. These organizations were continuously staging provocative demonstrations and inducing clashes with the Moscow police in hopes that the violence would escalate throughout the city and eventually force Yeltsin to resign from the presidency. The stage was set for the tragic events of October 3–4 and the Battle for Moscow, described at the start of this chapter. These events halted the progress toward democracy made in the first two years of Russia's independence.

■ ■ ■

Having devoted this chapter to developments in the largest of the post-Soviet countries, we turn in the next to an assessment of events in the other countries since 1991. Then we conclude this part with an analysis of the political situation in Russia after the Battle for Moscow, capped by the ratification of a new Russian constitution and election of a new Russian parliament on December 12, 1993.

36

Policy-Making Structures and Policy Alternatives in Central Eurasia

> There is no security, no stability, no law, no food, and no money. What do I need freedom for? If we have a choice only between anarchy and dictatorship, I choose dictatorship. Let a strong leader restore order.
>
> *Azerbaijani academic*
> Time *Magazine*
> *July 5, 1993*

Contradictory as political development in Russia has been since independence, the other fourteen countries in Central Eurasia have been no more able to progress consistently toward greater democracy. Five countries have actually regressed politically since 1991. In Uzbekistan and Turkmenistan, the former republic Communist party leaders—Islam Karimov and Saparmurad Niyazov—rule unchallenged as Presidents. Opposition parties have been banned, the media have been censored, and the public has been silenced by the secret police. In many ways, Uzbekistan's and Turkmenistan's political systems are even more autocratic than they had been as Communist republics of the Soviet Union.

In Tbilisi, the capital of Georgia, a national government under Eduard Shevardnadze, the chair of the State Council, existed in name only by the end of 1993. The separatist South Ossetians and Abkhazians effectively defeated or fought to a standoff the Georgian national army. They had fought in league with guerilla forces still loyal to the ousted Georgian president, Zviad Gamsakhurdia. Although Gamsakhurdia committed suicide in January 1994, his armed supporters still refused to surrender to the Georgian government and remained a continuing threat to Shevardnadze.

Tajikistan and Azerbaijan were also torn by ongoing civil wars that put both countries on the brink of disintegrating like Georgia or reverting to Communist autocracies like Uzbekistan and Turkmenistan. The origins and consequences of the civil wars in Tajikistan and Azerbaijan, summarized in the following section, are illustrative of all five countries' problems since independence.

■ *POLITICAL AUTOCRACIES: TAJIKISTAN AND AZERBAIJAN*

In Tajikistan and Azerbaijan, the civil wars (discussed in Chapters 31 and 33) have rendered the central governments and parliaments almost powerless to rule their countries or command very much authority outside of their capitals. The national governments have been taken over by mobs and armies in coups, instigated by the contending sides in these civil wars. By the fall of 1993, the weak national governments in Tajikistan and Azerbaijan had become little more than fronts for one side to legitimate the suppression and murder of the other.

Tajikistan

The deterioration of the national government in Tajikistan contrasts greatly with the hopeful beginning in 1990.[1] If nothing else, Tajikistan's nationalist movement had mutated into something of a consensual multiparty system. Four national political parties—Democratic Party, Rebirth Party, Islamic Renaissance Party, and Badakhshan Ruby Party—all opposed retention of Communist rule and commanded sizable support among the major ethnic and religious groups in the country. The problem was that all four parties had formed after the 1990 elections for the Tajik parliament, in which 94 percent of the deputies elected were hard-line and pro-Soviet Communist party members.

Things went quickly downhill politically after independence in Tajikistan. Directly elected as national President in November 1991 was Rakhmon Nabiev, the former Communist party leader of the Tajik republic. The four opposition parties shut out of the national parliament accused Nabiev and his followers of having rigged the election. They blamed his election on widespread vote fraud and on the biased pre-election coverage by the Communist-run state television and radio stations in the capital Dushanbe. Nabiev did make an indirect overture to the four opposition parties. The individual he appointed Prime Minister gave the four parties one-third of the positions in a national coalition government formed in May 1992.

Nabiev's overture, however, was rebuffed by the more hard-line Communists in the parliament and by the ruling Communist political establishment in the northern Tajik province of Leninabad. The Leninabad Communist political establishment had run Tajikistan throughout the Soviet era and still controlled the levers of political power behind the scenes in Dushanbe. With the outbreak of the civil war between the northern and southern provinces, ideologically a clash between secular Communists and Islamic democrats, Nabiev's attempts at reconciliation with the four opposing parties collapsed in September 1992.

---

[1]The generalizations about Tajikistan in this section are based on Keith Martin, "Tajikistan: Civil War without End?" *RFE/RL Research Report*, vol. 2, no. 33 (August 20, 1993), pp. 18–29, and *Human Rights and Democratization in the Newly Independent Countries of the Former Soviet Union*, compiled by the staff of the Commission on Security and Cooperation in Europe, U.S. Congress (Washington, D.C.: U.S. Government Printing Office, 1993), pp. 222–232.

Nabiev was forced to resign by armed mobs in Dushanbe, who kidnapped fifty senior government officials. The mobs captured Nabiev at the airport trying to flee the capital and threatened to kill him if he didn't step down as President. The national parliament reacted by eliminating the office of President. Under the dictate of the Leninabad Communist establishment, the parliament reconvened in Leninabad's capital in November 1992 and elected Imomali Rakhmonov chair of the parliament and head of state.

Rakhmonov's first action was to ban the four anti-Communist opposition parties, some of whose members joined forces with those waging civil war in southern Tajikistan against the continuing domination of the country by the Leninabad Communists. The national government of Rakhmonov and the hard-line Communist majority in the parliament became almost completely dependent for political survival on the Leninabad Communist establishment and on the contingents of soldiers on loan from the governments of Uzbekistan and Russia. The Uzbek and Russian soldiers and their airplanes have been employed by the government in Dushanbe in attacks on outposts of the Islamic democrats.

Rakhmonov was widely assumed to be a protégé of Sangak Safarov, a local warlord in southern Tajikistan. Safarov had been a notorious bank robber and local bandit leader. Since 1991 his gangs have plundered and terrorized villages in southern Tajik provinces at will, on the payroll and under the orders of the government in Dushanbe. The government has employed Safarov and his gangs to intimidate the southern villages to prevent them from joining the Islamic democrats in waging civil war against the Communist-dominated national government. As the political front man for the Leninabad establishment and warlords such as Safarov, Rakhmonov has appointed members of both groups to all the top positions in his government ministries and integrated Safarov's irregulars into the Tajik national armed forces.

Since Rakhmonov has banned all opposition political parties, his major rival is Ali Akhbar Turadzhonzoda, the leader of the Islamic-democratic southerners. Turadzhonzoda, the supreme religious authority (*kazikalon*) of all Muslims in Tajikistan, has formed a government-in-exile, across the border in Afghanistan. His government claims to be the legitimate national government of Tajikistan. Turadzhonzoda directs the anti-government southerners, who are armed by local military commanders in Afghanistan and effectively control most of southeast Tajikistan as an autonomous region in the Pamir Mountains.

By the fall of 1993, clashes between Russian soldiers defending the Dushanbe government and Afghan soldiers allied with Turadzhonzoda had become almost daily occurences along Tajikistan's southwest border with Afghanistan. Since 1991, the human toll from the almost complete breakdown in any legitimate civilian authority due to the civil war has been an estimated 50,000 killed, countless more terrorized by warlords such as Safarov, and hundreds of thousands driven from their homes by the fighting.

Azerbaijan

In Azerbaijan by 1994, the six-year civil war waged by Armenians in the province of Nagorno-Karabakh seeking to reunite with Armenia produced a lawless state similar to that in Tajikistan.[2] Mobs and military coups have dictated the choice of the national leadership and ruling government in the capital of Baku.

Since 1991, Azerbaijan has had three different Presidents. The first was Ayaz Mutalibov, the former Communist party leader of the republic, who was forced to resign in March 1992 after protesting mobs in the streets of Baku had surrounded the parliament building. The bloodless coup by the mobs was instigated and led by the Azerbaijani Popular Front. The second President was Abulfaz Elchibey, a dissident historian and leader of the Popular Front, directly elected on June 7, 1992, when he easily defeated four other contenders with over 90 percent of the vote. He was forced to flee Baku on June 17, 1993 under threat of a military coup led by 32-year-old Surat Guseinov.

Guseinov was the director of a state wool mill, who had recruited and equipped his own private army to fight the Armenians in Nagorno-Karabakh. He financed this army with a fortune he had amassed since 1990 selling textiles for hard currency to Turkey. In the summer of 1992, Elchibey had appointed Guseinov, with his private army, as the plenipotentiary military and political leader of Nagorno-Karabakh. By February 1993, all of Nagorno-Karabakh and several outlying provinces of Azerbaijan had fallen under the control of the Armenian Karabakhs and a force made up of the invading Armenian national army and Armenian mercenaries. Elchibey dismissed Guseinov as plenipotentiary, expelling him from the Popular Front and charging him with intending to overthrow the national government by a military coup. Refusing to accept responsibility for his military defeats or his dismissal, Guseinov began to lead his private army in a march on Baku, demanding Elchibey's resignation and his own election by the parliament as Azerbaijan's President.

The third President, Geidar Aliyev, was the former head of the Azerbaijan KGB and Communist party from 1969 to 1982, a close personal friend of the late Soviet Communist leader, Leonid Brezhnev, and mentioned previously for his brutality and corruption. Aliyev had rebounded from political obscurity to win election as chair of the parliament and acting President on June 19, 1993, following Elchibey's flight from the capital, for three reasons. First, he was not Elchibey. Aliyev had organized the most popular political party (New Azerbaijan) in the country. By May 1993, the Popular Front had become entirely disillusioned with the incompetency and corruption of Elchibey's government and was seeking a new national figure who could mobilize the population against Armenia. Second, Aliyev was trusted and endorsed by Russian officials in Moscow. If Aliyev were elected, those officials implied that they would intervene diplomatically or militarily to stop the Armenian invasion of the country. And, third, Aliyev was not Guseinov. In June 1993, Guseinov had brought his private army to the outskirts of Baku and was threatening to invade the capital and take over the entire national government by force. Aliyev alone had the authority, due to his

---

[2]The generalizations about Azerbaijan in this section are based on Elizabeth Fuller, "Azerbaijan's June Revolution," *RFE/RL Research Report,* vol. 2, no. 32 (August 13, 1993), pp. 24–29, and *Human Rights and Democratization,* pp. 109–122.

national party and the endorsement of Russian officials in Moscow, needed to stand up to Guseinov.

To placate Guseinov, Aliyev appointed him Prime Minister. To consolidate his own power, Aliyev then arrested and jailed the most prominent leaders of the Popular Front. The parliament (called the National Assembly) that elected Aliyev as chair and acting President was itself created by the Popular Front in May 1992, following its coup against President Mutalibov. The Popular Front had simply dissolved the previous national parliament (called the Supreme Soviet) elected in 1990 and designated fifty pro-Front deputies to be the National Assembly. Despite Elchibey's promises, no national parliamentary elections had been held prior to his own forced ouster as President in June 1993.

Aliyev and Guseinov tenuously lead a country in which over 10 percent of the population have been driven from their homes by Armenian Karabakhs, the Armenian national army, and Armenian mercenaries, who control the western half of Azerbaijan. The first major government policy instituted by Aliyev and Guseinov was to install military roadblocks on the highways leading into Baku to prevent more than 1 million Azerbaijani refugees from flooding into the capital. On October 3, 1993, Aliyev was directly elected President of Azerbaijan in true Soviet Communist fashion. According to official published results, 98.8 percent of all Azerbaijanis voted for Aliyev, who trounced two other nominal candidates in an election characterized by Western human rights observers as undemocratic and staged.

■ TRANSITIONAL DEMOCRACIES: UKRAINE

Tajikistan and Azerbaijan represent one extreme of lawless states, but national governments in Armenia, Belarus, Estonia, Kazakhstan, Kyrgyzstan, Latvia, Lithuania, Moldova, and Ukraine show the beginning signs of political transition toward democracy. Like Russia, all have adopted features of a mixed presidential and parliamentary system, in many ways similar to France under the Fifth Republic. The head of state (President or chair of the parliament) oversees foreign and defense policy and appoints the head of government (Prime Minister) and the cabinet. The parliament has some limited authority to hold the ruling government accountable through votes of no confidence, forcing the resignation of the Prime Minister and cabinet. Legislation includes both laws passed by the parliament and decrees issued by the heads of state and government. The parliaments have granted the heads of state and government special emergency powers to institute economic reforms by decree without the requirement of having the reforms passed as parliamentary laws.

As in Russia, the foundations of democracy have evolved in all nine countries. Factions and coalitions influence the legislative process in their parliaments, parliaments challenge the authority of the heads of state and government, political parties have formed in their societies, and the executive and legislative branches of government have gradually adapted to interacting with each other along the lines of certain constitutional procedures and rules. In 1992 or 1993 the three Baltic states of Lithuania, Latvia, and Estonia successfully held their first post-Soviet national elections, freely contested by political parties. The incumbent heads of government in all three countries lost the elections, but gave up their leadership positions to those who won, thus effecting a peaceful transfer of power—a critical stage in the transition to democratic governance.

Democratic political change in all nine countries has advanced and receded, often stalling for the same reasons that led to the dramatic violence in Moscow in October 1993. Among the nine countries, the closest parallel to Russia—although without the violent confrontation in its capital—has been Ukraine. In Ukraine, the national parliament and President have been deadlocked since independence over economic reforms and foreign policy. As in Russia, they have been unable to overcome their differences to adopt a post-Communist Ukrainian constitution or even to hold local and parliamentary elections since independence.

The Foundations of Ukrainian Democracy

The first year of independence for Ukraine began with a democratic turning point. Recall that Ukraine had brought about the end of the Soviet Union on December 1, 1991, when over 90 percent of all Ukrainian voters had approved in a referendum independence and statehood for their republic.[3] With this development, Yeltsin hastily convened the meeting with the leaders of Ukraine and Belarus the next week to draft and sign their collective declaration officially dissolving the Soviet Union.

On the same ballot, 62 percent had elected Leonid Kravchuk to a five-year term as the first President of Ukraine. Kravchuk's margin of victory even exceeded Yeltsin's in his direct election as Russian President in June 1991, and Kravchuk had won over four candidates, two of whom had been nominated by wings of *Rukh*, the umbrella organization uniting all of the various Ukrainian nationalists and anti-Communists. Like Yeltsin, Kravchuk was a former career Communist party official whose public image had dramatically changed by 1991. As chair of the Ukrainian republic parliament in 1990–1991, Kravchuk had outspokenly embraced anti-Soviet and anti-Communist positions. He had advocated the economic and political sovereignty of Ukraine. He had criticized the crackdown of the Soviet military in Latvia and Lithuania in January 1991. And he had appointed a constitutional commission to draft a new democratic constitution for the republic.

Kravchuk won as President for two reasons. First, he was the most popular candidate. His popularity stemmed from his advocacy of statehood for the republic and from his conversion to nationalistic and democratic ideals after a career as a Communist official. For many voters, his conversion implied less opportunism than pragmatism, a trait valued in someone to be entrusted with so much authority as the first Ukrainian President. Second, his pragmatic image contrasted with that of the two candidates running against him from *Rukh*, who managed to frighten some of the 11.3 million ethnic Russians and 5 million Russophones (Ukrainians, Jews,

---

[3]The generalizations about Ukraine in this section are based on Roman Solchanyk, "Ukraine: A Year of Transition," *RFE/RL Research Report,* vol. 2, no. 1 (January 1, 1993), pp. 58–63, and *Human Rights and Democratization,* pp. 50–75.

and others who spoke Russian as their first language) with the highly Ukrainian nationalistic tenor of that umbrella organization. Ethnic Russians and Russophones feared a *Rukh* presidency would impose requirements for Ukrainian-language use in schools and otherwise institute policies discriminatory against non-Ukrainians. Although Kravchuk was an ethnic Ukrainian, who since 1991 spoke publicly only in the Ukrainian language despite his fluency in Russian, he was clearly by temperament not a radical Ukrainian nationalist.

The euphoria of independence and the broad public mandate for Kravchuk did not last longer than the summer of 1992. One problem confronting Kravchuk, as it had Yeltsin in Russia, was that the Ukrainian parliament had been elected in March 1990. Like the two-tiered Russian parliament (Congress and Supreme Soviet), the single-chamber Ukrainian Supreme Council responsible for legislating democratic and economic reforms under Kravchuk's aegis in 1992 contained a sizable bloc of hard-line former Communist party officials and state managers associated with the Ukrainian military-industrial complex. This so-called Bloc of 239 (among the 450 deputies in the Supreme Council) generally opposed any radical reforms to denationalize state factories and privatize land ownership. Although the Bloc of 239 lacked the unity to defeat reform legislation, the remaining 211 Ukrainian deputies quickly split into several factions and caucuses, unable to agree on the kinds of reforms and the pace at which they should be implemented.

The factions and caucuses in the parliament reflected the ideological and political differences that had already emerged in Ukrainian civil society by 1992. There were fifteen national registered political parties, at least twenty-one unregistered parties, and hundreds of political organizations and mass movements. The Ukrainian multiparty system in its infancy has experienced continuous change and realignment. Moderate and radical factions of the political parties, led by nationally prominent and ambitious leaders, are constantly splitting off and forming new coalition parties. Ukrainian political pluralism evolved out of the civic activeness aroused by *Rukh*, the umbrella Ukrainian nationalist organization founded in 1989, which prior to independence had organized and led the mass movement against the Ukrainian Communist autocracy and against Ukraine's inclusion in a Soviet Union.

The various Ukrainian political parties and movements cluster into four ideological blocs:

1. *National democratic*—*Rukh* and political parties spun off by former leaders of *Rukh*
2. *Mainstream democratic*—social-democratic parties, the Green party, and several party coalitions such as New Ukraine, which unite liberal former Communist officials and former *Rukh* leaders
3. *Radical nationalist*—parties and movements spun off from the nationalist wing of *Rukh,* including coalitions such as the Ukrainian National Front, which has ties to fascist-racist parties in Europe
4. *Radical leftist*—socialist and communist, headed by the Ukrainian Socialist Party as the acknowledged successor to the Ukrainian Communist party, which was banned in 1991 and only re-legalized in late 1993

The four blocs differ both among themselves and between parties and factions within each bloc on the three overriding and interconnected issues of Ukrainian politics since independence: Kravchuk, Russia, and reform.

By 1993, *Rukh* remained the largest mass political organization in Ukraine, with 150,000 full and associate members. National in the scope of its support and membership, *Rukh* is especially popular in the central Ukrainian regions contiguous to the capital of Kiev and in the western regions annexed at the end of World War II. Like the Russian Communist party by 1993, the Ukrainian Socialist Party was the single largest party—as distinct from mass organization—by actual membership. Ethnic Russians from the southeastern coal-mining regions of Ukraine account for the largest number of Socialist Party members and those who support various parties in the radical leftist bloc.

Especially in the national democratic and radical nationalist blocs, some parties and movements completely distrust Kravchuk because of his background as a Communist official and his tendency to appoint many former Communist officials to presidential staff and cabinet positions. They believe that Ukraine's real independence will not be achieved until a new constitution is adopted and elections are held for both the parliament and the presidency. Without a new constitution and elections, they contend that the old Communist establishment—through Kravchuk and the Bloc of 239 in the Ukrainian parliament—still in effect controls political power in the country.

Other parties and leaders support Kravchuk as a necessary evil of the first stage of transition toward democracy. They view Kravchuk as a nation builder and a state builder. For them, he is a strong political leader with the instincts and skills to unite the nation, to institute market reforms and democratic changes, including adoption of a new constitution, and to defend the country's national interests with Russia and Western countries. Kravchuk responded by appointing several of the leaders from the mainstream democratic bloc to the State Council in 1992–1993. These appointees included some who, as former leaders of *Rukh*, had been among Kravchuk's harshest critics and political opponents a short time before. The members of the State Council meet weekly with Kravchuk as a consultative cabinet, advising him on the course of actions that he should undertake as President. At times in 1992 and 1993, Kravchuk attempted to elevate the status of the State Council as a decision-making body above that of the cabinet under his own Prime Minister.

On foreign policy, political parties and movements have split over the fundamental issue of Ukraine's relations with Russia. Some question whether even a Russia led by Yeltsin will accept Ukraine's independence as a country. They accuse the Russian government of economic imperialism and political blackmail against Ukraine, designed to force the collapse of the Ukrainian government and the reannexation of Ukraine into a single state under Russia. They have strongly resisted turning over to Russia any nuclear missiles or any portion of the formerly Soviet Black Sea fleet ported in the Crimea.

They also charge the Russian government and military with instigating separatist movements in Ukrainian regions that have large ethnic Russian populations (Crimea and Donetsk) and among Russians in the breakaway Transdniester republic in Moldova on Ukraine's southwestern border. They believe the Russian government finances and aids the separatist movements to weaken the national Ukrainian government and to effect the demise of the country. The radical Ukrainian nationalists have been the most bitter in their attacks on Russia as the major threat to Ukraine. Their paramilitary organizations have provoked clashes between ethnic Russians and Ukrainians in various parts of the country.

On the other side are those, mostly in the mainstream democratic bloc, who argue for pragmatism in Ukraine's relations with Russia and an acceptance of Ukraine's ineluctable ties to Russia. They contend that Ukraine cannot survive as an independent country without reintegrating its economy with Russia through some form of economic confederation. Almost all Ukrainian industry and agriculture remain vitally dependent on supplies and markets in Russia. The proposed confederation, forging a common market under the auspices of the Commonwealth of Independent States, would be modeled after the economic linkages uniting the twelve independent countries of the EC. This side considers the anti-Russia sentiments of its opponents economically suicidal, politically paranoid, and militarily provocative. In turn, the radical Ukrainian nationalist opponents view the advocacy of an economic union with Russia in a confederation as a betrayal of the Ukrainian nation, equivalent to outright treason.

As a consequence, Kravchuk and his first Prime Minister in 1992, Vitol'd Fokin, lacked a clear majority in the Ukrainian parliament for economic or foreign policies. Their bills had to be compromised to meet the divergent positions among reformist factions and those in the Bloc of 239. In Russia, Yeltsin had already begun to institute comprehensive market reforms on January 1, 1992, with the special authority to legislate through presidential decree granted him by the Russian Congress. Kravchuk did not receive the equivalent authority from his parliament to legislate economic reforms by presidential decree or through decrees of his appointed Prime Minister until November 1992.

In the interim, while Yeltsin's decrees were creating a private sector of farms, factories, and commercial outlets, which accounted for 10–15 percent of the Russian economy by 1993, very little of Ukraine's state-owned and state-run economy was privatized in the first two years of independence. Without any private sector, the Ukrainian economy collapsed into both hyperinflation and widespread shortages far worse than in the other countries. The worse conditions became in Ukraine, the more Kravchuk, Fokin, and a majority of the Ukrainian parliament vacillated on whether to denationalize state industries and privatize agriculture. The longer they delayed reforms, the more reluctant they became to make them, fearing it would set the economy into a complete tailspin, with millions of Ukrainians losing their jobs from the closing of unprofitable state factories and farms.

In the Ukrainian parliament, the opposition was united in blaming Kravchuk and Fokin for the country's economic woes. In late September 1992, Kravchuk removed Fokin as Prime Minister on the eve of a vote of no confidence in the entire ruling government by the Ukrainian parliament. In his place, Kravchuk appointed Leonid Kuchma, the director of one of the largest state-run defense factories in Ukraine. Despite Kuchma's promise to privatize the Ukrainian economy, his career as a state manager in the defense sector raised serious questions about the degree of his commitment to do so. Under the standing Ukrainian constitution, Kuchma had to be approved as Prime Minister by a majority of the Ukrainian parliament. Those who voted for him in the Ukrainian parliament were just as ambivalent over whether and how quickly the Ukrainian economy could be denationalized.

A Political Impasse

By late summer of 1993, little had changed under the Kuchma government, and the Ukrainian economy further deteriorated. Kravchuk blamed the parliament for not really wanting comprehensive market reforms. The parliament blamed Kravchuk for lack of leadership in appointing as Prime Minister someone ambivalent about market reforms. Kuchma blamed Kravchuk for undermining his authority and blamed the parliament for blocking all of his attempts to institute reforms gradually. In politics "Ukrainian style," Kuchma resigned as Prime Minister, only to have Kravchuk refuse to accept his resignation and the parliament vote against it. By the end of September 1993, Kuchma had again submitted his resignation. This time, Kravchuk accepted it, but followed up by issuing a presidential decree that eliminated the position of Prime Minister and assuming for himself all powers as the head of government.

The deadlock in the national government and the conflict over Kravchuk, foreign policy, and economic reform have stalled Ukrainian political development. Parallels to Russia in the spring of 1993 are striking.

Despite the appointment of a constitutional commission in 1990, Ukraine still has no new constitution. The national government functions under powers of the parliament and President added as amendments to the Ukrainian republic constitution adopted in 1978. The constitutional commission has been deadlocked over the issue of federalism. Strong sentiment exists for making Ukraine a federation, with the twenty-five regions of the country being sovereign states. Those favoring Ukrainian federalism contend that only strong local state governments in a federal system like that of Germany or the United States can prevent the national government in Kiev from reverting to authoritarianism.

There is just as strong support on the commission and among prominent Ukrainian officials for keeping Ukraine as a unitary state under a new constitution. Kravchuk, who ran for President in 1991 on a platform vaguely endorsing a form of limited federalism for Ukraine, has since become a strong defender of the unitary state. Kravchuk, commission members, and others favor a centralized unitary state because they fear that a federation would lead to the country's dismemberment. They assume that under a federation, Ukrainian regions bordering Russia that have large ethnic Russian populations would be clandestinely encouraged by the Russian government to declare their complete independence from Ukraine and be incorporated into the Russian Federation.

No national or local elections have been held in Ukraine since independence. Kravchuk and the parliament approved an election moratorium after independence for the same reason Yeltsin and the Russian Congress suspended elections. Kravchuk and the parliament feared that elections would only further polarize a

Ukrainian society and set back any momentum to implement market reforms, which were likely to increase unemployment and economic suffering over the next few years.

Like Yeltsin in Russia, Kravchuk was authorized by his parliament to appoint plenipotentiaries ("presidential representatives") to administer all of the twenty-five Ukrainian provinces. The presidential representatives are unaccountable to the populations in these jurisdictions but empowered to override decisions of the regional councils that were elected in 1990. Several appointed by Kravchuk to these positions were formerly Communist party or state officials from these regions. Their appointment only confirmed the belief among those in the national democratic and radical nationalist blocs that Kravchuk remains at heart a Communist and that through him the former Ukrainian Communist establishment still rules the country behind the scenes.

Like President Yeltsin, who found himself locked in political crisis with his own Vice-President and chair of the Russian parliament, by the fall of 1993 Kravchuk had become embroiled with a majority of his parliament and his Foreign and Defense Ministers. In September 1993 Kravchuk agreed at a meeting with Yeltsin in the Crimea to transfer Ukraine's nuclear weapons to Russia and to give up Ukraine's share of the Black Sea fleet to Russia. In return, Yeltsin agreed to forgive billions owed to Russian state firms by Ukrainian firms and to count the Black Sea fleet as Ukraine's down payment for the cost of gas and oil shipped to it from Russian refineries.

The Ukrainian parliament passed resolutions disavowing the agreements, and Kravchuk's own Foreign Minister repudiated them publicly. Kravchuk's Defense Minister was forced to resign by the parliament in early October 1993, both because he supported Kravchuk's agreement to give up nuclear weapons and because he opposed Ukraine's military cooperation with other CIS countries. Kravchuk's inability to control his own foreign and defense ministries and follow through on his own agreements not only undermined his own authority, it worsened relations between Ukraine and the United States. The U.S. government has criticized the Ukrainian government for reneging on its pledge to turn over its nuclear missiles to Russia.

The U.S. government was already greatly displeased with the failure of the Ukrainian parliament to ratify nuclear-arms reduction treaties signed by Gorbachev as the head of the Soviet Union in 1991. Under international law, the treaties cannot go into effect unless all four nuclear states of the former Soviet Union—Russia, Kazakhstan, Belarus, and Ukraine—ratify them. The United States is vital to Ukraine's economic future because it is a key participant in and greatly influences the other nations in the international lending agencies that finance loans to Ukraine.

By the fall of 1993, journalists in Kiev reported a mounting sense of isolation, desperation, and crisis among the top leaders at the national level in Ukraine, topped by the fear of being cut off from international loans by the United States. The Ukrainian parliament and Kravchuk's own ministers were rebelling against him and giving him little room to negotiate with the West or to reform the economy. Feelings of isolation, desperation, and crisis felt by national leaders in Russia and Central Eurasia since 1991 all too often have led to the imposition of emergency rule and the justification of anti-democratic measures. An overview of Ukraine by a commission of the U.S. Congress in 1993 concluded:

> A state based on the rule of law has yet to be firmly rooted . . . Totalitarianism has passed in Ukraine; it is not yet clear whether authoritarianism has as well. Ukraine is not the oppressed country it was under Soviet domination. Neither is it by any means a full-fledged democracy.[4]

To the credit of both Kravchuk and the Ukrainian parliament, common sense has appeared to prevail. With inflation increasing at more than 100 percent monthly and with an estimated 85 percent of the Ukrainian population living below the poverty level, the political impasse was threatening the very survivability of Ukraine as a country. To break the impasse, both sides agreed in November 1993 to dissolve the parliament and to elect a new legislature from single-member districts in March 1994. A national presidential election would also be held in June 1994. The parliamentary election would occur one year before and the presidential election would occur two years before required under the standing Soviet-era Ukrainian constitution. Both sides hoped that a newly elected parliament and President would have a public mandate to adopt a new constitution and to legislate a coherent program of political and economic reforms for the country.

■ CONCLUSION: A KIND OF RUSSIAN DEMOCRACY

One month after the storming of the Russian parliament building (described in Chapter 35) and two years after the demise of the Soviet Union, people were again crowding into Moscow's Red Square in the first week of November 1993.[5] A decade before they would have been there anticipating the upcoming national holiday of the Bolshevik Revolution of 1917, held every November 7 throughout the country. A decade ago, the November 7th celebration would have been crowned nationally with a parade in Moscow, past the mausoleum on Red Square containing the embalmed corpse of Lenin inside its walled enclosure. The marchers streaming through Red Square would have been saluted by all of the Communist party's Politburo members standing atop the mausoleum.

In 1993, the people had not come to commemorate the Bolshevik Revolution or to pay homage to Lenin. A week after crushing the early October rebellion of the hard-line Communists and Russian nationalists, Boris Yeltsin had ordered the military honor guard removed from Lenin's mausoleum and the entrance to Lenin's tomb sealed as the last remaining vestige of the former Communist system. The people in Red Square in 1993 were asking passers-by to sign petitions to place polit-

---

[4]*Human Rights and Democratization,* p. 75.

[5]The following generalizations about the election campaign in Russia are based partly on Serge Schmemann, "Russians Scramble to Fill an Unformed Parliament," *The New York Times,* November 1, 1993, p. A3.

ical parties and candidates on the ballot for the election of a new national Russian parliament.

On December 12, Russians would elect deputies to both chambers of a new national parliament called the Federal Assembly. The scene in Red Square was being played out throughout Russia, as the political parties rushed to gather 100,000 names from seven of the eighty-nine Russian administrative-geographical subdivisions (republics, provinces, territories) in order to be placed on the national electoral list for the lower chamber of the Federal Assembly. The deadline to register their parties and coalitions, set by the national electoral commission, was November 7.

On December 12, voters were to elect 450 deputies to the lower chamber of the Assembly, called the State Duma. Russian voters elected the Duma deputies by a hybrid voting procedure of direct and proportional representation, similar to the manner in which deputies to the German Bundestag have been elected since 1949. On one ballot would be included a list of individual names, and on a second ballot a list of political parties. Like Germans, Russians voted twice—on the first ballot for the candidate to represent their district and on the second ballot for the political party or party bloc they preferred.

Half of the 450 seats would go to the candidates winning the most votes in each district. For the election Russia had been divided into 225 districts of approximately 500,000 voters. To qualify, candidates needed the signatures of approximately 10 percent of the eligible voters in their district. The petitions with the signatures had to be submitted to the electoral districts no later than November 15. The other 225 seats in the Duma would be distributed proportionately to those parties or blocs receiving at least 5 percent of the national vote on the second, or party-list, ballot. Only parties that met the November 7th deadline for registering with 100,000 signatures collected in at least seven of the eighty-nine Russian administrative-geographical subdivisions would qualify to have their names included on the party-list ballot for the State Duma.

On December 12, Russians would also elect the 178 deputies to the upper chamber of the Federal Assembly, called the Federation Council. Two members were to be directly elected from each of the eighty-nine Russian administrative-geographical subdivisions. Candidates for the Federation Council needed the signatures of at least 1 percent of eligible voters in their subdivision, and the petitions had to be submitted to their local electoral commission by the same November 7th deadline. Thus, Russian voters would be given three separate ballots before entering the booths on December 12: one with the candidates for the two seats to the Federation Council from their administrative-geographical subdivision; the second with the candidates for the individually contested seat in the State Duma; and the third with the list of political parties and party blocs for the party-list seats proportionally distributed in the State Duma.

For the election to be considered valid, a minimum of two registered candidates had to qualify in contesting each of the 225 single-mandate seats for the State Duma. A minimum of three registered candidates had to qualify for the election to be held in any of the eighty-nine constituencies of the Federation Council. If an area failed to meet the November 15th and November 7th deadlines for registering at least two candidates for the State Duma or three candidates for the Federation Council, the election would be postponed until March 1994. At that time, a special election among the total number of candidates who had registered would be held.

By midnight on November 19, the Russian Central Electoral Commission reported that a total of slightly over 2,000 candidates had been registered to run for the Federal Assembly. Of these, 490 were slated to contest one of the seats in the upper chamber of the Federation Council and 1,567 to contest one of the single-mandate seats constituting half of the 450 seats in the lower chamber of the State Duma. Elections to two Russian administrative subdivisions for the Federation Council and one State Duma district were postponed until March 1994 because an insufficient number of candidates had registered for each before the deadline.

Thirteen parties and party bloc coalitions wound up qualifying for the party-list ballot for the State Duma. The number was surprising for three reasons. First, only 7 percent of all Russians even belonged to a political party or political organization. Second, a number of political parties had been permanently or temporarily banned by President Yeltsin in the two weeks of emergency rule that he had imposed after October 4. Third, the actual electoral rules on the composition of the two chambers and the procedures to register candidates and political parties had been drafted and published in the third week of October as edicts of President Yeltsin. In the three weeks given to qualify for the three ballots, candidates and political parties had to scramble to collect the necessary number of signatures on their petitions before their deadlines. Political parties and party coalitions had hastily convened conferences in the last week of October to adopt policy platforms and to select the individuals and their order for the party-list ballot.

Despite these complications, four reformist party coalitions on the political left had qualified and were expected to garner the largest number of seats to both the Federation Council and the State Duma. All four were expected to prevail, not so much because of public support for their hastily written programs and platforms than because of public recognition of their leaders by most Russian voters. Their leaders—Yegor Gaidar, Sergei Shakhrai, Anatolii Sobchak, Gavriil Popov, and Grigorii Yavlinskii—were the five most nationally prominent post-Communist politicians among democratic reformists and potential future candidates for Russian President. Many Russians viewed skeptically these leaders' political parties, which differed little ideologically and shared a common advocacy of democratic and market reforms, as attempts to create national organizations to support likely future runs for the Russian presidency in 1995 or 1996.

The front-running party coalition was Russia's Choice. It was led by several top ministers of the Yeltsin government under Yeltsin's former Prime Minister and recently reapppointed First Deputy Prime Minister, Yegor Gaidar. With the high name-visibility of its leading candidates among the Russian voters, Russia's Choice was expected to win a plurality of seats in the State Duma.

Its major rivals among the democratic reformist parties were the Russian Party of Unity and Accord and the Movement for Democratic Reforms. Unity and Accord was led by Deputy Prime Minister and Yeltsin confidant, Sergei Shakhrai. The one distinctive position of Shakhrai's party was its advocacy of devolving more powers to the eighty-nine administrative subdivisions in a reconstituted Russian Federation. The Movement, formed in 1991 by political liberals who had quit the Communist party, was led by a triumvirate: Anatolii Sobchak, the mayor of St. Petersburg; Gavriil Popov, the former mayor of Moscow and current chair of the party; and Aleksandr Yakovlev, the former close confidant of Gorbachev and architect of many of his perestroika reforms in 1985–1991.

The fourth democratic reformist coalition on the ballot—the Yavlinskii-Boldyrev-Lukin party bloc—was named after its three founders (and renamed Apple for the ballot). Yurii Boldyrev had been director of the Control Administration for Russian locales under President Yeltsin until the spring of 1993, when he was fired for criticizing Yeltsin's actions and his tendency to make decisions in an authoritarian manner. Vladimir Lukin was the Russian ambassador to the United States and a career diplomat, who had not been reluctant to criticize the Yeltsin-Gaidar market reforms publicly before American audiences and journalists. The actual leader and founder of this ad-hoc party coalition was Grigorii Yavlinskii. Yavlinskii had been the architect of the 500 days program to transform the Soviet command economy, which was aborted by Gorbachev in 1991. Since Russian independence, Yavlinskii had held no official political offices under President Yeltsin, and ironically benefited from not being associated with any of the policies and programs of Yeltsin's government over those two years. Public opinion polls rated him among the most popular political figures in Russia and a prime candidate for Russian President, if Yeltsin followed through with his pledge to schedule the election on June 12, 1995, a year earlier than required. Yavlinskii and Yegor Gaidar had belonged to the same Republican party, until Yavlinskii broke off to form his own political bloc for the election.

Six political parties made up the political center for the December 12 election, led by the Civic Union. With Aleksandr Rutskoi in the Lefortovo prison since October 4, the Civic Union was being led by Arkadii Volskii, the founder of the Union of Industrialists and Entrepreneurs. Whether it was politically helpful or not, Mikhail Gorbachev, in an interview before the election, had personally endorsed the Civic Union and hinted that he would not be averse to running in a future election as its candidate for Russian President.[6] The center of the political spectrum also included Nikolai Travkin's Democratic Party of Russia; the youth wing of the Civic Union, running separately as Russia's Future–New Names; a party for the elderly and poor calling itself Dignity and Charity; the environmental coalition Cedar; and a Women of Russia bloc. Women of Russia attempted to attract voters with a platform denouncing "extreme feminism" while advocating more women in national political offices as its major goal.

The radical and anti-reform left and right would be represented on the ballot for the December 12 election by three different political parties. The most well-known on the radical left was the Russian Communist Party. Still the single largest

---

[6]Serge Schmemann, "Gorbachev, Energetic, Chatty, but Not Yet Political," *The New York Times*, November 3, 1993, p. A3.

party by membership in the country, the Russian Communist Party had been re-legalized for the second time in two years by Yeltsin, who had banned it for two weeks following the October storming of the Russian parliament building. The Russian Communists put up their tables and solicited signatures for their petitions at the northeast side of Red Square in Moscow, near the portico of the Lenin Museum. It was almost as if they drew some spiritual karma from the Communist founder's artifacts in the building.

Also considered as being on the radical political left for the December 12 election was the Agrarian Party coalition, advocating retention of the collective-state farm system. One party aligned with this coalition was led by Vasilii Starodubtsev, who was one of the original eight members of the Emergency Committee, which had plotted the coup against Gorbachev in August 1991, and whose trial had been continuously delayed. The Agrarian Party coalition was projected to win at least 5 percent of the party-list vote in several Russian rural regions and earn a share of the 225 seats in the State Duma. Starodubtsev's candidacy was ironic in that he could win a seat in the Federal Assembly at the same time as his trial for treason as a member of the Emergency Committee was scheduled to resume in Moscow.

Radical right-wing candidates on the ballot were led by the Liberal Democratic Party. The Liberal Democrats, and like-minded candidates among the independents registered for the single-member seats in the State Duma and Federation Council, rooted their appeal and ideology in Russian nationalism and hard-core opposition to democratic and free-market reforms. These Russian nationalist candidates were anticipated to do especially well in the December 12th election in regions of Siberia and the conservative farmbelt of the central Black Earth Zone. The Liberal Democratic Party emerged under mysterious circumstances as the very first political party registered in March 1990, after the Soviet national parliament had legalized political parties. The party's founder and leader since 1990 was Vladimir Zhirinovskii. A graduate of Moscow State University's Institute of Oriental Languages—notorious as a principal recruiting base for the KGB—Zhirinovskii had never even been a member of the Communist party. Nor was there any hard evidence that he had ever been employed by the KGB. Nonetheless, before 1990, he had a checkered career in organizations generally assumed to have been KGB front groups (the Soviet Peace Council and the Soviet Confederation of Jewish Organizations). Given his background and his sudden emergence from total political obscurity with the money to form a political party, many democratic reformists in 1990 suspected that Zhirinovskii was a KGB stooge. They considered his party a ploy by hard-liners in the Communist party and KGB to infiltrate and discredit their own movements and parties that were attempting to democratize Soviet society.

Using his party base, Zhirinovskii had run for Russian President on June 12, 1991, placing third behind Boris Yeltsin and Nikolai Ryzhkov, with 6 million votes. Since 1991, Zhirinovskii had organized local branches of the Liberal Democratic Party in several areas of Russia, financing them from still unknown contributors and recruiting an enthusiastic core of party members under thirty years of age. By November 1993, Zhirinovskii claimed that his Liberal Democratic Party had 100,000 members.

Party membership was closely identified with Zhirinovskii himself. With ominous parallels to the National Socialists of Adolf Hitler in Germany before 1933, young party recruits of the Liberal Democratic Party in Russia of 1993 dressed in paramilitary uniforms and called themselves "Zhirinovskii's Falcons." The newspapers of the party were called *Zhirinovskii's Truth* and *Zhirinovskii's Falcon.* Party members were required to send dues equal to 1 percent of their monthly income to Zhirinovskii personally at his Moscow headquarters. Its finances, local branches, and devoted young recruits allowed the Liberal Democratic Party to be the very first political party to gather the 100,000 signatures required to register for the party-list ballot for the State Duma.

Many were drawn by Zhirinovskii's anti-establishment populist and racist rhetoric. An extremely effective campaigner and charismatic speaker before crowds or on television, Zhirinovskii encouraged the very worst prejudices, fears, and insecurities of his audiences. He singled out and denounced as the particular "enemy" of the country all ethnic non-Russians—especially Jews. He alleged that they, in a murky relationship with Russian organized criminal syndicates, were conspiring against ethnic Russians and were attempting through privatization of the economy to take over the country. Despite his own half-Jewish origins (his father was Jewish) and the fact that he had once applied to emigrate to Israel, Zhirinovskii by implication blamed Jews and other ethnic non-Russians, in league with organized crime, for the economic collapse of the country since 1991 and for all of the suffering experienced by many Russians. Zhirinovskii refuted the reports of his father's Jewishness and his own application to Israel as slanderous lies spread by these conspiratorial forces.

Zhirinovskii's economic platform was simple and precise. Russia under the Liberal Democrats would refuse to pay any of its foreign debts, cut off all aid to the "near abroad," limit privatization of the economy, continue to subsidize state-owned industries, and suspend any further conversion of its huge military-industrial complex to civilian production. Russia would economically recover by becoming a major arms merchant to the world, selling its military goods to some of its former best customers, such as Saddam Hussein of Iraq.

No less appealing to Zhirinovskii's party recruits was his nationalistic platform, advocating the restoration, if necessary by military force, of all the territory of the Russian Empire before 1917 (including Ukraine, Finland, Poland, and Alaska!). Zhirinovskii was very clear in his ultimate political goal. Before December 12, he openly announced his intention to run for Russian President in 1995 or 1996 as the candidate of the Liberal Democratic Party.

Despite the appearance of democracy in the month before December 12, the context of the election itself showed how very little Russia and the other countries in Central Eurasia had changed politically since 1991. Russian political parties were organizing and gathering signatures on petitions for candidates to a parliament whose powers and role were still completely unknown. The relevant articles on the parliament were to be included in a new Russian constitution that Russian voters would be asked to approve in principle on a fourth ballot they would be given on entering the voting booths on December 12.

The problem was that by November no one had yet seen a draft of the constitution to be approved in principle by voters on December 12. In the last three weeks before the election, the draft was finally published, but little serious discussion and debate of its articles occurred. President Yeltsin had lifted the censorship of the media imposed during the emergency rule he had declared for two weeks after October 4, but the Russian Ministry of Information still retained censors in the editorial offices of all newspapers and journals, who had the right to order seizure of any issues considered offensive. The individual appointed by Yeltsin to oversee the censors and to order the seizure of newspapers or journals considered politically offensive had been a former top-ranking official in *Glavlit*, the Communist party agency that censored all media and publications in the Soviet Union until 1990.

Yeltsin's unconstitutional declaration of emergency rule and the storming of the Russian parliament building had left an indelible autocratic chill on Russian democracy. Despite the democratic bustle in Red Square of parties registering to compete for seats in a new national parliament, Russia had reverted to an autocracy under President Yeltsin. Russia's Choice—likely to be the leading political party of a parliament whose powers were unknown—was Yeltsin's personal party, organized and led by his closest supporters in the government, who themselves had drafted the electoral rules after October 4. The lessons of October 1993 could not but inhibit any real democratic interaction between the Federal Assembly and the executive branch under Yeltsin after December 12. Which opposition parties in the new Federal Assembly would dare to defy the President with the recent memory of his ordering the storming of the parliament building on October 4?

▪ *EPILOGUE: DECEMBER 1993 RUSSIAN ELECTION*

Only 55 percent of the registered voters in Russia participated in the country's first post-Communist election on December 12, 1993.[7] This was the lowest turnout of registered Russian voters for any election since the first relatively free elections to the All-Union Congress of People's Deputies were held in 1989. The new Russian constitution was adopted by a margin of 58 percent to 42 percent, but the endorsement was less than a resounding public mandate. Adding the 25 million who voted against the constitution to the 48 million who failed to vote means that less than one-third of the 106 million eligible Russian voters approved the constitution. Public apathy and voter disillusionment with the new national democratic leaders and economic market reforms affected the turnout and outcome of the races to both chambers of the Federal Assembly.

The four democratic reform parties, expected to win a majority in both chambers, instead suffered a qualified defeat. Russia's Choice (Yeltsin's party) did win the largest combined number of single-member and party-list seats in the State

---

[7]On the results of the December 12th election, see Vera Tolz, "Russia's Parliamentary Elections: What Happened and Why," *RFE/RL Research Report*, vol. 3, no. 2 (January 14, 1994), pp. 1–8.

Duma—96. The other three reform parties won a total of only 68 single-member and party-list seats. The total number of seats in the State Duma held by the four reform parties after the election was 164, or 36.9 percent.[8] The Apple bloc (Yavlinskii-Boldyrev-Lukin party) received only 7.8 percent of the national party-list vote (20 seats). Shakhrai's Party of Russian Unity and Accord barely qualified for party-list seats with 6.8 percent (18 seats). And the Movement for Democratic Reforms failed to qualify, obtaining less than 5 percent of the party-list vote, although its candidates did win 18 single-member seats.

The reform parties did much better in the upper chamber of the Federation Council. Very few of the candidates contesting Federation Council seats ran on party labels, and voters tended to support the candidates who were the most well-known locally. Approximately half of the 178 who won were expected to support the general policies and positions of the four reform parties. These individuals were the executive heads and plenipotentiaries of their provinces and territories in Russia. They had won in great part because of their name recognition among the voters in their administrative locales. They were expected to support reform, if for no other reason than political obligation and loyalty. They had originally been appointed to their positions between 1991 and 1993 by President Yeltsin, and they had consistently supported him in his numerous political confrontations and stand-offs with the parliament in 1992 and 1993.

The real winners on December 12 turned out to be the three anti-reform parties of the radical right and radical left: the Liberal Democratic Party, the Russian Communist Party, and the Agrarian Party. Even though Russia's Choice gained the largest single bloc of 96 seats in the State Duma, Zhirinovskii's Liberal Democratic Party unofficially "won" the election based on the vote totals for the party-list ballot. The Liberal Democratic Party received the largest plurality (22.8 percent) of any party listed on the national party-list ballot and received 59 seats. When Zhirinovskii ran for Russian President on June 12, 1991, as the candidate of the Liberal Democratic Party, only 6 million Russians had voted for him and his party. On December 12, 1993, his party and its candidates were supported by approximately 15 million Russian voters. On the party-list ballot, the Russian Communist Party came in third behind Russia's Choice with 12.4 percent (32 seats), and the Agrarian Party came in fifth with 7.9 percent (21 seats).

With candidates of the three anti-reform parties winning an additional 70 single-member seats, the anti-reform bloc held the combined single largest plurality of 182 seats (41 percent) in the State Duma. The Liberal Democratic Party itself held 70 seats, second only to Russia's Choice in the State Duma. In the Federation Council, various deputies who had voiced sympathy during their own campaigns with the positions of communists and nationalists were expected to give the three

---

[8]Seats in the State Duma for 6 of the 225 single-member districts were not filled because less than 25 percent of the local registered voters required to validate the elections showed up to vote on December 12. The seats would remain vacant until new elections to fill them were held in March 1994.

anti-reform parties an equivalent of 40–50 percent of the upper chamber. This was expected to be a margin sufficient to challenge the Federation Council deputies likely to endorse reform policies.

Thirty independent deputies representing both reform and anti-reform views and 68 deputies affiliated with centrist parties won the remaining 22 percent of the seats in the State Duma. The Women of Russia party did unexpectedly well with its platform advocating more women in public office. It came in fourth among all parties on the party-list ballot with 8.1 percent of the national vote (21 seats) and a total of 25 Duma seats (including 4 single-member seats won by its affiliated candidates). Travkin's Democratic Party of Russia just barely qualified for party-list seats with 5.5 percent (for 14 seats) and a total of 21 seats (adding 7 won by its candidates in single-member districts). Civic Union failed to qualify with less than 5 percent of the party-list vote, but 18 of its best-known leaders won single-member seats in the State Duma.

The Russian voters may have been sending an underlying dual message with their election of three particular deputies to the Federal Assembly. The voters elected only one of ninety-five candidates who appeared on the ballot affiliated with the party that named itself Russia's Future–New Names. In contrast, they elected two independents with "old names"—Anatolii Lukyanov, to the State Duma, and Vasilii Starodubtsev, to the Federation Council. These were two of the eight original plotters of the abortive August 1991 coup.

With the support of enough centrist and independent deputies to constitute a majority, the three radical right and left parties in the State Duma elected Ivan Rybkin speaker of the lower chamber when the lower chamber convened for its first session in January 1994. Rybkin, who helped found the Russian Communist Party in 1990, was elected in December 1993 as a deputy of the Agrarian Party. Yeltsin reappointed Viktor Chernomyrdin as Prime Minister. Chernomyrdin—confronting a parliament in which communists, nationalists, and centrists held 63 percent of the seats in the lower chamber and an estimated 40–50 percent of the seats in the upper chamber—chose a relatively conservative and anti-reform cabinet. The few remaining free-market advocates from his last cabinet resigned in protest, issuing dire warnings that a reversal of economic policies would lead to a resurgence of hyperinflation and the collapse of the entire economy by the summer of 1994. The ultimate irony of the December 12th election is that the percentages of democratic reformers, nationalists and communists, and centrists in the new Federal Assembly almost exactly parallel the percentages of deputies aligned with the same three political groups in the previous Russian parliament, disbanded by President Yeltsin on September 21, 1993.

As its first major legislative action, the State Duma approved a sweeping amnesty on February 23, 1994. The amnesty freed from prison Aleksandr Rutskoi, Ruslan Khasbulatov, and all those arrested for instigating the October 1993 violence in Moscow and dropped all criminal charges against both them and the original eight plotters of the abortive August 1991 coup. President Yeltsin was powerless to appeal the amnesty, because it could be constitutionally reversed only by a decision of the Constitutional Court. The Court under its former Chief Justice Valerii Zorkin had ruled unconstitutional Yeltsin's decree dissolving the former Russian parliament on September 21. In retaliation, Yeltsin had suspended the Court from meeting and acting since October 4.

With Vladimir Zhirinovskii buoyed by the victory of his party in the State Duma and running for Russian President in the next election, the confrontation between Yeltsin and the Russian parliament was likely to enter its second act in 1994. The first act had ended with Yeltsin ordering the seizure of the parliament building on October 4, 1993. Many Russians anticipated that the second act would end in much the same manner. Russia's progress toward democracy looked just as uncertain as it had been since the demise of the Soviet Union in 1991.

Yeltsin in Russia, Kravchuk in Ukraine, Rakhmonov in Tajikistan, Karimov in Uzbekistan, and others—despite the clear differences in the brutality and ruthlessness of their rule—all share something in common. They are autocratic leaders of political systems founded on weak national governments, commanding little political authority and legitimacy, and crippled in terms of nation building by almost insoluble economic and social problems. Government in many of the post-Soviet successor states has become personalized, not institutionalized. It is Yeltsin, Kravchuk, and the other top leaders who ultimately count in holding their national governments together and making decisions. The national legislatures—if no longer rubber stamps—remain "pocket parliaments" dominated by the executive branch and by the top leader personally.

The weakness in this system of personalized government was most graphically illustrated by the events in Russia culminating in Yeltsin's crushing of the rebellion in the parliament. Had Yeltsin failed, civil war would likely have ensued. In Ukraine, as suggested earlier in this chapter, the national government also has become predominantly an extension of the personality and prerogatives of the President. The political stalemate between Kravchuk and the Ukrainian parliament has threatened to lead to the same presidential autocracy under Kravchuk as has been associated with Yeltsin in Russia since October 1993. The only difference in Uzbekistan, Turkmenistan, Tajikistan, and Azerbaijan is the absence of any democratic pretense on the part of their top leaders, who rule dictatorially and are retained in power by the forces that they can mobilize as mobs in the streets or as private armies.

Democracy is a system of governance based on constitutionalism, accountability, a rule of law, and democratic pluralism. None of these attributes have prevailed in Russia or many of the other countries of Central Eurasia since 1991. Over the next several decades, the countries are fated to remain at best presidential dictatorships under democratic facades—different more in form than in nature from the Soviet Communist autocracy. The Soviet autocracy, too, concentrated power in the executive branch of ruling party organs and in the individual holding the office of General Secretary.

In completing our analysis of Russia and Central Eurasia, we return to Mikhail Gorbachev, someone with particular insights into the difficulties of transforming an autocracy into a democracy. Gorbachev admonished Yeltsin a few weeks before the December 12, 1993 election, in words also relevant for the top leaders in many other Central Eurasian countries:

> I would like this thought to reach them. Democracy is not convenient, it's not fun to be shoved, controlled, required to give accounts, continually questioned. I know—I myself introduced pluralism. I caught hell from it, but I kept silent because this was kasha I cooked myself. But if the Parliament does not reflect society, its mood, then it will be Communist, neo-Bolshevik, it will allow one scheme. This will be an imposition again. And what kind of democracy is that?[9]

---

[9]Schmemann, loc. cit.

..... Part Six

Prospects for European Democracy

IRELAND

DENMARK

UNITED
KINGDOM

NETHERLANDS

London•

Berlin•

GERMANY

BELGIUM

LUX.

•Paris

FRANCE

ITALY

PORTUGAL

•Madrid

•Rome

•Lisbon

SPAIN

GREECE

European Union members

.....37

Durability and Change: Europe in Flux ___

Historically, the great majority of people have had to endure life under repressive governments. One of the major quests of the human experience has been for free government—government that, at the least, recognized and didn't abuse the intrinsic worth of every individual and, at the best, facilitated each individual's efforts to realize as fully as possible his or her potential. Various benefits and services are necessary to facilitate that struggle for self-attainment. The most basic of these boons is defense against those so strong or uncivilized as to try to take advantage of others. The most essential assistance is to provide a means of resolving conflict between individuals justly and without violence. The problem is how to allocate to government the power necessary to perform its tasks without giving it the ability to exploit and suppress individuals itself. Power, yes, but limited, accountable power, or the individual would be no better off than he or she was in the state of nature before government existed, when life was "poor, nasty, brutish, and short" because it was little more than a war of every person against every other person. The age-old dilemma is the proper balance, the proper mix of concentrated power and accountability. Solutions have emphasized two themes: limits on the scope of power and mechanisms for preventing its abuse.

■ ACCOUNTABILITY VERSUS CONCENTRATED POWER

Two centuries ago the so-called American Founding Fathers had to confront this dilemma. Like Alexander the Great's solution to the puzzle of untying the Gordian knot, they slashed through to the heart of the problem and fractionalized power—within the central level of government and between the central and subnational levels of government. They decided to forgo many of the potential benefits of untrammeled concentrated power, relying on their own individual self-efforts to provide these. They knew, however, that they could not travel that road all the way to its ultimate destination. They nearly had done so under their initial effort—the Articles of Confederation—and had found the product too ineffective to work in peacetime when no external enemy forced some measure of decisive action to avoid extinction. (To a considerable extent, the flaws of that initial effort resembled those of the Third and Fourth Republics of France.) The limits on the scope of governmental power had to be relaxed; relinquishing more power to the government couldn't be avoided. This broader power would be fractionalized, however, to create a system of checks and balances—the executive, the legislature, the courts, the central government, and the states all would constrain each other to keep any element from getting out of hand and abusing power. With the exception of the courts, each element would be accountable to the people periodically in elections. Since power was fractionalized, a more frequent calling to account wasn't required.

Such a solution is not surprising. The American system had originated in a rebellion against concentrated power. Furthermore, the settling of a "new world" and the successful establishment of an efficient economy demanded a great deal of individual self-reliance. However normal or natural the solution may seem to Americans, especially two centuries later, the essential point to recognize is the extent to which the American path diverged from the European experience. In this, as in other ways, the United States was, as a prominent social scientist pointed out, "the first new nation."

For most Europeans (the Swiss are the chief exceptions), monarchy remained the governmental tradition much longer than it did for Americans. Therefore, the European approach is *not* to fractionalize power, but to avoid abuse of power by making it accountable. In contrast to the American separation-of-powers system, the European tradition features the parliamentary system, in which executive politicians serving as the monarch's agents can be removed from office as a means of constraining the monarch's (which really is to say, the government's) powers. Removing the executive was the ultimate sanction. In the interim the executive would have to account regularly for its actions so an assessment could be made concerning whether removal might be needed. Accountability was enforced on the executive by the legislature; the courts had little role in keeping the executive within the legitimate scope of power. The legislature performed its function in trust for the people. There was constant, rather than periodic, accountability, and it was enforced by "professionals" who were not distracted by having to pursue the everyday tasks and interests of life.

Turning to specific instances within the European tradition, Britain long has practiced constitutionalism—limits on the scope of power. Some would date this from Magna Carta in 1215, whereas others go back only as far as the Glorious Revolution of 1688 and the subsequent Bill of Rights. Despite such constraints, the scope of power remained broad and, in contrast to the route taken by the United States, wasn't fractionalized. Therefore, the necessity—a recurrent theme in Part Two—of accountability. So long as accountability is maintained, the British have been content to allow political leaders to exercise political power relatively unencumbered. No written constitution limits power; nor does an elaborate system of checks and balances among governmental institutions restrain those who wield authority. The British rely instead on accountability.

This concept is the key to understanding the power structure of British government. Neither the monarch nor the House of Lords is accountable; thus, neither can be allowed to exercise any real power. The judiciary is somewhat more accountable—its members are appointed by the executive and can be removed by Parliament—but in practice it is subject to little control. Therefore, its power must be circumscribed as well. British courts lack the power of American ones to invalidate legislation. The British civil service at the upper levels clearly does exercise power and must, therefore, be accountable. This accountability must be accomplished, however, without jeopardizing the benefits of efficiency and merit-based selection. In an effort to do so, the British developed the doctrines of the political neutrality of the civil service and of ministerial responsibility.

In the traditional view, the linchpin of this system was Parliament. The people are unable to call all the government's officials to account. The job is too vast; it requires full-time effort. Therefore, the people delegate the task to elected legislative representatives. All governmental bodies must account to these representatives, who in turn are responsible to the people. British parties, because they are unified and cohesive, do not blur the locus of responsibility as American parties typically do. Thus, the British party system assists the electorate in calling their representatives to account.

Since it is the most powerful organ of government, the Cabinet must be accountable. That is why the Cabinet is required to keep Parliament informed of its plans and actions, why these must be debated fully there, why an official Opposition must exist, why that Opposition is consulted in planning the Commons' agenda, why the Cabinet allows time for censure debates, and why the Cabinet submits daily to Parliamentary questioning of its actions and policies. Such procedures make the Cabinet more accountable, more responsive to what the people want, as expressed through their representatives.

Although accountability was enforced daily by the people's legislative representatives, the ultimate responsibility still lay with the people. The voters possessed the power to determine who would govern. Should they decide that the party currently entrusted with this task was doing a bad job, then at the next election they could sweep it from office and get a change in policy. No other rascals needed to be turned out, no other strongholds of power had to be assaulted. The party in power had no excuse for failure because the power structure contained no obstacles to thwart a Cabinet from carrying out its program.

This summary of how the British political system is supposed to operate has come to be recognized as highly idealized. The atrophy of the doctrine of ministerial responsibility has weakened the accountability of both the political leaders and the top bureaucrats. The cautious attitude of the civil service militates against utilizing new methods and knowledge that may be essential to coping with contemporary problems. British membership in the European Union has further complicated the maintenance of accountability. As you will see in the next chapter, many aspects of British social and economic policy are now decided by EU organs. Despite attempts to create procedures for monitoring these agencies, Parliament quite simply lacks effective control over them.

Most fundamental, Parliament's ability to call the Cabinet to account has seemed to attenuate. Cohesive parties *do* focus responsibility. Precisely because British parties are quite unified in their voting in the legislature, however, the ability of Parliament to control the Cabinet weakened in the decades following World War

II. The reassertiveness of Parliament in the 1970s seemed a temporary aberration, attributable to an extended period of minority Government. Margaret Thatcher's dominance during the 1980s tended to obscure an increase in MPs' willingness to vote against their party's line on occasion.

The importance of this development didn't become obvious until the 1990s. Although the Conservatives retained what appeared to be a working majority in the House of Commons, the executive's policies were vulnerable because of weakened party discipline. One issue in particular epitomized how much things had changed. In December 1991 Prime Minister John Major signed the EC's Maastricht Treaty. He was hailed as a triumphant negotiator because he obtained the agreement of the other eleven members of the EC that Britain did not have to follow the treaty's provisions on monetary union or labor regulations. Before ratifying the treaty, he needed to obtain certain changes in British domestic law. The bill making those changes did not get through the "rubber stamp" Parliament until nearly the end of July 1993—a year and a half after the signing of the treaty. Only after two successive days of debate and four separate divisions of the House (one of which he lost) was Major able to get the support he needed—and then only because he made the ultimate vote a matter of confidence and threatened to call a general election if he were defeated on it. Did John Major feel accountable to the House of Commons? You'd better believe it!

Even then—amazingly, given the nature of the British system—Major still had to fight a challenge to the legislation in the courts. The judicial branch would determine whether the procedure he used for ratification of the treaty was constitutional. In short, not only was accountability live and well in Britain, but a measure of checks and balances might be hatching as well. The judges did endorse Major's procedure for ratification, so his action in some senses was not checked. The fact that their approval was necessary, however, did involve a constraint.

We suggested earlier some similarity between the American Articles of Confederation and the French Third and Fourth Republics. Perhaps a better comparison would be with the United States of the 1980s. American government suffered from gridlock, not only because the Presidency was controlled by the Republicans while the Democrats controlled Congress, but also because of the inability of Congress to act decisively on anything. Contrasting partisan control was irrelevant to the French situation because the President in the Third and Fourth Republics had nothing like the power of the American President. Nonetheless, the typical state of affairs in France was a stalemate similar to American gridlock. Power was concentrated in the French legislature, but precisely because it was, government was not very responsive to citizen concerns. The power that appeared concentrated was, in fact, fractionalized by the party system. No single party could command a majority in the legislature; often not even a coalition of parties could do so. Opposition was similarly fractionalized. Thus, when the Cabinet was defeated in the legislature, as often happened, no alternative existed—no cohesive group of leaders with some other coherent set of policies was available. Political groups combined readily to oust a Cabinet, but could not agree on what should be done thereafter. The legislature was unable to formulate a program of action. Affairs simply drifted until the problems reached crisis proportions, when the system would be galvanized into a spasm of frenzied activity, none of which dealt with the long-term problems. Instead of providing for accountability, this was a system in which one of the basic operational rules of the game was to avoid responsibility at all costs.

The French legislature was accountable to the voters; the electorate decided who would represent them. American voters choose both representatives and the chief executive. In neither country, however, could the electorate actually decide who was really in charge. Who should take the blame for failures or inaction? The executive and the legislature could blame each other. In the United States, both of these branches could blame the judiciary as well. The result in France was a general malaise that so lowered commitment to the system that few objected to its replacement in a less than legitimate fashion. Although matters did not reach that level in the United States, apathy and cynicism about the political process became common.

Charles de Gaulle's adulation of his country made him determined to transform this state of affairs. So successful was he in bringing strong leadership to France that many people felt that the executive had come to dominate the policy process. Such a concern was not unique to France. Despite the contrasting American and European responses to the dilemma of power and accountability, a good deal was heard in the United States, simultaneous with de Gaulle's heyday in France, about an "imperial presidency." Elsewhere in Europe—in Britain, for example—some scholars argued that the country's political system was becoming presidential, that the Prime Minister completely overshadowed the Cabinet, that any element of collective decision making had been lost. Some political trends cross national boundaries and produce similar issues and concerns despite basic differences in governmental structure.

De Gaulle was disinclined (some would say with good reason, given the history of the Third and Fourth Republics) to involve the legislature and the parties in the tasks of governing. Those who held positions of power did so not because they led significant groups in the legislature, but because they enjoyed his confidence. In some ways his system resembled Germany under the Second Empire, a period that, as you saw in Part Four, did little to nurture the values essential to parliamentary democracy.

De Gaulle granted little value to the partisan competition essential to a democracy; he refused to be beholden to or even to lead any political party. He sought to project an image of rising above trivial political bickering to concentrate on lofty principles. Devising means to achieve his goals could be left to the administrative structure. Don't be too quick to dismiss his attitude as autocratic; the description wouldn't have to be changed too much to be applicable to George Washington. (When George actually went to the Senate to consult with them about a treaty, he was subjected to such hostile questioning that when he left, he was heard to say he'd "be damned if I'll come back here again.")

De Gaulle shifted France so far toward concentrated power that accountability suffered. He was in for a seven-year term and the legislature, the fountainhead of accountability, had no way to get at him. When he was so bold as to amend the constitution unconstitutionally, the legislature was enraged. All that it could do, however, was to censure the hapless Prime Minister and his Cabinet. Not only did de

Gaulle go right ahead with his amendment, but he also dissolved parliament and called for elections, which resulted in his having more legislative support than he had had before the confrontation. The lesson was "I do what I damn well please."

Important as de Gaulle's constitutional changes were, the key element in his success was that he could count on support in the legislature. As you have seen, the legislature's support was the reason for the dominance of the British executive in the years after World War II. What would happen to the Fifth Republic, however, were control of the legislature and the Presidency in different partisan hands? Would such divided control produce gridlock as it did in the United States? The first instance of cohabitation—divided control—in the late 1980s supported two interesting conclusions. One, the system could continue to work effectively and, two, it took on some aspects of American checks and balances. Although executive power was divided between the President and the Prime Minister, stalemate wasn't the result. Neither executive, however, had as free a hand to act as the British Prime Minister typically did. Relations between President Mitterrand and Prime Minister Chirac bore some resemblance to those between Presidents Reagan and Bush and the Speakers of the House of Representatives.

The second period of cohabitation in the early 1990s seemed likely to reinforce these conclusions. Prime Minister Balladur had a much larger majority in the National Assembly than had Prime Minister Chirac. President Mitterrand was several years older than he had been in the first cohabitation, in ill health, and certain not to run for another term. For the second time during the Fifth Republic a Prime Minister had an excellent opportunity to truly be the equal of the President. Depending on the precedents established by this experience, the lack of accountability that causes concern about the French Fifth Republic may be remedied with a dose of separation of powers, even if not exactly the American form of that constraint.

Germany has gone even further than France in adopting portions of the American approach to the dilemma of concentrated power and accountability. Germany more clearly is a parliamentary system than is the French hybrid. Nonetheless, the German Chancellor is entrenched. Although he or she *can* be called to account by the legislature, almost always a Chancellor can anticipate a fixed term in office, highly unusual in any parliamentary system. Thus, the accountability/power balance has not been skewed so far to the former as to produce the ineffectiveness of the Weimar Republic. Power is constrained not so much by the threat of removal from office as by the need for consent from a partially separate power center.

As in France, the constitutional changes in Germany are important, but more significant is the shift from a fractionalized party system. Unlike the situation during the Weimar Republic, the leading German parties no longer are narrow sectional organizations, but broad groupings of diverse interests. Concentration of political forces makes avoiding weak, deadlocked Cabinets easier. That is to say, concentration of political powers tends to concentrate government power, regardless of constitutional provisions.

An even more notable example of checks and balances in Germany is the development of the Federal Constitutional Court. The Court has a major role in ensuring that the limits on the scope of governmental power are observed. Furthermore, its public policy decisions make it an active participant, just like the U.S. Supreme Court, in calling both the executive and the legislative branches to account. In fact, the ability of the Federal Constitutional Court to issue advisory opinions, which the U.S. Supreme Court doesn't have, means that it can be regarded as an even more active check.

A final element of checks and balances in Germany is the federal system, which both Britain and France lack. The allocation of power between the central and state levels of government, reinforced as it is by administrative arrangements, also serves to constrain government. We argued in Part Four that the Bundestag didn't do a very good job in legitimating government policy. Judged from the standard of the typical parliamentary system, that is true. But perhaps that shortcoming is less serious in Germany because accountability is not the only means employed there to prevent abuse of power. A fair measure of checks and balances also offers an effective weapon.

These comparisons should not be taken to imply that Europeans made a mistake in not employing the American means of controlling power and are gradually learning their lesson. The point is to understand the extent to which more than one solution to the problem is available. Comparative analysis of governmental systems requires that you be able to distinguish between different types of system, to be familiar with their basic characteristics. Different systems operate in different ways. Assumptions made about the likely impact of certain actions that are valid in one type of system may be irrelevant or misleading in another. And yet the different types of systems are just that—types. Real-world examples never correspond exactly to the pure type. This discussion has noted a number of instances in which the British, French, and German parliamentary systems depart from the pure type.

The same can be said about American government. The essence of the parliamentary type is day-to-day legislative monitoring of the executive. In contrast, the separation-of-powers system doesn't require the legislature to call the executive to account. Congressional committees, however, do precisely that. Congressional committees engage in a surveillance of the executive much more stringent than anything that occurs in Britain. The British, in fact, have been trying to import elements of Congressional committees in an effort to strengthen the ability of the House of Commons to call the Cabinet to account. Beyond these arrangements, the requirement in the United States for Senate approval of presidential appointments contains an element of accountability. True, the House of Commons can censure a member of the Cabinet and force him or her out of office, a power not possessed by the U.S. Senate. But the House of Commons has *no* initial say over whom the Prime Minister may appoint to the Cabinet, a power that the Senate has been willing to wield to thwart the President's plans. Who is to say that the one procedure is a truer example of accountability than the other? Yes, the American experience does differ from the European. The United States *did* choose a different means of seeking to prevent abuse of power. In practice, however, each alternative has incorporated some elements of the other.

What, then, of each country's existing mix? What is the likelihood of further borrowings or changes in constitutional arrangements? In Germany, virtually nil. So satisfied were West Germans with their Basic Law that when unification with East

Germany came, the provision that that event would require a new constitution to be drafted was ignored. A poverty-stricken cousin simply was added to the firm as a very junior partner. A commission has been studying the Basic Law to ascertain whether changes should be recommended, but little of importance seems likely to come of it. A change that would make the calling of elections easier might result, but nothing more significant than that. To the extent that there is a constitutional debate in Germany, it has concerned asylum for immigrants and use of military forces abroad. Although these are major issues, they don't suggest any constitutional instability in Germany or likelihood of fundamental change.

For all the controversy caused by its launch in the late 1950s, the French Fifth Republic has won remarkable acceptance. Traditionally a major element in French politics was constitutional debate. In the 1990s, however, constitutional questions are of less popular concern than they have been for over a half century. If the cohabitation between President Mitterrand and Prime Minister Balladur continues as smoothly as it began, the case for constitutional change will be even less compelling. The President's term might be shortened by two or three years; that hardly is a fundamental reform.

Rather surprisingly, possible constitutional change is a livelier issue in Britain than in either Germany or France. Traditionally, the British have not been much interested in such matters. Not having a written constitution and being disposed to practice incremental muddling-through, the British have been reluctant to tackle fundamental structural questions. Early in the twentieth century an attempt by the House of Lords to thwart the Government's economic plans caused what was termed a constitutional crisis and resulted in legislation deemed to be part of the unwritten constitution. No such events have occurred since then.

In recent years, however, a few fundamental issues have been injected into the political debate. Relations between the United Kingdom's constituent elements can't be regarded as settled. Although Prime Minister John Major protested vehemently during the 1992 election campaign against any change, nationalist forces continue to press for at least some form of devolution, if not outright independence. The question of a written bill of rights raises other fundamental issues. Although such a document seems unlikely to be adopted any time soon, the interest group Charter 88 continues to agitate for action. Electoral reform would have such significant impact that any change could be deemed constitutional in nature. Here, again, the ruling Conservatives would oppose any change. Only if they fell from power might some coalition of Labour and Liberal Democrats make a change. Nonetheless, electoral reform is discussed more seriously than it has been for many years. One never should expect quick action in Britain on fundamental issues, but the ongoing debate on these constitutional issues may produce change sooner than in either France or Germany.

British debate is as nothing compared to the ferment occurring in the fifteen countries of Russia and Central Eurasia. There the search for a workable balance between concentrated power and accountability is crucial. Whether under the tsars or the Communists, the Russian and Central Eurasian people have known little other than the repression of concentrated power. Soviet leaders for seven decades rejected governmental accountability and the separation of powers in Western democracies as shams employed by the ruling capitalist class to perpetuate its hegemony and divide the powerless working class. Soviet leaders defended the monolithic power of the Communist party autocracy as a higher form of real democracy, directly representing the real interests of all peoples in the Soviet Union and protecting them against internal and external enemies. Soviet government was merely the tool the Communist party utilized to bring about the ultimate goal of Communism. In Communist society, government itself would cease to exist, material abundance and economic morality having eliminated the source of all conflicts.

Only under Gorbachev were the principles of liberal democracy and representative government even nominally accepted and the first tentative reforms instituted to realize them. The demise of the Soviet Union before those reforms could have much lasting effect left a political vacuum. As you saw in Part Five, the extent to which the fifteen post-Soviet countries have repudiated their Communist past and taken tentative steps toward democracy varies considerably. All too often since 1991, the newly independent countries of Russia and Central Eurasia have reverted to autocracies little different from the past Soviet Communist system. Their heads of government have balked at accepting any real constitutional limitations on their authority, rejecting these as ploys by parliaments still dominated by deputies from the Soviet Communist era to undermine any democratic and free-market reform. The political deadlock between the heads of government and their parliaments has prevented almost all of the countries from adopting new post-Soviet constitutions, because they cannot agree on how, or even whether, ruling governments should be held accountable for their actions.

Operating under Soviet-era constitutions, many heads of government have justified repressive measures as essential to consolidate weak national authority in new countries on the brink of anarchy and civil war. National parliaments resisting the imposition of executive dictate and asserting a right to hold their ruling governments accountable have sparked violent conflicts. The most graphic instance has been the assault on the Russian parliament building ordered by President Boris Yeltsin on October 4, 1993, when he was challenged by the hard-line Communists and nationalists in the parliament. Yeltsin's clash with parliament stemmed from a fundamental constitutional disagreement. He insisted that the future Russian constitution and political system be modeled after the French Fifth Republic, investing supreme authority in the office of President and insulating it from any direct accountability to parliament. A plurality of the parliament, under the leadership of its Speaker Ruslan Khasbulatov, wanted a constitution and political system patterned more like the U.S. Constitution and its separation of powers and checks and balances between the legislative and executive branches. By the summer of 1993, a minority of hard-line Communists and nationalists in the parliament had escalated the constitutional crisis into a political standoff between Yeltsin and the parliament. They intended the crisis to force his resignation, permitting them to seize control of the government.

Yeltsin prevailed by means of military force, but his doing so, combined with the equally unconstitutional action of dissolving parliament, could not resolve the real crisis facing Russia and many other countries of Central Eurasia. Democracies are founded on widespread societal consensus rooted in public trust and certain basic values, attitudes, and beliefs. Leaders can't just impose democracy by reforming institutions, can't invoke public trust and democratic political culture by force, can't ordain constitutionalism simply by writing constitutions. Since 1991, the governments in Russia and Central Eurasia rule, rather than govern, highly polarized societies. These societies do not comprehend the balance required in a democracy between concentrated power and accountability. In repudiating the decades of Soviet Communism, the citizens of Russia and Central Eurasia viscerally distrust all governments. They equate democracy almost entirely with an ability to remove political leaders at will. In turn, the political leaders have overreacted to the threat of widespread civil chaos by imposing dictatorships, defending such extreme measures as necessary if a free-market economy and constitutional democracy are to be achieved.

What both sides fail to recognize is that the constitutional crisis in Russia and Central Eurasia entails more than the short-term disputes over alternative constitutions or power arrangements. Adopting a system of government patterned after that of the United States or France will alter little, unless leaders succeed in fostering the long-term societal consensus and public trust—the values and beliefs—underlying democracy. However justified Yeltsin's use of force against parliament may have been, his unconstitutional actions, like those taken by other leaders in Central Eurasia, have established a dangerous precedent. Subsequent leaders now can more easily base their rule on force, even if such action provokes widespread opposition and civil war. The failure of governments to foster a democratic political culture will remain the real constitutional crisis facing Russia and Central Eurasia over the next several decades.

You should not think that former communist countries are the only ones in which the constitutional debate has come to the forefront of politics. At the same time that constitutional democracy is struggling to emerge in Russia and Central Eurasia, it may be enduring the struggles of disintegration in Italy. Italy provides a compelling example of what happens when the holders of concentrated power become so arrogant as to deny any accountability. The Italian system bears some similarity to Third and Fourth Republic France—a figurehead President, a weak Prime Minister, and a dominant parliament. Although the party system was fractionalized, one party (the Christian Democrats) so overshadowed the others that it could, usually with some coalition allies, control parliament. The Christian Democrats ran the state as though it were their personal fief. They were unaccountable and could expect to remain in power forever, because the leading alternative to them was the Italian Communist party. For forty years the Christian Democrats operated an extraordinarily successful con job. Then communism collapsed throughout the world. The Christian Democrats were deprived of the bogeyman they had used to frighten voters into retaining them in office election after election. The voters decided they no longer had to put up with the corruption that infested not only the Christian Democrats, but also almost every other party, as any possible serious opposition to those in power had been bought off.

If so much of the legislature and the party system is corrupt, how does a system break free? The answer lies in both accountability and checks and balances. The framers of the Italian constitution back in the late 1940s (foolish idealists that they were) had included a provision on referenda. Minor, gadfly political groups in Italy were able to obtain the popular support required to force change in the electoral system and to initiate a process of fundamental reform. While this was occurring, the quasi-independent Italian judiciary began investigating official corruption. A virtual flood of politicians and business leaders swept through the courts. A major portion of the legislature was either being investigated or under indictment. The judiciary was checking the executive's and the legislature's abuse of power.

Meanwhile, regional parties—especially the Lombard League in the north— won support at an astounding rate. The corruption of the existing parties encouraged such a shift in voter loyalties, but the crucial factor was internal xenophobia. Wealthy northerners decided—in their view—that they were tired of supporting lazy southerners. Why should they continue to generate funds that the government would tax and use to buy support in the south? Many *Wessis* in Germany might say, "I know the feeling." In Italy, well over a century of unification had failed to produce a shared sense of Italian identity. More so than in the United Kingdom, with its English, Scottish, Welsh, and Irish nations, breakup was possible in Italy. Germany, so recently unified, was hardly likely to refragment. Italy, however, provided further worrying evidence of the regional strains that exist even among people who appear to share a common language and culture.

Italy also demonstrated that in the end accountability is not to be denied. Eventually the bill for abuse of power comes due. If the idea ever occurred to political leaders in Britain, France, and Germany that they could escape accountability, Italy provided the cautionary example of what such conduct ultimately would do to the country. Abraham Lincoln said it best: "You can fool some of the people all of the time and all of the people some of the time, but you can't fool all of the people all of the time." The hope in the quest for free government is that that insight applies in repressive, as well as democratic, regimes. The experience of what once was the Soviet Union suggests that it does. Thus far, however, it has not proven valid in China. And, yet, some argue that even China has had to accommodate some aspects of the free-market economy. They assert that economic change is beginning to occur in China and that this, in turn, ultimately will produce political change. Pollyannish? Perhaps, but who other than a naive optimist would have predicted in 1985 that five years later the Soviet Union would collapse? The fallout from that collapse is still settling. We cannot foresee how it will end. Nonetheless, humanity's quest for limited, accountable power continues.

■ ECONOMIC FACTORS

We just alluded to the hope that economic change in China will produce political reform. What about the interplay of politics and economics in Europe? Economics may well be the policy area having the greatest impact on citizens' ratings of governmental performance and, therefore, clearly has some relevance to questions of durability and change.

Of the three countries that had free-market economies throughout the post– World War II period, all had established a prosperous, peacetime economy by the end of the 1950s. The grim conditions of the late 1940s in Britain, including food rationing and shortages of basic necessities (insufficient coal to heat one's home, for example), were gradually remedied. By the 1959 election campaign, Prime Minister Harold Macmillan could tell the people that they never had had it so good (and be more correct than his Labour opponent, Harold Wilson, who rejoined that the people had never been had so good).

As for West Germany, few can doubt that its initial economic success was the overriding reason for the health of its democratic system. Within a generation West Germany went from desolation to recovery to prosperity as one of the major economic powers of the world. In contrast to the Weimar experience, unemployment and inflation were not excessive. The incredible inflation of the Weimar regime, when restaurant meals literally changed in price while they were being eaten, was not repeated after World War II. Instead, prosperity provided a climate in which democracy could take root and flourish. Had economic affairs gone wrong, democracy would have had no chance in postwar Germany, despite all the effort put into drafting a democratic constitution. The Weimar experience had demonstrated the futility of relying on legal defenses alone.

The case of France demonstrates, however, that economic success is not a panacea. Despite making substantial economic progress during the first decade after World War II, the Fourth Republic was vulnerable to fundamental challenge. The crucial policy failure was in "foreign" affairs. (However curious it may seem, Algeria was considered to be part of France and thus not really foreign.) The long indecisive struggle in Algeria, following the military failures of World War II and the humiliating withdrawal from Indochina, proved too much for the constitutional regime's survival. (Americans who remember the 1960s know the strains that such "unwinnable" wars place on the political system, even though in the United States the effect was to topple a President rather than an entire political system.)

Under the new Fifth Republic, de Gaulle demonstrated that he had the courage for amputation. He was probably the only political leader who could have granted independence to Algeria without causing a full-scale civil war. Solving the problem, however, was not enough. Had de Gaulle's regime failed to maintain the economic success of the 1950s, the smoldering discontent with his Algerian solution might well have flared into a major blaze. Under the Fifth Republic, however, the French economy did even better than it had under the Fourth. France was converted to a belief—all too rare during the Third Republic—in growth and material progress; it became committed to efficiency and economic modernization. The stress that French leaders placed on these factors in the 1960s and 1970s resulted in a dramatic rise in industrial production and a mushrooming in the total value of exports. Rhetoric was supported by government-facilitated capital grants, tax exemptions, and interest-rate subsidies.

Although the parties in power varied from time to time and country to country, the period immediately following World War II could be called the zenith of social democracy in Europe. Government was accorded a major role in running the economy, not only to rebuild after the destruction of the war, but also to provide the central direction and planning that capitalism lacked. Government would ensure that everyone had a job and provide for those who could not support themselves.

Everyone would be protected from the uncertainties and disasters of life. Extensive ownership of previously private enterprise would enable government to fulfill its tasks. European countries had yet to face the question of how their citizens would react to privation that couldn't be blamed on war because, it was assumed, social democratic policies would prevent that from ever occurring.

The first country to have to cope with the tensions produced by unanticipated economic failure was Britain. Interest groups, especially the trade unions, seemed to have obtained such power that government was unable to maintain control of the economy. At one point in the 1970s, the rate of inflation in Britain surpassed 20 percent a year. High labor costs and productive inefficiencies lost Britain a substantial share of its export markets. While the rest of the industrialized world sped ahead, Britain experienced economic stagnation and relative decline. In the mid-1970s the country had to go cap in hand, like a Third-World country, to the International Monetary Fund and accept its policy prescriptions in order to obtain a loan to prevent national bankruptcy.

Given their traditional commitment to a venerable political system, Britons were unlikely to jettison it for a new constitutional order. Nonetheless, having tried both Conservative and Labour prescriptions for managing the economy in the 1960s and 1970s and found both wanting, the British people became less stable in voting behavior—party loyalties weakened. Not only did the traditional third party, the Liberals, increase its support, but parties advocating the breakup of the political system prospered in Wales and Scotland.

Part of the appeal of the Scottish Nationalists was that income from North Sea oil would make Scotland better off as an independent country than it would be as part of the United Kingdom. This was a plausible argument, since British development of gas and oil reserves in the North Sea kept economic conditions for the entire country from being even worse. This energy bonus, whose existence hadn't even been suspected a few years earlier, meant that the British economy was not battered to the extent that the economies of other Western industrial countries were by the rapidly rising petroleum prices of the 1970s, when the OPEC oil countries escalated the price of an essential energy resource. By 1980 Britain was able to produce virtually all of the oil it needed and most of the gas.

France and Germany lacked such resources and, as a result, began toward the close of the 1970s to experience the economic problems that Britain had lived with for a decade and a half. Growth and productivity rates fell; declining tax revenues forced cuts in public spending; inflation worsened (but without reaching the level it had in Britain). Western democracies seemed caught in a cruel dilemma: the trade-off for lower rates of inflation was higher rates of unemployment. In the early 1990s about a tenth of the work force was unemployed in Britain, and the rate was even higher in France. Unemployment was considerably lower than this in the western parts of Germany, but so high in the eastern parts that stimulating economic growth to create new jobs was a top policy priority in Germany, as well as in the other two countries.

Linked to the unemployment problem—by demagoguery, if not in truth—was the growing presence of racial, religious, and ethnic minorities in these three countries. In discussing tolerance in Britain, we mentioned the hostility that developed to the immigration of West Indians, Pakistanis, and Indians. As unemployment worsened, urban riots broke out in several British cities and continued night after night. White youths attacked blacks and Asians; Asian youths mobilized in aggressive self-defense. Black youths fought with police in anger at constantly being suspected of petty thefts. Looting and vandalism made some streets look as they had during the German bombing of England in World War II.

Some Britons wanted to ship all dark-skinned people "back where they came from"; others realized such action not only would be unjust but would be dealing more with symptoms than with causes. Former Prime Minister Edward Heath criticized his own Conservative party's governmental policies saying, "If you have half a million young people hanging around the streets all day you will have a massive increase in juvenile crime. Of course you will get racial tension when you have young blacks with less chance of getting jobs." In his view the problem was that the British people "lack any indication of whether there is any better sort of life for them at the end of these incomprehensible [economic] policies" being pursued by Prime Minister Thatcher's Cabinet.

As we noted in Part Four, Germany experienced labor shortages, particularly in the lower-paying, more menial occupations, as its economy expanded in the 1960s. Immigrants willing to clean the streets, dig graves, collect garbage, and perform other manual tasks at cheap wages were welcome then. Because these "guest workers" (*gastarbeiter)* were covered by government health and pension programs, they were resented by some as a drain on public funds. Although they were supposed to be only temporary residents, many brought their families to join them. They were producing a second generation of "immigrant" workers, whose social, economic, and political integration could easily be inflated into a major political issue, especially in economic hard times.

Similar tensions developed in France. There the immigrant workers came mainly from North Africa (especially Algeria), Portugal, Spain, and Italy. Leaders of respectable conservative parties sought to prevent a loss of votes to extreme right-wing parties by employing anti-immigrant rhetoric. Even the leader of the French Communist party advocated protecting the jobs of French workers from immigrants in language that was parochial, if not outrightly racist. (Apparently, even if all workers are brothers, as Marx said, they are not immune from sibling rivalry.)

In all three countries animosity toward people of different customs, language, and color raised the fundamental question of the tension between majority rule and minority rights in a democracy. Difficult to resolve in the best of times, the search for accommodation was hampered in the early and mid-1990s by high unemployment and low economic growth. Healthier economies would impede the efforts of extremist groups to make political capital out of public anxieties.

How were those healthier economies to be achieved? The sun of social democracy might not have set, but it was a great deal closer to the horizon than it had been. Few people believed any longer that the government knew how to run the economy. Cutting back its role seemed advisable so that the market could run itself without interference. Governments began to sell off many of the enterprises they owned. Government ownership supposedly had been essential for integrated direction of the economy, better service, and the lowest prices. Service often seemed worse, however, than in the private sector and, despite use of tax revenues to bail them out of economic problems, government enterprises' charges rarely seemed inexpensive. Therefore, selling government-owned enterprises back to the public could be expected to lose little and to generate a great deal of money at a time when increasing taxes seemed politically impossible.

Even if social democracy has had its day—and the state of the British Labour party, the French Socialist party, and the German SPD in the mid-1990s seemed to demonstrate that the voters thought it had—European politics has not returned to its pre–World War II attitudes. European governments now are expected to keep inflation and unemployment low and to generate at least a moderate rate of economic growth. Whether any government can manage all that may be questionable, but each is expected to try and is likely to suffer the electoral penalty for failure. Furthermore, citizens do not wish to relinquish the various services and protections that they obtained in the social democratic era; they simply don't want to pay for them. The goal is not so much to end programs as it is to try to deliver them more efficiently and less expensively. Whereas the social democrat expected the rational, highly trained civil servant to be able to do so better than the profit-seeking capitalist, the current trend is to push competitive tendering—private delivery of public services—to the maximum. Social democracy has not been so much extinguished as transformed. The scope and the role of European government have altered, but its tasks and its goals have changed little.

The same cannot be said of Russia and Central Eurasia, where the fifteen countries confront the formidable task of transforming entirely the former Soviet command economy into free-market systems. The former command economy owned, managed, and controlled every facet of economic life in the Soviet Union. The legacy of the command economy includes the most environmentally polluted cities in the world, industry geared to produce over two-thirds of its output in military goods for a Soviet armed force that no longer exists, and a level of technology at least twenty years behind that of Western countries. The fifteen countries are saddled with industrial managers who have been trained over decades not to act independently or to try to produce goods profitable in a competitive market. Soviet culture for generations fostered the belief that Western capitalist market economies exploited workers, that private ownership was the source of all evil. In the post-Soviet era, the trend is to free prices and privatize the economies by selling off state-owned industries. A small, but important, segment of 5–10 percent of the population has emerged as a new entrepreneurial class of private business-owners and farmers. Nonetheless, public opinion polls still find that many of their fellow citizens consider all private owners to be criminals.

With the freeing of prices from state regulation, hyperinflation in the fifteen countries has surpassed annual rates of 1000 percent. Wages have increased several-fold but lag well behind inflation. Economic output has declined 15–20 percent every year since independence, and each government faces financial crisis. Budget deficits have soared to 15–25 percent of the entire gross domestic product. Hyperinflation and economic collapse have reduced as many as half of these countries' populations to a standard of living below the poverty line. Pensioners, invalids, and others on fixed incomes have become impoverished almost as an entire social class. Under pressure by international lending agencies, their governments must sell off the many remaining unprofitable state-owned industries, almost all of which will just close down. As a consequence, citizens of these countries face the looming additional threat of widespread unemployment.

Opinion polls in Russia and Central Eurasia confirm an increasing sense of hopelessness and disillusionment with all political authorities among the citizens. The people had been told by those who led the movements to abolish the Soviet Communist system that the transition to a free-market economy would be relatively painless and easy. They had been promised that the free-market would dramatically improve the quality of their lives. Now the private sector has expanded several-fold, yet they see their own daily lives becoming even worse than they were under the former Soviet economy. Then, despite widespread shortages of consumer goods and a standard of living well below that of Western societies, they were at least assured stable, state-fixed prices and jobs. They blame the political parties, the haggling of elected officials, and the slowness of democratic processes and institutions. Populist demagogues, who have become more politically prominent in all of these countries, offer simpler explanations. They blame the economic problems on conspiracies, especially by ethnic minorities. Desperate populations in several of the countries have been turning in increasing numbers to these demagogues, who promise an end to the economic plight by reimposing a Soviet-style command economy and suspending democratic institutions and processes.

■ *SYMBOL, SUBSTANCE, AND DURABILITY*

In the mid-1990s three of the European governments we've covered, despite their contrasting ages, were institutionalized and durable. They had managed to respond to various challenges and appeared able to do so in the future. All were pressed by economic problems, but these were of the sort that might topple a Government— put one party out of power and bring another into office—not of the severity to overturn a constitutional structure.

Although government output—substance—is a major element in systemic durability, also crucial is symbolic value, the intrinsic attractiveness of the system. In Britain, tradition remains immensely important and provides an aid to durability, independent of substance. Such reliance on tradition could produce an immensely conservative society, resistant to all change. The British have shown great talent, however, in adapting old institutions to new functions, in shifting power and reforming society in generally acceptable, nondislocative ways. Their success demonstrates that retaining the legitimacy of a political system necessarily entails recognizing that the role of rationality in politics is limited. It is wiser, although intellectually less tidy, to allow for sentiment and tradition by means of piecemeal reform than to implement major structural changes recommended mainly by their abstract intellectual brilliance and the demands of some that all problems be solved immediately.

The British approach has not recommended itself to the French, who have preferred root-and-branch reform. This preference has produced, during the last two centuries of French history, a great deal more upheaval than has occurred during that same time in Britain. The result in France is competing symbols, competing governmental traditions, which make symbolic support less broad-based than in Britain. The Fifth Republic tends more toward the administrative tradition of attenuated accountability than to the assembly-government tradition of untrammeled power. Nonetheless, the current French system has survived sufficiently long to begin to generate a new mixed tradition of concentrated, but, in some respects, balanced power. It has won a respect that its predecessor lacked.

The Weimar Republic was forced to try to make do without any symbolic buttressing. Therefore, when it failed substantively, the regime had no symbolic support to fall back on until output could be improved. Now in Germany, as in France, longevity is creating a tradition that can provide symbolic support. Perhaps the forty-year delay in unification was just as well. Whether Germany could have coped with the strains, say, twenty years earlier is questionable. As it was, West Germans had ample time to develop loyalty to the constitutional system in itself. On the other hand, each year the West Germans had in which to develop democratic values was one year more East Germans lived without them. The ethnic commonality is misleading; the East Germans really are a different people and integrating them into a democratic system with a market economy will be difficult. They are going to need the positive economic experience that the West Germans enjoyed to weld them to their new democratic system.

As for the fifteen countries of Russia and Central Eurasia, their national leaders have little symbolic support or legitimacy other than their identification with the movements that toppled the former Soviet Union and brought about national independence. Since 1991, these leaders govern societies bitterly divided along the lines of various ethnic and religious groups. These groups accuse each other of attempting to gain control of the government in order to benefit themselves and to persecute everyone else. The collapse of the Soviet economy and the desperate economic plight in all of Russia and Central Eurasia have only encouraged the worst aspects of intolerance, bigotry, and tribalism derived from the former Russian imperial and Soviet Communist political cultures. The lack of any symbolic legitimacy for the new countries is but one factor in the numerous outbreaks of ethnic violence and outright civil wars described in Part Five.

Although the situation is most risky for Russia and Central Eurasia, even those systems with symbolic support to fall back on obviously desire the best possible economic results. Increasingly that may not be just a matter of their own policies. The countries of the world have become so interdependent that many problems can no longer be addressed by the individual action of one or another. A country may have the will and the insight to implement appropriate action, but its efforts may be thwarted by the contrary policies or inaction of others. We need to examine, therefore, the extent to which the economies of Britain, France, and Germany are being linked together in the EU and how likely that community is to include other members such as the countries of Russia and Central Eurasia.

......38

Europe as a Community _____

Chapter 37 compared and contrasted the leading European countries to evaluate their success in calling power to account and the likelihood that the arrangements they had worked out would endure without fundamental alteration. Although this was a comparative assessment, it still examined the countries as individual governmental systems. This chapter considers them as part of an international system.

Two centuries ago, few knowledgeable observers of politics would have rated highly the prospects for durability of a new entity that thirteen separate governmental units along the seaboard of the North American continent had created. None would have imagined that this entity would grow into the United States, survive a civil war close to the end of its first century, and become the most powerful country in the world before the end of its second.

In some respects, Europe now finds itself where the United States was two centuries ago. Granted that the residents of those thirteen governmental units were primarily British, although they might have thought of themselves as Virginians or New Yorkers, and were not encumbered with longstanding diverse national histories. To that extent, their task of producing a new united governmental system was not as monumental as that facing Europe today. In the past generation, despite the obstacles, Europe has progressed so far toward economic and, even more significant, political integration that the prospects for major European governments can't be discussed comprehensively without some attention to this international dimension. What has occurred goes beyond the ad hoc cooperation, alliances, or trade agreements familiar to students of international affairs. European developments involve such a high degree of political integration that common policies are made through newly created institutions. This chapter discusses this new entity—the European Union (originally known as the European Economic Community, or the Common Market, and later as the European Community).

■ THE GENESIS OF UNITY

Throughout history many wars have been fought across large geographic areas, but most have not been global conflicts. This is because, during most of human history, people in one part of the world were not aware that other people existed in other parts of the world. Even when they learned of such people, they lacked the logistical ability to transport and supply sizable armies across oceans. Then, a few centuries ago, the growth of technology and, even more important, the development of bureaucratic structures—which made possible systematic taxation and administration—began increasing considerably the geographic scope and destructive extent of war.

Despite this increase, wars remained limited in some senses. Battles tended to be fought by relatively small armies of professionals, men who made a career out of military service. Since men with the requisite skills and experience were hard to find, commanders often tried to avoid battle so as not to squander manpower. Wars frequently involved maneuvering as much as combat. As for the citizens, provided that they were not so unlucky as to be in the path of an army, they could live unaffected by any war their country happened to be fighting.

Total War as European Civil War

The Napoleonic wars at the start of the nineteenth century changed all this. Armies were composed of the population at large. Mobilization of citizen-soldiers produced vast military forces. Death and destruction reached new heights. Following Napoleon's defeat at Waterloo, conflict among European nations for the remainder of the nineteenth century seemed to be moving back to the limited wars of the past. On the other side of the Atlantic, the American Civil War demonstrated how annihilating war had become, but its geographic scope was not international.

Then, early in the twentieth century, disputes in the Balkans spread throughout Europe in a conflict eventually known as World War I. From Europe, fighting spilled over into Asia Minor and the Middle East. The combatants included troops from North America and the South Pacific, and an Asian nation—Japan—was one of the belligerents. Just over twenty years after this international conflict ended, another conflagration truly enveloped the entire globe, with fighting not only in Europe but also in Asia and Africa. This, the most destructive and widespread conflict in history, was deservedly labeled World War II.

This brief historical summary may seem rather provincial; it focuses mainly on Europe, as though the countries and people there are the only ones that matter. The reason for such a focus is that the principal international conflicts of the last three centuries, in particular those of the current century, have tended to be among European nations and to have spread from that continent to encompass a global battleground. Many of the political leaders of Europe were haunted by this knowledge in 1945 as they surveyed the ruins of their continent—cities in rubble, millions homeless, industry obliterated. The current problems of Western Europe discussed in Chapter 37 are as nothing compared to those of 1945, when few could envision how the masses of Europe would be able to obtain the food, clothing, and shelter they needed for survival and when the victorious countries were almost as badly off as the vanquished.

Seeing all this, European political leaders in 1945 vowed that it would never happen again. For the first time they perceived the past three centuries of international conflict as a *civil war*, occurring *within* a political entity—Europe. Of course,

Europe was not truly a single governmental system, but their goal was to make it such. They felt that the national rivalries that had produced three centuries of intermittent warfare, increasingly tending to spread throughout the world, could no longer be tolerated. The rivalry they regarded as most pernicious was that between France and Germany: three times (1870, 1914, and 1939) in less than a century these two countries had gone to war against each other. The only solution appeared to be to bind the economies of these two rivals so closely together that it would be impossible for them to fight each other again. This was what Europe's political leaders set out to do as they rebuilt their continent in the middle of the twentieth century.

The Supranational Remedy

Common disasters and common fears galvanized European leaders at mid-century. They also shared common ideals. European union was a goal worth questing for; it provided a new political faith to replace discredited nationalism and offered an alternative to Communist ideology, which appealed to many who admired the Soviet Union's contribution to the defeat of Nazism. Union might also be a means of revitalizing European culture and, thus, of resisting the increasing influence of "vulgar" American mass culture. Another common aspect that many of these leaders shared was a religious faith. Christian Democracy was at its zenith as a political movement in the immediate postwar period. At times, the foreign ministers of the six countries most fully involved in working for union shared a Catholic background.

The roll call of the key leaders in this process is extensive, but if any one person deserves to be called the founder of European unity, it is Jean Monnet (pronounced "jahn moh-nay"). Monnet was a French bureaucrat who had also been an international civil servant. Although he is often thought of as an idealist and a visionary, he was also a practical man of affairs who gave European unity a concrete beginning.

In May 1948, delegates from many countries founded the European Movement, which led a year later to the creation of the Council of Europe by ten countries. These steps made clear that those interested in uniting Europe were divided on a fundamental issue—what the union would be like. On the one hand, some—mainly the British, the Swiss, and the Scandinavians—favored a cooperative approach. They wanted union to be limited to a few, relatively marginal functions. Countries would consult each other regularly, but a unanimous vote would be required for any decision and it would not be binding. No new organizations would be created to implement, to say nothing of enforce, decisions. Opposed to the cooperative approach was the supranational approach, which favored some pooling of sovereignty, thus limiting national independence to some extent. The postwar constitutions of France, Germany, and Italy all specifically provided for such limits as a means of furthering European unity. The supranational approach involved creating international organs with some independent power. For the supranationalists, union was the first step toward a federal system, toward a United States of Europe. Like the United States, composed of a number of states with certain powers and a central government with other powers, a single political system would come to exist in Europe—composed of such states as France and Germany, along with a separate central government.

The supranationalists quickly became disillusioned with the Council of Europe. The cross-national contacts and discussions it facilitated rarely produced any decisive action. A new attempt at union was needed; something realistic enough to produce the progress that idealism had failed to obtain. The strategy the supranationalists opted for became known as "functional federalism," working toward union on a limited sector-by-sector or function-by-function basis. At some unspecified point, the accumulated weight of many separate functional integrations would, they thought, tip the balance over to a compelling drive for general integration.

Their first effort involved the pooling of coal and steel production to create a single market for those products. All existing national tariffs and quotas were eliminated, as were cartels and price fixing. The idealistic component of this plan was to so merge key elements of French and German industrial capacity that military conflict between the two countries would be extremely unlikely. Only Italy, the Netherlands, Belgium, and Luxembourg were willing to join France and Germany in this attempt. In 1952, these six countries established the European Coal and Steel Community (ECSC). The ECSC had a supranational structure. Some countries had agreed to limit their sovereignty, although only to a limited extent. An executive body (called the High Authority and presided over by Monnet, whose plan ECSC had been) was created to administer the agreement. Furthermore, a parliament (the Assembly) was established to provide a forum for consultative discussion, and a Court of Justice was empowered to settle disputes over implementing the agreement.

Five years later, functional federalism advanced much further when the six ECSC members agreed to establish two more communities: the European Atomic Energy Community (Euratom) and the European Economic Community (EEC, or Common Market). Originally, three separate executives existed, since the power granted to the executive varied from one community to another. Eventually these were merged into a single executive (there were always only one court and one parliament), and the organizations became a single one—the European Community (EC).

The British regarded these steps as impractical nonsense. Talk and some cooperation were fine, but nations had diverged too greatly over the centuries to be able to pool sovereignty, even to a limited degree. Furthermore, British tradition was to remain aloof from continental affairs, getting involved only when necessary to preserve a balance of power—to prevent any country or alliance from becoming so predominant as to pose a threat to British interests. In addition, Britain regarded France, Germany, and Italy as unreliable, as unstable political systems with little commitment to democracy. In short, union was, in British parlance, a "non-starter."

Although Britain could get away with disdaining the ECSC, doing the same with the EEC was more risky. The EEC was going to not only eliminate trade barriers among its members, but also construct a common barrier against nonmembers. The common external tariff would put British businesses at a disadvantage in competing with enterprises within the EEC; Britain might well be cut off from a major market for its products. Since Britain can afford to import the food and raw materials it lacks only by selling manufactured goods abroad in volume, the potential danger was serious. Britain's response was to create its own trade organization, one lacking any hint of the EEC's supranationalism. The European Free Trade

Association (EFTA), launched in 1960, included Britain and six other countries on the periphery of the EEC. EFTA removed trade barriers among its members entirely by voluntary cooperation. It had no consultative assembly, no court to settle disputes, and, most important, no supranational executive to implement the agreement. All that the organization involved was regular meetings of representatives from the member countries to discuss trade policy and other relevant matters.

By linking at least some European countries with itself through EFTA, Britain sought to avoid being left in the lurch should any EEC success entice others to think of joining the original six members. Hardly had HMS EFTA left port, however, when perfidious Albion itself sought to jump ship—Britain opened negotiations for EEC membership. The British assumed, of course, that if and when they decided to cast their lot with the EEC, they would be welcomed with open arms. Little did they anticipate the hostility of President de Gaulle of France. After France had fallen to the Nazis in World War II, de Gaulle had been given a base of operation in London and had been consulted regularly throughout the struggle to free Europe. But there is no loathing like that produced by being forced to accept charity, especially when the recipient is inordinately proud. De Gaulle now saw an opportunity to spite the British. In January 1963 he announced that France would block British membership in the EEC because Britain was insufficiently European. As was often true of de Gaulle's high-handed actions, this charge was not entirely implausible. As we noted already, Britain had remained as aloof from the Continent as possible and regarded itself as more advanced politically than the countries there. Furthermore, Britain felt it possessed a unique "special relationship" with the United States. De Gaulle's dislike of the United States was even greater than his dislike of Britain; he was not about to allow into the EEC a British Trojan horse that would smuggle in U.S. influence. After all, France was supposed to dominate the EEC.

Expanding Membership

In 1967 Britain again applied for membership, and again de Gaulle said no. Eventually, after his death, Britain tried once more and was accepted. At the start of 1973, Britain—along with two other EFTA members, Denmark and Ireland—joined what was now the EC. During the 1980s Greece, Spain, and Portugal were admitted. The organization had doubled in size, to twelve members.

In the 1990s enlargement issues again became pressing problems. With the collapse of communism in Eastern Europe, the question of links between countries there and the EC was raised. Some of these countries had potentially thriving economies, but others had been so mismanaged by Communists that they resembled Third-World countries more than European ones. Associate membership in the EC, such as Greece had had before being granted full membership, was a possible, but by no means simple, solution. Even as associates, the Eastern European countries would make the EC even more diverse and thus impede attempts at tighter integration of the separate national economies.

The expansion question has produced some unusual political alliances. On the one hand, some idealistic Europeans are enamored with the idea of a community encompassing all of Europe. They seem willing to embrace all comers, perhaps even Russia and Ukraine. The nationalists, who, like many in Britain, oppose any limit on sovereignty, are inclined to support the idealists. This is not because they have been converted, but because they calculate that breadth of membership is the enemy of depth of integration. Admitting more members increases diversity—an excellent way to narrow the range of areas where common policies are feasible. Furthermore, in the meantime, no steps should be taken to integrate the existing organization more tightly because that would make the subsequent forging of links with the newly freed Eastern European nations much more difficult. Those supranationalists who are more practical than idealistic certainly don't want to turn their backs on Eastern Europe, but neither do they want the somewhat bogus concerns of the nationalists to impede European integration at just the time when advancing to a higher level of integration might be possible.

The Maastricht Treaty, whose ratification by Britain was described in Chapter 37, was intended to play a crucial role in pushing integration further. Following formal approval by all twelve member countries, the treaty became effective at the start of November 1993, and the EC became the European Union (EU).

■ THE EUROPEAN UNION

Community Institutions

The European Union (EU) is composed of five principal structures. The Commission is headquartered in Brussels, the Council of Ministers in Luxembourg, and the Court of Justice in Strasbourg, France. As for the European Parliament, it holds a plenary session in Strasbourg about once a month, its committees meet in Brussels, and its staff is located in Luxembourg. Yes, this is a ridiculous arrangement, but several countries wanted to be certain that they got a good share of the money to be spent locally in accommodating the various institutions. The European Council has no home or regular meeting place.

The Commission The Commission has seventeen members—two each from the five largest countries and one from each of the other seven. Commissioners serve simultaneous four-year terms and can be reappointed. Commissioners are appointed with the general consent of all member states, but the established practice is to allow each country to designate whomever it wishes to fill "its" position(s). Once appointed, however, Commissioners are supposed to be autonomous. They take an oath renouncing national interests and are expected to seek the general welfare of the EU.

The Commission chooses its own presiding officer. This official is simply the president of the Commission but is sometimes referred to as the president of the European Union. Jacques Delors of France, who became president in 1985, has been an extremely dynamic executive, constantly pushing for greater unity.

The Council of Ministers In contrast to the Commission, the Council of Ministers is intended to defend the interests of the member states, each of which has a single representative. The Council is not so much a single institution as a collection of separate bodies. Depending on the topic to be discussed, different ministers from the Cabinets of the member countries attend. If, for example, the subject is food, then each country would send its Minister of Agriculture to the meeting. A gathering of Foreign Ministers is probably the most important of the Council's meetings, since their scope for action is so broad. Given the Council's composition, its members have no fixed term; membership changes whenever a country decides to send someone else.

Assisting the Council is the Committee of Permanent Representatives (Coreper). Each country appoints an ambassador to the EU, just as to any foreign country. The twelve ambassadors that make up Coreper try to resolve as many issues as they can through regular discussions. Thus, only major controversies on which the contrasting views have been well-defined need to be handled by Council meetings. Coreper prepares the necessary materials for those meetings so that business can be transacted efficiently.

The European Parliament Perhaps the most visible, although least powerful, of the EU's institutions is the European Parliament. Its powers are primarily consultative. It is empowered, however, to reject the Union's budget by a two-thirds vote. Furthermore, it can remove the entire Commission from office (rather like a motion of no confidence in one of the national parliaments), again by a two-thirds vote. The latter has never occurred, but the Parliament has rejected the budget twice. In addition, the Parliament can direct questions to the Commission and the Council of Ministers.

Composed of 567 members, allocated as indicated in Table 38–1, the Parliament conducts business in ten languages by means of simultaneous translation. Members of the European Parliament (MEPs, or Euro-MPs, as they are also known) serve five-year terms. Originally appointed by their governments, they have been popularly elected since 1979. That year, during the same week in early June, voters in all the member countries went to the polls to choose their representatives. Except in Britain, which clung to its traditional single-member, simple-plurality system, proportional representation was used. Elections were held again in 1984 and in 1989. Unfortunately, these do not seem to have stirred up any great popular interest. In the first elections, just over three-fifths of those eligible went to the polls. Five years later the turnout dropped by 3 percentage points, and in 1989 it remained at that level. (A participation rate of 59 percent may sound pretty good by American standards, but Europeans normally vote in greater numbers than do Americans.)

Although the various parties contest elections only within their own national borders, typically, parties of similar type will issue a joint, cross-national manifesto for a Euro-election. Nonetheless, Euro-elections are not truly international. Parties tend to fight their campaigns much more on domestic political issues than on European ones. In some instances in 1989, national elections were held on the same day as the Euro-election. Even where that didn't occur, the Euro-election tended to be treated as a referendum on the parties in power in a particular country, and so national politics were the overriding influence on voting behavior.

Some of the Italian parties did make a gesture toward internationalism in 1989 by inviting people from other countries to run for the European Parliament in

Table 38–1

National Representation in the European Parliament

Germany	99
Britain	87
France	87
Italy	87
Spain	64
Netherlands	31
Belgium	25
Greece	25
Portugal	25
Denmark	16
Ireland	15
Luxembourg	6

Table 38–2

Results of 1989 Euro-Elections Compared to Those of 1984

Group	Seats	Change
Communists	41	–7
Rainbow Group	39	+19
Socialists	181	+15
European Peoples' Party	123	+11
European Democratic Group	34	–32
Liberals	44	–1
European Democratic Alliance	19	–11
Right	22	+6
Independents	15	0
Total	518	

Italian constituencies. The Italian Communists, for example, had as one of their candidates a prominent French political scientist, and a centrist grouping of Italian parties offered a slate including the former leader of the British Liberal party.

The 1989 Euro-elections showed a modest swing to the left. (See the results in Table 38–2. Prior to 1994 the Parliament had 518 members.) The Socialists, who already had been the largest single group in Parliament, increased their strength by more than a dozen seats. This gain was due almost entirely to the strong performance of the British Labour party. More remarkable was the success achieved by the Rainbow Group (this group has nothing to do with Jesse Jackson's Rainbow Coalition). The members of the Rainbow Group are primarily ecologists, or Greens. This group nearly doubled its previous strength to win almost as many seats as the Communists did. The gains would have been even greater had it not been for the British electoral system. In Britain, the Greens won 15 percent of the vote and finished third—ahead of the Liberal Democrats. Given what you have learned about the single-member, simple-plurality electoral system, you shouldn't be surprised to learn that despite their achievements, the Greens failed to elect a single MEP.

The European Peoples' Party (EPP), composed primarily of Christian Democrats, was the other chief gainer and maintained its position as the second-largest group in the Parliament. The EPP's additional strength did not result from increased support among the voters. The Spanish Popular party left the group to which it had belonged previously and joined the EPP. The sharp decline of the centrist European Democratic Group was due to the departure of the Spanish Popular party and the loss to Labour of a number of seats the British Conservatives had held. Two aspects of the 1989 results concerning the far right are worth noting. In France, the National Front managed to hold its ten seats, receiving just about the same share of the vote as it had in 1984, although less than its leader, Jean-Marie Le Pen, had polled in the 1988 French presidential election. In Germany, the far-right Republican party followed up some of its recent successes at the state level and outpolled the FDP, to win six seats. Nonetheless, its share of the vote in Germany was only two-thirds of that obtained by the National Front in France.

When the MEPs reach Strasbourg, they form international groups. That is, they do not sit in separate delegations by country, but join to form cross-national partisan groups, such as Communists and Socialists. The organizational rules of the Parliament encourage such cooperation across national boundaries. To be officially recognized as a group (and thus receive debate time, committee seats, and the like) requires twenty-three MEPs if all are from the same country, but only eighteen if the MEPs are from two countries, and only twelve if they are from three.

The Court of Justice   The Court of Justice has thirteen justices serving overlapping six-year terms, with reappointment permitted. Although the justices are supposed to be appointed by general consent among the member states, each country is entitled to a justice and its choice is automatically approved. Thus, only the thirteenth justice is truly appointed by agreement among all the countries, and even in this instance the practice is to rotate the position among the five largest countries. The justices select one of their number as president to preside over and organize their activities. All decisions of the Court must be unanimous; no dissenting opinions are issued. (The Court should not be confused with the European Court of Human Rights located in Strasbourg. That court was created under the Council of Europe and has nothing to do with the EU.)

Cases reach the Court of Justice in several ways. One member state may charge another with violating the EU's basic treaty, but this rarely occurs. More commonly, the Commission will charge a member with violating the treaty, or a member will file a complaint against the Commission or the Council. Also, the Parliament, the Commission, and the Council may seek to overturn one another's actions. Most interesting from a supranational perspective is the fact that, in some limited circumstances, private individuals may bring suit against the Commission or the Council in the Court.

In addition to hearing actual cases, the Court can provide advisory opinions. Either the Council or the Commission can ask it to indicate whether an international agreement being considered by the EU is compatible with the basic treaty. Even more important, judges in the various member states can seek advisory opinions on the proper interpretation of EU law when such questions arise in the cases being tried in their courts. When such a request is made, the Court's opinion is binding on the judge who made the inquiry.

At the start of the 1970s, the Court typically heard less than 100 cases a year. By the close of the 1980s, it was dealing with over 400. Furthermore, it was taking much longer to process a case. A case typically had been disposed of in nine months, but this grew to an average of twenty-one months. These work-load figures are a bit misleading, in that about two-fifths of all the cases were of limited importance, involving the staff of the EU's institutions. Since these "Eurocrats" have expatriate status, they cannot pursue their complaints in national courts.

To ease the work load, in 1989 the Community set up a junior Court of First Instance to handle lesser cases. All of the cases initiated by Eurocrats now go to this court. The Court of First Instance also handles competition cases. In 1993 the EU moved even further toward creating a two-level court system. Jurisdiction for cases brought by natural and legal persons (corporations) was shifted to the Court of First Instance. This change should help to ensure that the Court of Justice deals primarily with broad legal questions concerning the provisions of the EU's treaties and the relations between member countries and the EU.

The Court lacks any means of implementing its decisions; that is, it has no way to impose its sanctions. Nonetheless, most member states have observed their treaty obligation to comply with decisions—even when these go against their wishes. More than half of the members—Britain, Denmark, Ireland, Luxembourg, the Netherlands, Portugal, and Spain—had failed to comply with no more than four of the Court's decisions by the end of 1991. Although the other five members of the EU have not done as well, only one has been truly derelict. Italy had not implemented three dozen of the Court's judgments.

Perhaps the most significant of the Court's decisions was its holding in a 1964 case that Community law takes precedence over conflicting national law, just as the supremacy clause of the U.S. Constitution permits laws enacted by the national government to override state legislation. Despite this holding, many people in Britain were shocked in 1991 when the Court voided a British law for conflicting with a Community regulation. Since, as you know, Parliament is supreme in Britain, the idea that some court could throw out one of its acts was a revolutionary idea. Clearly, sovereignty, long regarded as the hallmark of national independence, is to some extent limited for those countries belonging to the EU.

The European Council The four institutions just discussed were originally provided for; another structure was subsequently added. You have seen how the conflict between the nationalists and the supranationalists was institutionalized in a Council of Ministers and a Commission. The Council of Ministers would ensure that the EU did not get too far out of step with national policies. Nonetheless, it was not entirely satisfactory. A President of a country is not a member of its Cabinet. The Prime Minister of whatever country seldom heads a particular government department in that country. Therefore, neither Presidents nor Prime Ministers attended the Council of Ministers. The chief executive in any EU country could instruct a national delegate to the meetings, but would not personally attend to participate in decision making. To a considerable extent, those who participated in meetings of the Council of Ministers had to speak on someone else's authority.

The national chief executives—the various heads of government and heads of state —could, of course, get together whenever they wished to hold something of a European summit and occasionally did so. In 1974 they formally agreed to meet regularly. A 1987 addition, known as the Single European Act, to the original treaties made these gatherings part of the Community's constitution. Each member country in its turn provides a presiding officer, known as the president of the European Council (not to be confused with the president of the Commission). The term lasts for six months. Shortly before a term ends, the European Council is convened in the country of the president. Some of the twice yearly meetings amount to little more than an opportunity for the heads of government and heads of state to get to know each other better. At times, however, the executives do make broad policy decisions concerning EU goals and priorities.

The Community in Action

The preceding description of the EU's structure may have made it sound rather like the American system—three branches of government (legislative, executive, and judicial) and a central government predominant over the constituent units. Were that true, those who wanted a supranational Europe would have triumphed. To see why they have not, we need to look at how the Community operated in practice during the 1970s and much of the 1980s.

The basic decision-making procedure was for the Commission to submit a proposal to Coreper. After extensive discussion, the ambassadors recommended a response to the Council. The Council could issue a directive (binding on member states with respect to the goals of action, but permitting each country to use whatever means it wished to obtain these ends) or a regulation (covering both ends and means and having the same status as laws passed by a country's legislature). The Council had to consult with the Parliament before acting, but could ignore any views that that body expressed. In practice, however, about two-thirds of all of the Parliament's suggested changes in proposed EC laws were accepted to some extent.

The Commission prepared the EC's budget, which was submitted to the Council before being sent on to the Parliament. After the Parliament had discussed it, the budget was returned to the Council for revision before being sent back to the Parliament for final action. Parliament's power lay primarily in that portion of the budget (about a quarter) providing funds for programs that were not specifically required by the EC's treaties. Each year the Commission set a ceiling on the increase the Parliament could make in this portion of the budget. Should the Council disagree with the specific increases that Parliament favored, it could reject them. When the budget returned to the Parliament from the Council, only a vote on the entire spending plan was permitted. Thus, if the Parliament had failed to persuade the Council to accept its wishes for a different allocation of funds, its only recourse was to vote down the entire budget (or accept the Council's decision). Such a threat lacked credibility since, typically, the Parliament would be trying to get the Council to agree to *greater* expenditures for particular programs, and the rules provide that if the budget is rejected, spending continues *at the same level* as in the preceding year. As we mentioned earlier, only twice did Parliament reject the budget. The result was to make the Council the EC's true law-making body.

Furthermore, the Council was the true executive as well. The Commission administered the EC in accord with instructions from the Council. The relation between the two executives that had existed under the ECSC was altered fundamentally. The High Authority of the ECSC had been empowered to act directly on the coal and steel firms in the member states, without having to go through their national governments. Not only could it issue binding, detailed decisions, but it could also fine companies for not complying and levy taxes. Furthermore, the High Authority decided issues on the basis of simple majority vote—there was no national veto. When the ECSC, Euratom, and the EEC merged into one community, the executive became more like the arrangement for the Common Market than that for the Coal and Steel Community. In contrast to the ECSC Treaty, the agreement for the EEC tended to lodge supranational powers not with the autonomous executive, but with the intergovernmental Council of Ministers. The Commission could act on its own only in matters of competition policy and farm policy. Its chief power lay in the fact that the Council needed a unanimous vote to modify one of the Commission's proposals.

The institutional change for the merged executive was of great significance, but what ensured a change in the Community's power structure was the immovable object encountered before—Charles de Gaulle. In the mid-1960s two changes were at issue. The EEC Treaty had provided that, following a transitional period, the Council of Ministers would cease to reach decisions by unanimity and start voting by weighted, or even simple, majority. Whatever de Gaulle may have thought about the British, he was even more adamant than they were in defending national sovereignty. He was not about to accept a voting procedure that could result in France's being required to implement an action that he opposed. The second issue involved the Commission's ill-judged decision to push for greater supranational arrangements in financial matters. Sizable sums were being raised for the EEC from the common external tariff. The Commission proposed that the Parliament should control the spending of this income. The red flag had been waved in front of the bull, who, naturally, charged. Using a tactic he had found to be quite effective in French politics, de Gaulle picked up his marbles and went home—literally. France boycotted EEC meetings, indicating that it would continue to do so until such time as everyone else came to their senses (that is, came to see things as de Gaulle did). The EEC and the process of economic integration ground to a halt.

The "compromise" that resolved this stalemate was to abandon any thought of the Parliament's controlling the Community's financial resources or of majority voting. It was accepted that on matters of vital interest to any member state, action could be taken only by unanimity—a national veto had been reimposed on decision making. In practice, rather than trying to distinguish between vital and trivial matters and to avoid further rancor, unanimity came to be the decision-making rule for all action in the Council. The Commission retained the power to formulate proposals for Community action, but the change in voting procedure meant a considerable shift in power to the Council (which in practice meant to Coreper).

By the 1980s European unity seem becalmed. In terms of both the breadth and depth of linkage among the economies of the EC countries, little progress was being made. European unity needed a new impetus. An EC internal study identified about 300 specific actions required to complete the process of transforming the members' separate economies into a single market. With this goal in mind, the members agreed in 1985 to the Single European Act (SEA), which, ratified by all, went into effect in mid-1987 (and as mentioned earlier codified the European Council). The SEA set the end of 1992 as the date for achieving a barrier-free, internal market, "an area without internal frontiers, in which the free movement of goods, persons, services and capital is assured." The Community was seeking to move beyond merely eliminating tariffs and quotas that hamper trade among members (this had largely been accomplished already) to removing all impediments to commerce.

The complexity of this task may not be immediately apparent. It included, for example, determining the professional qualifications required for people to practice as doctors and lawyers, accounting regulations for corporations, restrictions on manufacturing procedures (such as safety standards for workers and product contents), and rights for holders of patents, trademarks, and copyrights. What, to take a mundane example, were to be the standards for lawn-mower noise, and could an Italian company be permitted to make a lawn mower less quiet than a British company's? Could British sausages, which contain more filler and less meat than German ones, be sold in Germany? Could a French liqueur be kept out of Germany because its alcoholic content was too low to meet German standards for such drinks?

This was not the first time that the Community had grappled with such questions. In the past it had tried to resolve such problems through "harmonization." This process involved extensive haggling among the members in an effort to agree on a common regulation to be applied by all. The result all too often fully justified the old saying that a camel is a horse put together by a committee. Not only was the process inordinately time-consuming, but it produced extremely detailed regulations that were almost unworkable, if not incomprehensible.

The SEA tried a new approach—deregulation. The essence of this process was "mutual recognition," an arrangement similar to what is known as interstate comity under the U.S. federal system. In brief, mutual recognition means that what is legal in one of the member states should be legal in the others; safe products should be allowed to cross national borders, regardless of whether those products comply with the specifications typically prevailing in the destination country. Italy can require domestic producers of pasta to use a certain type and quality of flour, but it can't bar from sale in Italy pasta made in other member countries with different contents. France can continue to enact strict banking regulations, but it can't use these to keep less-restricted British bankers from doing business in France.

Permitting competition from products that do not meet national standards was only part of the concern. Member countries with high sales tax feared that they might have to lower them. If there are to be absolutely no border checks on nationals from member states, then what is to stop a Dane from popping over the border into Germany to buy a car there and escaping the high Danish tax on such a purchase? The U.S. federal system has had its own fascinating experiences with such questions. For example, when Wisconsin ("the dairy state") prohibited the sale of margarine that was colored yellow to resemble butter, residents in the southern part of the state used to make regular trips into Illinois to smuggle colored margarine back into the state under the noses of the state police. You might think the solution for the Danish case would be for Denmark to lower sales taxes to equal the German. But then the Danish government would be forced to raise some other taxes to make up for the shortfall in revenues; obviously, no government wants to do that.

To expedite action in building the single market, the SEA made important institutional changes. Only the Commission can initial proposals for new laws. Most of its proposals related to achieving the single market were freed from needing unanimous endorsement by the Council (Charles de Gaulle is dead at the present time);

they can be passed by a weighted majority. Each country's delegate to the Council of Ministers was given a number of votes roughly proportional to its population. Only fifty-four out of the total seventy-six votes is needed to decide an issue. Thus, the Commission no longer has to draw up proposals that will be acceptable to all the members. Since the five largest member states control forty-eight votes and the seven smallest twenty-eight, neither group can impose its will on the other. A minimal coalition for blocking action (twenty-three votes) requires cooperation among two of the four largest members and at least one of the small ones (other than Luxembourg—having only two votes, its cooperation would still leave the group a vote short). The new voting procedure greatly reduced the Council's decision-making time. Unanimity continues to be required for some subjects, primarily fiscal harmonization, border controls to prevent crime, and stringent standards on working conditions and environmental protection. In the latter case, however, the requirement is eased by allowing members wishing to adhere to higher standards than those of the Community to enact their own measures, as long as these do not impede trade.

Another important change made by the SEA concerns the role of the Parliament. Under the "assent procedure," it must approve any agreements between the EU and other countries. This means that new members can be admitted only if the European Parliament assents. The same procedure applies to renewal of existing agreements. Since the EU has a number of such agreements and they all have time limits on them, the role of the Parliament in its external affairs has been expanded.

Even more significant is the Parliament's enhanced policy role under the new "consent procedure." Commission proposals go first to the Parliament. Parliament passes them on to the Council of Ministers, along with its suggested amendments. In the first three years after this new procedure came into effect, the Council accepted nearly half of the proposed changes. The Council decides on a "common position" and returns the proposal to Parliament. If this is satisfactory to Parliament, then the Council enacts it.

Parliament can, however, amend or even reject a common position. If Parliament votes to reject, then the Council can enact the proposal only by unanimous vote. Should at least half of the members of Parliament vote to amend the proposal, then it is returned to the Commission. When the Commission accepts Parliament's amendment (which occurs more than half the time), the Council can enact the proposal by a weighted majority. The Parliament, backed by the Commission, is freed from needing every country's approval in the Council to enact its preferences. When the Commission rejects Parliament's amendment, the proposal can be implemented *only* by unanimous vote of the Council. An internally divided Council would either have to accept the amendments or drop the issue. Parliament's views have ceased to be simply advisory and easily ignorable.

The original EEC Treaty was concerned, you will recall, primarily with economic integration; it did not include foreign policy matters, except in so far as trade agreements might be made with other countries and economic aid provided. The SEA formalized the existing European Political Cooperation (EPC), intended to coordinate the member countries' international actions, as a means of achieving a

"European foreign policy." Despite the objections of the Danes, the Irish, and the Greeks, this is said to include security policy. Those meetings of the Council of Ministers involving the members' Foreign Ministers regularly include a representa-. tive from the Commission and seek to devise common positions on international affairs, as well as both political and economic aspects of security policy. EPC is serviced by a small secretariat in Brussels.

■ *E PLURIBUS UNUM?*

The year 1993 was to have been the one in which the EC came to full fruition. Instead it amply demonstrated that the comments of the Scottish poet Robert Burns concerning the best intentions were applicable not only to small rodents and people of male gender but also to the EC. The irony was that on the eve of the preparatory year the leaders of the member countries were congratulating themselves on having put into place the piece essential to complete the puzzle of integration. The Dutch presidency had concluded with a meeting of the European Council in December 1991 in the town of Maastricht. There the heads of state and of government signed a treaty making major changes in the Treaty of Rome, the framework agreement for the EC. The Maastricht Treaty was intended to tie together all the loose ends left by the SEA and make specific the procedures and criteria for the single market that had been left vague. The treaty had much grander goals than this, however; it was to launch a new drive for supranationalism. A European Union was to exist. One pillar of this new development would be economic and monetary integration occurring under the EU. A new second pillar would be political integration. European Political Cooperation (EPC), mentioned above, would be the core of this pillar. It would work to create common foreign policies. These would be complemented by defense and security actions organized through Western European Union (WEU), the organization devised in the 1950s as a means of making German rearmament acceptable to the French. Despite the fact that three (Denmark, Ireland, and Greece) of the EU's members don't belong to WEU, that organization was proclaimed to be the EU's defense component. Britain and France disagreed on whether this made WEU "subordinate" to the EC.

For the first few months of 1992 this new initiative for supranationalism seemed to be on track. Then in June the Danes made Europe tremble just as the Northmen had some nine centuries earlier. They voted against the Maastricht Treaty in a referendum. Not by much—49.3 percent in favor to 50.7 percent against; but no it was. Hagar the Horrible had struck again. A quick shove and a cry of "man overboard" wasn't a viable solution since the Maastricht Treaty required ratification by all twelve EC members. Only three months later, France reported some good news and some bad. The good news was that the French electorate had voted *in favor* of the Maastricht Treaty in a referendum; the bad was that the results were almost precisely the reverse of those of the Danish referendum—support had been expressed by the narrowest of margins.

In Britain, Prime Minister John Major refused to risk putting the treaty to a referendum, despite many calls for one. Denmark's vote, by putting the treaty at risk, made passage of the bill needed to give the treaty effect in Britain even more difficult. Parliamentary action preliminary to ratification had been anticipated by the summer of 1992; instead the process dragged on for another year. Even then the cloud of a legal challenge in the courts delayed ratification a bit longer. Britain was not unique in that regard. A legal challenge to the Maastricht Treaty had been filed as well with the Federal Constitutional Court in Germany. Since the FCC's judgment was not delivered until the fall of 1993, Germany was the last country to ratify the treaty.

While the Maastricht wars continued, the whole idea of economic unity suffered major blows: first, in mid-September 1992 both Britain and Italy withdrew from the Exchange Rate Mechanism (ERM), the procedure for linking together the currencies of the member countries en route to a common currency. Many harsh words were exchanged and fingers were pointed in all directions about whose economic policies had forced Britain to pull out. The widely held view in Europe was that Britain had behaved true to type: whenever it comes to the crunch, perfidious Albion will back away from tight economic and political integration with other countries.

Ten months later the British found it hard not to smirk openly behind the backs of their hands when France, in particular, and Denmark encountered precisely the same strains from international speculation in their currencies. If the French left, ERM would be stone-cold dead in the market. This second blow looked like a knockout punch. The anchor, or base, for ERM is the Deutsche Mark, or mark, which is the strongest currency in the EC in part because Germany—like the United States but in contrast to Britain and France—has an independent central bank. That means that German monetary policy is more likely to be determined by insulated public servants in accord with economic considerations than by politicians influenced by electoral benefits. These officials are even more frightened by inflation than is the typical German—remember the horrendous inflation of Weimar. Therefore, international financiers feel comfortable assuming that the value of the mark will fluctuate only modestly.

The other participants in ERM undertake to follow whatever policies and take whatever actions are needed to keep the value of their currencies within a relatively narrow range above and below the mark. When Britain found that trying to do so would cause huge and continuing losses of its currency reserves, it withdrew. To keep France from doing the same less than a year later, ERM was modified. The allowed range of value around the mark was greatly expanded. The pressure on the French franc was made manageable. The cost, however, was virtually ERM itself. The fluctuation range now was so great that ERM could contribute little to the convergence of national currencies that was essential to achieve a common currency. And, had the leaders of the EC been willing to take such drastic action the previous year, Britain would not have felt compelled to withdraw. It obviously was a case of too much, too late.

Despite all the turmoil, all twelve EC members eventually did ratify the Maastricht Treaty. By that time, however, the treaty seemed not so much the launching of a new initiative as a defiant protest against the idea that the EC was falling apart. Nonetheless, evidence of continued progress toward economic union could be cited. Over 200 EC regulations required enactment into national law to complete the single market. By March 1993 even Greece, which had made the least progress, had implemented about 75 percent of them. The Danes, who had the best record, had enacted about 90 percent.

The potential gains of economic integration remain great. The EU has a third again as many people as does the United States; its GDP is a sixth larger; the value of its exports a quarter greater. To make a market this size truly a single one, to have no greater internal barriers to commence than those that exist among the American states would be to create an economic giant. Studies of the potential effect of eliminating existing barriers within the EU estimate an increase in the value of its GDP of from 5 to 7 percent.

The potential was exciting, but the reality depressing. The European economy was stagnating in the mid-1990s. The EC's GDP grew each year during the 1980s, reaching a peak of a 4-percent increase over the previous year in 1988. Each year since then growth has been less than it had been in the previous year. By 1993 the EC's GDP actually contracted. At the start of the 1980s, EC unemployment was 6 percent. The rate rose to 11 percent before declining toward the end of the decade. Unfortunately, it fell no lower than 8 percent before climbing once again. By 1993, it was back to 11 percent and continuing to climb. Even with an integrated market, Europe has not been able to create new jobs in anything like the number that have been generated in the United States.

The economic problems probably account for the EC's declining popularity. In 1991 nearly three-fourths of those polled in EC member countries thought that membership was "a good thing." Two years later only three-fifths thought so. Even worse, in 1991 three-fifths had thought that EC membership had benefited their country; two years later fewer than half thought so.

Efforts to improve economic performance could be complicated in the near future by expanded membership. Austria, Finland, Norway, and Sweden could be admitted to the EU as early as 1996. Although their economies are sound, working out the details of economic integration could cause difficulties. Then comes the really hard part. Also anxious for admission are Poland, the Czech Republic, Hungary, and the Baltic States. If these are granted membership, could applications from Russia and Ukraine be refused? You saw in Part Four the strains placed on the West German economy in trying to integrate economically derelict East Germany. The EU soon may face an even more demanding challenge.

Beyond any economic strains, expanded membership would kill any idea of political union. Even the admission of the Scandinavian contingent and Austria may force a halt to such developments. Already the EU has shown little ability to formulate common policies on major international issues. The collapse of communism not only made the North Atlantic Treaty Organization (NATO) seem less essential for security, but also encouraged those Europeans who did not believe that their interests were identical with those of the United States. The first attempt to formulate an independent EU foreign and security policy, however, proved to be "an enormous setback for the European idea," according to an anonymous integration "enthusiast," despite dealing with what clearly was a European matter. Britain's leading weekly newsmagazine, *The Economist,* reported: "Wimps, bunglers, insouciants, appeasers. Those are some of the kinder descriptions of the Europeans' record in the Balkans. Bosnia has been generally judged a bad example of limp, uncoordinated, lowest-common-denominator policy." It went on to conclude that a "common European defense is a long way off. The Europeans have neither the military structure nor the unity of purpose for such a thing."[1] Add a traditionally neutral country, Sweden, to the EU membership and unity on security policy becomes even less likely. The political pillar of the projected European Union looks rickety.

Given the EU's various problems, two ideas are gaining support. One is to push ahead with subsidiarity. Under this approach, the EU would make regulations only for those matters that absolutely require a common policy. Everything else would be left to the separate regulation of the individual member countries. The other idea is to embark on variable geometry, or Europe *à la carte*. The precedent for such an approach is the opt-outs that Britain and Denmark were permitted for some provisions of the Maastricht Treaty. Under variable geometry, the mix of countries working together would vary from one policy sphere to another. In each case a country would decide whether the benefits of a common policy surpassed for it the loss of decision-making autonomy.

Subsidiarity could be accommodated within the existing EU structure. Variable geometry, however, would transform the EU, making it little more than an umbrella or framework organization. Variable geometry reverses the functional federalism argument explained early in this chapter. Instead of function-by-function integration, ultimately producing overarching federalism, the lack of sufficient desire for federalism is recognized to permit no more than a variety of functional integrations. If you recall what you learned about British and French political culture, you will understand why variable geometry is more popular in Britain than in France. What could be more pragmatic and gradual than a number of contrasting groupings being formed over time as need be, without preconceptions about membership and procedures? What, equally, could be any more intellectually sloppy and at odds with any grand theoretical conception of European unity? Twenty miles of water in the English Channel makes a lot of difference.

Perhaps because the European Community seemed such an innovation in world affairs, too much was expected of it. The optimistic hopes that it generated seem unlikely to be fulfilled. The disappointments are all too obvious. Yet we can conclude on a positive note by briefly summarizing what the Community *has* accomplished. It has achieved a customs union. Tariff and quota barriers to trade among the members have been eliminated, and all of the members apply a common tariff to goods imported from outside countries. In the 1960s trade within the EC accounted for about a quarter of GDP in Belgium and Luxembourg, ranging down to only about 3 percent in Spain. At the close of the 1980s intra-EC trade produced nearly 45 percent of GDP in Belgium and Luxembourg and in Spain was up to about a tenth.

A Common Agricultural Policy exists to make farming a viable sector of the economy. The Community is also actively involved in competition policy. The

---

[1] *The Economist,* "A Survey of the European Community," July 3, 1993, p. 16.

Commission can investigate apparent cases of price fixing or unfair price cutting and has fined many companies for violations. Its jurisdiction extends not just to firms headquartered within member states but also to foreign enterprises that do business within them, such as IBM and Pioneer, the Japanese electronics company (both of which have been fined). Should companies believe they have been penalized improperly, their recourse is to appeal to the Court of Justice. That supranational court has exercised its power to invalidate national laws. Thus, whether the national arrangement is parliamentary supremacy as in Britain or judicial review as in Germany, the final word on the power of national policy makers rests, in some instances, with the EU Court. By the standards of nation states, the EU's budget is small; that it has any independent revenues of its own, however, is remarkable. One of the factors that caused the Articles of Confederation to fail in the United States and be replaced by the Constitution was the absence of any taxing power for the central government. In the EU each member is required to pass on to the Community a stated share of all of the revenues it raises through the VAT (rather like a sales tax). Furthermore, the payments that the common external tariff imposes on foreign goods go to the EU, not to the country through whose port the goods entered the EC.

In these and many other ways the economies of a dozen Western European countries have been linked. Many crucial social and economic policies for these countries are formulated to some extent by an international organization, only partially subject to separate national interests. Further dramatic progress seems unlikely, but what has been achieved in the second half of the twentieth century means that the political systems of Britain, France, and Germany (as well, of course, as the other nine members not included in this book) operate in a fundamentally different context than they did forty years ago.

Regardless of whether any of the countries of the former Soviet Union eventually are admitted to the EU, several of them may seek a measure of international integration in another way. Under terms of a new charter membership in the Commonwealth of Independent States (the old Soviet Union) to become effective in December 1994, permanent integrative organs are to be established in Minsk. CIS members will be obligated to act under the auspices and authority of a Commonwealth bank, a Commonwealth court, and other interstate institutions. The bank will set a common monetary policy for member countries by controlling the issue of a common currency for the CIS. The court, like the International Court at the Hague, will adjudicate disputes among CIS member countries. A coordinating council of full-time officials, similar in power and composition to the EC's Commission, will be appointed by the member countries. Any of the fifteen countries formerly part of the Soviet Union, as well as countries in Eastern Europe, can seek to join.

When he was President of the Soviet Union in 1990–1991, Mikhail Gorbachev used to address British, French, and German audiences on his visits to their countries as citizens of "our common European home." The Soviet Union no longer exists, but the search for European community and that "common European home" continues to link the more than one-half billion people of the Continent.

Index _____